# CULTURAL
# SOCIOLOGY

## AN INTRODUCTORY READER

# RECENT SOCIOLOGY TITLES
# FROM W. W. NORTON

# CULTURAL SOCIOLOGY

## AN INTRODUCTORY READER

EDITED BY

## MATT WRAY

TEMPLE UNIVERSITY

FOREWORD BY

## MICHÈLE LAMONT

HARVARD UNIVERSITY

W. W. NORTON & COMPANY

New York · London

W. W. Norton & Company has been independent since its founding in 1923, when William
Warder Norton and Mary D. Herter Norton first published lectures delivered at the People's
Institute, the adult education division of New York City's Cooper Union. The Nortons soon
expanded their program beyond the Institute, publishing books by celebrated academics from
America and abroad. By mid-century, the two major pillars of Norton's publishing program—
trade books and college texts—were firmly established. In the 1950s, the Norton family
transferred control of the company to its employees, and today—with a staff of four hundred and
a comparable number of trade, college, and professional titles published each year—W. W. Norton
& Company stands as the largest and oldest publishing house owned wholly by its employees.

Book design by Chris Welch
Composition by Westchester Book Composition
Manufacturing by Maple-Vail Book Group
Book design by Chris Welch
Production manager: Ashley Horna

Library of Congress Cataloging-in-Publication Data

Cultural sociology : an introduction / edited by Matt Wray, Temple University;
foreword by Michèle Lamont, Harvard University.—First edition.
pages cm
Includes bibliographical references.
ISBN 978-0-393-93413-7 (pbk.)
1. Sociology.   2. Culture.   I. Wray, Matt, 1964–   II. Lamont, Michèle, 1957–
HM585.C854 2014
306—dc23

2012051180

W. W. Norton & Company, Inc., 500 Fifth Avenue, New York, N.Y. 10110-0017
www.wwnorton.com
W. W. Norton & Company Ltd., Castle House, 75/76 Wells Street. London WIT 3QT

1  2  3  4  5  6  7  8  9  0

# CONTENTS

## PART THREE  PRODUCTION, STABILITY, & CHANGE

## PART FOUR  ANALYZING CULTURE

# FOREWORD

MICHÈLE LAMONT

To produce a good reader is not an easy task. By definition, the intended audience is made up of undergraduates studying in English-speaking colleges and universities. Typically, the imagined conversation partners have little interest in disciplinary traditions. Instead, they are intrigued by the world at hand, and are seeking answers and tools for thinking through both ordinary and challenging experiences. The best readers provide these tools, as well as new puzzles and some answers.

A good reader also offers a distinctive cut into a field of research. It identifies key elements of an ongoing conversation that brings together researchers across a few generations, where the classics inspire the young, and where in selected cases, younger scholars keep older research questions and agendas alive.

The best readers also make a case for a set of questions, or an integrated field of knowledge, by offering evidence of its dynamism and liveliness, of the process by which one line of inquiry opens up to the next, while also providing at least provisional conclusions concerning burning issues. Such readers make the audience want to know more, to purchase the books that extend and amplify ten-page offerings of Clifford Geertz or Pierre Bourdieu. They speak to the audience by tackling real world problems, questions that are significant to the lives of the public—for instance, why is upward mobility so difficult for those at the bottom? And what determines musical tastes?

By these various standards, the present volume is a successful experiment. But it is more than that. It is also *de facto* a reflection on the conditions of production of knowledge as well as on the current or ideal ("the best of the best") state of a subfield.

By some respects, research problems change over time not because they are solved as much as because they no longer remain puzzling or "interesting." What items figure in a grouping of authors and contributions is predicated by where the field stands now as much as by what each individual scholar brought to past conversations. Knowledge does not advance so much as it moves to novel questions and new approaches. The cumulation of knowledge is accomplished practically when generations of scholars perform the moral duty of acknowledging what comes from where and what is the added value of their contribution given the current state of a field.

For the past thirty years I have taught cultural sociology to undergraduate and graduate students, moving from a large public university to elite institutions, where I have spent most of my professional life. During these years, I have attempted to use my teaching to alert promising young people to the existence of analytical tools that can make a difference to their ability to apprehend the world systematically and critically, and to help them gain a better understanding of how people, institutions, and resources hang together (or not).

Most of the authors brought together in this reader by Matt Wray have figured on my syllabi over time. For many colleagues and for me, they represent "the best of the best" that cultural sociology has to offer not only to our discipline, but also to neighboring fields. At the end, the proof is in the pudding, i.e. success can be measured by whether authors have been successful at creating disciplinary and supra-disciplinary conversations (as manifested in citation rates, for instance). Of course, others who are not included here have been influential as well. But at the very least, the present reader offers one very well-informed take on what American cultural sociology has stood for over the past exceptionally dynamic decades.

In the broader intellectual landscape, many characteristics differentiate cultural sociology from neighboring disciplines. It is more multi-method and cumulative in orientation than cultural anthropology, and less influenced by Foucault and by post modernism. It is less exclusively textual than cultural studies, more attuned to institutions, and it is concerned with explanation as well as with description. It is also more skeptical of explicit political involvement than other areas of critical studies, including queer, race, or legal theory.

Within sociology, cultural sociology has grown to exercise a deep influence on other subfields over the last forty years, on areas such as the study of race and ethnicity, education, social movements, economic sociology, and political sociology. And indeed, in a context where the American Sociological Association (ASA) is organized around substantively-based sections *qua* subfields, "Culture" is currently the largest section of all the sections, ahead of historically more popular areas such as medical sociology and the sociology of gender. This is an indubitable measure of the success of the enterprise, particularly among younger generations, as this section also includes more graduate students than any other section of the ASA.

Finally, by some accounts, cultural sociology has brought about a revolution within American mainstream sociology, which has moved from being largely conducted as a quantitative enterprise concerned with structural changes, to being a multi-method endeavor often concerned with the various social processes participating social change, including processes that are largely meaning-based (such as evaluation or racialization). As such, cultural sociology has facilitated a cross-Atlantic dialogue among American sociology and other sociological traditions, including the more hermeneutic and interpretative traditions found in Germany and France (as well as on other continents, Latin America especially).

These are just a few of the reasons we can celebrate the publication of Matt Wray's exceptional reader. Not only should it prove to be a useful tool in the education of younger generations, but it should also become a powerful arm against the balkanization of American sociology. Finally, may it also help experts and lay people alike move beyond a strict dichotomy between culture and structure and come to comprehend how meaning making is indeed a crucial collective enterprise, on par with the competition for material and symbolic resources.

# INTRODUCTION

It's hot. 105 degrees in the shade. Unfortunately, there isn't much shade to speak of, just the still heat under the shadow of the shelter we've made. It's a minor work of art, this shelter, with a frame made of jute and bamboo, covered with nylon and burlap. Bill dreamt it up after studying rough drawings of Bedouin tents. Right now, it's the only thing keeping us from crisping in the desert sun. We lie about in lawn chairs and try not to move, waiting for a breeze, the slightest breath of cooling wind. We had spent the cooler hours of the morning wandering and making chilled coffee drinks for the artists and creatives who stumbled into our camp, some bleary-eyed and wobbly from the night before, others clear-headed and voluble, spinning detailed descriptions about artworks, installations, and strange performances scattered across the desert. But now the heat makes us all retreat and scramble for shade.

As evening falls, the wind finally comes up, but brings a dust storm with it, and we have to abandon the sturdy shelter quickly. The dust, incredibly fine and whiter than snow, drives us choking into the stifling death heat of our cars. My friend Lincoln isn't having a very good time of it. The dust has brought on a fierce asthma attack (who knew he had asthma?), and he's sick, puking bile and white dust out through his nose. He looks like he's vomiting yellow plaster. In the car, the dust puffs in through the cracks in the doors and windows as gusts of wind rock us violently. Outside, our half-prepared pasta dinner is lost in the swirl of whiteness. I look into the rearview mirror and ask myself what the hell we are doing here.

My first thought was that it was Sky King's fault. Sky King, a.k.a. Richard Dillman, was the intrepid radio man in charge of coordinating communications for all of the protests, demos, banner hangings, direct actions, and other forms of guerrilla theater undertaken by Greenpeace, San Francisco, where I worked at the time. A year before, on a Tuesday morning in September 1992, I found Sky King in his office, his visage burnt red, his black hair and beard coated in fine white dust. He looked like he had just come down from the mountain after an appointment with God. "Geez," I asked, "what did you do over the weekend?"

He proceeded to tell me about his trip to an event called Burning Man and recounted the things he saw there. Burning Man now bills itself as an arts festival in the high mountain desert of northwest Nevada, but in 1993, it didn't really know what it was about and we just called it a gathering of the tribes. The focal point of the event, then as now, was a ritual burning of The Man, a 40-foot-tall figure constructed of wood, burlap, and neon and packed with explosives, fireworks, and diesel fuel. The burn takes place every Labor Day weekend in the Black Rock Desert, 70 miles outside of Reno. At over 1,000 square miles, it is one of the largest flat expanses of wilderness in North America. The reigning ethos of the event—if there was one—was that we were there not just to witness art, but to be the art we wanted to see. There was only one rule to guide our community: No Spectators!

Years later, Sky King's recollection of his arrival went something like this:

> We clamored into the VW microbus and off we went, cheek by jowl, crammed in there in this little can, creeping up over the mountains, past Dutchman flat, past Donner Pass, down towards Reno and out north into the wild country. Of course we had breakdowns, we had difficulties, we had delays. We didn't get there in the middle of the day as we expected. It was dark, it was night, past ten o'clock when we finally pulled into Gerlach and gassed up at Bruno's.
>
> Nobody around, just lights way off in the distance. You could see a train coming on an enormous train track that cut straight across like an arrow. We said, "We're trying to go to the Burning Man. What should we do?" There had been a couple of people who had come through earlier so they knew and they said, "Well, just go up the road. Up the road and turn right at the fork, then go another ten miles and turn right."
>
> Now, there was no road. It was turn right off the highway and directly onto the playa. Up until this point, we'd been having a good time. We'd been joking and kidding around. We'd been yapping and ribbing each other. Well, we made that right turn out onto the playa and the conversation became subdued because nobody had ever been in a place like this before.

It was pitch black and we'd heard about the quicksand, and we'd heard about the spots where you get stuck and nobody can get you out again, we'd heard about these things. But still . . . We kept going. We didn't know where we were going. The highway was long gone now . . . This was a wild area that we had no reference for . . .

When the sun came up in the morning it was an astounding sight. There's nothing there but somehow there's everything there. And when you stand up at dawn on that desert, your shadow goes on infinitely from your toes all the way out to the horizon and you see nothing. Not a blade, not an insect. Nothing. We had no idea where we were. We knew we were someplace on the face of this infinitely large, infinitely flat plane, but we didn't know where we were, really.

We got out the binoculars, looked around the horizon and saw this little whisker sticking up somewhere in the vast, vast distance. Just this one feature, the only thing we could see. Well, it had to be the Man that they had already erected so we struck the tents, got back into the microbus, and set a course towards that one little feature because it's not like driving, it's like navigating. It's like being at sea. You set up a course and you just hold it and eventually we got there and began a festival of drugs and alcohol and high explosives. Exactly what you're looking for. Add to that the most creative artwork, the most unbelievable displays and you really have something that nobody had ever experienced before, and there we were (Dillman 2012).

After hearing Sky King's tale, I vowed to go with him the following year. That's how I ended up at Black Rock Desert, Nevada, over Labor Day weekend in 1993, sweltering in my car in the middle of a ferocious dust storm. I had trekked out with 2,500 other hardy souls to experiment with community. We plunked ourselves down in the middle of this vast alkali playa, a prehistoric seabed surrounded by towering purple mountains. We had all come here to form an intentional but impermanent community, a kind of tempurban space.[1]

There are all sorts of people in Black Rock City, as the settlement has come to be called. Like all cities, it is a living, breathing encyclopedia of subcultures: desert survivalists, urban primitives and bohemians, artists, rocketeers, steampunks, aging hippies, queers, pyromaniacs, musicians, ranters, eco-freaks, acidheads, straight edgers, punks, gun lovers, goths,

---

1. For more on my early experiences at Burning Man, see Wray (1995). To hear Sky King's recollections, see Dillman (2012).

erotic dancers, S/M and bondage enthusiasts, nudists, swingers, metalheads, refugees from the men's movement, anarchists, hipsters, ravers, transgender types, Wiccans, and New Agers (and that's just the short list!).[2] Most gather in one of the hundreds of theme camps that form the basic social structure of the city. These camps are like mini-neighborhoods, communes dotting the tempurban landscape. In the course of the weekend, participants will, among other things, set up FM radio stations, print daily newspapers, build rave camps, and soak in the muddy heat of surrounding hot springs. Mostly they will build art projects, large and small, and then they will burn or otherwise destroy them.

I'm trying to describe Burning Man to you with words, but as the founders like to say, "trying to explain what Burning Man is to someone who has never been to the event is a bit like trying to explain what a particular color looks like to someone who is blind."[3] Even if I could nail the description—getting all the whos, whats, wheres, and whens just right—my words would probably still leave you wondering about the whys.

Why would anybody do this? Why all this high desert weirdness? Why are Burners (as participants are called) so devoted to and fulfilled by this event? Why the growing popularity of Black Rock City, which now attracts over 50,000 Burners every year? Why is this event happening and why is it happening now?

Of course, if you and I are going to answer these questions, then we have to have a theory that helps explain what drives human actions and behavior, especially when those behaviors are, well, a bit strange. We also need some theories about how groups organize themselves to work cooperatively and meet their collective goals, as well as some concepts that help us figure out how groups define goals for themselves in the first place. In short, to answer these questions, we need social theory.[4]

2. For a more complete list of the types of subcultures represented at Burning Man, see the archives of annual reports at http://afterburn.burningman.com/ (accessed September 24, 2012), which list thousands of camps.

3. www.burningman.com/whatisburningman/ (accessed September 25, 2012).

4. In recent years, Burning Man has attracted the attention of an increasing number of social theorists. The best sociological work to date is Chen (2009), which focuses on the organizational structures of Burners, and Turner (2009), which analyzes the event in relation to media studies. Other useful accounts focus on the political implications of the event (Doherty 2004); its ritualistic and spiritual dimensions (Gilmore 2010); and its relation to consumer culture and marketing (Kozinets 2002). See also the wide-ranging essays in Gilmore and Van Proyen (2005).

# FROM SOCIAL THEORY
# TO CULTURAL SOCIOLOGY

Social theorists try to understand the relationship between two big things: human action and social order. Usually, we call human action "agency" and social order "structure." These sound like they might be difficult concepts, but really, they refer to easy-to-understand things.

*Action* or *agency* refers to the things that individuals, groups, or organizations say and do. People make decisions, say and write words, and take actions, singly or collectively. Organizations and institutions do this too. All are active participants in the world. Theologians and philosophers have often referred to agency as "free will," and though it's not a term that sociologists use, the concept is analogous to agency.

*Order* or *structure* is the set of forces and facts that limit and constrain people's actions and agency. For instance, a system of laws is a structure, as are economic and political systems. Biological facts such as death also set limits to human will (making it not so free). These forces and facts give order to and shape patterns of action and behavior among individuals and groups. To use a common metaphor, order and structure are the rules of the game: They tell you and me what we can and cannot do, as well as how to win or succeed.

These two big things—action and order—fascinate sociologists for two reasons. One reason is that they are present in every society social scientists have ever observed. People do what they do (action), but seldom in conditions of their own choosing (order). Sometimes people's actions line up nicely with the structures they find themselves in and sometimes they don't. But order and action are always in play, be it in discord or in harmony.

The second reason is that—and here is where it gets really interesting—*structure* can be conceptualized as the historical result of previous actions. Structures are calcified residues of actions taken by people who came before us. They are built up over years and years of collective effort. Sometimes major shifts—wars, revolutions, famines, landmark court cases, fundamental shifts in policy, even major innovations in technology—alter structures relatively swiftly and in lasting ways. More typically, however, structures change incrementally, sometimes in measures so small that we are only aware of them retrospectively. In fact, an entire subfield called *historical sociology* has emerged to sharpen sociologists' focus on how structures and actions in the past have produced the outcome we call the present.

In either case, whether change comes quickly or slowly, people find ways to adapt their actions to the new structures, either conforming to or resisting them. And over time, these new actions lead to new structures. Do you see the circularity? Actions → structures → new actions → new structures. Around and around we go, in a ceaseless cycle.

This chicken-egg quality of the social world plays havoc with the logic of causation and often leaves sociologists feeling like we are chasing our own tails. But it is an exhilarating chase, this business of trying to understand the complex relationships between social order and human action. For the past 150 years or so, sociological theorists have been engaged in a quest to produce coherent systems of concepts and methods to solve the puzzles of structure and agency. Consequently, we have built up a very large body of sociological theory and methods.

So if that is what sociologists do, what do cultural sociologists do? How is our objective different from general sociology?

One very obvious reply to this question is that while not all sociologists are interested in studying culture, cultural sociologists definitely are. We're certainly not the only scholars interested in doing this, nor were we the first. Anthropologists pioneered the study of culture in the early decades of the twentieth century and invented many of the methods we use; historians turned to the study of culture in the late 1980s and taught us how to take the long view, tracking cultural developments and changes over decades and centuries; and cultural psychologists show us how the ways humans think about the world are deeply influenced by the cultures they inhabit.

Culture fascinates people across disciplines because it has the potential to explain a lot. But what sets cultural sociologists apart from other students of culture like anthropologists and cultural historians? One answer is: Not much. Cultural sociologists are often very interdisciplinary, drawing upon insights from anthropologists, historians, psychologists, and political scientists to get a grip on this thing we call culture. But another, more satisfying answer is that sociologists' objects of study tend to be different from what those in other disciplines tend to choose. Furthermore, the ways that we study culture—our preferred methods—tend to be different as well. So, if cultural sociologists differ from other students of culture (to the extent that we actually *are* different) because of how we define culture and how we study it, let's begin with that.

# DEFINING CULTURE

There is no agreed upon sociological definition of culture. My own definition starts with the point I mentioned earlier, that human actions always have local contexts. Human agency doesn't happen in a vacuum. Typically, people don't just do any random thing. Everyone has routines, rituals, preferences, and habits that they stick to. We have predictable behaviors that we share in common with people like us.

Of course, there are other people with different sets of behaviors. The way "we" do things is different from the way "they" do things. Routines, rituals, preferences, habits, and everyday behaviors vary quite a lot from place to place. Explaining this variation is one of the major tasks of cultural analysis. The consensus of social scientists is that differences in everyday habits, behaviors, and preferences arise from different ways of seeing the world, different social circumstances, and different historical traditions which are all related to different social structures. These different ways of seeing and doing things are called *cultures*.

Cultures sit in the space between order and action, structure and agency. Culture is not the same as structure, but structure is deeply influenced by culture. Neither is culture the same as agency, although agency is strongly shaped by culture. Sociologists like to say that *culture mediates both structure and agency*. That is, it acts as a kind of go-between, a bridge that joins these two major concepts.

Culture can be seen as the soft tissue that connects muscle (action) to bone (structure). Culture is the ligament, tendon, and cartilage of the social body. Without it, agency would be disconnected from structure, and structure from agency. When culture (connective tissue) ages and hardens into a durable shape, it is more or less indistinguishable from structure (bone). When it is new and flexible, it is more or less indistinguishable from agency (muscle). At a quick glance, muscles, bones, and connective tissues seem very distinct from each other, but when studied under a microscope, one discovers that they are composed of the same basic building blocks—cells. Something similar happens when sociologists study culture, structure, and agency. In most cases, we have no trouble distinguishing them from one another, but at times, a great deal of confusion arises from the difficulties of drawing precise lines between them.

But what exactly are the building blocks of culture, structure, and agency? What are the cellular elements of culture? There is no definitive list, but a broad survey of sociological work on culture, past and present, reveals six elements that are commonly identified as core components of cultural sociology. I detail these six elements below, but before discussing them, it will be helpful to say a few words about how the discipline of sociology has characterized the concept of culture in the three major theoretical traditions of the discipline: functionalism, conflict theory, and symbolic interactionism.[5]

## Culture in Functionalism

Functionalism is a branch of sociological theory that views society as a complex system of individuals and organizations that work together to promote the stability and functioning of the whole. Émile Durkheim was an early proponent of this view, positing that culture played a key role in social functioning by providing shared norms and values that bound people into groups, and groups into societies. Social systems could be stable and productive (i.e., functional) only if individuals and institutions adapted to the needs of the system. Culture was the means for accomplishing this adaptation in each successive generation, through a process called socialization.

In the 1950s, the structural functionalist theory of Talcott Parsons furthered this basic concept by viewing culture as an implicit feature of social life, one that provides the moral underpinnings for human behavior and social action. Parsons believed the major task of sociology was to observe objective things like social actions, roles, and institutions, which reside in social space. His theory did not leave much room for the consideration of subjective things like norms and values, which reside in people's hearts and minds. How these consensual norms and values developed is of less interest to Parsonian functionalism. Instead, the important questions concern how norms and values work to support the larger social whole. Seen through the lens of functionalism, culture plays an important role in sus-

---

5. These three theoretical traditions are by no means the only major traditions within the discipline, but most undergraduate sociology majors will be familiar with them. For a useful overview of the many theoretical approaches enlivening the discipline today, see Turner (2001).

taining consensus and solidarity in society, but it is never allowed to take center stage in sociological analysis.[6] As a school of thought, functionalism was eclipsed in the 1960s by conflict theory, but it still has adherents today.

## Culture in Conflict Theory

Conflict theory has its classical roots in Karl Marx and Max Weber (see pp. 7 and 37), but in the 20th century, this tradition is more closely aligned with Marxist theories of class struggle and economic determinism. Rather than seeing society as a functioning whole, conflict theory paints a picture of different groups struggling to assert and maintain dominance and power over each other. In the 20th century, this viewpoint was best represented by C. Wright Mills, whose books on the American class system are widely regarded as sociological classics (Mills 1948; 1951; 1956).

Mills and other conflict theorists also relegated culture to a supporting role in society, but unlike the functionalist view of culture as a widely shared set of values and norms, conflict theorists viewed culture as a set of ideologies and beliefs that tended to shore up the power of dominant classes. Culture was not an implicit system of values and norms, but an intentional product of organized efforts by groups struggling for power. This viewpoint echoed the classic statement by Marx (p. 8) that "the ideas of the ruling class are in every epoch the ruling ideas." Cultures were ideological and the norms and values they expressed were not based on broad, collective consensus, but rather on narrow class interests like money, power, and prestige. Culture, then, reflected the ideologies of dominant groups and were little more than a sideshow that distracted people from the real operations of power—the manipulation of economic and political systems by elites.

Beginning in the 1970s and '80s, the work of Marxists like Raymond Williams (p. 51) and other scholars at the Birmingham Center for Contemporary Cultural Studies in the UK led conflict theorists to take a deeper interest in culture, seeing it not just as a reflection of class ideologies, but as one of the arenas where class struggle occurred.[7] Working class people had culture too, it was argued, and they often used their cultures as symbolic

---

6. An important exception is Alexander (2003), who has argued for a neofunctionalist theory that places culture and cultural activity at the center of all sociological analysis.

7. For overviews of the intersection of cultural studies and cultural sociology, see Long (1997); Wolff (1999); and Calhoun and Sennett (2007).

weapons to fight back against the elite and middle classes. With this shift, culture was seen not only as an explicit product of class struggle, but also as a force that could potentially create oppositional identities and counter-cultural movements (see Willis and MacLeod, pp. 483 and 507). As conflict theory rose to prominence in the 1970s and '80s, its newfound respect for culture as a social force inspired a new generation of sociologists to refine their theories and methods for studying culture. In 1986, the American Sociological Association formally recognized cultural sociology as an important subfield by creating a special section of its membership devoted to the study of culture.

## Culture in Symbolic Interactionism

Symbolic interactionism is a branch of sociological theory that views interactions between individuals and groups as the building blocks of society. It has classical roots in Georg Simmel (p. 22) and George Herbert Mead, both of whom placed individual human interaction at the center of their theories. In contemporary sociological theory, this tradition is best represented by Erving Goffman (p. 80) and Herbert Blumer. In an influential summary, Blumer described symbolic interactionism as consisting of three core premises. First, that human beings act toward things in the world (objects, people, institutions) on the basis of the meaning those things have for them; second, that the meaning of those things (i.e., how individuals personally symbolize them) is not inherent in the things themselves, but arises out of interactions with other people; and third, that these symbolic meanings are subject to and modified by an interpretive process people use as they encounter things in the world (Blumer 1969). Symbolic interactionism places subjective meanings and their interpretations at the heart of social life.

Where does culture fit in symbolic interactionism? Inasmuch as culture is, among other things, a set of symbols and meanings about the world, one can say that culture is a focal point for symbolic interactionism. Far more than functionalism or conflict theory, interactionism sees the major tasks of sociology to be the investigation of meaning-making as it happens between people, and the examination of what people do and how they act based on those meanings. While functionalism and conflict theory are lenses that bring into sharp focus the objective social facts and constraints of the social world (i.e., structure), the lens of symbolic interactionism highlights the subjective responses and reactions (i.e., agency) of individuals and groups as they encounter that structure. Symbolic interactionist theory continues to inspire cultural sociologists today because it provides concepts and methods that render meaning-making visible for analysis and interpretation.

The changing fortunes of the culture concept within sociology can be summarized by noting three points: First, there are traditions of sociological thought that effectively relegate culture to the margins of sociological inquiry, seeing it as immaterial and, to use a word common in these circles, epiphenomenal. Second, while values and norms remain an important area of inquiry for cultural sociologists, conflict theory and symbolic interactionism have proven to be much more fruitful, yielding a greater number of insights and concepts widely used by cultural sociologists today. Finally, while functionalism and conflict theory view culture in its objective form (as shared values and norms or class ideologies) and treat it as a social product that has observable effects, symbolic interactionism views culture in its subjective form (as intersubjective meanings and symbols) and treats it as a social process with effects that must be interpreted rather than measured.

# THE BUILDING BLOCKS OF CULTURE

To return to the questions posed above: What are the building blocks of culture? What does culture look like at a cellular level? Given that *culture* means different things to different thinkers, it is prudent to offer a set of overlapping factors that together constitute culture. I have identified six elements, although there are other important factors that I do not consider here.[8]

8. For instance, there is important scholarship on "material culture"—the everyday objects, artifacts, and technologies that are present in all cultures, but that vary in form and function from one culture to the next. For key works on the sociology of material culture, see Mukerji (1994); Molotch (2003); and Epstein (2008). Likewise, there is a growing body of work, mostly derived from Pierre Bourdieu, that attends to culture as practices and strategies. Bourdieu's concepts of *habitus* and *field* are central to this work—called practice theory—but since his theories are not often taught at the undergraduate level, I do not attempt to explain them in this volume. For an introduction, see Bourdieu (1990). For broader introduction to practice theory, see Calhoun and Sennett (2007). To distill these six elements of culture, I drew upon a multitude of sources. Primary among these were Lee and Linnenberg (2000); Griswold (2008); Holt (2005); Jacobs and Hanrahan (2005); and Small, Harding, and Lamont (2010).

Taken alone, each specifies a distinctive—albeit more restricted—piece of culture. Together, they reveal the breadth and scope of contemporary scholarship in cultural sociology.

# I. Norms, Values, Attitudes, and Beliefs

Norms and values are shared beliefs that serve to guide individual and collective behavior along paths that a community deems appropriate and acceptable. Laws and rules are not norms or values, although they do resemble each other. The difference is that laws and rules are more formal and the consequences of violating them are quite serious. Norms and values are informal and flexible and the consequences of violating them are usually less severe. Examples of norms and values in mainstream American culture are hard work, individual responsibility, and being a good citizen.

There has been a great deal of sociological debate about how much norms actually influence behavior. The theory (typically associated with structural functionalism) that they do so predictably and reliably has received little empirical support (see Swidler, p. 111). While we don't always follow norms and we don't always live up to our own values, we nonetheless share them with other Americans. Americans who don't share widely accepted norms and values are usually viewed by those in the mainstream as "weird" or "immoral," or to use an old-fashioned term, "deviant." For example, many Americans would consider some of the behaviors that occur at Burning Man to be quite deviant, despite the fact that most Burners see themselves as adhering to a well-developed moral code.

## Values at Burning Man

According to its founders, the community has come to recognize ten core principles that serve as a set of guiding norms and values for participants:

- **Radical Inclusion**—Anyone may be a part of Burning Man. We welcome and respect the stranger. No prerequisites exist for participation in our community.

- **Gifting**—Burning Man is devoted to acts of gift-giving. The value of a gift is unconditional. Gifting does not contemplate a return or an exchange for something of equal value.
- **Decommodification**—In order to preserve the spirit of gifting, our community seeks to create social environments that are unmediated by commercial sponsorships, transactions, or advertising. We stand ready to protect our culture from such exploitation. We resist the substitution of consumption for participatory experience.
- **Radical Self-reliance**—Burning Man encourages the individual to discover, exercise, and rely on his or her inner resources.
- **Radical Self-expression**—Radical self-expression arises from the unique gifts of the individual. No one other than the individual or a collaborating group can determine its content. It is offered as a gift to others. In this spirit, the giver should respect the rights and liberties of the recipient.
- **Communal Effort**—Our community values creative cooperation and collaboration. We strive to produce, promote, and protect social networks, public spaces, works of art, and methods of communication that support such interaction.
- **Civic Responsibility**—We value civil society. Community members who organize events should assume responsibility for public welfare and endeavor to communicate civic responsibilities to participants. They must also assume responsibility for conducting events in accordance with local, state, and federal laws.
- **Leaving No Trace**—Our community respects the environment. We are committed to leaving no physical trace of our activities wherever we gather. We clean up after ourselves and endeavor, whenever possible, to leave such places in a better state than we found them.
- **Participation**—Our community is committed to a radically participatory ethic. We believe that transformative change, whether in the individual or in society, can occur only through the medium of deeply personal participation. We achieve being through doing. Everyone is invited to work. Everyone is invited to play. We make the world real through actions that open the heart.
- **Immediacy**—Immediate experience is, in many ways, the most important touchstone of value in our culture. We seek to overcome barriers

that stand between us and a recognition of our inner selves, the reality of those around us, participation in society, and contact with a natural world exceeding human powers. No idea can substitute for this experience.[9]

Larry Harvey, the creative visionary behind the event, has played a key role in formulating this ethos and creed.

Norms, values, attitudes, and beliefs remain important to cultural sociologists in large part because they are part of the cultural criteria that help define belonging in mainstream groups. Even those excluded from the mainstream may aspire to the values and goals of the mainstream (see MacLeod, p. 507). As sources of inspiration and aspiration and as indicators of inclusion and exclusion, norms and values have key sociological significance.

## II. Frames and Symbolic Boundaries

If norms and values orient people toward common goals and influence—however weakly—their actions, then frames and symbolic boundaries are the ways that individuals define their social situations. The basic idea behind frames is twofold: first, how a person acts toward others depends on his understanding of the social context, and second, different people from different backgrounds will define the same social situation differently. This often leads to misunderstandings, controversies, and conflicts as people regard others as behaving inappropriately according to their own definitions of appropriateness.

If frames are commonly agreed upon ways of looking at the world, symbolic boundaries are the ways humans define themselves in relation to others, especially those we perceive to be above and below us in the social hierarchy. Symbolic boundaries are essentially schemes of classification (see Durkheim and Mauss, p. 12) that people use to distinguish themselves and people like them from others. At their core, symbolic boundaries are moral distinctions, assigning finely graded categories of worthiness

---

9. From www.burningman.com/whatisburningman/about_burningman/principles.html (accessed September 25, 2012).

to individuals and groups. When individuals engage in this sort of differentiation and categorization of self and other, they are doing what cultural sociologists call *boundary work* (see Bryson, p. 387).

Cultural sociologists are in wide agreement that people use frames and symbolic boundaries to define their situations and locate themselves in social spaces. As their names imply, frames and boundaries draw lines and

## Symbolic Boundaries at Burning Man

Subcultures have a reputation—deserved or not—for being quite factional and splintery. Like dividing cells, subcultures often spin off other groups due to conflicting and divergent identities. Frequently, the conflict is over questions of authenticity, like "What does it mean to be a real ____ ?" This is a classic example of symbolic boundary work—defining "us" and "them" in oppositional or conflictual terms. Questions of authenticity are alive and well at Burning Man, as Katherine Chen's (2006, 2009) research has shown:

> During my years studying the organizing activities behind Burning Man, I've noticed that attendees, or Burners, struggle with a conundrum. At one sunset during the 2008 event, while I strolled back to my camp along a temporary street pressed into the desert's dusty surface, a banner caught my attention. Large, hand-written letters proclaimed the camp's theme: "The Museum of It Was Better Last Year." It captured the simultaneous joy and angst evident in Burners' accounts of their event experiences. When Burners long for the wonder and novelty of their first year participating in the festival, they may embark on a trip down memory lane. Their experiences every year after their first pose invidious and revealing comparisons about authenticity.
>
> To validate worth or confer esteem, people seek out what sociologists call authenticity—that sense of meaning and dignity, or a connection with other people and experiences. People pursue authenticity in their workplaces and neighborhoods, or through consumption and relationships, and as their experiences change, so too do their perceptions of authenticity.
>
> As Burning Man enters its third decade, several changes to the event have challenged hard-core Burners' conceptions of its authenticity.

> Some believe the event's longevity, exponential population growth, and increasingly complex rules and regulations have eroded its authenticity. In contrast, more supportive attendees uphold a dynamic conceptualization of authenticity: they view change as a creative process crucial to the event's rejuvenation.[10]

mark off borders and edges. They are the natural tools humans use to make mental maps of the social world.[11]

# III. Repertoires and Rituals

The concept of cultural repertoires is simple: individuals keep catalogues of how to do things in their heads. Everyone has ideas about how to behave in specific situations and how to accomplish specific things, but these can vary remarkably depending on people's backgrounds and life histories. Swidler (p. 300) analogized repertoires to toolkits from which people select tools for the job at hand, but others have proposed concepts like *cognitive schemas* (DiMaggio 1997) and *situated learning* (Lave and Wenger 1991) that pose sharp challenges to the toolkit approach. Regardless of which approach is used, the idea of repertoires is meant to counter the functionalist idea of norms and values as determinants of action.

Rituals are key aspects of cultural life and they are among the most obvious markers of cultural difference. Culture influences common, everyday rituals like how people greet one another as well as less common rituals like baptisms and funerals. Wedding rituals are likewise governed by codes and customs that can vary dramatically from one culture to the next, yet they often have a common function: they are performed at major life transitions and often mark changes in social status (such as the shift from being single) by requiring a brief separation (such as a honeymoon) from the usual routines before assuming the new status (married). Rituals

10. Chen (2006) p. 65.

11. Goffman (p. 80 in this volume), drawing directly from tenets of symbolic interactionism, provides key theorization of the framing concept. Lamont and Molnàr (2002) offer a broad survey of symbolic boundary theory. For more on symbolic boundary theory, see Wray (2006), especially pp. 1–17.

are designed to guide individuals, their friends, their families, and their communities safely as they navigate these disorienting life changes.

## IV. Arts, Ideas, and Cultural Capital

One commonsense understanding of the word "culture" has to do with the creative arts and humanities. Culture, in this sense, means the world of theater and performance, music and dance, poetry and literature. It conjures up thoughts of museums and bookstores, and visions of a highly cultivated appreciation of the finer things in life. These are cultural habits, preferences, and tastes associated with membership in the upper class. Indeed, these are regular features of all modern societies. Cultural sociologists are deeply interested in these forms of human expression, but not because we believe them to be worthwhile in and of themselves (although many surely are) and not because we take aesthetic pleasure in consuming them (although many of us surely do). Instead, we're interested in cultural expression in the realm of arts and ideas because of what they can tell us about the societies that produce and consume them. How does culture of this sort get produced? Who consumes it and who doesn't? Why does it exist? To what ends is this sort of high status culture put? What social functions and purposes does it serve aside from providing education, entertainment, or aesthetic pleasure?

One answer to these questions is that knowledge about arts and ideas—and the ability to appreciate their significance—is a kind of marketable currency. *Cultural capital* is the term we use to designate this feature of high-status culture: middle- and upper-class parents pass it along to their children, investing them with the knowledge they need to appear sophisticated and mannered, but parents in working-class and poor families do not. As Lareau (p. 518) demonstrates, one consequence is that kids with the right cultural capital are poised for success at an early age. Cultural capital is one of the most widely used concepts in cultural sociology today, in part because it links culture to social inequality in measurable ways.

## V. Discourses & Narratives

One of the key premises of symbolic interactionism is that humans are symbolizing beings—we tell ourselves stories about the world all of the time. Cultural sociologists embrace this notion and pay particular attention to two kinds of stories: discourses and narratives. Discourses are like meta-stories. They are ways of describing things (like social problems or categories of people) that follow their own set of observable rules, conventions, and terminologies. There is, for instance, a well-developed and ever-changing discourse on criminality. By labeling those who have served sentences as convicts or felons, labelers create a discourse that separates "them" from "us," in effect alienating "them" from society, and drawing "us" closer together in shared condemnation of the other. The concept of discourse is most often associated with the work of Michel Foucault (1926–1984), who drew attention to the ways that discourses tend to construct and produce the objects that they purport merely to describe. Discourses, he pointed out, reflect hidden cultural norms and frame social objects in powerful and subtle ways, dictating what can be thought or said about a given issue at any particular historical moment. Cultural sociologists find this and other, related ways of thinking about the power of discourse to be quite useful, as Bourdieu (p. 495) shows.

Narratives focus on how people describe themselves and understand their personal histories and social situations. Narratives reveal people's self-perceptions and social identities. They are important to cultural sociologists because, following symbolic interactionism, we believe that people are likely to act and behave in ways that are consistent with their personal narratives. Thus, capturing and understanding narratives is one more key to understanding human agency.

## VI. Institutions & Identities

The concept of institutions is central to sociological inquiry (Powell and DiMaggio 1991). In fact, when sociologists refer to structure, we most often have various kinds of institutions in mind. For instance, the state is a vast complex of institutions composed of other institutions such as our legal, educational, and health care systems, which are themselves composed of institutions like courts, jails, prisons, schools, and hospitals. On a smaller scale, the family is an institution. For sociologists, institutions are those established organizations or regular patterns of interaction that play important and decisive roles in the lives of people in a given society. As I have noted several times, institutions (structures) can be conceptualized as products of human agency, past and present, and they are of great interest to cultural sociologists because they forcefully shape how people act and interact with one another and interpret those actions.

Institutions are important shapers of people's personal and collective identities. For example, families are primary influences on who a person will become as she grows up, schools shape people's minds and social selves, and religious institutions shape individuals' beliefs and moral identities. Institutions like the state also set the official terms of group membership. Racial and gender identities, for instance, are assigned by the state at birth, a process sociologists call *ascription*. Institutions write people into specific identities and social categories that typically stay with them for the rest of their lives. Institutions are, therefore, incredibly powerful forces shaping people's personal and collective destinies.

## Institutions of Burning Man

Rather than just being a utopian wish list, the core principles of Burning Man have instilled in many Burners a sense of real possibilities for social change. They return from the playa with fire in their hearts—engaging their local communities, and seeking to make their off-playa communities conform to their on-playa worlds:

> The impact of the Burning Man experience has been so profound that a culture has formed around it. This culture pushes the limits of Burning Man and has led to people banding together nationwide, and putting on their own events, in attempt to rekindle that magic feeling that only being part of this community can provide. The Black Rock Arts Foundation (BRAF) promotes interactive art by supporting public art that exists outside the event, and has a special interest in supporting art at regional events. Additionally, Burning Man has over two thousand volunteers who work before, during and after the event (many who work year-round) to make the event a reality.[12]

In addition to BRAF, Burning Man has given birth to other institutions like Black Rock Solar, a nonprofit organization dedicated to installing solar panels and promoting renewable energy sources in poor and underserved communities—for free.

12. From www.burningman.com/what is burningman/ (accessed September 26, 2012).

Black Rock Solar starts by focusing on the social—rather than financial—bottom line. We look at who needs help the most and how we can best help them. We find ways to save money on installations and provide our services at the lowest cost possible, relying partly on donations and fundraising efforts. . . . Just to be clear, we're not interested in competing with anyone who does this for a living, and that's why we only take on projects that aren't viable otherwise. That way, we can increase the amount of solar power on the ground while still growing the market for high-paying "green collar" jobs.[13]

That Burning Man did not start out as an effort to create a movement makes it all the more interesting to study its evolution from a weekend gathering to a year-round commitment to social change. The trajectory suggests that temporary communities can have lasting effects through the process of cultural diffusion.

# STUDYING CULTURE

Having identified some of the major elements of culture, how do sociologists go about studying them? What methods are best for capturing the data that will become evidence, and what are the best kinds of evidence to draw upon?

The answers, of course, depend on which of the six elements you choose to emphasize in your research. Studying institutions and identities often requires examining historical details about the emergence of groups and their formal organization, while studying discourses and narratives often involves paying close attention to written texts, popular media, and oral life histories. Generally speaking, however, there are a limited number of methods that cultural sociologists frequently employ. Examples of several of these methods can be found in "Analyzing Culture," Section 4 of this volume, but I will briefly define a few of them here, as you will encounter them throughout the reader.

- Content analysis—a method of analysis for discovering the content of human communications. Content analysis has been used extensively

13. From www.blackrocksolar.org/about (accessed September 26, 2012).

to analyze news media, interview data, films, and other forms of popular culture. Typically, it involves *coding*, which is the process of systematically identifying recurring themes or memes in the data. Historically, coding was done manually by the researcher, but increasingly, researchers are assisted by specialized software.

- Ethnographic fieldwork—the process of learning about a group of people or a community through direct, personal observation. Typically, this involves *participant observation*, in which the researcher strives to gain familiarity and intimacy with the research subjects by becoming a trusted and engaged member of the group or community for an extended period of time. Ethnographers typically combine this method with other methods such as interviews and focus groups, content analysis, and historical and archival research. Often, the goal is to understand how group members understand themselves and the world around them.

- Historical and archival research—this approach typically involves locating, retrieving, and analyzing documents and images from the past. The sources, called *primary sources,* are often located in archives, special collections, and libraries, but they may be found anywhere. Researchers comb through sources to identify evidence that supports or contradicts a theory or argument. Cultural sociologists doing historical research frequently rely upon *secondary sources*, which are studies produced by other researchers using primary sources.

- Interviews and focus groups—an interview is the most direct and personal method for collecting data. Interviews can be *informal*, resembling casual conversation, or *formal*, with the interviewer following a structured protocol. They can be conducted in-person or by using some form of telecommunication, such as the telephone or Internet. A focus group is an interview with several interviewees at once. Focus groups allow the researcher to examine group dynamics that are not present in one-on-one settings.

- Mixed methods—not a method per se, but rather any methodology that combines both qualitative and quantitative methods in a single study. Examples would include combining statistical analysis of neighborhood-level demographic data with in-depth interviews with residents of those neighborhoods; or conducting ethnographic fieldwork in a community beset by job loss and measuring changes in income and status using quantitative data.

- Statistical analysis—a large group of quantitative methods for comparing one or more variables in a data set. Statistical analyses can be *descriptive,* used to describe data, such as calculating averages or conducting a frequency analysis, or they can be *inferential,* used to make estimates, predictions, and generalizations based on samples of populations.
- Survey research—in its most general form, this method involves asking questions of respondents and recording their answers. Interviews and focus groups are one kind of survey. The other most common form is the questionnaire. When surveying small numbers of respondents, results are most often handled with qualitative methods. When the number of respondents is large, results are typically handled through statistical analysis.

Given the variety of methods available, how does one know which to choose? *Study design* is the term that sociologists use to describe how they select a method or methods appropriate for their chosen research topic. A well-designed study is one where the logic and rationale for selecting the methods are clearly defined and persuasive. Generally speaking, sociologists want to know that the chosen method offers the best chance of capturing data that will answer the research question.[14]

## CULTURE AS MEANING MAKING

What the six elements of culture share, despite their obvious differences, is that they all involve meaning and meaning-making of one kind or another. If one had to offer a short definition of cultural sociology, most cultural sociologists could agree to this one: *Cultural sociology is the study of meaning-making.*

What, then, is meaning-making? This seemingly simple and direct question is anything but. Answering it thoroughly would require wading into deep philosophical waters and pondering vexing questions about episte-

---

14. Readers with prior knowledge of social science methodology will have noticed that the methods listed above tend to be more qualitative than quantitative. This is largely because many of the variables cultural sociologists wish to observe are not easily captured by numerical measurement. However, there is a new generation of cultural sociologists who have argued strenuously for the incorporation of quantitative analysis into the cultural sociologist's methodological toolkit. See, for example, Mohr (1998) and Perrin (2004).

mology (how we know what we know) and ontology (the nature of existence and being in the world).[15]

So let me answer in a more simplified way: meaning-making involves reflecting on one's experiences and creating *symbols*, *categories*, and *interpretations* to make sense of those experiences. *Symbols* are what people use to represent things to themselves and to others. For instance, words are symbols that people use to reference things and communicate ideas. There are, of course, many other kinds of symbols, such as images and icons. *Categories* are bounded sets of things that appear to be more similar than different. When people encounter new experiences and things, they create new categories by drawing symbolic boundaries that set up the systems of formal and informal classification used to bring order to the chaos of the world. When things in the world change, some categories and classifications become outdated, but if they remain useful and practical for making sense of the world, they persist.

*Interpretations* are the stories and narratives people devise, individually and in concert with others, to make sense of the symbols and categories used to represent the world. When people can't make sense of them they become confused and disoriented.

Why is meaning-making important? Think of the alternative. A life without meaning would be extremely difficult to live, wouldn't it? People must have reasons to get up every day and go to school or work, to fulfill obligations to themselves and to others, and to sacrifice their time and energy in pursuit of sometimes intangible goals. We do these things because we find them meaningful and if we begin to find them meaningless, we stop doing them if we can. Sometimes—and this is perhaps most often the case with our jobs—we can't stop doing them because of constraints (everybody needs money). In that case, we are stuck with going through the motions, which is depressing and demoralizing for everyone involved.

The meanings we assign to actions and structures in our lives are crucial for helping us feel that we lead satisfying and fulfilling lives. Without meanings that sustain us, we can be overcome by distress, anxiety, depression, fear, and other negative emotions that can contribute to illness and

---

15. Sociologists George Herbert Mead and Charles Cooley addressed these questions within the philosophical context of American pragmatism. For more on the sociological significance of this philosophical tradition, see Shalin (2007) and Gross (2008).

early death (Berkman et al. 2000; Kubzansky & Kawachi 2000). It is not stretching things too far to say that meaning-making can be a matter of life and death. For this reason alone, understanding how meanings are made and the strategies for using them are important questions, the answers to which can help contribute to our individual well-being (see Hall & Lamont, p. 532).

But meanings are not just important to us as individuals. Meanings are essential sources of group belonging and help to establish what sociologists call social cohesion. They are like a glue that binds us to those who have assigned the same meanings to the world that we have. Groups need that glue to attract and retain members, to grow in size, and subsequently, to grow in power and influence. If a group becomes powerful and influential enough, its meanings may sustain a social movement—a mass mobilization of individuals who recognize they are taking part in something larger than themselves. If the movement gains enough social power, it becomes not just popular, but dominant, and will seek to reform old institutions or create new ones devoted to perpetuating and further popularizing its particular worldviews, a process called *cultural diffusion* (see Kaufman and Patterson, p. 218).

Individuals form small groups that can grow into social institutions by putting meaning-making into action and practicing what they preach until enough converts emerge to create a movement; this can eventually produce an institution or a new structure. Maybe one day Burning Man—conceived some 25 years ago by an unemployed landscape gardener named Larry Harvey—will become large enough and influential enough to effect lasting social change.[16] Many of its participants would say it already has.

As you read through this volume, you'll encounter numerous affirmations, refinements, and outright rebuttals to the simple model of cultural sociology I've drawn here; namely, that it is the study of how human agency is linked to social structure by cultural elements, and how yesterday's cultural elements can become the structures of today. There are many ways of conceptualizing the field. I have merely tried to do my job as a teacher, which is to provide a heuristic—a way of discovering something new—that

16. Anyone interested in Burning Man would do well to get acquainted with the writings of Larry Harvey. Many of his most influential ideas are crystallized in Harvey (2000). See also his other writings collected at www.burningman.com/whatisburningman/lectures/la_vie.html (accessed September 21, 2012).

will serve you as you explore the intellectual landscape of cultural sociology. Your job as a student is not simply to watch and observe how cultural sociologists do their work, but to engage in the process of discovery on your own. As we Burners like to say, "No Spectators!"

## References

Alexander, Jeffrey. 2003. *The Meanings of Social Life: A Cultural Sociology.* New York: Oxford University Press.

Berkman, Lisa, Thomas Glass, Ian Brissette, and Teresa Seeman. 2000. "From Social Integration to Health: Durkheim in the New Millenium." *Social Science & Medicine* 51: 843–857.

Blumer, Herbert. 1969. *Symbolic Interactionism: Perspective and Method.* Berkeley: University of California Press.

Bourdieu, Pierre. 1990. *The Logic of Practice.* Stanford: Stanford University Press.

Calhoun, Craig and Richard Sennett, eds. 2007. *Practicing Culture.* New York: Routledge.

Chen, Katherine. 2006. "Authenticity at Burning Man." *Contexts* 8(3): 65–67.

———. 2009. *Enabling Creative Chaos: The Organization Behind the Burning Man Event.* Chicago: University of Chicago Press.

Dillman, Richard. 2012. "Incredible Radio Tales." www.kwmr.org/show/260. Accessed September, 26 2012.

DiMaggio, Paul. 1997. "Culture and Cognition." *Annual Review of Sociology* 23: 263–287.

Doherty, Brian. 2004. *This Is Burning Man: The Rise of a New American Underground.* Boston: Little, Brown and Co.

Epstein, Stephen. 2008. "Culture and Science/Technology: Rethinking Knowledge, Power, Materiality, and Nature." *Annals of the American Academy of Political and Social Science* 619 (September): 165–182.

Gilmore, Lee. 2010. *Theater in a Crowded Fire: Ritual and Spirituality at Burning Man.* Berkeley: University of California Press.

Gilmore, Lee and Mark Van Proyen, eds. 2005. *Afterburn: Reflections on Burning Man.* Albuquerque: University of New Mexico Press.

Griswold, Wendy. 2008. *Culture and Societies in a Changing World.* 3rd ed. Thousand Oaks: Sage.

Gross, Neil. 2008. *Richard Rorty: The Making of an American Philosopher.* Chicago: University of Chicago Press.

Holt, William G., ed. 2005. *Sociology of Culture: A Teaching Guide.* American Sociological Association, Washington, DC.

Jacobs, Mark and Nancy Weiss Hanrahan, eds. 2005. *The Blackwell Companion to the Sociology of Culture*. London: Blackwell.

Kozinets, Robert. 2002. "Can Consumers Escape the Market? Emancipatory Illuminations from Burning Man," *Journal of Consumer Research* 29 (June): 20–38.

Kubzansky, Laura and Ichiro Kawachi. 2000. "Going to the Heart of the Matter: Negative Emotions and Coronary Heart Disease." *Psychosomatic Research* 48:323–337.

Lamont, Michèle and Virag Molnàr. 2002. "The Study of Boundaries in the Social Sciences" *Annual Review of Sociology* 28:167–95.

Lave, Jean and Etienne Wenger. 1991. *Situated Learning: Legitimate Peripheral Participation*. Cambridge: Cambridge University Press.

Lee, Orville and Kate Lennenberg, eds. 2000. *Course Syllabi on the Sociology of Culture*. American Sociological Association, Washington, DC.

Long, Elizabeth, ed. 1997. *From Sociology to Cultural Studies: New Perspectives*. New York: Blackwell Publishers.

Mills, C. Wright. 1948. *The New Men of Power: America's Labor Leaders* (with the assistance of Helen Schneider). New York: Harcourt Brace and Co.

———. 1951. *White Collar: The American Middle Classes*. New York: Oxford University Press.

———. 1956. *The Power Elite*. New York: Oxford University Press.

Mohr, John. 1998. "Measuring Meaning Structures." *Annual Review of Sociology* 24:345–70.

Molotch, Harvey. 2003. *Where Stuff Comes From: How Toasters, Toilets, Cars, Computers, and Many Other Things Come to Be As They Are*. New York: Routledge.

Mukerji, Chandra. 1994. "Towards a Sociology of Material Culture: Science Studies, Cultural Studies, and the Meanings of Things." Pp. 143–62 in *The Sociology of Culture: Emerging Perspectives*, edited by Diana Crane. New York: Blackwell.

Perrin, Andrew. 2004. "Who's Afraid of Linear Regression?" *Culture* (newsletter of the Sociology of Culture section of the ASA) 18:3 (Spring), and reply to critics, *Culture* 19:1 (Autumn).

Powell, Walter W. and Paul J. DiMaggio. 1991. *The New Institutionalism in Organizational Analysis*. Chicago: Chicago International Press.

Shalin. Dmitri. 2007. "Signing in the Flesh: Notes on a Pragmatist Hermeneutics." *Sociological Theory* 25: 193–224.

Small, Mario, David Harding, and Michèle Lamont. 2010. "Reconsidering Culture and Poverty." *Annals of the American Academy of Political and Social Science* 629:6, 6–27.

Turner, Fred. 2009. "Burning Man at Google: A Cultural Infrastructure for New Media Production." *New Media and Society* 11(1&2, April): 145–166.

Tuner, Jonathan, ed. 2001. *Handbook of Sociological Theory*. New York: Springer.

Wolff, Janet. 1999. "Cultural Studies and the Sociology of Culture." *Invisible Culture*. www.rochester.edu/in_visible_culture/issue1/wolff/wolff.html. Accessed October 1, 2012.

Wray, Matt. 1995. "Burning Man and the Rituals of Capitalism." *Bad Subjects*. http://bad.eserver.org/issues/1995/21/wray.html. Accessed October 1, 2012.

———. 2006. *Not Quite White: White Trash and the Boundaries of Whiteness*. Durham: Duke University Press.

# ACKNOWLEDGMENTS

In 2008, when Karl Bakeman, Norton's sociology editor extraordinaire, first approached me about this project, I didn't hesitate. I had been teaching my sociology students about culture for years and had been frustrated at the relative lack of cultural sociology readers and textbooks. In the years it has taken to complete this reader, new readers and textbooks have appeared, as well as two new academic journals of cultural sociology. Springtime for cultural sociology has arrived and the field is blossoming. Karl's apparently limitless enthusiasm for cultural sociology reflects this changing landscape, to be sure, but more than that, his enthusiasm and unflagging support are major reasons why anthologies like this come to flower the field in the first place.

Special thanks go out to the staff at Norton, who have been wonderful to work with every step of the way. Megan Jackson did heroic work on permissions, Rebecca Charney offered initial guidance in compiling the manuscript, and Kate Feighery and Melissa Atkin shepherded my untidy pages through the finishing stages.

At Temple, I benefitted from the assistance of several talented students. In the early stages of the project, Laura Martin helped identify and vet dozens of candidate articles and excerpts and also drafted examples of study questions, many of which survived multiple rounds of edits and are included in the book. Jorge Ballanas provided key research assistance during the middle stage of the project and Ashley Mang proved to be up to the task of helping me complete the reader. Ashley's keen editorial eye and sharp mind took off lots of the rough edges. Thanks also go to Rosario Espinal and Robert Kaufman, successive chairs of the department of sociology at Temple, for their moral support. Special thanks are also due to Magali Sarfatti Larson for early encouragement and for sharing course materials originally developed by Diana Crane at the University of Pennsylvania. Robin Pacifici-Wagner offered key words of advice, as did Eric Klinenberg and David Grazian. Additional thanks are due to Laura Grindstaff, Jason Kaufman, Michèle Lamont, and Dustin Kidd for sharing their course syllabi and to the twenty-nine anonymous reviewers who responded to a survey about the initial proposal with excellent comments and suggestions, a great number of which have been incorporated into the final manuscript.

This project was conceived and developed when I was a Robert Wood Johnson Foundation Health and Society Scholar at Harvard University. I'm grateful to the foundation and to my Harvard mentors: Lisa Berkman, Allan Brandt, Ichiro Kawachi, Matthew Miller, and Charles Rosenberg. I'm especially grateful to Michèle Lamont, who taught me a great deal about cultural sociology and who graciously agreed to pen the foreword for this anthology.

Finally, my greatest thanks go to my family, Maxine, Zack, and Jill, who grew tired of hearing me say I still had work to do, but never once complained (not loudly enough for me to hear, anyway). You make the search for meaning meaningful.

# CULTURAL SOCIOLOGY

## AN INTRODUCTORY READER

# PART ONE

# FOUNDATIONS AND DEFINITIONS

O N A SEPTEMBER day in London in 1854, a British doctor named John Snow watched anxiously as city officials removed the handle from a public water pump located on Broad Street in the overcrowded and impoverished area of the city known as Soho. Snow was convinced that the well was contaminated and that it was the source of a deadly outbreak of cholera that had killed hundreds of residents in just a few weeks. City health officials remained deeply skeptical, but they went along with his plan.

In the 1850s, the prevailing scientific consensus was that cholera and other diseases, like fevers, were caused by the inhalation of miasma, or foul-smelling odors caused by filth. The idea that something invisible called "germs" was responsible for the origins and spread of infectious diseases was considered highly speculative and unscientific. Snow represented the fringe viewpoint that whatever the origins of cholera, it was being spread not by miasma, but by water. Over the course of the outbreak, which began in late August, he worked diligently to prove his idea, accumulating evidence about the number of cases that could be tied to exposure to the Broad Street pump water. By September, Snow had built enough evidence to persuade reluctant officials to remove the pump handle. Within days, the number of new cases of cholera plummeted.

Amazingly, the scientific community remained unconvinced of the connection and resisted the contagionist theory that Snow's intervention seemed to have proved. The miasmatist viewpoint continued to dominate medical and scientific explanations for a few more decades before finally being discredited in the late nineteenth century. Despite the fact that he had no theory about germs or bacteria to explain exactly how cholera worked to kill its victims, Snow is, to this day, regarded as the founder of modern epidemiology, the science of diseases and the populations they afflict.

Alfred North Whitehead, the British mathematician and philosopher, once famously remarked that "A science that hesitates to forget its founders is lost." By "science," he meant the natural sciences like physics, biology, and chemistry, but do his words apply to the social sciences? To cultural sociology? If so, what's the point of reading what founding sociologists thought and said about culture? Shouldn't sociologists just follow Whitehead's advice and forget them? In other words: Do students really need to know all this stuff? This is a perennial question and it's a fair one. Whitehead questioned the value in returning to the founding figures of a discipline, so why is your professor not listening?

It is true that sociologists sometimes talk about our founders and their theories in reverent tones, as if we were tour guides in the cathedral of sociological knowledge, where every image, icon, and relic is supposedly laden with hidden meanings and insights that only the properly initiated can grasp. But when we talk that way, we have stopped being sociologists and have instead become intellectual historians. That is all well and good, but it means we are apt to lose sight of the real value of the sociological tradition for us today.

The value lies not in the fact that the tradition contains theories, concepts, and methods that help you and me understand the past (although surely it does), nor in helping us comprehend the singular genius of the founders (although that too is a worthy goal). The real value of the sociological tradition lies instead in helping us to make sense of the present. It serves as a model for coming to grips with an ever-changing social world where the principles and laws of the natural sciences seldom seem to apply. We should read the classics not to divine what Marx, Durkheim, Weber, and others thought about the changes wrought by the advent of capitalism, modernism, urbanism, and secularism in their time. Rather, we should read them in order to find tools that enable us to think about the changes wrought by advanced capitalism, postmodernism, globalism, and the rise of religious fundamentalism in our time. We should try viewing our world through their eyes.

On the other hand, understanding how basic concepts in science change over time is important. The classic work on this question is Thomas Kuhn's *The Structure of Scientific Revolutions* (1970). Kuhn argued that while science is designed to be a contentious way of knowing, with scientists pitting their arguments and evidence against other scientists, the historical evolution of scientific thought and practice regularly produced periods and lines of consensus. At such times, the scientific community agrees on the important questions that must be asked, as well as the appropriate methods and techniques for asking them. Kuhn called these periods and lines of consensus "paradigms." Well-established paradigms governed what he called "normal" science, research that was widely recognized as important and mainstream. Normal science was good at producing basic scientific facts and accumulating coherent descriptions of the natural world, but incapable of producing new scientific breakthroughs or revolutions. Scientific knowledge advanced not only through the linear accumulation of facts, but through revolutionary shifts in the paradigms that governed the production of scientific knowledge. Some of what is today considered "fringe" science will become the paradigmatic normal science of tomorrow, just as the miasma paradigm gave way to the contagion-germ paradigm, and the idea that foul odors can kill us has become a laughingstock.

Kuhn's arguments, like Whitehead's before him, were focused on the natural sciences. Can they be applied to social science as well? They can and should be, with one important caveat. In Kuhn's formulation, new paradigms not only displace, but often discredit older science. The new paradigm supplants the old and the old ways are consigned to history. In contrast, the founders of sociology—Marx, Durkheim, Weber, and Simmel—asked questions and defined ways of thinking about the social world that remain central to the ways that sociologists look at the world today. Their foundational theories—and those of others included here, like Horkheimer and Adorno—are paradigms in the sense that each offers very specific definitions, asks very specific kinds of questions, and presents a challenge to other paradigms. But they are not like Kuhn's paradigms because, typically, they do not supplant and discredit each other over time. So how should students think about them? To invoke a common metaphor, the social theories of the founders are "lenses" that can be used to view different aspects of the social world.

In the 2011 Steven Soderbergh film, *Contagion,* a deadly new virus makes the leap from bat to pig to human, inflicting flu-like symptoms that quickly turn lethal as the potent pathogen runs its biological course. The heroes of Soderbergh's cautionary tale are the epidemiologists, molecular biologists, and geneticists who track the virus to its origin, decode its genetic structure, and produce an effective vaccine. Like John Snow and their real-life counterparts, these scientists worked feverishly during the course of an outbreak to isolate causal agents, map the timing and location of deaths, and discover interventions and cures to stop the disease in its tracks. They succeed in real life, as they do in the film, not because they adhere to the principles of the discredited theory of miasma, but because they have embraced the theoretical lens of John Snow's epidemiology. Their search for the pump handle—the elusive source of the disease—pays off. The epidemic is conquered.

What lessons are there for students of cultural sociology as they read these foundational thinkers? First, the ways that the founders think about culture are, in the long run, often more important than the specific things they say about culture. It is the way they posed questions that remains influential, rather than the answers they gave. Second, if Kuhn is right, one can predict that new paradigms in cultural sociology will emerge over time, just as one can be confident that the new paradigms will not fully supplant the old. Revolutions in social scientific thought are few and far between. Third, the only way to recognize new paradigms is knowing what the older paradigms were. If it is true that in order to advance, cultural sociology should "forget" its founders, it's equally true that you can never forget something you did not know. Take the time to immerse yourself in these readings, soaking up what you can of the theories, concepts, and ideas. The point lies in understanding both what existed before and how what followed is different and why.

# 1

# THE GERMAN IDEOLOGY

KARL MARX AND FRIEDRICH ENGELS

"The ideas of the ruling class are in every epoch the ruling ideas." With this simple phrase, Karl Marx (1818–1883) sought to undermine a common way of thinking about culture in the nineteenth century. For the educated classes, "culture" referred to the very best ideas, values, and artistic expressions handed down over the ages, the kinds of things one found celebrated in books, museums, and symphony halls. "Cultured" people were expected to know and revere these cultural treasures and to recognize in them the very best of civilization. Marx's point was that these "ruling ideas" should be seen for what they really were: ideas and values that tended to reflect the collective self-image of elites and to affirm and legitimate the existing social order. Far from being a sacred tradition that elevated everyone through intellectual and spiritual edification, culture in Marx's view was a self-serving belief system installed by each new ruling class. Their ideas become common ideas and, over time, appear to be the natural order of things, "just the way things are." By accepting the elite cultural mindset as natural, people miss the fact that it does not reflect or speak to everyone's interests, only the elite's. What was needed, Marx, argued, was for non-elites to reject the ideas of the ruling class and develop a class consciousness of their own.

While Marx is regarded as one of sociology's founding figures, his influence is not limited to this discipline. His intellectual work spans across philosophy, history, and the social sciences, and his political writings helped spark revolutions around the world. As explained in

**the Introduction, his ideas were central to the development of forms of cultural analysis such as Cultural Studies. While few cultural sociologists today would identify as Marxists, his work remains a touchstone for cultural sociologists who focus on the cultural production of ideas, knowledge, and ideology.**

The ideas of the ruling class are in every epoch the ruling ideas: i.e., the class which is the ruling *material* force of society, is at the same time its ruling *intellectual* force. The class which has the means of material production at its disposal, has control at the same time over the means of mental production, so that thereby, generally speaking, the ideas of those who lack the means of mental production are subject to it. The ruling ideas are nothing more than the ideal expression of the dominant material relationships, the dominant material relationships grasped as ideas; hence of the relationships which make the one class the ruling one, therefore, the ideas of its dominance. The individuals composing the ruling class possess among other things consciousness, and therefore think. Insofar, therefore, as they rule as a class and determine the extent and compass of an epoch, it is self-evident that they do this in its whole range, hence among other things rule also as thinkers, as producers of ideas, and regulate the production and distribution of the ideas of their age: thus their ideas are the ruling ideas of the epoch. For instance, in an age and in a country where royal power, aristocracy and bourgeoisie are contending for mastery and where, therefore, mastery is shared, the doctrine of the separation of powers proves to be the dominant idea and is expressed as an "eternal law."

The division of labour, which we have already seen above as one of the chief forces of history up till now, manifests itself also in the ruling class as the division of mental and material labour, so that inside this class one part appears as the thinkers of the class (its active, conceptive ideologists, who make the perfecting of the illusion of the class about itself their chief source of livelihood), while the others' attitude to these ideas and illusions is more passive and receptive, because they are in reality the active members of this class and have less time to make up illusions and ideas about themselves. Within this class this cleavage can even develop into a certain opposition and hostility between the two parts, which, however, in the case of a practical collision, in which the class itself is endangered, automatically comes to nothing, in which case there also vanishes the semblance that the ruling ideas were not the ideas of the ruling class and had a power distinct from the power of this class. . . .

If now in considering the course of history we detach the ideas of the ruling class from the ruling class itself and attribute to them an independent existence, if we confine ourselves to saying that these or those ideas were dominant at a given time, without bothering ourselves about the conditions of production and the producers of these ideas, if we thus ignore the individuals and world conditions which are the source of the ideas, we can say, for instance, that during the time that the aristocracy was dominant, the concepts honour, loyalty, etc., were dominant, during the dominance of the bourgeoisie the concepts freedom, equality, etc. The ruling class itself on the whole imagines this to be so. This conception of history, which is common to all historians, particularly since the eighteenth century, will necessarily come up against the phenomenon that increasingly abstract ideas hold sway, i.e., ideas which increasingly take on the form of universality. For each new class which puts itself in the place of one ruling before it, is compelled, merely in order to carry through its aim, to represent its interest as the common interest of all the members of society, that is, expressed in ideal form: it has to give its ideas the form of universality, and represent them as the only rational, universally valid ones. The class making a revolution appears from the very start, if only because it is opposed to a *class*, not as a class but as the representative of the whole of society; it appears as the whole mass of society confronting the one ruling class.[1] It can do this because, to start with, its interest really is more connected with the common interest of all other non-ruling classes, because under the pressure of hitherto existing conditions its interest has not yet been able to develop as the particular interest of a particular class. Its victory, therefore, benefits also many individuals of the other classes which are not winning a dominant position, but only insofar as it now puts these individuals in a position to raise themselves into the ruling class. When the French bourgeoisie overthrew the power of the aristocracy, it thereby made it possible for many proletarians to raise themselves above the proletariat, but only insofar as they became bourgeois. Every new class, therefore, achieves its hegemony only on a broader basis than that of the class ruling previously, whereas the opposition of the

---

1. Marginal note by Marx: "Universality corresponds to (1) the class versus the estate, (2) the competition, world-wide intercourse, etc., (3) the great numerical strength of the ruling class, (4) the illusion of the *common* interests (in the beginning this illusion is true), (5) the delusion of the ideologists and the division of labour."

non-ruling class against the new ruling class later develops all the more sharply and profoundly. Both these things determine the fact that the struggle to be waged against this new ruling class, in its turn, aims at a more decided and radical negation of the previous conditions of society than could all previous classes which sought to rule.

This whole semblance, that the rule of a certain class is only the rule of certain ideas, comes to a natural end, of course, as soon as class rule in general ceases to be the form in which society is organised, that is to say, as soon as it is no longer necessary to represent a particular interest as general or the "general interest" as ruling.

Once the ruling ideas have been separated from the ruling individuals and, above all, from the relationships which result from a given stage of the mode of production, and in this way the conclusion has been reached that history is always under the sway of ideas, it is very easy to abstract from these various ideas "*the* idea," the notion, etc., as the dominant force in history, and thus to understand all these separate ideas and concepts as "forms of self-determination" on the part of *the* concept developing in history. It follows then naturally, too, that all the relationships of men can be derived from the concept of man, man as conceived, the essence of man, *Man*. This has been done by the speculative philosophers. Hegel himself confesses at the end of the *Geschichtsphilosophie* that he "has considered the progress of the *concept* only" and has represented in history the "true *theodicy*." Now one can go back again to the producers of the "concept," to the theorists, ideologists and philosophers, and one comes then to the conclusion that the philosophers, the thinkers as such, have at all times been dominant in history: a conclusion, as we see, already expressed by Hegel. The whole trick of proving the hegemony of the spirit in history (hierarchy Stirner calls it) is thus confined to the following three efforts.

No. 1. One must separate the ideas of those ruling for empirical reasons, under empirical conditions and as empirical individuals, from these actual rulers, and thus recognise the rule of ideas or illusions in history.

No. 2. One must bring an order into this rule of ideas, prove a mystical connection among the successive ruling ideas, which is managed by understanding them as "acts of self-determination on the part of the concept" (this is possible because by virtue of their empirical basis these ideas are really connected with one another and because, conceived as *mere* ideas, they become self-distinctions, distinctions made by thought).

No. 3. To remove the mystical appearance of this "self-determining concept" it is changed into a person—"Self-Consciousness"—or, to appear thoroughly materialistic, into a series of persons, who represent the "concept" in history, into the "thinkers," the "philosophers," the ideologists, who again are understood as the manufacturers of history, as the "council of guardians," as the rulers.[2] Thus the whole body of materialistic elements has been removed from history and now full rein can be given to the speculative steed.

Whilst in ordinary life every shopkeeper is very well able to distinguish between what somebody professes to be and what he really is, our historians have not yet won even this trivial insight. They take every epoch at its word and believe that everything it says and imagines about itself is true.

This historical method which reigned in Germany and especially the reason why, must be understood from its connection with the illusion of ideologists in general, e.g., the illusions of the jurists, politicians (of the practical statesmen among them, too), from the dogmatic dreamings and distortions of these fellows; this is explained perfectly easily from their practical position in life, their job, and the division of labour.

# STUDY QUESTIONS

1. Marx writes about a split in the ruling class—shared by all classes—that follows the basic division of labor between mental and material (or manual) labor. What does he mean and why is this important for his argument?
2. Why does each new ruling class come to believe that its interests are common to all members of society?

---

2. Marginal note by Marx: "Man = the 'rational human spirit.'"

# 2

# CLASSIFYING THINGS FROM
## *PRIMITIVE CLASSIFICATION*

ÉMILE DURKHEIM AND MARCEL MAUSS

"One of these things is not like the other. One of these things just doesn't belong." Remember that classic *Sesame Street* bit? In one episode, Cookie Monster is surrounded by four plates, three of which have two cookies and one of which has three cookies. "Can you guess which one of these things is not like the other thing," he sings, "before I finish my song?" Of course, before he can finish the song, he gobbles up all the cookies.

This regular segment of the show was devoted to helping kids learn about different classes of objects and how to group things together and exclude things that don't logically fit. Classification is an issue in philosophy and a foundational problem in psychology (and now, neuroscience) because it goes right to the heart of basic questions: How do people make sense of the world? How do individuals create order and structure out of the chaotic flow of information coming from our senses? In this reading, Émile Durkheim (1858–1917) and Marcel Mauss (1872–1950) argue that far from being something that individual minds construct for themselves, human classification schemes are built up collectively, by groups of individuals working together to arrive at agreed-upon systems for categorizing things. They are built up over hundreds and thousands of years and are the result of a complex and dynamic process of making distinctions that allow for meaningful comparisons. Different groups of people have developed very different classification schemes, and this is one of the things sociologists mean when we refer to "cultural differences." You've probably heard that Eskimos have over two hundred words for snow. That's not true, but the larger point remains: People from different parts of the world have different ways of grouping things. Durkheim and Mauss argue, in effect, that to understand the basic operations of culture, one needs to understand the social nature of "the classificatory function."

# THE PROBLEM

The discoveries of contemporary psychology have thrown into promi-nence the frequent illusion that we regard certain mental operations as simple and elementary when they are really very complex. We now know what a multiplicity of elements make up the mechanism by virtue of which we construct, project, and localize in space our representations of the tangible world. But this operation of dissociation has been only very rarely applied as yet to operations which are properly speaking logi-cal. The faculties of definition, deduction, and induction are generally considered as immediately given in the constitution of the individual understanding. Admittedly, it has been known for a long time that, in the course of history, men have learned to use these diverse functions better and better. But it is thought that there have been no important changes except in the way of employing them; that in their essential fea-tures they have been fully formed as long as mankind has existed. It has not even been imagined that they might have been formed by a painful combination of elements borrowed from extremely different sources, quite foreign to logic, and laboriously organized. And this conception of the matter was not at all surprising so long as the development of logical faculties was thought to belong simply to individual psychology, so long as no one had the idea of seeing in these methods of scientific thought veritable social institutions whose origin sociology alone can retrace and explain.

The preceding remarks apply particularly to what we might call the classificatory function. Logicians and even psychologists commonly regard the procedure which consists in classifying things, events, and facts about the world into kinds and species, subsuming them one under the other, and determining their relations of inclusion or exclusion, as being simple, innate, or at least as instituted by the powers of the individual alone. Logicians consider the hierarchy of concepts as given in things and as directly expressible by the infinite chain of syllogisms. Psychologists think that the simple play of the association of ideas, and of the laws of contiguity and similarity between mental states, suffice to explain the binding together of images, their organization into concepts, and into concepts classed in relation to each other. It is true that recently a less simple theory of psychological development has come to the fore. The hypothesis has been put forward, namely, that ideas are grouped not only according to their mutual affinities but also according to the relations they bear to movements. Nevertheless, whatever may be the superiority of this explanation, it still represents classification as a product of individual activity.

There is however one fact which in itself would suffice to indicate that this operation has other origins: it is that the way in which we understand it and practise it is relatively recent. For us, in fact, to classify things is to arrange them in groups which are distinct from each other, and are separated by clearly determined lines of demarcation. From the fact that modern evolutionism denies that there is an insuperable abyss between them, it does not follow that it so merges them as to claim the right to deduce one from the other. At the bottom of our conception of class there is the idea of a circumscription with fixed and definite outlines. Now one could almost say that this conception of classification does not go back before Aristotle. Aristotle was the first to proclaim the existence and the reality of specific differences, to show that the means was cause, and that there was no direct passage from one genus to another. Plato had far less sense of this distinction and this hierarchical organization, since for him genera were in a way homogeneous and could be reduced to each other by dialectic.

Not only has our present notion of classification a history, but this history itself implies a considerable prehistory. It would be impossible to exaggerate, in fact, the state of indistinction from which the human mind developed. Even today a considerable part of our popular literature, our myths, and our religions is based on a fundamental confusion of all images and ideas. They are not separated from each other, as it were, with any clarity. Metamorphoses, the transmission of qualities, the substitution of persons, souls, and bodies, beliefs about the materialization of spirits and the spiritualization of material objects, are the elements of religious thought or of folklore. Now the very idea of such transmutations could not arise if things were represented by delimited and classified concepts. The Christian dogma of transubstantiation is a consequence of this state of mind and may serve to prove its generality.

However, this way of thinking exists today only as a survival, and even in this form it is found only in certain distinctly localized functions of collective thought. But there are innumerable societies whose entire natural history lies in etiological tales, all their speculation about vegetable and animal species in metamorphoses, all scientific conjecture in divinatory cycles, magical circles and squares. In China, in all the Far East, and in modern India, as well as in ancient Greece and Rome, ideas about sympathetic actions, symbolic correspondences, and astrological influences not only were or are very widespread, but exhausted or still exhaust collective knowledge. They all presuppose the belief in the possibility of the transformation of the most heterogeneous things one into another, and consequently the more or less complete absence of definite concepts.

If we descend to the least evolved societies known, those which the Germans call by the rather vague term *Naturvölker*, we shall find an even more general mental confusion. Here, the individual himself loses his personality. There is a complete lack of distinction between him and his exterior soul or his totem. He and his "fellow-animal" together compose a single personality. The identification is such that the man assumes the characteristics of the thing or animal with which he is thus united. For example, on Mabuiag Island people of the crocodile clan are thought to have the temperament of the crocodile: they are proud, cruel, always ready for battle. Among certain Sioux, there is a section of the tribe which is called red, and which comprises the clans of the mountain lion, buffalo, and elk, all animals characterized by their violent instincts; the members of these clans are from birth warriors, whereas the farmers, people who are naturally peaceful, belong to clans of which the totems are essentially pacific animals.

If it is thus with people, all the more reason that it should be the same with things. Not only is there complete indifferentiation between sign and thing, name and person, places and inhabitants, but, to adopt a very exact remark made by von den Steinen concerning the Bakairi and the Bororo, for the primitive the principle of *generatio aequivoca* is proved. The Bororo sincerely imagines himself to be a parrot; at least, though he assumes the characteristic form only after he is dead, in this life he is to that animal what the caterpillar is to the butterfly. . . . Animals, people, and inanimate objects were originally almost always conceived as standing in relations of the most perfect identity to each other. The relations between the black cow and rain, between the white or red horse and the sun, are characteristic traits of the Indo-European tradition; and examples could be multiplied infinitely.

Besides, this state of mind does not differ appreciably from that which still, in each generation, serves as point of departure for the development of the individual. Consciousness at this point is only a continuous flow of representations which are lost one in another, and when distinctions begin to appear they are quite fragmentary. This is to the right, that to the left; that is past, this is present; this resembles that, this accompanies that. This is about all that even the adult mind could produce if education did not inculcate ways of thinking which it could never have established by its own efforts and which are the result of an entire historical development. It is obvious what a great difference there is between these rudimentary distinctions and groupings and what truly constitutes a classification.

Far, then, from man classifying spontaneously and by a sort of natural necessity, humanity in the beginning lacks the most indispensable conditions for the classificatory function. Further, it is enough to examine the very idea of classification to understand that man could not have found its essential elements in himself. A class is a group of things; and things do not present themselves to observation grouped in such a way. We may well perceive, more or less vaguely, their resemblances. But the simple fact of these resemblances is not enough to explain how we are led to group things which thus resemble each other, to bring them together in a sort of ideal sphere, enclosed by definite limits, which we call a class, a species, etc. We have no justification for supposing that our mind bears within it at birth, completely formed, the prototype of this elementary framework of all classification. Certainly, the word can help us to give a greater unity and consistency to the assemblage thus formed; but though the word is a means of realizing this grouping the better once its possibility has been conceived, it could not by itself suggest the idea of it. From another angle, to classify is not only to form groups; it means arranging these groups according to particular relations. We imagine them as co-ordinated, or subordinate one to the other, we say that some (the species) are included in others (the genera), that the former are subsumed under the latter. There are some which are dominant, others which are dominated, still others which are independent of each other. Every classification implies a hierarchical order for which neither the tangible world nor our mind gives us the model. We therefore have reason to ask where it was found. The very terms which we use in order to characterize it allow us to presume that all these logical notions have an extra-logical origin. We say that species of the same genera are connected by relations of kinship; we call certain classes "families"; did not the very word genus (*genre*) itself originally designate a group of relatives (γἐνος)? These facts lead us to the conjecture that the scheme of classification is not the spontaneous product of abstract understanding, but results from a process into which all sorts of foreign elements enter.

Naturally, these preliminary observations are in no way intended to resolve the problem, or even to prejudge its solution, but merely to show that there is a problem which must be posed. Far from being able to say that men classify quite naturally, by a sort of necessity of their individual understandings, we must on the contrary ask ourselves what could have led them to arrange their ideas in this way, and where they could have found the plan of this remarkable disposition. We cannot even dream of tackling this question in all its ramifications. But, having posed it, we should like to adduce certain evidences which, we believe, may elucidate it. The only way to answer it is to investigate the most rudimentary classifications made by mankind, in order to see with what elements they have been constructed.

# CONCLUSIONS

Primitive classifications are therefore not singular or exceptional, having no analogy with those employed by more civilized peoples; on the contrary, they seem to be connected, with no break in continuity, to the first scientific classifications. In fact, however different they may be in certain respects from the latter, they nevertheless have all their essential characteristics. First of all, like all sophisticated classifications, they are systems of hierarchized notions. Things are not simply arranged by them in the form of isolated groups, but these groups stand in fixed relationships to each other and together form a single whole. Moreover, these systems, like those of science, have a purely speculative purpose. Their object is not to facilitate action, but to advance understanding, to make intelligible the relations which exist between things. Given certain concepts which are considered to be fundamental, the mind feels the need to connect to them the ideas which it forms about other things. Such classifications are thus intended, above all, to connect ideas, to unify knowledge; as such, they may be said without inexactitude to be scientific, and to constitute a first philosophy of nature. The Australian does not divide the universe between the totems of his tribe with a view to regulating his conduct or even to justify his practice; it is because, the idea of the totem being cardinal for him, he is under a necessity to place everything else that he knows in relation to it. We may therefore think that the conditions on which these very ancient classifications depend may have played an important part in the genesis of the classificatory function in general.

Now it results from this study that the nature of these conditions is social. Far from it being the case, as Frazer seems to think, that the social relations of men are based on logical relations between things, in reality it is the former which have provided the prototype for the latter. According to him, men were divided into clans by a pre-existing classification of things; but, quite on the contrary, they classified things because they were divided by clans.

We have seen, indeed, how these classifications were modelled on the closest and most fundamental form of social organization. This, however, is not going far enough. Society was not simply a model which classificatory thought followed; it was its own divisions which served as divisions for the system of classification. The first logical categories were social categories; the first classes of things were classes of men, into which these things were integrated. It was because men were grouped, and thought of themselves in the form of groups, that in their ideas they grouped other things, and in the beginning the two modes of grouping were merged to the point of being indistinct. Moieties were the first genera; clans, the first species. Things were thought to be integral parts of society, and it was their place in society which determined their place in nature. We may even wonder whether the schematic manner in which genera are ordinarily conceived may not have depended in part on the same influences. It is a fact of current observation that the things which they comprise are generally imagined as situated in a sort of ideational milieu, with a more or less clearly delimited spatial circumscription. It is certainly not without cause that concepts and their interrelations have so often been represented by concentric and eccentric circles, interior and exterior to each other, etc. Might it not be that this tendency to imagine purely logical groupings in a form contrasting so much with their true nature originated in the fact that at first they were conceived in the form of social groups occupying, consequently, definite positions in space? And have we not in fact seen this spatial localization of genus and species in a fairly large number of very different societies?

Not only the external form of classes, but also the relations uniting them to each other, are of social origin. It is because human groups fit one into another—the sub-clan into the clan, the clan into the moiety, the moiety into the tribe—that groups of things are ordered in the same way. Their regular diminution in span, from genus to species, species to variety, and so on, comes from the equally diminishing extent presented by social groups as one leaves the largest and oldest and approaches the more recent and the more derivative. And if the totality of things is conceived as a single system, this is because society itself is seen in the same way. It is a whole, or rather it is *the* unique whole to which everything is related. Thus logical hierarchy is only another aspect of social hierarchy, and the unity of knowledge is nothing else than the very unity of the collectivity, extended to the universe.

Furthermore, the ties which unite things of the same group or different groups to each other are themselves conceived as social ties. We recalled in the beginning that the expressions by which we refer to these relations still have a moral significance; but whereas for us they are hardly more than metaphors, originally they meant what they said. Things of the same class were really considered as relatives of the individuals of the same social group, and consequently of each other. They are of "the same flesh," the same family. Logical relations are thus, in a sense, domestic relations. Sometimes, too, as we have seen, they are comparable at all points with those which exist between a master and an object possessed, between a chief and his subjects. We may even wonder whether the idea of the pre-eminence of genus over species, which is so strange from a positivistic point of view, may not be seen here in its rudimentary form. Just as, for the realist, the general idea dominates the individual, so the clan totem dominates those of the sub-clans and, still more, the personal totems of individuals; and wherever the moiety has retained its original stability it has a sort of primacy over the divisions of which it is composed and the particular things which are included in them. Though he may be essentially Wartwut and partially Moiwiluk, the Wotjobaluk described by Howitt is above all a Krokitch or a Gamutch. Among the Zuñi, the animals symbolizing the six main clans are set in sovereign charge over their respective subclans and over creatures of all kinds which are grouped with them.

But if the foregoing has allowed us to understand how the notion of classes, linked to each other in a single system, could have been born, we still do not know what the forces were which induced men to divide things as they did between the classes. From the fact that the external form of the classification was furnished by society, it does not necessarily follow that the way in which the framework was used is due to reasons of the same origin. *A priori* it is very possible that motives of a quite different order should have determined the way in which things were connected and merged, or else, on the contrary, distinguished and opposed.

The particular conception of logical connexions which we now have permits us to reject this hypothesis. We have just seen, in fact, that they are represented in the form of familial connexions, or as relations of economic or political subordination; so that the same sentiments which are the basis of domestic, social, and other kinds of organization have been effective in this logical division of things also. The latter are attracted or opposed to each other in the same way as men are bound by kinship or opposed in the vendetta. They are merged as members of the same family are merged by common sentiment. That some are subordinate to others is analogous in every respect to the fact that an object possessed appears inferior to its owner, and likewise the subject to his master. It is thus states of the collective mind (*âme*) which gave birth to these groupings, and these states moreover are manifestly affective. There are sentimental affinities between things as between individuals, and they are classed according to these affinities.

We thus arrive at this conclusion: it is possible to classify other things than concepts, and otherwise than in accordance with the laws of pure understanding. For in order for it to be possible for ideas to be systematically arranged for reasons of sentiment, it is necessary that they should not be pure ideas, but that they should themselves be products of sentiment. And in fact, for those who are called primitives, a species of things is not a simple object of knowledge but corresponds above all to a certain sentimental attitude. All kinds of affective elements combine in the representation made of it. Religious emotions, notably, not only give it a special tinge, but attribute to it the most essential properties of which it is constituted. Things are above all sacred or profane, pure or impure, friends or enemies, favourable or unfavourable; i.e. their most fundamental characteristics are only expressions of the way in which they affect social sensibility. The differences and resemblances which determine the fashion in which they are grouped are more affective than intellectual. This is how it happens that things change their nature, in a way, from society to society; it is because they affect the sentiments of groups differently. What is conceived in one as perfectly homogeneous is represented elsewhere as essentially heterogeneous. For us, space is formed of similar parts which are substitutable one for the other. We have seen, however, that for many peoples it is profoundly differentiated according to regions. This is because each region has its own affective value. Under the influence of diverse sentiments, it is connected with a special religious principle, and consequently it is endowed with virtues *sui generis* which distinguish it from all others. And it is this emotional value of notions which plays the preponderant part in the manner in which ideas are connected or separated. It is the dominant characteristic in classification.

# STUDY QUESTIONS

1. Durkheim and Mauss argue that classification systems are based on the structure of social groups. Why are classification systems important to cultural sociologists?
2. The relationship between the classification system and social organization is an example of how even very abstract ideas like time and space are closely connected with the ways we organize ourselves into groups. What other abstract concepts are influenced by social forms?

# 3

# THE METROPOLIS AND MENTAL LIFE

GEORG SIMMEL

If you were raised in an urban setting, you probably don't find the hustle and bustle of busy city streets to be particularly frightening or confusing. If, however, you grew up in a woodsy rural setting or a quiet, leafy suburb, chances are you'd find a visit to New York City's Times Square to be both thrilling and exhausting. Surrounded by tall buildings, thousands of pedestrians, massive billboards full of blinking lights, and taxis with blaring horns, you might be quickly overwhelmed and disoriented by the constant barrage of stimulation. It's like your mental apparatus isn't equipped to handle the scene. Indeed, Times Square can be too much for even seasoned New Yorkers.

In this famous essay, German sociologist Georg Simmel (1858–1918) ruminates on the meaning and emotional significance of the growth of cities. The effects, large and small, were of rapid urbanization in nineteenth-century Europe was of central concern to the founders of sociology. They noted that the mass transition from small, traditional, and rural agricultural communities to large, modern, and urban industrial cities was a source of major disruptions and transformations in how individuals saw themselves in relation to society. After all, cities grew by attracting millions of people from those rural, traditional places, none of whom had any idea about how to live comfortably in such density and proximity to strangers. Those who manage to assimilate successfully to the rigors of city life do so, Simmel suggests, by adopting a kind of emotional coldness, a reserved attitude that comes off as impersonal and flat to the newcomer. This flatness of affect and emotion, he goes on to say, was important in bringing about the historical rise of finance and money, as it both enabled and required urbanites to develop a kind of calculating rationality with respect to the strangers around them. Most significantly, Simmel says, the mental life of city dwellers is marked by greater freedom from the demands of the small group. City living is a condition of relative anonymity, but also one of greater autonomy. In this way, he suggests, the story of the rise of the city is also the story of the rise of the modern self: more socially disconnected, more calculating, and more rational compared to the pre-modern self.

The deepest problems of modern life derive from the claim of the individual to preserve the autonomy and individuality of his existence in the face of overwhelming social forces, of historical heritage, of external culture, and of the technique of life. The fight with nature which primitive man has to wage for his *bodily* existence attains in this modern form its latest transformation. The eighteenth century called upon man to free himself of all the historical bonds in the state and in religion, in morals and in economics. Man's nature, originally good and common to all, should develop unhampered. In addition to more liberty, the nineteenth century demanded the functional specialization of man and his work; this specialization makes one individual incomparable to another, and each of them indispensable to the highest possible extent. However, this specialization makes each man the more directly dependent upon the supplementary activities of all others. Nietzsche sees the full development of the individual conditioned by the most ruthless struggle of individuals; socialism believes in the suppression of all competition for the same reason. Be that as it may, in all these positions the same basic motive is at work: the person resists to being leveled down and worn out by a social-technological mechanism. An inquiry into the inner meaning of specifically modern life and its products, into the soul of the cultural body, so to speak, must seek to solve the equation which structures like the metropolis set up between the individual and the super-individual contents of life. Such an inquiry must answer the question of how the personality accommodates itself in the adjustments to external forces. This will be my task today.

The psychological basis of the metropolitan type of individuality consists in the *intensification of nervous stimulation* which results from the
swift and uninterrupted change of outer and inner stimuli. Man is a differentiating creature. His mind is stimulated by the difference between a
momentary impression and the one which preceded it. Lasting impressions,
impressions which differ only slightly from one another, impressions which
take a regular and habitual course and show regular and habitual contrasts—
all these use up, so to speak, less consciousness than does the rapid crowd-
ing of changing images, the sharp discontinuity in the grasp of a single
glance, and the unexpectedness of onrushing impressions. These are the
psychological conditions which the metropolis creates. With each crossing
of the street, with the tempo and multiplicity of economic, occupational
and social life, the city sets up a deep contrast with small town and rural
life with reference to the sensory foundations of psychic life. The metropolis exacts from man as a discriminating creature a different amount of
consciousness than does rural life. Here the rhythm of life and sensory
mental imagery flows more slowly, more habitually, and more evenly. Precisely in this connection the sophisticated character of metropolitan psychic life becomes understandable—as over against small town life which
rests more upon deeply felt and emotional relationships. These latter are
rooted in the more unconscious layers of the psyche and grow most readily
in the steady rhythm of uninterrupted habituations. The intellect, however, has its locus in the transparent, conscious, higher layers of the psyche;
it is the most adaptable of our inner forces. In order to accommodate to
change and to the contrast of phenomena, the intellect does not require
any shocks and inner upheavals; it is only through such upheavals that the
more conservative mind could accommodate to the metropolitan rhythm
of events. Thus the metropolitan type of man—which, of course, exists in
a thousand individual variants—develops an organ protecting him against
the threatening currents and discrepancies of his external environment
which would uproot him. He reacts with his head instead of his heart. In
this an increased awareness assumes the psychic prerogative. Metropolitan
life, thus, underlies a heightened awareness and a predominance of intelligence in metropolitan man. The reaction to metropolitan phenomena is
shifted to that organ which is least sensitive and quite remote from the
depth of the personality. Intellectuality is thus seen to preserve subjective
life against the overwhelming power of metropolitan life, and intellectual-

ity branches out in many directions and is integrated with numerous discrete phenomena.

The metropolis has always been the seat of the money economy. Here the multiplicity and concentration of economic exchange gives an importance to the means of exchange which the scantiness of rural commerce would not have allowed. Money economy and the dominance of the intellect are intrinsically connected. They share a matter-of-fact attitude in dealing with men and with things; and, in this attitude, a formal justice is often coupled with an inconsiderate hardness. The intellectually sophisticated person is indifferent to all genuine individuality, because relationships and reactions result from it which cannot be exhausted with logical operations. In the same manner, the individuality of phenomena is not commensurate with the pecuniary principle. Money is concerned only with what is common to all: it asks for the exchange value, it reduces all quality and individuality to the question: How much? All intimate emotional relations between persons are founded in their individuality, whereas in rational relations man is reckoned with like a number, like an element which is in itself indifferent. Only the objective measurable achievement is of interest. Thus metropolitan man reckons with his merchants and customers, his domestic servants and often even with persons with whom he is obliged to have social intercourse. These features of intellectuality contrast with the nature of the small circle in which the inevitable knowledge of individuality as inevitably produces a warmer tone of behavior, a behavior which is beyond a mere objective balancing of service and return. In the sphere of the economic psychology of the small group it is of importance that under primitive conditions production serves the customer who orders the good, so that the producer and the consumer are acquainted. The modern metropolis, however, is supplied almost entirely by production for the market, that is, for entirely unknown purchasers who never personally enter the producer's actual field of vision. Through this anonymity the interests of each party acquire an unmerciful matter-of-factness; and the intellectually calculating economic egoisms of both parties need not fear any deflection because of the imponderables of personal relationships. The money economy dominates the metropolis; it has displaced the last survivals of domestic production and the direct barter of goods; it minimizes, from day to day, the amount of work ordered by customers. The matter-of-fact attitude is obviously so intimately interrelated with the money economy, which is dominant in the metropolis, that nobody can say whether the intellectualistic mentality first promoted the money economy or whether the latter determined the former. The metropolitan way of life is certainly the most fertile soil for this reciprocity, a point which I shall document merely by citing the dictum of the most eminent English constitutional historian: throughout the whole course of English history, London has never acted as England's heart but often as England's intellect and always as her moneybag!

In certain seemingly insignificant traits, which lie upon the surface of life, the same psychic currents characteristically unite. Modern mind has become more and more calculating. The calculative exactness of practical life which the money economy has brought about corresponds to the ideal of natural science: to transform the world into an arithmetic problem, to fix every part of the world by mathematical formulas. Only money economy has filled the days of so many people with weighing, calculating, with numerical determinations, with a reduction of qualitative values to quantitative ones. Through the calculative nature of money a new precision, a certainty in the definition of identities and differences, an unambiguousness in agreements and arrangements has been brought about in the relations of life-elements—just as externally this precision has been effected by the universal diffusion of pocket watches. However, the conditions of metropolitan life are at once cause and effect of this trait. The relationships and affairs of the typical metropolitan usually are so varied and complex that without the strictest punctuality in promises and services the whole structure would break down into an inextricable chaos. Above all, this necessity is brought about by the aggregation of so many people with such differentiated interests, who must integrate their relations and activities into a highly complex organism. If all clocks and watches in Berlin would suddenly go wrong in different ways, even if only by one hour, all economic life and communication of the city would be disrupted for a long time. In addition an apparently mere external factor: long distances, would make all waiting and broken appointments result in an ill-afforded waste of time. Thus, the technique of metropolitan life is unimaginable without the most punctual integration of all activities and mutual relations into a stable and impersonal time schedule. Here again the general conclusions of this entire task of reflection become obvious, namely, that from each point on the surface of existence—however closely attached to the surface alone—one may drop a sounding into the depth of the psyche so that all the most banal externalities of life finally are connected with the ultimate decisions concerning the meaning and style of life. Punctuality, calculability, exactness are forced upon life by the complexity and extension of metropolitan existence and are not only most intimately connected with its money economy and intellectualistic character. These traits must also color the contents of life and favor the exclusion of those irrational, instinctive, sovereign traits and impulses which aim at determining the mode of life from within, instead of receiving the general and precisely schematized form of life from without. Even though sovereign types of personality, characterized by irrational impulses, are by no means impossible in the city, they are, nevertheless, opposed to typical city life. The passionate hatred of men like Ruskin and Nietzsche for the metropolis is understandable in these terms. Their natures discovered the value of life alone in the unschematized existence which cannot be defined with precision for all alike. From the same source of this hatred of the metropolis surged their hatred of money economy and of the intellectualism of modern existence.

The same factors which have thus coalesced into the exactness and minute precision of the form of life have coalesced into a structure of the highest impersonality; on the other hand, they have promoted a highly personal subjectivity. There is perhaps no psychic phenomenon which has been so unconditionally reserved to the metropolis as has the blasé attitude. The blasé attitude results first from the rapidly changing and closely compressed contrasting stimulations of the nerves. From this, the enhancement of metropolitan intellectuality, also, seems originally to stem. Therefore, stupid people who are not intellectually alive in the first place usually are not exactly blasé. A life in boundless pursuit of pleasure makes one blasé because it agitates the nerves to their strongest reactivity for such a long time that they finally cease to react at all. In the same way, through the rapidity and contradictoriness of their changes, more harmless impressions force such violent responses, tearing the nerves so brutally hither and thither that their last reserves of strength are spent; and if one remains in the same milieu they have no time to gather new strength. An incapacity thus emerges to react to new sensations with the appropriate energy. This constitutes that blasé attitude which, in fact, every metropolitan child shows when compared with children of quieter and less changeable milieus.

This physiological source of the metropolitan blasé attitude is joined by another source which flows from the money economy. The essence of the blasé attitude consists in the blunting of discrimination. This does not mean that the objects are not perceived, as is the case with the half-wit, but rather that the meaning and differing values of things, and thereby the things themselves, are experienced as insubstantial. They appear to the blasé person in an evenly flat and gray tone; no one object deserves preference over any other. This mood is the faithful subjective reflection of the completely internalized money economy. By being the equivalent to all the manifold things in one and the same way, money becomes the most frightful leveler. For money expresses all qualitative differences of things in terms of "how much?" Money, with all its colorlessness and indifference, becomes the common denominator of all values; irreparably it hollows out the core of things, their individuality, their specific value, and their incomparability. All things float with equal specific gravity in the constantly moving stream of money. All things lie on the same level and differ from one another only in the size of the area which they cover. In the individual case this coloration, or rather discoloration, of things through their money equivalence may be unnoticeably minute. However, through the relations of the rich to the objects to be had for money, perhaps even through the total character which the mentality of the contemporary public everywhere imparts to these objects, the exclusively pecuniary evaluation of objects has become quite considerable. The large cities, the main seats of the money exchange, bring the purchasability of things to the fore much more impressively than do smaller localities. That is why cities are also the genuine locale of the blasé attitude. In the blasé attitude the concentration of men and things stimulate the nervous system of the individual to its highest achievement so that it attains its peak. Through the mere quantitative intensification of the same conditioning factors this achievement is transformed into its opposite and appears in the peculiar adjustment of the blasé attitude. In this phenomenon the nerves find in the refusal to react to their stimulation the last possibility of accommodating to the contents and forms of metropolitan life. The self-preservation of certain personalities is brought at the price of devaluating the whole objective world, a devaluation which in the end unavoidably drags one's own personality down into a feeling of the same worthlessness.

Whereas the subject of this form of existence has to come to terms with it entirely for himself, his self-preservation in the face of the large city demands from him a no less negative behavior of a social nature. This mental attitude of metropolitans toward one another we may designate, from a formal point of view, as reserve. If so many inner reactions were responses to the continuous external contacts with innumerable people as are those in the small town, where one knows almost everybody one meets and where one has a positive relation to almost everyone, one would be completely atomized internally and come to an unimaginable psychic state. Partly this psychological fact, partly the right to distrust which men have in the face of the touch-and-go elements of metropolitan life, necessitates our reserve. As a result of this reserve we frequently do not even know by sight those who have been our neighbors for years. And it is this reserve which in the eyes of the small-town people makes us appear to be cold and heartless. Indeed, if I do not deceive myself, the inner aspect of this outer reserve is not only indifference but, more often than we are aware, it is a slight aversion, a mutual strangeness and repulsion, which will break into hatred and fight at the moment of a closer contact, however caused. The whole inner organization of such an extensive communicative life rests upon an extremely varied hierarchy of sympathies, indifferences, and aversions of the briefest as well as of the most permanent nature. The sphere of indifference in this hierarchy is not as large as might appear on the surface. Our psychic activity still responds to almost every impression of somebody else with a somewhat distinct feeling. The unconscious, fluid and changing character of this impression seems to result in a state of indifference. Actually this indifference would be just as unnatural as the diffusion of indiscriminate mutual suggestion would be unbearable. From both these typical dangers of the metropolis, indifference and indiscriminate suggestibility, antipathy protects us. A latent antipathy and the preparatory stage of practical antagonism effect the distances and aversions without which this mode of life could not at all be led. The extent and the mixture of this style of life, the rhythm of its emergence and disappearance, the forms in which it is satisfied—all these, with the unifying motives in the narrower sense, form the inseparable whole of the metropolitan style of life. What appears in the metropolitan style of life directly as dissociation is in reality only one of its elemental forms of socialization.

This reserve with its overtone of hidden aversion appears in turn as the form or the cloak of a more general mental phenomenon of the metropolis: it grants to the individual a kind and an amount of personal freedom which has no analogy whatsoever under other conditions. The metropolis goes back to one of the large developmental tendencies of social life as such, to one of the few tendencies for which an approximately universal formula can be discovered. The earliest phase of social formations found in historical as well as in contemporary social structures is this: a relatively small circle firmly closed against neighboring, strange, or in some way antagonistic circles. However, this circle is closely coherent and allows its individual members only a narrow field for the development of unique qualities and free, self-responsible movements. Political and kinship groups, parties and religious associations begin in this way. The self-preservation of very young associations requires the establishment of strict boundaries and a centripetal unity. Therefore they cannot allow the individual freedom and unique inner and outer development. From this stage social development proceeds at once in two different, yet corresponding, directions. To the extent to which the group grows—numerically, spatially, in significance and in content of life—to the same degree the group's direct, inner unity loosens, and the rigidity of the original demarcation against others is softened through mutual relations and connections. At the same time, the individual gains freedom of movement, far beyond the first jealous delimitation. The individual also gains a specific individuality to which the division of labor in the enlarged group gives both occasion and necessity. The state and Christianity, guilds and political parties, and innumerable other groups have developed according to this formula, however much, of course, the special conditions and forces of the respective groups have modified the general scheme. This scheme seems to me distinctly recognizable also in the evolution of individuality within urban life. The small-town life in Antiquity and in the Middle Ages set barriers against movement and relations of the individual toward the outside, and it set up barriers against individual independence and differentiation within the individual self. These barriers were such that under them modern man could not have breathed. Even today a metropolitan man who is placed in a small town feels a restriction similar, at least, in kind. The smaller the circle which forms our milieu is, and the more restricted those relations to others are which dissolve the boundaries of the individual, the more anxiously the circle guards the achievements, the conduct of life, and the outlook of the individual, and the more readily a quantitative and qualitative specialization would break up the framework of the whole little circle.

The ancient *polis* in this respect seems to have had the very character of a small town. The constant threat to its existence at the hands of enemies from near and afar effected strict coherence in political and military respects, a supervision of the citizen by the citizen, a jealousy of the whole against the individual whose particular life was suppressed to such a degree that he could compensate only by acting as a despot in his own household. The tremendous agitation and excitement, the unique colorfulness of Athenian life, can perhaps be understood in terms of the fact that a people of incomparably individualized personalities struggled against the constant inner and outer pressure of a de-individualizing small town. This produced a tense atmosphere in which the weaker individuals were suppressed and those of stronger natures were incited to prove themselves in the most passionate manner. This is precisely why it was that there blossomed in Athens what must be called, without defining it exactly, "the general human character" in the intellectual development of our species. For we maintain factual as well as historical validity for the following connection: the most extensive and the most general contents and forms of life are most intimately connected with the most individual ones. They have a preparatory stage in common, that is, they find their enemy in narrow formations and groupings the maintenance of which places both of them into a state of defense against expanse and generality lying without and the freely moving individuality within. Just as in the feudal age, the "free" man was the one who stood under the law of the land, that is, under the law of the largest social orbit, and the unfree man was the one who derived his right merely from the narrow circle of a feudal association and was excluded from the larger social orbit—so today metropolitan man is "free" in a spiritualized and refined sense, in contrast to the pettiness and prejudices which hem in the small-town man. For the reciprocal reserve and indifference and the intellectual life conditions of large circles are never felt more strongly by the individual in their impact upon his independence than in the thickest crowd of the big city. This is because the bodily proximity and narrowness of space makes the mental distance only the more visible. It is obviously only the obverse of this freedom if, under certain circumstances, one nowhere feels as lonely and lost as in the metropolitan crowd. For here as elsewhere it is by no means necessary that the freedom of man be reflected in his emotional life as comfort.

It is not only the immediate size of the area and the number of persons which, because of the universal historical correlation between the enlargement of the circle and the personal inner and outer freedom, has made the metropolis the locale of freedom. It is rather in transcending this visible expanse that any given city becomes the seat of cosmopolitanism. The horizon of the city expands in a manner comparable to the way in which wealth develops; a certain amount of property increases in a quasi-automatical way in ever more rapid progression. As soon as a certain limit has been passed, the economic, personal, and intellectual relations of the citizenry, the sphere of intellectual predominance of the city over its hinterland, grow as in geometrical progression. Every gain in dynamic extension becomes a step, not for an equal, but for a new and larger extension. From every thread spinning out of the city, ever new threads grow as if by themselves, just as within the city the unearned increment of ground rent, through the mere increase in communication, brings the owner automatically increasing profits. At this point, the quantitative aspect of life is transformed directly into qualitative traits of character. The sphere of life of the small town is, in the main, self-contained and autarchic. For it is the decisive nature of the metropolis that its inner life overflows by waves into a far-flung national or international area. Weimar is not an example to the contrary, since its significance was hinged upon individual personalities and died with them; whereas the metropolis is indeed characterized by its essential independence even from the most eminent individual personalities. This is the counterpart to the independence, and it is the price the individual pays for the independence, which he enjoys in the metropolis. The most significant characteristic of the metropolis is this functional extension beyond its physical boundaries. And this efficacy reacts in turn and gives weight, importance, and responsibility to metropolitan life. Man does not end with the limits of his body or the area comprising his immediate activity. Rather is the range of the person constituted by the sum of effects emanating from him temporally and spatially. In the same way, a city consists of its total effects which extend beyond its immediate confines. Only this range is the city's actual extent in which its existence is expressed. This fact makes it obvious that individual freedom, the logical and historical complement of such extension, is not to be understood only in the negative sense of mere freedom of mobility and elimination of prejudices and petty philistinism. The essential point is that the particularity and incomparability, which ultimately every human being possesses, be somehow expressed in the working-out of a way of life. That we follow the laws of our own nature—and this after all is freedom—becomes obvious and convincing to ourselves and to others only if the expressions of this nature differ from the expressions of others. Only our unmistakability proves that our way of life has not been superimposed by others.

Cities are, first of all, seats of the highest economic division of labor. They produce thereby such extreme phenomena as in Paris the renumerative occupation of the *quatorzième*. They are persons who identify themselves by signs on their residences and who are ready at the dinner hour in correct attire, so that they can be quickly called upon if a dinner party should consist of thirteen persons. In the measure of its expansion, the city offers more and more the decisive conditions of the division of labor. It offers a circle which through its size can absorb a highly diverse variety of services. At the same time, the concentration of individuals and their struggle for customers compel the individual to specialize in a function from which he cannot be readily displaced by another. It is decisive that city life has transformed the struggle with nature for livelihood into an inter-human struggle for gain, which here is not granted by nature but by other men. For specialization does not flow only from the competition for gain but also from the underlying fact that the seller must always seek to call forth new and differentiated needs of the lured customer. In order to find a source of income which is not yet exhausted, and to find a function which cannot readily be displaced, it is necessary to specialize in one's services. This process promotes differentiation, refinement, and the enrichment of the public's needs, which obviously must lead to growing personal differences within this public.

All this forms the transition to the individualization of mental and psychic traits which the city occasions in proportion to its size. There is a whole series of obvious causes underlying this process. First, one must meet the difficulty of asserting his own peronality within the dimensions of metropolitan life. Where the quantitative increase in importance and the expense of energy reach their limits, one seizes upon qualitative differentiation in order somehow to attract the attention of the social circle by playing upon its sensitivity for differences. Finally, man is tempted to adopt the most tendentious peculiarities, that is, the specifically metropolitan extravagances of mannerism, caprice, and preciousness. Now, the meaning of these extravagances does not at all lie in the contents of such behavior, but rather in its form of "being different," of standing out in a striking manner and thereby attracting attention. For many character types, ultimately the only means of saving for themselves some modicum of self-esteem and the sense of filling a position is indirect, through the awareness of others. In the same sense a seemingly insignificant factor is operating, the cumulative effects of which are, however, still noticeable. I refer to the brevity and scarcity of the inter-human contacts granted to the metropolitan man, as compared with social intercourse in the small town. The temptation to appear "to the point," to appear concentrated and strikingly characteristic, lies much closer to the individual in brief metropolitan contacts than in an atmosphere in which frequent and prolonged association assures the personality of an unambiguous image of himself in the eyes of the other.

The most profound reason, however, why the metropolis conduces to the urge for the most individual personal existence—no matter whether justified and successful—appears to me to be the following: the development of modern culture is characterized by the preponderance of what one may call the "objective spirit" over the "subjective spirit." This is to say, in language as well as in law, in the technique of production as well as in art, in science as well as in the objects of the domestic environment, there is embodied a sum of spirit. The individual in his intellectual development follows the growth of this spirit very imperfectly and at an ever increasing distance. If, for instance, we view the immense culture which for the last hundred years has been embodied in things and in knowledge, in institutions and in comforts, and if we compare all this with the cultural progress of the individual during the same period—at least in high status groups— a frightful disproportion in growth between the two becomes evident. Indeed, at some points we notice a retrogression in the culture of the individual with reference to spirituality, delicacy, and idealism. This discrepancy results essentially from the growing division of labor. For the division of labor demands from the individual an ever more one-sided accomplishment, and the greatest advance in a one-sided pursuit only too frequently means dearth to the personality of the individual. In any case, he can cope less and less with the overgrowth of objective culture. The individual is reduced to a negligible quantity, perhaps less in his consciousness than in his practice and in the totality of his obscure emotional states that are derived from this practice. The individual has become a mere cog in an enormous organization of things and powers which tear from his hands all progress, spirituality, and value in order to transform them from their subjective form into the form of a purely objective life. It needs merely to be pointed out that the metropolis is the genuine arena of this culture which outgrows all personal life. Here in buildings and educational institutions, in the wonders and comforts of space-conquering technology, in the formations of community life, and in the visible institutions of the state, is offered such an overwhelming fullness of crystallized and impersonalized spirit that the personality, so to speak, cannot maintain itself under its impact. On the one hand, life is made infinitely easy for the personality in that stimulations, interests, uses of time and consciousness are offered to it from all sides. They carry the person as if in a stream, and one needs hardly to swim for oneself. On the other hand, however, life is composed more and more of these impersonal contents and offerings which tend to displace the genuine personal colorations and incomparabilities. This results in the individual's summoning the utmost in uniqueness and particularization, in order to preserve his most personal core. He has to exaggerate this personal element in order to remain audible even to himself. The atrophy of individual culture through the hypertrophy of objective culture is one reason for the bitter hatred which the preachers of the most extreme individualism, above all Nietzsche, harbor against the metropolis. But it is, indeed, also a reason why these preachers are so passionately loved in the metropolis and why they appear to the metropolitan man as the prophets and saviors of his most unsatisfied yearnings.

If one asks for the historical position of these two forms of individualism which are nourished by the quantitative relation of the metropolis, namely, individual independence and the elaboration of individuality itself, then the metropolis assumes an entirely new rank order in the world history of the spirit. The eighteenth century found the individual in oppressive bonds which had become meaningless—bonds of a political, agrarian, guild, and religious character. They were restraints which, so to speak, forced upon man an unnatural form and outmoded, unjust inequalities. In this situation the cry for liberty and equality arose, the belief in the individual's full freedom of movement in all social and intellectual relationships. Freedom would at once permit the noble substance common to all to come to the fore, a substance which nature had deposited in every man and which society and history had only deformed. Besides this eighteenth-century ideal of liberalism, in the nineteenth century, through Goethe and Romanticism, on the one hand, and through the economic division of labor, on the other hand, another ideal arose: individuals liberated from historical bonds now wished to distinguish themselves from one another. The carrier of man's values is no longer the "general human being" in every individual, but rather man's qualitative uniqueness and irreplaceability. The external and internal history of our time takes its course within the struggle and in the changing entanglements of these two ways of defining the individual's role in the whole of society. It is the function of the metropolis to provide the arena for this struggle and its reconciliation. For the metropolis presents the peculiar conditions which are revealed to us as the opportunities and the stimuli for the development of both these ways of allocating roles to men. Therewith these conditions gain a unique place, pregnant with inestimable meanings for the development of psychic existence. The metropolis reveals itself as one of those great historical formations in which opposing streams which enclose life unfold, as well as join one another with equal right. However, in this process the currents of life, whether their individual phenomena touch us sympathetically or antipathetically, entirely transcend the sphere for which the judge's attitude is appropriate. Since such forces of life have grown into the roots and into the crown of the whole of the historical life in which we, in our fleeting existence, as a cell, belong only as a part, it is not our task either to accuse or to pardon, but only to understand.

# STUDY QUESTIONS

1. What is Simmel saying about how the money economy of cities differs from that in rural areas and why is this important?
2. How does the city shape individuality and emotional relationships between people and how does this differ from what happens in small towns?

# BASIC SOCIOLOGICAL CONCEPTS FROM *ECONOMY AND SOCIETY: AN OUTLINE OF INTERPRETIVE SOCIOLOGY*

MAX WEBER

Among the simplest definitions of sociology is this: sociology is the study of social action and its causes. In this reading, Max Weber (1864–1920) takes this as his starting point and offers a series of basic concepts and definitions that demonstrate his clear vision of sociology as the study of how meaning guides "social action," defined as any meaningful behavior that is oriented toward others. The major task of sociology, in Weber's view, is to understand the social world by interpreting the meanings people attach to their actions and their situations. He charges sociologists with the difficult task of ferreting out the motives, interests, and intentions of people, groups, institutions, and societies as they interact with one another. While it is necessary for sociologists to observe statistical regularities or patterns in populations large or small, Weber contends this is not enough. Sociologists must also take account of how shared meanings—or contests over meanings—help produce those regularities and patterns in human interaction.

This interpretive approach, along with a set of strategies and tools for carrying it out, has made Weberian sociology a fountainhead for generations of cultural sociologists as they seek to understand the role of culture in producing and reproducing the social world. The excerpt below does not touch directly on Weber's ideas about culture—interested readers can find those ideas in his writings that examine the role of religion in the historical development of different economic systems. Instead, the focus of the passage below is pressing the argument that sociology must grasp meaning-making as a complex process that occurs *intersubjectively* (between two or more people). The resulting understanding gained by sociologists, while often short of a full understanding of causal factors, enables us to gauge the impact and force that seemingly immaterial things like ideas, values, morals, emotions, and meanings exert in the material world.

# 1. THE DEFINITION OF SOCIOLOGY AND OF SOCIAL ACTION

Sociology (in the sense in which this highly ambiguous word is used here) is a science concerning itself with the interpretive understanding of social action and thereby with a causal explanation of its course and consequences. We shall speak of "action" insofar as the acting individual attaches a subjective meaning to his behavior—be it overt or covert, omission or acquiescence. Action is "social" insofar as its subjective meaning takes account of the behavior of others and is thereby oriented in its course.

## A. Methodological Foundations

1. "Meaning" may be of two kinds. The term may refer first to the actual existing meaning in the given concrete case of a particular actor, or to the average or approximate meaning attributable to a given plurality of actors; or secondly to the theoretically conceived *pure type* of subjective meaning attributed to the hypothetical actor or actors in a given type of action. In no case does it refer to an objectively "correct" meaning or one which is "true" in some metaphysical sense. It is this which distinguishes the empirical sciences of action, such as sociology and history, from the dogmatic disciplines in that area, such as jurisprudence, logic, ethics, and

esthetics, which seek to ascertain the "true" and "valid" meanings associated with the objects of their investigation.

2. The line between meaningful action and merely reactive behavior to which no subjective meaning is attached, cannot be sharply drawn empirically. A very considerable part of all sociologically relevant behavior, especially purely traditional behavior, is marginal between the two. In the case of some psychophysical processes, meaningful, i.e., subjectively understandable, action is not to be found at all; in others it is discernible only by the psychologist. Many mystical experiences which cannot be adequately communicated in words are, for a person who is not susceptible to such experiences, not fully understandable. At the same time the ability to perform a similar action is not a necessary prerequisite to understanding; "one need not have been Caesar in order to understand Caesar." "Recapturing an experience" is important for accurate understanding, but not an absolute precondition for its interpretation. Understandable and non-understandable components of a process are often intermingled and bound up together.

3. All interpretation of meaning, like all scientific observations, strives for clarity and verifiable accuracy of insight and comprehension. The basis for certainty in understanding can be either rational, which can be further subdivided into logical and mathematical, or it can be of an emotionally empathic or artistically appreciative quality. Action is rationally evident chiefly when we attain a completely clear intellectual grasp of the action-elements in their intended context of meaning. Empathic or appreciative accuracy is attained when, through sympathetic participation, we can adequately grasp the emotional context in which the action took place. The highest degree of rational understanding is attained in cases involving the meanings of logically or mathematically related propositions; their meaning may be immediately and unambiguously intelligible. We have a perfectly clear understanding of what it means when somebody employs the proposition $2 \times 2 = 4$ or the Pythagorean theorem in reasoning or argument, or when someone correctly carries out a logical train of reasoning according to our accepted modes of thinking. In the same way we also understand what a person is doing when he tries to achieve certain ends by choosing appropriate means on the basis of the facts of the situation, as experience has accustomed us to interpret them. The interpretation of such rationally purposeful action possesses, for the understanding of the choice of means,

the highest degree of verifiable certainty. With a lower degree of certainty, which is, however, adequate for most purposes of explanation, we are able to understand errors, including confusion of problems of the sort that we ourselves are liable to, or the origin of which we can detect by sympathetic self-analysis.

On the other hand, many ultimate ends or values toward which experience shows that human action may be oriented, often cannot be understood completely, though sometimes we are able to grasp them intellectually. The more radically they differ from our own ultimate values, however, the more difficult it is for us to understand them empathically. Depending upon the circumstances of the particular case we must be content either with a purely intellectual understanding of such values or when even that fails, sometimes we must simply accept them as given data. Then we can try to understand the action motivated by them on the basis of whatever opportunities for approximate emotional and intellectual interpretation seem to be available at different points in its course. These difficulties confront, for instance, people not susceptible to unusual acts of religious and charitable zeal, or persons who abhor extreme rationalist fanaticism (such as the fanatic advocacy of the "rights of man").

The more we ourselves are susceptible to such emotional reactions as anxiety, anger, ambition, envy, jealousy, love, enthusiasm, pride, vengefulness, loyalty, devotion, and appetites of all sorts, and to the "irrational" conduct which grows out of them, the more readily can we empathize with them. Even when such emotions are found in a degree of intensity of which the observer himself is completely incapable, he can still have a significant degree of emotional understanding of their meaning and can interpret intellectually their influence on the course of action and the selection of means.

For the purposes of a typological scientific analysis it is convenient to treat all irrational, affectually determined elements of behavior as factors of deviation from a conceptually pure type of rational action. For example a panic on the stock exchange can be most conveniently analysed by attempting to determine first what the course of action would have been if it had not been influenced by irrational affects; it is then possible to introduce the irrational components as accounting for the observed deviations from this hypothetical course. Similarly, in analysing a political or military campaign it is convenient to determine in the first place what would have been a rational course, given the ends of the participants and adequate knowledge of all the circumstances. Only in this way is it possible to assess the causal significance of irrational factors as accounting for the deviations from this type. The construction of a purely rational course of action in such cases serves the sociologist as a type (ideal type) which has the merit of clear understandability and lack of ambiguity. By comparison with this it is possible to understand the ways in which actual action is influenced by irrational factors of all sorts, such as affects and errors, in that they account for the deviation from the line of conduct which would be expected on the hypothesis that the action were purely rational.

Only in this respect and for these reasons of methodological convenience is the method of sociology "rationalistic." It is naturally not legitimate to interpret this procedure as involving a rationalistic bias of sociology, but only as a methodological device. It certainly does not involve a belief in the actual predominance of rational elements in human life, for on the question of how far this predominance does or does not exist, nothing whatever has been said. That there is, however, a danger of rationalistic interpretations where they are out of place cannot be denied. All experience unfortunately confirms the existence of this danger.

4. In all the sciences of human action, account must be taken of processes and phenomena which are devoid of subjective meaning, in the role of stimuli, results, favoring or hindering circumstances. To be devoid of meaning is not identical with being lifeless or non-human; every artifact, such as for example a machine, can be understood only in terms of the meaning which its production and use have had or were intended to have; a meaning which may derive from a relation to exceedingly various purposes. Without reference to this meaning such an object remains wholly unintelligible. That which is intelligible or understandable about it is thus its relation to human action in the role either of means or of end; a relation of which the actor or actors can be said to have been aware and to which their action has been oriented. Only in terms of such categories is it possible to "understand" objects of this kind. On the other hand processes or conditions, whether they are animate or inanimate, human or non-human, are in the present sense devoid of meaning in so far as they cannot be related to an intended purpose. That is to say they are devoid of meaning if they cannot be related to action in the role of means or ends but constitute only the stimulus, the favoring or hindering circumstances. It may be that the

flooding of the Dollart [at the mouth of the Ems river near the Dutch-German border] in 1277 had historical significance as a stimulus to the beginning of certain migrations of considerable importance. Human mortality, indeed the organic life cycle from the helplessness of infancy to that of old age, is naturally of the very greatest sociological importance through the various ways in which human action has been oriented to these facts. To still another category of facts devoid of meaning belong certain psychic or psychophysical phenomena such as fatigue, habituation, memory, etc.; also certain typical states of euphoria under some conditions of ascetic mortification; finally, typical variations in the reactions of individuals according to reaction-time, precision, and other modes. But in the last analysis the same principle applies to these as to other phenomena which are devoid of meaning. Both the actor and the sociologist must accept them as data to be taken into account.

It is possible that future research may be able to discover non-interpretable uniformities underlying what has appeared to be specifically meaningful action, though little has been accomplished in this direction thus far. Thus, for example, differences in hereditary biological constitution, as of "races," would have to be treated by sociology as given data in the same way as the physiological facts of the need of nutrition or the effect of senescence on action. This would be the case if, and insofar as, we had statistically conclusive proof of their influence on sociologically relevant behavior. The recognition of the causal significance of such factors would not in the least alter the specific task of sociological analysis or of that of the other sciences of action, which is the interpretation of action in terms of its subjective meaning. The effect would be only to introduce certain non-interpretable data of the same order as others which are already present, into the complex of subjectively understandable motivation at certain points. (Thus it may come to be known that there are typical relations between the frequency of certain types of teleological orientation of action or of the degree of certain kinds of rationality and the cephalic index or skin color or any other biologically inherited characteristic.)

5. Understanding may be of two kinds: the first is the direct observational understanding of the subjective meaning of a given act as such, including verbal utterances. We thus understand by direct observation, in this case, the meaning of the proposition $2 \times 2 = 4$ when we hear or read it. This is a case of the direct rational understanding of ideas. We also understand an outbreak of anger as manifested by facial expression, exclamations or

irrational movements. This is direct observational understanding of irrational emotional reactions. We can understand in a similar observational way the action of a woodcutter or of somebody who reaches for the knob to shut a door or who aims a gun at an animal. This is rational observational understanding of actions.

Understanding may, however, be of another sort, namely explanatory understanding. Thus we understand in terms of *motive* the meaning an actor attaches to the proposition twice two equals four, when he states it or writes it down, in that we understand what makes him do this at precisely this moment and in these circumstances. Understanding in this sense is attained if we know that he is engaged in balancing a ledger or in making a scientific demonstration, or is engaged in some other task of which this particular act would be an appropriate part. This is rational understanding of motivation, which consists in placing the act in an intelligible and more inclusive context of meaning. Thus we understand the chopping of wood or aiming of a gun in terms of motive in addition to direct observation if we know that the woodchopper is working for a wage or is chopping a supply of firewood for his own use or possibly is doing it for recreation. But he might also be working off a fit of rage, an irrational case. Similarly we understand the motive of a person aiming a gun if we know that he has been commanded to shoot as a member of a firing squad, that he is fighting against an enemy, or that he is doing it for revenge. The last is affectually determined and thus in a certain sense irrational. Finally we have a motivational understanding of the outburst of anger if we know that it has been provoked by jealousy, injured pride, or an insult. The last examples are all affectually determined and hence derived from irrational motives. In all the above cases the particular act has been placed in an understandable sequence of motivation, the understanding of which can be treated as an explanation of the actual course of behavior. Thus for a science which is concerned with the subjective meaning of action, explanation requires a grasp of the complex of meaning in which an actual course of understandable action thus interpreted belongs. In all such cases, even where the processes are largely affectual, the subjective meaning of the action, including that also of the relevant meaning complexes, will be called the intended meaning. (This involves a departure from ordinary usage, which speaks of intention in this sense only in the case of rationally purposive action.)

6. In all these cases understanding involves the interpretive grasp of the meaning present in one of the following contexts: (a) as in the histori-

cal approach, the actually intended meaning for concrete individual action; or (b) as in cases of sociological mass phenomena, the average of, or an approximation to, the actually intended meaning; or (c) the meaning appropriate to a scientifically formulated pure type (an ideal type) of a common phenomenon. The concepts and "laws" of pure economic theory are examples of this kind of ideal type. They state what course a given type of human action would take if it were strictly rational, unaffected by errors or emotional factors and if, furthermore, it were completely and unequivocally directed to a single end, the maximization of economic advantage. In reality, action takes exactly this course only in unusual cases, as sometimes on the stock exchange; and even then there is usually only an approximation to the ideal type.

Every interpretation attempts to attain clarity and certainty, but no matter how clear an interpretation as such appears to be from the point of view of meaning, it cannot on this account claim to be the causally valid interpretation. On this level it must remain only a peculiarly plausible hypothesis. In the first place the "conscious motives" may well, even to the actor himself, conceal the various "motives" and "repressions" which constitute the real driving force of his action. Thus in such cases even subjectively honest self-analysis has only a relative value. Then it is the task of the sociologist to be aware of this motivational situation and to describe and analyse it, even though it has not actually been concretely part of the conscious intention of the actor; possibly not at all, at least not fully. This is a borderline case of the interpretation of meaning. Secondly, processes of action which seem to an observer to be the same or similar may fit into exceedingly various complexes of motive in the case of the actual actor. Then even though the situations appear superficially to be very similar we must actually understand them or interpret them as very different, perhaps, in terms of meaning, directly opposed. (Simmel, in his *Probleme der Geschichtsphilosophie*, gives a number of examples.) Third, the actors in any given situation are often subject to opposing and conflicting impulses, all of which we are able to understand. In a large number of cases we know from experience it is not possible to arrive at even an approximate estimate of the relative strength of conflicting motives and very often we cannot be certain of our interpretation. Only the actual outcome of the conflict gives a solid basis of judgment.

# B. Social Action

1. Social action, which includes both failure to act and passive acquiescence, may be oriented to the past, present, or expected future behavior of others. Thus it may be motivated by revenge for a past attack, defence against present, or measures of defence against future aggression. The "others" may be individual persons, and may be known to the actor as such, or may constitute an indefinite plurality and may be entirely unknown as individuals. (Thus, money is a means of exchange which the actor accepts in payment because he orients his action to the expectation that a large but unknown number of individuals he is personally unacquainted with will be ready to accept it in exchange on some future occasion.)

2. Not every kind of action, even of overt action, is "social" in the sense of the present discussion. Overt action is non-social if it is oriented solely to the behavior of inanimate objects. Subjective attitudes constitute social action only so far as they are oriented to the behavior of others. For example, religious behavior is not social if it is simply a matter of contemplation or of solitary prayer. The economic activity of an individual is social only if it takes account of the behavior of someone else. Thus very generally it becomes social insofar as the actor assumes that others will respect his actual control over economic goods. Concretely it is social, for instance, if in relation to the actor's own consumption the future wants of others are taken into account and this becomes one consideration affecting the actor's own saving. Or, in another connexion, production may be oriented to the future wants of other people.

3. Not every type of contact of human beings has a social character; this is rather confined to cases where the actor's behavior is meaningfully oriented to that of others. For example, a mere collision of two cyclists may be compared to a natural event. On the other hand, their attempt to avoid hitting each other, or whatever insults, blows, or friendly discussion might follow the collision, would constitute "social action."

4. Social action is not identical either with the similar actions of many persons or with every action influenced by other persons. Thus, if at the beginning of a shower a number of people on the street put up their umbrellas at the same time, this would not ordinarily be a case of action mutually oriented to that of each other, but rather of all reacting in the same way to the like need of protection from the rain. It is well known that the actions of the individual are strongly influenced by the mere fact that

he is a member of a crowd confined within a limited space. Thus, the sub-ject matter of studies of "crowd psychology," such as those of Le Bon, will be called "action conditioned by crowds." It is also possible for large num-bers, though dispersed, to be influenced simultaneously or successively by a source of influence operating similarly on all the individuals, as by means of the press. Here also the behavior of an individual is influenced by his membership in a "mass" and by the fact that he is aware of being a mem-ber. Some types of reaction are only made possible by the mere fact that the individual acts as part of a crowd. Others become more difficult under these conditions. Hence it is possible that a particular event or mode of human behavior can give rise to the most diverse kinds of feeling—gaiety, anger, enthusiasm, despair, and passions of all sorts—in a crowd situation which would not occur at all or not nearly so readily if the individual were alone. But for this to happen there need not, at least in many cases, be any meaningful relation between the behavior of the individual and the fact that he is a member of a crowd. It is not proposed in the present sense to call action "social" when it is merely a result of the effect on the individual of the existence of a crowd as such and the action is not oriented to that fact on the level of meaning. At the same time the borderline is naturally highly indefinite. In such cases as that of the influence of the demagogue, there may be a wide variation in the extent to which his mass clientele is affected by a meaningful reaction to the fact of its large numbers; and whatever this relation may be, it is open to varying interpretations.

But furthermore, mere "imitation" of the action of others, . . . will not be considered a case of specifically social action if it is purely reactive so that there is no meaningful orientation to the actor imitated. The borderline is, however, so indefinite that it is often hardly possible to discriminate. The mere fact that a person is found to employ some apparently useful proce-dure which he learned from someone else does not, however, constitute, in the present sense, social action. Action such as this is not oriented to the action of the other person, but the actor has, through observing the other, become acquainted with certain objective facts; and it is these to which his action is oriented. His action is then *causally* determined by the action of others, but not meaningfully. On the other hand, if the action of others is imitated because it is fashionable or traditional or exemplary, or lends social distinction, or on similar grounds, it is meaningfully oriented either to the behavior of the source of imitation or of third persons or of both. There are

of course all manner of transitional cases between the two types of imitation. Both the phenomena discussed above, the behavior of crowds and
imitation, stand on the indefinite borderline of social action. The same is
true, as will often appear, of traditionalism and charisma. The reason for
the indefiniteness of the line in these and other cases lies in the fact that
both the orientation to the behavior of others and the meaning which can
be imputed by the actor himself, are by no means always capable of clear
determination and are often altogether unconscious and seldom fully self-
conscious. Mere "influence" and meaningful orientation cannot therefore
always be clearly differentiated on the empirical level. But conceptually it is
essential to distinguish them, even though merely reactive imitation may
well have a degree of sociological importance at least equal to that of the
type which can be called social action in the strict sense. Sociology, it goes
without saying, is by no means confined to the study of social action; this is
only, at least for the kind of sociology being developed here, its central subject matter, that which may be said to be decisive for its status as a science.
But this does not imply any judgment on the comparative importance of
this and other factors.

# 2. TYPES OF SOCIAL ACTION

Social action, like all action, may be oriented in four ways. It may be:

(1) *instrumentally rational (zweckrational)*, that is, determined by expectations as to the behavior of objects in the environment and of other human
beings; these expectations are used as "conditions" or "means" for the attainment of the actor's own rationally pursued and calculated ends;

(2) *value-rational (wertrational)*, that is, determined by a conscious belief
in the value for its own sake of some ethical, aesthetic, religious, or other
form of behavior, independently of its prospects of success;

(3) *affectual* (especially emotional), that is, determined by the actor's
specific affects and feeling states;

(4) *traditional*, that is, determined by ingrained habituation.

1. Strictly traditional behavior, like the reactive type of imitation discussed
   above, lies very close to the borderline of what can justifiably be called
   meaningfully oriented action, and indeed often on the other side. For it

is very often a matter of almost automatic reaction to habitual stimuli which guide behavior in a course which has been repeatedly followed. The great bulk of all everyday action to which people have become habitually accustomed approaches this type. Hence, its place in a systematic classification is not merely that of a limiting case because, as will be shown later, attachment to habitual forms can be upheld with varying degrees of self-consciousness and in a variety of senses. In this case the type may shade over into value rationality (*Wertrationalität*).

2. Purely affectual behavior also stands on the borderline of what can be considered "meaningfully" oriented, and often it, too, goes over the line. It may, for instance, consist in an uncontrolled reaction to some exceptional stimulus. It is a case of sublimation when affectually determined action occurs in the form of conscious release of emotional tension. When this happens it is usually well on the road to rationalization in one or the other or both of the above senses.

3. The orientation of value-rational action is distinguished from the affectual type by its clearly self-conscious formulation of the ultimate values governing the action and the consistently planned orientation of its detailed course to these values. At the same time the two types have a common element, namely that the meaning of the action does not lie in the achievement of a result ulterior to it, but in carrying out the specific type of action for its own sake. Action is affectual if it satisfies a need for revenge, sensual gratification, devotion, contemplative bliss, or for working off emotional tensions (irrespective of the level of sublimation).

Examples of pure value-rational orientation would be the actions of persons who, regardless of possible cost to themselves, act to put into practice their convictions of what seems to them to be required by duty, honor, the pursuit of beauty, a religious call, personal loyalty, or the importance of some "cause" no matter in what it consists. In our terminology, value-rational action always involves "commands" or "demands" which, in the actor's opinion, are binding on him. It is only in cases where human action is motivated by the fulfillment of such unconditional demands that it will be called value-rational. This is the case in widely varying degrees, but for the most part only to a relatively slight extent. Nevertheless, it will be shown that the occurrence of this mode of action is important enough to justify its formulation as a distinct type; though it may be remarked that there is no intention here of attempting to formulate in any sense an exhaustive classification of types of action.

4. Action is instrumentally rational (*zweckrational*) when the end, the means, and the secondary results are all rationally taken into account and weighed. This involves rational consideration of alternative means to the end, of the relations of the end to the secondary consequences, and finally of the relative importance of different possible ends. Determination of action either in affectual or in traditional terms is thus incompatible with this type. Choice between alternative and conflicting ends and results may well be determined in a value-rational manner. In that case, action is instrumentally rational only in respect to the choice of means. On the other hand, the actor may, instead of deciding between alternative and conflicting ends in terms of a rational orientation to a system of values, simply take them as given subjective wants and arrange them in a scale of consciously assessed relative urgency. He may then orient his action to this scale in such a way that they are satisfied as far as possible in order of urgency, as formulated in the principle of "marginal utility." Value-rational action may thus have various different relations to the instrumentally rational action. From the latter point of view, however, value-rationality is always irrational. Indeed, the more the value to which action is oriented is elevated to the status of an absolute value, the more "irrational" in this sense the corresponding action is. For, the more unconditionally the actor devotes himself to this value for its own sake, to pure sentiment or beauty, to absolute goodness or devotion to duty, the less is he influenced by considerations of the consequences of his action. The orientation of action wholly to the rational achievement of ends without relation to fundamental values is, to be sure, essentially only a limiting case.

5. It would be very unusual to find concrete cases of action, especially of social action, which were oriented *only* in one or another of these ways. Furthermore, this classification of the modes of orientation of action is in no sense meant to exhaust the possibilities of the field, but only to formulate in conceptually pure form certain sociologically important types to which actual action is more or less closely approximated or, in much the more common case, which constitute its elements. The usefulness of the classification for the purposes of this investigation can only be judged in terms of its results.

# STUDY QUESTIONS

1. Why are the subjective meanings in social action so important to Weber and his definition of sociology?
2. What are the four types of social action that Weber outlines? Give an example of each from your own life.

# 5

# THE MEANINGS OF "CULTURE"

RAYMOND WILLIAMS

If your classificatory function is working, you might begin to suspect that this essay is not like the others in this section. You'd be correct. Raymond Williams (1921–1988) was not a sociologist and this reading does not introduce fundamental ideas or theories about the nature of culture. Instead, Williams, who was a professor of drama at Cambridge University, takes on the meanings of the word *culture* itself.

Williams is widely recognized as one of the founders of the field of Cultural Studies, an interdisciplinary approach to cultural analysis that combines literary studies and social theory. His writings laid the groundwork for a kind of Marxist approach to culture called *cultural materialism.* This reading offers a brief analysis of culture as a "keyword" in the western intellectual tradition, one whose meaning has changed repeatedly over time. His observations are included here because they offer insight into how and why the concept of culture remains so fuzzy and confusing. He shows us that as each new era (abbreviated, for example, as "eC19" for early nineteenth century) redefined the term, some of the older definitions, far from becoming obsolete, remained popular and meaningful. Over time, as these different layers of meanings and definitions piled onto the word, it became *polysemous*—many different meanings for the word coexisted. This makes culture a very slippery concept and frustrates some social scientists, but rather than try to define the term precisely, Williams argues, we ought to recognize that "it is the range and overlap of meanings that is significant."

Williams is also careful to show us that changes in the meaning of the word were not just random or happenstance. New meanings arose in part through the influence and diffusion of new intellectual movements, as well as social and economic shifts. For instance, the shift from pre-modern agricultural to modern industrial economies signaled a shift toward a more class-based definition of the word, where "culture" came to mean that which only the higher classes possessed. Williams's tracking of the wide range of meanings helps us understand why the field of cultural sociology is so broad and complex: the concept itself encompasses many different realms of human experience.

# CULTURE

**C** **ulture** is one of the two or three most complicated words in the English language. This is so partly because of its intricate historical development, in several European languages, but mainly because it has now come to be used for important concepts in several distinct intellectual disciplines and in several distinct and incompatible systems of thought.

The fw is *cultura*, L, from rw *colere*, L. *Colere* had a range of meanings: inhabit, cultivate, protect, honour with worship. Some of these meanings eventually separated, though still with occasional overlapping, in the derived nouns. Thus "inhabit" developed through *colonus*, L to *colony*. "Honour with worship" developed through *cultus*, L to *cult*. *Cultura* took on the main meaning of cultivation or tending, including, as in Cicero, *cultura animi*, though with subsidiary medieval meanings of honour and worship (cf. in English **culture** as "worship" in Caxton (1483)). The French forms of *cultura* were *couture*, oF, which has since developed its own specialized meaning, and later *culture*, which by eC15 had passed into English. The primary meaning was then in husbandry, the tending of natural growth.

**Culture** in all its early uses was a noun of process: the tending *of* something, basically crops or animals. The subsidiary *coulter*–ploughshare, had travelled by a different linguistic route, from *culter*, L–ploughshare, *culter*, oE, to the variant English spellings *culter*, *colter*, *coulter* and as late as eC17 **culture** (Webster, *Duchess of Malfi*, III, ii: "hot burning cultures"). This provided a further basis for the important next stage of meaning, by metaphor. From eC16 the tending of natural growth was extended to a process of human development, and this, alongside the original meaning in husbandry, was the main sense until lC18 and eC19. Thus More: "to the culture and profit of their minds"; Bacon: "the culture and manurance of minds" (1605); Hobbes: "a culture of their minds" (1651); Johnson: "she neglected the culture of her understanding" (1759). At various points in this development two crucial changes occurred: first, a degree of habituation to the metaphor, which made the sense of human tending direct; second, an extension of particular processes to a general process, which the word could abstractly carry. It is of course from the latter development that the independent noun **culture** began its complicated modern history, but the process of change is so intricate, and the latencies of meaning are at times so close, that it is not possible to give any definite date. **Culture** as an independent noun, an abstract process or the product of such a process, is not important before lC18 and is not common before mC19. But the early stages of this development were not sudden. There is an interesting use in Milton, in the second (revised) edition of *The Readie and Easie Way to Establish a Free Commonwealth* (1660): "spread much more Knowledg and Civility, yea, Religion, through all parts of the Land, by communicating the natural heat of Government and Culture more distributively to all extreme parts, which now lie num and neglected." Here the metaphorical sense ("natural heat") still appears to be present, and *civility* (cf. CIVILIZATION) is still written, where in C19 we would normally expect **culture**. Yet we can also read "government and culture" in a quite modern sense. Milton, from the tenor of his whole argument, is writing about a general social process, and this is a definite stage of development. In C18 England this general process acquired definite class associations though **cultivation** and **cultivated** were more commonly used for this. But there is a letter of 1730 (Bishop of Killala, to Mrs Clayton; cit Plumb, *England in the Eighteenth Century*) which has this clear sense: "It has not been customary for persons of either birth or culture to breed up their children to the Church." Akenside (*Pleasures of Imagination*, 1744) wrote: ". . . nor purple state nor culture can bestow." Wordsworth wrote "where grace of culture hath been utterly unknown" (1805), and Jane Austen (*Emma*, 1816) "every advantage of discipline and culture."

It is thus clear that culture was developing in English towards some of its modern senses before the decisive effects of a new social and intellectual movement. But to follow the development through this movement, in lC18 and eC19, we have to look also at developments in other languages and especially in German.

In French, until C18, **culture** was always accompanied by a grammatical form indicating the matter being cultivated, as in the English usage already noted. Its occasional use as an independent noun dates from mC18, rather later than similar occasional uses in English. The independent noun *civilization* also emerged in mC18; its relationship to **culture** has since been very complicated (cf. CIVILIZATION and discussion below). There was at this point an important development in German: the word was borrowed from French, spelled first (lC18) *Cultur* and from C19 *Kultur*. Its main use was still as a synonym for *civilization*: first in the abstract sense of a general process of becoming "civilized" or "cultivated," second, in the sense which had already been established for *civilization* by the historians of the Enlightenment, in the popular C18 form of the universal histories, as a description of the secular process of human development. There was then a decisive change of use in Herder. In his unfinished *Ideas, on the Philosophy of the History of Mankind* (1784–91) he wrote of *Cultur*: "nothing is more indeterminate than this word, and nothing more deceptive than its application to all nations and periods." He attacked the assumption of the universal histories that "civilization" or "culture"—the historical self-development of humanity—was what we would now call a unilinear process, leading to the high and dominant point of C18 European culture. Indeed he attacked what he called European subjugation and domination of the four quarters of the globe, and wrote:

> Men of all the quarters of the globe, who have perished over the ages, you have not lived solely to manure the earth with your ashes, so that at the end of time your posterity should be made happy by European culture. The very thought of a superior European culture is a blatant insult to the majesty of Nature.

It is then necessary, he argued, in a decisive innovation, to speak of "cultures" in the plural: the specific and variable cultures of different nations and periods, but also the specific and variable cultures of social and economic groups within a nation. This sense was widely developed, in the Romantic movement, as an alternative to the orthodox and dominant "*civilization*." It was first used to emphasize national and traditional cultures, including the new concept of **folk-culture** (cf. FOLK). It was later used to attack what was seen as the "MECHANICAL" (q.v.) character of the new civilization then emerging: both for its abstract rationalism and for the "inhumanity" of current industrial development. It was used to distinguish between "human" and "material" development. Politically, as so often in this period, it veered between radicalism and reaction and very often, in the confusion of major social change, fused elements of both. (It should also be noted, though it adds to the real complication, that the same kind of distinction, especially between "material" and "spiritual" development, was made by von Humboldt and others, until as late as 1900, with a reversal of the terms, **culture** being material and *civilization* spiritual. In general, however, the opposite distinction was dominant.)

On the other hand, from the 1840s in Germany, *Kultur* was being used in very much the sense in which *civilization* had been used in C18 universal histories. The decisive innovation is G. F. Klemm's *Allgemeine Kulturgeschichte der Menschheit*—"General Cultural History of Mankind" (1843–52)—which traced human development from savagery through domestication to freedom. Although the American anthropologist Morgan, tracing comparable stages, used "Ancient *Society*," with a culmination in *Civilization*, Klemm's sense was sustained, and was directly followed in English by Tylor in *Primitive Culture* (1870). It is along this line of reference that the dominant sense in modern social sciences has to be traced.

The complexity of the modern development of the word, and of its modern usage, can then be appreciated. We can easily distinguish the sense which depends on a literal continuity of physical process as now in "sugar-beet culture" or, in the specialized physical application in bacteriology since the 1880s, "germ culture." But once we go beyond the physical reference, we have to recognize three broad active categories of usage. The sources of two of these we have already discussed: (i) the independent and abstract noun which describes a general process of intellectual, spiritual and aesthetic development, from C18; (ii) the independent noun, whether used generally or specifically, which indicates a particular way of life, whether of a people, a period, a group, or humanity in general, from Herder and Klemm. But we have also to recognize (iii) the independent and abstract noun which describes the works and practices of intellectual and especially artistic activity. This seems often now the most widespread use: **culture** is music, literature, painting and sculpture, theatre and film. A **Ministry of**

**Culture** refers to these specific activities, sometimes with the addition of philosophy, scholarship, history. This use, (iii), is in fact relatively late. It is difficult to date precisely because it is in origin an applied form of sense (i): the idea of a general process of intellectual, spiritual and aesthetic development was applied and effectively transferred to the works and practices which represent and sustain it. But it also developed from the earlier sense of process; cf. "progressive culture of fine arts," Millar, *Historical View of the English Government*, IV, 314 (1812). In English (i) and (iii) are still close; at times, for internal reasons, they are indistinguishable as in Arnold, *Culture and Anarchy* (1867); while sense (ii) was decisively introduced into English by Tylor, *Primitive Culture* (1870), following Klemm. The decisive development of sense (iii) in English was in lC19 and eC20.

Faced by this complex and still active history of the word, it is easy to react by selecting one "true" or "proper" or "scientific" sense and dismissing other senses as loose or confused. There is evidence of this reaction even in the excellent study by Kroeber and Kluckhohn, *Culture: a Critical Review of Concepts and Definitions*, where usage in North American anthropology is in effect taken as a norm. It is clear that, within a discipline, conceptual usage has to be clarified. But in general it is the range and overlap of meanings that is significant. The complex of senses indicates a complex argument about the relations between general human development and a particular way of life, and between both and the works and practices of art and intelligence. It is especially interesting that in archaeology and in *cultural anthropology* the reference to **culture** or **a culture** is primarily to *material* production, while in history and *cultural studies* the reference is primarily to *signifying* or *symbolic* systems. This often confuses but even more often conceals the central question of the relations between "material" and "symbolic" production, which in some recent argument—cf. my own *Culture*— have always to be related rather than contrasted. Within this complex argument there are fundamentally opposed as well as effectively overlapping positions; there are also, understandably, many unresolved questions and confused answers. But these arguments and questions cannot be resolved by reducing the complexity of actual usage. This point is relevant also to uses of forms of the word in languages other than English, where there is considerable variation. The anthropological use is common in the German, Scandinavian and Slavonic language groups, but it is distinctly subordinate to the senses of art and learning, or of a general process of human development, in Italian and French. Between languages as within a language, the range and complexity of sense and reference indicate both difference of intellectual position and some blurring or overlapping. These variations, of whatever kind, necessarily involve alternative views of the activities, relationships and processes which this complex word indicates. The complexity, that is to say, is not finally in the word but in the problems which its variations of use significantly indicate.

It is necessary to look also at some associated and derived words. **Cultivation** and **cultivated** went through the same metaphorical extension from a physical to a social or educational sense in C17, and were especially significant words in C18. Coleridge, making a classical eC19 distinction between civilization and culture, wrote (1830): "the permanent distinction, and occasional contrast, between cultivation and civilization." The noun in this sense has effectively disappeared but the adjective is still quite common, especially in relation to manners and tastes. The important adjective **cultural** appears to date from the 1870s; it became common by the 1890s. The word is only available, in its modern sense, when the independent noun, in the artistic and intellectual or anthropological senses, has become familiar. Hostility to the word **culture** in English appears to date from the controversy around Arnold's views. It gathered force in 1C19 and eC20, in association with a comparable hostility to *aesthete* and AESTHETIC (q.v.). Its association with class distinction produced the mime-word *culchah*. There was also an area of hostility associated with anti-German feeling, during and after the 1914–18 War, in relation to propaganda about *Kultur*. The central area of hostility has lasted, and one element of it has been emphasized by the recent American phrase **culture-vulture.** It is significant that virtually all the hostility (with the sole exception of the temporary anti-German association) has been connected with uses involving claims to superior knowledge (cf. the noun INTELLECTUAL), refinement (*culchah*) and distinctions between "high" art (**culture**) and popular art and entertainment. It thus records a real social history and a very difficult and confused phase of social and cultural development. It is interesting that the steadily extending social and anthropological use of **culture** and **cultural** and such formations as **sub-culture** (the culture of a distinguishable smaller group) has, except in certain areas (notably popular entertainment), either bypassed or effectively diminished the hostility and its associated unease and embarrassment. The recent use of *culturalism*, to indicate a methodological contrast with *structuralism* in social analysis, retains many of the earlier difficulties, and does not always bypass the hostility.

# STUDY QUESTIONS

1. Of the many different senses of the word *culture* that Williams discusses, which one is most familiar to you and why? Which is least familiar?
2. Given the different ways in which *culture* has been used, what challenges might cultural sociologists face when we set out to do our work?

# PART TWO

# FRAMES, ACTIONS, AND EFFECTS

I N THE ACCLAIMED television show, *The Wire*, Wallace and Bodie, a couple of corner-boys (street level drug dealers, typically teenage boys, who stand on corners and sell drugs supplied by higher-ups) are playing chess outside on a bright, autumn day. They are approached by D'Angelo Barksdale, the nephew of the local drug kingpin, Avon Barksdale, for whom all three work. D'Angelo watches the game for a moment and interrupts the boys: "Yo, what was that?" he exclaims. "Castle can't move like that." "Nah, we ain't playing that," Bodie replies.

Confused, D'Angelo looks on and realizes the boys aren't actually playing chess. They are playing checkers, but using chess pieces. He laughs and teases the boys mercilessly, but then offers to show them the rules of the game and how each piece moves. What follows is both funny and heartbreaking as D'Angelo explains to Wallace and Bodie that chess is not like checkers, even though they are played on the same board. There is a King (like Avon the kingpin) who doesn't do much, but who has all the power. He has a partner (the Queen) who "has all the moves" and directs the dirty work. There is also the Castle, which is like the drug stash. Each time it moves, a little muscle in the form of Knights and Pawns (in Bodie's memorable phrase, "those little bald-headed bitches") get moved along with it. "The pawns in the game, they get capped quick," D'Angelo warns.

But the boys, now seeing themselves as pawns, resist this lesson.

"But if I make it to the other side," Bodie asks, "I win, right?" He is clearly thinking of checkers, where if you make it to the other side of the board, you get kinged. D'Angelo patiently explains that in chess, if one of the pawns makes it to other side of the board, it becomes a queen. But "the king stays the king" and the pawns never become "top dog." "They outta the game early," D'Angelo warns him.

"Unless they some smart-ass pawns," Bodie calmly retorts, again refusing to accept D'Angelo's implications about his fate.

There is much to be said about this powerful scene, including the way it wryly compares drug dealing to the art of playing chess, elevating a criminal enterprise to the favored game of ancient kings and nobles. It is also worth noting the sad irony that these low-level drug dealers think they are playing one game when in fact they are playing another, one with rules and outcomes completely unknown to them. The scene is emblematic of how different frames can affect people's perceptions of their situations and because of this, can influence how they react. If you think you're playing checkers, one set of actions, strategies, and out-comes is expected. But if chess is the game, an entirely different set of actions, strategies, and outcomes comes into play. Onlookers who see you and me at play (or work, or engaged in any kind of behavior) might conclude from the scene that we are acting according to one set of rules with which they are familiar, when we are in fact playing according to our own rules, which we collectively defined for ourselves. In the eyes of the outsider, we misunderstand our situation and the actions appropriate to it. In our eyes, it is the outsider who misunderstands. Of course, con-flicts can and often do arise precisely because of such misunderstand-ings. Different people frame their actions in different ways.

This framing dynamic points to a fundamental sociological insight, best articulated by W. I. Thomas: "If men define situations as real, they are real in their consequences." This insight underpins much sociological research, including the work of cultural sociologists seeking to interpret the meanings people assign to human behavior, both their own and that of others. The Thomas Theorem, as it is called, posits that a person's interpretation of his situation guides the actions he takes in response to the situation. The way that people frame their circumstances is an important cause of their behavior. Sociologist Robert Merton took the Thomas Theorem one step further with his idea of the "self-fulfilling prophecy," noting that people's expectation that something is going to happen—or is already happening—can bring that reality to be.

It follows from these insights that if sociologists want to understand people's behavior, we first need to understand how they perceive their situation. If we want to understand Bodie and Wallace's actions, we first need to understand that they think they are playing checkers, not chess.

If we want to understand their persistent belief that they can rise up through the ranks to become drug kingpins, we need to know that they don't understand chess well enough to estimate their chances of survival as mere pawns.

The readings in this section illustrate that frames have powerful influences on collective human actions, which in turn powerfully shape outcomes and events. The essays here cover a wide variety of topics, from basic social interactions between two people, to the nature of public memory and history, to the ways that different forms of music develop over time. But they share a common preoccupation with discovering and illuminating how humans come to understand our experiences as much more than raw, disconnected bits of sensory perceptions or a seamless roar of indiscriminate white noise. Instead, we think about our lives as being composed of discrete blocks of meaningful moments, or memorable instances. All of us use symbols, signs, and representations that society makes available to organize these blocks of time into categories, the meanings of which we somehow work out with others around us. Both formally and informally, we assemble these categories into classification systems that we use to make distinctions between right and wrong, good and bad, us and them. We use these basic distinctions to orient ourselves in social space and to navigate our social worlds. We use them to guide our actions and to judge the actions of others. And we use them to understand the consequences of those actions and the outcomes and events that arise from such actions.

What these readings argue, then, is that understanding how people come to notice some things and not others and how individuals learn to make sense out of the things they notice is far from just an act of cognition that occurs within the brain. It is best viewed instead as a cultural process, whereby one's perceptions of reality are shaped to a very large degree by the social and cultural environments and by the understandings of different situations that are available for making sense of those environments.

Thinking back on that scene from The Wire, it is tempting to ask whose definition of the situation is correct. Bodie and Wallace happily play checkers using chess pieces. Does this mean they are competent (even innovative) checkers players? Or are they incompetent chess players? The answer, of course, depends on your point of view, though D'Angelo does not see it that way.

Ultimately, cultural sociologists don't seek to sort answers into right and wrong. Instead, we concern ourselves with discovering what happens when certain situations are framed one way versus another. We focus on documenting how defining situations as "real" results in real consequences, whether or not the shared definitions of the situation seem correct to us or not. Sometimes, we try to generalize from a limited number of cases where the outcomes of frames are known to predict what will happen in similarly framed situations, where outcomes are yet unknown. Our point is simple: if you want to understand people's actions and their effects, you must first understand the meanings of the frames they use. Otherwise, you might mistake a checkers game for chess.

# 6

# MASS DECEPTION

MAX HORKHEIMER AND THEODOR ADORNO

In the animated science-fiction film *WALL-E,* a lone robot toils ceaselessly, cleaning up a despoiled earth. An apocalyptic, ecological collapse has rendered the planet uninhabitable and humanity has retreated to outer space aboard vast, cruise-ship-like vessels that periodically send out probes in search of viable plant life. Aboard the ship, humans enjoy every conceivable convenience, whizzing around in hovercraft chaise lounges, slurping giant soft-drinks, and consuming seemingly endless quantities of fast food. As a species, humans have become grossly obese, mired in complacency and apathetic about the fate of earth and their own destinies. Everywhere they go, flat screen TVs distract them from their problems, soothe their troubled thoughts, and entertain them with promises of a better tomorrow.

Max Horkheimer (1895–1973) and Theodor Adorno (1903–1969) would no doubt see this fictional society as an apt metaphor for the effects of mass culture on human consciousness. Members of the influential circle of German Marxist intellectuals known as the *Frankfurt School,* Horkheimer and Adorno decried the rise of a *culture industry* that existed to profit from the production of cultural objects like films, music, and TV shows. They saw deeply pernicious effects emanating from pop culture, which they believed lulled people into a state of political passivity and false contentment. The culture industry, they argued, did not serve human needs, but rather the needs of the postwar capitalist system, which required fresh hordes of eager consumers willing to buy shiny new products (whether they need them or not). But it was not just the rise of advertising and commercialization that bothered Horkheimer and Adorno. They linked the effects of the culture industry to the rise of fascism and totalitarianism. Their broad, sweeping, and controversial condemnation of the effects of pop culture has criticized been by cultural sociologists for its overly deterministic view. But their theory remains an important touchstone for students seeking to understand how power works through cultural forms.

# THE CULTURE INDUSTRY: ENLIGHTENMENT AS MASS DECEPTION

The sociological theory that the loss of the support of objectively established religion, the dissolution of the last remnants of precapitalism, together with technological and social differentiation or specialization, have led to cultural chaos is disproved every day; for culture now impresses the same stamp on everything. Films, radio and magazines make up a system which is uniform as a whole and in every part. Even the aesthetic activities of political opposites are one in their enthusiastic obedience to the rhythm of the iron system. The decorative industrial management buildings and exhibition centers in authoritarian countries are much the same as anywhere else. The huge gleaming towers that shoot up everywhere are outward signs of the ingenious planning of international concerns, toward which the unleashed entrepreneurial system (whose monuments are a mass of gloomy houses and business premises in grimy, spiritless cities) was already hastening. Even now the older houses just outside the concrete city centers look like slums, and the new bungalows on the outskirts are at one with the flimsy structures of world fairs in their praise of technical progress and their built-in demand to be discarded after a short while like empty food cans. Yet the city housing projects designed to perpetuate the individual as a supposedly independent unit in a small hygienic dwelling make him all the more subservient to his adversary—the absolute power of capitalism. Because the inhabitants, as producers and as consumers, are drawn into the center in search of work and pleasure, all the living units crystallize into well-organized complexes. The striking unity of microcosm and mac-

rocosm presents men with a model of their culture: the false identity of
the general and the particular. Under monopoly all mass culture is identical, and the lines of its artificial framework begin to show through. The
people at the top are no longer so interested in concealing monopoly: as
its violence becomes more open, so its power grows. Movies and radio
need no longer pretend to be art. The truth that they are just business is
made into an ideology in order to justify the rubbish they deliberately
produce. They call themselves industries; and when their directors'
incomes are published, any doubt about the social utility of the finished
products is removed.

Interested parties explain the culture industry in technological terms.
It is alleged that because millions participate in it, certain reproduction
processes are necessary that inevitably require identical needs in innumerable places to be satisfied with identical goods. The technical contrast
between the few production centers and the large number of widely dispersed consumption points is said to demand organization and planning
by management. Furthermore, it is claimed that standards were based in
the first place on consumers' needs, and for that reason were accepted
with so little resistance. The result is the circle of manipulation and retro-
active need in which the unity of the system grows ever stronger. No mention is made of the fact that the basis on which technology acquires power
over society is the power of those whose economic hold over society is
greatest. A technological rationale is the rationale of domination itself. It
is the coercive nature of society alienated from itself. Automobiles, bombs,
and movies keep the whole thing together until their leveling element shows
its strength in the very wrong which it furthered. It has made the technology
of the culture industry no more than the achievement of standardization
and mass production, sacrificing whatever involved a distinction between
the logic of the work and that of the social system. This is the result not
of a law of movement in technology as such but of its function in today's
economy. The need which might resist central control has already been
suppressed by the control of the individual consciousness. The step from
the telephone to the radio has clearly distinguished the roles. The former
still allowed the subscriber to play the role of subject, and was liberal. The
latter is democratic: it turns all participants into listeners and authorita-
tively subjects them to broadcast programs which are all exactly the same.
No machinery of rejoinder has been devised, and private broadcasters are

denied any freedom. They are confined to the apocryphal field of the "amateur," and also have to accept organization from above. But any trace of spontaneity from the public in official broadcasting is controlled and absorbed by talent scouts, studio competitions and official programs of every kind selected by professionals. Talented performers belong to the industry long before it displays them; otherwise they would not be so eager to fit in. The attitude of the public, which ostensibly and actually favors the system of the culture industry, is a part of the system and not an excuse for it. If one branch of art follows the same formula as one with a very different medium and content; if the dramatic intrigue of broadcast soap operas becomes no more than useful material for showing how to master technical problems at both ends of the scale of musical experience—real jazz or a cheap imitation; or if a movement from a Beethoven symphony is crudely "adapted" for a film sound-track in the same way as a Tolstoy novel is garbled in a film script: then the claim that this is done to satisfy the spontaneous wishes of the public is no more than hot air. We are closer to the facts if we explain these phenomena as inherent in the technical and personnel apparatus which, down to its last cog, itself forms part of the economic mechanism of selection. In addition there is the agreement—or at least the determination—of all executive authorities not to produce or sanction anything that in any way differs from their own rules, their own ideas about consumers, or above all themselves.

In our age the objective social tendency is incarnate in the hidden subjective purposes of company directors, the foremost among whom are in the most powerful sectors of industry—steel, petroleum, electricity, and chemicals. Culture monopolies are weak and dependent in comparison. They cannot afford to neglect their appeasement of the real holders of power if their sphere of activity in mass society (a sphere producing a specific type of commodity which anyhow is still too closely bound up with easygoing liberalism and Jewish intellectuals) is not to undergo a series of purges. The dependence of the most powerful broadcasting company on the electrical industry, or of the motion picture industry on the banks, is characteristic of the whole sphere, whose individual branches are themselves economically interwoven. All are in such close contact that the extreme concentration of mental forces allows demarcation lines between different firms and technical branches to be ignored. The ruthless unity in the culture industry is evidence of what will happen in politics. Marked differentiations such as those of A and B films, or of stories in magazines

in different price ranges, depend not so much on subject matter as on classifying, organizing, and labeling consumers. Something is provided for all
so that none may escape; the distinctions are emphasized and extended.
The public is catered for with a hierarchical range of mass-produced products of varying quality, thus advancing the rule of complete quantification.
Everybody must behave (as if spontaneously) in accordance with his previously determined and indexed level, and choose the category of mass product turned out for his type. Consumers appear as statistics on research
organization charts, and are divided by income groups into red, green, and
blue areas; the technique is that used for any type of propaganda.

How formalized the procedure is can be seen when the mechanically
differentiated products prove to be all alike in the end. That the difference
between the Chrysler range and General Motors products is basically illusory strikes every child with a keen interest in varieties. What connoisseurs discuss as good or bad points serve only to perpetuate the semblance
of competition and range of choice. The same applies to the Warner Brothers
and Metro Goldwyn Mayer productions. But even the differences between
the more expensive and cheaper models put out by the same firm steadily
diminish: for automobiles, there are such differences as the number of cyl-
inders, cubic capacity, details of patented gadgets; and for films there are
the number of stars, the extravagant use of technology, labor, and equipment, and the introduction of the latest psychological formulas. The universal criterion of merit is the amount of "conspicuous production," of blatant
cash investment. The varying budgets in the culture industry do not bear
the slightest relation to factual values, to the meaning of the products themselves. Even the technical media are relentlessly forced into uniformity. Television aims at a synthesis of radio and film, and is held up only because the
interested parties have not yet reached agreement, but its consequences
will be quite enormous and promise to intensify the impoverishment of
aesthetic matter so drastically, that by tomorrow the thinly veiled identity
of all industrial culture products can come triumphantly out into the open,
derisively fulfilling the Wagnerian dream of the *Gesamtkunstwerk*—the
fusion of all the arts in one work.

The man with leisure has to accept what the culture manufacturers offer
him. Kant's formalism still expected a contribution from the individual,

who was thought to relate the varied experiences of the senses to fundamental concepts; but industry robs the individual of his function. Its prime
service to the customer is to do his schematizing for him. Kant said that
there was a secret mechanism in the soul which prepared direct intuitions
in such a way that they could be fitted into the system of pure reason. But
today that secret has been deciphered. While the mechanism is to all appearances planned by those who serve up the data of experience, that is, by the
culture industry, it is in fact forced upon the latter by the power of society,
which remains irrational, however we may try to rationalize it; and this
inescapable force is processed by commercial agencies so that they give an
artificial impression of being in command. There is nothing left for the
consumer to classify. Producers have done it for him. Art for the masses
has destroyed the dream but still conforms to the tenets of that dreaming
idealism which critical idealism balked at. Everything derives from consciousness: for Malebranche and Berkeley, from the consciousness of God;
in mass art, from the consciousness of the production team. Not only are
the hit songs, stars, and soap operas cyclically recurrent and rigidly invari-
able types, but the specific content of the entertainment itself is derived
from them and only appears to change. The details are interchangeable.
The short interval sequence which was effective in a hit song, the hero's
momentary fall from grace (which he accepts as good sport), the rough
treatment which the beloved gets from the male star, the latter's rugged
defiance of the spoilt heiress, are, like all the other details, ready-made
clichés to be slotted in anywhere; they never do anything more than fulfill
the purpose allotted them in the overall plan. Their whole *raison d'être* is to
confirm it by being its constituent parts. As soon as the film begins, it is
quite clear how it will end, and who will be rewarded, punished, or forgotten. In light music, once the trained ear has heard the first notes of the hit
song, it can guess what is coming and feel flattered when it does come.
The average length of the short story has to be rigidly adhered to. Even
gags, effects, and jokes are calculated like the setting in which they are
placed. They are the responsibility of special experts and their narrow
range makes it easy for them to be apportioned in the office. The development of the culture industry has led to the predominance of the effect, the
obvious touch, and the technical detail over the work itself—which once
expressed an idea, but was liquidated together with the idea. When the
detail won its freedom, it became rebellious and, in the period from Romanticism to Expressionism, asserted itself as free expression, as a vehicle of

protest against the organization. In music the single harmonic effect obliterated the awareness of form as a whole; in painting the individual color was stressed at the expense of pictorial composition; and in the novel psychology became more important than structure. The totality of the culture industry has put an end to this. Though concerned exclusively with effects, it crushes their insubordination and makes them subserve the formula, which replaces the work. The same fate is inflicted on whole and parts alike. The whole inevitably bears no relation to the details—just like the career of a successful man into which everything is made to fit as an illustration or a proof, whereas it is nothing more than the sum of all those idiotic events. The so-called dominant idea is like a file which ensures order but not coherence. The whole and the parts are alike; there is no antithesis and no connection. Their prearranged harmony is a mockery of what had to be striven after in the great bourgeois works of art. In Germany the graveyard stillness of the dictatorship already hung over the gayest films of the democratic era.

The whole world is made to pass through the filter of the culture industry. The old experience of the movie-goer, who sees the world outside as an extension of the film he has just left (because the latter is intent upon reproducing the world of everyday perceptions), is now the producer's guideline. The more intensely and flawlessly his techniques duplicate empirical objects, the easier it is today for the illusion to prevail that the outside world is the straightforward continuation of that presented on the screen. This purpose has been furthered by mechanical reproduction since the lightning takeover by the sound film.

Real life is becoming indistinguishable from the movies. The sound film, far surpassing the theater of illusion, leaves no room for imagination or reflection on the part of the audience, who is unable to respond within the structure of the film, yet deviate from its precise detail without losing the thread of the story; hence the film forces its victims to equate it directly with reality. The stunting of the mass-media consumer's powers of imagination and spontaneity does not have to be traced back to any psychological mechanisms; he must ascribe the loss of those attributes to the objective nature of the products themselves, especially to the most characteristic of them, the sound film. They are so designed that quickness, powers of observation, and experience are undeniably needed to apprehend them at all; yet sustained thought is out of the question if the spectator is not to miss the relentless rush of facts. Even though the effort required for his response is semi-automatic, no scope is left for the imagination. Those who are so absorbed by the world of the movie—by its images, gestures, and words— that they are unable to supply what really makes it a world, do not have to dwell on particular points of its mechanics during a screening. All the other films and products of the entertainment industry which they have seen have taught them what to expect; they react automatically. The might of industrial society is lodged in men's minds. The entertainments manu- facturers know that their products will be consumed with alertness even when the customer is distraught, for each of them is a model of the huge economic machinery which has always sustained the masses, whether at work or at leisure—which is akin to work. From every sound film and every broadcast program the social effect can be inferred which is exclusive to none but is shared by all alike. The culture industry as a whole has molded men as a type unfailingly reproduced in every product. All the agents of this process, from the producer to the women's clubs, take good care that the simple reproduction of this mental state is not nuanced or extended in any way.

The art historians and guardians of culture who complain of the extinc- tion in the West of a basic style-determining power are wrong. The stereo- typed appropriation of everything, even the inchoate, for the purposes of mechanical reproduction surpasses the rigor and general currency of any "real style," in the sense in which cultural *cognoscenti* celebrate the organic pre-capitalist past.

A constant sameness governs the relationship to the past as well. What is new about the phase of mass culture compared with the late liberal stage is the exclusion of the new. The machine rotates on the same spot. While determining consumption it excludes the untried as a risk. The movie- makers distrust any manuscript which is not reassuringly backed by a bestseller. Yet for this very reason there is never-ending talk of ideas, nov- elty, and surprise, of what is taken for granted but has never existed. Tempo and dynamics serve this trend. Nothing remains as of old; every- thing has to run incessantly, to keep moving. For only the universal tri- umph of the rhythm of mechanical production and reproduction promises that nothing changes, and nothing unsuitable will appear. Any additions to the well-proven culture inventory are too much of a speculation. The

ossified forms—such as the sketch, short story, problem film, or hit song—
are the standardized average of late liberal taste, dictated with threats
from above. The people at the top in the culture agencies, who work in
harmony as only one manager can with another, whether he comes from
the rag trade or from college, have long since reorganized and rationalized
the objective spirit. One might think that an omnipresent authority had
sifted the material and drawn up an official catalog of cultural commodities to provide a smooth supply of available mass-produced lines. The
ideas are written in the cultural firmament where they had already been
numbered by Plato—and were indeed numbers, incapable of increase and
immutable.

Amusement and all the elements of the culture industry existed long
before the latter came into existence. Now they are taken over from above
and brought up to date. The culture industry can pride itself on having ener-
getically executed the previously clumsy transposition of art into the sphere
of consumption, on making this a principle, on divesting amusement of its
obtrusive naïvetés and improving the type of commodities. The more absolute it became, the more ruthless it was in forcing every outsider either into
bankruptcy or into a syndicate, and became more refined and elevated—
until it ended up as a synthesis of Beethoven and the Casino de Paris. It
enjoys a double victory: the truth it extinguishes without it can reproduce
at will as a lie within. "Light" art as such, distraction, is not a decadent form.
Anyone who complains that it is a betrayal of the ideal of pure expression
is under an illusion about society. The purity of bourgeois art, which
hypostasized itself as a world of freedom in contrast to what was happening in the material world, was from the beginning bought with the exclusion of the lower classes—with whose cause, the real universality, art keeps
faith precisely by its freedom from the ends of the false universality. Serious
art has been withheld from those for whom the hardship and oppression of
life make a mockery of seriousness, and who must be glad if they can use
time not spent at the production line just to keep going. Light art has been
the shadow of autonomous art. It is the social bad conscience of serious
art. The truth which the latter necessarily lacked because of its social
premises gives the other the semblance of legitimacy. The division itself is
the truth: it does at least express the negativity of the culture which the
different spheres constitute. Least of all can the antithesis be reconciled
by absorbing light into serious art, or vice versa. But that is what the culture industry attempts.

Nevertheless the culture industry remains the entertainment business. Its influence over the consumers is established by entertainment; that will ultimately be broken not by an outright decree, but by the hostility inherent in the principle of entertainment to what is greater than itself. Since all the trends of the culture industry are profoundly embedded in the public by the whole social process, they are encouraged by the survival of the market in this area. Demand has not yet been replaced by simple obedience. As is well known, the major reorganization of the film industry shortly before World War I, the material prerequisite of its expansion, was precisely its deliberate acceptance of the public's needs as recorded at the box-office—a procedure which was hardly thought necessary in the pioneering days of the screen. The same opinion is held today by the captains of the film industry, who take as their criterion the more or less phenomenal song hits but wisely never have recourse to the judgment of truth, the opposite criterion. Business is their ideology. It is quite correct that the power of the culture industry resides in its identification with a manufactured need, and not in simple contrast to it, even if this contrast were one of complete power and complete powerlessness. Amusement under late capitalism is the prolongation of work. It is sought after as an escape from the mechanized work process, and to recruit strength in order to be able to cope with it again. But at the same time mechanization has such power over a man's leisure and happiness, and so profoundly determines the manufacture of amusement goods, that his experiences are inevitably after-images of the work process itself. The ostensible content is merely a faded foreground; what sinks in is the automatic succession of standardized operations. What happens at work, in the factory, or in the office can only be escaped from by approximation to it in one's leisure time. All amusement suffers from this incurable malady.

The culture industry perpetually cheats its consumers of what it perpetually promises. The promissory note which, with its plots and staging, it draws on pleasure is endlessly prolonged; the promise, which is actually all the spectacle consists of, is illusory: all it actually confirms is that the real point will never be reached, that the diner must be satisfied with the menu. In front of the appetite stimulated by all those brilliant names and images there is finally set no more than a commendation of the depressing everyday world it sought to escape. Of course works of art were not sexual exhibitions either. However, by representing deprivation as negative, they retracted, as it were, the prostitution of the impulse and rescued by mediation what was denied. The secret of aesthetic sublimation is its representation of fulfillment as a broken promise. The culture industry does not sublimate; it represses. By repeatedly exposing the objects of desire, breasts in a clinging sweater or the naked torso of the athletic hero, it only stimulates the unsublimated forepleasure which habitual deprivation has long since reduced to a masochistic semblance. There is no erotic situation which, while insinuating and exciting, does not fail to indicate unmistakably that things can never go that far. The Hays Office merely confirms the ritual of Tantalus that the culture industry has established anyway. Works of art are ascetic and unashamed; the culture industry is pornographic and prudish. Love is downgraded to romance. And, after the descent, much is permitted; even license as a marketable speciality has its quota bearing the trade description "daring." The mass production of the sexual automatically achieves its repression. Because of his ubiquity, the film star with whom one is meant to fall in love is from the outset a copy of himself. Every tenor voice comes to sound like a Caruso record, and the "natural" faces of Texas girls are like the successful models by whom Hollywood has typecast them. The mechanical reproduction of beauty, which reactionary cultural fanaticism wholeheartedly serves in its methodical idolization of individuality, leaves no room for that unconscious idolatry which was once essential to beauty. The triumph over beauty is celebrated by humor—the *Schadenfreude* that every successful deprivation calls forth. There is laughter because there is nothing to laugh at. Laughter, whether conciliatory or terrible, always occurs when some fear passes. It indicates liberation either from physical danger or from the grip of logic. Conciliatory laughter is heard as the echo of an escape from power; the wrong kind overcomes fear by capitulating to the forces which are to be feared. It is the echo of power as something inescapable. Fun is a medicinal bath. The pleasure industry never fails to prescribe it. It makes laughter the instrument of the fraud practised on happiness. Moments of happiness are without laughter; only operettas and films portray sex to the accompaniment of resounding laughter.

The stronger the positions of the culture industry become, the more summarily it can deal with consumers' needs, producing them, controlling them, disciplining them, and even withdrawing amusement: no limits are set to cultural progress of this kind. But the tendency is immanent in the principle of amusement itself, which is enlightened in a bourgeois sense. If the need for amusement was in large measure the creation of industry, which used the subject as a means of recommending the work to the masses—the oleograph by the dainty morsel it depicted, or the cake mix by a picture of a cake—amusement always reveals the influence of business, the sales talk, the quack's spiel. But the original affinity of business and amusement is shown in the latter's specific significance: to defend society. To be pleased means to say Yes. It is possible only by insulation from the totality of the social process, by desensitization and, from the first, by senselessly sacrificing the inescapable claim of every work, however inane, within its limits to reflect the whole. Pleasure always means not to think about anything, to forget suffering even where it is shown. Basically it is helplessness. It is flight; not, as is asserted, flight from a wretched reality, but from the last remaining thought of resistance. The liberation which amusement promises is freedom from thought and from negation. The effrontery of the rhetorical question, "What do people want?" lies in the fact that it is addressed—as if to reflective individuals—to those very people who are deliberately to be deprived of this individuality. Even when the public does—exceptionally—rebel against the pleasure industry, all it can muster is that feeble resistance which that very industry has inculcated in it. Nevertheless, it has become increasingly difficult to keep people in this condition. The rate at which they are reduced to stupidity must not fall behind the rate at which their intelligence is increasing. In this age of statistics the masses are too sharp to identify themselves with the millionaire on the screen, and too slow-witted to ignore the law of the largest number. Ideology conceals itself in the calculation of probabilities. Not everyone will be lucky one day—but the person who draws the winning ticket, or rather the one who is marked out to do so by a higher power—usually by the pleasure industry itself, which is represented as unceasingly in search of talent. Those discovered by talent scouts and then publicized on a vast scale by the studio are ideal types of the new dependent average. Of course, the starlet is meant to symbolize the typist in such a way that the splendid evening dress seems meant for the actress as distinct from the real girl. The girls in the audience not only feel that they could be on the screen, but realize the great gulf separating them from it.

Only one girl can draw the lucky ticket, only one man can win the prize, and if, mathematically, all have the same chance, yet this is so infinitesimal for each one that he or she will do best to write it off and rejoice in the other's success, which might just as well have been his or hers, and somehow never is. Whenever the culture industry still issues an invitation naïvely to identify, it is immediately withdrawn. No one can escape from himself any more. Once a member of the audience could see his own wedding in the one shown in the film. Now the lucky actors on the screen are copies of the same category as every member of the public, but such equality only demonstrates the insurmountable separation of the human elements. The perfect similarity is the absolute difference. The identity of the category forbids that of the individual cases. Ironically, man as a member of a species has been made a reality by the culture industry. Now any person signifies only those attributes by which he can replace everybody else: he is interchangeable, a copy. As an individual he is completely expendable and utterly insignificant, and this is just what he finds out when time deprives him of this similarity. This changes the inner structure of the religion of success—otherwise strictly maintained. Increasing emphasis is laid not on the path *per aspera ad astra* (which presupposes hardship and effort), but on winning a prize. The element of blind chance in the routine decision about which song deserves to be a hit and which extra a heroine is stressed by the ideology. Movies emphasize chance. By stopping at nothing to ensure that all the characters are essentially alike, with the exception of the villain, and by excluding non-conforming faces (for example, those which, like Garbo's, do not look as if you could say "Hello sister!" to them), life is made easier for movie-goers at first. They are assured that they are all right as they are, that they could do just as well and that nothing beyond their powers will be asked of them. But at the same time they are given a hint that any effort would be useless because even bourgeois luck no longer has any connection with the calculable effect of their own work. They take the hint. Fundamentally they all recognize chance (by which one occasionally makes his fortune) as the other side of planning. Precisely because the forces of society are so deployed in the direction of rationality that anyone might become an engineer or manager, it has ceased entirely to be a rational matter who the one will be in whom society will invest training or confidence for such functions. Chance and planning become one and the same thing, because, given men's equality, individual success and failure—right up to the top—lose any economic meaning. Chance itself is planned, not because it affects any particular individual but precisely because it is believed to play a vital part. It serves the planners as an alibi, and makes it seem that the complex of transactions and measures into which life has been transformed leaves scope for spontaneous and direct relations between man. This freedom is symbolized in the various media of the culture industry by the arbitrary selection of average individuals. In a magazine's detailed accounts of the modestly magnificent pleasure-trips it has arranged for the lucky person, preferably a stenotypist (who has probably won the competition because of her contacts with local bigwigs), the powerlessness of all is reflected. They are mere matter—so much so that those in control can take someone up into their heaven and throw him out again: his rights and his work count for nothing. Industry is interested in people merely as customers and employees, and has in fact reduced mankind as a whole and each of its elements to this all-embracing formula. According to the ruling aspect at the time, ideology emphasizes plan or chance, technology or life, civilization or nature. As employees, men are reminded of the rational organization and urged to fit in like sensible people. As customers, the freedom of choice, the charm of novelty, is demonstrated to them on the screen or in the press by means of the human and personal anecdote. In either case they remain objects.

The less the culture industry has to promise, the less it can offer a meaningful explanation of life, and the emptier is the ideology it disseminates. Even the abstract ideals of the harmony and beneficence of society are too concrete in this age of universal publicity. We have even learned how to identify abstract concepts as sales propaganda. Language based entirely on truth simply arouses impatience to get on with the business deal it is probably advancing. The words that are not means appear senseless; the others seem to be fiction, untrue. Value judgments are taken either as advertising or as empty talk. Accordingly ideology has been made vague and noncommittal, and thus neither clearer nor weaker. Its very vagueness, its almost scientific aversion from committing itself to anything which cannot be verified, acts as an instrument of domination. It becomes a vigorous and prearranged promulgation of the status quo. The culture industry tends to make itself the embodiment of authoritative pronouncements, and thus the irrefutable prophet of the prevailing order. It skilfully steers a winding course between the cliffs of demonstrable misinformation and manifest truth, faithfully reproducing the phenomenon whose opaqueness blocks any insight and installs the ubiquitous and intact phenomenon as ideal. Ideology is split into the photograph of stubborn life and the naked lie about its meaning—which is not expressed but suggested and yet drummed in. To demonstrate its divine nature, reality is always repeated in a purely cynical way. Such a photological proof is of course not stringent, but it is overpowering.

———

Today the culture industry has taken over the civilizing inheritance of the entrepreneurial and frontier democracy—whose appreciation of intellectual deviations was never very finely attuned. All are free to dance and enjoy themselves, just as they have been free, since the historical neutralization of religion, to join any of the innumerable sects. But freedom to choose an ideology—since ideology always reflects economic coercion—everywhere proves to be freedom to choose what is always the same. The way in which a girl accepts and keeps the obligatory date, the inflection on the telephone or in the most intimate situation, the choice of words in conversation, and the whole inner life as classified by the now somewhat devalued depth psychology, bear witness to man's attempt to make himself a proficient apparatus, similar (even in emotions) to the model served up by the culture industry. The most intimate reactions of human beings have been so thoroughly reified that the idea of anything specific to themselves now persists only as an utterly abstract notion: personality scarcely signifies anything more than shining white teeth and freedom from body odor and emotions. The triumph of advertising in the culture industry is that consumers feel compelled to buy and use its products even though they see through them.

## STUDY QUESTIONS

1. According to Horkheimer and Adorno, what have been some of the major effects of mass culture on society? On individuals?
2. Horkheimer and Adorno state that, "Amusement under late capitalism is the prolongation of work." Explain what they mean and offer an example from your own life of how this might be true.

# 7

# FRAMES

ERVING GOFFMAN

Erving Goffman (1922–1982) was a Canadian-born sociologist noted for his close observations of everyday social life. His insights and theories furthered a tradition of sociological thinking known as symbolic interactionism, which focuses attention on how people collectively produce and use meanings to guide their behavior and interactions with each other. Within that tradition, Goffman's major contribution was to illuminate the theatrical or staged elements of social interactions. People perform the roles that society expects them to play, whether it be in subtle or obvious ways, he argued, and the sum of these performances gives social life a dramaturgical quality.

In this excerpt, Goffman takes up fundamental questions that have preoccupied philosophers for centuries: how do we decide what is real? How do we come to accept certain perceptions about the world as factual, while refusing other perceptions as incorrect or irrelevant? While Goffman is interested in the kinds of answers to these questions that philosophers and psychologists have given, he insists that sociology offers something at once more direct and more concrete. What matters to people, he says, is that they are able to answer the question, "What is going on here?" when confronted with a new or unfamiliar situation or event. Frames, he argues, are the devices individuals use to organize their experiences, but those frames are initiated not by the individual's mind, but rather by larger social collectives and the cultures they produce.

**The significance of Goffman's approach for cultural sociology is that he provides a set of concepts and some tools for observing and cataloguing "the basic frameworks of understanding available in our society for making sense out of events." He wants to show how these conventional understandings impose meanings on situations and events— meanings that are open to interpretation. Interestingly, he also wants to show how these frameworks can fail, opening the door to other possibilities, which are in effect alternate social realities.**

# FRAME ANALYSIS: AN ESSAY ON THE ORGANIZATION OF EXPERIENCE

My perspective is situational, meaning here a concern for what one individual can be alive to at a particular moment, this often involving a few other particular individuals and not necessarily restricted to the mutually monitored arena of a face-to-face gathering. I assume that when individuals attend to any current situation, they face the question: "What is it that's going on here?" Whether asked explicitly, as in times of confusion and doubt, or tacitly, during occasions of usual certitude, the question is put and the answer to it is presumed by the way the individuals then proceed to get on with the affairs at hand. Starting, then, with that question, this volume attempts to limn out a framework that could be appealed to for the answer.

Let me say at once that the question "What is it that's going on here?" is considerably suspect. Any event can be described in terms of a focus that includes a wide swath or a narrow one and—as a related but not identical matter—in terms of a focus that is close-up or distant. And no one has a theory as to what particular span and level will come to be the ones employed. To begin with, I must be allowed to proceed by picking my span and level arbitrarily, without special justification.

―――――

My aim is to try to isolate some of the basic frameworks of understanding available in our society for making sense out of events and to analyze the special vulnerabilities to which these frames of reference are subject. I start with the fact that from an individual's particular point of view, while one thing may momentarily appear to be what is really going on, in fact what is actually happening is plainly a joke, or a dream, or an accident, or a mistake, or a misunderstanding, or a deception, or a theatrical performance, and so forth. And attention will be directed to what it is about our sense of what is going on that makes it so vulnerable to the need for these various rereadings.

Elementary terms required by the subject matter to be dealt with are provided first. My treatment of these initial terms is abstract, and I am afraid the formulations provided are crude indeed by the standards of modern philosophy. The reader must initially bestow the benefit of mere doubt in order for us both to get to matters that (I feel) are less dubious.

The term "strip" will be used to refer to any arbitrary slice or cut from the stream of ongoing activity, including here sequences of happenings, real or fictive, as seen from the perspective of those subjectively involved in sustaining an interest in them. A strip is not meant to reflect a natural division made by the subjects of inquiry or an analytical division made by students who inquire; it will be used only to refer to any raw batch of occurrences (of whatever status in reality) that one wants to draw attention to as a starting point for analysis.

. . . I assume that definitions of a situation are built up in accordance with principles of organization which govern events—at least social ones— and our subjective involvement in them; frame is the word I use to refer to such of these basic elements as I am able to identify. That is my definition of frame. My phrase "frame analysis" is a slogan to refer to the examination in these terms of the organization of experience.

━━━━━

A further caveat. There are lots of good grounds for doubting the kind of analysis about to be presented. I would do so myself if it weren't my own. It is too bookish, too general, too removed from fieldwork to have a good chance of being anything more than another mentalistic adumbration. And, as will be noted throughout, there are certainly things that cannot be nicely dealt with in the arguments that follow. (I coin a series of terms— some "basic"; but writers have been doing that to not much avail for years.)

Nonetheless, some of the things in this world seem to urge the analysis I am here attempting, and the compulsion is strong to try to outline the framework that will perform this job, even if this means some other tasks get handled badly.

Another disclaimer. This book is about the organization of experience—something that an individual actor can take into his mind—and not the organization of society. I make no claim whatsoever to be talking about the core matters of sociology—social organization and social structure. Those matters have been and can continue to be quite nicely studied without reference to frame at all. I am not addressing the structure of social life but the structure of experience individuals have at any moment of their social lives. I personally hold society to be first in every way and any individual's current involvements to be second; this report deals only with matters that are second. This book will have weaknesses enough in the areas it claims to deal with; there is no need to find limitations in regard to what it does not set about to cover. Of course, it can be argued that to focus on the nature of personal experiencing—with the implication this can have for giving equally serious consideration to all matters that might momentarily concern the individual—is itself a standpoint with marked political implications, and that these are conservative ones. The analysis developed does not catch at the differences between the advantaged and disadvantaged classes and can be said to direct attention away from such matters. I think that is true. I can only suggest that he who would combat false consciousness and awaken people to their true interests has much to do, because the sleep is very deep. And I do not intend here to provide a lullaby but merely to sneak in and watch the way the people snore.

# PRIMARY FRAMEWORKS

## I

. . . A primary framework is one that is seen as rendering what would otherwise be a meaningless aspect of the scene into something that is meaningful.

Primary frameworks vary in degree of organization. Some are neatly presentable as a system of entities, postulates, and rules; others—indeed, most others—appear to have no apparent articulated shape, providing only a lore of understanding, an approach, a perspective. Whatever the degree of organization, however, each primary framework allows its user to locate, perceive, identify, and label a seemingly infinite number of concrete occurrences defined in its terms. He is likely to be unaware of such organized features as the framework has and unable to describe the framework with any completeness if asked, yet these handicaps are no bar to his easily and fully applying it.

In daily life in our society a tolerably clear distinction is sensed, if not made, between two broad classes of primary frameworks: natural and social. Natural frameworks identify occurrences seen as undirected, unoriented, unanimated, unguided, "purely physical." Such unguided events are ones understood to be due totally, from start to finish, to "natural" determinants. It is seen that no willful agency causally and intentionally interferes, that no actor continuously guides the outcome. Success or failure in regard to these events is not imaginable; no negative or positive sanctions are involved. Full determinism and determinateness prevail. There is some understanding that events perceived in one such schema can be reductively translated into ones perceived in a more "fundamental" framework and that some premises, such as the notion of the conservation of energy or that of a single, irreversible time, will be shared by all. Elegant versions of these natural frameworks are found, of course, in the physical and biological sciences. An ordinary example would be the state of the weather as given in a report.

Social frameworks, on the other hand, provide background understanding for events that incorporate the will, aim, and controlling effort of an intelligence, a live agency, the chief one being the human being. Such an agency is anything but implacable; it can be coaxed, flattered, affronted, and threatened. What it does can be described as "guided doings." These doings subject the doer to "standards," to social appraisal of his action based on its honesty, efficiency, economy, safety, elegance, tactfulness, good taste, and so forth. A serial management of consequentiality is sustained, that is, continuous corrective control, becoming most apparent when action is unexpectedly blocked or deflected and special compensatory effort is required. Motive and intent are involved, and their imputation helps select which of the various social frameworks of understanding is to be applied. An example of a guided doing would be the newscast reporting of the weather. So one deals here with deeds, not mere events. (We support some perceivedly basic distinctions within the social sphere, such as that between human and animal purposiveness, but more of this later.) We use the same term, "causality," to refer to the blind effect of nature and the intended effect of man, the first seen as an infinitely extended chain of caused and causing effects and the second something that somehow begins with a mental decision.

In our society we feel that intelligent agents have the capacity to gear into the ongoing natural world and exploit its determinacy, providing only that natural design is respected. Moreover, it is felt that, with the possible exception of pure fantasy or thought, whatever an agent seeks to do will be continuously conditioned by natural constraints, and that effective doing will require the exploitation, not the neglect, of this condition. Even when two persons play checkers by keeping the board in their heads, they will still have to convey information concerning moves, this exchange requiring physically competent, willful use of the voice in speech or the hand in writing. The assumption is, then, that although natural events occur without intelligent intervention, intelligent doings cannot be accomplished effectively without entrance into the natural order. Thus any segment of a socially guided doing can be partly analyzed within a natural schema.

Guided doings appear, then, to allow for two kinds of understanding. One, more or less common to all doings, pertains to the patent manipulation of the natural world in accordance with the special constraints that natural occurrings impose; the other understanding pertains to the special worlds in which the actor can become involved, which, of course, vary considerably. Thus each play in checkers involves two radically different bases for guidance: one pertains to quite physical matters—to the physical management of the vehicle, not the sign; the other pertains to the very social world of opposing positions that the play has generated, wherein a move can equally well be made by voice, gesture, or the mails, or by physically shifting a checker by the fist, any combination of fingers, or the right elbow. Behavior at the board can easily be separated into making moves and shifting checkers. And an easy distinction can be drawn between a clumsy move, one that ill considers the strategic positions of the two players, and a move made clumsily, one that has been badly executed according to local social standards for accomplishing physical acts. Observe that although an adult with a newly acquired prosthetic device might play checkers fully mindful of the physical task involved, ordinary players do not. Decisions as to which move to make are problematic and significant;

pushing the checker once the decision is made is neither. On the other hand, there are guided doings such as fixing a sink or clearing a sidewalk in which sustained, conscious effort is given to manipulating the physical world, the doing itself taking on the identity of an "instrumental procedure," a task, a "purely utilitarian" activity—a doing the purpose of which cannot be easily separated from the physical means employed to accomplish it.

All social frameworks involve rules, but differently. For example, a checker move is informed by rules of the game, most of which will be applied in any one complete playing through of the game; the physical manipulation of a checker, on the other hand, involves a framework informing small bodily movements, and this framework, if indeed it is possible to speak in terms of *a* or *one* framework, might well be manifest only partially during the playing of a game. So, too, although the rules for checkers and the rules of vehicular traffic can be (and are) well enough explicated within the confines of a small booklet, there is a difference: the game of checkers incorporates an understanding of the governing purpose of the participants, whereas the traffic code does not establish where we are to travel or why we should want to, but merely the restraints we are to observe in getting there.

In sum, then, we tend to perceive events in terms of primary frameworks, and the type of framework we employ provides a way of describing the event to which it is applied. When the sun comes up, a natural event; when the blind is pulled down in order to avoid what has come up, a guided doing. When a coroner asks the *cause* of death, he wants an answer phrased in the natural schema of physiology; when he asks the *manner* of death, he wants a dramatically social answer, one that describes what is quite possibly part of an intent.

## II

Taken all together, the primary frameworks of a particular social group constitute a central element of its culture, especially insofar as understandings emerge concerning principal classes of schemata, the relations of these classes to one another, and the sum total of forces and agents that these interpretive designs acknowledge to be loose in the world. One must try to form an image of a group's framework of frameworks—its belief system, its "cosmology"—even though this is a domain that close students of contemporary social life have usually been happy to give over to others. And note that across a territory like the United States there is an incomplete sharing of these cognitive resources. Persons otherwise quite similar in their beliefs may yet differ in regard to a few assumptions, such as the existence of second sight, divine intervention, and the like. (Belief in God and in the sacredness of His local representatives seems to constitute currently one of the largest bases of dissensus in our society concerning ultimate forces. Tact ordinarily prevents social scientists from discussing the matter.)

## III

The notion of primary framework, unsatisfactory as it is, does allow one immediately to consider five distinctive matters and to appreciate something of their bearing on our overall understanding of the workings of the world.

1. First, the "astounding complex." An event occurs, or is made to occur, that leads observers to doubt their overall approach to events, for it seems that to account for the occurrence, new kinds of natural forces will have to be allowed or new kinds of guiding capacities, the latter involving, perhaps, new kinds of active agents. Here are included what appear to be visitations and communications from outer space, religious healing miracles, sightings of monsters from the deep, levitations, horses that are mathematically inclined, fortune-telling, contacting the dead, and so forth. As suggested, these astonishing occurrences imply the existence of extraordinary natural forces and guidance capacities: for example, astrological influences, second sight, extrasensory perception, and so on. Believe-it-or-not books are available detailing events that are "still unexplained." Occasionally scientists themselves make news by giving what is defined as serious attention to ESP, UFOs, influences deriving from the phases of the moon, and the like. Many private persons can call to mind at least one event which they themselves have never quite been able to account for reasonably. Yet in general, when an astounding event occurs, individuals in our society expect that a "simple" or "natural" explanation will soon be discovered, one that will clear up the mystery and restore them to the range of forces and agents that they are accustomed to and to the line they ordinarily draw between natural phenomena and guided doings. Certainly individuals exhibit considerable

resistance to changing their framework of frameworks. A public stir—or at least a ripple—is caused by any event that apparently cannot be managed within the traditional cosmology. . . . Let me repeat: in our society the very significant assumption is generally made that all events—without exception—can be contained and managed within the conventional system of beliefs. We tolerate the unexplained but not the inexplicable.

2. Cosmological interests, in some ways the largest we can have, support a humble entertainment: the exhibition of stunts, that is, the maintenance of guidance and control by some willed agency under what are seen as nearly impossible conditions. Here is found the doings of jugglers, tightrope walkers, equestrians, surfers, trick skiers, knife throwers, high divers, daredevil drivers, and, currently, astronauts, these last having the greatest act of all, albeit one for which they must share credits with American technology. One might also include the stunts that individuals can learn to perform with their physiology, as when a function like blood pressure or pain response is brought under voluntary control. Note that "animal acts" play an important role in regard to stunting. Trained seals, sociable porpoises, dancing elephants, and acrobatic lions all exemplify the possibility of ordinary guided doings done by alien agents, thus drawing attention to the cosmological line drawn in our society between human agents and animal ones. So, too, when animals are shown to have been pressed into doing the sort of utilitarian tasks that are felt to be the exclusive province of man, as when a chimp causes deep consternation on the highway because her trainer has taught her to steer an open sports car while he appears to be asleep in the next seat, or a troop of chimps is employed by a farmer in Australia to help with the harvesting.

═══════

3. Consider now "muffings," namely, occasions when the body, or some other object assumed to be under assured guidance, unexpectedly breaks free, deviates from course, or otherwise slips from control, becoming totally subject to—not merely conditioned by—natural forces, with consequent disruption of orderly life. Thus, "flubs," "goofs," and—when the guidance of meaning in talk should have occurred—"gaffes." (The limiting case would be where no blame whatsoever attaches, as when an earthquake is given full responsibility for a person's having spilled a cup of tea.) The body

here retains its capacity as a natural, causal force, but not as an intentioned, social one. . . .

Note, a stunt occurs when we might well expect and even condone a loss of control, a muffing when exemplary effort is not felt to be needed to maintain control, but nonetheless control is lost.

═══════

4. Next to consider is "fortuitousness," meaning here that a significant event can come to be seen as incidentally produced. An individual, properly guiding his doings, meets with the natural workings of the world in a way he could not be expected to anticipate, with consequential results. Or two or more unconnected and mutually unoriented individuals, each properly guiding his own doings, jointly bring about an unanticipated event that is significant—and these actors have this effect even though their contributed doings remain fully under control. We speak here of happenstance, coincidence, good and bad luck, accident, and so forth. Because no responsibility is imputed, one has something like a natural framework, except that the ingredients upon which the natural forces operate are here socially guided doings. Note, too, fortuitous consequences may be felt to be desirable or undesirable. I cite an instance of the latter:

> Amman, Jordan—A ceremonial salvo was fatal to a Palestinian commando yesterday. He was killed by a stray bullet as guerrilla units fired their rifles in the air at burial services for casualties of an Israeli air raid Sunday.[1]

The notion of fortuitous connection is obviously delicate, as though those who put it forward as an account had some doubts about using so pat a solution or were concerned that another might have these doubts. This precariousness becomes especially evident when a particular kind of happenstance occurs a second or third time to the same object or individual or category of individuals. So, too, meaningfulness will be hard to avoid when the beneficiary or victim of the fortuitousness is in a prominent class of persons containing only one member.

1. *San Francisco Chronicle*, August 6, 1968.

The concepts of muffings and fortuitousness have considerable cosmological significance. Given our belief that the world can be totally perceived in terms of either natural events or guided doings and that every event can be comfortably lodged in one or the other category, it becomes apparent that a means must be at hand to deal with slippage and looseness. The cultural notions of muffing and fortuitousness serve in this way, enabling the citizenry to come to terms with events that would otherwise be an embarrassment to its system of analysis.

5. The final matter to consider bears upon the segregation issue expressed in "tension" and joking. As will be argued throughout, individuals can rather fully constitute what they see in accordance with the framework that officially applies. But there is a limit to this capacity. Certain effects carry over from one perspective in which events could easily be seen to a radically different one, the latter the one which officially applies. The best documented case, perhaps, is the slow development of the easy right of medical people to approach the human naked body with a natural instead of a social perspective. Thus, it was only at the end of the eighteenth century in Britain that childbirth could benefit from an obstetric examination, an undarkened operating room, and delivery—if a male physician was to do it—unencumbered by its having to be performed under covers. The gynecological examination is even today a matter of some concern, special effort being taken to infuse the procedure with terms and actions that keep sexual readings in check. Another example is the difficulty faced by those who would promote the practice of rescue breathing; mouth-to-mouth contact apparently cannot easily be dissociated from its ritual implications. Similarly, we manage to let orthopedists and shoe salesmen touch our feet, but first we make sure to clean what might ritually contaminate. . . .

It should be obvious that the human body and touchings of it will figure in the issue of frame maintenance, just as the body's various waste products and involuntary movements will figure in tensions regarding boundaries. For it seems that the body is too constantly present as a resource to be managed in accordance with only one primary framework. It seems inevitable that our interpretive competency will allow us to come to distinguish, say, between an arm waved to signal a car on and an arm waved to greet a friend, and that both wavings will be distinguished from what we are seen as doing when we dispel flies or increase circulation. These discernments in turn seem linked to the fact that each kind of event is but one element in a whole idiom of events, each idiom being part of a distinctive framework. And here what is true of Western society is probably also true of all other societies.

# STUDY QUESTIONS

1. Why does Goffman think that the question, "What is it that's going on here?" is significant for sociologists?
2. Goffman writes that "the primary frameworks of a particular social group constitute a central element of its culture." How so?

# HIGHBROW AND
# LOWBROW CULTURE

PAUL DIMAGGIO

Given a choice, which would you prefer: tickets to a museum and a play or tickets to a football game and a hip-hop show? The difference is clear: museums and plays are examples of what is sometimes called *high culture* or *the arts.* Football games and hip-hop belong to the world of *popular*—or *pop*—and *mass culture.* What, if anything, does it say about you as an individual that you would choose one over the other?

Not much, you may answer, as some of us enjoy both. But at one time the distinction between pop culture and high culture carried great social and political significance, as high culture was widely perceived to be the exclusive domain of the wealthy and powerful, while pop culture was meant for everyone else. This period in America, from the 1900s to the 1960s, saw the emergence and development of individuals, organizations, and institutions devoted to guarding high culture from what were thought to be the effects of pop culture, which came to be seen as coarse, vulgar, and unrefined. Naturally, pop culture was thought by many elites to be fit only for "the great unwashed," the lower classes of workers and immigrants whose dull lives and duller intelligence rendered them incapable of truly appreciating the higher arts. Today's pop culture was synonymous with low culture.

As Paul DiMaggio points out, it hadn't always been this way in America. As late as the 1890s, the line between high and low culture was fuzzy and dim, if it even existed at all. Variety shows mixed Shakespearean theater with bawdy vaudeville skits, while the finest museums featured serious painters alongside circus sideshow exhibits of dwarves and taxidermied models of two-headed fish. Something happened at the turn of the century that allowed for the high/low culture distinction to emerge and to gain social force, such that today many people think of opera and ballet—and the people who like them—as *high class.* DiMaggio explains how this distinction was created and why, and reveals its lasting effects.

# CULTURAL ENTREPRENEURSHIP IN NINETEENTH-CENTURY BOSTON: THE CREATION OF AN ORGANIZATIONAL BASE FOR HIGH CULTURE IN AMERICA

Sociological and political discussions of culture have been predicated on a strong dichotomy between high culture—what goes on in museums, opera houses, symphony halls and theatres—and popular culture, of both the folk and commercial varieties. Such culture critics as Dwight McDonald (1957) and Theodor Adorno (1941) have based on this dichotomy thoroughgoing critiques of popular culture and the mass media. Defenders of popular culture (Lowenthal, 1961; Gans, 1974) have questioned the normative aspect of the critique of popular culture, but have, for the most part, accepted the basic categories. The distinction between high and popular culture has been implicit, as well, in the discussion of public policy towards culture in both the United States and Great Britain (DiMaggio and Useem, 1978).

Yet high and popular culture can be defined neither by qualities inherent to the work of art, nor, as some have argued, by simple reference to the class character of their publics. The distinction between high and popular culture, in its American version, emerged in the period between 1850 and 1900 out of the efforts of urban elites to build organizational forms that, first, isolated high culture and, second, differentiated it from popular culture. Americans did not merely adopt available European models. Instead they groped their way to a workable distinction. Not until two distinct organizational forms—the private or semi-private, non-profit cultural institution and the commercial popular-culture industry—took shape did the high/popular-culture dichotomy emerge in its modern form. Once these organizational models developed, the first in the bosom of elite urban status communities, the second in the relative impersonality of emerging regional and national markets, they shaped the role that cultural institutions would play, the careers of artists, the nature of the works created and performed, and the purposes and publics that cultural organizations would serve.

In this paper I will address only one side of this process of classification, the institutionalization of high culture and the creation of distinctly high-cultural organizations. While high culture could be defined only in opposition to popular culture, it is the process by which urban elites forged an institutional system embodying their ideas about the high arts that will engage us here. In order to grasp the extent to which the creation of modern high-cultural institutions was a task that involved elites as an organic group, we will focus on that process in one American city. Boston in the nineteenth century was the most active center of American culture; and its elite—the Boston Brahmins—constituted the most well defined status group of any of the urban upper classes of this period. For this reason the processes with which I am concerned appear here in particularly clear relief.[1]

When we look at Boston before 1850 we see a culture defined by the pulpit, the lectern and a collection of artistic efforts, amateurish by modern standards, in which effort rarely was made to distinguish between an and entertainment, or between culture and commerce. The arts in Boston were not self-conscious; they drew few boundaries. While intellectuals and ministers distinguished culture that elevated the spirit from that which debased it, there was relatively little agreement on what works or genres constituted which (see Hatch, 1962; Harris, 1966). Harvard's Pierian Sodality mixed popular songs with student compositions and works by European fine-arts composers. The Philharmonic Society played classical concerts, but also backed visiting popular vocalists. Throughout this period, most of Boston music was in the hands of commercial entrepreneurs. Gottlieb Graupner, the city's leading impresario in the 1830s, sold sheet music and instruments, published songs and promoted concerts at which religious, classical and popular tunes mingled freely. (One typical performance included a bit of Italian opera, a devotional song by Mrs Graupner, a piece by Verdi. "Bluebell of Scotland" and "The Origin of Common Nails," recited by Mr Bernard, a comedian.) The two exceptions, the Handel and Haydn Society and the Harvard Musical Association, founded in the 1840s and

1850s respectively, were associations of amateurs and professionals that appealed only to a relatively narrow segment of the elite.

The visual arts were also organized on a largely commercial basis in this era. In the 1840s, the American Art Union sold paintings by national lottery (Lynnes, 1953). These lotteries were succeeded, in Boston, New York and Philadelphia, by private galleries. Museums were modelled on Barnum's (Barnum, 1879; Harris, 1973): fine art was interspersed among such curiosities as bearded women and mutant animals, and popular entertainments were offered for the price of admission to a clientele that included working people as well as the upper middle class. Founded as a commercial venture in 1841, Moses Kemball's Boston Museum exhibited works by such painters as Sully and Peale alongside Chinese curiosities, stuffed animals, mermaids and dwarves. For the entrance fee visitors could also attend the Boston Museum Theatre, which presented works by Dickens and Shakespeare as well as performances by gymnasts and contortionists, and brought to Boston the leading players of the American and British stage (McGlinchee, 1940). The promiscuous combination of genres that later would be considered incompatible was not uncommon. As late as the 1880s, American circuses employed Shakespearian clowns who recited the bard's lines in full clown make-up (Fellows and Freeman, 1936).

By 1910, high and popular culture were encountered far less frequently in the same settings. The distinction towards which Boston's clerics and critics had groped 50 years before had emerged in institutional form. The Boston Symphony Orchestra was a permanent aggregation, wresting the favor of Boston's upper class decisively from the commercial and co-operative ensembles with which it first competed. The Museum of Fine Arts, founded in 1873, was at the center of the city's artistic life, its exhibitions complemented by those of Harvard and the eccentric Mrs Gardner. Music and art critics might disagree on the merits of individual conductors or painters; but they were united in an aesthetic ideology that distinguished sharply between the nobility of art and the vulgarity of mere entertainment. The distinction between true art, distributed by not-for-profit corporations managed by artistic professionals and governed closely by prosperous and influential trustees, and popular entertainment, sponsored by entrepreneurs and distributed via the market to whomever would buy it, had taken a form that has persisted to the present. So, too, had the social distinctions that would differentiate the publics for high and popular culture.

The sacralization of art, the definition of high culture and its opposite, popular culture and the institutionalization of this classification, was the work of men and women whom I refer to as *cultural capitalists*. I use the term in two senses to describe the capitalists (and the professionals whose wealth came from the participation of their families in the industrial ventures—textiles, railroads and mining—of the day) who founded the museums and the symphony orchestras that embodied and elaborated the high-cultural ideal. They were capitalists in the sense that their wealth came from the management of industrial enterprises from which they extracted a profit, and cultural capitalists in that they invested some of these profits in the foundation and maintenance of distinctly cultural enterprises. They also—and this is the second sense in which I use the term— were collectors of what Bourdieu has called "cultural capital," knowledge and familiarity with styles and genres that are socially valued and that confer prestige upon those who have mastered them (Bourdieu and Passeron, 1977, 1979). It was the vision of the founders of the institutions that have become, in effect, the treasuries of cultural capital upon which their descendants have drawn that defined the nature of cultural capital in American society.[2]

To create an institutional high culture, Boston's upper class had to accomplish three concurrent, but analytically distinct, projects: entrepreneurship, classification and framing. By entrepreneurship, I mean the creation of an organizational form that members of the elite could control and govern. By classification, I refer to the erection of strong and clearly defined boundaries between an and entertainment, the definition of a high art that elites and segments of the middle class could appropriate as their own cultural property; and the acknowledgment of that classification's legitimacy by other classes and the state. Finally, I use the term framing to refer to the development of a new etiquette of appropriation, a new relationship between the audience and the work of art.[3] The focus of this paper will be on the first of these three processes.

## The predecessors: organizational models before the Gilded Age

High culture (and by this I mean a strongly classified, consensually defined body of art distinct from "popular" fare) failed to develop in Boston prior to the 1870s because the organizational models through which art was distributed were not equipped to define and sustain such a body and a view of an. Each of the three major models for organizing the distribution of aesthetic experience before 1870—the for-profit firm, the co-operative enterprise and the communal association—was flawed in some important way.

The problems of the privately owned, for-profit firm are most obvious. As Weber (1968, vol. 2, sec. 9: 937) has argued, the market declassifies culture: presenters of cultural events mix genres and cross boundaries to reach out to larger audiences. The Boston Museum, founded in the 1840s, mixed fine art and side-show oddities, Shakespeare and theatrical ephemerata. For-profit galleries exhibited art as spectacle: when James Jackson Jarves showed his fine collection of Italian primitives at Derby's Institute of Fine Arts in New York, "the decor of this . . . dazzlingly ornate commercial emporium . . . caused much more favorable comment than Jarves' queer old pictures" (Burt, 1977: 57).

If anything, commerce was even less favorable to the insulation of high art in the performance media. Fine-art theatre in Boston never seems to have got off the ground. And the numerous commercial orchestras that either resided in or toured Boston during this period mixed fine-arts and light music indiscriminately. A memoir of the period recalls a concert of the Germania Society (one of the better orchestras of this type):

> One of the numbers was the "Railway Gallop,"—composer forgotten—during the playing of which a little mock steam-engine kept scooting about the floor of the hall, with black cotton wool smoke coming out of the funnel.

The same writer describes the memorable

> evening when a fantasia on themes from Wallace's "Maritana" was played as a duet for mouth harmonica and the Great Organ; a combination, as the program informed us, "never before attempted in the history of music!" (William F. Apthorp, quoted in Howe, 1914).

As with the visual arts, the commercial treatment of serious music tended to the extravagant rather than to the sacred. In 1869, an entrepreneur organized a Peace Jubilee to celebrate the end of the Civil War. A structure large enough to accommodate 30,000 people was built (at what would later be the first site of the Museum of Fine Arts) and "star" instrumentalists and vocalists were contracted to perform along with an orchestra of 1,000 and a chorus of 10,000. As a finale, the orchestra (which included 330 strings, 75 drums and 83 tubas) played the anvil chorus with accompaniment from a squadron of firemen beating anvils, and the firing of live cannon (Fisher, 1918: 45–46).

An alternative form of organization, embraced by some musical societies, was the workers' co-operative, in which each member had a vote, shared in the profits of the enterprise and elected a conductor from among their number.[4] The cooperative was vulnerable to market incentives. Perhaps more important, however, it was (also like its privately owned counterpart) unable to secure the complete allegiance of its members, who supported themselves by playing many different kinds of music in a wide range of settings. The early New York Philharmonic, for example, performed as a group only monthly. Members anticipated the concert

> as a pleasant relief from more remunerative occupational duties, and the rehearsal periods were cluttered up with routine business matters, from which members could absent themselves with relative impunity (Mueller, 1951: 41).

The lines dividing non-profit, co-operative, for-profit and public enterprise were not as strong in the nineteenth century as they would become in the twentieth. Civic-minded guarantors might hold stock in commercial ventures with no hope of gaining a profit (e.g. Symphony Hall at the end of the century). The goals of the charitable corporation were usually defined into its charter, but otherwise it legally resembled its for-profit counterpart. Even less clearly defined was what I call the voluntary association: closed associations of individuals (sometimes incorporated, sometimes not) to further the aims of the participating members, rather than of the community as a whole. For associations like the Handel and Haydn Society, which might give public concerts, or the Athenaeum, which took an active role in public affairs, privateness was relative. But, ultimately, each was a voluntary and exclusive instrument of its members.

Why were these communal associations ill-suited to serve as the organizational bases for high culture in Boston? Why could the Athenaeum, a private library, or the Boston Art Club, which sponsored contemporary art shows (Boston Art Club, 1878), not have developed continuous programs of public exhibitions? Could not the Handel and Haydn Society, the Harvard Musical Association (formed by Harvard graduates who wished to pursue after graduation musical interests developed in the College's Pierian Sodality) or one of the numerous singing circles have developed into a permanent orchestra? They faced no commercial temptations to study, exhibit or perform any but the highest art. (Indeed, the Harvard Musical Association's performances were so austere as to give rise to the proverb "dull as a symphony concert" (Howe, 1914: 8)).

None of them, however, could, by the late nineteenth century, claim to speak for the community as a whole, even if they chose to. Each represented only a fraction (although, in the case of Athenaeum, a very large and potent fraction) of the elite; and, in the case of the musical associations and the Art Club, members of the middle class and artistic professionals were active as well. The culture of an elite status group must be monopolized, it must be legitimate and it must be sacralized. Boston's cultural capitalists would have to find a form able to achieve all these aims: a single organizational base for each art form; institutions that could claim to serve the community, even as they defined the community to include only the elite and the upper-middle classes; and enough social distance between artist and audience, between performer and public, to permit the mystification necessary to define a body of artistic work as sacred.

This they did in the period between 1870 and 1900. By the end of the century, in art and music (but not in theatre (see Twentieth Century Club, 1919; Poggi, 1968)), the differences between high- and popular-culture artists and performers were becoming distinct, as were the physical settings in which high and popular art were presented.

The form that the distribution of high culture would take was the non-profit corporation, governed by a self-perpetuating board of trustees who, eventually, would delegate most artistic decisions to professional artists or art historians (Zolberg, 1974; 1981). The charitable corporation was not designed to define a high culture that elites could monopolize; nor are non-profit organizations by their nature exclusive. But the non-profit corporation had five virtues that enabled it to play a key role in this instance. First, the corporation was a familiar and successful tool by which nineteenth-century elites organized their affairs (see Frederickson, 1965; Story, 1980; Hall, 1984). In the economic realm it enabled them to raise capital for such profitable ventures as the Calumet and Hecla Mines, the western railroads and the telephone company. In the non-profit arena, it had been a useful instrument for elite communal governance at Harvard, the Massachusetts General Hospital and a host of charitable institutions (Story, 1980). Second, by entrusting governance decisions to trustees who were committed either to providing financial support or to soliciting it from their peers, the non-profit form effectively (if not completely) insulated museums and orchestras from the pressures of the market. Third, by vesting control in a well integrated social and financial elite, the charitable corporation enabled its governors to rule without interference from the state or from other social classes. Fourth, those organizations whose trustees were able to enlist the support of the greater part of the elite could provide the stability needed for a necessarily lengthy process of defining art and developing ancillary institutions to insulate high-cultural from popular-cultural work, performance and careers. Finally, and less obviously, the goals of the charitable corporation, unlike those of the profit-seeking firm, are diffuse and ambiguous enough to accommodate a range of conflicting purposes and changing ends. The broad charters of Boston's major cultural organizations permitted their missions to be redefined with time, and enabled their governors to claim (and to believe) that they pursued communitarian goals even as they institutionalized a view and vision of art that made elite culture less and less accessible to the vast majority of Boston's citizens.

## The context of cultural capitalism

In almost every literate society, dominant status groups or classes eventually have developed their own styles of art and the institutional means of supporting them. It was predictable that this would happen in the United States, despite the absence of an hereditary aristocracy. It is more difficult, however, to explain the timing of this process. Dwight and others wished (but failed) to start a permanent professional symphony orchestra from at least the late 1840s. The Athenaeum's proprietors tried to raise a public subscription to purchase the Jarves collection in the late 1850s, but they failed. What had changed?

Consider, first, the simple increase in scale and wealth between 1800 and 1870. At the time of the revolution, Boston's population was under

10,000. By 1800 it had risen to 25,000; by 1846 it was 120,000. By 1870, over a quarter of a million people lived in Boston (Lane, 1975). The increase in the size of the local cultural market facilitated a boom in theatre building in the 1830s (Nye, 1960: 264), a rise in the number and stability of book and music stores (Fisher, 1918: 30) and the growth of markets for theatre, music, opera, dancing and equestrian shows (Nye, 1960: 143). The growth of population was accompanied by an increase in wealth. . . .

With growth came challenges to the stability of the community and to the cultural authority (Starr, 1982) of elites. Irish immigrants flowed into Boston from the 1840s to work in the city's industrial enterprises (Handlin, 1972; Thernstrom, 1972); industrial employment roles doubled between 1845 and 1855 (Handlin, 1972). With industry and immigration came disease, pauperism, alcoholism, rising infant mortality and vice. The Catholic Irish were, by provenance and religion, outside the consensus that the Brahmins had established. By 1900, 30% of Boston's residents were foreign-born and 70% were of foreign parentage (Green, 1966: 102). By the close of the Civil War, Boston's immigrants were organizing to challenge the native elite in the political arena (Solomon, 1956).

If immigration and industrialization wrought traumatic changes in the city's social fabric, the political assault on Brahmin institutions by native populists proved even more frightening. The Know-Nothings who captured state government in the 1850s attacked the social exclusivity of Harvard College frontally, amending its charter and threatening state control over its governance, hiring and admissions policies (Story, 1980). Scalded by these attacks, Boston's leadership retreated from the public sector to found a system of non-profit organizations that permitted them to maintain some control over the community even as they lost their command of its political institutions.[5]

Story (1980) argues persuasively that this political challenge, and the wave of institution-building that followed it, transformed the Brahmins from an elite into a social class.[6] As a social class, the Brahmins built institutions (schools, almshouses and charitable societies) aimed at securing control over the city's social life (Huggins, 1971; Vogel, 1981). As a status group, they constructed organizations (clubs, prep schools and cultural institutions) to seal themselves off from their increasingly unruly environment. Thus Vernon Parrington's only partially accurate observation that

"The Brahmins conceived the great business of life to be the erection of barriers against the intrusion of the unpleasant" (quoted in Shiverick, 1970: 129). The creation of a network of private institutions that could define and monopolize high art was an essential part of this process of building cultural boundaries.

The Brahmin class, however, was neither large enough to constitute a public for large-scale arts organizations, nor was it content to keep its cultural achievements solely to itself. Alongside of, and complicating, the Brahmins' drive towards exclusivity was a conflicting desire, as they saw it, to educate the community. The growth of the middle class during this period—a class that was economically and socially closer to the working class and thus in greater need of differentiating itself from it culturally—provided a natural clientele for Boston's inchoate high culture. . . .

## Cultural entrepreneurship: the Museum of Fine Arts and the Boston Symphony Orchestra

The first step in the creation of a high culture was the centralization of artistic activities within institutions controlled by Boston's cultural capitalists. This was accomplished with the foundings of the Museum of Fine Arts and the Boston Symphony Orchestra. These institutions were to provide a framework, in the visual arts and music, respectively, for the definition of high art, for its segregation from popular forms and for the elaboration of an etiquette of appropriation.

The initial aspirations of the Museum founders were somewhat modest. The key figure in the founding was Charles Callahan Perkins, great-nephew of a China-trade magnate, kinsman of the chairman of the Athenaeum's Fine Arts Committee and himself President of the Boston Art Club. Perkins wrote two books on Italian sculpture in the 1860s, championed arts education in Boston's public schools and served as head of the American Social Science Association's arts-education panel in 1869. (He had studied painting and sculpture in Europe for almost 10 years, before concluding that he lacked the creativity to be a good artist.) Perkins, in a report to the ASSA had asserted "the feasibility of establishing a regular Museum of Art at moderate expense," with primarily educational aims. Since Boston's collections had few originals, he recommended that the new collection consist of reproductions, primarily plaster casts of sculpture and architecture.

———

One reason for the breadth of early support was that the Museum, although in private hands, was to be a professedly communitarian and educational venture. The Board of Trustees contained a large segment of the Brahmin class: All but one of the first 23 trustees were proprietors of the Athenaeum; 11 were members of the Saturday Club, while many others were members of the Somerset and St Botolph's clubs; most were graduates of Harvard and many were active in its affairs. The public nature of the Board was further emphasized by the inclusion on it of permanent and *ex-officio* appointments: from Harvard, MIT and the Athenaeum; the Mayor, the Chairman of the Boston Public Library's board, the trustee of the Lowell Institute, the Secretary of the State Board of Education and the Superintendent of Boston's schools. The trustees dedicated the institution to education; one hoped that the breadth of the board's membership would ensure that the Museum's managers would be "prevented from squandering their funds upon the private fancies of would-be connoisseurs." Indeed, the articles of incorporation required that the Museum be open free of charge at least four times a month. The public responded by flooding the Museum on free weekend days in the early years (Harris, 1962: 48–52).

The centralization of the visual arts around a museum required only the provision of a building and an institution controlled by a board of civic-minded members of the elite. The Museum functioned on a relatively small budget in its early years, under the direction of Charles Greely Loring, a Harvard graduate and Civil War general, who had studied Egyptology when his physician sent him to the banks of the Nile. The Museum's founders, facing the need to raise substantial funds, organized both private and public support carefully, mobilizing a consensus in favor of their project from the onset.

By contrast, the Boston Symphony Orchestra was, for its first years at least, a one-man operation, forced to wrest hegemony over Boston's musical life from several contenders, each with its own coterie of elite support. That Henry Lee Higginson, a partner in the brokerage firm of Lee, Higginson, was able to do so was a consequence of the soundness of his organizational vision, the firmness of his commitment, and, equally important, his centrality to Boston's economic and social elite.

———

Despite a measure of public incredulity, and some resentment at Higginson's choice of European conductor, George Henschel, over local candidates, the BSO opened in December 1881 to the enthusiastic response of the musical public. (The demand for tickets was great; lines formed outside the box office the evening before they went on sale.) The social complexion of the first night's audience is indicated by a report in a Boston newspaper that "the spirit of the music so affected the audience that when the English national air was recognized in Weber's Festival Overture, the people arose en masse and remained standing until the close." By employing local musicians and permitting them to play with the Philharmonic Society and the Harvard Musical Association (both of which, like the BSO, offered about 20 concerts that season), Higginson earned the gratitude of the city's music lovers.

The trouble began in February 1882, when the players received Higginson's terms for the following season. To continue to work for the Symphony, they would be required to make themselves available for rehearsals and performances from October through April, four days a week, and to play for no other conductor or musical association. (The Handel and Haydn Society, which had strong ties to the Athenaeum, was exempted from this prohibition.) The implications of the contract, which the players resisted unsuccessfully, were clear: Boston's other orchestras, lacking the salaries that Higginson's subsidies permitted, would be unable to compete for the services of Boston's musicians. (To make matters worse, a number of the city's journeymen musicians received no offers from Higginson at all.)

———

Higginson and his orchestra weathered the storm. Attendance stayed up and, within a year, his was the only orchestral association in Boston, coexisting peacefully with the smaller Handel and Haydn Society. In order to achieve the kind of ensemble he desired, however, Higginson had to ensure that his musicians would commit their time and their attention to the BSO alone, and accept his (and his agent's, the conductor's) authority as inviolate. Since, in the past, all musicians, whatever their affiliations, were freelancers upon whom no single obligation weighed supreme, accomplishing these aspirations required a fundamental change in the relationship between musicians and their employers.

In part, effecting this internal monopolization of attention was simply a matter of gaining an external monopoly of classical-music performance. With the surrender of the Philharmonic Society and the Harvard Musical Association, two major competitors for the working time of Boston's musicians disappeared. Nonetheless, while his musicians were now more dependent upon the BSO for their livelihoods, and thus more amenable to his demands, his control over the work force was still challenged by the availability of light-music or dance engagements, teaching commitments and the tradition of lax discipline to which the players were accustomed.

## The Brahmins as an organization-forming class

The Museum of Fine Arts and the Boston Symphony Orchestra were both organizations embedded in a social class, formal organizations whose official structure was draped around the ongoing life of the group that governed, patronized, and staffed them.[7] They were not separate products of different segments of an elite; or of artists and critics who mobilized wealthy men to bankroll their causes. Rather they were the creations of a densely connected self-conscious social group intensely unified by multiple ties among its members based in kinship, commerce, club life and participation in a wide range of philanthropic associations. Indeed, if, as Stinchcombe (1965) has argued, there are "organization-forming organizations"—organizations that spawn off other organizations in profusion—there are also organization-forming status groups, and the Brahmins were one of these. This they could be not just because of their cultural or religious convictions (to which Green [1966], Baltzell [1979] and Hall [1984] have called attention), but because they were integrated by their families' marriages, their Harvard educations, their joint business ventures, their memberships in a web of social clubs and their trusteeships of charitable and cultural organizations. This integration is exemplified in the associations of Higginson, and in the ties between the Museum and the Orchestra during the last 20 years of the nineteenth century.

## Conclusions

The Museum of Fine Arts and the Boston Symphony Orchestra were creations of the Brahmins, and the Brahmins alone. As such, their origins are easier to understand than were British or Continental efforts in which aristocrats and bourgeoisie played complex and interrelated roles (Wolff, 1982). The Brahmins were a status group, and as such they strove towards exclusivity, towards the definition of a prestigious culture that they could monopolize as their own. Yet they were also a social class, and they were concerned, as is any dominant social class, with establishing hegemony over those they dominated. Some Marxist students of culture have misinterpreted the cultural institutions as efforts to dictate taste or to inculcate the masses with the ideas of elites. Certainly, the cultural capitalists, consummate organizers and intelligent men and women, were wise enough to understand the impossibility of socializing the masses in institutions from which they effectively were barred. Their concern with education, however, was not simply window-dressing or an effort at public relations. Higginson, for example, devoted much of his fortune to American universities and secondary schools. He once wrote a kinsman, from whom he sought a donation of $100,000 for Harvard, "Educate, and save ourselves and our families and our money from the mobs!" (Perry, 1921: 329). Moreover, a secret or thoroughly esoteric culture could not have served to legitimate the status of American elites; it would be necessary to share it, at least partially. The tension between monopolization and hegemony, between exclusivity and legitimation, was a constant counterpoint to the efforts at classification of American urban elites.

This explains, in part, the initial emphasis on education at the Museum of Fine Arts. Yet, from the first, the Museum managers sought to educate through distinguishing true from vulgar art—at first, cautiously, later with more confidence. In the years that followed they would place increased emphasis on the original art that became available to them, until they abandoned reproductions altogether and with them their emphasis on education. In a less dramatic way, the Orchestra, which began with an artistic mandate, would further classify the contents of its programs and frame the aesthetic experience in the years to come.

In structure, however, the Museum and the Orchestra were similar innovations. Each was private, controlled by members of the Brahmin class, and established on the corporate model, dependent on private philanthropy and relatively long-range financial planning; each was sparsely staffed and relied for much of its management on elite volunteers; and each counted among its founders wealthy men with considerable scholarly or artistic credentials who were centrally located in Boston's elite social structure. The Museum was established under broad auspices for the education of the community as a whole; the Orchestra was created by one man in the service of art and of those in the community with the sophistication or motivation to appreciate it. Within 40 years, the logic of cultural capitalism would moderate sharply, if not eliminate, these historically grounded differences. The Symphony would come to resemble the Museum in charter and governance, and the Museum would abandon its broad social mission in favor of aestheticism and an elite clientele.

The creation of the MFA, the BSO and similar organizations throughout the United States created a base through which the ideal of high culture could be given institutional flesh. The alliance between class and culture that emerged was defined by, and thus inseparable from, its organizational mediation. As a consequence, the classification "high culture/popular culture" is comprehensible only in its dual sense as characterizing both a ritual classification and the organizational systems that give that classification meaning.

# References

Adorno, T. W. 1941. On popular music, *Studies in Philosophy and Social Science*, vol. 9, no. 1.

Baltzell, E. D. 1979. *Puritan Boston and Quaker Philadelphia*. New York, Free Press.

Barnum, P. T. 1879. *Struggles and Triumphs; or Forty Years Recollections*. Buffalo, New York, The Courier Company.

Bernstein, B. 1975a. On the classification and framing of educational knowledge, in *Class, Codes and Control*, vol. 3. London, Routledge and Kegan Paul.

———. 1975b. Ritual in education in *Class, Codes and Control*, vol. 3. London, Routledge and Kegan Paul.

Boston Art Club. 1878. Constitution and By-Laws of the Boston Art Club. With a Sketch of its History. Boston. E. H. Trulan.

Bourdieu, P. and Passeron, J. C. 1977. *Reproduction in Education, Society and Culture*. Beverly Hills, Sage.

———. 1979. *The Inheritors: French Students and Their Relation to Culture*. Chicago, University of Chicago Press.

Burt, N. 1977. *Palaces for the People*. Boston, Little, Brown and Co.

Couch, S. R. 1976a. Class, politics and symphony orchestras. *Society*, vol. 14. no. 1.

Couch, S. R. 1976b. The symphony orchestra in London and New York: some political considerations, presented at the Third Annual Conference on Social Theory and the Arts, Albany, New York.

DiMaggio, P. and Useem, M. 1978. Cultural property and public policy: Emerging tensions in government support for the arts. *Social Research*, vol. 45, Summer.

Douglas, M. 1966. *Purity and Danger: An Analysis of Pollution and Taboo.* London, Routledge and Kegan Paul.

Fellows, D. W. and Freeman, A. A. 1936. *This Way to the Big Show: The Life of Dexter Fellows.* New York, Viking Press.

Fisher, W. A. 1918. *Notes on Music in Old Boston.* Boston, Oliver Ditson.

Fredrickson, G. M. 1965. *The Inner Civil War: Northern Intellectuals and the Crisis of the Union.* New York, Harper and Row.

Gans, H. J. 1974. *Popular Culture and High Culture.* New York, Basic Books.

Green, M. 1966. *The Problem of Boston.* New York, Norton.

Hall, P. D. 1984. *Institutions and the Making of American Culture.* Westport, Connecticut, Greenwood.

Handlin, O. 1972. *Boston's Immigrants, 1790–1880.* New York, Atheneum.

Harris, N. 1962. The Gilded Age revisited: Boston and the museum movement. *American Quarterly*, vol. 14, Winter.

———. 1966. *The Artist in American Society: The Formative Years, 1790–1860.* New York, George Braziller.

———. 1973. *Humbug: The Art of P. T. Barnum.* Boston, Little, Brown and Co.

Hatch, C. 1962. Music for America: A cultural controversy of the 1850s. *American Quarterly*, vol. 14, Winter.

Howe, M. A. D. 1914. *The Boston Symphony Orchestra: An Historical Sketch.* Boston, Houghton Mifflin.

Huggins, N. J. 1971. *Protestants against Poverty: Boston's Charities, 1870–1900.* Westport, Connecticut, Greenwood.

Lane, R. 1975. *Policing the City: Boston, 1822–85.* New York, Atheneum.

Lowenthal, L. 1961. *Literature, Popular Culture, and Society.* Englewood Cliffs, Prentice-Hall.

Lynnes, R. 1953. *The Tastemaker.* New York, Grosset and Dunlap.

McDonald, D. 1957. A theory of mass culture, in Rosenberg, B. and White, D. M., eds., *Mass Culture: The Popular Arts in America.* Glencoe, Illinois, Free Press.

McGlinchee, C. 1940. *The First Decade of the Boston Museum.* Boston, Bruce Humphries.

Mueller, J. H. 1951. *The American Symphony Orchestra: A Social History of Musical Taste.* Bloomington, Indiana University Press.

Nye, R. B. 1960. *The Cultural Life of the New Nation, 1776–1830.* New York, Harper and Row.

Perry, B. 1921. *Life and Letters of Henry Lee Higginson.* Boston, Atlantic Monthly Press.

Poggi, J. 1968. *Theater in America: The Impact of Economic Forces, 1870–1967.* Ithaca, Cornell University Press.

Shiverick, N. C. 1970. The social reorganization of Boston, in Williams, A. W., *A Social History of the Greater Boston Clubs.* New York, Barre.

Solomon, B. M. 1956. *Ancestors and Immigrants.* New York, John Wiley.

Starr, P. 1982. *The Social Transformation of American Medicine.* New York, Basic Books.

Stinchcombe, A. L. 1965. Social structure and organizations, in March, J. G., ed., *Handbook of Organizations.* Chicago, Rand McNally.

Story, R. 1980. *The Forging of an Aristocracy: Harvard and the Boston Upper Class, 1800–1870.* Middletown, Connecticut, Wesleyan University Press.

Thernstrom, S. 1972. *Poverty and Progress: Social Mobility in a Nineteenth-Century City.* New York, Atheneum.

Thompson, E. P. 1966. *The Making of the English Working Class.* New York, Random House.

Thompson, J. D. 1967. *Organization in Action.* New York, McGraw-Hill.

Twentieth Century Club. 1910. *The Amusement Situation in Boston.* Boston.

Vogel, M. 1981. *The Invention of the Modern Hospital.* Chicago, University of Chicago Press.

Weber, M. 1968. *Economy and Society*, 3 volumes. New York, Bedminster Press.

Wolff, J. 1982. The problem of ideology in the sociology of art: a case study of Manchester in the nineteenth century. *Media, Culture and Society*, vol. 4, no. 1.

Zolberg, V. L. 1974. The art institute of Chicago: the sociology of a cultural institution, Ph.D. Dissertation, Department of Sociology, University of Chicago.

Zolberg, V. L. 1981. Conflicting visions of American art museums. *Theory and Society*, vol. 10, January.

# End Notes

1. The process, in other American cities, was to a large extent influenced by the Boston model. A final, more mundane, consideration recommends Boston as the focus for this study. The work in this paper is still in an exploratory stage, at which I am plundering history rather than writing it: the prolixity of nineteenth-century Boston's men and women of letters and the dedication and quality of her local historians makes Boston an ideal site for such an enterprise.

2. In a third sense, "cultural capital" might refer to the entrepreneurs of popular culture—the Barnums, the Keiths, the Shuberts and others—who turned culture into profits. While we will not consider this group at any length, we must remember that it was in opposition to their activities that the former defined their own.

3. My debt to Bernstein (1975*a, b*) and to Mary Douglas (1966) is evident here. My use of the terms "classification" and "framing" is similar to Bernstein's.

4. See Couch (1976*a, b*) and Mueller (1951: 37ff.) for more detailed descriptions of this form.

5. Shiverick (1970) notes the contrast between the founding of the public library in the 1850s and that of the private art museum 20 years later, both enterprises in which Athenaeum members were central.

6. I use the term "class" to refer to a self-conscious elite united by bonds of economic interest, kinship and culture (see Thompson, 1966: 8; Story, 1980: xi).

7. In James Thompson's terms, they were organizations whose resource dependencies all coincided. For their financial support, for their governance and for their clients, they looked to a class whose members were "functionally interdependent and interact[ed] regularly with respect to religious, economic, recreational, and governmental matters" (Thompson, 1967: 27).

# STUDY QUESTIONS

1. Why, according to DiMaggio, was the creation of the nonprofit corporation so essential to creating a distinction between high and low culture?

2. Do you think that the distinction between high and low culture is as useful or relevant today as DiMaggio claims it was in the past? Why or why not?

# 9

# CULTURE AS A TOOLKIT

ANN SWIDLER

The foundation of cultural sociology was built on the notion that culture was a set of meanings, values, ideals, and morals that served to guide individual and collective action. Values were conceptualized as the ultimate ends served by human actions. And to the extent that human actions resulted in those ends being served, culture could be said to be the "cause" of action. For example, Weber famously argued that asceticism and self-denial, central values of Protestant Christianity, caused northern Europeans to devote themselves to working hard and investing their money. Their culturally driven accumulation of wealth altered the development of the economic system because without Protestant wealth fueling its growth, Weber argued, capitalist development would have sputtered and stalled. This line of thinking runs contrary to Marx's argument that a society's culture arises from and reflects its economic structure. In effect, Weber turned Marx on his head.

Ann Swidler believes that thinking about culture as a set of ultimate values served by individual and collective actions is misleading. It is, she argues, much more complicated than that. Culture matters not because of why people use it but rather because of how they use it. After all, Swidler notes, the same practices, habits and behaviors can be used for different ends. Culture is best understood not as the agreed-upon ends (or goals), but rather as the agreed-upon *means*. Shared culture thus allows for individuals to pursue very different life courses in the same way, while conversely allowing individuals to

**pursue similar life goals in different ways. Moreover, historical context matters: in times of relative stability, there is little change in the daily toolkit of practices, habits, and behaviors. But unsettled, tumultuous times give rise to innovations and new strategies. Consequently, people's tools for daily living change as well.**

# CULTURE IN ACTION: SYMBOLS AND STRATEGIES

The reigning model used to understand culture's effects on action is fundamentally misleading. It assumes that culture shapes action by supplying ultimate ends or values toward which action is directed, thus making values the central causal element of culture. This paper analyzes the conceptual difficulties into which this traditional view of culture leads and offers an alternative model.

Among sociologists and anthropologists, debate has raged for several academic generations over defining the term "culture." Since the seminal work of Clifford Geertz (1973a), the older definition of culture as the entire way of life of a people, including their technology and material artifacts, or that (associated with the name of Ward Goodenough) as everything one would need to know to become a functioning member of a society, have been displaced in favor of defining culture as the publicly available symbolic forms through which people experience and express meaning (see Keesing, 1974). For purposes of this paper, culture consists of such symbolic vehicles of meaning, including beliefs, ritual practices, art forms, and ceremonies, as well as informal cultural practices such as language, gossip, stories, and rituals of daily life. These symbolic forms are the means through which "social processes of sharing modes of behavior and outlook within [a] community" (Hannerz, 1969:184) take place.

The recent resurgence of cultural studies has skirted the causal issues of greatest interest to sociologists. Interpretive approaches drawn from anthropology (Clifford Geertz, Victor Turner, Mary Douglas, and Claude Levi-Strauss) and literary criticism (Kenneth Burke, Roland Barthes) allow us better to describe the features of cultural products and experiences.

Pierre Bourdieu and Michel Foucault have offered new ways of thinking about culture's relationship to social stratification and power. For those interested in cultural *explanation* (as opposed to "thick description" [Geertz, 1973a] or interpretive social science [Rabinow and Sullivan, 1979]), however, values remain the major link between culture and action. This is not because sociologists really believe in the values paradigm. Indeed, it has been thoroughly criticized.[1] But without an alternative formulation of culture's causal significance, scholars either avoid causal questions or admit the values paradigm through the back door.

The alternative analysis of culture proposed here consists of three steps. First, it offers an image of culture as a "tool kit" of symbols, stories, rituals, and world-views, which people may use in varying configurations to solve different kinds of problems. Second, to analyze culture's causal effects, it focuses on "strategies of action," persistent ways of ordering action through time. Third, it sees culture's causal significance not in defining ends of action, but in providing cultural components that are used to construct strategies of action.

## Culture as Values

Our underlying view of culture derives from Max Weber. For Weber, human beings are motivated by ideal and material interests. Ideal interests, such as the desire to be saved from the torments of hell, are also ends-oriented, except that these ends are derived from symbolic realities. In Weber's (1946a [1922–3]:280) famous "switchmen" metaphor:

> Not ideas, but material and ideal interests, directly govern men's conduct. Yet very frequently the "world images" that have been created by "ideas" have, like switchmen, determined the tracks along which action has been pushed by the dynamic of interest.

Interests are the engine of action, pushing it along, but ideas define the destinations human beings seek to reach (inner-worldly versus other-worldly

---

1. See Blake and Davis (1964) and the empirical and theoretical critique in Cancian (1975).

possibilities of salvation, for example) and the means for getting there (mystical versus ascetic techniques of salvation).

Talcott Parsons adopted Weber's model, but blunted its explanatory thrust.

=====

A "cultural tradition," according to Parsons (1951:11–12), provides "value orientations," a "value" defined as "an element of a shared symbolic system which serves as a criterion or standard for selection among the alternatives of orientation which are intrinsically open in a situation." Culture thus affects human action through values that direct it to some ends rather than others.

The theory of values survives in part, no doubt, because of the intuitive plausibility in our own culture of the assumption that all action is ultimately governed by some means–ends schema. Culture shapes action by defining what people want.

What people want, however, is of little help in explaining their action.

=====

## THE PROTESTANT ETHIC

Causal issues appear again when we turn to the paradigmatic sociological argument for the importance of culture in human action—Max Weber's *The Protestant Ethic and the Spirit of Capitalism* (1958a [1904–51]). Weber sought to explain rational, capitalist economic behavior by arguing that culture, in the shape of Calvinist doctrine, created a distinctive frame of mind which encouraged rationalized, ascetic behavior. The doctrine of predestination channeled the desire to be saved into a quest for proof of salvation in worldly conduct, thus stimulating anxious self-examination and relentless self-discipline. Ends created by ideas (that is, the desire for salvation) powerfully influenced conduct.

If we take seriously the causal model Weber offers (both in *The Protestant Ethic* and in his theoretical writings on religion), however, we cannot understand his larger claim: that the ethos of Protestantism endured even after the spur of the Calvinist quest for proof of salvation had been lost. If ideas shape ethos, why did the ethos of ascetic Protestantism outlast its ideas?

Weber argues for continuity between the desire of early Calvinists to know whether they were saved or damned and the secular ethic of Benjamin Franklin. We recognize other continuities as well: in the Methodist demand for sobriety, humility, and self-control among the working class; and even in the anxious self-scrutiny of contemporary Americans seeking psychological health, material success, or personal authenticity.

How, then, should we understand continuity in the style or ethos of action, even when ideas (and the ends of action they advocate) change? This continuity suggests that what endures is *the way action is organized*, not its ends. In the Protestant West (and especially in Puritan America), for example, action is assumed to depend on the choices of individual persons, so that before an individual acts he or she must ask: What kind of self do I have? Saved or damned? Righteous or dissolute? Go-getter or plodder? Authentic or false?

Collective action is also understood to rest on the choices of individual actors. Groups are thus seen as collections of like-minded individuals who come together to pursue their common interests (Varenne, 1977). Even large-scale social purposes are presumed best accomplished through movements of moral reform or education that transform individuals (McLoughlin, 1978; Boyer, 1978; Gusfield, 1981). To call this cultural approach to action the "value" of individualism, as is often done, misses the point, since this individualistic way of organizing action can be directed to many values, among them the establishment of "community" (Varenne, 1977; Bellah, et al., 1985). This reliance on moral "work" on the self to organize action has, then, been a more enduring feature of Protestant culture than the particular ends toward which this work has been directed. Such examples underline the need for new ways of thinking about cultural explanation.

These two cases illustrate the chronic difficulties with traditional efforts to use culture as an explanatory variable and suggest why many have written off the effort altogether.

## Cultural Explanation

If values have little explanatory power, why expect culture to play any causal role in human action? Why not explain action as the result of interests and structural constraints, with only a rational, interest-maximizing actor to link the two?

The view that action is governed by "interests" is inadequate in the same way as the view that action is governed by non-rational values. Both models have a common explanatory logic, differing only in assuming different ends of action: either individualistic, arbitrary "tastes" or consenual, cultural "values."

Both views are flawed by an excessive emphasis on the "unit act," the notion that people choose their actions one at a time according to their interests or values. But people do not, indeed cannot, build up a sequence of actions piece by piece, striving with each act to maximize a given outcome. Action is necessarily integrated into larger assemblages, called here "strategies of action." Culture has an independent causal role because it shapes the capacities from which such strategies of action are constructed.

The term "strategy" is not used here in the conventional sense of a plan consciously devised to attain a goal. It is, rather, a general way of organizing action (depending upon a network of kin and friends, for example, or relying on selling one's skills in a market) that might allow one to reach several different life goals. Strategies of action incorporate, and thus depend on, habits, moods, sensibilities, and views of the world (Geertz, 1973a). People do not build lines of action from scratch, choosing actions one at a time as efficient means to given ends. Instead, they construct chains of action beginning with at least some pre-fabricated links. Culture influences action through the shape and organization of those links, not by determining the ends to which they are put.

Our alternative model also rests on the fact that all real cultures contain diverse, often conflicting symbols, rituals, stories, and guides to action. The reader of the Bible can find a passage to justify almost any act, and traditional wisdom usually comes in paired adages counseling opposite behaviors. A culture is not a unified system that pushes action in a consistent direction. Rather, it is more like a "tool kit" or repertoire (Hannerz, 1969:186–88) from which actors select differing pieces for constructing lines of action. Both individuals and groups know how to do different kinds of things in different circumstances (see, for example, Gilbert and Mulkay, 1984). People may have in readiness cultural capacities they rarely employ; and all people know more culture than they use (if only in the sense that they ignore much that they hear). A realistic cultural theory should lead us to expect not passive "cultural dopes" (Garfinkel, 1967; Wrong, 1961), but rather the active, sometimes skilled users of culture whom we actually observe.

If culture influences action through end values, people in changing circumstances should hold on to their preferred ends while altering their strategies for attaining them. But if culture provides the tools with which persons construct lines of action, then styles or strategies of action will be more persistent than the ends people seek to attain. Indeed, people will come to value ends for which their cultural equipment is well suited (cf. Mancini, 1980). To return to the culture of poverty example, a ghetto youth who can expertly "read" signs of friendship and loyalty (Hannerz, 1969), or who can recognize with practised acuity threats to turf or dignity (Horowitz, 1983), may pursue ends that place group loyalty above individual achievement, not because he disdains what individual achievement could bring, but because the cultural meanings and social skills necessary for playing *that* game well would require drastic and costly cultural retooling.

This revised imagery—culture as a "tool kit" for constructing "strategies of action," rather than as a switchman directing an engine propelled by interests—turns our attention toward different causal issues than do traditional perspectives in the sociology of culture.

## TWO MODELS OF CULTURAL INFLUENCE

We need two different models to understand two situations in which culture works very differently. In one case, culture accounts for continuities in "settled lives." In settled lives, culture is intimately integrated with action; it is here that we are most tempted to see values as organizing and anchoring patterns of action; and here it is most difficult to disentangle what is uniquely "cultural," since culture and structural circumstance seem to reinforce each other. This is the situation about which a theorist like Clifford Geertz (1973b) writes so persuasively: culture is a model of and a model for experience; and cultural symbols reinforce an ethos, making plausible a world-view which in turn justifies the ethos.

The second case is that of "unsettled lives." The distinction is less between settled and unsettled lives, however, than between culture's role in sustaining existing strategies of action and its role in constructing new ones. This contrast is not, of course, absolute. Even when they lead settled lives, people do active cultural work to maintain or refine their cultural capacities. Conversely, even the most fanatical ideological movement, which seeks to remake completely the cultural capacities of its members, will inevitably draw on many tacit assumptions from the existing culture. There are, nonetheless, more and less settled lives, and more and less settled cultural periods. Individuals in certain phases of their lives, and groups or entire societies in certain historical periods, are involved in constructing new strategies of action. It is for the latter situation that our usual models of culture's effects are most inadequate.

## UNSETTLED LIVES

Periods of social transformation seem to provide simultaneously the best and the worst evidence for culture's influence on social action. Established cultural ends are jettisoned with apparent ease, and yet explicitly articulated cultural models, such as ideologies, play a powerful role in organizing social life (see, for examples, Geertz, 1968; Schurmann, 1970; Eisenstadt, 1970b; Walzer, 1974; Madsen, 1984; Hunt, 1984).

In such periods, ideologies—explicit, articulated, highly organized meaning systems (both political and religious)—*establish* new styles or strategies of action. When people are learning new ways of organizing individual and collective action, practicing unfamiliar habits until they become familiar, then doctrine, symbol, and ritual directly shape action.

Assumed here is a continuum from *ideology* to *tradition* to *common sense* (see Stromberg, 1985). An "ideology" is a highly articulated, self-conscious belief and ritual system, aspiring to offer a unified answer to problems of social action. Ideology may be thought of as a phase in the development of a system of cultural meaning. "Traditions," on the other hand, are articulated cultural beliefs and practices, but ones taken for granted so that they seem inevitable parts of life. Diverse, rather than unified, partial rather than all-embracing, they do not always inspire enthusiastic assent. (A wedding, in our own culture, may seem odd, forced, or unnatural when we actually attend one, for example. But it will still seem the natural way to get married, so that going to a justice of the peace requires special explanation.) Traditions, whether the routine ones of daily life or the extraordinary ones of communal ceremony, nonetheless seem ordained in the order of things, so that people may rest in the certainty that they exist, without necessarily participating in them. The same belief system—a religion, for example—may be held by some people as an ideology and by others as tradition; and what has been tradition may under certain historical circumstances become ideology. (This is the distinction Geertz [1968:61] makes when he writes about a loss of traditional religious certainty in modern "ideologized" Islam—coming to "hold" rather than be "held by" one's beliefs.) "Common sense," finally, is the set of assumptions so unselfconscious as to seem a natural, transparent, undeniable part of the structure of the world (Geertz, 1975).

Bursts of ideological activism occur in periods when competing ways of organizing action are developing or contending for dominance. People formulate, flesh out, and put into practice new habits of action. In such situations, culture may indeed be said to directly shape action. Members of a religious cult wear orange, or share their property, or dissolve their marriages because their beliefs tell them to. Protestants simplify worship, read the Bible, and work in a calling because of their faith. Doctrine and casuistry tell people how to act and provide blueprints for community life.

During such periods, differences in ritual practice or doctrine may become highly charged, so that statuary in churches (Baxandall, 1980), the clothing and preaching styles of ministers (Davis, 1975; Zaret, 1985), or the style and decoration of religious objects are fraught with significance.

Ritual acquires such significance in unsettled lives because ritual changes reorganize taken-for-granted habits and modes of experience. People developing new strategies of action depend on cultural models to learn styles of self, relationship, cooperation, authority, and so forth. Commitment to such an ideology, originating perhaps in conversion, is more conscious than is the embeddedness of individuals in settled cultures, representing a break with some alternative way of life.

These explicit cultures might well be called "systems." While not perfectly consistent, they aspire to offer not multiple answers, but one unified answer to the question of how human beings should live. In conflict with other cultural models, these cultures are coherent because they must battle to dominate the world-views, assumptions, and habits of their members.

———

Culture has independent causal influence in unsettled cultural periods because it makes possible new strategies of action—constructing entities that can act (selves, families, corporations), shaping the styles and skills with which they act, and modeling forms of authority and cooperation. It is, however, the concrete situations in which these cultural models are enacted that determine which take root and thrive, and which wither and die.

## SETTLED LIVES

The causal connections between culture and action are very different in settled cultural periods. Culture provides the materials from which individuals and groups construct strategies of action. Such cultural resources are diverse, however, and normally groups and individuals call upon these resources selectively, bringing to bear different styles and habits of action in different situations. Settled cultures thus support varied patterns of action, obscuring culture's independent influence.

Specifying culture's causal role is made more difficult in settled cultural periods by the "loose coupling" between culture and action. People profess ideals they do not follow, utter platitudes without examining their validity, or fall into cynicism or indifference with the assurance that the world will go on just the same. Such gaps between the explicit norms, worldviews, and rules of conduct individuals espouse and the ways they habitually act create little difficulty within settled strategies of action. People naturally "know" how to act. Cultural experience may reinforce or refine the skills, habits, and attitudes important for common strategies of action, but established ways of acting do not depend upon such immediate cultural support.

In settled cultural periods, then, culture and social structure are simultaneously too fused and too disconnected for easy analysis. On the one hand, people in settled periods can live with great discontinuity between talk and action. On the other hand, in settled lives it is particularly difficult to disentangle cultural and structural influences on action. That is because ideology has both diversified, by being adapted to varied life circumstances, and gone underground, so pervading ordinary experience as to blend imperceptibly into common-sense assumptions about what is true. Settled cultures are thus more encompassing then are ideologies, in that they are not in open competition with alternative models for organizing experience. Instead, they have the undisputed authority of habit, normality, and common sense. Such culture does not impose a single, unified pattern on action, in the sense of imposing norms, styles, values, or ends on individual actors. Rather, settled cultures constrain action by providing a limited set of resources out of which individuals and groups construct strategies of action.

There is nonetheless a distinctive kind of cultural explanation appropriate to settled cultures. First, while such cultures provide a "tool kit" of resources from which people can construct diverse strategies of action, to construct such a strategy means selecting certain cultural elements (both such tacit culture as attitudes and styles and, sometimes, such explicit cultural materials as rituals and beliefs) and investing them with particular meanings in concrete life circumstances. An example might [be] young adults who become more church-going when they marry and have children, and who then, in turn, find themselves with reawakened religious feelings. In such cases culture cannot be said to have "caused" the choices people make, in the sense that both the cultural elements and the life strategy are, in effect, chosen simultaneously. Indeed, the meanings of particular cultural elements depend, in part, on the strategy of action in which they are embedded (so, for example, religious ritual may have special meaning as part of a family's weekly routine). Nonetheless, culture has an effect in that the ability to put together such a strategy depends on the available set of cultural resources. Furthermore, as certain cultural resources become more central in a given life, and become more fully invested with meaning, they anchor the strategies of action people have developed.

Such cultural influence can be observed in "cultural lag." People do not readily take advantage of new structural opportunities which would require them to abandon established ways of life. This is not because they cling to cultural values, but because they are reluctant to abandon familiar strategies of action for which they have the cultural equipment. Because cultural expertise underlies the ability of both individuals and groups to construct effective strategies of action, such matters as the style or ethos of action and related ways of organizing authority and cooperation are enduring aspects of individual, and especially of collective, life.

Second, the influence of culture in settled lives is especially strong in structuring those uninstitutionalized, but recurrent situations in which people act in concert. When Americans try to get something done, they are likely to create voluntarist social movements—from religious revivals (McLoughlin, 1978), to reform campaigns (Boyer, 1978), to the voluntary local initiatives that created much of American public schooling (Meyer, et al., 1979). Such strategies of action rest on the cultural assumption that social groups—indeed, society itself—are constituted by the voluntary choices of individuals. Yet such voluntarism does *not*, in fact, dominate most of our institutional life. A bureaucratic state, large corporations, and an impersonal market run many spheres of American life without voluntary individual cooperation. American voluntarism persists, nonetheless, as the predominant collective way of dealing with situations that are not taken care of by institutions.[2]

Culture affects action, but in different ways in settled versus unsettled periods. Disentangling these two modes of culture's influence and specifying more clearly how culture works in the two situations, creates new possibilities for cultural explanation. The following schematic diagram summarizes the two models of cultural explanation proposed here. Neither model looks like the Parsonian theory of values, the Weberian model of how ideas influence action, or the Marxian model of the relationship of ideas and interests. However, between them the two models account for much of what has been persuasive about these earlier images of cultural influence while avoiding those expectations that cannot be supported by evidence.

# Conclusion

The approach developed here may seem at first to relegate culture to a subordinate, purely instrumental role in social life. The attentive reader will see, though, that what this paper has suggested is precisely the opposite. Strategies of action are cultural products; the symbolic experiences, mythic lore, and ritual practices of a group or society create moods and motivations, ways of organizing experience and evaluating reality, modes of regulating conduct, and ways of forming social bonds, which provide resources for constructing strategies of action. When we notice cultural differences we recognize that people do not all go about their business in the same ways; how they approach life is shaped by their culture.

The problem, however, is to develop more sophisticated theoretical ways of thinking about how culture shapes or constrains action, and more generally, how culture interacts with social structure. This paper has argued that

2. Renato Rosaldo (1985) has written provocatively of anthropology's overreliance on images of culture as sets of plans or rules. He argues that culture is better thought of as providing resources for dealing with the unexpected, for improvising. While my argument stays close to the culture as plan imagery, it nonetheless stresses that what is culturally regulated is that part of social life which has to be continually created and recreated, not that part which is so institutionalized that it requires little active support by those it regulates.

**FIGURE 1  Two Models of Culture**

|  | **Characteristics** | **Short-Term Effects** | **Long-Term Effects** |
|---|---|---|---|
| Settled Culture (traditions and common sense) | Low coherence, consistency | Weak direct control over action | Provides resources for constructing strategies of action |
|  | Encapsulates | Refines and reinforces skills, habits, modes of experience | Creates continuities in style or ethos, and especially in organization of strategies of action |
| Unsettled Culture (ideology) | High coherence, consistency | Strong control over action | Creates new strategies of action, but long-term influence depends on structural opportunities for survival of competing ideologies |
|  | Competes with other cultural views | Teaches new modes of action | |

these relationships vary across time and historical situation. Within established modes of life, culture provides a repertoire of capacities from which varying strategies of action may be constructed. Thus culture appears to shape action only in that the cultural repertoire limits the available range of strategies of action. Such "settled cultures" are nonetheless constraining. Although internally diverse and often contradictory, they provide the ritual traditions that regulate ordinary patterns of authority and cooperation, and they so define common sense that alternative ways of organizing action seem unimaginable, or at least implausible. Settled cultures constrain action over time because of the high costs of cultural retooling to adopt new patterns of action.

In unsettled periods, in contrast, cultural meanings are more highly articulated and explicit, because they model patterns of action that do not "come naturally." Belief and ritual practice directly shape action for the community that adheres to a given ideology. Such ideologies are, however, in competition with other sets of cultural assumptions. Ultimately, structural and historical opportunities determine which strategies, and thus which cultural systems, succeed.

In neither case is it cultural end-values that shape action in the long run. Indeed, a culture has enduring effects on those who hold it, not by shaping the ends they pursue, but by providing the characteristic repertoire from which they build lines of action.

A focus on cultural values was attractive for sociology because it suggested that culture, not material circumstances, was determinative "in the last instance." In Parsons' (1966) ingenious "cybernetic model," social structure may have constrained opportunities for action, but cultural ends directed it. The challenge for the contemporary sociology of culture is not, however, to try to estimate how *much* culture shapes action. Instead, sociologists should search for new analytic perspectives that will allow more effective concrete analyses of how culture is used by actors, how cultural elements constrain or facilitate patterns of action, what aspects of a cultural heritage have enduring effects on action, and what specific historical changes undermine the vitality of some cultural patterns and give rise to others. The suggestion that both the influence and the fate of cultural meanings depend on the strategies of action they support is made in an attempt to fill this gap. Such attempts at more systematic, differentiated causal models may help to restore the study of culture to a central place in contemporary social science.

# References

Baxandall, Michael. 1980. *The Limewood Sculptors of Renaissance Germany, 1475–1525: Images and Circumstances.* New Haven: Yale University Press.

Bellah, Robert N., Richard Madsen, William M. Sullivan, Ann Swidler, and Steven M. Tipton. 1985. *Habits of the Heart: Individualism and Commitment in American Life.* Berkeley: University of California Press.

Blake, Judith and Kingsley Davis. 1964. "Norms, Values and Sanctions," Pp. 456–84 in *Handbook of Modern Sociology,* edited by Robert L. Paris. Chicago: Rand-McNally.

Boyer, Paul. 1978. *Urban Masses and Moral Order in America, 1820–1920.* Cambridge, MA: Harvard University Press.

Cancian, Francesca M. 1975. *What Are Norms? A Study of Beliefs and Action in a Maya Community.* London: Cambridge University Press.

Davis, Natalie Zemon. 1975. "The Rites of Violence." Pp. 152–87 in *Society and Culture in Early Modern France.* Stanford: Stanford University Press.

Eisenstadt, S. N., ed. 1970b. "The Protestant Ethic Thesis in an Analytical and Comparative Framework." Pp. 3–45 in *The Protestant Ethic and Modernization*, edited by S. N. Eisenstadt.

Garfinkel, Harold. 1967. *Studies in Ethnomethodology*. Englewood Cliffs, NJ: Prentice-Hall.

Geertz, Clifford. 1968. *Islam Observed: Religious Development in Morocco and Indonesia*. New Haven: Yale University Press.

———. 1973a. *The Interpretation of Cultures*. New York: Basic Books.

———. 1973b. "Religion as a Cultural System." Pp. 87–125 in *The Interpretation of Cultures*.

———. 1975. "Common Sense as a Cultural System." *Antioch Review* 33:5–26.

Gilbert, G. Nigel and Michael Mulkay. 1984. *Opening Pandora's Box: A Sociological Analysis of Scientists' Discourse*. Cambridge. England: Cambridge University Press.

Gusfield, Joseph R. 1981. *The Culture of Public Problems: Drinking–Driving and the Symbolic Order*. Chicago: University of Chicago Press:

Hannerz, Ulf. 1969. *Soulside: Inquiries into Ghetto Culture and Community,* New York: Columbia University Press.

Horowitz, Ruth. 1983. *Honor and the American Dream: Culture and Identity in a Chicano Community*. New Brunswick, NJ: Rutgers University Press.

Hunt, Lynn. 1984. *Politics, Culture, and Class in the French Revolution*. Berkeley: University of California Press.

Keesing, Roger M. 1974. *Theories of Culture*. Pp. 73–97 in *Annual Review of Anthropology 3*. Palo Alto: Annual Reviews, Inc.

McLoughlin, William G. 1978. *Revivals, Awakenings, and Reform: An Essay on Religion and Social Change in America, 1607–1977*. Chicago: University of Chicago Press.

Madsen, Richard. 1984. *Morality and Power in a Chinese Village*. Berkeley: University of California Press.

Mancini, Janet K. 1980. *Strategic Styles: Coping in the Inner City*. Hanover, NH: University Press of New England.

Meyer, John W., David Tyack, Joane Nagel, and Audri Gordon. 1979. "Public Education as Nation-Building in America: Enrollments and Bureaucratization in the American States, 1870–1930." *American Journal of Sociology* 85:591–613.

Parsons, Telcott. 1951. *The Social System*. New York: Free Press.

———. 1966. *Societies: Evolutionary and Comparative Perspectives*. Englewood Cliffs, NJ: Prentice-Hall.

Rabinow, Paul and William M. Sullivan, eds. 1979. *Interpretive Social Science: A Reader*. Berkeley: University of California Press.

Rosaldo, Renato. 1985. "While Making Other Plans." *Southern California Law Review* 58:19–28.

Schurmann, Franz. 1970. *Ideology and Organization in Communist China.* 2nd edition. Berkeley: University of California Press.

Stromberg, Peter G. 1985. "Ideology and Culture: A Critique of Semiotic Approaches in Anthropology." Unpublished paper, Department of Anthropology, University of Arizona.

Varenne, Hervé. 1977. *Americans Together: Structured Diversity in a Midwestern Town.* New York: Teacher's College Press.

Walzer, Michael. 1974. *The Revolution of the Saints.* New York: Atheneum.

Weber, Max. 1946a [1922–23]. "The Social Psychology of the World Religions." Pp. 267–301 in *From Max Weber*, edited by H.H. Gerth and C. Wright Mills. New York: Oxford University Press.

———. 1958a [1904–05]. *The Protestant Ethic and the Spirit of Capitalism.* New York: Charles Scribner and Sons.

Wrong, Dennis. 1961. "The Oversocialized Conception of Man in Modern Sociology." *American Sociological Review* 26:183–93.

Zaret, David. 1985. *The Heavenly Contract: Ideology and Organization in Pre-Revolutionary Puritanism.* Chicago: University of Chicago Press.

# STUDY QUESTIONS

1. How does Swidler define culture? How does her definition differ from Weber's?

2. Why does Swidler distinguish between settled and unsettled lives? Why is this distinction important for her argument?

# 10

# MEDIA EFFECTS

MICHAEL SCHUDSON

On April 20, 1999, Eric Harris and Dylan Klebold armed themselves with guns and bombs, entered their high school, and opened fire. They killed 12 students and 1 teacher and wounded 21 others before killing themselves. The Columbine massacre, as it came to be known, sparked national debates about the possible factors that caused Harris and Klebold's killing spree. Some blamed Goth culture, others blamed America's gun culture, still others the adolescent cultures of the Internet. Much attention was given to the "culture of violence" exhibited in films and video games, especially the ultra-violent first-person shooter games of which Harris and Klebold were fans. Was that what made them do it? Too much time playing *Doom?* Whatever the ultimate motives and causes were, Americans seemed to be seeking answers that had something to do with culture. But such explanations beg the question: How does culture influence us?

What work does culture do and how does it do it? Alternatively, what if culture doesn't work? That is, what if culture doesn't really have the kind of power we've long presumed it does? These are the central questions with which sociologist Michael Schudson's article grapples. He begins by reviewing fundamental debates about idealism versus materialism in social theory and then focuses on the area he knows best, the sociology of mass media. In order for mass-media objects like a song, a movie, a news story, a television show, or a video game to be effective, he says, there are certain conditions which must be met. First, people have to know about it. It must be accessible and

**it has to reach people. Second, it has to be forceful or seductive, or memorable in some way. Third, it has to resonate with a larger public issue or concern. Fourth, it must become valued by an influential group or institution. It must have relevance for a set of stakeholders who care about it and nurture its survival. Fifth, it must be able to mobilize people to take action or to make a decision. Cultural objects can exert real-world effects without meeting all of these conditions, but when all five are present, the object gains significant power and efficacy.**

# HOW CULTURE WORKS

## Perspectives from Media Studies on the Efficacy of Symbols

How does culture work? That is, what influence do particular symbols have on what people think and how they act?

An anthropologist might find the question bizarre, one that by the asking reveals a fundamental misunderstanding. Culture is not something that works or fails to work. It is not something imposed on or done to a person; it is constitutive of the person. It is the precondition and the condition of human-ness. The meanings people incorporate in their lives are not separate from their activities; activities are made of meanings. Culture, as Clifford Geertz says, "is not a power, something to which social events, behaviors, institutions, or processes can be causally attributed; it is a context, something within which they can be intelligibly—that is, thickly—described."[1] Insofar as this is true, the question of the "impact" of culture is not answerable because culture is not separable from social structure, economics, politics, and other features of human activity.

And yet, even Clifford Geertz and other symbolic anthropologists are far from having given up efforts at causal attribution when it comes to culture. If we think of culture as the symbolic dimension of human activity and if we conceive its study, somewhat arbitrarily, as the study of discrete symbolic objects (art, literature, sermons, ideologies, advertisements, maps, street signs) and how they function in social life, then the question of what work culture does and how it does it is not self-evidently foolish.

Indeed, it can then be understood as a key question in sociology, anthropology, and history, closely related to the central question in Western social thought since Marx (as James Fernandez has asserted)—the debate between cultural idealism and historical materialism.[2] It is the problem raised by Max Weber's essay on the Protestant ethic: do systems of ideas or beliefs have causal significance in human affairs over against forces? It is the problem suggested by the debates in Marxism about the relation of "superstructure" to "base."

———

In history and the social sciences, answers to the question of the efficacy of cultural symbols or objects cluster around two poles. At one end, cultural objects are seen as enormously powerful in shaping human action—even if the cultural objects themselves are shown to be rather simply derived from the interests of powerful social groups. Ideas or symbols or propaganda successfully manipulate people. "Ideology" (or the somewhat more slippery term "hegemony") is viewed as a potent agent of powerful ruling groups, successfully molding the ideas and expectations and presuppositions of the general population and making people deferent and pliable. This position, which in its Marxist formulation has been dubbed "the dominant ideology thesis," is equally consistent with what David Laitin identifies as a conventional, social-system, rather than social-action, view, or the "first face" of culture.

At the other end, concepts of culture cluster around a more optimistic view of human activity, a voluntaristic sense in which culture is seen not as a program but as a "tool kit" (in Ann Swidler's words, although she is not herself a tool-kit theorist) or "equipment for living" (in Kenneth Burke's).[3] Culture is not a set of ideas imposed but a set of ideas and symbols available for use. Individuals select the meanings they need for particular purposes and occasions from the limited but nonetheless varied cultural menu a given society provides. In this view, culture is a resource for social action more than a structure to limit social action. It serves a variety of purposes because symbols are "polysemic" and can be variously interpreted; because communication is inherently ambiguous and people will read into messages what they please; or because meaning is at the service of individual interest. Symbols, not people, are pliable. This is what Laitin calls the "second face" of culture in which culture is largely an ambiguous set of symbols that are usable as a resource for rational actors in society pursuing their own interests. Taken to its logical extreme, this position assigns culture no efficacy in social action at all. It suggests that while people may need a symbolic object to define, explain, or galvanize a course of action they have already decided on an appropriate object will always be found to clothe the pre-existing intention.

———

. . . To understand the efficacy of culture, it is essential to recognize simultaneously that (1) human beings make their own history and (2) they do not make it according to circumstances of their own choosing.

It is not surprising that a good many thinkers have sought some kind of middle position that recognizes both the constraining force of culture (thereby supporting the social mold or hegemonic position) and the instrumental and voluntaristic uses of culture by individuals (thus lending weight to the tool-kit position). . . .

I want to pursue a middle position myself here. . . .

I focus especially on the influence of the mass media because this is the field I am most familiar with. I am most of all interested in the direct influence of cultural objects. Does TV lead to a more violent society or a more fearful society? Do romance novels buy off potential feminist unrest? Does advertising make people materialistic? Do cockfights in Bali provide an emotional training ground for the Balinese? Did Harriet Beecher Stowe help start the Civil War? Did Wagner give aid and comfort to the rise of Fascism? These are naive questions. They are, nonetheless, recurrent questions, popular questions, and publicly significant ones. (Should advertisements on children's television programs be banned? Should pornography be forbidden? What impact do sex education classes have? Or warning labels on cigarette packages?) There are a variety of more subtle questions concerning the role of culture in social life, but these questions of whether "exposure" to certain symbols or messages in various media actually lead people to change how they think about the world or act in it are powerful and central.

———

Does culture "work"? Instead of asking whether it does, I ask about the conditions—both of the cultural object and its environment—that are likely to make the culture or cultural object work more or less. I will try to do this without bowdlerizing the concept of culture—but I recognize a tendency in this enterprise to reduce culture to information, to neglect the emotional and psychological dimensions of meaning, to ignore culture that is unconsciously transmitted or received, to focus on the most discrete and propositional forms of culture. The examples I present here draw primarily from media studies and so do not represent all of what one might mean by "culture," but I think they set the general questions clearly.

I want to examine five dimensions of the potency of a cultural object. I call these, for the sake of alliteration, retrievability, rhetorical force, resonance, institutional retention, and resolution.

## Retrievability

If culture is to influence a person, it must reach the person. An advertisement is of little use to the manufacturer if a consumer never sees it; it is equally of little use if the person sees the ad but cannot locate the product in a store or find out how to order it by mail. Advertising agencies spend time and energy learning to place ads where they are most likely to be seen by the people most likely to be in the market for the product they announce. Cosmetic ads appear more frequently in *Vogue* than in *Field & Stream* because more cosmetic purchasers read *Vogue* than read *Field & Stream.*

In the language of marketing, we can call this "reach," in the language of cognitive psychology, we can refer to it as "availability," but the general term I will use, to suggest more easily the sociological dimension of the phenomenon, is "retrievability."

===

From the individual's perspective, then, some elements of experience are more readily drawn upon as bases for action than other elements. From the perspective of someone who would seek to manipulate cultural objects to advantage, the question is how to make some key elements of culture more available to audiences.

What puts a cultural object in the presence of (and therefore potentially in the mind and memory of) an individual in an audience? Sociologically, there are a variety of dimensions of retrievability. A cultural object or cultural information is more *economically* retrievable if it is cheaper for people to retrieve. Marketers know that price is a barrier to customers' trying out a new product, so they distribute free samples or announce low introductory price offers, reducing the economic barrier to direct, experiential knowledge of the product. Libraries send bookmobiles to neighborhoods to attract readers who would find getting to the nearest library inconvenient or expensive.

Culture can be socially as well as economically retrievable. Books in a library's general collection are socially more retrievable than books in the Rare Book Room where a person must go through a librarian and show some identification or announce a special purpose for examining a book. It is as much the etiquette of the Rare Book Room as its formal constraints that erects a barrier to its use. Working-class parents get more information about their children's public schools from school newsletters than from parent-teacher conferences while middle-class parents make better use of the conferences. The working-class parent often feels socially awkward or inadequate talking with teachers and finds it difficult to breach the social barrier to the school system's personnel directly.[4]

There are other categories of retrievability—ways in which a part of culture becomes more or less accessible to the awareness, mind, or memory of an individual. All the categories concern the retrievability of culture either in space or in time. The examples of social and economic retrievability I have already mentioned have to do with the availability of culture in space—whether a cultural object or piece of information is geographically in the presence of the individual. There are also ways that cultural retrievability may be expanded or limited temporally. A written message lasts longer than a verbal one, other things being equal (which is not to say it will be as rhetorically potent as the verbal message). If a cultural object is connected to a culturally salient event institutionalized on the cultural calendar, it will be more available—not only more present, that is, but more easily remembered over time.

## Rhetorical Force

Even if a cultural object, be it advertisement or ritual or novel, is within reach, what will lead someone to be mindful of it? Even if it is in view, what will make viewing it memorable and powerful?

Different cultural objects have different degrees of rhetorical force or effectiveness. What makes one novel more powerful than another, one advertisement more memorable than another, one ritual more moving than another, is a matter that does not afford easy answers. . . .

If the cultural object is taken to be a communicative act, there may be a rhetorical aspect to each of its analytically distinct features. There may be a rhetorical aspect of the sender (higher-status speakers will be more persuasive to an audience than lower-status speakers); of the receiving audience (messages that flatter the audience without arousing suspicion of the speaker's insincerity will be more persuasive than messages that do not flatter); of the medium (people in a given culture may find one medium, say, television, generally more credible than another, say, radio); of the form or format (a whispered confidence is more persuasive than a public, joking insinuation); of the cultural situation (a painting in a museum more easily wins attention and respect than a painting in an antique store or on a bathroom wall); and of the message itself.

———

. . . Cultural objects do not exist by themselves. Each new one enters a field already occupied. If it is to gain attention, it must do so by displacing others or by entering into a conversation with others. The power of a cultural object or message exists by virtue of contrastive relationships to other objects in its field. A new painting can be understood only as it follows from or departs from traditions of painting that have gone before, both in the artist's own work and in the history of art to which the artist's efforts are some kind of new response. Even the lowly advertisement speaks within a field of advertisements and, indeed, is designed with contemporaneous rival advertisements in mind. Whether an advertisement or a painting or a novel appears striking to an audience will depend very much on how skillfully the object draws from the general culture and from the specific cultural field it is a part of.

———

## Resonance

The importance of the conventions of the subcommunity brings me to the third feature of cultural power: the degree to which the cultural object is resonant with the audience. A rhetorically effective object must be relevant to and resonant with the life of the audience. This is a simple and familiar point. It is made, for instance, by George Mosse when he argues in a study of the power of political ideology and ritual that rulers cannot successfully impose culture on people unless the political symbolism they choose connects to underlying native traditions.[5] So far as this is true, an analysis of cultural power inevitably leans toward the second face of culture, the "tool-kit" sense of culture as a set of resources from which people choose, depending on their "interests." . . .

. . . People not only attend to media selectively but perceive selectively from what they attend to. Obviously, then, people normally participate in culture-making; as some literary theorists would say today, readers are co-authors, "writing" the texts they read. This can be taken too far, I think—and does go too far if it falls altogether into the tool-kit view of culture—but there is a great deal of truth in it.

For producers of mass media culture, the issue of "resonance" will be experienced as a central problem. Whether a new television show, book, or record album will be a "hit" is notoriously difficult for the "culture industry" to predict.[6] The broader the audience a message reaches, the less likely the message is to be specifically relevant to a given individual receiving it. Media reports of crime, for example, apparently have little influence on people's fear of crime and less influence still on the kinds of crime-preventing precautions people take. Why? Because, it has been suggested, the media report on spectacular crimes—which people rarely encounter in their own or their acquaintances' lives—and because the crimes reported rarely take place in the neighborhoods where most of the media audience lives.[7]

The relevance of a cultural object to its audience, its utility, if you will, is a property not only of the object's content or nature and the audience's interest in it but of the position of the object in the cultural tradition of the society the audience is a part of. That is, the uses to which an audience puts a cultural object are not necessarily personal or idiosyncratic; the needs or interests of an audience are socially and culturally constituted. What is "resonant" is not a matter of how "culture" connects to individual "interests" but a matter of how culture connects to interests that are themselves constituted in a cultural frame. . . .

. . . One of the reasons a symbol becomes powerful is that—sometimes more or less by chance—it has been settled on, it has won out over other symbols as a representation of some valued entity and it comes to have an aura. The aura generates its own power and what might originally have been a very modest advantage (or even lucky coincidence) of a symbol becomes, with the accumulation of the aura of tradition over time, a major feature.[8]

Relevance or resonance, then, is not a private relation between cultural object and individual, not even a social relation between cultural object and audience, but a public and cultural relation among object, tradition, and audience.

## Institutional Retention

Culture interpenetrates with institutions as well as with interests. It exists not only as a set of meanings people share but as a set of concrete social relations in which meaning is enacted, in which it is, in a sense, tied down. If you tie a string around your finger to remember to water the house plants, and fail to heed the string, you may suffer social consequences. It may take a few days or a week for the leaves on your house plants to turn brown, but it may take only a few hours after you return home for your spouse or roommate to be angry with you for failing to remember your chore. To take up the example of Homer, you may well believe that the Bhagavad Gita is as great an epic as the Iliad, but this judgment will not receive social or institutional support in the West. You will have some difficulty getting your friends to read the Gita if they have a choice of reading the Iliad instead because there are no social sanctions, apart from your own disapproval, if they fail to read it. There are sanctions, however, (or there used to be—culture does change, after all) for not knowing Homer. You might, for instance, fail high school English. That is tied-down, institutionalized culture.

A good many cultural objects may be widely available, rhetorically effective, and culturally resonant, but fail of institutionalization. If they never turn up in a school classroom, never become a part of common reference, never enter into the knowledge formally required for citizenship or job-holding or social acceptability, their power will be limited. A "fad" is the phenomenon that epitomizes this situation: a fad is a cultural object that makes its ways into public awareness and use, is widely adopted, and then fades completely or almost completely from view.

Powerful culture is reinforced in and through social institutions that have carrots and sticks of their own. Some culture—say, popular entertainment—is only modestly institutionalized. For certain social groups—notably, teenagers—familiarity with popular entertainment is a key element in social life and there are serious sanctions for lack of knowledge or lack of caring about it. For most adults, popular entertainment is framed as "this is fun" or, in other words, "this does not matter." That is quite different from the social-cultural framework for "serious" art where the culture—and a whole series of powerful institutions from schools to museums to government funding agencies—tell us "this is relevant." It may be fun but it is fun that bears on the meaning of an individual's life—or, so the frame tells us, it should.

————

The more thoroughly a cultural object is institutionalized—in the educational system or economic and social system or in the dynamics of family life, the more opportunity there is for it to exercise influence. This is not the same thing as retrievability. If an object is retrievable, it can still be disregarded with impunity; if an object is institutionally retained, there are sanctions, social or economic or legal, for disregard.

## Resolution

Some elements in culture are more likely to influence action than others because they are better situated at a point of action or because they are by nature directives for action. An advertisement is a cultural text of high "resolution" in that it normally tells the audience precisely what to do to respond. It says: go out and buy. Books of advice or instruction—Jane Fonda's exercise books, a cookbook, Dr. Spock, the Boy Scout Handbook also give precise directions and can usually be readily enacted. Sacred texts are highly resolved in another sense—they are performative cultural acts, that is, the very act of reading them is itself part of the desired response; reading the book is itself an enactment of the devotional behavior the text urges. But most cultural texts are not imperatives in so clear a fashion or, indeed, in any fashion. They may be powerful in a variety of ways but their low "resolution" means that they are unlikely to stimulate action in concrete, visible, immediate, and measurable ways. (It may be that culture achieves its end precisely when it keeps action from happening; the aim of art may be to inflict waiting and reflection, and Auden's claim that "poetry makes nothing happen" might be read—though I do not think he intended this—as a strong claim about something poetry does, not a statement that poetry does nothing.)

James Lemert has studied what he calls "mobilizing information" in the news media. Mobilizing information tells the reader how to respond in action to the news story. A news story on a 4th of July parade might include information on the parade route. This is more likely to get someone to the parade than a story that gives no indication of how a person might actually observe the parade. The American news media have an unwritten policy that it is acceptable, even desirable, to print mobilizing information about topics on which there is a cultural consensus—the 4th of July parade or a charity drive at Christmas, but not to print mobilizing information about topics of controversy (the parade route for a political demonstration, for instance). The news media thereby choose a path of low resolution in a way that demobilizes or depoliticizes the public over issues of political controversy. This is another case where a cultural producer—here a news organization—acts to limit the direct cultural power of its own creation.

# Notes

1. Clifford Geertz, *The Interpretation of Cultures* (New York: Basic Books, 1973), 14.
2. Wendy Griswold offers a nice definition of a cultural object as "shared significance embodied in form." Wendy Griswold, *Renaissance Revivals: City Comedy and Revenge Tragedy in the London Theatre 1576–1980* (Chicago: University of Chicago Press, 1986) 5. Fernandez's remark is in "Macrothought," *American Ethnologist* 12 (November, 1985), 749.
3. Ann Swidler, "Culture in Action: Symbols and Strategies," *American Sociological Review* 51 (1986) 273–286. Kenneth Burke, "Literature as Equipment for Living," in Kenneth Burke, *The Philosophy of Literary Form* (Berkeley: University of California Press, 1973), 293–304.
4. Steve Chaffee, "The Public View of the Media as Carriers of Information Between School and Community," *Journalism Quarterly* 44 (Winter, 1967) 732.
5. George Mosse, "Caesarism, Circuses, and Monuments," *Journal of Contemporary History* 6 (1971) 167–182.

6. See Paul Hirsch, "Processing Fads and Fashions: An Organization-Set Analysis of Cultural Industry Systems," *American Journal of Sociology* 77 (1972) 639–659 on books and records; Todd Gitlin, *Inside Prime Time* (New York: Pantheon Books, 1981) on television; and Michael Schudson, *Advertising, the Uneasy Persuasion* (New York: Basic Books, 1984) on consumer goods generally.

7. Tom R. Tyler, "Assessing the Risk of Crime Victimization: The Integration of Personal Victimization Experience and Socially Transmitted Information," *Journal of Social Issues* 40 (1984) 27–38 at 34.

8. See Lynn Hunt, *Politics, Culture, and Class in the French Revolution* (Berkeley: University of California Press, 1984). Edward Shils has tried to get at the social meaning of tradition in *Tradition* (Chicago: University of Chicago Press, 1981).

# STUDY QUESTIONS

1. What is a cultural object, according to Schudson?
2. Give examples of cultural objects that illustrate the four ways culture can influence people (large influence on a large group, large influence on a small group, a small influence on a large group, small influence on a small group).

# 11

# COLLECTIVE MEMORY

ROBIN WAGNER-PACIFICI AND BARRY SCHWARTZ

Do you remember where you were when you heard that the Twin Towers had fallen? For most Americans, that memory is seared into our consciousness, such that we can recall, in sharp detail, not only where we were, but a series of moments just before and after, along with the range of emotions we experienced as the tragedy unfolded. September 11, 2001, like December 7, 1941, jolted us with the realization that the United States was vulnerable to a devastating attack. Americans were momentarily united in shared grief for lives lost and in shared anger toward the terrorists.

As the dust settled on Ground Zero, however, the unity quickly began to fray, with some Americans calling for swift retaliation against Al Qaeda and others urging moderation and diplomacy. A few more radical voices of dissent seemed to take a kind of satisfaction from the attacks, arguing that 9/11 was payback for decades of American imperialism and global domination of the weak and oppressed. Justice, in their view, was being served. Voices of dissent, however, were drowned out by the drums of war. Nearly a decade later, we remained embroiled in military occupations in Afghanistan and Iraq, even though these wars were more unpopular than ever before. Troop withdrawals finally began in the region in late 2011.

How does our ambivalence toward these wars against terrorism affect our perception of 9/11 itself? This ambivalence seems to have played out in the stark dilemmas over what to do with empty space where the towers once stood. A memorial to the towers, to 9/11, and to the American lives lost there remained mired in controversy for years before finally opening in 2011.

How does a society come to terms with a difficult past? What meanings and symbols arise to allow citizens to cope with, for instance, the losses of war? While sociologists Robin Wagner-Pacifici and Barry Schwartz do not address our questions about 9/11, they light a path for us to do so by examining the public controversy, official discourse, and private sentiments and emotions that swirl around another site of commemoration, the Vietnam Veterans Memorial in Washington, DC.

# THE VIETNAM VETERANS MEMORIAL: COMMEMORATING A DIFFICULT PAST

In this article, we address two problems, one general and one particular, and claim that they are best approached by referring each to the other. The first, general, problem is that of discovering the processes by which culture and cultural meaning are produced. Collective memory, moral and political entrepreneurship, dominant ideologies, and representational genres are all refracted through these processes and must all be sociologically identified and gauged. The second, particular, problem is the Vietnam Veterans Memorial. This unusual monument grew out of a delayed realization that some public symbol was needed to recognize the men and women who died in the Vietnam War. But its makers faced a task for which American history furnished no precedent—the task of commemorating a divisive defeat.

By dealing with the problem of commemoration in this case study of the Vietnam Veterans Memorial, we can address general concerns in the sociology of culture. Our concentration on the details of a particular case follows Clifford Geertz's maxim that "the essential task of theory building . . . is not to codify abstract regularities but to make thick description possible, not to generalize across cases but to generalize within them"

(1973, p. 26). However, we are also concerned to locate commemorative formulas as they are repeated across cases. Thus we will be moving from the case of the Vietnam Veterans Memorial to monuments that have similarly vexed commemorative missions, seeking to bring together the resemblances and differences under a single analytic framework.

We take up our subject by tracing the social, political, and cultural trajectories of the negotiation process that resulted in the Vietnam Veterans Memorial. That process confronted several distinct, but related, problems: (1) the social problems of fixing painful parts of the past (a military defeat, a generation of unredeemed veterans) in the public consciousness, (2) the political problem of commemorating an event for which there is no national consensus, and (3) the cultural problem of working through and against traditional expectations about the war memorial genre.

## Dilemmas of Commemoration

The memory of the Vietnam War and its epoch takes place within a culture of commemoration. Current analytic approaches to culture define commemorative objects, and cultural objects in general, as "shared significance embodied in form" (Griswold 1987, p. 13). However, our concern is in formulating an approach to those kinds of commemoration for which significance is not shared.

One of the most influential perspectives on the social functions of commemoration is Émile Durkheim's. Commemorative rites and symbols, Durkheim tells us (1965, p. 420), preserve and celebrate traditional beliefs; they "serve to sustain the vitality of these beliefs, to keep them from being effaced from memory and, in sum, to revivify the most essential elements of the collective consciousness. Through [commemoration] the group periodically renews the sentiment which it has of itself and of its unity." . . . In this view, commemoration is governed by a kind of pleasure principle that produces a unified, positive image of the past. But suppose a society is divided over the very event it selects for commemoration. Suppose that event constitutes a painful moment for society, such as a military defeat or an era of domestic oppression. What kinds of "traditional beliefs" and "essential elements," and what kind of monuments, if any, can crystallize these moments and unify the society around them? How is commemoration without consensus, or without pride, possible?

The Vietnam Veterans Memorial provides a good case to use in thinking about these issues. The succession of events that led to the Memorial's creation and public reception was a culture-producing process. In that process, contrasting moral evaluations of the Vietnam War and its participants were affirmed. The process itself consisted of seven stages, each defined by the activity of different individuals and different institutions: (1) the Pentagon's decision to mark the war by an inconspicuous plaque in Arlington Cemetery; (2) congressional activity culminating in a Vietnam Veterans Week and a series of veterans' support programs; (3) a former Vietnam soldier's conception and promotion of a tangible monument; (4) intense controversy over the nontraditional monument design selected by the United States Commission of Fine Arts; (5) modification of this original design by the incorporation of traditional symbols; (6) the public's extraordinary and unexpected reaction to the Memorial; and (7) the ongoing controversy over its further modification. Our analysis will pass through these stages as we chart the Vietnam Veterans Memorial's development.

## COMMEMORATION AS A GENRE PROBLEM

Controversies over the merits of a war are expressed at some point in debates over measures taken to commemorate it. The stages in the Vietnam Memorial's construction reveal, on the one hand, the desire for a design that reflects the uniqueness of the Vietnam War and, on the other, the desire for a design that recognizes the sense in which the Vietnam War was similar to previous wars. The Vietnam War differed from other wars because it was controversial, morally questionable, and unsuccessful. It resembled other wars because it called forth in its participants the traditional virtues of self-sacrifice, courage, loyalty, and honor. Tension between alternative commemorative designs centers on the problem of incorporating these contrasting features into a single monument.

Distinctions among war monuments are, like all generic distinctions, produced by "sorting, seeing the similarities in different . . . objects, abstracting the common elements from a welter of particular variations" (Griswold 1987, p. 17). Genre, in Wendy Griswold's view, is a kind of schema that organizes perception. Griswold asserts, however, that literary and artistic genres are impermanent and express the changing character of their creators, audiences, and contexts. This conception of genre is relevant to our present problem: What kind of monument can be built in the context of changes in traditional beliefs about what war monuments should look like and represent? Since no slate of tradition can be wiped totally clean, however, definite limits to the negotiability of commemorative genres must be assumed. To generalize this assumption, any analysis of a cultural object must chart and interpret its generic limitations. When, for example, is a tragedy no longer a tragedy? When is a war memorial no longer a war memorial? This matter, the negotiability of genre, is germane to our study. Is there some essence of "war memorialness" and can people identify it? Most important, how does this generic essence translate conflicting ideas about the Vietnam War into the monument-making process? How does it contribute to the task of incorporating painful events into the collective memory?

———

Attitudes and interests are translated into commemorative forms through enterprise. Before any event can be regarded as worth remembering, and before any class of people can be recognized for having participated in that event, some individual, and eventually some group, must deem both event and participants commemorable and must have the influence to get others to agree. Memorial devices are not self-created; they are conceived and built by those who wish to bring to consciousness the events and people that others are more inclined to forget. To understand memorial making in this way is to understand it as a construction process wherein competing "moral entrepreneurs" seek public arenas and support for their interpretations of the past. These interpretations are embodied in the memorial's symbolic structure.

———

## A Nation's Gratitude: Search for a Genre

The first official recognition of the Vietnam veteran was not bestowed until 1978, three years after the last American was flown out of Saigon. The recognition itself was hesitant and uncertain. A Vietnam War crypt had already been prepared in the Tomb of the Unknown Soldier, but the Army determined that neither of its two unidentified bodies (only 30% of the remains in either case) made for a decent corpse. Instead of honoring its Vietnam battle dead by symbolically joining them, through entombment of unknown soldiers' remains, with men fallen in earlier wars, the army recommended that a plaque and display of medals be set apart behind the tomb, along with the following inscription: "Let all know that the United States of America pays tribute to the members of the Armed Forces who answered their country's call." This strange declaration bears no reference at all to the Vietnam War, and it required an act of the Veterans Affairs sub-committee to make it more specific: "Let all people know that the United States pays tribute to those members of the Armed Forces who served hon-orably in Southeast Asia during the Vietnam era." In even this second, stronger statement, three things are noteworthy: (1) although revised in Congress, the statement was initiated by the military; (2) it received little publicity; and (3) it designated the conflict in Vietnam by the word "era" rather than "war." Thus the recognition came from only a small part of the society for whose interests and values the war was fought; it was communi-cated to that society without conspicuous ceremony; and it betrayed confu-sion about the meaning of the war by its failure to find a word to describe it. This last point is the most noteworthy of all. Although a war had not been officially declared, many congressional resolutions during the 1980s referred to the hostilities in Vietnam as "the Vietnam war." Touchiness during the late 1970s about what to call the conflict stemmed from social, not legal, con-cerns. To name an event is to categorize it morally and to provide an identity for its participants. Anomalous names betray ambiguity about an event's nature and uncertainty about how to react to the men who take part in it.

The first solution to the war's commemorative genre problem was thus halting and uncertain. The fighters were honored but not by an imposing monument. They were honored by a plaque, inconspicuously placed, whose inscription was, itself, indirect and muted. Undeclared wars are usually fought with restraint, however violent they might be. The Vietnam War's first official commemoration mirrored this restraint, marking the cause without really drawing attention to it.

Official ambivalence toward the Vietnam War showed up next in the activities of Congress. It was in Congress, in fall 1978, that the work cul-minating in the Veterans Memorial began. The plan then discussed, how-ever, was not to commemorate those who had died in the war, but to set aside a special "Vietnam Veterans Week" for its survivors. Thus evolved a second solution to the problem of finding a genre to commemorate the Vietnam War. Time, rather than granite, the dedication of a week rather than the dedication of a tangible monument, sufficed to honor the Vietnam fighting man. This plan's principal entrepreneurs were the members of the Vietnam-Era Caucus, 19 U.S. representatives and senators who had served in the military during the Vietnam War years. They meant to achieve two goals: to unify a nation divided by war and to induce Congress to recognize that many war veterans were suffering from unmet needs. Before anything could actually be accomplished, however, certain obstacles had to be overcome, obstacles inherent in the object of commemoration itself.

To promote unity by separating the event from its men was Congress's first concern. In Congressman Grisham's words, "We may still have differing opinions about our involvement in the Vietnam War, but we are no longer divided in our attitudes toward those who served in Vietnam" (U.S. House of Representatives 1979, p. 12588). At one time, however, the division was deep. Grisham himself acknowledged that the veterans were stigmatized or, at best, ignored on their return from the battlefront. No ceremony dramatized and ennobled their sacrifices. Most of the other congressmen knew this, and they wanted to upgrade the veterans' status. Transforming the Vietnam soldier from an Ugly American into a patriot who innocently carried out the policy of elected leaders, Congress tried to create a positive image that all Americans could accept.

However, the very attempt to improve the veterans' status raised unsettling questions. Congressmen openly recognized that America's lower-income minorities were disproportionately represented in the armed forces and that the trauma of war bore more heavily on them, economically and psychologically, than it would have on a middle-class army. An uncomplimentary view of the returning soldier accompanied this recognition. The congressmen made no mention of the crimes allegedly committed by American soldiers in Vietnam; however, they did recognize publicly "statistics such as the fact that 25 percent of the persons incarcerated in correctional institutions in America are veterans of the Vietnam War," along with the veterans' need for "an expanded drug and alcohol abuse treatment and rehabilitation program." Family counseling needs were also described: "Of those veterans married before going to Vietnam almost 40 percent were divorced within six months of their return" (U.S. House of Representatives 1979, pp. 12589, 12593, 12584; for details, see Johnson [1976, 1980]; U.S. House Committee on Veterans' Affairs 1981). Congresswoman Mikulski recognized the veterans' social marginality by pleading for the government to "be responsive to the unique problems which they face . . . so that they will be better able to fill their roles in society." Congressman Mikva spoke to the same point. Existing veterans' programs, he explained, are not enough for this group. "We must back up this symbolic recognition of their efforts for our country with . . . educational and rehabilitative programs geared to their special needs" (U.S. House of Representatives 1979, pp. 12583, 12588). Here, as elsewhere, the emphasis is on the veterans' shortcomings, and this emphasis reflects society's desire to reconstitute them morally.

## Entrepreneurs and Sponsors

Negative characterizations of the Vietnam veteran might have eventually undermined his positive recognition were it not for a new development, one that was oriented less to the living than to the dead. During the time that the Vietnam-Era Caucus worked on its legislation, a former army corporal from a working-class family, Jan Scruggs, had independently decided on a plan of his own. As noted above, one of the premises of Vietnam Veterans Week was that the soldier must be separated from the cause. This separation is precisely what Scruggs aimed to celebrate publicly. At first, his idea attracted little notice, but it eventually overshadowed Vietnam Veterans Week in commemorative significance. He would build a memorial to the men who served in Vietnam and would inscribe on it the names of all the war dead. The plan represented a different solution to the commemorative genre problem than those previously proposed. It was different in that it combined the traditional idea of a stone monument to the war dead with the radical idea of excluding from it any prominent symbol of national honor and glory. In place of such a symbol would appear a list of the dead soliders' names—58,000 of them. On May 28, 1979, Scruggs announced the formation of the Vietnam Veterans Memorial Fund to raise money to build the monument.

The accumulation of money to build the Veterans Memorial did not automatically follow from the desire to build it. What needed to be overcome was not only opposition from the still vocal critics of the war but more important, a sense of uncertainty in the public at large as to what the monument would look like and what it would represent. These suspicions and uncertainties were relieved when the Memorial's original framing rule—"Honor the solider, not the cause"—was reiterated in the very selection of its sponsors. Chosen were men and women who differed visibly and widely on many political questions but shared the desire to honor the Vietnam veterans. The sponsoring leaders and celebrities included Vernon Jordan, president of the National Urban League; Ruben Bonilla, national president of the League of United Latin American Citizens; Carol Burnett, the actress who played the mother of a soldier killed in the war in the television drama, *Friendly Fire;* First Lady Rosalynn Carter and former First Lady Betty Ford; Father Theodore Hesburgh, president of the University of Notre Dame; Bob Hope; Rocky Bleir, described as a "wounded Vietnam veteran who came back to star with the Pittsburgh Steelers"; and Admiral James B. Stockdale, formerly a prisoner of war and now president of The Citadel. These individuals represented many sectors of society: blacks, Hispanics, women, religious and academic figures, entertainment and sports celebrities, and military men. With the support of this noncontroversial coalition of sponsors, funds were quickly raised to pay for design and construction costs and, by July 4, 1980, a few days after the proclamation of Vietnam Veterans' Week, President Carter signed a joint resolution that reserved a two-acre site in Constitution Gardens, between the Washington Monument and Lincoln Memorial, for the Veterans Memorial's placement.

It was the redemptive qualities of Scruggs's project—precisely, its embodiment of gratitude, the only currency for paying off a moral debt—that congressional supporters emphasized. As President Carter approved Congress's resolution, he expressed his belief that the formal honoring of the veteran would also promote the healing of a nation divided by war. To this end, the Memorial fund's directors continued to avoid political statements in both fund-raising efforts and in contemplation of the Memorial design. The universal support of the Senate and strong support of the House were based on this same requirement: that the Memorial make no reference to the war, only to the men who fought it.

## Uses of Genre: The Enshrinement Process

The meaning of the Vietnam Veterans Memorial is defined by the way people behave in reference to it. Some monuments are rarely talked about or visited and never put to ceremonial use. Other monuments, like the Tomb of the Unknown Soldier, are used often as formal ceremonial sites and visited year after year by large numbers of people. Between the Vietnam Veterans Memorial and its visitors, a very different relationship obtains. Not only is the Memorial an object of frequent ceremony and frequent visitation (more than 2.5 million visitors and 1,100–1,500 reunions per year),[1] it is also an object with which visitors enter into active and affective relationships. These relationships have thwarted all original intentions as to what the Memorial should be and represent.

Conceived as something to be passively looked at and contemplated, the Vietnam Memorial has become an object of emotion. This is not the case for the Memorial site as a whole, just the wall and its names. The names on the wall are touched, their letters traced by the moving finger. The names are caressed. The names are reproduced on paper by pencil rubbing and taken home. And something is left from home itself—a material object bearing special significance to the deceased or a written statement by the visitor or mourner.

The dedications of the aggrieved are a spectacle that to many is more moving than the Memorial wall itself. More goes into spectators' reactions, however, than morbid curiosity, for the scenes of mourning are not altogether private affairs. These scenes make palpable a collective loss known to all. Not only, therefore, do friends and family bring their personal grief to the Memorial wall, but society exercises a moral pressure over those not directly affected by loss to add their presence to the situation and to align their sentiments with it.

———

1. Personal communication from Duery Felton, Jr., curator, Vietnam Veterans Memorial Collection Museum and Archeological Regional Storage Facility, National Park Service.

## Uses of Genre: The Representation of Ambivalence

All nonperishable articles left at the Vietnam Veterans Memorial are collected each day and kept at the Museum and Archeological Regional Storage Facility. Row after row of airtight shelters preserve these "gifts" for the future, thus extending the Memorial in space and in time. This part of the Veterans Memorial complex is the most populist, for its contents, in accordance with Interior Department policy, are determined by the people who visit the Memorial and not by professional curators. . . .

The most colorful objects left by visitors are flowers, taped to the wall or placed on the ground beneath a loved one's name. Nothing of a political nature is embodied in these floral displays; however, the Park Service's inventory of other (nonperishable) items does convey a coherent political message. This inventory shows that the one object most frequently left by the wall is a small American flag attached to a stick and set in the ground below the name that the visitor desired to mark. Through this offering, visitors uttered a political statement that was not supposed to be made. They asserted their patriotism, their loyalty to a nation. Whether they got the idea themselves or copied it from one another, they could think of no better way to dignify their loved one's memory than to associate his name with his country's emblem.

These assertions are amplified by other objects. The largest category of objects, almost a third of everything that has been deposited by the visitors, consists of military items, mostly patches and insignias marking military-unit membership, as well as parts of uniforms, dog tags, identification bracelets, medals, awards, and certificates. The memorial site was thus decorated by symbols of the roles through which living veterans once enacted their commitment to the nation. These symbols began to appear in great profusion as soon as the Memorial was dedicated and continued to appear two years later when the statue of the three soldiers was unveiled. Designed to draw attention to the individual and away from the nation and its cause, the Memorial's wall turns out to be a most dramatic locus of patriotic feeling. The wall's use moved it toward that traditional war monument genre that opponents and supporters alike once believed it deviated from.

When profusely decorated with patriotic emblems, the wall alone may enhance our idea of the traditional war monument, but it cannot embody that idea. This is because patriotism is not the only response that the wall excites. The Memorial wall has in fact become a kind of debating forum—a repository of diverse opinions about the very war that occasioned its construction. Traditional war monuments serve no such reflexive function.

That the Vietnam Memorial itself is deemed a sacred site and is an object of frequent ritual also conforms to our assumption that the paramount source of its meaning is operational. The rituals that take place there, however, are not the kind Durkheim would have understood. These are not rituals that strengthen common sentiments by bringing together those who hold them and putting them into closer and more active relations with one another (1965, p. 241). We are dealing with ritual assemblies that are intense even though, or perhaps because, the volume of common thoughts and sentiments about their object is so sparse. In studying the Vietnam Memorial, we have come to believe that people may need more ritual to face a painful and controversial part of the past than to deal with a painful part of the past about whose cause and meaning there is agreement. Rituals, however, do not resolve historical controversies; they only articulate them, making their memory public and dramatic. Unable to convince one another about what went wrong in Vietnam, therefore, the men and women who assemble at the Vietnam Memorial do so with more gravity than is displayed at shrines commemorating any other war.

In the end, contexts and meanings change. A day will come when the names that appear on the Vietnam Memorial's wall are known to few living persons. On this day, the intensity of feeling evoked by the wall will be less acute; the flags and objects that decorate the wall will be less dense; the solemnity that now grips those who enter the Memorial site will be diluted by an air of casualness; the ritual relation that now links shrine and pilgrim will become a mundane relation that links attraction and tourist. On this day, the Vietnam War will have become a less fitful part of American history. But the Vietnam Veterans Memorial, its several parts continuing to reflect different aspects of and beliefs about the war, will echo the ambivalence with which that war was first commemorated.

# References

Durkheim, Émile. 1965. *The Elementary Forms of the Religious Life*. New York: Free Press.

Geertz, Clifford. 1973. *The Interpretation of Cultures*. New York: Basic.

Griswold, Wendy. 1987. "A Methodological Framework for the Sociology of Culture." Pp. 1–35 in *Sociological Methodology,* vol. 17. Edited by Clifford Clogg.

Johnson, Loch. 1976. "Political Alienation among Vietnam Veterans." *Western
Political Quarterly* 29:398–410.

U.S. House Committee on Veterans' Affairs. 1981. *Legacies of Vietnam: Comparative Adjustment of Veterans and Their Peers.* Report no. 14. March 9. Washington, D.C.: Government Printing Office.

U.S. House of Representatives. 1979. *Congressional Record.* May 24. Washington,
D.C.: Government Printing Office.

# STUDY QUESTIONS

1. What is another example, besides the Vietnam Veterans Memorial or
Ground Zero, of a national symbol that reflects conflicts over how to
commemorate the past?
2. How do you think the events of 9/11 may have shifted popular perceptions of the Vietnam Veterans Memorial and the Vietnam War?

# PART THREE

# PRODUCTION, STABILITY, AND CHANGE

O N SUNDAY AFTERNOONS every fall, Americans huddle around their TVs watching professional football. Some watch alone, others with family or friends. Millions of American households engage in this ritual. It is so utterly normal and taken-for-granted that it seems rude to ask: Why do people do this? What's the attraction?

Football fans have no shortage of answers. It's fun and exciting, they'll say, and the best games are suspenseful and dramatic. It's inspiring watching superstar athletes compete, they'll add, and for them, it's a way of bringing friends and families closer together. Well, who can argue with that?

Meanwhile, in the rest of the world, American football has very little appeal. But *futbol*? That's another story. Soccer is the most globalized sport, enjoying huge numbers of fans and highly professionalized teams, along with amateur and semi-professional leagues in virtually every nation on earth. The oddity is that America is one of the few places that watching professional soccer has not become a national pastime.

Why is this so? Historians of sport give one kind of answer, based on their carefully accumulated knowledge of when and where specific sports like football and soccer originated, as well as the deeper connections these sports have to older, obsolete games. But if sociologists want to know why football has flourished in America instead of soccer, we need more than descriptive facts. We need to know why Americans prefer football over soccer and, as noted in the Introduction, when we ask ourselves what forces are shaping people's preferences, we find ourselves in the middle of the playing field called culture.

The readings in this section grapple with questions about how cultural objects are made and how and why they propagate, spreading outside their original contexts to new people, places, and societies. For example, where do fads come from? How does a new show become a hit? How and why has music changed over time and why do some people prefer country music over other kinds? What roles do individual and group preferences play in shaping the success or failure of specific cultural products?

The readings here also focus on the industries that invent new cultural objects for the public to consume and how, in doing so, they aren't simply giving people what they want. They are hoping to actively shape and mold people's wants and desires through advertising and selling techniques, like commercials, billboards, and product placement. When they are successful at this, people embrace these cultural products (hit songs, new diets, trendy ideas, and yes, football) at least in part because other people—friends, acquaintances, people they admire—are embracing them as well. In fact, people sometimes find themselves wanting things they did not know they wanted, in part because others want them. When this happens at a large-enough scale, the demand for any given cultural product becomes more or less stable and consistent. The fad becomes a tradition, a shared ritual, like spending Sunday afternoons watching NFL games.

What's puzzling is how people sometimes stop wanting what they used to desire and move on to something new. The fad or fashion begins to fade and seems old and tired, even obsolete. Some honored traditions and rituals are devalued and discarded by a generation that no longer sees the point nor cares enough to continue them. The pattern is familiar and easy enough to observe, but it still remains somewhat mysterious, doesn't it? How does this kind of large-scale cultural change actually play out? To put it more concretely, will football ever decline and become a less popular sport? Will soccer ever join the ranks of marquee American sports like baseball, basketball, and football? If so, how might that happen? (And, by the way, how come jai alai never took off in America?)

Cultural sociologists often seek answers to these questions by finding representative case studies, examples of how these processes worked out in specific places and social settings. We try to learn as much as possible about the social and historical context in which the culture change occurred by identifying the significant people and institutions responsible for initiating the change and then tracing the sequence of events leading up to it. By making before and after comparisons, we aim to document the extent and consequences of the change. We then think about how general and widespread these processes might be in other contexts and situations where change occurs and craft some general theories that we think will cover other, as yet unexplored cases. The goal is less about making theories that have the power to predict change and more about making theories that illuminate the hidden and mysterious processes that result in change, while giving us a sense of what kinds of change are likely to occur based on past patterns.

These questions are important to sociologists because they are connected to larger issues about how people's preferences and tastes are influenced by society and how, over time, those preferences and tastes can change or remain relatively stable. Sociological theories that emphasized how dominant groups impose their cultural preferences on less dominant groups—most notably, Marxist theories about cultural domination discussed in the Introduction and in Part 1—have given way to more flexible theories. These newer theories highlight the interplay of structural determinism and individual agency at work in the production, reception, and diffusion of culture. The more subtle and nuanced versions of accounting for cultural change are well represented in the readings that follow. And for those American students reading this who love soccer, remember this: cultural sociology holds out hope that in the future, generations of Americans will huddle around the TV watching *Monday Night Soccer*.

# 12

# ART WORLDS

HOWARD S. BECKER

Think of the lonely artist, devoted to his muses, toiling away in obscurity, until the day his work is discovered. If he is gifted enough, fame and fortune will follow and, if he is lucky, some kind of scandalous behavior will bestow lasting notoriety upon him. The aura of infamy reassures us that for all the attention and riches society lavishes upon him, the wild artist remains untamed. He might be an author, a playwright, a painter, a sculptor, or an architect—the medium of artistic expression scarcely matters. Instead, what moves us is his ability to endure isolation, impoverishment, and even public scorn as he single-mindedly pursues his creative and aesthetic vision. In the end, we find pleasure in his pain and take joy in his sorrows because the artist does for us what we cannot do for ourselves: He sets us free, even if only for a moment, from the cages that society builds around us.

But is this really how art is made? Or is this just a romantic fiction we tell ourselves about what it takes to be a creative genius? Come to think of it, how do most artists actually produce their art? Is it really so solitary an affair? Where and how do they learn their craft? Who buys and sells their stuff? How do they come to earn reputations and status in the art world? And what, exactly, is the art world?

Howard Becker, one of the most prolific and influential sociologists of the twentieth century, takes on and takes apart the romantic fiction of the artist as genius and demonstrates that the production of art is, at its core, a collective process. Art exists in a social world that shares many features with the non-art world: a well-developed struc-

**ture of occupations, roles, and organizations that somehow facilitates both the cooperation of individuals and the coordination of their actions. Becker argues that art as we know it does not exist outside of the networks of individuals that produce it. This doesn't mean there are not creative and skilled artistic geniuses—only that without the skill and genius of others, the work of the artist would never be known.**

# ART AS COLLECTIVE ACTION

## Cooperation and Cooperative Links

Think, with respect to any work of art, of all the activities that must be carried on for that work to appear as it finally does. For a symphony orchestra to give a concert, for instance, instruments must have been invented, manufactured and maintained, a notation must have been devised and music composed using that notation, people must have learned to play the notated notes on the instruments, times and places for rehearsal must have been provided, ads for the concert must have been placed, publicity arranged and tickets sold, and an audience capable of listening to and in some way understanding and responding to the performance must have been recruited. A similar list can be compiled for any of the performing arts. With minor variations (substitute materials for instruments and exhibition for performance), the list applies to the visual and (substituting language and print for materials and publication for exhibition) literary arts. Generally speaking, the necessary activities typically include conceiving the idea for the work, making the necessary physical artifacts, creating a conventional language of expression, training artistic personnel and audiences to use the conventional language to create and experience, and providing the necessary mixture of those ingredients for a particular work or performance.

Imagine, as an extreme case, one person who did all these things: made everything, invented everything, performed, created and experienced the result, all without the assistance or cooperation of anyone else. In fact, we can barely imagine such a thing, for all the arts we know about involve elaborate networks of cooperation. A division of the labor required takes place. Typically, many people participate in the work without which the performance or artifact could not be produced. A sociological analysis of any art therefore looks for that division of labor. How are the various tasks divided among the people who do them?

Nothing in the technology of any art makes one division of tasks more "natural" than another. Consider the relations between the composition and performance of music. In conventional symphonic and chamber music, the two activities occur separately; although many composers perform, and many performers compose, we recognize no necessary connection between the two and see them as two separate roles which may occasionally coincide in one person. In jazz, composition is not important, the standard tune merely furnishing a framework on which the performer builds the improvisation listeners consider important. In contemporary rock music, the performer ideally composes his own music; rock groups who play other people's music (Bennett, 1972) carry the derogatory title of "copy bands." Similarly, some art photographers always make their own prints; others seldom do. Poets writing in the Western tradition do not think it necessary to incorporate their handwriting into the work, leaving it to printers to put the material in readable form, but Oriental calligraphers count the actual writing an integral part of the poetry. In no case does the character of the art impose a natural division of labor; the division always results from a consensual definition of the situation. Once that has been achieved, of course, participants in the world of art regard it as natural and resist attempts to change it as unnatural, unwise or immoral.

Participants in an art world regard some of the activities necessary to the production of that form of art as "artistic," requiring the special gift or sensibility of an artist. The remaining activities seem to them a matter of craft, business acumen or some other ability less rare, less characteristic of art, less necessary to the success of the work, and less worthy of respect. They define the people who perform these special activities as artists, and everyone else as (to borrow a military term) support personnel. Art worlds differ in how they allocate the honorific title of artist and in the mechanisms by which they choose who gets it and who doesn't. At one extreme, a guild or academy (Pevsner, 1940) may require long apprenticeship and prevent those it does not license from practicing. At the other, the choice may be left to the lay public that consumes the work, whoever they accept being ipso facto an artist. An activity's status as art or non-art may change, in either direction. Kealy (1974) notes that the recording engineer has, when new technical possibilities arose that artists could use expressively, been regarded as something of an artist. When the effects he can produce become commonplace, capable of being produced on demand by any competent worker, he loses that status.

How little of the activity necessary for the art can a person do and still claim the title of artist? The amount the composer contributes to the material contained in the final work has varied greatly. Virtuoso performers from the Renaissance through the nineteenth century embellished and improvised on the score the composer provided (Dart, 1967, and Reese, 1959), so it is not unprecedented for contemporary composers to prepare scores which give only the sketchiest directions to the performer (though the counter-tendency, for composers to restrict the interpretative freedom of the performer by giving increasingly detailed directions, has until recently been more prominent). John Cage and Karlheinz Stockhausen (Wörner, 1973) are regarded as composers in the world of contemporary music, though many of their scores leave much of the material to be played to the decision of the player. Artists need not handle the materials from which the art work is made to remain artists; architects seldom build what they design. The same practice raises questions, however, when sculptors construct a piece by sending a set of specifications to a machine shop; and many people balk at awarding the title of artist to authors of conceptual works consisting of specifications which are never actually embodied in an artifact. Marcel Duchamp outraged many people by insisting that he created a valid work of art when he signed a commercially produced snowshovel or signed a reproduction of the Mona Lisa on which he had drawn a mustache, thus classifying Leonardo as support personnel along with the snowshovel's designer and manufacturer. Outrageous as that idea may seem, something like it is standard in making collages, in which the entire work may be constructed of things made by other people. The point of these examples is that what is taken, in any world of art, to be the quintessential artistic act, the act whose performance marks one as an artist, is a matter of consensual definition.

Whatever the artist, so defined, does not do himself must be done by someone else. The artist thus works in the center of a large network of cooperating people, all of whose work is essential to the final outcome. Wherever he depends on others, a cooperative link exists. The people with whom he cooperates may share in every particular his idea of how their work is to be done. This consensus is likely when everyone involved can perform any of the necessary activities, so that while a division of labor exists, no specialized functional groups develop. This situation might occur in simple communally shared art forms like the square dance or in segments of a society whose ordinary members are trained in artistic activities. A well-bred nineteenth century American, for instance, knew enough music to take part in performing the parlor songs of Stephen Foster just as his Renaissance counterpart could participate in performing madrigal. In such cases, cooperation occurs simply and readily.

When specialized professional groups take over the performance of the activities necessary to an art work's production, however, their members tend to develop specialized aesthetic, financial and career interests which differ substantially from the artist's. Orchestral musicians, for instance, are notoriously more concerned with how they sound in performance than with the success of a particular work; with good reason, for their own success depends in part on impressing those who hire them with their competence (Faulkner, 1973a, 1973b). They may sabotage a new work which can make them sound bad because of its difficulty, their career interests lying at cross-purposes to the composer's.

Aesthetic conflicts between support personnel and the artist also occur. A sculptor friend of mine was invited to use the services of a group of master lithographic printers. Knowing little of the technique of lithography, he was glad to have these master craftsmen do the actual printing, this division of labor being customary and having generated a highly specialized craft of printing. He drew designs containing large areas of solid colors, thinking to simplify the printer's job. Instead, he made it more difficult. When the printer rolls ink onto the stone, a large area will require more than one rolling to be fully inked and may thus exhibit roller marks. The printers, who prided themselves on being the greatest in the world, explained to my friend that while they could print his designs, the areas of solid color could cause difficulty with roller marks. He had not known about roller marks and talked of using them as part of his design. The printers said, no, he could not do that, because roller marks were an obvious sign (to other printers) of poor craftsmanship and no print exhibiting roller marks was allowed to leave their shop. His artistic curiosity fell victim to the printers' craft standards, a neat example of how specialized support groups develop their own standards and interests.

My friend was at the mercy of the printers because he did not know how to print lithographs himself. His experience exemplified the choice that faces the artist at every cooperative link. He can do things the way established groups of support personnel are prepared to do them; he can try to make them do it his way: he can train others to do it his way; or he can do it himself. Any choice but the first requires an additional investment of time and energy to do what could be done less expensively if done the standard way. The artist's involvement with and dependence on cooperative links thus constrains the kind of art he can produce.

Similar examples can be found in any field of art. e.e. cummings had trouble getting his first book of poetry published because printers were afraid to set his bizarre layouts (Norman, 1958). Producing a motion picture involves multiple difficulties of this kind: actors who will only be photographed in flattering ways, writers who don't want a word changed, cameramen who will not use unfamiliar processes.

Artists often create works which existing facilities for production or exhibition cannot accommodate. Sculptors build constructions too large and heavy for existing museums. Composers write music which requires more performers than existing organizations can furnish. Playwrights write plays too long for their audience's taste. When they go beyond the capacities of existing institutions, their works are not exhibited or performed: that reminds us that most artists make sculptures which are not too big or heavy, compose music which uses a comfortable number of players, or write plays which run a reasonable length of time. By accommodating their conceptions to available resources, conventional artists accept the constraints arising from their dependence on the cooperation of members of the existing art world. Wherever the artist depends on others for some necessary component he must either accept the constraints they impose or expend the time and energy necessary to provide it some other way.

To say that the artist must have the cooperation of others *for the art work to occur as it finally does* does not mean that he cannot work without that cooperation. The art work, after all, need not occur as it does, but can take many other forms, including those which allow it to be done without others' help. Thus, though poets do depend on printers and publishers (as cummings' example indicates), one can produce poetry without them. Russian poets whose work circulates in privately copied typescripts do that, as did Emily Dickinson (Johnson, 1955). In both cases, the poetry does not circulate in conventional print because the artist would not accept the censorship or rewriting imposed by those who would publish the work. The poet either has to reproduce and circulate his work himself or not have it circulated. But he can still write poetry. My argument thus differs from a functionalism that asserts that the artist must have cooperation, ignoring the possibility that the cooperation can be foregone, though at a price.

The examples given so far emphasize matters more or less external to the art work—exhibition space, printing or musical notation. Relations of cooperation and constraint, however, penetrate the entire process of artistic creation and composition, as will become clear in looking at the nature and function of artistic conventions.

## Conventions

Producing art works requires elaborate modes of cooperation among specialized personnel. How do these people arrive at the terms on which they will cooperate? They could, of course, decide everything fresh on each occasion. A group of musicians could discuss and agree on such matters as which sounds would be used as tonal resources, what instruments might be constructed to make those sounds, how those sounds would be combined to create a musical language, how the language would be used to create works of a particular length requiring a given number of instruments and playable for audiences of a certain size recruited in a certain way. Something like that sometimes happens in, for instance, the creation of a new theatrical group, although in most cases only a small number of the questions to be decided are actually considered anew.

People who cooperate to produce a work of art usually do not decide things afresh. Instead, they rely on earlier agreements now become customary, agreements that have become part of the conventional way of doing things in that art. Artistic conventions cover all the decisions that must be made with respect to works produced in a given art world, even though a particular convention may be revised for a given work. Thus, conventions dictate the materials to be used, as when musicians agree to base their music on the notes contained in a set of modes, or on the diatonic, pentatonic or chromatic scales with their associated harmonies. Conventions dictate the abstractions to be used to convey particular ideas or experiences, as when painters use the laws of perspective to convey the illusion of three dimensions or photographers use black, white and shades of gray to convey the interplay of light and color. Conventions dictate the form in which materials and abstractions will be combined, as in the musical use of the sonata form or the poetic use of the sonnet. Conventions suggest the appropriate dimensions of a work, the proper length for a musical or dramatic event, the proper size and shape of a painting or sculpture. Conventions regulate the relations between artists and audience, specifying the rights and obligations of both.

Humanistic scholars—art historians, musicologists and literary critics—have found the concept of the artistic convention useful in accounting for artists' ability to produce art works which produce an emotional response in audiences. By using such a conventional organization of tones as a scale, the composer can create and manipulate the listener's expectations as to what sounds will follow. He can then delay and frustrate the satisfaction of those expectations, generating tension and release as the expectation is ultimately satisfied (Meyer, 1956, 1973; Cooper and Meyer, 1960). Only because artist and audience share knowledge of and experience with the conventions invoked does the art work produce an emotional effect. Smith (1968) has shown how poets manipulate conventional means embodied in poetic forms and diction to bring poems to a clear and satisfying conclusion, in which the expectations produced early in the lyric are simultaneously and satisfactorily resolved. Gombrich (1960) has analyzed the visual conventions artists use to create the illusion for viewers that they are seeing a realistic depiction of some aspect of the world. In all these cases (and in others like stage design, dance, and film), the possibility of artistic experience arises from the existence of a body of conventions that artists and audiences can refer to in making sense of the work.

Conventions make art possible in another sense. Because decisions can be made quickly, because plans can be made simply by referring to a conventional way of doing things, artists can devote more time to actually doing their work. Conventions thus make possible the easy and efficient coordination of activity among artists and support personnel. Ivins (1953), for instance, shows how, by using a conventionalized scheme for rendering shadows, modeling and other effects, several graphic artists could collaborate in producing a single plate. The same conventions made it possible for viewers to read what were essentially arbitrary marks as shadows and modeling. Seen this way, the concept of convention provides a point of contact between humanists and sociologists, being interchangeable with such familiar sociological ideas as norm, rule, shared understanding, custom or folkway, all referring in one way or another to the ideas and understandings people hold in common and through which they effect cooperative activity. Burlesque comedians could stage elaborate three man skits without rehearsal because they had only to refer to a conventional body of skits they all knew, pick one and assign the parts. Dance musicians who are total strangers can play all night with no more prearrangement than to mention a title ("Sunny Side of the Street," in C) and count off four beats to give the tempo; the title indicates a melody, its accompanying harmony and perhaps even customary background figures. The conventions of character and dramatic structure, in the one case, and of melody, harmony and tempo, in the other, are familiar enough that audiences have no difficulty in responding appropriately.

Though standardized, conventions are seldom rigid and unchanging. They do not specify an inviolate set of rules everyone must refer to in settling questions of what to do. Even where the directions seem quite specific, they leave much unsettled which gets resolved by reference to customary modes of interpretation on the one hand and by negotiation on the other. A tradition of performance practice, often codified in book form, tells performers how to interpret the musical scores or dramatic scripts they perform. Seventeenth century scores, for instance, contained relatively little information; but contemporary books explained how to deal with questions of instrumentation, note values, extemporization and the realization of embellishments and ornaments. Performers read their music in the light of all these customary styles of interpretation and thus were able to coordinate their activities (Dart, 1967). The same thing occurs in the visual arts. Much of the content, symbolism and coloring of Italian Renaissance religious painting was conventionally given; but a multitude of decisions remained for the artist, so that even within those strict conventions different works could be produced. Adhering to the conventional materials, however, allowed viewers to read much emotion and meaning into the picture. Even where customary interpretations of conventions exist, having become conventions themselves, artists can agree to do things differently, negotiation making change possible.

Conventions place strong constraints on the artist. They are particularly constraining because they do not exist in isolation, but come in complexly interdependent systems, so that making one small change often requires making changes in a variety of other activities. A system of conventions gets embodied in equipment, materials, training, available facilities and sites, systems of notation and the like, all of which must be changed if any one segment is.

Consider what a change from the conventional western chromatic musical scale of twelve tones to one including forty-two tones between the octaves entails. Such a change characterizes the compositions of Harry Partch (1949). Western musical instruments cannot produce these micro-tones easily and some cannot produce them at all, so conventional instruments must be reconstructed (as Partch does) or new instruments must be invented and built. Since the instruments are new, no one knows how to play them, and players must train themselves. Conventional Western nota-tion is inadequate to score forty-two tone music, so a new notation must be devised, and players must learn to read it. (Comparable resources can be taken as given by anyone who writes for the conventional twelve chro-matic tones). Consequently, whereas a performance of music scored for the conventional set of tones can be performed adequately after relatively few hours of rehearsal, forty-two tone music requires much more work, time, effort and resources. Partch's music has typically come to be performed in the following way: a university invites him to spend a year. In the fall, he recruits a group of interested students, who build the instruments (which he has already invented) under his direction. In the winter, they learn to play the instruments and read the notation he has devised. In the spring, they rehearse several works and finally give a performance. Seven or eight months of work finally result in two hours of music, hours which could have been filled with other music after eight to ten hours of rehearsal by trained symphonic musicians playing the standard repertoire. The differ-ence in the resources required measures the strength of the constraint imposed by the conventional system.

Similarly, conventions specifying what a good photograph should look like are embodied not only in an aesthetic more or less accepted in the world of art photography (Rosenblum, 1973), but also in the acceptance of the constraints built into the neatly interwoven complex of standardized equipment and materials made by major manufacturers. Available lenses, camera bodies, shutter speeds, apertures, films, and printing paper all con-stitute a tiny fraction of the things that could be made, a selection that can be used together to produce acceptable prints; with ingenuity they can also be used to produce effects their purveyors did not have in mind. But some kinds of prints, once common, can now only be produced with great difficulty because the materials are no longer available. Specifically, the photosensitive material in conventional papers is a silver salt, which produces a characteristic look. Photographers once printed on paper sensitized with platinum salts, until it went off the market in 1937 (Newhall, 1964, p. 117). You can still make platinum prints, which have a distinctively softer look, but only by making your own paper. Not surprisingly, most photographers accept the constraint and learn to maximize the effects that can be obtained from available silver-based materials. They likewise prize the standardization and dependability of mass-produced materials; a roll of Kodak Tri-X film purchased anywhere in the world has approximately the same characteristics and will produce the same results as any other roll, that being the opportunity that is the obverse of the constraint.

The limitations of conventional practice, clearly, are not total. One can always do things differently if one is prepared to pay the price in increased effort or decreased circulation of one's work. The experience of composer Charles Ives exemplifies the latter possibility. He experimented with polytonality and polyrhythms before they became part of the ordinary performer's competence. The New York players who tried to play his chamber and orchestral music told him that it was unplayable, that their instruments could not make those sounds, that the scores could not be played in any practical way. Ives finally accepted their judgment, but continued to compose such music. What makes his case interesting is that, according to his biographers (Cowell and Cowell, 1954), though he was also bitter about it, he experienced this as a great liberation. If no one could play his music, then he no longer had to write music that musicians could play, no longer had to accept the constraints imposed by the conventions that regulated cooperation between contemporary composer and player. Since, for instance, his music would not be played, he never needed to finish it; he was quite unwilling to confirm John Kirkpatrick's pioneer reading of the *Concord Sonata* as a correct one because that would mean that he could no longer change it. Nor did he have to accommodate his writing to the practical constraints of what could be financed by conventional means, and so he wrote his Fourth Symphony for three orchestras. (That impracticality lessened with time; Leonard Bernstein premiered the work in 1958 and it has been played many times since.)

In general, breaking with existing conventions and their manifestations in social structure and material artifacts increases the artist's trouble and decreases the circulation of his work, on the one hand, but at the same time increases his freedom to choose unconventional alternatives and to depart substantially from customary practice. If that is true, we can understand any work as the product of a choice between conventional ease and success and unconventional trouble and lack of recognition, looking for the experiences and situational and structural elements that dispose artists in one direction or the other.

Interdependent systems of conventions and structures of cooperative links appear very stable and difficult to change. In fact, though arts sometimes experience periods of stasis, that does not mean that no change or innovation occurs (Meyer, 1967). Small innovations occur constantly, as conventional means of creating expectations and delaying their satisfaction become so well-known as to become conventional expectations in their own right. Meyer (1956) analyzes this process and gives a nice example in the use of vibrato by string instrument players. At one time, string players used no vibrato, introducing it on rare occasions as a deviation from convention which heightened tension and created emotional response by virtue of its rarity. String players who wished to excite such an emotional response began using vibrato more and more often until the way to excite the emotional response it had once produced was to play without vibrato, a device that Bartok and other composers exploited. Meyer describes the process by which deviations from convention become accepted conventions in their own right as a common one.

Such changes are a kind of gradualist reform in a persisting artistic tradition. Broader, more disruptive changes also occur, bearing a marked resemblance to political and scientific revolutions (Kuhn, 1962). Any major change necessarily attacks some of the existing conventions of the art directly, as when the Impressionists or Cubists changed the existing visual language of painting, the way one read paint on canvas as a representation of something. An attack on convention does not merely mean an attack on the particular item to be changed. Every convention carries with it an aesthetic, according to which what is conventional becomes the standard by which artistic beauty and effectiveness is judged. A play which violates the classical unities is not merely different, it is distasteful, barbaric and ugly to those for whom the classical unities represent a fixed criterion of dramatic worth. An attack on a convention becomes an attack on the aesthetic related to it. But people do not experience their aesthetic beliefs as merely arbitrary and conventional; they feel that they are natural, proper and moral. An attack on a convention and an aesthetic is also an attack on a morality. The regularity with which audiences greet major changes in dramatic, musical and visual conventions with vituperative hostility indicates the close relation between aesthetic and moral belief (Kubler, 1962).

An attack on sacred aesthetic beliefs as embodied in particular conventions is, finally, an attack on an existing arrangement of ranked statuses, a stratification system. Remember that the conventional way of doing things in any art utilizes an existing cooperative network, an organized art world which rewards those who manipulate the existing conventions appropriately in light of the associated sacred aesthetic. Suppose that a dance world is organized around the conventions and skills embodied in classical ballet. If I then learn those conventions and skills, I become eligible for positions in the best ballet companies; the finest choreographers will create ballets for me that are just the kind I know how to dance and will look good in; the best composers will write scores for me; theaters will be available; I will earn as good a living as a dancer can earn; audiences will love me and I will be famous. Anyone who successfully promotes a new convention in which he is skilled and I am not attacks not only my aesthetic but also my high position in the world of dance. So the resistance to the new expresses the anger of those who will lose materially by the change, in the form of aesthetic outrage.

Others than the artist have something invested in the status quo which a change in accepted conventions will lose them. Consider earthworks made, for instance, by a bulldozer in a square mile of pasture. Such a sculpture cannot be collected (though a patron can pay for its construction and receive signed plans or photographs as a document of his patronage), or put in museums (though the mementos the collector receives can be displayed). If earthworks become an important art form, the museum personnel whose evaluations of museum-collectable art have had important consequences for the careers of artists and art movements lose the power to choose which works will be displayed, for their museums are unnecessary for displaying those works. Everyone involved in the museum-collectable kind of art (collectors, museum curators, galleries, dealers, artists) loses something. We might say that every cooperative network that constitutes an art world creates value by the agreement of its members as to what is valuable (Levine, 1972; Christopherson, 1974). When new people successfully create a new world which defines other conventions as embodying artistic value, all the participants in the old world who cannot make a place in the new one lose out.

Every art world develops standardized modes of support and artists who support their work through those conventional means develop an aesthetic which accepts the constraints embedded in those forms of cooperation. Rosenblum (1973) has shown that the aesthetic of photographers varies with the economic channels through which their work is distributed in the same way that their customary work styles do, and Lyon (1974) has analyzed the interdependence of aesthetic decisions and the means by which resources are gathered in a semi-professional theater group. One example will illustrate the nature of the dependence. The group depended on volunteer help to get necessary work done. But people volunteered for non-artistic kinds of work largely because they hoped eventually to get a part in a play and gain some acting experience. The people who ran the company soon accumulated many such debts and were constrained to choose plays with relatively large casts to pay them off.

## Conclusion

If we focus on a specific art work, it proves useful to think of social organization as a network of people who cooperate to produce that work. We see that the same people often cooperate repeatedly, even routinely, in similar ways to produce similar works. They organize their cooperation by referring to the conventions current among those who participate in the production and consumption of such works. If the same people do not actually act together in every case, their replacements are also familiar with and proficient in the use of the same conventions, so that the cooperation can go on without difficulty. Conventions make collective action simpler and less costly in time, energy and other resources; but they do not make unconventional work impossible, only more costly and more difficult. Change can occur, as it often does, whenever someone devises a way to gather the greater resources required. Thus, the conventional modes of cooperation and collective action need not recur because people constantly devise new modes of action and discover the resources necessary to put them into practice.

To say all this goes beyond the assertion that art is social and beyond demonstrations of the congruence between forms of social organization and artistic styles or subjects. It shows that art is social in the sense that it is created by networks of people acting together, and proposes a framework in which differing modes of collective action, mediated by accepted or newly developed conventions, can be studied. It places a number of traditional questions in the field in a context in which their similarity to other forms of collective action can be used for comparative theoretical work.

The discussion of art as collective action suggests a general approach to the analysis of social organization. We can focus on any event (the more general term which encompasses the production of an art work as a special case) and look for the network of people, however large or extended, whose collective activity made it possible for the event to occur as it did. We can look for networks whose cooperative activity recurs or has become routine and specify the conventions by which their constituent members coordinate their separate lines of action.

We might want to use such terms as social organization or social structure as a metaphorical way of referring to those recurring networks and their activities. In doing so, however, we should not forget their metaphorical character and inadvertently assert as a fact implied in the metaphor what can only be discovered through research. When sociologists speak of social structure or social systems, the metaphor implies (though its user neither proves nor argues the point) that the collective action involved occurs "regularly" or "often" (the quantifier, being implicit, is non-specific) and, further, that the people involved act together to produce a large variety of events. But we should recognize generally, as the empirical materials require us to do in the study of the arts, that whether a mode of collective action is recurrent or routine enough to warrant such description must be decided by investigation, not by definition. Some forms of collective action recur often, others occasionally, some very seldom. Similarly, people who participate in the network that produces one event or kind of event may not act together in art works producing other events. That question, too, must be decided by investigation.

Collective actions and the events they produce are the basic unit of sociological investigation. Social organization consists of the special case in which the same people act together to produce a variety of different events in a recurring way. Social organization (and its cognates) are not only concepts, then, but also empirical findings. Whether we speak of the collective acts of a few people—a family or a friendship—or of a much larger number—a profession or a class system—we need always to ask exactly who is joining together to produce what events. To pursue the generalization from the theory developed for artistic activities, we can study social organizations of all kinds by looking for the networks responsible for producing specific events, the overlaps among such cooperative networks, the way participants use conventions to coordinate their activities, how existing conventions simultaneously make coordinated action possible and limit the forms it can take, and how the development of new forms of acquiring resources makes change possible. (I should point out that, while this point of view is not exactly commonplace, neither is it novel. It can be found in the writings of, among others, Simmel [1898], Park [1950, 1952, 1955 passim], Blumer [1966] and Hughes [1971, esp. pp 5–13 and 52–64]).

# Bibliography

Bennett, H. S. 1972. "Other People's Music." Unpublished doctoral dissertation, Northwestern University.

Blumer, Herbert. 1966. "Sociological implications of the thought of George Herbert Mead." *American Journal of Sociology* 71:535–44.

Christopherson, Richard. 1974. "Making art with machines: photography's institutional inadequacies." *Urban Life and Culture* 3(1):3–34.

Cooper, Grosvenor W. and Leonard B. Meyer. 1960. *The Rhythmic Structure of Music.* Chicago: University of Chicago Press.

Cowell, Henry and Sidney Cowell. 1954. *Charles Ives and His Music.* New York: Oxford University Press.

Dart, Thurston. 1967. *The Interpretation of Music.* 4th ed. London: Hutchinson.

Faulkner, Robert R. 1973a. "Orchestra interaction: some features of communication and authority in an artistic organization." *Sociological Quarterly* 14:147–57.

———. 1973b. "Career concerns and mobility motivations of orchestra musicians." *Sociological Quarterly.* 14:334–49.

Gombrich, E. H. 1960. *Art and Illusion.* New York: Bollingen.

Hughes, Everett C. 1971. *The Sociological Eye.* New York: Free Press.

Ivins, W. 1953. *Prints and Visual Communication.* Cambridge: MIT Press.

Johnson, Thomas. 1955. *Emily Dickinson.* Cambridge: Harvard University Press.

Kealy, Edward. 1974. "The Real Rock Revolution: Sound Mixers, their Work, and the Aesthetics of Popular Music Production." Unpublished doctoral dissertation, Northwestern University.

———. 1974. "The Recording Engineer." Doctoral dissertation in progress, Northwestern University.

Kubler, George. 1962. *The Shape of Time.* New Haven: Yale University Press.

Kuhn, Thomas. 1962. *The Structure of Scientific Revolution.* Chicago: University of Chicago Press.

Levine, Edward M. 1972. "Chicago's art world." *Urban Life and Culture* 1:292–322.

Lyon, Eleanor. 1974. "Work and play: resource constraints in a small theater." *Urban Life and Culture* 3(1):71–97.

Meyer, L. B. 1956. *Emotion and Meaning in Music.* Chicago: University of Chicago.

———. 1967. *Music, the Arts and Ideas.* Chicago: University of Chicago.

———. 1973. *Explaining Music.* Berkeley: University of California.

Newhall, Beaumont. 1964. *The History of Photography.* New York: Museum of Modern Art.

Norman, Charles. 1958. *The Magic-maker, e. e. cummings.* New York: MacMillan.

Park, Robert E. 1950. *Race and Culture.* New York: Free Press.

———. 1952. *Human Communities.* New York: Free Press.

———. 1955. *Society.* New York: Free Press.

Partch, Harry. 1949. *Genesis of a Music.* Madison: University of Wisconsin Press.

Pevsner, Nikolaus. 1940. *Academies of Art: Past and Present.* Cambridge: Cambridge University Press.

Reese, Gustave. 1959. *Music in the Renaissance.* Revised ed. New York: W. W. Norton.

Rosenblum, Barbara. 1973. "Photographers and their Photographs." Unpublished doctoral dissertation, Northwestern University.

Smith, B. H. 1968. *Poetic Closure.* Chicago: University of Chicago Press.

Wörner, Karl H. 1973. *Stockhausen: Life and Work.* Berkeley: University of California Press.

# STUDY QUESTIONS

1. According to Becker, how and when do artistic innovations occur? What makes this process of innovation difficult?
2. What are some implications of Becker's argument for thinking about how other forms of collective action, besides art, are organized?

# 13

# AGENCY AND STRUCTURAL CHANGE

WILLIAM H. SEWELL, JR.

Does your sociology professor use the phrase *social structure* a lot? Like, maybe, too much? The next time she uses it, ask her for a definition. Oh, and don't be surprised if you stump her with this one! Sociology professors love this phrase and we are not the only ones. Most social scientists use it over and over again, without ever bothering to define it. So what exactly do sociologists mean by social structure and how do we conceptualize it? Is social structure the same thing as social pattern? If not, how do these differ? Where do social structures come from and how do they change? More importantly, why do they change?

William Sewell, a historian and social scientist, addresses these questions because, in his view, it is important that social scientists have some well thought out concepts that explain how and why social transformations are possible. This is especially true because so much sociological theory points to the remarkable power that social structures have to reproduce themselves and endure, despite efforts by people to change them. Human efforts to change or challenge these structures—our *agency*—often seem to fall flat in the face of implacable social realities. The structures seem to win time and time again. Yet—and this is the puzzling part—societies do change over time. Sometimes they transform suddenly and violently, as we witnessed in the Arab Spring of 2011, and sometimes more gradually, as

**happened in America when the staid and placid 1950s gave way to the tumultuous and riotous 1960s. The key to solving this puzzle, Sewell says, is to recognize how structures contain within themselves the agents of change that eventually transform them.**

# A THEORY OF STRUCTURE: DUALITY, AGENCY, AND TRANSFORMATION

"Structure" is one of the most important and most elusive terms in the vocabulary of current social science. The concept is central not only in such eponymous schools as structural functionalism, structuralism, and poststructuralism, but in virtually all tendencies of social scientific thought. But if social scientists find it impossible to do without the term "structure," we also find it nearly impossible to define it adequately. Many of us have surely had the experience of being asked by a "naive" student what we mean by structure, and then finding it embarrassingly difficult to define the term without using the word "structure" or one of its variants in its own definition. Sometimes we find what seems to be an acceptable synonym—for example, "pattern"—but all such synonyms lack the original's rhetorical force. When it comes to indicating that a relation is powerful or important it is certainly more convincing to designate it as "structural" than as "patterning."

The term structure empowers what it designates. Structure, in its nominative sense, always implies structure in its transitive verbal sense. Whatever aspect of social life we designate as structure is posited as "structuring" some other aspect of social existence—whether it is class that structures politics, gender that structures employment opportunities, rhetorical conventions that structure texts or utterances, or modes of production that structure social formations. Structure operates in social scientific discourse as a powerful metonymic device, identifying some part of a complex social reality as explaining the whole. It is a word to conjure with in the social sciences. In fact, structure is less a precise concept than a kind of founding or epistemic metaphor of social scientific—and scientific—discourse. For this reason, no formal definition can succeed in fixing the term's meaning: the metaphor of structure continues its essential if somewhat mysterious work in the constitution of social scientific knowledge despite theorists' definitional efforts.

There are, nevertheless, three problems in the current use of the term that make self-conscious theorizing about the meanings of structure seem worthwhile. The most fundamental problem is that structural or structuralist arguments tend to assume a far too rigid causal determinism in social life. Those features of social existence denominated as structures tend to be reified and treated as primary, hard, and immutable, like the girders of a building, while the events or social processes they structure tend to be seen as secondary and superficial, like the outer "skin" of a skyscraper, or as mutable within "hard" structural constraints, like the layout of offices on floors defined by a skeleton of girders. What tends to get lost in the language of structure is the efficacy of human action—or "agency," to use the currently favored term. Structures tend to appear in social scientific discourse as impervious to human agency, to exist apart from, but nevertheless to determine the essential shape of, the strivings and motivated transactions that constitute the experienced surface of social life. A social science trapped in an unexamined metaphor of structure tends to reduce actors to cleverly programmed automatons. A second and closely related problem with the notion of structure is that it makes dealing with change awkward. The metaphor of structure implies stability. For this reason, structural language lends itself readily to explanations of how social life is shaped into consistent patterns, but not to explanations of how these patterns change over time. In structural discourse, change is commonly located outside of structures, either in a telos of history, in notions of breakdown, or in influences exogenous to the system in question. Consequently, moving from questions of stability to questions of change tends to involve awkward epistemological shifts.

The third problem is of a rather different order: the term structure is used in apparently contradictory senses in different social scientific discourses, particularly in sociology and anthropology. Sociologists typically contrast "structure" to "culture." Structure, in normal sociological usage, is thought of as "hard" or "material" and therefore as primary and determining, whereas culture is regarded as "soft" or "mental" and therefore as secondary or derived. By contrast, semiotically inclined social scientists, most particularly anthropologists, regard culture as the preeminent site of structure. In typical anthropological usage, the term structure is assumed to refer to the realm of culture, except when it is modified by the adjective "social." As a consequence, social scientists as different in outlook as Theda Skocpol and Marshall Sahlins can be designated as "structuralists" by their respective disciplines. Sociologists and anthropologists, in short, tend to visualize the nature and location of structure in sharply discrepant, indeed mutually incompatible, ways.

In view of all these problems with the notion of structure, it is tempting to conclude that the term should simply be discarded. But this, I think, is impossible: structure is so rhetorically powerful and pervasive a term that any attempt to legislate its abolition would be futile. Moreover, the notion of structure does denominate, however problematically, something very important about social relations: the tendency of patterns of relations to be reproduced, even when actors engaging in the relations are unaware of the patterns or do not desire their reproduction. In my opinion, the notion of structure neither could nor should be banished from the discourse of social science. But it does need extensive rethinking. This article will attempt to develop a theory of structure that overcomes the three cardinal weaknesses of the concept as it is normally employed in social science. The theory will attempt (1) to recognize the agency of social actors, (2) to build the possibility of change into the concept of structure, and (3) to overcome the divide between semiotic and materialist visions of structure.

## Why Structural Change Is Possible

. . . It is my conviction that a theory of change cannot be built into a theory of structure unless we adopt a far more multiple, contingent, and fractured conception of society—and of structure. What is needed is a conceptual vocabulary that makes it possible to show how the ordinary operations of structures can generate transformations. To this end, I propose five key axioms: the multiplicity of structures, the transposability of schemas, the unpredictability of resource accumulation, the polysemy of resources, and the intersection of structures.

*The multiplicity of structures.*—Societies are based on practices that derive from many distinct structures, which exist at different levels, operate in different modalities, and are themselves based on widely varying types and quantities of resources. While it is common for a certain range of these structures to be homologous, like those described by Bourdieu in *Outline of a Theory of Practice*, it is never true that all of them are homologous. Structures tend to vary significantly between different institutional spheres, so that

kinship structures will have different logics and dynamics than those possessed by religious structures, productive structures, aesthetic structures,
educational structures, and so on. There is, moreover, important variation
even within a given sphere. For example, the structures that shape and constrain religion in Christian societies include authoritarian, prophetic, ritual,
and theoretical modes. These may sometimes operate in harmony, but they
can also lead to sharply conflicting claims and empowerments. The multiplicity of structures means that the knowledgeble social actors whose practices constitute a society are far more versatile than Bourdieu's account of a
universally homologous habitus would imply: social actors are capable of
applying a wide range of different and even incompatible schemas and have
access to heterogeneous arrays of resources.

   *The transposability of schemas.*—Moroever, the schemas to which actors
have access can be applied across a wide range of circumstances. This is
actually recognized by Bourdieu, but he has not, in my opinion, drawn the
correct conclusions from his insight. Schemas were defined above as generalizable or transposable procedures applied in the enactment of social life.
The term "generalizable" is taken from Giddens; the term "transposable,"
which I prefer, is taken from Bourdieu. At one point Bourdieu defines habitus as "a system of lasting transposable dispositions which, integrating past
experiences, functions at every moment as a *matrix of perceptions, apprecia-
tions, and actions* and makes possible the achievement of infinitely diversified tasks, thanks to analogical transfers of schemes permitting the solution
of similarly shaped problems" (1977, p. 83; emphasis in original).

   The slippage in this passage occurs in the final phrase, "permitting the
solution of similarly shaped problems." Whether a given problem is similarly shaped enough to be solved by analogical transfers of schemes cannot
be decided in advance by social scientific analysts, but must be determined
case by case by the actors, which means that there is no fixed limit to the
possible transpositions. This is in fact implied by the earlier phrase, "makes
possible the achievement of infinitely diversified tasks." To say that schemas are transposable, in other words, is to say that they can be applied to
a wide and not fully predictable range of cases outside the context in which
they are initially learned. This fits with what we usually mean by knowledge
of a rule or of some other learned procedure. In ordinary speech one cannot be said to really *know* a rule simply because one can apply it mechanically
to repeated instances of the same case. Whether we are speaking of rules of
grammar, mathematics, law, etiquette, or carpentry, the real test of know-

ing a rule is to be able to apply it successfully in *unfamiliar* cases. Knowledge of a rule or a schema by definition means the ability to transpose or extend it—that is, to apply it creatively. If this is so, then *agency*, which I would define as entailing the capacity to transpose and extend schemas to new contexts, is inherent in the knowledge of cultural schemas that characterizes all minimally competent members of society.

*The unpredictability of resource accumulation.*—But the very fact that schemas are by definition capable of being transposed or extended means that the resource consequences of the enactment of cultural schemas is never entirely predictable. A joke told to a new audience, an investment made in a new market, an offer of marriage made to a new patriline, a cavalry attack made on a new terrain, a crop planted in a newly cleared field or in a familiar field in a new spring—the effect of these actions on the resources of the actors is never quite certain. Investment in a new market may make the entrepreneur a pauper or a millionaire, negotiation of a marriage with a new patriline may result in a family's elevation in status or its extinction in a feud, planting a crop in the familiar field may result in subsistence, starvation, or plenty. Moreover, if the enactment of schemas creates unpredictable quantities and qualities of resources, and if the reproduction of schemas depends on their continuing validation by resources, this implies that schemas will in fact be differentially validated when they are put into action and therefore will potentially be subject to modification. A brilliantly successful cavalry attack on a new terrain may change the battle plans of subsequent campaigns or even theories of military tactics; a joke that draws rotten tomatoes rather than laughter may result in the suppression of a category of jokes from the comedian's repertoire; a succession of crop failures may modify routines of planting or plowing.

*The polysemy of resources.*—The term polysemy (or multiplicity of meaning) is normally applied to symbols, language, or texts. Its application to resources sounds like a contradiction in terms. But, given the concept of resources I am advocating here, it is not. Resources, I have insisted, embody cultural schemas. Like texts or ritual performances, however, their meaning is never entirely unambiguous. The form of the factory embodies and therefore teaches capitalist notions of property relations. But, as Marx points out, it can also teach the necessarily social and collective character of production and thereby undermine the capitalist notion of private property. The new prestige, wealth, and territory gained from the brilliant success of a cavalry charge may be attributed to the superior discipline and élan of the cavalry officers and thereby enhance the power of an aristocratic officer corps, or it may be attributed to the commanding general and thereby result in the increasing subordination of officers to a charismatic leader. Any array of resources is capable of being interpreted in varying ways and, therefore, of empowering different actors and teaching different schemas. Again, this seems to me inherent in a definition of agency as the capacity to transpose and extend schemas to new contexts. Agency, to put it differently, is the actor's capacity to reinterpret and mobilize an array of resources in terms of cultural schemas other than those that initially constituted the array.

*The intersection of structures.*—One reason arrays of resources can be interpreted in more than one way is that structures or structural complexes intersect and overlap. The structures of capitalist society include both a mode of production based on private property and profit and a mode of labor organization based on workplace solidarity. The factory figures as a crucial resource in both of these structures, and its meaning and consequences for both workers and managers is therefore open and contested. The intersection of structures, in fact, takes place in both the schema and the resource dimensions. Not only can a given array of resources be claimed by different actors embedded in different structural complexes (or differentially claimed by the same actor embedded in different structural complexes), but schemas can be borrowed or appropriated from one structural complex and applied to another. Not only do workers and factory owners struggle for control of the factory, but Marx appropriates political economy for the advancement of socialism.

Structures, then, are sets of mutually sustaining schemas and resources that empower and constrain social action and that tend to be reproduced by that social action. But their reproduction is never automatic. Structures are at risk, at least to some extent, in all of the social encounters they shape—because structures are multiple and intersecting, because schemas are transposable, and because resources are polysemic and accumulate unpredictably. Placing the relationship between resources and cultural schemas at the center of a concept of structure makes it possible to show how social change, no less than social stasis, can be generated by the enactment of structures in social life.

## AGENCY

Such enactments of structures imply a particular concept of agency—one that sees agency not as opposed to, but as constituent of, structure. To be an agent means to be capable of exerting some degree of control over the social relations in which one is enmeshed, which in turn implies the ability to transform those social relations to some degree. As I see it, agents are empowered to act with and against others by structures: they have knowledge of the schemas that inform social life and have access to some measure of human and nonhuman resources. Agency arises from the actor's knowledge of schemas, which means the ability to apply them to new contexts. Or, to put the same thing the other way around, agency arises from the actor's control of resources, which means the capacity to reinterpret or mobilize an array of resources in terms of schemas other than those that constituted the array. Agency is implied by the existence of structures.

I would argue that a capacity for agency—for desiring, for forming intentions, and for acting creatively—is inherent in all humans. But I would also argue that humans are born with only a highly generalized capacity for agency, analogous to their capacity to use language. Just as linguistic capacity takes the form of becoming a competent speaker of some particular language—French, or Arabic, or Swahili, or Urdu—agency is formed by a specific range of cultural schemas and resources available in a person's particular social milieu. The specific forms that agency will take consequently vary enormously and are culturally and historically determined. But a capacity for agency is as much a given for humans as the capacity for respiration.

That all humans actually exercise agency in practice is demonstrated to my satisfaction by the work of Erving Goffman (1959, 1967). Goffman shows that all members of society employ complex repertoires of interaction skills to control and sustain ongoing social relations. He also shows that small transformative actions—for example, intervening to save the face of an interactant who has misread the situation—turn out to be necessary to sustain even the most ordinary intercourse of daily life (Goffman 1967, pp. 5–46). Once again, knowledge of cultural schemas (in this case of interaction rituals) implies the ability to act creatively. Actors, of course, vary in the extent of their control of social relations and in the scope of their transformative powers, but all members of society exercise some measure of agency in the conduct of their daily lives.

It is equally important, however, to insist that the agency exercised by different persons is far from uniform, that agency differs enormously in both kind and extent. What kinds of desires people can have, what intentions they can form, and what sorts of creative transpositions they can carry out vary dramatically from one social world to another depending on the nature of the particular structures that inform those social worlds. Without a notion of heaven and hell a person cannot strive for admission into paradise; only in a modern capitalist economy can one attempt to make a killing on the futures market; if they are denied access to the public sphere, women's ambitions will be focused on private life. Agency also differs in extent, both between and within societies. Occupancy of different social positions—as defined, for example, by gender, wealth, social prestige, class, ethnicity, occupation, generation, sexual preference, or education—gives people knowledge of different schemas and access to different kinds and amounts of resources and hence different possibilities for transformative action. And the scope or extent of agency also varies enormously between different social systems, even for occupants of analogous positions. The owner of the biggest art gallery in St. Louis has far less influence on American artistic taste than the owner of the biggest gallery in Los Angeles; the president of Chad has far less power over global environmental policy than the president of Russia. Structures, in short, empower agents differentially, which also implies that they embody the desires, intentions, and knowledge of agents differentially as well. Structures, and the human agencies they endow, are laden with differences in power.

Finally, I would insist that agency is collective as well as individual. I do not agree with Barry Hindess (1986) that the term "agent" must be applied in the same sense to collectivities that act as corporate units in social life—political parties, firms, families, states, clubs, or trade unions—as it is applied to individuals. But I do see agency as profoundly social or collective. The transpositions of schemas and remobilizations of resources that constitute agency are always acts of communication with others. Agency entails an ability to coordinate one's actions with others and against others, to form collective projects, to persuade, to coerce, and to monitor the simultaneous effects of one's own and others' activities. Moreover, the extent of the agency exercised by individual persons depends profoundly on their positions in collective organizations. To take the extreme case, a monarch's personal whims or quarrels may affect the lives of thousands (see, e.g., Sahlins 1991). But it is also true that the agency of fathers, executives, or professors is greatly expanded by the places they occupy in patriarchal families, corporations, or universities and by their consequent authority to bind the collectivity by their actions. Agency, then, characterizes all persons. But the agency exercised by persons is collective in both its sources and its mode of exercise. Personal agency is, therefore, laden with collectively produced differences of power and implicated in collective struggles and resistances.

# References

Bourdieu, Pierre. 1977. *Outline of a Theory of Practice.* Cambridge: Cambridge University Press.

Goffman, Erving. 1959. *The Presentation of Self in Everyday Life.* New York: Doubleday.

———. 1967. *Interaction Ritual: Essays on Face to Face Behavior.* New York: Pantheon.

Hindess, Barry. 1986. "Actors and Social Relations." Pp. 113–26 in *Social Theory in Transition*, edited by Mark L. Wordell and Stephen P. Turner. London: Allen & Unwin.

Sahlins, Marshall. 1991. "The Return of the Event, Again; With Reflections on the Beginnings of the Great Fijian War of 1843 to 1855 between the Kingdoms of Bau and Rewa." Pp. 37–100 in *Clio in Oceania: Toward a Historical Anthropology,* edited by A. Biersack. Washington, D.C.: Smithsonian.

# STUDY QUESTIONS

1. How does Sewell define *agency* and what does it have to do with resources?
2. Why do you think Sewell's work has been so important for cultural sociologists?

# 14

# MAKING HITS

WILLIAM T. BIELBY AND DENISE D. BIELBY

Ever watch *American Idol*? I'm guessing you have. The reality TV show, which premiered in June of 2002, remains one of the most watched shows on TV. An estimated 25 million viewers watch the show each week and winners can garner upwards of 65 million or more votes (viewers can vote multiple times). When you consider that President Barack Obama won the 2008 presidential election with 65 million votes, the show's popularity becomes clear.

*American Idol* is a massive hit, by any measure. But what is the secret of its success? Every TV executive in the world is asking the same question. William and Denise Bielby aren't TV executives, but they also wanted to know how hit shows are made. Television is one of the *culture industries* that Horkheimer and Adorno (p. 65) wrote about so critically. The Bielbys set aside criticisms and concerns about the *effects* of mass culture and ask instead: How is it *made*?

Their answers are illuminating. TV executives don't have a crystal ball that tells them what will work, so every year they consider thousands of possible ideas for new shows, selecting about 600 or so for development. Producers decide which shows to pilot based on the genre of the show (e.g., sitcom or reality), the reputation of the producers and creative talent involved, and how well they think it can imitate other successful shows. They consider all these factors because of the inherent risk and uncertainty involved in predicting what makes a hit. Ironically, while there is no formula for making hits, the industry takes a fairly formulaic approach in order to justify,

**to themselves and to others, that they know what they are doing. What makes a hit remains a bit of a mystery.**

# "ALL HITS ARE FLUKES": INSTITUTIONALIZED DECISION MAKING AND THE RHETORIC OF NETWORK PRIME-TIME PROGRAM DEVELOPMENT

## Interdependence Among Suppliers, Networks, and Markets

Each year, the four networks evaluate thousands of concepts for new series and purchase approximately 600 pilot scripts. From these, the networks select about 20% to be produced as pilots at the networks' expense (CBS Inc. 1990). About one-third of the pilots eventually appear on the prime-time schedule. For example, of the 112 pilots commissioned by ABC, CBS, NBC, and Fox for 1991, 23 debuted in the fall and another 15 were scheduled as midseason replacements.

Until very recently, the FCC's Financial Interest and Syndication Rules (the "Fin-Syn" rules) have placed strict limits on the amount of prime-time programming that can be produced by the networks themselves, so most prime-time pilots and series are supplied by independent writer-producers working for outside production companies. Program suppliers include small independent companies and the television subsidiaries of the major film studios. Either as sole producers or in joint ventures with smaller companies, the major studios account for a majority of the series produced for network prime time. Program suppliers retain ownership of the series and license networks to one first-run and one rerun broadcast of each episode (Bielby and Bielby 1990; Cantor and Cantor 1992).

Since (with a few exceptions) the networks do not own the shows they broadcast, advertising revenues from network broadcasts are their primary source of profit from prime-time series. At the same time, the licensing fees received by the program suppliers typically do not cover the cost of production. A typical sitcom costs about $600,000 per episode to produce and is licensed to the network for about $500,000. An episode of a typical one-hour drama costs about $1.2–$1.3 million to produce and is licensed to the network for $250,000–$300,000 less than the cost of production (*Channels* 1990). Program suppliers incur these short-term losses in anticipation of substantial profits from eventual syndication of successful series.

Thus, program suppliers and network programmers are mutually dependent. On the one hand, a writer-producer who creates a new series seeks access to a network's prime-time schedule. The supplier is hoping for a network run of at least three or four seasons, so that enough episodes will be produced to make the series profitable in subsequent syndication. On the other hand, the network programmer is dependent upon program suppliers for new series that will attract audiences that advertisers want to reach. A series that fails to deliver a sizable audience with a desirable demographic composition will be unprofitable for the network and its affiliates. However, participants in network program development are not simply interacting in a product market. They are also embedded in an institutional context that introduces a symbolic dimension that they manage and enact through their decisions.

## Decision Making Amid Ambiguity and Uncertainty

"Institutions" are routinely reproduced, taken-for-granted social practices that have "rule-like status." in thought and action (Meyer and Rowan 1977; Jepperson 1991). Network prime-time program development is an institution in this sense, and decisions about introducing new series are made in an "institutionalized" context. In such contexts, decision makers cope with ambiguity and uncertainty by substituting imitation, routines, and rules of thumb for rational calculation as decision criteria (March and Olsen 1976). To maintain legitimacy, they are likely to engage in activities that have "ritual significance" to outsiders, providing "prudent, rational, and legitimate accounts" of their actions (Meyer and Rowan 1977).

Highly institutionalized decision contexts exhibit two distinctive features: (1) technologies are poorly understood; and (2) actions are evaluated according to multiple, ambiguous, and contradictory criteria by external constituencies (Meyer and Rowan 1977). The context for decisions about new prime-time series is highly institutionalized in both respects. First, network programmers are making decisions about productions for which there are no agreed-upon standards of competence. An experienced programmer can probably distinguish well-crafted from mediocre scripts and make informed judgments about the quality of acting, editing, and direction of a pilot. Nevertheless, the programmer has no reliable basis for predicting whether audiences, advertisers, and critics will accept the series. In the words of Jeff Sagansky, president of CBS Entertainment, "All hits are flukes" (Frank 1991, p. 1; also see Cantor and Cantor 1992, p. 70). Gitlin (1983) found network executives consistently expressing views like these and concluded that the "problem of knowing" is a key feature of program development decisions.

Second network programmers are making decisions that are subject to multiple, ambiguous, and often conflicting assessment criteria. Least ambiguous are criteria of commercial success. A commercially successful series is one that delivers a large audience with a demographic composition valued by advertisers. However, feedback from ratings comes months after the decision is made to schedule a series, and even that feedback can be misleading for a series that slowly builds an audience over the course of one or two seasons.

Criteria for critical acclaim are more varied, and critics often reserve their most favorable assessments for so-called quality series that the networks have dropped from their prime-time schedules. Critics' "obituaries" for their favorite canceled series often reveal the conflicting criteria that underlie judgments about aesthetic versus commercial success. For example, at the end of the 1990–91 season, *Wall Street Journal* critic Robert Goldberg (1991) celebrated the qualities of "subtlety in depicting relationships," "solid writing," and "innovative ideas" among canceled shows on his "Best of 1990–91" list, while *Los Angeles Times* critic Rick Du Brow (1991) recently lamented the loss of "humanistic ensemble dramas," "well-crafted TV fiction," and "work of major social import."

Dozens of special interest groups also monitor network executives' programming decisions. They evaluate network series on issues as diverse as representations of race, age, gender, drug use, violence, birth control, and "traditional" family values (Montgomery 1989). In short, as a cultural object, a television series has a range of meanings attributed to it (Griswold 1987). A decision to develop a series for prime time is simultaneously a choice about a commercial commodity, an aesthetic endeavor, and a social institution. As a result, those making programming decisions will be variously evaluated according to perceptions of their business judgment, their aesthetic tastes, and the values they impart.

Because the industry is so highly centralized, programmers are more directly accountable to commercial interests than to other constituencies. DiMaggio (1977) has described such an industry context as a "centralized brokerage system." Network programmers mediate the business relationship between creative personnel employed by independent production companies and advertisers who bear the costs of distribution. The programmer "brokers" the inherent conflict between the creative interests of the writer-producers who create and supply programs and the commercial interests of advertisers. Programmers perform the monitoring function that would otherwise reside in the authority relations of a bureaucratic structure or in the professional standards and contractually mandated product specifications of a craft structure.

In mediating the relationship between writer-producers and the networks, programmers do not give equal weight to creative and commercial concerns. Writer-producers have almost no alternative to the four networks as distribution channels for their creations, despite the growth of cable and first-run syndication in recent years. Most are also dependent upon one of the seven major studios for financing, and, of course, series creators have their own interests in commercial success. Thus, as DiMaggio (1977) has theorized, in a mass-culture industry with a high level of market concentration such as network television, brokers are more directly accountable to commercial interests than to creative interests.

## Rhetorical Strategies for Introducing New Series

### "FRAMING" PRIME-TIME PROGRAM DEVELOPMENT

A "frame" is a central organizing idea for making sense of events (Gamson 1988; Gamson and Modigliani 1989). Gamson (1988) and Snow and Benford (1988; Benford 1993) have applied the concept to represent how social movement elites develop rhetorical strategies to mobilize constituencies and shape understandings. According to Gamson and Modigliani, meaning in media discourse is managed by assembling frames into "interpretive packages." A package "offers a number of different condensing symbols that suggest the core frame and positions in shorthand, making it possible to display the package as a whole with a deft metaphor, catchphrase, or other symbolic device" (Gamson and Modigliani 1989, p. 3).

We apply the frame concept to the vocabularies articulated by decision makers to justify their actions in highly institutionalized contexts. In developing new prime-time series, network programmers are compelled to provide legitimate accounts for their decisions (Meyer and Rowan 1977). We argue that they do so by organizing discourse around widely accepted frames. Specifically, in describing series in development, network executives invoke the framing devices of *genre*, *reputation*, and *imitation*.

## GENRE, REPUTATION, AND IMITATION

*Genre.*—Television genres are conventions regarding the content of television series—formulas that prescribe format, themes, premises, characterizations, etc. In contemporary television, consensus among writers, producers, programmers, advertisers, and audiences over the boundaries of genres is probably greater than in any other area of popular culture. Ideas for new series are "pitched" in terms of widely recognized genres, while network scheduling decisions, advertisers' purchasing decisions, and audience viewing patterns are all based, to some extent, upon shared understandings about program categories.

Since the late 1950s the television industry has recognized two basic genres for prime-time network series: the half-hour situation comedy ("sitcom") and the one-hour drama. These genres are recognized and reproduced in the industry's organizational structures. Since the late 1970s the entertainment divisions of ABC, CBS, and NBC have contained separate units for comedy development and drama development, and corresponding units exist in the television divisions of the major studios. Pilots for new sitcoms and dramas are easily recognized and labeled as such.

Over the past several years the "reality" series has become recognized as a third basic prime-time genre. The reality genre label is typically applied to inexpensively produced half-hour nonfiction series other than programs produced by the network news divisions. The reality genre is less established than the sitcom and drama categories. Nevertheless, the reality series' existence as a distinct genre is recognized as such by programmers, producers, creative personnel, advertisers, critics, the industry press, and, increasingly, audiences.

As industry conventions, genres can be viewed as forms of social organization that facilitate the coordination of production. Work outside of established genres disrupts shared understandings and requires more effort to coordinate and promote (Becker 1982). Accordingly, a writer-producer seeking to sell a pilot that defies the conventions of established genres can expect resistance from network programmers. Moreover, a programmer seeking to place such a series on the network schedule can expect advertisers and local affiliates (who sell local advertising time) to demand reassurance that despite—or because of—its innovative elements, the new series will be accessible to audiences and commercially viable.

Genres are more than just shared understandings that economize on the costs of doing business. They are taken-for-granted categories that guide thought and action, serving to rationalize and legitimate decisions made in a context that is characterized by a high degree of ambiguity and uncertainty. As such, they are readily available as a framing device. Thus, locating a series pilot with respect to an established genre provides an immediate frame of reference for the new and unknown cultural product. Even before the pilot is produced, the potential new series is linked to a category that is widely perceived as familiar, understandable, and appropriate.

*Reputation.*—In culture industries the success of new products cannot be known a priori. As a result, those who propose new products are likely to be evaluated on the basis of reputations built upon prior successes (DiMaggio 1977, p. 442). The importance of reputation has been documented in studies of studio musicians (Faulkner 1983), filmmakers (Baker and Faulkner 1991), and television writers (Bielby and Bielby 1993; Gitlin 1983). Accordingly, we expect reputation to figure prominently in programmers' rhetoric about series in development. Linking new series to producers' prior hits reassures commercial constituencies that well-crafted episodes will be produced in an orderly and timely manner and will contain elements proven successful with audiences in the past. Similarly, linking a new series to a well-known celebrity establishes an association with a familiar and successful commodity.

*Imitation.*—When decisions are made under conditions of ambiguity and uncertainty, decision makers often attempt to establish legitimacy by imitating the successful efforts of others (March and Olsen 1976; DiMaggio and Powell 1983). Accordingly, we expect network programmers to rely upon imitation as a rhetorical strategy in their discourse about series in development. A new production can be described as similar to another hit series, even if it is supplied by a different production team. In addition, network executives can emphasize a series' similarity to or origins in a product from another popular medium, such as a hit film, play, comic book, or novel.

In sum, in a context where formulas for producing successful products do not exist and "all hits are flukes," decision makers rely on rhetorical strategies to demonstrate that their actions are rational and appropriate. Network executives construct succinct interpretive packages by linking new series to established genres, to reputable producers, and to other popular and successful cultural commodities. If the series is successful, external constituencies will view the executives' actions as understandable and familiar (Hirsch 1986).

## Discussion

Overall, what is most striking about our findings is the importance of claims about linkages to established writer-producers in the program development process. For the 1991–92 season, the framing device of linking a potential new series to established writer-producers is invoked much more frequently than any other rhetorical strategy, and it is the only one positively associated with the likelihood of a series being selected for a network's prime-time schedule. Other framing devices appear to be strictly symbolic, designed to shape perceptions of constituencies with conflicting assessment criteria in a context characterized by uncertainty and ambiguity. In an industry where all hits are flukes, decision makers use rhetorical strategies to reassure others that their decisions are rational, appropriate, and legitimate.

If anything, our statistical findings understate the importance of actual links (as opposed to claims about links) between networks and established writer-producers. Not reflected in our statistical analysis are several new series from veteran producers selected for the network schedules without going through the normal development process of pilot production and evaluation. For example, *Flesh 'n' Blood*, from the producers of *Cheers*, was scheduled by NBC based on a six-minute presentation to network executives (de Moraes 1991c), while Gary David Goldberg's *Brooklyn Bridge* was sold to CBS on the basis of a script alone (Lowry 1991b).

The commitments to these shows reflect a recent change in the network development process. The networks are increasingly making multiyear, multiseries commitments to the most sought-after producers. For example, the network may commit to ordering a specific number of episodes of a series before seeing a pilot, or even a script, or it may agree to pay a financial penalty to the producer if the network fails to order a fixed number of episodes (CBS Inc. 1990, p. 26). At least six of the series in our data, all linked to established producers, had such commitments from the networks at the time the development slates were announced in March.

As the level of risk and uncertainty facing the industry increases (Marich 1991), these kinds of arrangements are likely to proliferate. Reliance on established writer-producers is likely to intensify, which should be reflected in the discourse framing the program development process in the future. In terms of the defining characteristics of a centralized brokerage system, (1) it is becoming more difficult to predict the success of a new series a priori, (2) pressures for commercial success are increasing, and (3) network programmers are becoming more dependent on contributions of the creative personnel who supply series. As a result, actively managing the reception of new series through carefully organized rhetorical strategies will become increasingly important, but doing so successfully will become more difficult.

## Conclusions

Our study provides an explanation for the organization and content of discourse that introduces new cultural objects marketed to a mass audience. Our research extends Griswold's (1987) methodological framework for the sociology of culture by emphasizing how social agents actively manage the reception of new cultural objects through rhetorical strategies. Our analysis of prime-time television suggests that three factors shape the content of rhetorical strategies for introducing new cultural objects: (1) the degree of centralization in social arrangements that mediate the relationship among creators, audiences, critics, and commercial constituencies; (2) the degree to which the commercial viability of a new product can be unambiguously evaluated based on measurable features of the clinical object; and (3) the degree to which commercial and critical assessment of a new cultural object are successfully decoupled from one another. Our case study of prime-time television applies to a context in which the brokered relationship between creators and business interests is highly centralized, commercial and critical success cannot be predicted in advance, and critical and commercial assessment are decoupled from one another. We found that in such circumstances, decision-making brokers use linguistic framing devices of reputation, imitation, and genre to reassure commercial and creative constituencies that their actions are appropriate, legitimate, and rational. Because of the primacy of commercial viability in evaluating success, claims regarding the reputation of creators are emphasized over other rhetorical strategies.

Variation along these three dimensions should have consequences for the discourse used to introduce new cultural objects. For example, when the brokerage between creators and business interests is less centralized and success is more predictable, less emphasis should be placed on reputational claims about creators. In such circumstances, claims about creators' reputations should also be less strongly associated with access to channels of distribution. Furthermore, when critical and commercial assessments are more tightly coupled, linguistic claims about aesthetic qualities of the product should receive greater emphasis relative to claims about reputation and imitation.

The validity of our explanatory scheme for understanding the management of the introduction of new cultural objects can be assessed empirically in two ways. One is through historical analysis of the discourse in a specific culture industry. For example, in the early years of network prime-time television, critical acceptance should have been more important for establishing the legitimacy of the new medium as a profit-making enterprise (Boddy 1990). Accordingly, we should find claims about aesthetic quality to be more common in programmers' discourse about new prime-time series in the late 1940s and early 1950s. Similarly, if attacks on the values imparted by contemporary television begin to seriously threaten the legitimacy of the industry, we can expect programmers' claims to increasingly emphasize the positive social values of the series they broadcast.

A second way to assess our approach to the management of the introduction of new cultural objects is through comparative analysis across culture industries. Prime-time television, feature film, popular fiction, and popular music differ in the organization of production, in levels of risk, uncertainty, and ambiguity, and in the relative importance of critical reception for commercial success. They also differ in features of the product life cycle such as the length of time between creation, production, and distribution and the duration of popularity with audiences. These industry traits should be systematically related to the kinds of rhetorical strategies invoked by brokers and their effectiveness for shaping the reception of new cultural objects by business interests, critics, and audiences.

In sum, we have analyzed how language is used to manage uncertainty and ambiguity in a highly centralized and institutionalized culture industry. By specifying how institutional context and industry structure shape interaction among those engaged in the production, distribution, and consumption of popular culture, we have demonstrated the importance of three phenomena. First, we show that when confronted with high levels of ambiguity and uncertainty and conflicting assessment criteria, it is incumbent upon decision makers to develop rhetorical strategies that provide legitimate accounts of their actions. Second, we demonstrate that the content of that discourse will be organized around widely shared categories and symbols that have meaning to varied constituencies. Third, we show that in centralized culture industries, brokers' rhetorical strategies have consequences for creators' access to product markets and audiences. Others have shown how the structure of industries and markets constrain innovation in culture industries (Peterson and Berger 1975; DiMaggio 1977). Our analysis suggests that the strategic use of language and categories to manage commercial and creative interests can also have a causal impact on the sources and diversity of cultural objects reaching the marketplace.

# References

Baker, Wayne E. and Robert R. Faulkner. 1991. "Role as Resource in the Hollywood Film Industry." *American Journal of Sociology* 97:279–309.

Becker, Howard S. 1982. *Art Worlds*. Berkeley and Los Angeles: University of California Press.

Benford, Robert D. 1993. "Frame Disputes within the Nuclear Disarmament Movement." *Social Forces* 71:677–701.

Bielby, Denise D. and William T. Bielby. 1993. "The Hollywood 'Graylist'? Audience Demographics and Age Stratification among Television Writers." Pp. 141–70 in *Creators of Culture*, edited by Muriel G. Cantor and Cheryl Zollars. Vol. 8 of *Current Research on Occupations and Professions*. Greenwich, CT: JAI Press.

Bielby, William T. and Denise D. Bielby. 1990. "Producing Prime Time: Organizational Concentration and the Diversity of Network Television Programming." Paper presented at the annual meeting of the American Sociological Association, Washington, D.C.

Boddy, William. 1990. *Fifties Television: The Industry and Its Critics*. Urbana: University of Illinois Press.

Cantor, Muriel G. and Joel M. Cantor. 1992. *Prime-Time Television: Content and Control*. 2d ed. Newbury Park, CA: Sage.

CBS, Inc. 1990. "Comments of CBS Inc." *In the Matter of Evaluation of the Syndication and Financial Interest Rules.* Federal Communications Commission, Docket no. 90–162. June 14.

*Channels.* 1990. "Primetime's Price Tag." *Channels* 10 (September 10): 50–51.

de Moraes, Lisa. 1991c. "NBC to Bow Six Comedies, Two Dramas in Fall Shake-up." *Hollywood Reporter* (May 21), pp. 1, 78.

DiMaggio, Paul J. 1977. "Market Structure, the Creative Process, and Popular Culture: Toward an Organizational Reinterpretation of Mass Culture Theory." *Journal of Popular Culture* 11:433–51.

DiMaggio, Paul J. and Walter W. Powell. 1983. "The Iron Cage Revisited: Institutional Isomorphism and Collective Rationality in Organizational Fields." *American Sociological Review* 48:147–60.

Du Brow, Rick. 1991. "Humanity Loses to Reality." *Los Angeles Times* (March 30), pp. F1, F12.

Faulkner, Robert R. 1983. *Music on Demand: Composers and Careers in the Hollywood Film Industry.* New Brunswick, NJ: Transaction.

Frank, Betsy. 1991. *On Air: Primetime Program Development, 1991–92.* New York: Saatchi & Saatchi Advertising.

Gamson, William A. 1988. "Political Discourse and Collective Action." Pp. 219–44 in *From Structure to Action: Social Movement Participation across Cultures,* edited by Bert Klandermans, Hanspeter Kriesi, and Sidney Tarrow. Greenwich, CT: JAI Press.

Gamson, William A. and Andre Modigliani. 1989. "Media Discourse and Public Opinion on Nuclear Power: A Constructionist Approach." *American Journal of Sociology* 95:1–37.

Gitlin, Todd. 1983. *Inside Prime Time.* New York: Pantheon.

Goldberg, Robert. 1991. "TV: Winners That Were Losers." *Wall Street Journal* (June 24), p. A9.

Griswold, Wendy. 1987. "A Methodological Framework for the Sociology of Culture." Pp. 1–35 in *Sociological Methodology 1987,* edited by Clifford C. Clogg. Washington, D.C.: American Sociological Association.

Hirsch, Paul M. 1986. "From Ambushes to Golden Parachutes: Corporate Takeovers as an Instance of Cultural Framing and Institutional Integration." *American Journal of Sociology* 91:800–37.

Jepperson, Ronald L. 1991. "Institutions, Institutional Effects, and Institutionalism." Pp. 143–63 in *The New Institutionalism in Organizational Analysis,* edited by Walter W. Powell and Paul J. DiMaggio. Chicago: University of Chicago Press.

Lowry, Brian. 1991b. "Pilots Lighted for Fall." *Daily Variety* 231 (March 20): 1, 14, 18.

March, James G. and Johan P. Olsen. 1976. *Ambiguity and Choice in Organizations.* Bergen: Universitetsforlaget.

Marich, Robert. 1991. "Networks Suffer 61% Profit Drop in 5-Year Period." *Hollywood Reporter* (May 24), pp. 1, 8.

Meyer, John W. and Brian Rowan. 1977. "Institutionalized Organizations: Formal Structure as Myth and Ceremony." *American Journal of Sociology* 83:340–63.

Montgomery, Kathryn C. 1989. *Target Prime Time: Advocacy Groups and the Struggle over Entertainment Television.* New York: Oxford University Press.

Peterson, Richard A. and David G. Berger. 1975. "Cycles of Symbol Production: The Case of Popular Music." *American Sociological Review* 40:158–73.

Snow, David A. and Robert D. Benford. 1988. "Ideology, Frame Resonance, and Participant Mobilization." Pp. 197–217 in *From Structure to Action: Social Movement Participation across Cultures*, edited by Bert Klandermans, Hanspeter Kriesi, and Sidney Tarrow. Greenwich, CT: JAI Press.

# STUDY QUESTIONS

1. How do Bielby and Bielby define a "frame" and why is it important in this discussion of producing and programming TV?
2. This article was written many years ago. Do you think the television industry has changed since then and if so, how? Have other framing techniques become more prominent?

# 15

# THE ENDURING STRUCTURE OF CIVIL DISCOURSE

JEFFREY C. ALEXANDER AND PHILIP SMITH

The more things change, the more they remain the same. It sounds better in French, but in any language the meaning is clear: history is full of "changes" that on closer inspection don't seem to have altered anything in a fundamental way. This observation applies particularly well to politics. New parties, new leaders, and new promises end up delivering the same set of limited options and familiar constraints. It is almost as if the superficial "changes" allow people, over time, to recognize the deeper, underlying structure. The more frequent the changes, the more quickly individuals discern what remains unchanged.

Jeffrey Alexander and Philip Smith propose a way of looking at the continuities beneath the surface of changes in American politics. They uncover a single set of oppositions that, in their view, have operated as a strong force in structuring political debates and events for more than a century. This durable and influential structure is not the economy, nor is it racial or gender inequality. It is a cultural structure, a system of symbolic codes that organizes meanings, shared definitions, and ways of thinking into what cultural analysts call a *discourse*. This discourse influences human behavior and action in two primary ways: First, individuals internalize these codes, which then become the foundation for personal morality, and second, the codes serve as publicly available yard-sticks by which the actions and behaviors of political leaders (and others) are judged to be moral or immoral. What Alexander and Smith are advancing is a way of looking at culture as a strong, struc-turing force in social life, one that molds itself to current times, and which helps account for the fact that, so often, history repeats itself.

# THE DISCOURSE OF AMERICAN CIVIL SOCIETY: A NEW PROPOSAL FOR CULTURAL STUDIES

## Value Analysis and Its Critics

From the 1940s to the 1960s, "culture" played a fundamental part in social science theory and research. Primarily by employing the concept of "values," sociologists, political scientists, anthropologists, and even psy-chologists continued a modified version of the hermeneutic tradition that Max Weber had introduced into social science.[1]

In the period that followed those early postwar decades, it is fair to say that value analysis, and what was taken to be the "cultural approach" more generally, was forcefully rejected. It was convicted, sometimes more and sometimes less justifiably, of idealism. There were two main dimensions to the accusation. On the one hand it was argued that, in both theoretical and empirical work, values had been accorded an illegitimate primacy over other types of social structures. On the other, it was asserted that value analysis was idealistic in that it failed to heed the complexity and contingency of human action.

These critiques, however, merely led to one-sided approaches in turn. Idealism was defeated at the cost of reductionism, and this time it was culture itself that played the subordinate role. Those sensitive to the fail-ure of value analysis to record the significance of social structure recast culture as an adaptive, if creative and expressive response, to ecological and organizational demands. Meanwhile, those concerned with the problem of action reduced culture to the product of action and interaction or aggregate individual behavior. Social structural and actor-centered understandings of culture remain today the dominant trends in mainstream social science.

We take this movement from culture to social structure and action to be premature: It has solved the problems of value analysis at the expense of a consideration of meaning itself. While the careful correlation of culture with social structure represents a real advance over the more idealistic versions of value analysis, the "new institutionalist"[2] focus on practical action and objectification at the expense of representation and internalization and, more importantly, at the expense of internal symbolic logic and cultural process. While we sometimes find in this work the formal language of codes, myths, narratives, and symbols, we do not find the referents of these terms in a substantive sense. Too often, cultural forms are presented as empty boxes to be filled in by structural needs, with the result that the internal content of representations exercises little explanatory power.

═══════

Bringing contingency and institutional effects back into our understanding of how culture works is a vital task. In achieving this micro-macro link, however, one must not overlook the reality of emergent properties, which demands that the integrity of different levels of analysis be maintained. Neither the importance of attitudes and actions, nor the significance of organization and environment, negates the existence at still another level of a cultural system. The recent approaches to culture have not provided a satisfactory alternative to the value analysis that was discredited decades ago. They have provided for more subjectivity, more organizational responsiveness, more contingency, and sometimes more empirical pay-off in a traditional causal or predictive sense. They have not, however, provided a model that achieves these advances while allowing for a continuing, formative reference to the cultural order.

═══════

## An Alternative Model

Beginning from Parsons's insistence on the merely analytic distinction between culture and social system, we draw upon semiotics and poststructuralism and their elaboration in the new cultural history. We also draw from the hermeneutical tradition, which suggests that meaningful action can be considered as a text,[3] and, of course, from symbolic anthropology. We bind these together in a manner that may, for want of a better term, be understood as late-Durkheimian.[4]

Definitions have an arbitrary quality, but they do have the virtue of offering a place to begin. We would like to propose that culture be thought of as a structure composed of symbolic sets. Symbols are signs that have a generalized status and provide categories for understanding the elements of social, individual and organic life. Although symbols take as referents elements of these other systems, they define and interrelate them in an "arbitrary" manner, that is, in a manner that cannot be deduced from exigencies at these other levels. This is to say that, when they are interrelated, symbols provide a nonmaterial structure. They represent a level of organization that patterns action as surely as structures of a more visible, material kind. They do so by creating patterned order, lines of consistency in human actions. The action of an individual does not create this pattern; at the same time, as we will see, cultural structures do not create the action itself.

We may think of a cultural system as composed of these structures and may think of these structures themselves as being of several different kinds. One important kind of "cultural structure" is the narrative. People, groups, and nations understand their progress through time in terms of stories, plots which have beginnings, middles, and ends, heroes and antiheroes, epiphanies and denouements, dramatic, comic, and tragic forms. This mythical dimension of even the most secular societies has been vastly underestimated in empirical social science and, until recently, in most cultural theory. . . .

As Levi-Strauss and Barthes have suggested, however, beneath narrative there lie structures of a more basic kind which organize concepts and objects into symbolic patterns and convert them into signs.[5] Complex cultural logics of analogy and metaphor, feeding on differences, enable extended codes to be built up from simple binary structures. Because meaning is produced by the internal play of signifiers, the formal autonomy of culture from social structural determination is assured. To paraphrase Saussure in a sociological way, the arbitrary status of a sign means that its meaning is derived not from its social referent—the signified—but from its relation to other symbols, or signifiers within a discursive code. It is only difference that defines meaning, not an ontological or verifiable linkage to extra-symbolic reality. Symbols, then, are located in sets of binary relations. When meaningful action is considered as a text, the cultural life of society can be visualized as a web of intertwining sets of binary relations.

Taking our leave from Foucault, on the one hand, and from Parsons and Durkheim on the other, we assert that signs sets are organized into discourses.[6] These discourses not only communicate information, structuring reality in a cognitive way, but also perform a forceful evaluative task. Binary sets do so when they are charged by the "religious" symbology of the sacred and profane.[7] In this situation, analogies are not simply relations of sterile signs; they set off the good from the bad, the desirable from the detested, the sainted from the demonic. Sacred symbols provide images of purity and they charge those who are committed to them with protecting their referents from harm. Profane symbols embody this harm; they provide images of pollution, identifying actions, groups, and processes that must be defended against.

## The Discourse of American Civil Society

We proceed now to develop this alternative conception of cultural organization in a more substantive form. We describe what might be called the "discourse of civil society." In formulating this ideal-type, we draw upon historical notions of civilization and civility[8] and also upon the tradition of liberal political theory in which democracy is defined by the distinction between the state and an independent, legally-regulated civil order. Because we conceive the goal of civil society to be the moral regulation of social life, it is a concept that lends itself particularly well to our project per se. While any detailed discussion of the structure of civil society is impossible here, it certainly has institutions of its own—parliaments, courts, voluntary associations and the media—through which this regulation is administered. These institutions provide the forum in which crises and problems are resolved. Their decisions are not only binding, but also exemplary. Most important from our perspective, however, is the fact that the institutions of civil society, and their decisions, are informed by a unique set of cultural codes.

These codes, we are convinced, show marked similarities from one national society to another; not only broad pressures of Western cultural history but also the very structures of civil society, and its ability to interpenetrate with other social spheres, mandate a cultural structure that regulates civil life in similar ways. Such a homogeneity of core structures, however, does not preclude substantial and important variations in national form. Every civil society develops in an historically specific way. *Bürgerliche Gesellschaft, société,* and "society" name variations in the relations among state, economy, culture, and community in different national civil societies, just as they can be seen to suggest variations on widely-shared cultural themes. In the present article, we concentrate on only the discourse of civil society in its American form. We concentrate on America for two reasons. First, detailed, thick description tends to be the most persuasive in cultural studies; one must fight against the tendency (tempting in comparative work) for interpretation to engage in a broad brush-stroke portrayal of general themes. Second, America has typically been considered the closest approximation to a democratic nation-state. Here, if anywhere, we would expect to find the discourse of civil society in its most pristine form.

Civil society, at the social structural level, consists of actors, relationships between actors, and institutions. At the very heart of the culture of American civil society is a set of binary codes which discuss and interrelate these three dimensions of social-structural reality in a patterned and coherent way. In the United States, there is a "democratic code" that creates the discourse of liberty. It specifies the characteristics of actors, social relationships and institutions that are appropriate in a democratically functioning society. Its antithesis is a "counter-democratic code" that specifies the same features for an authoritarian society. The presence of two such contrasting codes is no accident: the elements that create the discourse of liberty can signify democracy only by virtue of the presence of antonymic "partners" in an accompanying discourse of repression.

Democratic and counter-democratic codes provide radically divergent models of actors and their motivations. Democratically minded persons are symbolically constructed as rational, reasonable, calm and realistic in their decision making, and are thought to be motivated by conscience and a sense of honor. In contrast, the repressive code posits that anti-democratically minded persons are motivated by pathological greed and self-interest. They are deemed incapable of rational decision making, and conceived of as exhibiting a tendency towards hysterical behavior by virtue of an excitable personality from which unrealistic plans are often born. Whereas the democratic person is characterized by action and autonomy, the counter-democratic person is perceived of as having little free-will, and, if not a leader, as a passive figure who follows the dictates of others.

## The Discursive Structure of Actors

| Democratic Code | Counter-Democratic Code |
| --- | --- |
| Active | Passive |
| Autonomous | Dependent |
| Rational | Irrational |
| Reasonable | Hysterical |
| Calm | Excitable |
| Controlled | Passionate |
| Realistic | Unrealistic |
| Sane | Mad |

Accompanying this discourse on actors and their motivations is another directed to the social relationships that are presumed to follow from such personal needs. The qualities of the democratic personality are constructed as those which permit open, trusting, and straightforward relationships. They encourage critical and reflective, rather than deferential, relations among people. In contrast, counter-democratic persons are associated with secretive, conspirational dealings in which deceit and Machiavellian calculation play a key role. The irrational and essentially dependent character of such persons, however, means that they still tend to be deferential toward authority.

**The Discursive Structure of Social Relationships**

| Democratic Code | Counter-Democratic Code |
| --- | --- |
| Open | Secret |
| Trusting | Suspicious |
| Critical | Deferential |
| Truthful | Deceitful |
| Straightforward | Calculating |
| Citizen | Enemy |

Given the discursive structure of motives and civil relationships, it should not be surprising that the implied homologies and antimonies extend to social, political and economic institutions. Where members of the community are irrational in motivation and distrusting in their social relationships, they will "naturally" create institutions that are arbitrary rather than rule governed, that use brute power rather than law, and that exercise hierarchy over equality. Such institutions will tend to be exclusive rather than inclusive and to promote personal loyalty over impersonal and contractual obligations. They will tend to favor the interests of small factions rather than the needs of the community as a whole.

**The Discursive Structure of Social Institutions**

| Democratic Code | Counter-Democratic Code |
| --- | --- |
| Rule regulated | Arbitrary |
| Law | Power |
| Equality | Hierarchy |
| Inclusive | Exclusive |
| Impersonal | Personal |
| Contractual | Ascriptive |
| Groups | Factions |
| Office | Personality |

The elements in the civil discourses on motives, relationships, and institutions are tied closely together. "Common sense" seems to dictate that certain kinds of motivations are associated with certain kinds of institutions and relationships. After all, it is hard to conceive of a dictator who trusts his minions, is open and honest, and who rigorously follows the law in an attempt to extend equality to all his subjects. The semiologics of the codes, then, associate and bind individual elements on each side of a particular code to the other elements on the same side of the discourse as a whole. "Rule regulated," for example, is considered homologous with "truthful" and "open," terms that define social relationships, and with "reasonable" and "autonomous," elements from the symbolic set that stipulate democratic motives. In the same manner, any element from any set on one side is taken to be antithetical to any element from any set on the other side. Thus, hierarchy is thought to be inimical to "critical" and "open" and also to "active" and "self-controlled."

The formal logic of homology and opposition through which meaning is created, and which we have outlined above, is the guarantor of the autonomy of the cultural codes—despite the fact that they are associated with a particular social-structural domain. However, despite the formal grammars at work in the codes, which turn the arbitrary relationships between the elements into a set of relationships characterized by what Levi-Strauss has termed an "a posteriori necessity," it would be a mistake to conceive of the discourse of civil society as merely an abstract cognitive system of quasi-mathematical relationships. To the contrary, the codes have an evaluative dimension that enables them to play a key role in the determination of political outcomes. In American civil society, the democratic code has a sacred status, whereas the counter-democratic code is considered profane. The elements of the counter-democratic code are dangerous and polluting, held to threaten the sacred center of civil society, which is identified with the democratic code. To protect the center, and the sacred discourse that embodies its symbolic aspirations, the persons, institutions, and objects identified with the profane have to be isolated and marginalized at the boundaries of civil society, and sometimes even destroyed.

It is because of this evaluative dimension that the codes of civil society become critical in determining the outcomes of political processes. Actors are obsessed with sorting out empirical reality and, typifying from code to event, with attributing moral qualities to concrete "facts." Persons, groups, institutions, and communities who consider themselves worthy members of the national community identify themselves with the symbolic elements associated with the sacred side of the divide. Their membership in civil society is morally assured by the homology that they are able to draw between their motives and actions and the sacred elements of the semiotic structure. Indeed, if called upon, members who identify themselves as in good standing in civil society must make all their actions "accountable" in terms of the discourse of liberty. They must also be competent to account for those who are thought to be unworthy of civic membership—who are or should be excluded from it—in terms of the alternative discourse of repression. It is through the concept of accountability that the strategic aspects of action come back into the picture, for differing accounts of actors, relationships and institutions can, if successfully disseminated, have powerful consequences in terms of the allocation of resources and power. Strategically, this dual capacity will typically result in efforts by competing actors to tar each other with the brush of the counter-democratic code, while attempting to shield themselves behind the discourse of democracy. This process is clearest in the courts, where lawyers attempt to sway the opinion of the jury by providing differing accounts of the plaintiffs and defendants in terms of the discourses of civil society.

## A MODERN SCANDAL: THE IRAN-CONTRA AFFAIR

The Iran-Contra affair of the late-1980s provides evidence of the continuing importance of the cultural codes that we have identified as central in the social definition of scandal. . . . In late 1986 information emerged that a small team in the Reagan administration, spearheaded by Lieutenant-Colonel Oliver North, had sold arms to Iran in return for which Iran was to use its influence to obtain the release of American hostages held by various Islamic groups in the Middle-East. As a further twist in the tale, the money raised from the sale was used to support a secret operation in Central America backing the anti-communist "Contra" guerrillas in Nicaragua. Once the action came to light, a process of generalization rapidly occurred in which the motivations, relationships, and institutions of North and his associates became the subject of intense public scrutiny.

The week-long session of the Joint Congressional Inquiry in which North was the key witness is a useful place to examine this cultural process, which centered around dramatically different interpretations by North and his detractors of the same empirical events. Of the greatest importance to those who denounced the affair were the social relationships involved, which they described in terms of the counter-democratic code. The administration officials involved were perceived by their critics as an elite "secret team," operating clandestinely and furthering their own particularistic and illegal aims through a web of lies.

> Foreign policies were created and carried out by a tiny circle of persons, apparently without the involvement of even some of the highest officials of our government. The administration tried to do secretly what the Congress sought to prevent it from doing. The administration did secretly what it claimed to all the world it was not doing.[9]
>
> But I am impressed that policy was driven by a series of lies—lies to the Iranians, lies to the Central Intelligence Agency, lies to the Attorney General, lies to our friends and allies, lies to the Congress, and lies to the American people.[10]
>
> It has been chilling, and, in fact, frightening. I'm not talking just about your part in this, but the entire scenario—about government officials who plotted and conspired, who set up a straw man, a fall guy [North]. Officials who lied, misrepresented and deceived. Officials who planned to superimpose upon our government a layer outside of our government, shrouded in secrecy and only accountable to the conspirators.[11]

Such "conspirators" could not be expected to trust other institutions and persons in government; according to the semiotic foundations of common sense reasoning, they could treat them only as enemies, not as friends. This attitude was understood as antithetical to the democratic ideal.

> Your opening statement made the analogy to a baseball game. You said the playing field here was uneven and the Congress would declare itself the winner. [But we] are not engaged in a game of winners and losers. That approach, if I may say so, is self-serving and ultimately self-defeating. We all lost. The interests of the United States have been damaged by what happened.[12]

These kinds of relationships were taken not only to confound the possibility of open and free political institutions, but they were also perceived as leading to inevitably foolish and self-defeating policies.

A great power cannot base its policy on an untruth without a loss of credibility. . . . In the Middle-East, mutual trust with some friends was dam-
aged, even shattered. The policy of arms for hostages sent a clear message
to the States of the Persian Gulf, and that message was, that the United
States is helping Iran in its war effort, and making an accommodation
with the Iranian revolution, and Iran's neighbors should do the same. The
policy provided the Soviets with an opportunity they have now grasped,
with which we are struggling to deal. The policy achieved none of the
goals it sought. The Ayatollah got his arms, more Americans are held
hostage today than when this policy began, subversion of U.S. interests
throughout the region by Iran continues. Moderates in Iran, if any there
were, did not come forward.[13]

In dealing with attacks on his motives and the relationships in which
he was involved, North used several strategies. At a mundane level he
denied the illegality of his actions, pointing not only to various historical
precedents, but also to the legal justification of the "Hostage Act," which
had given the American executive vast autonomy over policy in recovering American hostages. North also drew upon aspects of the generalized
codes to defend and interpret not only his own actions but those of Congress. First, he argued that while the methods he employed and the relationships he developed could be characterized within the discourse of
repression, they were necessary means in order more effectively to promote the cause of the good. Second, North argued that his own motivations were, in fact, compatible with the discourse of liberty. Finally,
North suggested that it was actually the policies of Congress that could
best be construed in terms of the discourse of repression, not the administration's own.

In defending the secrecy of his operations, and his lies to Congress,
North denied particularistic motivations and drew attention to his higher,
more universal aims. He argued in strongly patriotic terms that secrecy
and lies were necessary in a world threatened by antidemocratic Soviet
power, that dealings with polluted terrorist parties were necessary in order
to protect the purity of American civic life, and that his policies in Central
America had the extension of democracy as their noble aim.

If we could [find] a way to insulate with a bubble over these hearings that
are being broadcast in Moscow, and talk about covert operations to the

American people without it getting into the hands of our adversaries, I'm sure we would do that. But we haven't found the way to do it.[14]

Much has been made of, "How callous could North be, to deal with the very people who killed his fellow Marines?" The fact is we were trying to keep more Marines in places like El Salvador from being killed.[15]

I worked hard on the political military strategy for restoring and sustaining democracy in Central America, and in particular El Salvador. We sought to achieve the democratic outcome in Nicaragua that this administration still supports, which involved keeping the Contras together in both body and soul.[16]

As long as democratically motivated, rational individuals were involved, North argued, counter-democratic methods would be legitimate and safe.

There are certainly times for patience and prudence, and there are certainly times when one has to cut through the tape. And I think the hope is that one can find that there are good and prudent men who are judicious in the application of their understanding of the law, and understanding of what was right. And I think we had that.[17]

With great success North argued that he was just such a man. Public discourse before the trial had portrayed North as a counter-democratic figure. It was argued, on the one hand, that he was a passive zombie blindly following the dictates of his superiors, and on the other that he was a Machiavellian maverick pursuing his own "gung-ho" policies. In the symbolic work of the Hearings, North managed to refute these characterizations, drawing attention to his dynamic patriotism and the autonomy of his White House role, while at the same time demonstrating a sense of his officially regulated position on the White House team.

I did not engage in fantasy that I was President or Vice President or Cabinet member, or even Director of the National Security Council. I was simply a staff member, with a demonstrated ability to get the job done. My authority to act always flowed, I believe, from my superiors. My military training inculcated in me a strong belief in the chain of command. And so far as I can recall, I always acted on major matters with specific approval, after informing my superiors of the facts, as I knew them, the risks, and the potential benefits. I readily admit that I was counted upon as a man who got the job done. . . . There were times when my superiors, confronted with accomplishing goals or difficult tasks, would simply say, "Fix it, Ollie," or "Take care of it."[18]

Although he was a "patriot" who understood his own actions and motivations as informed by the discourse of liberty, North did not feel that the actions of some other Americans could be constituted in the same way. Notably, he asserted that he had been driven to his own actions by a weak and uncertain Congress, which had first decided to support, then to withdraw support from the "Contras." North described this Congressional action as arbitrary and irrational, as a betrayal of persons who were fighting for liberty and against repression in Central America.

> I suggest to you that it is the Congress which must accept at least some of the blame in the Nicaraguan freedom fighters matter. Plain and simple, the Congress is to blame because of the fickle, vacillating, unpredictable, on-again off-again policy toward the Nicaraguan Democratic Resistance—the so called, Contras. I do not believe that the support of the Nicaraguan freedom fighters can be treated as the passage of a budget. . . . [They] are people—living, breathing, young men and women who have had to suffer a desperate struggle for liberty with sporadic and confusing support from the United States of America.[19]

North understood Congress to be repressive not only in its treatment of the Contras, but also in its investigation of himself and his associates. In denying that he would receive a fair hearing North drew attention to what he saw as the arbitrary use of power by Congress, and its deceit in making the executive branch into a scapegoat for its own foolish policies. Far from being the case that he had treated Congress without trust, it was members of the Congressional investigation who had treated him as an enemy, declaring him to be guilty and announcing that they would refuse to believe his testimony even before he had spoken. The actions of the Congressional Committee were threatening to pollute the universal, timeless rules of the American "game."

> You dissect that testimony to find inconsistencies and declare some to be truthful and others to be liars. You make the rulings as to what is proper and what is not proper. You put the testimony which you think is helpful to your goals up before the people and leave others out. It's sort of like a baseball game in which you are both the player and the umpire.[20]

The Congress of the United States left soldiers in the field unsup-
ported and vulnerable to their communist enemies. When the executive
branch did everything possible within the law to prevent them from
being wiped out by Moscow's surrogates in Havana and Managua, you
then had this investigation to blame the problem on the executive branch.
It does not make sense to me.[21]

As a result of rumor and speculation and innuendo, I have been
accused of almost every crime imaginable—wild rumours have abound.[22]

## Conclusions

We do not claim to provide in this article anything approaching a complete
theory of the relationship between culture and behavior. An adequate
account would have to involve a detailed consideration of the psychological, not merely the cultural environment of action, an account of socialization, motivation, and personality that is beyond the scope of our essay. Nor
do we claim to provide here an exhaustive account of the interaction between
culture and social structure. A full investigation of this linkage would
involve the examination of such phenomena as ritualization, the relationship between differing social groups, their typifications and the semiotic
system, and the role of power and resources in mobilizing and changing
typifications according to political and economic interests.

Our aims have been more restricted. We limited ourselves to developing and illustrating a new approach to culture, one that avoids the pitfalls
of reductionism which have characterized most recent theorizing. We
argue that culture should be conceived as a system of symbolic codes
which specify the good and the evil. Conceptualizing culture in this way
allows it causal autonomy—by virtue of its internal semi-logics—and also
affords the possibility for generalizing from and between specific localities
and historical contexts. Yet, at the same time, our formulation allows for
individual action and social-structural factors to be included in the analytical frame. The codes, we have argued, inform action in two ways. Firstly,
they are internalized, and hence provide the foundations for a strong moral
imperative. Secondly, they constitute publicly available resources against
which the actions of particular individual actors are typified and held morally accountable. By acknowledging the importance of phenomenological

processes in channeling symbolic inputs, our model shows that it is precisely these contingent processes that allow codes to make sense in specific situations for specific actors and their interests.

In addition to this claim about action, our model takes account of social structure. We have argued, in theoretical terms, that autonomous cultural codes may be specified to sub-systems and institutions. Their content, we have suggested, reflects and refracts upon the empirical dimensions in which institutions are embedded. Our studies, indeed, provide crucial empirical insights into the relationship between culture and social structure, and more specifically, into the relationship between civil society and the state in American society. They demonstrate that conflicts at the social-structural level need not necessarily be accompanied by divergent values, or "ideologies," at the ideational level. To the contrary, in the American context at least, conflicting parties within the civil society have drawn upon the same symbolic code to formulate their particular understandings and to advance their competing claims.

The very structured quality of this civil culture, and its impressive scope and breadth, help to underscore a paradoxical fact: differences of opinion between contending groups cannot be explained simply as the automatic product of divergent sub-cultures and value sets. In many cases, especially those which respond to new historical conditions, divergent cultural understandings are in part an emergent property of individual and group-level typifications from code to event. This is not to posit a radically individualist theory, but rather to suggest a more interactive conception of the link between cultural and social structures, on the one hand, and the actors, groups, and movements who have to improvise understandings always for "another first time," on the other. Because worthiness can be achieved only by association to the discourse of liberty or by active opposition to the discourse of repression, political legitimacy and political action in the "real world" are critically dependent upon the processes by which contingent events and persons are arrayed in relation to the "imagined" one. In light of these relations among culture, structure, and typification, we can credit the role of political tactics and strategies without falling into the instrumentalist reductions of "institutionalism," on the one hand, or elusive concepts like "structuration" or "habitus" on the other.

Although in this article our studies were drawn from spheres of life that may be considered "political" in a narrow sense, we are confident that the discourses and processes we have discovered provide insights into other domains in which questions of citizenship, inclusion, and exclusion within civil society are at stake. Women and Afro-Americans, for example, were for a long time excluded from full citizenship (and to some extent still are) in part because of a negative coding. In these cases the discourse of motivation was mobilized to identify purported intellectual deficiencies. These deficiencies were variously attributed to a naturally emotive and fickle disposition and to a lack of the education necessary to become an informed and responsible member of the civil society. Similarly, schizophrenics and the mentally ill, to take another example, have long been marginalized on the basis of alleged qualities such as lack of self-control, deficient moral sensibility, or inability to function autonomously, and the lack of a realistic and accurate world view. Since the 1960s their champions have asserted that this view is mistaken. They argue that the mentally ill have a unique insight into the true condition of society. In general this counterattack has used the discourse of institutions and relationships to assault the psychiatric professions and their practices. Take as a final example, during the 1950s in the United States the persecution and marginalization of "communists" was legitimated through a discourse which drew upon the counter-democratic codes of relationships and institutions.

Our studies have established the remarkable durability and continuity of a single culture structure over time, which is able to reproduce itself discursively in various highly contingent contexts. On the basis of this discovery, it seems plausible to suggest that this culture structure must be considered a "necessary cause" in all political events that are subject to the scrutiny of American civil society. The wide-ranging nature of our survey, however, also has distinctive drawbacks, for only by developing a more elaborated case study would we be able to detail the shifts in typifications that allow culture to operate not only as a generalized input but also as an efficient cause. Even if we could show this to be the case, however, we would not wish to suggest that cultural forces are cause enough alone. We merely argue that to understand American politics, one must understand the culture of its civil society, and that the best way to understand that political culture is to understand its symbolic codes.

# Notes

1. Seminal works in the tradition of value analysis include Parsons and Shils, "Values, Motives, and Systems of Action" in *Towards a General Theory of Action* (Cambridge: Harvard University Press, 1951), 47–243; Gabriel Almond and Sidney Verba, *The Civic Culture: Political Attitudes and Democracy in Five Nations* (Princeton, N.J.: Princeton University Press, 1963); Clyde Kluckhohn, "The Evolution of Contemporary American Values," *Daedalus* 87 (1958): 78–109; Floyd Allport, *Theories of Perception and the Concept of Structure* (New York: Wiley, 1955); and Milton Rokeach, *Beliefs, Attitudes and Values: A Theory of Organization and Change* (San Francisco: Josey Bass, 1968), and *The Nature of Human Values* (New York: Free Press, 1973).

2. Cf. Paul DiMaggio and Walter Powell, editors, *The New Institutionalism in Organizational Analysis* (Chicago: University of Chicago Press, 1991), and particularly the editors' introduction.

3. Cf. Paul Ricoeur, "The Model of a Text: Meaningful Action Considered as a Text," *Social Research* 38 (1971): 529–562; Wilhelm Dilthey, "The Construction of the Historical World in the Human Studies," in *Dilthey: Selected Writings* (New York and Cambridge: Cambridge University Press, 1976), 168–245.

4. Cf. Jeffrey C. Alexander, "Three Models of Culture and the Social System" in Alexander, editor, *Durkheimian Sociology: Cultural Studies* (Berkeley: University of California Press, 1989); Philip Smith, "Codes and Conflict: Towards a Theory of War as Ritual," *Theory and Society* 20/1 (1991): 103–138.

5. Claude Levi-Strauss, *The Savage Mind* (Chicago: University of Chicago Press, 1966); Roland Barthes, "Introduction to the Structural Analysis of Narratives" in Barthes, *Image/Music/Text* (London: Fontana, 1977).

6. Michel Foucault, *The Archaeology of Knowledge* (New York: Pantheon, 1972); Talcott Parsons and Edward Shils, *Towards a General Theory of Action*; Émile Durkheim *The Elementary Forms of Religious Life* (New York: Free Press, 1965 [1912]).

7. Mircea Eliade, *The Sacred and the Profane.* (New York: Harper, 1957); Edward Shils, *Center and Periphery: Essays in Macrosociology* (Chicago: University of Chicago Press, 1975).

8. Cf. Norbert Elias, *The Civilizing Process* (New York: Urizen Books, 1978); Sigmund Freud, *Civilization and Its Discontents* (New York: Norton, 1961 [1930]); Edmund Shils, "Primordial, Personal, Sacred, and Civil Ties," in *Center and Periphery*; Michael Walzer, *Obligations: Essays on Disobedience, War, and Citizenship* (Cambridge, Mass.: Harvard University Press, 1970).

9. Chairman Hamilton, in *Taking the Stand: The Testimony of Lieutenant-Colonel Oliver C. North* (New York: Simon and Schuster, 1987), 742.

10. Ibid., 743.
11. Representative Stokes, ibid., 695.
12. Chairman Hamilton, ibid., 745.
13. Chairman Hamilton, ibid., 741.
14. North, ibid., 9.
15. North, ibid., 504.
16. North, ibid., 264.
17. North, ibid., 510.
18. North, ibid., 262–263.
19. North, ibid., 266.
20. North, ibid., 264.
21. North, ibid., 266.
22. North, ibid., 267.

# STUDY QUESTIONS

1. How do the authors define *discourse* and why is this concept important for cultural analysis?
2. How are the cultural codes of American civil discourse applied in the political arena today? Choose a current political issue and discuss how it exemplifies the authors' argument.

# 16

# CULTURAL DIFFUSION

JASON KAUFMAN AND ORLANDO PATTERSON

On February 5, 2012, in a crowded arena in Las Vegas, two professional football teams battled it out for the national championship. It was a bit of a blow-out. The defending champions from Los Angeles soundly defeated their top-ranked opponents from Philadelphia in a 28–6 rout. For the third year in a row, the head coach from Los Angeles joined her players in hoisting the famed Ring of Champions, the glittering trophy cup of the LFL.

What's the LFL? The Lingerie Football League, of course. Billed as "true fantasy football," the league consists of twelve franchises scattered across North America whose teams play 7-on-7 arena football dressed in, well, very little. The sport is weathering the economic recession reasonably well, with Commissioner Mitchell Mortaza announcing plans to launch ten new expansion teams over the next few years. Will the LFL evolve into a serious sport? Or is it a mere novelty, just the latest way to objectify women's bodies for the male gaze, as its many critics charge?

As a cultural sociologist, I don't dare to predict. While we have good studies about how fads become popular over time (several of which are featured in this section of the book), we know much less about how and why some remain fashionable while others become passé. My guess is that in ten years, lingerie football will be history, but I could easily be wrong. To strengthen my prediction, I'd want to make a study of the LFL using cultural diffusion theories—theories that help sociologists make good guesses about how cultural phenomena rise and fall in popularity, status, and esteem.

Kaufman and Patterson, in their influential study of international diffusion, advance a new theory of cultural diffusion based on a detailed examination of cricket. Their careful analysis tracks the spread of cricket through ten regions on five continents over a period of about 300 years, amassing data on whether or not cricket was, by the end of the study, adopted or rejected by the host nation. Their research led them to conclude that current sociological theories of cultural diffusion are inadequate to explain what they found.

# CROSS-NATIONAL CULTURAL DIFFUSION: THE GLOBAL SPREAD OF CRICKET

Why do some foreign practices take rest while others either arrive dead in the water or take hold only to wither and die? Modern diffusion studies have focused primarily on the structural aspects of diffusion, or the existence of tangible points of contact between adopters and adoptees, as well as the environmental contexts that modulate such interactions. But as Strang and Soule (1998:276) note, "[S]tructural opportunities for meaningful contact cannot tell us what sorts of practices are likely to diffuse," whereas an "analysis of the cultural bases of diffusion speaks more directly to what spreads, replacing a theory of connections with a theory of connecting." According to this more culturally minded approach, diffusing practices are most likely to be adopted when they are first made congruent with local cultural frames or understandings, and are thus "rendered salient, familiar and compelling" (Strang and Soule 1998:276; see also Gottdiener 1985; Rogers 1995). In other cases, however, more than just "congruence" is needed for successful adoption; institutional support, repeated exposure, and/or active instruction in the new practice are required for it to "take hold" in new settings. The original cultural profile of that practice is often transformed in the process (e.g., Appadurai 1996; Bhabha 1994; Guillén 2001; Watson 2002). Sometimes, moreover, it is the very difference in social, cultural, and political power between change agents and adopters that accounts for successful long-term diffusion.

One case that encompasses all of these factors is the cross-national diffusion of cricket. Cricket originated in England as an informal rural game, though it quickly emerged into a highly competitive sport. Over time, cricket evolved into an English national pastime, along with soccer, rugby, and horse racing (Allen 1990). Cricket began diffusing to other countries when British soldiers and settlers brought it with them to the various colonies of the empire, and today, most Commonwealth countries support active cricket cultures, though not all.

The case of Canada is particularly striking in this regard. Cricket was popular in Canada and the United States in the mid-nineteenth century—in fact, the first official international cricket match in the world took place between American and Canadian "elevens" in 1844 (Boller 1994a:23). The game's popularity rivaled that of baseball until the late nineteenth century, after which interest declined sharply. The game languished in both countries until quite recently, when new immigrants from the Caribbean and South Asia began arriving in North America in significant numbers (Gunaratnam 1993; Steen 1999). This pattern of adoption-then-rejection poses important substantive and theoretical issues regarding the cross-national diffusion of cultural practices. Given Canada's—and to a lesser degree, America's—demographic, cultural, and sociopolitical connections to Britain, the game's unexpected demise there is puzzling, especially in contrast to its successful diffusion in far less "British" parts of the Commonwealth. At the same time, this disjuncture also seems at odds with several important perspectives in the sociological study of diffusion.

## Situating Cricket in Diffusion Theory

There is widespread agreement that diffusion is the transmission, adoption, and eventual acculturation of an innovation by a recipient population (Coleman, Katz, and Menzel 1966; Rogers 1995; Wejnert 2002; cf. Palloni 2001). Most sociological studies of the diffusion process aim to identify the mechanisms by which an innovation spreads as well as the rate at which it does so in a given population. Although there is now a rich body of important findings about this process, several major problems and gaps still exist.

One major failing of the diffusion literature is the tendency to overlook cases where innovations are transmitted but eventually rejected, as well as cases where adoption might have been expected but did not occur. Palloni (2001: 73–75) highlights two aspects of this problem in his important recent review of the field. First, he notes the common failure to try and account for the persistence of diffused practices in their new surroundings—how and why, in other words, do diffused practices become part of the lived experience of those who have adopted them? Second, he notes the obverse: that after the initial adoption of an innovation, mechanisms might arise that undermine its retention. Palloni (2001:73) adds that, "Despite the fact that this is a key part of a diffusion process, it is rarely mentioned and almost never explicitly modeled or studied." The problem, we suspect, is that many diffusion studies track cultural practices that are not commonly rejected, such as the adoption of new, time-tested medical or agricultural practices. Strang and Soule (1998: 268) observe, for example, that there is "a strong selection bias in diffusion research, where investigators choose ultimately popular [i.e., widely diffused] practices as appropriate candidates for study." Issues such as the persistence and rejection of diffused practices are thus generally overlooked in the literature.

Another shortcoming of diffusion studies is highlighted by Wejnert (2002:299–302), who notes a tendency in the literature to ignore the role of characteristics unique to the practice or thing being diffused. Specific features of the innovation being adopted, such as its potential for replication and change, play an important but often overlooked role in the ultimate success or failure of diffusion. By confining their studies to simple physical objects or cultural routines that are diffused at the micro-social level, diffusion scholars have tended to create advanced formal models that overlook real-world obstacles to diffusion—those posed by the nature, complexity, continuity, and potential mutability of the innovations themselves. Wejnert (2002) also notes the often overlooked distinction between innovations that are diffused at the macro- and micro-social levels. Those involving large collective actors such as countries and industries likely have different consequences and diffusion mechanisms than those that involve mainly individuals or firms.

The dominant "relational" approach to diffusion research in sociology has improved our knowledge of the role of social networks in the transmission of information and ideas (e.g. Buskens and Yamaguchi 1999), but it tends to underspecify the role of social structural factors such as class, status, and power in the adoption or rejection of innovations. In this light, Burt (1987), Marsden and Podolny (1990), and Van don Bulte and Lilien (2001) have revised Coleman, Katz, and Menzel's (1966) classic study of the adoption of a new antibiotic drug among a community of Midwestern doctors, but diffusion research has otherwise largely neglected these topics. It is significant, note Mizruchi and Fein (1999), that sociologists have widely overlooked the role of power in DiMaggio and Powell's (1983) celebrated study of the diffusion of organizational forms. Inequality, in particular, seems to be a neglected subject in the diffusion literature. Rogers (1995:7) makes a distinction between homophilous and heterophilous diffusion processes—that is, those in which the change agents and adopters either share or do not share comparable social positions—but fails to explore the ramifications of the latter situation in detail. As we will see in the case of cricket, status differences and the attendant mechanisms of distancing and inclusion can be decisive variables in explaining the adoption of cross-nationally diffused cultural practices. It will be shown that a top-down, or vertically heterophilous, process of diffusion best explains diffusionary success in some cases.

Some sociologists who work within the institutional framework of diffusion studies have, happily, attempted to address these concerns (see, e.g., Clemens and Cook 1999; Cole 1989; Dobbin and Sutton 1998; Guillén 1994; Lillrank 1995; Meyer and Hannan 1979; Molotch, Freudenberg, and Paulsen 2000; Patterson 1994; Strang 1990; Strang and Meyer, 1993; Starr 1989). While we applaud the temporal and causal acuity of these studies, we think there are further insights to be gained from case studies that explore the cultural and structural complexities of the diffusion process in broad socio-historical terms.

The case study presented here will focus on a Western social practice that is, by any measure, an internally complex cultural entity with powerful symbolic and political consequences (Appadurai 1996; Beckles and Stoddart 1995; Bourdieu 1978; Malcolm 2001; Miller et al. 2001; Nandy 2000; Patterson 1995; Stoddart 1988). It involves cross-national diffusion among large collective entities engaging bread arrays of both practitioners and spectators. It illustrates both the successful diffusion of a politically potent national cultural practice and the potential for such diffusion to be discontinued midstream. Finally, the case of cricket highlights the roles of social structure and "cultural power" in the diffusion process.

We first dispense with several common explanations of the diffusion of cricket, each of which hinges on one or another argument about national culture. Instead, we demonstrate the need to consider four aspects of the adopting countries' social systems that appear to mitigate the potential diffusion of a cultural practice from a "dominant" power to its "subordinates": *social stratification, secondary education, entrepreneurship/network-building,* and *indexical nationalism,* or the frame of reference in which citizens measure their own national accomplishments. Of the four, social stratification seems to have had the most widespread (i.e., generalizable) impact on the global diffusion of cricket, though this occurred at least partially through indirect effects related to the other three. Before explaining any of this in more detail, however, we will enumerate our study population, evaluate evidence relating to the popularity of cricket and other sports in various countries, and outline the criteria by which we measure national sports cultures.

## Cricket's Universe: The Study Population

One reason the global diffusion of cricket is of particular sociological interest is that it is so strongly associated with a specific country of origin. Cricket was first played in England, and since its earliest years, global diffusion of the game has been controlled by Englishmen and their cricket clubs. C.L.R. James (1963:164), the great West Indian social analyst, once wrote, for example, "Cricket was one of the most complete products of that previous age to which a man like Dickens always looked back with such nostalgia. . . . It is the only contribution of the English educational system of the nineteenth century to the general education of Western civilization." Similarly, J. A. Mangan (1986: 153), author of *The Games Ethic and Imperialism,* wrote, "Cricket was the umbilical cord of Empire linking the mother country with her children." Moreover, the game was deliberately "exported" to the British colonies as part of British colonial policy. According to one historian of the game, Brian Stoddart (1988: 658), "Cricket was considered the main vehicle for transferring the appropriate British moral code from the messengers of empire to the local populations."

International cricket has long since been dominated by ten core constituencies, each of which is officially recognized by the International Cricket Council (ICC) as "qualified to play official Test matches." The ICC was founded in England in 1909 and originally comprised just three member countries: England, Australia, and South Africa. (South Africa was expelled from the Commonwealth, and thus the ICC, in 1961 but was reappointed to the ICC as a "full member" nation in 1991.) In 1926, India, New Zealand,

**TABLE 1  The Study Population in Brief**

| Potential Adopter Nations | Key Period of "Populariza-tion" | "Successful" Adopters | "Failed" Adopters | References |
|---|---|---|---|---|
| Australia | 1850s–70s | **** | | Cashman 1998a; Mandle 1973; Pollard 1987 |
| British Caribbean (West Indies) | 1830s–60s | **** | | Beckles 1998a, 1998b; James 1963; Stoddart 1998a |
| Canada | 1860s–90s | | **** | Boller 1994b; Hall and McCulloch 1895; Metcalfe 1987 |
| England | 17th–18th centuries | **** | | Allen 1990; Brookes 1978; Dunning and Sheard 1979; Mandle 1973; Sandiford 1998a |
| India (including Bangladesh & Pakistan) | 1880s–1900s | **** | | Appadurai 1996; Bose 1990; Cashman 1980, 1998b; Nandy 2000 |
| New Zealand | 1860s–90s | **** | | Ryan 1998; Reese 1927 |
| South Africa | 1860s–80s | **** | | Merritt and Nauright 1998; Stoddart 1998b |
| Sri Lanka | 1880s–90s | **** | | Cashman 1998b; Perera 1998, 1999 |

(continued)

**TABLE 1** (continued)

| Potential Adopter Nations | Key Period of "Populariza-tion" | "Successful" Adopters | "Failed" Adopters | References |
|---|---|---|---|---|
| United States | 1860s–90s | | **** | Boller 1994b; Kirsch 1989, 1991; Mrozek 1983 |
| Zimbabwe | 1890s–1900s | **** | | Stoddart 1998; Winch 1983 |

and a conglomeration of British Caribbean islands (the West Indies) were added to the ICC's membership, allowing them to compete in global competition at the highest level. The remaining four full-member nations are Bangladesh, Pakistan, Sri Lanka, and Zimbabwe. These ten countries thus make up what one might view as those parts of the world in which cricket has in fact attained the status of "hegemonic sports culture." Note the conspicuous absence of Canada, itself a major Commonwealth country. The United States is excluded as well. These twelve nations—the world's ten major cricketing countries plus the United States and Canada—constitute the primary set of cases analyzed here (see Table 1).

## Traditional Explanations of the Failure of Cricket in Canada and the United States

In trying to explain the virtual absence of popular interest in cricket in the US and Canada, we encountered several common arguments. The most obvious, having to do with climate, is tempting but ultimately unsatisfactory. True, Canadians are fanatical about ice hockey, a decidedly cold-weather sport; and true, most of the leading cricket-playing nations do not suffer particularly cold winters. On the other hand, Canadians enjoy a wide variety of warm-weather sports, including not only baseball but also field hockey, football, and lacrosse. Furthermore, England, where the game was invented, is hardly a "warm" country itself. Indeed, the game is played there only in the summer season, which is subject to more rain than many parts of Canada. Nor has cricket survived in the more temperate parts of the United States or Canada. Weather, obviously, is not the answer.

Some historians of cricket in the United States have suggested that the sport is not more popular among Americans because it is inconsistent with their cultural worldview (Adelman 1986; Kirsch 1989, 1991). Cricket is a long, slow, tightly regimented game, they argue, whereas Americans are always in a hurry and anxious for results. According to nineteenth-century sportswriter Henry Chadwick (1868:52, quoted in Kirsch 1991:12), for example, "We fast people of America, call cricket slow and tedious; while the leisurely, take-your-time-my-boy people of England think our game of baseball too fast. Each game, however, just suits the people of the two nations." True, cricket matches are generally longer than baseball games; nevertheless, time itself does not appear to be a sufficient explanation. While international test matches can last up to five days, many local matches are only one day in duration. In Australia, for example, an abbreviated "limited overs" version of cricket is popular with television audiences (Cashman 1998a). Anthropologist Arjun Appadurai (1996: 101) even argues that, "Cricket is perfectly suited for television, with its many pauses, its spatial concentration of action, and its extended format. . . . It is the perfect television sport." Moreover, when played by amateurs, among whom wickets fall quickly, the game easily adapts to a spirited afternoon "knock" no longer than amateur soccer or baseball games. Note, too, that such perceptions are as much an effect of the differential status of sports as a cause thereof: Americans' pejorative descriptions of cricket are a product, as well as a cause of, the sport's wider failure to reach "hegemonic" status in the United States.

Similarly, cricket has been described by some as a sport that requires too much submission (i.e., orderly behavior) for Americans. Neither spitting nor swearing are officially condoned on the cricket field, for example, and disagreement with match officials is strictly forbidden.

Nonetheless, while some might criticize Americans for their ungainly habits, this would hardly appear to constitute a satisfactory sociological explanation, particularly when Americans are so attracted to other sports that make similar demands of players, such as tennis and golf. And, even if this is true of Americans, it still leaves the question of Canadian habits unaccounted for. Given the frequency with which one hears Canadians described as modest, well-mannered, and community-minded people (e.g., Frye 1971; Lipset 1996), one would expect cricket to be wildly popular in the Dominion. In fact, a Canadian, James Naismith, invented basketball (in Massachusetts, USA) with these very characteristics in mind: "If men will not be gentlemanly in their play," he said in introducing the game to its first players (Wise 1989:124), "it is our place to encourage them to games that may be played by gentlemen in a manly way, and show them that science is superior to brute force with a disregard for the feelings of others." So why didn't Dr. Naismith merely foist cricket on these "ungentle-manly" young Americans? Such explanations echo, in homely terms, the "cultural understanding" argument of diffusion scholars. We discount such explanations as overly simplistic and, in some cases, patently biased.

———

Despite its stodgy reputation in America, cricket was not originally an aristocratic game. In its earliest incarnation cricket was, in fact, an agrarian pastime for modest farmers and craftsmen. Though historical precedents exist as far back as the twelfth century, English cricket is commonly thought to have come into its own in the seventeenth century (Allen 1990: 16–17; also Brookes 1978; James 1963:164). According to most historical accounts, it was gambling that truly inspired enthusiasm for cricket among England's upper classes (e.g., Allen 1990; James 1963; Sandiford 1994). Country gentlemen found that they could field highly competitive teams by hiring skilled "players" (i.e., professionals) to work on their estates, thus inaugu-rating a long tradition of collaboration between "gentlemen and players," in which elites and commoners played cricket side-by-side (Warner 1950).

At the same time, English elites encouraged their colonial subjects to play cricket because of the game's professed ability to discipline and civi-lize men, English and native alike. . . .

## Adoption Followed by Failed Acculturation: Elite Versus Popular Sports in Canada and the United States

The most distinctive feature of the history of cricket in both the United States and Canada is its elevation to a pastime for elites only. In Canada, for example, cricket "gained a firm foothold among upper-class Canadians who were to perpetuate the game through the private schools. Cricket's longevity and persistence were directly related to its position within the highest levels of Canadian society" (Metcalfe 1987:8). Thus, one key to the rise and fall of Canadian cricket was the changing role of the game in Canada's elite universities and secondary schools . . .

. . . Translating these observations into sociological theory about diffusion failure requires some conjecture but is ultimately rather straightforward. As fewer Canadian elite schools devoted time to training young men in the finer points of cricket, the quantity and quality of play declined. Without fresh infusions of talent or widespread networks of league play, the game gradually took on the air of a marginal, old-fashioned pastime for antiquarians and Anglophiles. . . .

The central feature of the Canadian story is thus the isolation of cricket as a class-specific pastime. The clubby "Britishness" of Canadian elites may be one reason for this split, but the key causal factor remains the exclusivity of the sport, not its association with Britain per se. In looking at Canadian sports history of the late nineteenth and early twentieth centuries, one sees substantial evidence that cricket was an increasingly insular pastime, practiced only by those with the time and money to join exclusive clubs. . . .

## CRICKET IN THE UNITED STATES

The place of cricket in late-nineteenth-century American society could hardly be more different: Though cricket was originally popularized in the United States by working-class immigrants from the British Isles, it later became a sport practiced by only a select few Americans (Melville 1998: 16–17, 25). Note, moreover, that while the increasing popularity of baseball did present a formidable challenge to American cricket, the two games existed comfortably side-by-side throughout the 1850s and 60s. It was not uncommon, in fact, for cricket and baseball teams to challenge one another to matches in their rival's sport (Melville 1998:67). In truth, it was American elites' exclusivist attitude toward cricket that led to the sport's decline among the population at large. As in Canada, American cricket players increasingly retreated to small, elite clubs, and competition with rival "elevens" was quickly restricted to a small coterie of suitable teams (Kirsch 1989:221–22).

Over time, the sport's snooty image took a toll on the popularity of cricket among Americans at large, an image that elites sought to cultivate.

In contrast to the robust English tradition of "gentlemen and players," American cricket clubs strictly forbade professionals from play, even if it meant bitter defeat at the hands of traveling English and Australian teams. Melville (1998: 77; also 120–22) notes that, "As the old-line [American] competitive cricket clubs went into decline, their roles were assumed by cricket organizations dedicated to providing an environment of more socially selective participation upon strictly amateur lines." A 1907 *New York Times* story ("Cricket") quips, "Once more the game of cricket has been shown to be a languishing exotic in New York." It noted, "A visiting team of Englishmen have worked their will upon the local cricketers. . . . In the West, New York is supposed to be the seat and centre of Anglomania. But the West ought to be softened when it sees how very badly New York plays the Anglican national game. Cricketally [sic] speaking, Philadelphia is the Anglomaniacal town." Indeed, with the exception of a few New England college teams, cricket thrived only in Philadelphia by the end of the nineteenth century. As early as 1884, a *New York Times* story ("Philadelphia Cricketers") joked, "Residents of American cities where cricket is not played, except by a few homesick Englishmen, assert that it is played in Philadelphia because cricket is the slowest of games and Philadelphia the slowest of cities."

Regardless of the Philadelphians' supposed motives, it is true that a handful of Philadelphia-based teams provided the bulk of American training and participation in the sport during the late nineteenth and early twentieth centuries. One finds little evidence, furthermore, that the Philadelphians were concerned about the overall decline of interest in American cricket; in fact, they appear to have encouraged it. They confined the game to prestigious country clubs like the Merion and Belmont Cricket Clubs, founded in 1865 and 1874 respectively. Sports historian George Kirsch (1991:15) sums up the Philadelphia scene, and the American milieu more generally, by saying,

> "The upper-class 'Proper Philadelphians' who patronized the sport after the Civil War did not wish to convert the masses. They preferred their leisurely game because they were amateur sportsmen who had plenty of time for recreation. They supported the English game until the early twentieth century, when tennis and golf became more popular amusements for the upper class. Elite Boston cricketers and working-class English immigrants also kept the game going into the 1900s. But by the eve of the First World War very few were still alive who could recall the days when cricket had a chance to become America's national pastime."

Approximately 120 cricket clubs are said to have existed in the Philadelphia area at one time or another, at least ten of which still exist today. One might hypothesize that cricket thrived there in part because of the nature of elite Philadelphian society in the late nineteenth century. Says E. Digby Baltzell, a sociologist who has studied the American elite in detail, "[T]he flowering of New England was the product of an aristocratic social structure led by men with deep roots in the governing class of the society, going back to the glacial age; Philadelphia's Golden Age, on the other hand, was the product of a heterogeneous and democratic social structure whose leadership elites came largely from elsewhere and from all classes within the city" (Baltzell [1979] 1996:54). By our thinking, then, social mobility in Philadelphia might have prompted its "old-money" elite to look for ways to segregate themselves from the city's nouveau riche and upwardly mobile populations. Boston Brahmins had no such cause for status anxiety, given their long-standing dominance of the city's cultural and urban affairs, though they did establish other forms of elite cultural institution in their midst (DiMaggio 1982). Nor were social mobility and status anxiety unique to Philadelphia at this time: Thus, we think that there is a more salient explanation of the Philadelphia-phenomenon in American cricket, one that mirrors the success of American baseball at the national level.

Cricket seems to have survived in Philadelphia primarily because there was a critical mass of clubs ready to field competitive teams. Thus, though comparable numbers of elite men in other cities may have been interested in cricket, they failed to build (elite) cricket leagues that would sustain (elite) interest in the game over time. Put in more formal terms, the Philadelphians created a network "dense" enough to sustain a local cricket culture; they stayed above the "threshold" at which interest in collective pursuits risks extinction (Granovetter and Soong 1983). Haverford College, the University of Pennsylvania, and Princeton University dominated the late-nineteenth-century game largely because of their proximity to the "cricket nurseries" of Philadelphia (Lester 1951), and the former remains a central hub of American cricket to this day—Haverford not only pays a professional cricketer to instruct its current "elevens" but also maintains a special library collection devoted to the history of the sport. Elsewhere in the country (and in Canada), elite clubs failed to create viable leagues and thus faltered. The absence of a strong cricket culture in the notably stratified American South also makes sense in light of this explanation. The rural focus of late-nineteenth-century Southern elites seems to have predisposed them against team sports of any kind. Southern leisure activities were generally more grounded in agrarian pastimes like hunting, fishing, and riding. Only much later, following the rise of large state universities in the South, did team sports like football, basketball, and baseball become mainstays of sporting culture for Southern elites and non-elites alike.

Nonetheless, even with the exception of Philadelphia, it would appear that the popularity of cricket in both the United States and Canada suffered primarily from the exclusionism of its elite practitioners. North American cricket prevailed, though weakly, in places where status anxiety was high among wealthy families and where these families established and maintained multiple dense networks of rival cricket clubs. In both Canada and the United States, an egalitarian ethos encouraged economic elites to cultivate exclusive status-based activities with which to maintain their superior position in the social system. Cricket was not an inevitable response to this status anxiety, but it was one viable option.

At the same time, however, even elite tastes began changing in the early twentieth century. Increasingly, America's wealthiest families "placed maximum importance on the pleasuring of the individual sportsman taken as a consumer, albeit a wealthy one, and on gratification as a suitable goal in his life" (Mrozek 1983: 106). Country clubs, though still popular, increasingly built their reputations on the quality of their clubhouses, tennis tournaments, and golf courses. According to the sporting news of the day, even long-standing cricket clubs began hosting tennis and golf tournaments on their grounds. Cricket was languishing.

The obvious irony here is that elitism spelled the death of a once-popular pastime in two countries known for their exceptional egalitarianism. . . .

## Discussion

### CRICKET AND SOCIOLOGICAL MODELS OF CULTURAL DIFFUSION

Our analysis suggests an important extension of current diffusion theory. It is widely accepted among scholars in the field that diffusion is most likely to succeed where change agents and adoptees share the same culture and social category (especially the same socioeconomic status). Thus Rogers (1995:7) asserts as "an obvious principle of human communication that the transfer of ideas occurs most frequently between two individuals who are similar or homopholous," this being "the degree to which two or more individuals who interact are similar in certain attributes such as beliefs, education, social class, and the like. . . ." Rogers contrasts this with situations where relations are heterophilous (i.e., the social position of the change agent is different from that of the adopters) and notes that this can present a major obstacle to successful diffusion. The ideal situation in the initial adoption phase, he argues, is thus one in which change agents and potential adopters "would be homopholous on all other variables (education and social status, for example) even though they are heterophilous regarding the innovation" (Rogers 1995, 7; for similar views see Strang and Meyer 1993; Wejnert 2002).

We are inclined to agree that homopholous diffusion is indeed true in many, perhaps most, cases, especially those involving the intra-societal transfer of simple innovations among individuals. Our study, however, indicates that there is an important class of diffusion processes in which just the opposite might occur—i.e., cases in which a distinctly heterophilous relationship between change agents and would-be change-adopters promotes diffusion. In the case of cricket, it is precisely the stable status-inequality between those who brought the game from England and the lower-status colonial populations that adopted it that accounts for the successful diffusion of cricket. In such cases (i.e., top-down, or heterophilous, diffusion), it is the authority and high social status of change agents, combined with their willingness not simply to transmit but actively to participate in the promotion of the innovation, *and* their desire to continue their engagement with it even after it has begun to spread down and across the social hierarchy, that accounts for successful diffusion.

As shown in the case of cricket, all three elements are necessary for this kind of top-down diffusion to work: It is not enough for elites simply to introduce the innovation; they are required to promote it actively and to persist in lending it their prestige by continuing to practice it themselves. Where they do not, one of two outcomes, both fatal for the long-term acculturation of the innovation, is likely: One possibility is that the innovation becomes a fad, thereby enjoying a brief period of widespread popularity because of its upper-class origins, but later being abandoned by the elite transmitters because of this very popularity, thereby triggering a decline in overall popularity. The history of fashion is replete with examples of this (e.g., Crane 2000). Another possible "negative" outcome is that status-insecure first-adopters "capture" the innovation, thus preventing its diffusion into the population at large. Precisely this happened to cricket in Canada and the United States, as we have seen.

Naturally, the nature of social stratification in these Commonwealth countries is not sufficient to explain the success or failure of cricket in each country; nor does it fully explain the failed cases of Canada and the United States. Our earlier discussion of the rising popularity of baseball in the United States offers several keys to refining our explanation. Baseball was aggressively promoted throughout the United States by league-owners, sporting goods manufacturers, and "star" players. Inter-urban play helped promote widespread audiences. Youths were encouraged to play in and out of school, and the necessary equipment and playing grounds were made widely available. Similar efforts were made for football and basketball in the United States, and for cricket throughout much of the Commonwealth. Cross-class participation in such sports was supplemented, in other words, by intense efforts to recruit spectators, as well as new talent, to the games. At some point, such self-promotion seems to cross a threshold at which the game's popularity fuels itself: baseball was so popular and baseball rivalries so intense that even American elites flocked to it, thus leaving cricket virtually no following whatsoever. Absent celebrity players and careful marketing, crew and track and field, in contrast, lost momentum and popularity among American audiences.

The lessons here are rather simple: On the supply side, would-be audiences must be offered a steady stream of well-publicized events between evenly matched, talented teams. Annual matches, such as Thanksgiving Day college football games or "The Ashes," a biennial cricket match between England and Australia, help solidify a sport's place in the public mind (cf. Schudson 1989). On the demand side, a surfeit of opportunities whereby talented athletes can find selective incentives to devote time and effort to one sport over another also appears to make a difference. Such factors, it should be noted, can also erode support for a sport even after it has been successfully adopted. The popularity of professional rugby in the Antipodes, for example, and the spread of basketball to the Caribbean, both potentially represent threats to their nations' hegemonic cricket cultures.

The evolution of the game in each country, then, is the result not only of the relative status position of interested parties but also such intangibles as the rise of sports entrepreneurs devoted to the promotion of a specific sport; the rise of competitive league play, which helps draw regular "fans" from different strata of society; and the rise (or demise) of other seasonal sports competing for the same talent and audience base. Nonetheless, we feel that of these multiple factors, it is social stratification that lies most fundamentally at the heart of the matter. The extent to which an elite cultural practice like cricket was shared with or shielded from the general population was a direct result of elites' own sense of their place atop the social hierarchy. Had American elite cricketers felt less anxious about their social position, for example, they might have popularized the sport along the same lines as baseball (or golf and tennis).

# References

Adelman, Melvin L. 1986. *A Sporting Time: New York City and the Rise of Modern Athletics, 1820–1870.* Urbana, IL: University of Illinois Press.

Allen, David Rayvern. 1990. *Cricket: An Illustrated History.* Oxford, England: Phaidon Press.

Appadurai, Arjun. 1996. *Modernity at Large: Cultural Dimensions of Globalization.* Minneapolis, MN: University of Minnesota Press.

Baltzell, E. Digby. [1979] 1996. *Puritan Boston and Quaker Philadelphia.* New Brunswick, NJ: Transaction Publishers.

Beckles, Hilary McD. 1998a. *The Development of West Indies Cricket, vol. 1, The Age of Nationalism.* Barbados: Press of the University of the West Indies.

———. ed. 1998b. *A Spirit of Dominance: Cricket and Nationalism in the West Indies.* Barbados: Canoe Press.

Beckles, Hilary McD and Brian Stoddart, eds. 1995. *Liberation Cricket: West Indies Cricket Culture.* Manchester, England: Manchester University Press.

Bhabha, Homi. 1994. *The Location of Culture.* London, England: Routledge Press.

Boller, Kevin. 1994a. "International Cricket: Launched by a Hoax." *The Canadian Cricketer* 22:23.

———. 1994b. "The 49th Parallel Divide: The Story of Canada and the United States at Cricket." *The Canadian Cricketer* 22:24–25.

Bose, Mihir. 1990. *A History of Indian Cricket.* London, England: Deutsch.

Bourdieu, Pierre. 1978. "Sport and Social Class." *Social Science Information* 17:819–40.

Brookes, Christopher. 1978. *English Cricket: The Game and Its Players Throughout the Ages.* London, England: Weidenfeld and Nicholson.

Burt, Ronald. 1987. "Social Contagion and Innovation: Cohesion vs. Structural Equivalence." *American Journal of Sociology* 92:1287–335.

Buskens, Vincent and Kazuo Yamaguchi. 1999. "A New Model for Information Diffusion in Heterogeneous Social Networks." *Sociological Methodology* 29:281–325.

Cashman, Richard. 1980. *Patrons, Players, and the Crowd: The Phenomenon of Indian Cricket*. New Delhi, India: Orient Longman.

———. 1998a. "Australia." *The Imperial Game: Cricket, Culture and Society*, edited by Brian Stoddart and Keith A. P. Sandiford. Manchester, England: Manchester University Press.

———. 1998b. "The Subcontinent." *The Imperial Game: Cricket, Culture, and Society*, edited by Brian Stoddart and Keith A. P. Sandiford. Manchester, England: Manchester University Press.

Chadwick, Henry. 1868. *American Chronicle of Sports and Pastimes* 1:52.

Clemens, Elisabeth S. and James M. Cook. 1999. "Politics and Institutionalism: Explaining Durability and Change." *Annual Review of Sociology* 25:441–66.

Cole, Robert E. 1989. *Strategies for Learning: Small-Group Activities in American, Japanese, and Swedish Industry*. Berkeley, CA: University of California Press.

Coleman, James S., Elihu Katz, and Herbert Menzel. 1966. *Medical Innovation: A Diffusion Study*. Indianapolis, IN: Bobbs-Merrill.

Crane, Diana. 2000. *Fashion and Its Social Agendas! Class, Gender, and Identity in Clothing*. Chicago, IL: University of Chicago Press.

"Cricket" 1907. *New York Times*, Sept. 21.

DiMaggio, Paul J. 1982. "Cultural Entrepreneurship in Nineteenth-Century Boston." *Media, Culture, and Society* 4:33–50.

DiMaggio, Paul J. and Walter W. Powell. 1983. "The Iron Cage Revisited: Institutional Isomorphism and Collective Rationality in Organizational Fields." *American Sociological Review* 48:147–60.

Dobbin, Frank and John R. Sutton. 1998. "The Strength of a Weak State: The Rights Revolution and the Rise of Human Resources Management Divisions." *American Journal of Sociology* 104:441–76.

Dunning, Eric and Kenneth Sheard, 1979. *Barbarians, Gentlemen and Players: A Sociological Study of the Development of Rugby Football*. New York: New York University Press.

Frye, Northrop. 1971. *The Bush Garden: Essays on the Canadian Imagination*. Toronto, Canada: Anansi.

Gottdiener, M. 1985. "Hegemony and Mass Culture: A Semiotic Approach." *American Journal of Sociology* 90:979–1001.

Granovetter, Mark and Roland Soong. 1983. "Threshold Models of Diffusion and Collective Behavior." *Journal of Mathematical Sociology* 9:165–79.

Guillén, Mauro F. 1994. *Models of Management: Work, Authority, and Organization in a Comparative Perspective*. Chicago, IL: University of Chicago Press.

———. 2001. *The Limits of Convergence: Globalization and Organizational Change in Argentina, South Korea, and Spain.* Princeton, NJ: Princeton University Press.

Gunaratnam, Visva, 1993. "I Have a Dream." *The Canadian Cricketer* 21:11.

Hall, John E. and R. O. McCulloch. 1895. *Sixty Years of Canadian Cricket.* Toronto, Canada: Bryant.

James, C.L.R. 1963. *Beyond a Boundary.* London, England: Hutchinson.

Kirsch, George. 1991. "Massachusetts Baseball and Cricket, 1840–1870." Pp. 1–15 in *Sports in Massachusetts: Historical Essays,* edited by Ronald Story. Westfield, MA: Institute for Massachusetts Studies, Westfield State College.

———. 1989. *The Creation of American Team Sports: Baseball and Cricket, 1838–72.* Urbana, IL: University of Illinois Press.

Lester, John A., ed. 1951. *A Century of Philadelphia Cricket.* Philadelphia, PA: University of Pennsylvania Press.

Lillrank, Paul. 1995. "The Transfer of Management Innovations from Japan." *Organization Studies* 16:971–89.

Lipset, Seymour Martin. 1996. *American Exceptionalism: A Double-Edged Sword.* New York: Norton.

Malcolm, Dominic. 2001. "'It's Not Cricket': Colonial Legacies and Contemporary Inequalities." *Journal of Historical Sociology* 14:253–75.

Mandle, W. F. 1973. "Games People Played: Cricket and Football in England and Victoria in the Late Nineteenth Century." *Historical Studies* 15(60): 511–535.

Mangan, J. A. 1986. *The Games Ethic and Imperialism: Aspects of the Diffusion of an Ideal.* London, England: Frank Cass.

Marsden, Peter and Joel Podolny. 1990. "Dynamic Analysis of Network Diffusion Processes." *Social Networks Through Time,* edited by J. Weesie and H. Flap. Utrecht, Netherlands: ISOR.

Melville, Tom. 1998. *The Tented Field: A History of Cricket in America.* Bowling Green, IN: Bowling Green State University Popular Press.

Merrett, Christopher and John Nauright. 1998. "South Africa." Pp. 55–78 in *The Imperial Game: Cricket, Culture and Society,* edited by Brian Stoddart and Keith A. P. Sandiford. Manchester, England: Manchester University Press.

Metcalfe, Alan. 1987. *Canada Learns to Play: The Emergence of Organized Sport 1807–1914.* Toronto, Canada: McClelland and Stewart.

Meyer, John and Michael Hannan, eds. 1979. *National Development and the World System: Educational, Economic and Political Change, 1950–1970.* Chicago, IL: University of Chicago Press.

Miller, Toby, Geoffrey Lawrence, Jim McKay, and David Rowe. 2001. *Globalization and Sport,* London, England: Sage Publications.

Mizruchi, Mark S. and Lisa C. Fein. 1999. "The Social Construction of Organizational Knowledge: A Study of the Uses of Coercive, Mimetic, and Normative Isomorphism." *Administrative Science Quarterly* 44: 653–83.

Molotch, Harvey, William Freudenburg, and Krista E. Paulsen. 2000. "History Repeats Itself, but How? City Character, Urban Tradition, and the Accomplishment of Place." *American Sociological Review* 65:791–823.

Mrozek, Donald J. 1983. *Sport and American Mentality 1880–1910.* Knoxville, TN: University of Tennessee Press.

Nandy, Ashis. 2000. *The Tao of Cricket: On Games of Destiny and Destiny of Games.* New Delhi, India: Oxford University Press.

Palloni, Alberto. 2001. "Diffusion in Sociological Analysis." Pp. 67–114 in *Diffusion Processes and Fertility Transition: Selected Perspectives,* edited by John B. Casterline. Washington D.C.: National Academy Press.

Patterson, Orlando. 1994. "Ecumenical America: Global Culture and the American Cosmos." *World Policy Journal* 11:103–17.

———. 1995. "The Ritual of Cricket." Pp. 141–47 in *Liberation Cricket.* edited by Hilary McD Beckles and Brian Steddart. Kingston, Jamaica: Ian Randle Publishers.

Perera, S. S. 1998a. *The Janashakthi Book of Sri Lanka Cricket, 1832–1996.* Colombo: Janashakthi Insurance.

———. 1998b. "Notes on Sri Lanka's Cricket Heritage." *Crosscurrents: Sri Lanka and Australia at Cricket,* edited by Michael Roberts and Alfred James. Petersham, Australia: Walla Walla Press.

"The Philadelphia Cricketers." 1884. *New York Times,* July 15.

Pollard, Jack. 1987. *The Formative Years of Australian Cricket, 1803–1893.* North Ryde, Australia: Angus and Robertson.

Reese, T. W. 1927. *New Zealand Cricket, 1814–1914.* Christchurch, New Zealand: Simpson and Williams.

Rogers, Everett M. 1995. *Diffusion of Innovations.* 4th ed. New York: Free Press.

Ryan, Greg, 1998. "New Zealand." Pp. 93–115 in *The Imperial Game: Cricket, Culture and Society,* edited by Brian Stoddart and Keith A. P. Sandiford. Manchester, England: Manchester University Press.

Sandiford, Keith A. P. 1998a. "England." Pp. 9–33 in *The Imperial Game: Cricket, Culture and Society,* edited by Brian Stoddart and Keith A. P. Sandiford. Manchester, England: Manchester University Press.

———. 1994. *Cricket and the Victorians.* Alderahot, England: Scholar Press.

Schudson, Michael. 1989. "How Culture Works: Perspectives from Media Studies on the Efficacy of Symbols." *Theory and Society* 18:153–80.

Starr, Paul. 1989. "The Meaning of Privatization." Pp. 15–48 in *Privatization and the Welfare State,* edited by Sheila Kamerman and Alfred Kahn. Princeton, NJ: Princeton University Press.

Steen, Rob. 1999. *The Official Companion to the 1999 Cricket World Cup.* London: Boxtree.

Stoddart, Brian. 1988. "Sport, Cultural Imperialism, and Colonial Response in the British Empire." *Comparative Studies in Society and History* 30:649–73.

———. 1998a. "West Indies." *The Imperial Game: Cricket, Culture, and Society*, edited by Brian Stoddart and Keith A. P. Sandiford. Manchester, England: Manchester University Press.

———. 1998b. "Other Cultures." *The Imperial Game: Cricket, Culture and Society*, edited by Brian Stoddart and Keith A. P. Sandiford. Manchester, England: Manchester University Press.

Strang, David. 1990. "Form Dependency to Sovereignty: An Event History Analysis of Decolonization 1870–1987." *American Sociological Review* 55: 846–60.

Strang, David and John Meyer. 1993. "Institutional Conditions for Diffusion." *Theory and Society* 22:487–511.

Strang, David and Sarah Soule. 1998. "Diffusion in Organizations and Social Movements: From Hybrid Corn to Poison Pills." *Annual Review of Sociology* 24:265–90.

Van den Bulte, Christophe and Gary L. Lilien. 2001. "Medical Innovation Revisited: Social Contagion versus Marketing Effort." *American Journal of Sociology* 106:1409–35.

Warner, Sir Pelham. 1950. *Gentlemen v. Players, 1806–1949*. London: George G. Harrap.

Watson, James L. 2002. "Transnationalism, Localization, and Fast Foods in East Asia." Pp. 222–32 *McDonaldization: The Reader*, edited by George Ritzer. Thousand Oaks, CA: Pine Forge Press.

Wejnert, Barbara. 2002. "Integrating Models of Diffusion of Innovations: A Conceptual Framework." *Annual Review of Sociology* 28:297–326.

Winch, Jonty. 1983. *Cricket's Rich Heritage: A History of Rhodesian and Zimbabwean Cricket, 1890–1982*. (Bulawayo, Zimbabwe: Books of Zimbabwe).

Wise, S. F. 1989. "Sport and Class Values in Old Ontario and Quebec." Pp. 107–129 in *Sports in Canada: Historical Readings*, edited by Morris Mett. Toronto, Canada: Copp, Clark, Pitman.

# STUDY QUESTIONS

1. What two key factors help explain why cricket did not take hold in the United States and Canada, as it did in other countries with close ties to England?
2. Explain what the authors mean by the term *cultural entrepreneur.*

# 17

# CHANGING MUSICAL STYLES

JENNIFER C. LENA AND RICHARD A. PETERSON

Are you a fan of goth music? Emo? Screamo? If not, maybe you prefer shoegazer rock, or alt-country, or some other spin-off indie-rock
sound? None of the above, you say? Well, then how about grindcore
or speed metal? No? Maybe crunk? Hip-hop? Everybody likes hip-
hop, right?

We live in a world with dozens of contemporary musical genres
and scores upon scores of older forms that continue to inspire loyal
fans. What shapes our musical preferences is a combination of factors: the preferences of family, friends, and social circles; the different live music scenes to which we've been exposed; whatever is on
our local radio stations; and of course, the music industry—that vast
conglomeration of organizations and individuals that cooperate and
compete to turn our love of music into profits for companies and
artists.

Cultural sociologists have studied how musical styles emerge over
time and have tried to understand the processes of cultural production at work. In the following reading, Jennifer Lena and Richard
"Pete" Peterson (1933–2010) note that one of the more important
factors at work is the different cultural meanings expressed in different styles or genres of music. For sociologists, a musical genre refers
to a style of creative expression that unites musicians, their peers,
and their audiences, providing a kind of cohesion that ties together
artist, sound, and fan.

**Lena and Peterson use the notion of genre to track how new musics emerge and evolve. They describe common trajectories for musical styles, with some originating among avant-garde musicians, others in local music scenes, and others still in the corporate music industry. They trace the common pathways taken by 60 different musical genres in order to propose some new theories about how and why musical forms change over time.**

# CLASSIFICATION AS CULTURE: TYPES AND TRAJECTORIES OF MUSIC GENRES

Since its advent as a discipline, sociology has generated systems of sociocultural classification for a diverse set of phenomena, including forms of organization religious belief, fashion, gender, sexuality, art, race, and societies at large, to name but a few. The sociological concern with systemic change is venerable yet, as DiMaggio (1987) notes, there is no theory of the dynamic change in classificatory schemes, although efforts have been made in domains such as nation building (Anderson 1983), social movements (Traugott 1995), name-giving practices (Lieberson 2000), and French cuisine (Ferguson 2004). Analyses of such classificatory schemes, however, often relegate the cultural meanings of these categories to a secondary feature of the system. In contrast, the use of the concept of *genre* places cultural meaning at the forefront of any analysis of category construction and has potential and significant general utility across domains.

Genre is a conceptual tool most often used to classify varieties of cultural products, particularly in the fields of visual art, popular culture, video games, film, literature, and music. It describes a manner of expression that governs artists' work, their peer groups, and the audiences for their work (Becker 1982; Bourdieu 1993). In this article, we build on the theoretical and conceptual use of genre to better understand the dynamics of symbolic classification and change in order to identify recurrent sociocultural forms of music genres. To date, no one has published a systematic analysis of the characteristic forms that music-making communities take or how they change over time. Instead, historical surveys of popular music focus attention on charismatic performers, analyze works within the canon, and identify cultural factors that promote the growth of music genres (e.g., Garofalo 2002; Toynbee 2000). In addition, hundreds of social scientists have studied the structure of particular popular-music communities and the social contexts that shape them. We carefully examine these studies to find uniformities in the forms of music genres and regularities in their trajectories. We also identify the developmental sequences of these genres, rather than focus on the mechanisms that cause genres to transition from one form to the next. Although we examine the case of music genres in the twentieth-century United States in particular, our method of social and cultural analysis offers a more general sociological framework—a framework potentially applicable to all manner of phenomena where individuals and groups construct cultural boundaries. We conclude with a discussion of these more general implications.

## The Genre Idea

Genre organizes the production and consumption of cultural material including organizational procedures (Ahlkvist and Faulkner 2002; Ballard, Dodson, and Bazzini 1999; Becker 1982; Bielby and Bielby 1994; Griswold 1987; Hirsch 1972; Negus 1999), and influences tastes and the larger structures of stratification in which they are embedded (Bourdieu 1993, 1995; Lizardo 2006). Recently, organizational ecologists have deployed genre to understand the competitive success and restructuring of organizations (Hsu 2006; Hsu and Hannan 2006).

There are two dominant approaches to the study of genre. In the first, humanities scholars typically focus attention on the "text" of a cultural object, which is abstracted from the context in which it is made or consumed (Apperley 2006; Devitt 2004; Fowler 1982; Frow 2006; Hyon 1996; Swales 1990; C. Williams 2006). Most musicologists employ this textual approach to identify genre as a set of pieces of music that share a distinctive musical language (van der Merwe 1989). Some sociologists employ the use of genre-as-text, but they are careful to show how genre is influenced by the context in which it is made and consumed.[1]

1. Dowd (1992) shows the societal influences on the musicological structure of popular music, and Cerulo (1995) shows how national anthems mirror the societal contexts within which they are created. Other lines of work use genre without problematizing its content or development (Bourdieu 1984; Peterson and Kern 1996).

The second dominant approach defocalizes text and places the study of genre squarely in a social context. Some analysts apply the term to general marketing categories such as pop, classical, country, urban, and jazz (Negus 1999). Most studies of taste that analyze survey data to examine how groups of consumers use available genres to express their social identity or status (e.g., Mark 1998) look at very inclusive genres (e.g., rock, MOR, or classical), closer to Ennis's (1992) "streams" or Bourdieu's (1993) "fields." Others use the terms subculture (Thornton 1996), scene (Bennett 1997), or neo-tribe (Maffesoli 1996) in ways cognate with the meaning of genre here.

Alternatively, others highlight the set of cultural practices (Becker 1982) that a music community defines as a genre and view its texts as the product of social interactions in a specific sociocultural context (Frith 1996). This approach is found in Peterson's (1997) study of the creation of country music, as well as DeVeaux (1997) on bebop jazz, Garland (1970) on soul, Bennett (2004) on the Canterbury sound, Cantwell (1984) on bluegrass, and Kahn-Harris (2007) on the European varieties of heavy metal rock. Following these studies, and paraphrasing Neale's (1980:19) definition of genre in film, we define music genres as systems of orientations, expectations, and conventions that bind together an industry, performers, critics, and fans in making what they identify as a distinctive sort of music.

Given this definition, genres are numerous and boundary work is ongoing as genres emerge, evolve, and disappear (Lamont and Molnár 2002). Musicians often do not want to be confined by genre boundaries, but, as Becker (1982) notes, their freedom of expression is necessarily bounded by the expectations of other performers, audience members, critics, and the diverse others whose work is necessary to making, distributing, and consuming symbolic goods.[2] Walser (1993:4) provides an example of such boundary work: "'Heavy metal' is a term that is constantly debated and contested, primarily among fans, but also in dialogue with musicians, commercial marketing strategists, and outside critics and censors. Debates over which bands, which songs, sounds and sights get to count as heavy metal provide occasions for contesting musical and social prestige." These debates not only sort bands

---

2. "Free music" is an interesting limiting case because, as Toynbee (2000) notes, although its practitioners say that what they play is guided by the dictates of the musical sounds of the moment, and not by the expectations of other players, audiences, or critics, they nonetheless play within conventions well understood by progressive jazz musicians (Attali 1985; Lewis 1996).

and songs into groups, but they also distinguish individuals who are aware of current distinctions from those who are outsiders or hapless pretenders.

———

# Research Methods

This article builds on two prior works in which we closely examined the features of four twentieth-century U.S. musics that seemed to experience a complete developmental trajectory (Lena and Peterson 2006, 2007). We selected grunge from the rock stream, rap from the R&B stream, bebop from the jazz stream, and bluegrass from the country music stream. We then read extensively in the academic and popular press about each.

We found that over time each music took on different forms that were roughly comparable across the musics examined. We designate these as Avant-garde, Scene-based, Industry-based, and Traditionalist genre forms. Finally, we discovered that over the course of its history, each of these music communities began as an Avant-garde genre, became Scene-based, then Industry-based, and finally Traditionalist, a trajectory we abbreviate as AgSIT.

We chose the four cases in our initial analyses for their musical differences from each other and for the wealth of secondary material available on their histories. We did not choose them for their representativeness of a larger class of musics, nor for differences in their trajectories of growth. The strong similarities in the developmental patterns of the four musics led us to seek out a large set of musics that might not fit this trajectory. To bound our search we limited our study to genres established in the United States during the twentieth century. Because genre boundaries are contested and fluid, and no one has attempted to exhaustively and continually document all the music genres in the United States, it proved impossible to find a definitive universe of musics from which to choose a representative sample. Accordingly, we began with Ennis's (1992) list of music streams, which includes rock-n-roll, pop, Black pop, country pop, jazz, folk, and gospel. Ennis (1992) identified streams as such because each had distinctive institutional structures, aesthetics, and symbolic identities. His model is a good sociological examination of the popular music field, but it is dated. To include new kinds of U.S. music, we added musics that do not fit neatly into one of these seven streams.

Critics, fans, and music promoters regularly invent genre terms, but many of these are not widely used in the relevant music community. To form a set of genres, we consulted reference works and music-related magazines to find terms commonly in use. Because we needed enough information to make judgments about the forms and histories of genres, we limited our focus to musics for which we could find at least two reliable sources. Working independently, we coded types of music genres and then discussed them until we had agreement on the proper coding. We coded several hundred books and articles to get reliable data on 60 genres. We do not claim that these genres comprise a representative sample of all genres in the twentieth-century United States. We do, however, argue that the sample is sufficiently large, and the genres sampled sufficiently diverse, to illuminate patterns in genre forms and trajectories.

Based on the four preliminary case studies, the current analysis is designed to answer two questions: What are the attributes that organize musics into genres, and how are these genres organized into developmental trajectories? Our design is inductive, so our goal is to generate theory, not test it.

## Genre Forms and Attributes

Are the genre forms Avant-garde, Scene-based, Industry-based, and Traditionalist adequate to describe all the musics in our sample of 60 genres? We find that (1) all of the musics evince at least one of these genre forms, (2) with the exception of Scene-based genres, each of the genre forms is missing in some of the musics, and (3) none of the musics have genre forms other than these four.

To be sure that we examined all the relevant attributes of genres in each of the 60 sample genres, we created and iteratively refined a conceptual template to classify each of the 60 musics. Table 1 shows this template, with the four genre types represented in the columns. Each of the 12 rows represents a *dimension* common to all sample genres, and each cell represents the specific *attributes* characteristic of a genre type. So, for example, in the upper-left corner cell, "creative circle" is the representative organizational form of Avant-garde genres.

The entries in each column of Table 1 represent an ideal-typical construction of a genre type; they do not operate like entries in the periodic table of elements or the genetically-based taxonomies in biology. This is because each specific attribute is not both necessary and sufficient to code a music as a particular genre. This table of attributes should therefore be considered a conceptual tool for understanding genre. By making more detailed distinctions among attributes, it would be possible to create more than four genre types. However, the four–genre type by twelve-dimension resolution is the most parsimonious.

The first three dimensions in Table 1 identify the prototypical organizational form, scale, and locus of activity for genres. Genre ideal is the vision of the music held by those most involved in the genre, including the fundamental values they see embodied in the music. The next dimension describes the degree to which performance conventions are codified and the form of such conventions. These vary widely from being very open and experimental to rigidly codified. Technological features of music making, distribution, and enjoyment do much to constrain genre development, and changes in these features often augur the emergence of new genres. Through boundary work, genre members identify who is a member of a genre community and who is beyond its pale by cultivating distinctive dress, adornment, drug use, and argot.[3] The sources of income to artists and the amount and kind of press coverage a genre receives largely reflect the organizational form, locus, and goals of the genre. These factors are of specific interest to scholars working at the intersection of political economy, urban social dynamics, and cultural production. Finally, the source of a genre name can be used to distinguish genre types and reveal processes of collective memory and discursive structures that link nomenclature to genre forms. In the remainder of this section, we consider the attributes of each of the four genre types, starting with the Avant-garde.

## AVANT-GARDE GENRES

Avant-garde genres are quite small, having no more than a dozen participants who meet informally and irregularly. Borrowing a term from fine arts, we call such creative groups "circles." Circles are leaderless, fractious, and typically unravel in a matter of months from lack of recognition or because a subset of the participants gains wider recognition. These genres form around members' shared dislike of some aspect of the music of the day and the quest for music that is different. Members play together informally

---

3. There is not always a direct correspondence between different "styles" and musical difference; some argue that riot grrrl, straight edge, anarcho-punk, and White power music are differentiated by political and philosophical, not musical, distinctiveness (Schilt 2004; P. Williams 2006).

in an effort to create a genre ideal for the group. This ideal, and specifically the musical ideas that are central to it, may emerge from members taking lessons, carefully listening to records, and playing with different kinds of musicians. Alternatively, avant-gardists may assert that prevailing genres are predictable and emotionless and, flaunting the fact that they cannot play instruments in conventional ways, make what others consider loud and harsh sounds. This was the experience of both the thrash metal and punk Avant-garde genres (Kahn-Harris 2007; McNeil and McCain 1996). In crafting music that is "new," avant-gardists may combine elements of genres that are usually treated as distinct. Bauck (1997:232), for example, describes how Avant-garde grunge melded different genres together: "Grunge contained the energy, volume and distortion of hardcore punk, but was generally played at a far slower tempo. While borrowing the melodic lines and hooks of heavy metal, grunge left behind the macho posturing and gratuitous guitar solos."

The desire to produce a new music drives groups to engage in experimental practices, including playing standard instruments in unconventional ways, creating new musical instruments, and modifying objects that have not previously been used in the production of music. For example, in their early shows, Iggy and the Stooges, an Avant-grade punk band, "played" a food blender filled with water and a microphone, danced on a washboard wearing golf shoes, and drummed 50-gallon oil drums with hammers (McNeil and McCain 1996:41). The experimental ethos is often expressed through the idiosyncratic grooming, dress, demeanor, and argot of circle members, but these are not (yet) consolidated into a distinctive genre style.

Avant-garde genre members do not receive remuneration for their participation in genre related activities. They earn money for performing conventional types of music and from nonperformance employment. In addition, family, friends, and partners often contribute a range of resources. Avant-gardists commonly live with little recognition and many privations. These harsh conditions may retrospectively be romanticized as bohemian, but they contribute to the demise of many Avant-garde genres. The music and the people making it receive virtually no press coverage, which makes it exceedingly difficult for scholars to find accounts of Avant-garde musics that did not evolve into more institutionalized forms. The new music receives numerous appellations, but the eventual name is generally applied retrospectively by promoters, critics, and historians.

**TABLE 1 Genre Forms and Attributes**

| Attributes | Genre Forms | | | |
| --- | --- | --- | --- | --- |
| | Avant-Garde | Scene-Based | Industry-Based | Traditionalist |
| Organizational Form | Creative circle | Local scene | Established field | Clubs, associations |
| Organizational Scale | Local, some Internet | Local, Internet linked | National, worldwide | Local to international |
| Organization Locus | Homes, coffee shops, bars, empty spaces | Local, translocal, and virtual scenes | Industrial firms | Festivals, tours, academic settings |
| Genre Ideal or Member Goals | Create new music | Create community | Produce revenue, intellectual property | Preserve heritage and pass it on |
| Codification of Performance Conventions | Low: highly experimental | Medium: much attention to codifying style | High: shaped by industry categories | Hyper: great concern about deviation |
| Technology | Experimentation | Codifying technical innovations | Production tools that standardize sound | Idealized orthodoxy |
| Boundary Work | Against established music | Against rival musics | Market driven | Against deviants within |
| Dress, Adornment, Drugs | Eccentric | Emblematic of genre | Mass marketed "style" | Stereotypic and muted |
| Argot | Sporadic | Signals membership | Used to sell products | Stylized |
| Sources of Income for Artists | Self-contributed, partners, unknowing employers | Scene activities, self-contributed | Sales, licensing, merchandise, endorsements | Self contributed, heritage grants, festivals |
| Press Coverage | Virtually none | Community press | National press | Genre-based advocacy and critique |
| Source of Genre Name | Site or group specific | Scene members, genre-based media | Mass media or industry | Academics, critics |

## SCENE-BASED GENRES

For more than a decade, scholars analyzing music communities across the globe have used the concept of "scene" to refer to a community of spatially-situated artists, fans, record companies, and supporting small business people (see, e.g., Shank [1994] on rock and country in Austin, Texas; Cohen [1991] on the Liverpool scene; Becker [2004] on jazz in Kansas City; Grazian [2004] on blues in Chicago; and Urquia [2004] on salsa in London). These local scenes may be in communication with similar scenes in distant locales whose members enjoy the same kind of music and lifestyle. Such communities cohere through the exchange of information and music, which is made simpler with the advent of quick, small-parcel shipping companies and digital technologies such as the Internet (see Laing [1985] on punk, Kruse [2003] on alternative rock, Schilt [2004] on riot grrrl, and Kahn-Harris [2007] on death metal). Some scenes are essentially, if not entirely, virtual, fans, musicians, and critics find each other on the Internet through listservs and chat rooms (Bennett 2004; Kibby 2000; Lee and Peterson 2004). A Scene-based music genre may take any or all of these forms (Bennett and Peterson 2004), but here we focus primarily on the local form.

Scenes, musical and otherwise, commonly emerge in neighborhoods where rents are low, police supervision is lax, and residents tolerate diversity of all kinds (Florida 2002; Lloyd 2006). Such neighborhoods nurture a scene, and the lifestyle growing around it, by fostering constant interaction among scenesters (Gaines 1994; Thornton 1996; Urquia 2004; Walker 2006). Business entrepreneurs, often drawn from the ranks of scene-participants, become music promoters, club owners, and band managers. Some founded independent record companies, Scene-based fanzines, and Internet sites. Local newspapers, radio stations, and criminal elements often arrive in the area to support the scene and to derive profits from it. Scene musicians and ancillary creative people often cannot support themselves entirely from the music. They typically take low-skill service jobs in the community and depend on money and other support from partners, family, and friends. As scenes develop, these neighborhoods draw both more casual scenesters and merchandisers of the genre lifestyle, hastening the end of intensely local genres (Shank 1994).

Innovative technology often plays an important role in Scene-based genres. For example, the development of inexpensive, powerful, portable, and relatively compact sound amplifiers in the late 1930s was important in the development of bluegrass (Rosenberg 1985), urban blues (Grazian 2003), honky-tonk country music (Peterson 1997), and bebop (DeVeaux 1997). Technological innovations can also change the balance among elements of the music. In the early days of rap, DJs were the center of interest, but when Grandmaster Flash modified the turntable mixer, he solved the technical challenges of producing steady rhythm, and the next set of innovative practitioners turned their attention toward lyrical content and techniques of oral delivery. This effectively refocused crowd attention on the rapper, and DJs ceased to be the focus of innovation or attention (Chang 2005; Fricke and Ahearn 2002; Lena 2003, 2004).

Conventions of performance and presentation are rapidly codified in Scene-based genres. These conventions grow out of efforts to find the best way to express new musical ideas, but they often put performers in direct conflict with practitioners of other genres competing for the same resources. These frictions between rival scenes can be quite contentious and visible, as when bebop scene members fought with swing musicians (Lopes 2002), or when, urged on by a radio DJ, rock fans met in a Chicago stadium to break dance records and chant "disco sucks." Ornette Coleman even had his specially-made instrument smashed by fellow musicians who felt upstaged by his complex and aggressive way of playing hard bop (Rosenthal 1992).

Scene-based genres have a loose organizational form characterized by nested rings of varying commitment to the genre ideal. Clusters of those most responsible for the distinctive characteristics of the music are at the center. Next, there is a ring of committed activists whose identity, and sometimes means of employment, is tied to the scene. Outside of this is a ring of fans who participate in the scene more or less regularly. The outer ring is made up of "tourists" who enjoy activities within the scene without identifying with it. Such distinct rings are characteristic of mature scenes like the Chicago blues in the 1990s (Grazian 2004); newer scenes exhibit similar rings of commitment, but their structure is much more fluid (Cohen 1991).

## INDUSTRY-BASED GENRES

Industry-based music genres are so named because their primary organizational form is the industrial corporation. Some are multinational in scope, but others are independent companies organized to compete directly with the multinationals. Frith (1996:77) describes such genres as being located within the "market-based popular music field." Along with industrial firms, the prime actors in this field include singers and musicians who contract for their services, genre-targeted audiences, and a wide array of ancillary service providers, from song publishers to radio stations and diverse retail outlets.

For a genre to thrive for long in this large apparatus, its fans must number in the hundreds of thousands, and market logic demands ever larger numbers. Corporate interest in a particular genre lasts as long as its sales potential is increasing (Negus 1999). The otherwise highly competitive multinational entertainment conglomerates collectively fight the unauthorized use and distribution of their copyrighted music, doing whatever they can to frustrate the development of new genres (Peterson 1990). At the same time, industrial firms that are more closely linked to their markets, such as Motown, Rough Trade, and Sugar Hill Records, can be instrumental in the development of genres (Toynbee 2000).

Simplified genre conventions are codified in the interests of making, measuring, and marketing Industry-based genres. Firms train new artists to work within highly-codified performance conventions, and record producers regularly coach songwriters and artists to make simple music, clearly within genre bounds that will appeal to a mass audience. Such stereotyping strategies also facilitate sales because company personnel will know how to categorize and market the "product" (Longhurst 2007; Negus 1999), and potential consumers can be identified through analysis of marketing demographics data (Negus 1999). Over the past century, technological innovations have standardized and simplified the production of music to satisfy the needs of mass production. Trade magazines' weekly charts of song sales and Industry-based annual music awards help guide industry decisions about the relative success of individual songs and whole genres (Anand and Peterson 2000; Anand and Watson 2004; Watson and Anand 2006). In the process, genre names become more clearly fixed, but, at the same time, different Scene-based genres that were thought to be antithetical may be melded into one category (Peterson 1997).

Like the music, elements of dress, adornment, and lifestyle are exaggerated and mass-marketed to new fans of Industry-based genres. The "grunge aesthetic," for example, inspired fashion designer Marc Jacobs to incorporate flannel shirts, wool ski caps, and Doc Marten boots into Perry Ellis's 1992 spring collection (Moore 2005). Likewise, advertisers often capitalized upon the popularity of a genre to promote their products. In the early 1990s, for example, the moniker "alternative," commonly used to refer to grunge rock, was used to sell consumer products like Budweiser (the "alternative beer") and to describe the MTV program "Alternative Nation." A generation earlier, the popularity of political protest prompted a major company to pronounce, "Columbia Records brings you the revolution" (Santelli 1980).

New fans attracted to an Industry-based genre by intensive merchandising often raise the ire of more committed genre participants. New recruits argue over what constitutes authenticity in music, musicians, and signs of group affiliation (Grazian 2004; Peterson 1997), while committed, longer-term fans and performers engage in a discourse about lost authenticity (Cantwell 1984; Eyerman and Jamison 1998; Lopes 2002). This tension is sometimes divisive enough to propel some genre members into forming new genres, either Avant-garde or Traditionalist.

## TRADITIONALIST GENRES

Traditionalist genre participants' goal is to preserve a genre's musical heritage and inculcate the rising generation of devotees in the performance techniques, history, and rituals of the genre. Fans and organizations dedicated to perpetuating a genre put a great amount of effort into constructing its history and highlighting exemplary performers who they deem fit into the genre's emerging canon of exemplars (Lee 2007; Regev 1994; Rosenberg 1985).

Periodic gatherings of genre artists and fans at festivals, celebratory concerts, and reunions are characteristic of Traditionalist genres. These rituals give devotees the chance to gather and momentarily live in the spirit of the genre and reaffirm its continuity (Rosenberg 1985). New and old performers will often play together, enacting a ritual of renewal through the veneration of the old timers and the "discovery" of new talent. Performers and promoters commonly rely on employment outside the genre, so these gatherings provide the most significant proportion of their earnings from performing genre music. They may also earn additional money from selling records, musical instruments, and genre-related ephemera. Many fans sing, play an instrument, or act as promoters of genre events, so the division of labor is less distinct between fan, artist, and industry than in Industry-based or fully-developed Scene-based genres.

———

Committed Traditionalists expend a great deal of energy fighting with each other about the models they construct to represent a genre's music and the canon of its iconic performers. Traditionalists argue over which instruments and vocal stylings are appropriate, and they may even battle over the place and time that a genre originated. For example, Traditionalist U.S. punks claim that punk developed in New York and Detroit during the late 1960s and early 1970s, while British Traditionalists locate punk's founding in 1970s London (Longhurst 2007). Retrospectively, adherents of Traditionalist genres decry what they identify as the adulterating consequences of commercial exploitation of genre music, and they censure artists who are seen as catering to corporate interests or values. This censure can be seen in the denigration of "crossover" rap artists of the 1980s like Vanilla Ice or Digital Underground, who are derided for having "made Rap palatable to white, suburban youth across the country" (Light 2004:140).

Performers' race, class, educational attainment, and regional origins are often used as markers of authenticity. To play bluegrass, for example, it is said a musician must be White, working class, rural, and preferably from the Appalachian mountains (Rosenberg 1985); you must be young, White, and an underachiever to perform punk music in an exemplary fashion (Laing 1985); and to really play salsa, a musician must be Latin American (Urquia 2004). Even journalistic and academic accounts of Traditionalist genres engage in such demographic profiling (Kelley 2004). Other outsiders often conflate stories of a genre's exotic origin with its present Traditionalist form, and these stereotypes influence tourists who want to know something about the genre. Grazian (2003:13) reports that well-meaning tourists come to Chicago expecting to find blues played by "uneducated American black men afflicted with blindness or some other disability, playing in ramshackle joints that are dimly lit, unbearably smoky, and smelling as funky as their music sounds."

# Genre Trajectories

## AGSIT GENRE TRAJECTORIES

Based on our four case studies, we expected all genre trajectories to grow from Avant-garde circles, but just 40 of the 60 genres we sampled began this way, and only 16 experienced the full AgSIT trajectory. Bebop, a form of jazz that emerged in the early 1940s, exemplifies a genre that experienced the full trajectory. Like other Avant-garde genres, Bebop coalesced around a small group of experimentalists, including Charlie Parker and "Dizzy" Gillespie. They attracted the attention of other young jazz players, most notably Bud Powell, Thelonious Monk, and Charlie Christian, who were dissatisfied with the big-band swing of the time (DeVeaux 1997). Their collective stylistic innovations, dedication to creating Black art music, and charismatic leadership created a consensus around the Bop genre ideal (Lopes 2002). Genre music conventions coalesced as Bebop came to be played by small combos of musicians on acoustic instruments, usually led by a saxophone and trumpet, and characterized by a series of fast extended solos improvised on a song's harmonic structure rather than on its melody.

As the Avant-garde Beboppers began to experiment in small clubs, a Scene-based genre developed. Bop-dedicated clubs such as Birdland opened and several specialty record companies, like Blue Bird, were established. The always contentious jazz press hotly debated the music, politics, and behavioral "excesses" of the music's practitioners and devotees. A set of sartorial, linguistic, and behavioral markers developed, allowing Bopsters to identify each other and enact the circle's criticism of the status-quo music scene. Evoking the image of French bohemian artists, Dizzy Gillespie and other Boppers wore black berets, but the prime symbol of Bop group allegiance was the use of an elaborate vocabulary to describe themselves, swing players, ignorant fans, demanding managers, varieties of drugs, and the authorities. This rapidly evolving argot made it possible to deride outsiders in their presence, and the language made its way into a number of the genre's songs.

In the late 1940s, Bebop made the transition into an Industry-based genre as the major record companies bought the recording contracts of the leading Bop artists and began to promote the music to the general public. The national press regularly reported on the music, as well as Bop artists' and fans' antics. Many stories described the zoot suit fashions, argot, racial mixing, juvenile delinquency, and drug taking (Lopes 2002). Much of the national media attention initially derided Bop, but by the mid-1950s the media was increasingly positive, leading to a rapid swelling in the ranks of casual listeners who wanted to vicariously live the dangerous life of the "hepcat." Numerous marketers obliged with the mass production of distinctive emblems of scene status. The record companies, to draw more casual fans, began backing the star Bop performers with string sections, a move that signaled the Industry-based genre was reaching its end.

Genres that experience the explosive growth and aesthetic dilution characteristic of an Industry-based genre tend to suffer a crisis as their many casual fans find a new focus of attention. In this instance, the growth of both R&B and Rock music drew fans away from Bebop. Not surprisingly, the general media reduced its coverage of Bebop, and the major record companies reduced their marketing and financial support of genre artists, sometimes terminating their contracts altogether. Even the media supportive of Bebop increasingly saw it as music to review rather than as a newsworthy lifestyle.

In response, some musicians explore new ways to revitalize a genre ideal, and new Avant-garde genres emerge from these efforts. For example, Bebop artists helped to spawn Hard bop, Cool jazz, Free jazz, psychedelic jazz, and third stream genres. At the same time, hardcore Bebop fans, who were dismayed by the adulterations made in the Industry-based genre and by the hordes of touristic fans, took wry pleasure from Bebop's downfall and set about trying to recreate Bebop as it had been in the glory days when it was Scene-based. In time, these musicians, scholars, and fans created a set of institutions to preserve the memory and practice of the music through education in the schools, festivals, album reissues, and other features of Traditionalist genres. Increasingly, Bebop was interpreted as a modern art form worthy of scholarly attention and preservation in the major conservatories of classical music (Lopes 2002; Peterson 1972). The February 28, 1964 issue of *Time* magazine, for example, featured Thelonious Monk on its cover and described his eccentricities not as signs of madness but of creative genius.

Fifteen other genres followed the same AgSIT trajectory as Bebop: Bluegrass, Chicago jazz, Folk revival music, Gospel, Folk rock, Heavy metal, Honky-tonk country. Old-school rap, Punk rock, Rockabilly, Salsa, Urban blues, Western swing, Hillbilly, and Rock-n-roll (see Table 2). Of these, Bebop most closely resembles Heavy metal, Old-school rap, Punk rock, and Rockabilly in the spectacular and contentious Industry-based phase of their trajectories.

As Table 2 shows, nine musics in disparate streams, including Alternative country, Disco, Gangsta rap, Jump blues, Psychedelic rock, and Thrash metal, experienced Avant-garde, Scene-based, and Industry-based genres but have not formed a Traditionalist genre. Since there is often a gap of five or more years between the collapse of an Industry-based genre and the coalescence of a Traditionalist genre, it is possible that they may experience a "revival" in years to come. In several cases, the creative energies that might have gone into tradition-building went instead toward building new genres. Most conspicuously, Alternative country, Disco, Gangsta rap, and Psychedelic rock spawned, respectively, Americana; newer forms of dance music like Techno, House, and Jungle; top-40 rap; and glam rock (Brewster and Broughton 2000; Chang 2005; Curtis 1987; Lee and Peterson 2004; Lena 2006).

Three musics in our sample, Delta blues, Doowop, and New Orleans jazz, developed a Traditionalist genre without ever being an Industry-based genre. This may be due to particular features of the racialized system for music distribution in the first half of the twentieth century, which limited the accessibility of Black music. Beginning in the third quarter of the twentieth century, both Delta blues and New Orleans jazz experienced revivals as Traditionalist genres. The history of Doowop is a bit different. Doowop started in the 1950s when young African American vocal groups began to use their voices to simulate the Black pop music of the day. As the style became more popular, their vocal renditions were augmented by R&B bands, and Doowop merged into the Black pop-music stream (Pruter 1996).

We found 11 genre trajectories that were lively Scene-based genres but never became Industry-based genres nor formed a Traditionalist genre. Most of these communities purposively maintained their genre ideal, appealing to a narrow group. Death metal is an extreme example; its often violent, sexist, racist, and homophobic lyrics, as well as devotees' antisocial behavior, foreclosed any distribution by major music companies (Kahn-Harris 2007). Less extreme examples include Free jazz, Black metal, Garage, Grindcore, and South Texas polka. Country boogie and Hard bop were both absorbed into other genres, so they did not enjoy a separate Traditionalist period. At the end of the 1990s, three dance musics, House,

**TABLE 2  AgSIT Genre Trajectories**

| | Avant-Garde | Scene-Based | Industry-Based | Traditionalist |
|---|:---:|:---:|:---:|:---:|
| BeBop Jazz | x | x | x | x |
| Bluegrass | x | x | x | x |
| Chicago Jazz | x | x | x | x |
| Folk Revival | x | x | x | x |
| Folk Rock | x | x | x | x |
| Gospel | x | x | x | x |
| Heavy Metal | x | x | x | x |
| Hillbilly | x | x | x | x |
| Honky Tonk | x | x | x | x |
| Old-School Rap | x | x | x | x |
| Punk Rock | x | x | x | x |
| Rockabilly | x | x | x | x |
| Rock-n-Roll | x | x | x | x |
| Salsa | x | x | x | x |
| Urban Blues | x | x | x | x |
| Western Swing | x | x | x | x |
| Alternative Country | x | x | x | |
| Disco | x | x | x | |
| East Coast Gangsta Rap | x | x | x | |
| Grunge Rock | x | x | x | |
| Jazz Fusion | x | x | x | |
| Jump Blues | x | x | x | |
| Psychedelic Rock | x | x | x | |
| Thrash Metal | x | x | x | |
| West Coast Gangsta Rap | x | x | x | |
| Delta Blues | x | x | | x |
| DooWop | x | x | | x |

(continued)

**TABLE 2** (continued)

| | Avant-Garde | Scene-Based | Industry-Based | Traditionalist |
|---|---|---|---|---|
| New Orleans Jazz | x | x | | x |
| Black Metal | x | x | | |
| Country Boogie | x | x | | |
| Death Metal | x | x | | |
| Free Jazz | x | x | | |
| Garage | x | x | | |
| Grindcore | x | x | | |
| Hard Bop | x | x | | |
| House | x | x | | |
| Jungle | x | x | | |
| South Texas Polka | x | x | | |
| Techno | x | x | | |
| Laurel Canyon | x | | | |

Jungle, and Techno, enjoyed continuing vital development and produced numerous permutations through Scene-based media (McLeod 2001).

Finally, while most Avant-garde genres either wither or develop new scenes, from time to time an Avant-garde circle explodes, spawning several new genres. Such Avant-garde genres are usually labeled by the place they came together, such as the loose collection of singer-songwriter-musicians who gathered in the bucolic canyons above Los Angeles in the late 1960s and we identify as the "Laurel Canyon" circle. Like all Avant-garde genres, the artists associated with Laurel Canyon were quite eclectic, but they were united in their dislike of the music of the day, including pop, glam, and psychedelic rock. The Laurel Canyon circle did not develop a cohesive Scene-based genre, but its efforts were central to the flowering of several quite distinct genres, including the singer-songwriter style of James Taylor and Joni Mitchell, Folk rock led by the Byrds, cosmic country exemplified by the Flying Burrito Brothers, the country rock of the Eagles, and the psychedelic pop of The Mamas and The Papas (Hoskyns 2006; Walker 2006).

## SIT GENRE TRAJECTORIES

Among our 60 genre trajectories, 11 began as Scene-based genres and moved to an Industry-based or Traditionalist form (see Table 3). The first five genres in Table 3 grew out of preexisting domestic Scene-based genres, and six imports from abroad took on distinctive identities in the United States.

Swing is the only one of these 11 musics to go through the entire SIT trajectory in the twentieth century. It developed in the late 1920s when sweet dance bands incorporated elements of "hot jazz" into their music. Composers and arrangers orchestrated hot jazz improvisation over written dance-band parts, satisfying both dancers and jazz fans. In the hands of Duke Ellington, Glen Miller, Count Basie, and Benny Goodman, Swing became the dominant form of industrial pop music by the late 1930s. Its Industry-based form withered in the late 1940s, but a vigorous swing Traditionalist genre emerged a decade later (Magee 2005; Shipton 2001).

Contemporary Christian music grew out of young gospel musicians' efforts to incorporate elements of rock into their religiously-themed music (Darden 2004). Likewise, Conscious rap, Contemporary gospel, and Humor rap emerged from efforts to combine scenes (see Krims [2000]

**TABLE 3  SIT Genre Trajectories**

|  | Scene-Based | Industry-Based | Traditionalist |
|---|---|---|---|
| Swing | x | x | x |
| Contemporary Christian | x | x | |
| Conscious Rap | x | x | |
| Contemporary Gospel | x | x | |
| Humor Rap | x | x | |
| Reggae | x | x | |
| Soca | x | x | |
| Tango | x | x | |
| Chicago Polka | x | | x |
| Cleveland Polka | x | | x |
| Milwaukee Polka | x | | x |

and Rose [1994] on Rap; see Darden [2004], Heilbut [1997], and Thompson [2000] on Contemporary gospel). Reggae, Soca, and Tango, Caribbean and Latin music forms that came to the United States and developed distinctive attributes here, had no Traditionalist phase. Instead, each became part of the foundation for later forms of Latin, Rock, and Rap music (Dudley 2004; Roberts 1979; Shepherd et al. 2005). Finally, three forms of polka music coming from central Europe took on distinctive forms in Midwestern industrial cities, fostered by Scene-based institutions (Shepherd et al. 2005). None of the polka musics developed into Industry-based genres, but all sustained an extended Traditionalist genre.

## IST GENRE TRAJECTORIES

Nine of our 60 genre trajectories, as depicted in Table 4, began as Industry-based genres and then developed scenes; six then experienced Traditionalist phases. We did not anticipate this sort of trajectory but identified a number of cases that share this "anomaly." On close inspection, we found that most of these genres conspicuously share a source in the pooled efforts of a few creative musicians paired with arrangers, producers, and industry marketers working in the field of Industry-based music.

Soul is a good example of this pattern. African American religious singers had long borrowed from Black secular music and rhythms to give their sacred songs intensity and popular appeal. Following World War II, singers raised in the church reversed the process, bringing elements of energized

**TABLE 4  IST Genre Trajectories**

|  | Industry-Based | Scene-Based | Traditionalist |
|---|---|---|---|
| Cool Jazz | x | x | x |
| Funk | x | x | x |
| Movie Cowboy | x | x | x |
| New Jack Swing | x | x | x |
| Soul | x | x | x |
| Southern Gospel | x | x | x |
| Nashville Sound | x | x | |
| Nu Metal | x | x | |
| Outlaw Country | x | x | |

Gospel music into their secular songs. These efforts ranged widely, from the rocking songs of Little Richard and the shouts of James Brown to the ballads of numerous R&B quartets. This work coalesced as a coherent genre in the hands of Ray Charles and Ahmet Ertegun, the Atlantic Records owner and producer. In 1954, Charles had a huge hit when he transformed the well-known Gospel anthem "My Jesus Means the World to Me" into the secular "I Got a Woman (way over town that's good to me)." Over the next 10 years, many artists followed his lead, including Solomon Burke, Otis Redding, Aretha Franklin, Sam Cook, Jackie Wilson, and Wilson Picket (Garland 1970; Gillett 1974; Guralnick 1999). In the 1960s, Motown Records became very successful by crafting a line of "softer," "safer," soul songs. Cool jazz, Funk, New jack swing, and Nu metal likewise emerged from the efforts of successful artists working with industrial record company producers or arrangers.

Southern gospel developed quite differently. While the genre is highly inflected with Black influences, the designation "Southern" is used to clearly distinguish its predominantly White, close-harmony style from related trends in Black Gospel. Southern gospel was an unintended byproduct of marketing efforts begun in 1910 by the Vaughn Music Publishing Company to sell their new line of religious songbooks featuring four-part harmonies. The company hired a male quartet to perform works from the songbooks in churches across the South and the Midwest. Four-part quartets had not been popular previously, but they were the most cost efficient way to promote songbooks. Touring quartets rapidly became popular, and enterprising singers formed publishing companies and sent out singing quartets of their own. This created a great demand for new songs well suited to four-part harmonies. By 1940, performances were also held in town halls, theaters, schools, and under tents where theatricality was important to success. Several quartets recorded for RCA in the 1920s, but it wasn't until the 1960s that groups again obtained contracts with major labels. By the 1980s the old circuit no longer drew young fans, but the form has experienced a revival as a Traditionalist genre since the 1990s (Goff 2002; Murray 2005).

The Nashville sound was also an unintended byproduct of music industry actors. It was the work of major music corporation producers who were also accomplished musicians, most notably Owen Bradley, Herbert Long, and Chat Atkins. Beginning in the late 1950s, they created an assembly-line system of production in an effort to produce standard, high-quality country music at a low cost. Professional songwriters provided songs that were assigned to particular artists, and a set of professional "session" musicians created arrangements in the studio. What began as a system of production soon developed distinct musical qualities that collectively became known as the Nashville sound (Hemphill 1970). The genre flourished in the 1960s, was supplanted in the 1970s, and to date it has not had a Traditionalist form (Jensen 1998). Like the Nashville sound, Cowboy music was the byproduct of a system of creating recorded music; it was produced in the Hollywood movie lots devoted to making "B" Western films (Peterson 1997).

Outlaw country coalesced in the mid-1970s as a reaction to the growing banality of the Nashville sound, but it represented a long tradition of "hard country music," running from Jimmie Rodgers and Hank Williams to George Jones and Johnny Cash (Malone 2002). Led by Waylon Jennings and Willie Nelson, artists began to flaunt their drug use, write their own songs, choose their record producers, and record with their own road bands away from the large corporately-owned studios. This "outlaw" movement became a genre in 1976 when RCA repackaged previously-released material by Jennings, Nelson, Jessi Colter, and Tompall Glaser as "Wanted: The Outlaws," which became the first country music album to sell a million copies. Many artists followed in the wake of this success, but the music has not had a Traditionalist phase. Instead, the outlaw spirit and way of making records has animated loosely-organized Avant-garde movements, such as Texas country, Southern rock, Alternative country, and hellbilly (Ching 2001, Malone 2002).

Our sample genres suggest that not all industrial environments are equally congenial to the development of new musics. While the major companies (measured in a way appropriate to the time) accounted for most popular music production in the twentieth-century United States, six of the nine musics in our sample—Cool jazz, Funk, New jack swing, Soul, Southern gospel, and Nu metal—were developed in unaffiliated, independent record companies that were in competition with the major labels.

---

# References

Ahlkvist, Jarl A. and Robert Faulkner. 2002. "'Will This Record Work for Us?': Managing Music Formats in Commercial Radio." *Qualitative Sociology* 25(2):189–215.

Anand, N. and Richard A. Peterson. 2000. "When Market Information Consti-
    tutes Fields: Sensemaking of Markets in the Commercial Music Industry."
    *Organization Science* 11:270–84.

Anand, N. and Mary R. Watson. 2004. "Tournament Rituals in the Evolution of
    Fields: The Case of the Grammy Awards." *Academy of Management Journal*
    47:59–80.

Anderson, Benedict. 1983. *Imagined Communities.* London, UK: Verso.

Apperley, Thomas H. 2006. "Genre and Game Studies: Toward a Critical Approach
    to Video Game Genres." *Simulation & Gaming* 37:6–23.

Attali, Jacques. 1985. *Noise: The Political Economy of Music.* Manchester, UK:
    Manchester University Press.

Ballard, Mary E., Alan R. Dodson, and Doris G. Bazzini. 1999. "Genre of Music
    and Lyrical Content: Expectation Effects." *The Journal of Genetic Psychology*
    160(4):476–87.

Bauck, Andrew. 1997. "Review." *Popular Music* 16(2):231–34.

Becker, Howard S. 1982. *Art Worlds.* Berkeley, CA: University of California Press.

———. 2004. "Jazz Places." Pp. 17–29 in *Music Scenes,* edited by A. Bennett and
    R. A. Peterson. Nashville, TN: Vanderbilt University Press.

Bennett, Andrew. 1997. "'Going Down the Pub': The Pub Rock Scene." *Popular
    Music* 16:97–108.

———. 2004. "New Tales from Canterbury: The Making of a Virtual Scene." Pp.
    205–20 in *Music Scenes,* edited by A. Bennett and R. A. Peterson. Nashville,
    TN: Vanderbilt University Press.

Bennett, Andrew and Richard A. Peterson, eds. 2004. *Music Scenes: Local, Translo-
    cal and Virtual.* Nashville, TN: Vanderbilt University Press.

Bielby, William T. and Denise D. Bielby. 1994. "'All Hits are Flukes': Institutional-
    ized Decision-Making and the Rhetoric of Network Prime-Time Program
    Development." *American Journal of Sociology* 99:1287–1313.

Bourdieu, Pierre. 1984. *Distinction: A Social Critique of the Judgment of Taste.* Cam-
    bridge, MA: Harvard University Press.

———. 1993. *The Field of Cultural Production.* New York: Columbia University Press.

———. 1995. *The Rules of Art: Genesis and Structure of the Literary Field.* Translated
    by S. Emanuel. Stanford, CA: Stanford University Press.

Brewster, Bill and Frank Broughton. 2000. *Last Night a DJ Saved My Life.* New
    York: Grove.

Cantwell, Robert. 1984. *Bluegrass Breakdown: The Making of the Old Southern
    Sound.* Urbana, IL: University of Illinois Press.

Cerulo, Karen A. 1995. *Identity Designs: The Sights and Sounds of a Nation.* New
    Brunswick, NJ: Rutgers University Press.

Chang, Jeff. 2005. *Can't Stop Won't Stop: A History of the Hip-Hop Generation.* New
    York: Picador.

Ching, Barbara. 2001. *Wrong's What I Do Best: Hard Country Music and Contemporary Culture*. New York: Oxford University Press.

Cohen, Sara. 1991. *Rock Culture in Liverpool: Popular Music in the Making*. Oxford, UK: Clarendon Press.

Curtis, James. 1987. *Rock Eras*. Bowling Green, OH: Popular Press.

Darden, Robert. 2004. *People Get Ready!: A New History of Black Gospel Music*. New York: Continuum.

DeVeaux, Scott. 1997. *The Birth of BeBop: A Social and Musical History*. Berkeley, CA: University of California Press.

Devitt, Amy J. 2004. *Writing Genres: Rhetorical Philosophy and Theory*. Carbondale, IL: Southern Illinois Press.

DiMaggio, Paul. 1987. "Classification in Art." *American Sociological Review* 52(4):440–55.

Dowd, Timothy J. 1992. "The Musical Structure and Social Context of Number-One Songs, 1955 to 1988: An Exploratory Analysis." Pp. 130–57 in *Vocabularies of Public Life*, edited by R. Wuthnow. London, UK: Routledge.

Dudley, Shannon. 2004. *Carnival Music in Trinidad: Experiencing Music, Expressing Culture*. New York: Oxford University Press.

Ennis, Philip H. 1992. *The Seventh Stream: The Emergence of Rock-n-Roll in American Popular Music*. Middletown, CT: Wesleyan University Press.

Eyerman, Ron and Andrew Jamison. 1998. *Music and Social Movements*. Cambridge, UK: Cambridge University Press.

Ferguson, Priscilla Parkhurst. 2004. *Accounting for Taste: The Triumph of French Cuisine*. Chicago, IL: University of Chicago Press.

Florida, Richard. 2002. *The Rise of the Creative Class: And How It's Transforming Work, Leisure, Community and Everyday Life*. New York: Basic.

Fowler, Alastair. 1982. *Kinds of Literature: An Introduction to the Theory of Genres and Modes*. Cambridge, MA: Harvard University Press.

Fricke, Jim and Charlie Ahearn. 2002. *Yes, Yes Y'all: Oral History of Hip-Hop's First Decade*. New York: Da Capo Press.

Frith, Simon. 1996. *Performing Rites: On the Value of Popular Music*. Oxford, UK: Oxford University Press.

Frow, John. 2006. *Genre*. New York: Routledge.

Gaines, Donna. 1994. "The Local Economy of Suburban Scenes." Pp. 47–65 in *Adolescents and Their Music: If It Is Too Loud You Are Too Old*, edited by J. S. Epstein. New York: Garland.

Garland, Phyl. 1970. *The Sound of Soul*. Chicago, IL: Regenry.

Garofalo, Reebee. 2002. *Rockin' Out: Popular Music in the USA*. New York: Prentice Hall.

Gillett, Charlie. 1974. *Making Tracks: Atlantic Records and the Growth of a Multi-Billion-Dollar Industry*. New York: Dutton.

Goff, James R., Jr. 2002. *Close Harmony: A History of Southern Gospel.* Chapel Hill, NC: University of North Carolina Press.

Grazian, David. 2003. *Blue Chicago: The Search for Authenticity in Urban Blues Clubs.* Chicago, IL: University of Chicago Press.

———. 2004. "The Symbolic Economy of the Chicago Blues Scene." Pp. 31–47 in *Music Scenes,* edited by A. Bennett and R. A. Peterson. Nashville, TN: Vanderbilt University Press.

Griswold, Wendy. 1987. "The Fabrication of Meaning: Literary Interpretation in the United States, Great Britain, and the West Indies." *American Journal of Sociology* 92(5):1077–1117.

Guralnick, Peter. 1999. *Sweet Soul Music.* New York: Harper Collins.

Heilbut, Anthony. 1997. *The Gospel Sound: Good News and Bad Times.* 4th ed. New York: Limelight Editions.

Hemphill, Paul. 1970. *The Nashville Sound.* New York: Simon and Schuster.

Hirsch, Paul M. 1972. "Processing Fads and Fashions: An Organization-Set Analysis of Cultural Industry Systems." *American Journal of Sociology* 77(4):639–59.

Hoskyns, Barney. 2006. *Hotel California.* New York: Wiley.

Hsu, Greta. 2006. "Jacks of All Trades and Masters of None: Audiences' Reactions to Spanning Genres in Feature Film Production." *Administrative Science Quarterly* 51:420–50.

Hsu, Greta and Michael Hannan. 2005. "Identities, Genres, and Organizational Forms." *Organizational Science* 16:474–90.

Hyon, Sunny. 1996. "Genre in Three Traditions: Implications for ESL." *TESOL Quarterly* 30:693–722.

Jensen, Joli. 1998. *Nashville Sound: Authenticity, Commercialization, and Country Music.* Nashville, TN: Vanderbilt University Press.

Kahn-Harris, Keith. 2007. *Extreme Metal: Music and Culture on the Edge.* Oxford, UK: Berg Publishers.

Kelley, Robin D. G. 2004. "Looking for the 'Real' Nigga: Social Scientists Construct the Ghetto." Pp. 119–36 in *That's the Joint!: The Hip-Hop Studies Reader,* edited by M. Forman and M. A. Neal. New York: Routledge.

Kibby, Marjorie. 2000. "Home on the Page: A Virtual Place of Music Community." *Popular Music* 19:91–100.

Krims, Adam. 2000. *Rap Music and the Poetics of Identity.* New York: Cambridge University Press.

Kruse, Holly. 2003. *Sight and Sound: Understanding Independent Music Scenes.* New York: Peter Lang.

Laing, Dave. 1985. *One Chord Wonders: Power and Meaning in Punk Rock.* Milton Keynes: Open University Press.

Lamont, Michèle and Virág Molnár. 2002. "The Study of Boundaries in the Social Sciences." *Annual Review of Sociology* 28:167–95.

Lee, Steve S. 2007. "Musical Stratification: Explaining the Aesthetic Mobility among Music Genres." PhD Dissertation, Department of Sociology, Nashville, TN, Vanderbill University.

Lee, Steve S. and Richard A. Peterson. 2004. "Internet-Based Virtual Music Scenes: The Case of P2 in Alt. Country." Pp. 187–204 in *Music Scenes*, edited by A. Bennett and R. A. Peterson. Nashville, TN: Vanderbilt University Press.

Lena, Jennifer C. 2003. "From 'Flash' to 'Cash': Producing Rap Authenticity, 1979 to 1995." PhD dissertation, Department of Sociology, Columbia University, New York City, New York.

———. 2004. "Meaning and Membership: Samples in Rap Music, 1979 to 1995." *Poetics* 32(3–4):297–310.

———. 2006. "Social Context and Musical Content: Rap Music, 1979–1995." *Social Forces* 85(1):479–95.

Lena, Jennifer C. and Richard A. Peterson. 2006. "Movement-Made Music." Paper presented at the Thematic Session on Social Movements, the 101st annual meetings of the American Sociological Association, Montreal, Canada.

———. 2007. "Resources and Phases in Music Genre Formation." Paper presented at the panel on New Trends in the Sociology of the Arts, Culture Section, American Sociological Association Conference, New York City, New York.

Lewis, George E. 1996. "Improvised Music after 1950: Afrological and Eurological Perspectives." *Black Music Research Journal* 16:91–122.

Lieberson, Stanley. 2000. *A Matter of Taste: How Names, Fashions, and Culture Change.* New Haven, CT: Yale University Press.

Light, Alan. 2004. "About a Salary or Reality?—Rap's Recurrent Conflict" Pp. 137–46 in *That's the Joint!: The Hip-Hop Studies Reader*, edited by M. Forman and M. A. Neal. New York: Routledge.

Lizardo, Omar. 2006. "How Cultural Tastes Shape Personal Networks." *American Sociological Review* 71:778–807.

Lloyd, Richard. 2006. *Neo-Bohemia: Art and Commerce in the Postindustrial City.* New York: Routledge.

Longhurst, Brian. 2007. *Popular Music and Society.* Cambridge, UK: Polity.

Lopes, Paul. 2002. *The Rise of a Jazz Art World.* New York: Cambridge University Press.

Maffesoli, Michael. 1996. *The Time of Tribes: The Decline of Individualism in Mass Society.* Translated by D. Smith. London, UK: Sage.

Magee, Jeffrey. 2005. *The Uncrowned King of Swing: Fletcher Henderson and Big Band Jazz.* New York: Oxford University Press.

Malone, William C. 2002. *Don't Get Above Your Rasin': Country Music and the Southern Working Class.* Urbana, IL: University of Illinois Press.

Mark, Noah. 1998. "Birds of a Feather Sing Together." *Social Forces* 77(2):453–85.

McLeod, Kembrew. 2001. "Genres, Subgenres, and More: Musical and Social Differentiation within Electronic/Dance Music Communities." *Journal of Popular Music Studies* 13:59–76.

McNeil, Legs and Gillian McCain. 1996. *Please Kill Me: The Uncensored Oral History of Punk.* New York: Penguin.

Merwe, Peter van der. 1989. *Origins of Popular Style: The Antecedents of Twentieth-Century Popular Music.* Oxford, UK: Clarendon Press.

Moore, Ryan. 2005. "Alternative to What? Subcultural Capital and the Commercialization of a Music Scene." *Deviant Behavior* 26:229–52.

Murray, David B. 2005. *Encyclopedia of Southern Gospel Music.* Bostic, NC: MusicScribe Publishing.

Neale, Steve. 1980. *Genre.* London, UK: British Film Institute.

Negus, Keith. 1999. *Music Genres and Corporate Cultures.* New York: Routledge.

Peterson, Richard A. 1972. "A Process Model of the Folk, Pop and Fine Art Phases of Jazz." Pp. 135–51 in *American Music: From Storyville to Woodstock,* edited by C. Nanry. New Brunswick, NJ: Transaction Books.

———. 1990. "Why 1955? Explaining the Advent of Rock and Roll." *Popular Music* 9:97–116.

———. 1997. *Creating Country Music: Fabricating Authenticity.* Chicago, IL: University of Chicago Press.

Peterson, Richard A. and David Berger. 1975. "Cycles in Symbol Production: The Case of Popular Music." *American Sociological Review* 40:158–73.

Peterson, Richard A. and Roger Kern. 1996. "Changing Highbrow Taste: From Snob to Omnivore." *American Sociological Review* 61:900–907.

Pruter, Robert. 1996. *DooWop: The Chicago Scene.* Urbana, IL: University of Illinois Press.

Regev, Motti. 1994. "Producing Artistic Value: The Case of Rock Music." *The Sociological Quarterly* 35:85–102.

Roberts, John Storm. 1979. *The Latin Tinge: The Impact of Latin American Music on the United States.* New York: Oxford University Press.

Rose, Tricia. 1994. *Black Noise: Black Music and Black Culture in Contemporary America.* Hanover CT: Wesleyan University Press.

Rosenberg, Neil V. 1985. *Bluegrass: A History.* Urbana, IL: University of Illinois Press.

Rosenthal, David 1992. *Hard Bop.* New York: Oxford University Press.

Santelli, Robert. 1980. *Aquarius Rising: The Rock Festival Years.* New York: Delta.

Schilt, Kristin. 2004. "'Riot Grrrl is . . .' : Contestation Over Meaning in a Music Scene." Pp. 115–30 in *Music Scenes,* edited by A. Bennett and R. A. Peterson. Nashville, TN: Vanderbilt University Press.

Shank, Barry. 1994. *Dissonant Identities: The Rock 'n' Roll Scene in Austin, Texas.* Hanover, CT: Wesleyan University Press.

Shepherd, John, David Horn, and Dave Laing. 2005. *Continuum Encyclopedia of Popular Music of the World.* New York: Continuum.

Shipton, Alyn. 2001. *A New History of Jazz.* London, UK: Continuum.

Swales, John M. 1990. *Genre Analysis.* Cambridge, UK: Cambridge University Press.

Thompson, John J. 2000. *Raised by Wolves: The Story of Christian Rock & Roll.* Toronto, Canada: BCW Press.

Thornton, Sarah. 1996. *Club Cultures: Music, Media, and Subcultural Capital.* Hanover, CT: Wesleyan University Press.

Toynbee, Jason. 2000. *Making Popular Music: Musicians, Creativity and Institutions.* London, UK: Arnold.

Trougott, Mark, ed. 1995. *Repertoires and Cycles of Collective Action.* Durham, NC: Duke University Press.

Urquia, Norman. 2004. "'Doin' It Right': Contested Authenticity in London's Salsa Scene." Pp. 96–114 in *Music Scenes*, edited by A. Bennett and R. A. Peterson. Nashville, TN: Vanderbilt University Press.

Walker, Michael. 2006. *Laurel Canyon: Rock-and-Roll's Legendary Neighborhood.* New York: Faber and Faber.

Walser, Robert. 1993. *Running with the Devil: Power, Gender, and Madness in Heavy Metal Music.* Hanover, CT: Wesleyan University Press.

Watson, Mary and N. Anand. 2006. "Award Ceremony as an Arbiter of Commerce and Canon in the Popular Music Industry." *Popular Music* 25:41–56.

Williams, Caroline. 2006. "Genre Matters." *Victorian Studies* 48:295–304.

Williams, J. Patrick. 2006. "Authentic Identities: Straightedge Subculture, Music, and the Internet." *Journal of Contemporary Ethnography* 35(2):173–200.

# STUDY QUESTIONS

1. How do the authors define *genre forms* and how do they use this concept in their research? What applications might this concept have outside the world of music?

2. Of the 60 genres of music the authors discuss, choose one that you like. Where does it fit in the genre form table? What was its trajectory?

# PART FOUR

# ANALYZING CULTURE

WHEN I WAS a freshman in college, I took a summer job as a carpenter's helper. The first day, I was tasked with putting up sheetrock, a job I'd never done before. My boss gave me a few pointers, made me promise not to waste the sheetrock, and left me on my own to figure it out. Sheetrock is heavy wallboard that you screw into wooden studs to form walls. You begin by placing a single sheet against the wall, long edge on the floor, running perpendicular to the vertical studs. If there are no electrical outlets along the wall, it's easy. You just screw the sheet tight to the studs. But if there are outlets, you have to cut a hole in the sheetrock so that you don't cover them up.

Things were going fine for me until I encountered the first outlet. I figured I'd just measure exactly where the box was on the studs—how far from the corner? how far from the floor? how big is the box?—carefully transfer those measurements to the sheetrock, then draw and cut the hole. I'd just have to maneuver the heavy beast into place and the hole and the outlet would be perfectly aligned.

Needless to say, it wasn't so simple. My precision measurement and cutting job was off by about ½ inch on one side and ¼ inch on the other. I tried to correct this by reshaping the hole, but that only made things worse, as now there was a wide gap on one side and a too-tight fit on the other. I then tried trimming one end of the board and repositioning it, but that also failed to produce alignment. I decided to start over completely. I measured and cut again and to my dismay, found that again, I couldn't get outlet and hole to line up as they should. I was completely puzzled, not only about why my brilliant method wasn't working, but also why I couldn't think of another way to do it.

As I was puzzling over this, my boss walked in, immediately sized up the situation, and shook his head, amazed at my lack of progress. "Watch this," he said. He grabbed a chalk line out of his tool bag and rubbed the chalky twine all over the edges of the electrical outlet, leaving it covered in fine red dust. Then he positioned the uncut wallboard exactly into place, reached out with the palm of his hand and slapped the wallboard two times directly over spot where the box was located. He eased the wallboard back away from the wall and there, perfectly outlined in red chalk, was a direct transfer of the precise location of the outlet. "Cut just outside those lines with your knife," he advised, "and you'll have a perfect fit every time."

I had just learned what builders call a "trick of the trade," one of those clever methods used by experienced people to solve problems that stump beginners and novices. Once you know the trick, the solution seems obvious and simple. "Why didn't I think of that?" you're likely to say. Without knowing the trick, the solution can be very hard to see.

A recurring theme throughout this reader is that social scientists who study culture find it to be an endeavor fraught with difficulties. We don't always agree on how to best study culture, nor do we always agree on what it even is. The readings in this section don't dive deeply into these debates, but they do offer a variety of different approaches to solving some of the basic puzzles of cultural analysis. They explain some of the tricks of the trade that cultural sociologists have developed in order to produce sound and methodical studies of a wide variety of cultural phenomena. Some of these readings focus on developing a reliable method for evaluating cultural objects, others describe systematic ways of sizing up cultural frames, and still others focus on finding ways to marshal the specific kind of evidence that supports arguments about cultural effects. In most cases, these authors are trying to show the different kinds of logic—coherent ways of thinking about connections, causes, and effects—that can be useful to cultural sociologists as we puzzle over the problems we encounter in our research. Like my old boss, these authors teach their tricks by way of example. They present real-world applications of their advice and encourage students to think through how to apply these tricks to research puzzles.

Unlike the problems found in the heavy, solid realm of sheetrock and studs, where a trick of the trade can lead to perfect alignments and tight fits, the problems of the cultural realm often resist easy solutions. The same tricks of the trade don't work every time, nor have cultural sociologists found tricks to solve every problem. But if you fill your methodological toolbox with these ideas, you'll have much of what you need to tackle a wide variety of analytical jobs.

# 18

# THICK DESCRIPTION

CLIFFORD GEERTZ

What's in a wink? Physiologically, it's little more than a contraction of a tiny muscle above the eye. But we seldom think of it that way. Sure, if you get something stuck in your eyelash, you might wink. But, typically we wink for other reasons: to flirt; to signal irony; or, perhaps, to seal a minor conspiracy with a friend. Winks, it seems, are social things. We wink not for ourselves, but for others.

Clifford Geertz (1926–2006) was an American anthropologist who specialized in Indonesian cultures. For thirty years, he was a professor at the Institute for Advanced Study at Princeton University, where he produced the major works of scholarship that greatly influenced cultural sociologists of the 1970s–1990s. Geertz championed the Weberian ideal of interpretive social science and argued powerfully and persuasively that culture was essentially a system of inherited symbols and meanings that shape our attitudes and actions. The goal of cultural analysis, he argued, was to find the deeper meanings that lay beneath human behavior and action. The best available method, he contended, was *ethnography,* the practice of closely observing symbols, codes, and systems of signs, along with how people use them in their customs, practices, and everyday habits and behaviors. Ethographic descriptions are the basis for cultural analysis, which is the interpretation of those symbols, signs, and codes. For such descriptions to be useful, Geertz insisted, they must be *thick,* by which he meant complex, layered, and nuanced.

**Although he was interested in the meaning of winks and, famously, things like cockfights, Geertz was focused on bigger issues. He foresaw a time when cultural analysts might lose themselves in the maze of meanings surrounding minor things like games and, yes, winks. He urged ethnographers to focus instead on the "hard surfaces" of life: violence; wars and revolutions; status and ethnicity; even death. To offer thick descriptions of the symbolic dimensions of such matters, Geertz believed, was to probe the deepest mysteries of human existence.**

## FROM *THE INTERPRETATION OF CULTURES*

B elieving, with Max Weber, that man is an animal suspended in webs of significance he himself has spun, I take culture to be those webs, and the analysis of it to be therefore not an experimental science in search of law but an interpretive one in search of meaning. It is explication I am after, construing social expressions on their surface enigmatical. But this pronouncement, a doctrine in a clause, demands itself some explication.

## II

In anthropology, or anyway social anthropology, what the practioners do is ethnography. And it is in understanding what ethnography is, or more exactly *what doing ethnography is*, that a start can be made toward grasping what anthropological analysis amounts to as a form of knowledge. This, it must immediately be said, is not a matter of methods. From one point of view, that of the textbook, doing ethnography is establishing rapport, selecting informants, transcribing texts, taking genealogies, mapping fields, keeping a diary, and so on. But it is not these things, techniques and received procedures, that define the enterprise. What defines it is the kind of intellectual effort it is: an elaborate venture in, to borrow a notion from Gilbert Ryle, "thick description."

Ryle's discussion of "thick description" appears in two recent essays of his (now reprinted in the second volume of his *Collected Papers*) addressed to the general question of what, as he puts it, "*Le Penseur*" is doing: "Thinking and Reflecting" and "The Thinking of Thoughts." Consider, he says, two boys rapidly contracting the eyelids of their right eyes. In one, this is an involuntary twitch; in the other, a conspiratorial signal to a friend. The two movements are, as movements, identical; from an I-am-a-camera, "phenomenalistic" observation of them alone, one could not tell which was twitch and which was wink, or indeed whether both or either was twitch or wink. Yet the difference, however unphotographable, between a twitch and a wink is vast; as anyone unfortunate enough to have had the first taken for the second knows. The winker is communicating, and indeed communicating in a quite precise and special way: (1) deliberately, (2) to someone in particular, (3) to impart a particular message, (4) according to a socially established code, and (5) without cognizance of the rest of the company. As Ryle points out, the winker has not done two things, contracted his eyelids and winked, while the twitcher has done only one, contracted his eyelids. Contracting your eyelids on purpose when there exists a public code in which so doing counts as a conspiratorial signal *is* winking. That's all there is to it: a speck of behavior, a fleck of culture, and—*voilà*—a gesture.

That, however, is just the beginning. Suppose, he continues, there is a third boy, who, "to give malicious amusement to his cronies," parodies the first boy's wink, as amateurish, clumsy, obvious, and so on. He, of course, does this in the same way the second boy winked and the first twitched: by contracting his right eyelids. Only this boy is neither winking nor twitching, he is parodying someone else's, as he takes it, laughable, attempt at winking. Here, too, a socially established code exists (he will "wink" laboriously, overobviously, perhaps adding a grimace—the usual artifices of the clown); and so also does a message. Only now it is not conspiracy but ridicule that is in the air. If the others think he is actually winking, his whole project misfires as completely, though with somewhat different results, as if they think he is twitching. One can go further: uncertain of his mimicking abilities, the would-be satirist may practice at home before the mirror, in which case he is not twitching, winking, or parodying, but rehearsing; though so far as what a camera, a radical behaviorist, or a believer in protocol sentences would record he is just rapidly contracting his right eyelids like all the others. Complexities are possible, if not practically without end, at least logically so. The original winker might, for example, actually have been fake-winking, say, to mislead outsiders into imagining there was a conspiracy afoot when there in fact was not, in which case our descriptions of what the parodist is parodying and the rehearser rehearsing of course shift accordingly. But the point is that between what Ryle calls the "thin description" of what the rehearser (parodist, winker, twitcher . . . ) is doing ("rapidly contracting his right eyelids") and the "thick description" of what he is doing ("practicing a burlesque of a friend faking a wink to deceive an innocent into thinking a conspiracy is in motion") lies the object of ethnography: a stratified hierarchy of meaningful structures in terms of which twitches, winks, fake-winks, parodies, rehearsals of parodies are produced, perceived, and interpreted, and without which they would not (not even the zero-form twitches, which, *as a cultural category*, are as much nonwinks as winks are nontwitches) in fact exist, no matter what anyone did or didn't do with his eyelids.

Like so many of the little stories Oxford philosophers like to make up for themselves, all this winking, fake-winking, burlesque-fake-winking, rehearsed-burlesque-fake-winking, may seem a bit artificial. In way of adding a more empirical note, let me give, deliberately unpreceded by any prior explanatory comment at all, a not untypical excerpt from my own field journal to demonstrate that, however evened off for didactic purposes, Ryle's example presents an image only too exact of the sort of piled-up structures of inference and implication through which an ethnographer is continually trying to pick his way:

> The French [the informant said] had only just arrived. They set up twenty or so small forts between here, the town, and the Marmusha area up in the middle of the mountains, placing them on promontories so they could survey the countryside. But for all this they couldn't guarantee safety, especially at night, so although the *mezrag*, trade-pact, system was supposed to be legally abolished it in fact continued as before.
>
> One night, when Cohen (who speaks fluent Berber), was up there, at Marmusha, two other Jews who were traders to a neighboring tribe came by to purchase some goods from him. Some Berbers, from yet another neighboring tribe, tried to break into Cohen's place, but he fired his rifle in the air. (Traditionally, Jews were not allowed to carry weapons; but at this period things were so unsettled many did so anyway.) This attracted the attention of the French and the marauders fled.
>
> The next night, however, they came back, one of them disguised as a woman who knocked on the door with some sort of a story. Cohen was

suspicious and didn't want to let "her" in, but the other Jews said, "oh, it's all right, it's only a woman." So they opened the door and the whole lot came pouring in. They killed the two visiting Jews, but Cohen managed to barricade himself in an adjoining room. He heard the robbers planning to burn him alive in the shop after they removed his goods, and so he opened the door and, laying about him wildly with a club, managed to escape through a window.

He went up to the fort, then, to have his wounds dressed, and complained to the local commandant, one Captain Dumari, saying he wanted his 'ar—i.e., four or five times the value of the merchandise stolen from him. The robbers were from a tribe which had not yet submitted to French authority and were in open rebellion against it, and he wanted authorization to go with his *mezrag*-holder, the Marmusha tribal *sheikh*, to collect the indemnity that, under traditional rules, he had coming to him. Captain Dumari couldn't officially give him permission to do this, because of the French prohibition of the *mezrag* relationship, but he gave him verbal authorization, saying, "If you get killed, it's your problem."

So the *sheikh*, the Jew, and a small company of armed Marmushans went off ten or fifteen kilometers up into the rebellious area, where there were of course no French, and, sneaking up, captured the thief-tribe's shepherd and stole its herds. The other tribe soon came riding out on horses after them, armed with rifles and ready to attack. But when they saw who the "sheep thieves" were, they thought better of it and said, "all right, we'll talk." They couldn't really deny what had happened—that some of their men had robbed Cohen and killed the two visitors—and they weren't prepared to start the serious feud with the Marmusha a scuffle with the invading party would bring on. So the two groups talked, and talked, and talked, there on the plain amid the thousands of sheep, and decided finally on five-hundred-sheep damages. The two armed Berber groups then lined up on their horses at opposite ends of the plain, with the sheep herded between them, and Cohen, in his black gown, pillbox hat, and flapping slippers, went out alone among the sheep, picking out, one by one and at his own good speed, the best ones for his payment.

So Cohen got his sheep and drove them back to Marmusha. The French, up in their fort, heard them coming from some distance ("Ba, ba, ba" said Cohen, happily, recalling the image) and said, "What the hell is that?" And Cohen said, "That is my 'ar." The French couldn't believe he had actually done what he said he had done, and accused him of being a spy for the rebellious Berbers, put him in prison, and took his sheep. In the town, his family, not having heard from him in so long a time, thought he was dead. But after a while the French released him and he came back home, but without his sheep. He then went to the Colonel in the town, the Frenchman in charge of the whole region, to complain. But the Colonel said, "I can't do anything about the matter. It's not my problem."

Quoted raw, a note in a bottle, this passage conveys, as any similar one similarly presented would do, a fair sense of how much goes into ethnographic description of even the most elemental sort—how extraordinarily "thick" it is. In finished anthropological writings, including those collected here, this fact—that what we call our data are really our own constructions of other people's constructions of what they and their compatriots are up to—is obscured because most of what we need to comprehend a particular event, ritual, custom, idea, or whatever is insinuated as background information before the thing itself is directly examined. (Even to reveal that this little drama took place in the highlands of central Morocco in 1912—and was recounted there in 1968—is to determine much of our understanding of it.) There is nothing particularly wrong with this, and it is in any case inevitable. But it does lead to a view of anthropological research as rather more of an observational and rather less of an interpretive activity than it really is. Right down at the factual base, the hard rock, insofar as there is any, of the whole enterprise, we are already explicating: and worse, explicating explications. Winks upon winks upon winks.

Analysis, then, is sorting out the structures of signification—what Ryle called established codes, a somewhat misleading expression, for it makes the enterprise sound too much like that of the cipher clerk when it is much more like that of the literary critic—and determining their social ground and import. Here, in our text, such sorting would begin with distinguishing the three unlike frames of interpretation ingredient in the situation, Jewish, Berber, and French, and would then move on to show how (and why) at that time, in that place, their copresence produced a situation in which systematic misunderstanding reduced traditional form to social farce. What tripped Cohen up, and with him the whole, ancient pattern of social and economic relationships within which he functioned, was a confusion of tongues.

I shall come back to this too-compacted aphorism later, as well as to the details of the text itself. The point for now is only that ethnography is thick description. What the ethnographer is in fact faced with—except when (as, of course, he must do) he is pursuing the more automatized routines of data collection—is a multiplicity of complex conceptual structures, many of them superimposed upon or knotted into one another, which are at once strange, irregular, and inexplicit, and which he must contrive somehow first to grasp and then to render. And this is true at the most down-to-earth, jungle field work levels of his activity: interviewing informants, observing rituals, eliciting kin terms, tracing property lines, censusing households . . . writing his journal. Doing ethnography is like trying to read (in the sense of "construct a reading of") a manuscript—foreign, faded, full of ellipses, incoherencies, suspicious emendations, and tendentious commentaries, but written not in conventionalized graphs of sound but in transient examples of shaped behavior.

## III

Looked at in this way, the aim of anthropology is the enlargement of the universe of human discourse. That is not, of course, its only aim—instruction, amusement, practical counsel, moral advance, and the discovery of natural order in human behavior are others; nor is anthropology the only discipline which pursues it. But it is an aim to which a semiotic concept of culture is peculiarly well adapted. As interworked systems of construable signs (what, ignoring provincial usages, I would call symbols), culture is not a power, something to which social events, behaviors, institutions, or processes can be causally attributed; it is a context, something within which they can be intelligibly—that is, thickly—described.

The famous anthropological absorption with the (to us) exotic—Berber horsemen, Jewish peddlers, French Legionnaires—is, thus, essentially a device for displacing the dulling sense of familiarity with which the mysteriousness of our own ability to relate perceptively to one another is concealed from us. Looking at the ordinary in places where it takes unaccustomed forms brings out not, as has so often been claimed, the arbitrariness of human behavior (there is nothing especially arbitrary about taking sheep theft for insolence in Morocco), but the degree to which its meaning varies according to the pattern of life by which it is informed. Understanding a people's culture exposes their normalness without reducing their particularity. (The more I manage to follow what the Moroccans are up to, the more logical, and the more singular, they seem.) It renders them accessible: setting them in the frame of their own banalities, it dissolves their opacity.

It is this maneuver, usually too casually referred to as "seeing things from the actor's point of view," too bookishly as "the *verstehen* approach," or too technically as "emic analysis," that so often leads to the notion that anthropology is a variety of either long-distance mind reading or cannibalisle fantasizing, and which, for someone anxious to navigate past the wrecks of a dozen sunken philosophies, must therefore be executed with a great deal of care. Nothing is more necessary to comprehending what anthropological interpretation is, and the degree to which it *is* interpretation, than an exact understanding of what it means—and what it does not mean— to say that our formulations of other peoples' symbol systems must be actor-oriented.

# VIII

There is an Indian story—at least I heard it as an Indian story—about an Englishman who, having been told that the world rested on a platform which rested on the back of an elephant which rested in turn on the back of a turtle, asked (perhaps he was an ethnographer; it is the way they behave), what did the turtle rest on? Another turtle. And that turtle? "Ah, Sahib, after that it is turtles all the way down."

Such, indeed, is the condition of things. I do not know how long it would be profitable to meditate on the encounter of Cohen, the sheikh, and "Dumari" (the period has perhaps already been exceeded); but I do know that however long I did so I would not get anywhere near to the bottom of it. Nor have I ever gotten anywhere near to the bottom of anything I have ever written about, either in the essays below or elsewhere. Cultural analysis is intrinsically incomplete. And, worse than that, the more deeply it goes the less complete it is. It is a strange science whose most telling assertions are its most tremulously based, in which to get somewhere with the matter at hand is to intensify the suspicion, both your own and that of others, that you are not quite getting it right. But that, along with plaguing subtle people with obtuse questions, is what being an ethnographer is like.

There are a number of ways to escape this—turning culture into folklore and collecting it, turning it into traits and counting it, turning it into institutions and classifying it, turning it into structures and toying with it. But they *are* escapes. The fact is that to commit oneself to a semiotic concept of culture and an interpretive approach to the study of it is to commit oneself to a view of ethnographic assertion as, to borrow W. B. Gallie's by now famous phrase, "essentially contestable." Anthropology, or at least interpretive anthropology, is a science whose progress is marked less by a perfection of consensus than by a refinement of debate. What gets better is the precision with which we vex each other.

This is very difficult to see when one's attention is being monopolized by a single party to the argument. Monologues are of little value here, because there are no conclusions to be reported; there is merely a discussion to be sustained. Insofar as the essays here collected have any importance, it is less in what they say than what they are witness to: an enormous increase in interest, not only in anthropology, but in social studies generally, in the role of symbolic forms in human life. Meaning, that elusive and ill-defined pseudoentity we were once more than content to leave philosophers and literary critics to fumble with, has now come back into the heart of our discipline. Even Marxists are quoting Cassirer; even positivists, Kenneth Burke.

My own position in the midst of all this has been to try to resist subjectivism on the one hand and cabbalism on the other, to try to keep the analysis of symbolic forms as closely tied as I could to concrete social events and occasions, the public world of common life, and to organize it in such a way that the connections between theoretical formulations and descriptive interpretations were unobscured by appeals to dark sciences. I have never been impressed by the argument that, as complete objectivity is impossible in these matters (as, of course, it is), one might as well let one's sentiments run loose. As Robert Solow has remarked, that is like saying that as a perfectly aseptic environment is impossible, one might as well conduct surgery in a sewer. Nor, on the other hand, have I been impressed with claims that structural linguistics, computer engineering, or some other advanced form of thought is going to enable us to understand men without knowing them. Nothing will discredit a semiotic approach to culture more quickly than allowing it to drift into a combination of intuitionism and alchemy, no matter how elegantly the intuitions are expressed or how modern the alchemy is made to look.

The danger that cultural analysis, in search of all-too-deep-lying turtles, will lose touch with the hard surfaces of life—with the political, economic, stratificatory realities within which men are everywhere contained—and with the biological and physical necessities on which those surfaces rest, is an ever-present one. The only defense against it, and against, thus, turning cultural analysis into a kind of sociological aestheticism, is to train such analysis on such realities and such necessities in the first place. It is thus that I have written about nationalism, about violence, about identity, about human nature, about legitimacy, about revolution, about ethnicity, about urbanization, about status, about death, about time, and most of all about particular attempts by particular peoples to place these things in some sort of comprehensible, meaningful frame.

To look at the symbolic dimensions of social action—art, religion, ideology, science, law, morality, common sense—is not to turn away from the existential dilemmas of life for some empyrean realm of de-emotionalized forms; it is to plunge into the midst of them. The essential vocation of interpretive anthropology is not to answer our deepest questions, but to make available to us answers that others, guarding other sheep in other valleys, have given, and thus to include them in the consultable record of what man has said.

# STUDY QUESTIONS

1. What points does Geertz make about "thick description" with the story of the sheep?
2. Geertz's view is that culture is semiotic. What does he mean by this claim?

# 19

# METHOD

WENDY GRISWOLD

Most of the authors in this reader focus on one area of cultural analysis—cultural production or diffusion, for instance, or cultural change or transformation—and study it intensively. Consequently, students learn a great deal from them about relatively narrow aspects of culture. Griswold contends that with the proper method in place, one can broaden the analytical focus to include other aspects of culture that matter as much or more than those on which sociologists have previously focused. Her approach covers four key aspects of cultural objects: 1) the intentions of cultural producers and creators; 2) the different ways an object is received and interpreted by audiences; 3) the qualities and characteristics of a cultural object itself; and 4) the relation of an object to the larger social content in which it appears.

The four key aspects Griswold names call to mind Marx's insistence that any complete analysis of economic systems must deal with four processes: production, consumption, distribution, and exchange (or circulation). Marx suggested that if you want to discover something about the nature of capitalism, you should follow commodities as they move through these four distinct but related processes.

These basic guidelines for discovering broader aspects of culture are very abstract, as all outlines for methodologies must be. But Griswold fleshes out the abstractions and shows us the significance of each area of concern by offering examples drawn from the sociology of literature and the arts. Her many writings have exemplified this method, and she has simplified it over the years, labeling it the "cultural diamond" approach for the way it interrelates these four sides of cultural analysis. Griswold's approach is probably more often cited than followed, but her now-classic methodology has inspired a generation of cultural sociologists to look at the big picture.

# A METHODOLOGICAL FRAMEWORK FOR THE SOCIOLOGY OF CULTURE

A cultural methodology that does not throw meaning overboard in some sort of disciplinary triage begins by focusing cultural analysis on the point at which individuals interact with a cultural object. I use the term *cultural object* to refer to shared significance embodied in form, i.e., to an expression of social meanings that is tangible or can be put into words.[1] Thus, a religious doctrine, a belief about the racial characteristics of blacks, a sonnet, a hairstyle, and a quilt could all be analyzed as cultural objects; the analyst must designate just what the object in question is. The analysis centered on this interaction is thereby organized by four actions: intention, reception, comprehension, and explanation. One dimension of this typology is defined by the person performing the action—the social agent or the analyst. The other dimension is defined by the person's attitude toward the cultural object's meaning—constituted in the object or embedded in the social world. Thus, the social agent intends and receives; the analyst comprehends and explains. Intention and comprehension involve understanding the meaning of the cultural object as constituted by the object itself, internal to it, while reception and explanation involve framing the cultural object in relation to some larger, external system of meaning. Thus, the four actions

1. This definition of *cultural object*, and its pragmatic specification in analysis, is somewhat narrower than Talcott Parsons's use of the term. Parsons defined a cultural object as any pattern reproducible in the action of another person (see Alexander 1983, pp. 40–41). A cultural object and its partial meaning must be capable of being articulated by an agent, either a social actor or the analyst of social action; a pattern to which no particular meaning can be attached would not be included under my definition.

delineated by crossing the two dimensions involve the agent and the analyst in both the internal character and the external connectedness of the cultural object.

======

# Intention

Agents, particularly producing agents, have intentions. Central to the analytic framework proposed here is some social agent, or agents, interacting with some cultural object. Sociologists must not reduce intention to an agent's individual psychology or consciousness, but this does not mean that the concept is not analytically useful. While it is futile to try to get at the subjectivity of any particular individual, it is possible to reconstruct probable intentionality of any agent whose context and behavior are known.[2] The purpose of doing so is to separate the individually idiosyncratic from the socially influenced by determining the degree to which intentionality has been shaped by social elements, which may be shared, and the degree to which cultural outcomes are themselves shaped by intentions.

The simplest and most typical approach to intention is to attempt to connect a cultural object to its producing agent by asking, for example, why Piero della Francesca organized the elements of his painting *Baptism of Christ* in a certain way, or whether John Donne intended his poem "A Valediction: Forbidding Mourning" to be about death or departure. Taking the former as an illustrative problem, Baxandall (1985) suggests that the tracing of plausible intention amounts to the reconstruction of the "charge" and "brief" that an artist held at the time of his creation of some particular work. The charge, a general and immediate prompt for an agent to act, may be internally generated or may come from an external and quite explicit source. Piero was commissioned to paint an altarpiece for the church of Sansepolcro sometime around 1450; thus, in Baxandall's terms, Piero's client gave him the charge, "Altarpiece!" This charge entailed a set of social expectations (local wisdom about altarpieces) and the particular concerns of those wealthy enough to commission them: An altarpiece must represent a recognizable

---

2. Arguments for the necessity of determining intentionality in historical and sociological texts can be found in Skinner (1969) and Jones (1977).

scriptural passage, it must be instructive, it must be emotionally moving and able to instill reverence, it must be clear and memorable, and it must reflect the taste and wealth of the client who paid for it.

For any given charge, the analyst may construct a brief, which is a list of constraints and influences, clustered by their sources and types, that together constitute the artist's probable intention. Piero's brief would look something like this:[3]

*Immediate circumstances*: (1) church in Borgo Sansepolcro, Piero's native town; (2) altar width requires tall, narrow painting; (3) client requires that all, or almost all, of painting be done by Piero, not his students; (4) client requires that subject be Christ's baptism.

*Piero's training and experience*: (5) fifteenth-century Italian artists' familiarity with *commensurazione* (interdependent proportion and perspective); Piero's particular expertise (he wrote treatises on mathematics and perspective); (6) Piero's contract, which probably stipulated colors and amount of gilding to be used; (7) Piero's 1439 stay in Florence, when Donatello was finishing the Cantoria of the Cathedral, a monumental work of public art.

*Local conditions*: (8) community expectations regarding the didactic function of altarpieces; (9) familiarity of learned members of community with biblical narrative of Christ's baptism (Matthew 3); (10) shared assumptions regarding the mystery and cosmic significance of Christ's baptism as a historical event.

*Physical media and constraints*: (11) working on two-dimensional plane, using paint and gilding; (12) picture had to be organized vertically because of tall, narrow shape of central panel of the altarpiece imposed by small size of the altar.

*Aesthetic conditions*: (13) Piero's normal employment of rose color to denote importance; (14) Piero's normal representation of angels—statuesque, undifferentiated, no off-shoulder garments, no wreaths; (15) conventional representations of angels in Renaissance paintings of Christ's baptism, even though not found in biblical account; (16) other conventions of Renaissance religious painting.

---

3. The actual contract between Piero and his client for the *Baptism* no longer exists, but a 1445 contract for one of his similar commissions does. Baxandall does not set out the brief as a numerical list in his chapter on Piero, so I have followed the format he used in an earlier chapter (see pp. 26–32). I have constructed the brief only as it relates to one strand of Baxandall's analysis, that having to do with the spatial arrangement of the pictorial elements; the entire brief would be considerably longer.

Such a brief has several useful features: It includes constraints from the narrow, institutional market and from the broader, cultural market of ideas; it incorporates elements from the agent's biography, including information on other artists to whom he responded; and it draws on the mentalities of the artist's social group and the groups to which he had to appeal.

——

Notice that intention, represented by the agent's brief and the relationship of that brief to the cultural outcome, is discovered not by getting inside the agent's head—this naïve reductionism is repudiated by those who lay the greatest emphasis on intentionality—but by constructing probabilities to answer some questions about cultural objects. . . .

Nor is intention to be confused with consequences. A cultural object may fail to realize the intentions of its creative agent in two ways: Either the agent may be unable to formulate the object in accord with his intentions, or the object may not "work" as intended on its recipients because of an inappropriate setting, misunderstandings, interpretations at odds with the agent's own, and similar communicative infelicities. If Piero had been unable to obtain gold, he would have failed to carry out his intention of glorifying Christ with a heavenly spotlight; when the gilding wore off, his intention of indicating sacredness was no longer realized because of a material failure. His original intentions, as constructed by the analyst, are not altered by the subsequent reception of his work.

## Reception

As in the Donne example, a focus on intention usually involves the question, What made a cultural object the way it is, i.e., why did a social agent involved in its production give it its particular characteristics, which the analyst has specified in terms of structures, symbols, or patterns? A different type of question (or a different phase of the analysis) asks, How is the cultural object received? Varieties of this type of question might be concerned with the object's differential impact among different social categories or groups, its influence, its popularity, its meaning for those who appropriate it. For all such questions, the social agent is the receiver. (Of course, a receiver may also be a producer in a different agent/object interaction. Piero "received" Donatello's angels and incorporated them into his own intentional brief for the *Baptism*.) Hans Robert Jauss (1982, pp. 20–45) has described literary reception as a reader situating a text against his "horizon of expectations," a horizon based on his social and cultural experiences. For the analyst attempting to reconstruct such a horizon, Jauss offers seven suggestions (all of which may be extended beyond Jauss's specifically literary concerns): (1) take the past reader's point of view; (2) understand the history of the genre and the literary frame of reference at the time of the work's appearance (the initial horizon); (3) examine the effect of the work on its audiences; (4) find the question that the work originally addressed; (5) locate the work diachronically by understanding its historical position in literary history; (6) locate it synchronically by understanding the system of contemporary literary works at its historical moment; and (7) relate literary history to general history by showing, among other things, how literature affects its readers' social horizon of expectations. . . .

There are at least five types of reception, which are related but not congruent. These are interpretation (the meaning-construction produced by any particular agent or group of agents), market success (popularity, indicated by commercial success, by number of converts, or by some other measure of immediate esteem accorded to a cultural object), impact on fields of cultural reference (a cultural object's influence on the framing of other cultural objects), canonization (the acceptance of a cultural object by that elite group of specialists who may legitimately talk about value), and endurance (the persistence of a cultural object over time at either the elite or popular level). These forms are interactive, but their mutual relations are neither obvious nor inevitable. . . .

=====

A consideration of reception demonstrates the indispensable role comparison plays in elucidating cultural meanings for social actors. Comparison is useful even for developing hypotheses of originating intention (Donne's typical use of the term *valediction* compared with that of his contemporaries), but sociologists, although they must rely on intention as a tool for investigation, are usually more concerned with significance, i.e., with the relationship between a cultural object and some human beings beyond its creator. Here, neither an assumed objective meaning buried in a cultural object nor a hypothetical intentional context of a creative agent are as important as the constructions and reconstructions made by the recipients who interact with the object, and significant reconstructions are only obvious in comparison with other constructions. For example, according to Eugene Genovese (1974), slave owners believed Christianity taught their chattels the virtues of humility and service in expectation of an otherworldly reward, so they were tolerant of limited amounts of missionary activity (so long as the evangelists did not teach dangerous skills such as literacy). The slaves, on the other hand, constructed a gospel whose characteristics were quite different from those understood by their owners—a gospel emphasizing freedom, individual dignity, earthly salvation, and even a heavenly sanctioned deviousness ("steal away to Jesus"). Similarly, a recent study of my own demonstrates that three different groups of recipients regularly construed different meanings from George Lamming's novel *In the Castle of My Skin*: American readers believed it was about race, West Indian readers believed it was about identity and nation building, and British readers believed it was a poetic depiction of growing up, without a political or social message (Griswold 1987). . . .

So far, I have treated the interactions proceeding to and from a cultural object as if they were static, but this is only a convenient fiction. Because they are multivocal, cultural objects are never fixed, and the analyst must be able to treat a cultural phenomenon in terms of its characteristics as a process, as movement through space and time. The dynamic nature of a cultural object is perhaps most obvious in its reception, i.e., in its impact on a human agent. . . .

## Comprehension

For the analyst, comprehension means understanding those characteristics of the cultural object that bear on the investigation. Such understanding requires both inclusion—the analyst "takes in" the object—and utility—the analyst "grasps" the object, "gets a handle on it," in order to do something with it. But cultural objects seldom have handles, nor do they come in clearly demarcated units of meaning to be gathered up like apples. The analyst faces a figure/field problem: How is he to designate, even provisionally, those characteristics that will be helpful to his explorations of meaning and social connectedness and that will be available to the understanding of others, i.e., replicable? How is a scientific comprehension possible?

Comprehension entails apperception, the interpretation of a new cultural object in terms of what is already known. Thus, genre is the key to analytic comprehension. Genres, as they have been understood in literary theory, are classifications based on similarities and differences. Making generic distinctions involves sorting, seeing the similarities in different literary objects, abstracting the common elements from a welter of particular variations. Since the Renaissance, the dominant view among critics has been that genres are arbitrarily defined; such definitions are often practical, but the critic should not fall for the "superstition" that genres have any ontological status (Croce [1922] 1978, p. 449). Like the critic, the sociological analyst, being practical, may grasp cultural objects through the provisional construction of genre. Employing a convenient fiction for the time being, the analyst may treat genre as if it were a property of a cultural object, thereby emphasizing that object's similarity to and differences from other cultural objects. Thus construed, genre may be a variable or a constant in cultural analysis.

Two conceptions of genre that come from literary criticism—provided by Hirsch (1967) and by Rosmarin (1985)—clarify the link between comprehension and genre. In some respects, the two are explicitly opposed. Hirsch's primary interest in genre lies in its capacity to offer clues to an author's intended meaning, while Rosmarin sees genre as a pragmatic decision made by critics to facilitate their criticism. Hirsch advocates a method of probabilistic analysis to narrow the field toward an increasingly precise reconstruction of authorial intention ("intrinsic genre"), while Rosmarin looks for syllogistic expansiveness (the best genre decision by the critic is that which will lead to the longest and most fruitful chain of syllogisms). For the sociological analyst, however, their points of agreement are more significant. Both regard genre not as some property of the literary text but as an inherently social relationship. For Hirsch, the relationship is between the author and the interpreter; the author must work within the reader's set of generic expectations, or the author's meaning will not be communicated. Thus, genre is constitutive as well as heuristic. Rosmarin's concern is also with communication, although the agents she focuses on are critics and their readers. In addition to this shared concern with the social, both theorists emphasize the historical contingencies of genre, as opposed to some Aristotelian fixity. For Hirsch, history constitutes the background for the author's generic choices; for Rosmarin, history is the background for the critic's practical choices. In both cases, genre is neither obvious nor unchanging.

Previously, I pointed out that there are two types of social agents in relation to cultural objects: the producer (or originator, or creator) and the recipient. These may be better understood as phases of agency, and when the phase changes, the cultural object changes too: The recipient of a sonnet becomes the producer of another sonnet or of a critical essay.[4] The producing agent has some idea of what genre he is working in; that is, he intends his cultural object to fit into, or refer to, one or more known classifications having particular characteristics. This sense of genre, constitutive in Hirsch's typology, forms a part of the agent's brief; Piero knew that the genre of altarpieces implied certain things that all altarpieces had in common. In empirical cultural analysis, the analyst reconstructing the creative agent's brief attempts to understand his intrinsic genre. But to comprehend the cultural object for his own practical purposes, the analyst makes generic decisions of his own, treating genre as a heuristic in his attempt to get a comparative handle on the objects in question.

———

This process of comprehending the cultural object by establishing provisional, heuristic genres exemplifies Rosmarin's pragmatism. But I want to emphasize my agreement with Hirsch's contention that it is desirable to give temporal privilege to the producing agent's meanings, especially including his generic decisions. This helps the analyst elucidate parts of the cultural object in question, its distinctiveness and its affiliations, and it enables him to construct better genres of his own based on their analytical utility. Piero's reconstructed brief provides data on his intended genre (altarpiece), which can be used as evidence even when the analyst is focusing on a different genre (Piero's paintings) and asking why one particular work is different from his others. The sociologist may ultimately be more concerned with significance than with intention, but the latter is a way to the former.

4. For precision's sake, one should avoid thinking of an agent as a mediator. Mediation is simply the combination of the reception and production of different cultural objects. For example, the disk jockey, a classic gatekeeper, selects from a large number of records clamoring for attention and produces a "Pick of the Week" or "Top Ten." To say that the disk jockey mediates between recording artists and audiences is true enough, but it obscures the two separate actions involved.

# Explanation

While comprehension refers to the generic specification of the cultural object, and intention and reception refer to the interaction of objects and agents, explanation is the analyst's connection of cultural objects, through social agents, to the external world beyond the creative community. My consideration of explanation builds on the theories of two of the most astute analysts of cultural phenomena: Lucien Goldmann and Clifford Geertz. Goldmann ([1967] 1970), a Belgian Marxist sociologist influenced by Lukacs, postulated that over the course of their histories, social groups (by which he meant classes and class fractions) develop shared categories of understanding that transcend what any individual group member possesses. The artist, who is unusually though perhaps unconsciously receptive to the mental categories of his group, incorporates homologues of these categories in his artistic or literary works. In keeping with this program of "genetic structuralism," Goldmann defined the comprehension of cultural works more narrowly than I have in the discussion of genre. For him, comprehension was the elucidation of structures within the works. In the case of masterpieces, whose coherence is especially profound by definition, these structures organize most of the features of the work. Explanation then becomes a matter of finding homologies between these structures and the mental structures, or collective categories, of the artist's social group, which shares a historical position and predicament. . . .

Goldmann's explicit concern with method contrasts sharply with Geertz's equally explicit rejection of methodological specification beyond "thick description." But in spite of his vigorous denial of generalizing intent or systematic procedures, Geertz's actual practice in interpretive analysis may be schematically represented in similar fashion. As an anthropologist who has studied forms of collective expression from cockfights to funerary customs, Geertz has considered a broader range of cultural objects than Goldmann, and his research lacks Goldmann's special emphasis on masterpieces (although cultural endurance seems to weigh heavily). Geertz examines cultural performances for their enacted signs and symbols, not just structures, and he is particularly interested in the local cognitive styles that give meaning to these symbols. In his explanations, he argues that this cognitive style originates in the social and cultural experience of a society, without according primacy to the relations of conflict between classes (as required by Goldmann's Marxist assumptions). . . .

This parallel schematization brings out several differences between Geertz's and Goldmann's styles of cultural explanation. Geertz is not willing to generalize from one "local" result to another; Goldmann is, and he is confident about which variables have causal primacy. The two represent extremes that suggest the intermediate: the possibility of generalizing beyond the strictly local while remaining agnostic about ultimate causality in any particular case. Also, while Goldmann concentrates on artists and their class backgrounds, Geertz brings in a wider variety of human agents (poets, wedding guests, hosts who place certain demands on the poets) operating in and through a variety of institutions (the performance context of a wedding, an educational system that emphasizes memorization of texts). Such breadth seems desirable, at least as an initial strategy, in attempting to understand complex cultural phenomena without imposing preconceived ideas too hastily. Yet, while Geertz seems to imply a matrix of sensibility for an entire society (indeed, for all Islamic societies), Goldmann talks about the mental structures of distinguishable social categories or groups within the larger society. Goldmann's program more accurately represents sociological capacities than do the extremes of either psychological reductionism or the assumption that all members of a society share a common knowledge and sensibility.

Drawing what seems to be most useful from both methods, one arrives at a framework for cultural analysis that may be schematically represented as follows:

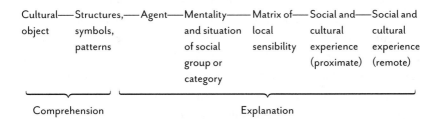

Several features of this framework require comment. First (moving from left to right), the cultural object under examination is identified by the analyst as anything that fits the general definition of shared significance embodied in form. The model does not assume that masterpieces are different from lesser works, that so-called high culture is different from popular culture, or that tangible cultural artifacts are different from systems of ideas, beliefs, values, or practices. Cultural objects are distinguished from their surrounding socioeconomic context not by their ontological status but by their analytic use. When the analyst attends to the significance, the meaning beyond itself, of a particular human artifact, idea, or piece of behavior, he may thereby consider it a cultural object; the same artifact, idea, or behavior might be considered a commodity or an element of the social structure in a different analysis.

Second, symbols, patterns of symbols or relations, and formal structures are available components for the comprehension of any cultural object. To comprehend a cultural object, one begins with the genres, distinctions, and comparisons used by the experts on the object in question. There are two types of experts: the academic specialist on the subject, and the local informant who actually interacts with the object in question. For example, sociologists studying a religious sect should determine the analytic and comparative categories used by theologians to talk about sects—beliefs and practices, eschatology, theodicy, liturgy, what the sect is grouped with and differentiated from—and examine the terminology and assumptions of sect members themselves. Sociologists studying novels should comprehend their data using the terms of literary critics—genres like "Gothic novel" or *Künstlerroman*, narrative structure, characterization, themes, imagery, moral content—and the terms authors or readers use to talk about novels. Experts' categories do not constitute the sociologist's final resting point, but in any unknown country, it pays to listen to what the natives have to say. Then, if the experts' conceptions of genre are inadequate for the social scientist's purposes, he may provisionally construct his own genre. Goldmann chose to group Pascal and Racine together regardless of their intentions, defining a genre of the tragic vision that he could then link to the politico-economic position of the *noblesse de robe*. Similarly, Geertz established an implicit genre of glorified agonistic language to illustrate the relationship between Moroccan wedding poems as cultural objects and the Quran as part of remote cultural experience.

Third, the pivot of the framework is the agent. The agent may be a cultural producer (prophet, artist), recipient (audience member, person operating in a particular ideological context), mediator (editor, preacher, impressario, media figure, arts administrator), or any other social actor. The essential point is that for a sociological analysis, there must be a specifiable, observable, behaving agent who interacts with a cultural object and for whom a probable structure of intention (a brief) can be constructed. This does not mean that the analyst must be able to ascertain subjective, let alone conscious, meaning at the individual agent's level, but it does mean that the analyst should know enough about the agent's social and historical context, and about his immediate productive or receptive conditions, to produce a justifiable reconstruction of his intentionality.

Fourth, the agent is understood as someone who subscribes to, participates in, or reacts to the mentality of some specific social categories or some more formally organized social groups. Such categories and groups constitute the intermediate variable between agent and society. *Categories* refers to divisions by class, sex, race, ethnicity, age, cohort, education, occupation, and geographic location, and to any combination of these typical sociological variables, as in studies of working-class teenage boys. *Groups* denotes formal membership or face-to-face contact. *Mentality* is a short-hand designation for cognitive style, orthodoxy-heterodoxy-doxa (Bourdieu 1977), shared knowledge, common sense, group consciousness, and the mental structures favored by Goldmann. Thus, intentions are influenced by an agent's concrete situation and by his membership in social categories and groups.

Fifth, the idea of local sensibility has been adopted from Geertz to distinguish the ways of thinking and behaving characteristic of the most immediate spatial and temporal context of groups and agents from those more distant. More than one social category and group participate in a given local sensibility, which sets the ideological context for the more particular concerns and attitudes of the group in question. Conversely, many social groupings cross localities, and in some types of analyses, this may be the more important consideration.

Sixth, the local sensibility, and any particular group's participation in it, is shaped by the social (especially economic and political) and cultural experience of the people in question. Such experience may be arbitrarily divided between the more proximate and the more remote, as in Geertz's interpretation of the remote influence of the Quran through the more proximate patterns of Islamic education.

Finally, it must be remembered that every element on the explanatory side of the heuristic is linked to or separated from its neighbors via

social institutions. Flows of influence are not automatic but are channeled and mediated. This is apparent, for example, in the transmission
of African cultural knowledge (social and cultural experience) to the
slaves of the New World (local sensibility). Since certain types of religious
knowledge were passed on only through the elders of the West African
peoples from which the slave trade drew, and since the slave trade was
largely restricted to teenagers and young adults, there was a rupture
between remote and proximate experience that made it institutionally
impossible for these elements of African culture, despite their significance, to reappear in the local sensibility of the New World. Similarly,
much sociological attention has been paid to the disproportionate representation of certain categories, and not others, among agents involved
in the actual production of cultural objects. The exploration of social
institutions need not be the ultimate goal of sociocultural analysis, but
such institutions do constitute indispensable variables in the explanation of cultural phenomena.

Now, taking the framework developed in the examination of the explanatory procedures of Goldmann and Geertz, one may add intention, reception, and comprehension in terms of genre. The final framework, applicable
to all modes of cultural analysis that aspire to deal with the cultural object
and at the same time provide a comprehensive explanation, now looks like
this:

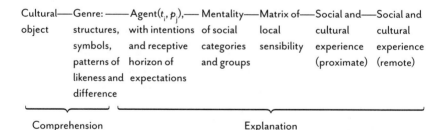

Cultural—Genre: ———Agent($t_i$, $p_j$),— Mentality—Matrix of—Social and—Social and
object      structures,   with intentions  of social     local        cultural      cultural
            symbols,      and receptive    categories    sensibility   experience    experience
            patterns of   horizon of       and groups                  (proximate)   (remote)
            likeness and  expectations
            difference

      Comprehension                                  Explanation

A cultural analysis that pays attention to the elements and connections of
this framework will produce findings that meet our criterion of sensitivity
to the specific characteristics of cultural phenomena and our scientific
desiderata of rigor and potential for generalization.

# References

Alexander, Jeffrey C. 1983. *Theoretical Logic in Sociology.* Vol. 4. Berkeley: University of California Press.

Baxandall, Michael. 1985. *Patterns of Intention: On the Historical Explanation of Pictures.* New Haven: Yale University Press.

Bourdieu, Pierre. 1977. *Outline of a Theory of Practice.* Translated by Richard Nice. Cambridge: Cambridge University Press.

Croce, Benedetto. (1922) 1978. *Aesthetic as Science of Expression and General Linguistic.* Translated by Douglas Ainslie. Boston: Nonpareil.

Genovese, Eugene D. 1974. *Roll, Jordon, Roll: The World the Slaves Made.* New York: Pantheon.

Goldmann, Lucien. (1967) 1970. "The Sociology of Literature: Status and Problems of Method." Pp. 582–609 in *The Sociology of Art and Literature: A Reader,* edited by Milton C. Albrecht, James H. Barnett, and Mason Griff. New York: Praeger.

Griswold, Wendy. 1987. "The Fabrication of Meaning." *American Journal of Sociology* 92:1077–117.

Hirsch, E. D., Jr. 1967. *Validity in Interpretation.* New Haven: Yale University Press.

Jauss, Hans Robert. 1982. *Toward an Aesthetic of Reception.* Translated by Timothy Bahti. Minneapolis: University of Minnesota Press.

Jones, Robert Alun. 1977. "On Understanding a Sociological Classic." *American Journal of Sociology* 83:279–319.

Rosmarin, Adena. 1985. *The Power of Genre.* Minneapolis: University of Minnesota Press.

Skinner, Quentin. 1969. "Meaning and Understanding in the History of Ideas." *History and Theory* 8:3–53.

# STUDY QUESTIONS

1. How does Griswold define a *cultural object*? Her definition is abstract. Make it concrete by offering an example of a cultural object which is familiar to you.
2. Why does Griswold include *comprehension* and *explanation* in her model and why are these components important?

# 20

# ANALYZING CODES, CONTEXTS, AND INSTITUTIONS

ANN SWIDLER

Throughout her book, *Talk of Love: How Culture Matters,* Ann Swidler argues that the usual ways sociologists think of culture as influencing human action are too simplistic. People don't just react to cultural inputs such as norms, values, symbols, and icons like robots processing electronic signals; their actions aren't dictated or programmed in that way. Instead, people can use cultural inputs in strategic and sometimes unpredictable ways. While there are very common patterns and repertoires of action and behavior that flow from shared cultural backgrounds, individuals can evade those patterns and defy the best predictions about how they will act. For these individuals, specific cultural inputs may have only weak significance, but generally speaking, culture manages to influence most people's behavior in quite predictable ways because they have so deeply internalized the cultures of which they are a part.

In this excerpt, Swidler addresses how and when culture takes on the power to constrain and guide people's actions and when it doesn't. In her theory, there are three key aspects of the social world that organize, focus, and enforce cultural meanings: codes, context, and institutions. She defines each of these and gives examples of how they act as decisive links between culture and action. Moreover, she indicates how these three elements work together to shape thoughts and behaviors, and draws on evidence ranging from case studies of social revolutions

to fieldwork on gift-giving in small-town America. Swidler's approach
serves up excellent examples of how local contexts influence the
power of culture, and in all of these cases, she takes pains to show
that culture can influence behavior even when people feel indifferent, ambivalent, or hostile to its meanings. In short, she offers both a
theory of what questions to ask as well as a method of how to look for
answers.

# CODES, CONTEXTS, AND INSTITUTIONS

In analyzing where and when culture actually affects action, I concentrate
on forces that focus, organize, and enforce cultural meanings: codes, contexts, and institutions. These operate "from the outside in," as, for example,
when cultural codes define what an individual's action means, independently of what the person intends it to mean. This differs from our earlier
exploration of when culture becomes meaningful for particular people or
when and how they apply culture to their life experience. In this chapter I
develop the argument that culture can have powerful influence on action
even when individuals do not deeply internalize its meanings, when it
remains a matter of indifference or antipathy, or even when they are
ambivalent or confused about its meanings. Codes, contexts, and institutions provide crucial links between culture and action. They do so by
structuring the external environment of meanings that surround actors,
giving those meanings coherence and direct implications for action that
they often lack in the thoughts and feelings of individuals.

## Codes

In a study of Christmas gift-giving in "Middletown," Caplow (1982, 1984)
offers a wonderful example of how culture can influence action from the
"outside," whether or not people deeply believe it. Caplow notes that Christmas gift-giving occupies an important place in Middletown's culture. People

spend a great deal of time and money buying gifts; they fret about finding the right gift; many plan all year to complete their gift-giving responsibilities by Christmas. But when Caplow and his associates interviewed people about giving Christmas gifts, they found great ambivalence. Many people felt that Christmas had become too commercialized, that gift-giving violated the real meaning of Christmas, and that retailers promoted Christmas giving only to stimulate sales. They found the process of both buying and receiving gifts unsatisfying, feeling that most of the things they gave and received were useless. In short, Middletowners were highly critical of Christmas gift-giving. Then why, Caplow asks, did they continue this ritual despite their disenchantment?

Caplow found the answer in an examination of actual gift-giving practices. Looking closely at what people gave, he found that a simple "semiotic code" was at work. The more important someone was to the giver, the more valuable the gift. Thus not to give a gift was to send a message: no gift would signal that the (non)recipient was not valued. Caplow argues that this system of meanings enforced conformity to gift-giving practices without "normative consent." By this he means that people gave gifts not because they themselves believed in the practice, found it meaningful, or even acted from unthinking habit. Rather people were constrained by their knowledge of *what their actions would mean to others.*

In recent years, terms like "semiotic code" and "discourse" have infiltrated the social sciences from the humanities. Such terms relocate culture in the public domain, focusing on publicly available systems of meaning, on the codes that define what it is possible to say, rather than on the particular thoughts or utterances of individual speakers. But following Caplow, I think of a semiotic code in a more limited way than many contemporary culture analysts. A semiotic code is a self-referential system of meanings in which each element in the system takes its meaning not from its inherent properties or from some external referent, but from the meanings created by the code itself. Thus if a school divides its students into two competing sports teams, the "Blues" and the "Golds," the meanings of Blue and Gold within that school are defined by the system of competing teams, the assignment of students to teams, and the rule that each student must be either a "Blue" or a "Gold." The system of Christmas gift-giving is a semiotic code in the sense that the "meaning" of a gift is defined in relative terms: the more valuable the gift, the more valued the recipient. Gifts are markers in a system of meanings, and thus whatever the "private" meanings individual givers and recipients hold, knowledge of the code defines the public meaning of the gift.

Semiotic codes are often thought of as the "deep structure" of a culture, by analogy with the deep structures of language, the general set of invisible but necessary rules that make it possible for people to generate and understand particular utterances. I argue, however, that semiotic codes can be culturally powerful even when they are of recent origin, lightly held, or even widely mistrusted. Extending Caplow's example of Christmas gift-giving, which might after all be regarded as a deeply embedded traditional practice despite recent cavils, we might consider the public pressure by florists and greeting-card companies to celebrate Mother's Day. The publicly promoted code is that if you love your mother you will remember her with a card, a gift, or flowers on Mothers Day. Whatever their cynicism about the holiday, many people, realizing that their mothers and their mothers' friends have probably seen the same deluge of advertising they have, conclude that, however much both they and their mothers know that a child's real love for a parent is expressed in other ways, it is prudent to send at least a token of that love on Mother's Day. For some, of course, Mother's Day may have special sentimental meanings; some families make it the occasion for a celebratory outing or breakfast-in-bed for Mom. But all know the public code, and if they do not follow it, they may need to negotiate a way around it.

———

Semiotic codes thus provide one answer to the question of how the welter of competing cultural meanings is actually brought to bear on action. Codes influence action by ordering the profusion of cultural information into a few simple categories and defining the signs of membership in each category. Actors are then constrained by their knowledge, often implicit, of how their action will be read by others. People may be especially constrained by cultural codes in impersonal, public contexts, and somewhat less constrained in intimate situations where they can more directly influence the ways their behavior will be read by others.

Of course, all social action involves awareness of the actions and responses of others. Indeed, Max Weber (1968:4–12) defined social action as action that is meaningfully oriented toward the action of others; and symbolic interactionists, such as George Herbert Mead (1967), see the internalization of a "generalized other," the ability to understand how our action will seem to others, as a fundamental capacity of all normal social actors. But this capacity differs from what I emphasize here. The way culture shapes our selves as we internalize knowledge of how others will perceive our actions is not the same as the more direct influence publicly enunciated codes can have on action, whether individuals internalize those codes or not.

=====

Some semiotic codes are narrow and specialized in their application (sending a Mother's Day card as a signal of filial loyalty); others seem deep and pervasive, like the code that makes autonomous choice the sign of authentic, reliable action. But I would caution against the assumption that deeper, more pervasive, more invisible culture is more powerful. For example, the code that signals reliable, consistent action through proclaiming autonomous choice is cross-cut by other codes, such as those through which people signal their friendly intentions (which may involve conveying an eager willingness to please), their loyalty, their social status (DiMaggio 1987), their honesty (see Lamont 1992), or their social power (Collins 1977, 1988).

=====

The power of semiotic codes comes from the actor's often implicit knowledge of how his conduct will be read by others. This is shared culture in the sense that the actor is influenced by his knowledge that particular codes are widely disseminated. But the shared culture need not be consensual in the sense that actors believe the code is "right" in some evaluative sense, or even that it is true in a cognitive sense. As with recent accounts of ethnic identity, categories may quickly become naturalized so that people really do seem to exist only in the varieties the code designates.

Codes can be powerful, however, even when they do not seem so inevitable or so important. Their sharedness is not a matter of common, consensual belief but of widespread publicity.

=====

# Contexts

The debate over whether or how much culture influences action obscures a crucial insight: that culture's influence varies by context. Max Weber is known as an "idealist" who stressed the influence of ideas on action. But Weber emphasized that the influence of ideas varies, and he sought in his substantive work to delineate the contexts that enhance the influence of ideas, such as an autonomous priesthood in an organizationally independent church (Weber 1993).

Few sociologists of culture have seriously explored the path opened by Weber, however (Wuthnow 1989 is an important exception). There is remarkably little analysis of the contexts in which culture is brought to bear on action. And the analysis of extreme contexts like cults, communes, and total institutions is rarely considered to have anything to do with the sociology of culture (Lifton 1989; Goffman 1961; Zablocki 1971; Kanter 1972).

. . . [Yet,] Social contexts make a difference because some contexts systematize and unify culture, magnifying its influence. Culture's effects are strongest where the context demands and enforces public cultural coherence.

Our usual stereotype is that public contexts—group meetings, for example—produce *in*coherence, because individual views, which may make perfect sense on their own, have to be trimmed, modified, or gutted to produce something like a group consensus. But some public settings clarify and organize cultural meanings.

———

In unstable, high-risk situations, people may seize on coherent ideologies, not because they deeply believe them but because they need some way to organize action when settled habit no longer suffices. This is especially true when people must mobilize and unify their allies, both among the general populace and, perhaps more important, within the core group of political actors (Palmer 1989). While in settled times the search for allies may lead people to soften their political disagreements, during dangerous crises people need to tighten their alliances, to know who is really with them.

One way of defining friends and enemies is to generate clear ideological disagreements that force people to choose sides. Leaders attempt to consolidate control over allies and keep opponents off balance by pushing ideological extremes, eliminating compromise positions, forcing allies to burn their bridges, and keeping opponents on the defensive.

=====

Even in less politically charged times, many of us know the experience of participating in a polarized meeting. Our personal views on the issues at stake may be confused, ambivalent, or even at odds with those of our allies. But when the issue becomes framed as a conflict between opposed factions, then that public arena and the semiotic code generated within it define the meaning of various positions, independent of their manifest content. To be feminist versus antifeminist, to support the union position or not, to be pro- or anti- the dominant faction, comes to be defined with respect to a coherent political "line." Whether participants start out with clearly defined views, whether they stretch their views to accommodate the evolving ideology, or whether they simply suppress qualms because they know which side they are on, the effect is to bring cultural meanings into public alignment, whatever private confusions remain.

Striking parallels to the ways political contexts affect cultural coherence come from a study of the ways members of divorcing couples transform uncertainty and ambivalence into coherent but opposed accounts in the polarizing context of a divorce. Joseph Hopper (1993) notes that divorcing couples develop roles as either the initiator of the divorce or the noninitiating partner. Once these identities emerge, they structure the ways people reconstruct their motives in the divorce.

> [T]he motives that divorcing people attributed to their actions cohered around their identities as either initiators or noninitiating partners: They described what led them to seek a divorce or, conversely, they described why they opposed a divorce. However, nothing prior to a divorce seemed to predict who would become the initiator and who the partner, (p. 805)

Hopper (p. 811) finds that before a divorce, the feelings of both partners are characterized by uncertainty, ambivalence, and confusion. There are plenty of "events, feelings, facts, and 'motives'" to explain any line of conduct. "But just as many events feelings, facts, and motives that would explain numerous other possible outcomes were there as well." In fact, Hopper

(p. 810) argues, "the motives by which divorcing people interpret their behaviors have less to do with actual events leading up to divorce and more to do with an emergent symbolic order structured around the initiator and noninitiator identities."

———

Particular contexts can make semiotic codes powerful even when these codes never become institutional common sense. The series of campaigns the Chinese Communists mounted from 1949 onward as they tacked back and forth from economic growth to political rectification (Schurmann 1970; Hinton 1966; Madsen, Chen, and Unger 1984; Madsen 1984) provide a dramatic example. During each campaign powerful new codes were promulgated—categorizing people by class background, defining enemies of the regime versus progressive elements, and so forth. Public meetings "criticizing" class enemies or, during the Cultural Revolution, "criticism-self-criticism" sessions directed against party leaders and officials, forced participants publicly to embrace these new terminologies. Such events made the slogans and categories real. Even those who remained privately skeptical had to learn to manipulate the new codes in order to survive. The power of the new codes rested on ideological mobilization in public contexts backed by threats of dire sanctions.

Neither the succession of ideological campaigns in China nor the periodic shifts of categories and slogans when interests at the center changed prevented these ideologies from exercising coherent cultural power. If individuals became more and more cynical with each succeeding wave of government sponsored enthusiasm, the cultural codes, as long as they were mobilized in public settings and backed by sanctions, powerfully influenced action. Each succeeding code organized a field of social meanings that defined the statuses and vulnerabilities of social actors. Each code was authoritative as long as it lasted; each disappeared when the context changed.

———

If some situations turn inchoate cultural images into clearly delineated public facts, we still understand very little about how the ordinary range of contexts might affect the power, coherence, or inescapability of cultural meanings. It is not even clear along what dimensions we might want to analyze contexts. I have suggested that situations of extreme polarization and acute uncertainty produce cultural coherence and that public meetings can make ideological loyalties highly visible. Weber (1993) suggested that where priests have an autonomous institutional base they are more likely to focus on logical problems in their doctrines. But we do not know whether small, recurrent gatherings are likely to produce less ideological consistency because meanings can continually be renegotiated in the meandering conversations of close intimates; or whether irregular, more anonymous situations might produce greater inconsistencies since what one says or does has few consequences (like confiding to a stranger on a plane). But without an analysis of contexts, we cannot understand why cultural logics sometimes matter, and why they matter more in some times and places than others.

## Institutions

Institutions also structure cultural meanings, giving them a coherent logic despite ambivalence or skepticism on the part of individuals. Indeed, chapters 6 and 7 focused on just such structuring, arguing that the institution of marriage organizes middle-class Americans' understandings of love, even when people find their experience in conflict with these understandings.

Institutional demands create cultural consistencies in two different ways. First, institutional constraints can give coherence to individuals' life strategies and thus to the cultural narratives, practices, or capacities they make use of. Thus individuals for whom marriage is central monitor their experience for (and soak up popular culture that describes) feelings that would sustain an enduring, exclusive, all-or-nothing, socially defining commitment like that of marriage. And they may suppress or rationalize away experiences that do not fit that institutionally anchored life strategy (see Quinn 1996:418).

Individuals participate in many such cultural complexes, because they participate in many institutional arenas. The culturally mediated strategies they develop to make their way through each institution, along with the relevant cultured capacities for action, may add up to a quite incoherent-seeming sum. But each set of cultural capacities may turn out to have its own logic, if only we can understand the institutional challenges that anchor its meaning. What sounded like inconsistent understandings of love in my interviews turned out to be ways of dealing with two different institutional aspects of marriage—the choice that commits people to a marriage and the negotiations that sustain ongoing relationships. (The culture that putatively helps sustain relationships is especially incoherent, with its never-ending flow of varied recommendations and recipes for happier, more fulfilling, or more exciting and challenging relationships.) There are, thus, powerful cultural consistencies, but they are less a consistent set of internalized beliefs than coherent orientations to the demands of institutions.

Institutions also create cultural consistencies in a second way—by providing the basis for a shared culture. It is because so many Americans deal with the institution of marriage that there is a shared culture of love. Consistencies across individuals come less from common inculcation by cultural authorities than from the common dilemmas institutional life poses in a given society. Not shared indoctrination but shared life-structuring institutions create the basis for a common culture. The myth of romantic love appears again and again, tailored for a new audience or with a twist to keep it fresh. It retains its vitality because it speaks to dilemmas created by the institutional structure of marriage.

Even when individuals consciously disbelieve dominant myths, they find themselves engaged with the very myths whose truths they reject—because the institutional dilemmas those myths capture are their dilemmas as well. The myths that sustain beliefs in American individualism are precisely of this sort. Survey and interview studies find that Americans do not really believe, for example, that their country provides equal opportunity for all or that ability and hard work account for success, especially when people think about concrete cases (see Mann 1970; Huber and Form 1973; Kluegel and Smith 1986; Swidler 1992). Yet these beliefs appear again and again, especially as general platitudes, even among the poor and disprivileged (see Lane 1962; Rainwater 1974; Reinarman 1987).

We may reconcile these puzzling findings by seeing that even when people know that the social deck is unfairly stacked, the major institutions they have to deal with are those of a market society (see Collier 1997). And a market society requires personal effort—a willingness to promote one's own virtues or to offer one's labor—while it repeatedly creates the experience that one's own "traits" (grades, test scores, or credentials, for example) determine one's options. Even a rich boy whose family pays for college and law school has the experience of putting forth his grades, test scores, recommendations, and essays as "reasons" why he should be admitted to a particular college or law school. And even the poor child, whose family and school experience have left her with few options, will be led to feel that her poor grades and lack of motivation in school account for her poor opportunities (see Clark 1960; Brint and Karabel 1989). If she wants a job, she will have to go out and look for one, making the best case for herself that she can. Thus the experience of living as a market actor continually reproduces the ethic of self-reliance, making it seem realistic even for those who know that it is a poor description of their own life chances or of the general distribution of opportunities and rewards among their fellows.

It may be, indeed, that a good deal of what we normally mean by culture is not an internalized set of beliefs or values, easily transportable from one institutional setting to another. Precisely the opposite: most culture sustains the symbolic capacities people develop to deal with institutions. The sense of cultural disjointedness one feels in moving to or through a foreign culture is primarily a sense of the misfit between one's cultural expectations and an alien set of institutions. Young Americans who consider themselves alienated from their own society may not realize how truly American they are until they go abroad—when they try to get routine paperwork done at a foreign airport, or when they discover that they lack the cultural skills to negotiate successfully (or at least, without feeling suspicious and resentful) in a market without fixed prices.

———

This formulation of how culture influences action calls for an approach different from those that prevail in much of the sociology and anthropology of culture. First, it suggests that rather than looking at cultural meanings in the abstract, it is crucial to attend to the contexts in which they are actually used. Ideas that are incoherent or inconsistent in the minds of individuals may acquire coherence and direction when they are mobilized in a particular context. Second, while ideas and cultural meanings come in many forms—evoking ethos and feeling tone, specifying modes of interaction, articulating values and norms for guiding daily life—I contend that "semiotic codes," systems of meaning that define what our actions will signify to others, have a special status. These meaning systems shape our action by becoming known, not necessarily by converting us. They derive their effectiveness from publicity and the power of public scrutiny.

Deployed in public settings and backed by sanctions, they solidify the cultural control of action.

Cultural meanings can be systematized and given coherence from the outside in, as well as through their inner logic. In polarized political contexts, from gang wars to revolutions, what one wears or how one walks, as well as what ideas one espouses, can become linked to one faction or side in a conflict. And through such polarization, matters of style and substance may become increasingly part of a coherent cultural package, unified by the conflicts in which they are invoked (Hebdige 1979). Thus the tight integration of a cultural system may come as much from cultural differentiation from enemies or competitors as from the unified inner logic of a system of ideas (Schneider 1976; LeVine 1984).

Finally, institutions can provide templates for the organization of particular cultural packages. To the degree that institutions structure major life strategies, the cultured capacities for action that individuals develop will be coherent not within an individual self but within a particular institutionally organized arena of action.

# Bibliography

Brint, Steven G. and Jerome Karabel. 1989. *The Diverted Dream: Community Colleges and the Promise of Educational Opportunity in America, 1900–1985.* New York: Oxford University Press.

Caplow, Theodore. 1982. "Christmas Gifts and Kin Networks." *American Sociological Review* 47:383–92.

———. 1984. "Rule Enforcement without Visible Means: Christmas Gift Giving in Middletown." *American Journal of Sociology* 89:1306–23.

Clark, Burton R. 1960. *The Open Door College.* New York: McGraw-Hill.

Collier, Jane Fishburne. 1997. *From Duty to Desire: Remaking Families in a Spanish Village.* Princeton: Princeton University Press.

Collins, Randall. 1977. *Conflict Sociology.* New York: Academic Press.

DiMaggio, Paul. 1987. "Classification in Art." *American Sociological Review* 52 (August): 440–55.

Goffman, Erving. 1961. *Asylums: Essays on the Social Situation of Mental Patients and Other Inmates.* Garden City, N.Y.: Anchor Books.

Hebdige, Dick. 1979. *Subculture: The Meaning of Style.* London: Routledge.

Hinton, William. 1966. *Fanshen: A Documentary of Revolution in a Chinese Village.* New York: Vintage Books.

Hopper, Joseph. 1993. "The Rhetoric of Motives in Divorce." *Journal of Marriage and the Family* 55 (November): 801–13.

Huber, Joan and William H. Form. 1973. *Income and Ideology.* New York: Free Press.

Kanter, Rosabeth Moss. 1972. *Commitment and Community: Communes and Utopias in Sociological Perspective.* Cambridge: Harvard University Press.

Kluegel, James R. and Eliot R. Smith. 1986. *Beliefs About Inequality: Americans' Views of What Is and What Ought to Be.* New York: Aldine de Gruyter.

Lamont, Michèle. 1992. *Money, Morals, and Manners: The Culture of the French and American Upper-Middle Class.* Chicago: University of Chicago Press.

Lane, Robert E. 1962. *Political Ideology: Why the American Common Man Believes What He Does.* New York: Free Press.

LeVine, Robert A. 1984. "Properties of Culture: An Ethnographic View." In *Culture Theory: Essays on Mind, Self, and Emotion*, ed. Richard A. Shweder and Robert A. LeVine, pp. 67–87. Cambridge: Cambridge University Press.

Lifton, Robert Jay. 1989. *Thought Reform and the Psychology of Totalism: The Study of "Brainwashing" in China.* Chapel Hill: University of North Carolina Press.

Madsen, Richard. 1984. *Morality and Power in A Chinese Village.* Berkeley: University of California Press.

Madsen, Richard, Anita Chen, and Jonathan Unger. 1984. *Chen Village: the Recent History of a Peasant Community in Mao's China.* Berkeley: University of California Press.

Mann, Michael. 1970. "The Social Cohesion of Liberal Democracy." *American Sociological Review* (June): 423–39.

Mead, George Herbert. 1967 [1934]. *Mind, Self and Society.* Chicago: University of Chicago Press.

Palmer, R. R. 1989 [1941]. *Twelve Who Ruled: The Year of the Terror in the French Revolution.* Princeton: Princeton University Press.

Quinn, Naomi. 1996. "Culture and Contradiction: The Case of Americans Reasoning about Marriage." *Ethos* 24(3): 391–425.

Rainwater, Lee. 1974. *What Money Buys: Inequality and the Social Meanings of Income.* New York: Basic Books.

Reinarman, Craig. 1987. *American States of Mind: Political Beliefs and Behavior Among Private and Public Workers.* New Haven: Yale University Press.

Schneider, David M. 1976. "Notes Toward a Theory of Culture." In *Meaning in Anthropology*, ed. Keith H. Basso and Henry A. Selby, pp. 197–220. Albuquerque: University of New Mexico Press.

Schurmann, Franz. 1970. *Ideology and Organization in Communist China*, 2nd edition. Berkeley: University of California Press.

Swidler, Ann. 1992. "Inequality in American Culture: The Persistence of Voluntarism." *American Behavioral Scientist* 35 (March/June): 606–29.

Weber, Max. 1968 [1920–22]. *Economy and Society: An Outline of Interpretive Sociology*, ed. Guenther Roth and Claus Wittich. Berkeley: University of California Press.

———. 1993 [1922]. *The Sociology of Religion*. Boston: Beacon Press.

Wuthnow, Robert. 1989. *Communities of Discourse: Ideology and Social Structure in the Reformation, the Enlightenment, and European Socialism*. Cambridge: Harvard University Press.

Zablocki, Benjamin. 1971. *The Joyful Community: An Account of the Bruderhof, a Communal Movement Now in Its Third Generation*. Baltimore: Penguin Books.

# STUDY QUESTIONS

1. What does Swidler mean by *semiotic codes*? Give an example of a semiotic code that influences your behavior. Why is personal belief unimportant in this circumstance?
2. How do institutions influence human behavior, according to Swidler?

# 21

# MAKING FILM INTO ART

SHYON BAUMANN

It's Friday night and you want to check out a flick, maybe the latest
giant robot epic. You call a friend, but she isn't interested; she wants
to see the critically acclaimed feel-good movie about two Hungar-
ian kids growing up during the Holocaust. It's playing at the art
house theater close to campus. You decline—art films are not really
your thing. After realizing you'll likely be watching the robot apoc-
alypse alone tonight, you start to wonder why art films exist in the
first place. What makes your friend's film artsy and your robot flick
not?

Shyon Baumann answers this question by tracing what he calls
the intellectualization of film over several decades in the United
States. In the early twentieth century, movies were regarded as
vulgar entertainment—cheap amusement to entertain the working
classes—but by the end of the century, audiences around the
world came to include film as a form of high art. Baumann demonstrates that in order for films to be considered art required much
more than directors simply aspiring to be taken seriously as artists. The elevation of movies to the status of art involved new
kinds of organizations (juried film festivals); transformations in
the way movies were made (from the studio system to the director
system); shifts in the language and discourse of film reviewers;
and the growth of college-educated audiences capable of interpreting films as deeply artistic achievements (as they would great
paintings or symphonies).

**Baumann's article is included here as a model method for displaying how larger social and historical trends can be illuminated by examining cultural artifacts. Exploring all facets of the film industry and its consumers—from production and reception, to distribution and exchange—allows him to offer a full account of the transformation from movies as tasteless entertainment to film as art.**

# INTELLECTUALIZATION AND ART WORLD DEVELOPMENT: FILM IN THE UNITED STATES

The concept of film as art is intriguing because during film's first decades, at the beginning of the twentieth century, film in the United States was considered popular entertainment and was strongly identified with working-class audiences. From its beginnings as a "suspect" entertainment medium fraught with technological, financial, and reputational difficulties (Canby 1971), the cinema has been transformed (Giannetti 1981; Lounsbury 1973; Mast 1981; Sinyard 1985). It is now widely recognized that a film can be appreciated and evaluated as a serious artistic endeavor and that filmmakers can be full-fledged artists (e.g., see Basinger 1994; Bordwell and Thompson 1986; Quart and Auster 1984; Sultanik 1986). Many organizations are now dedicated to the appreciation of film, and academic programs for the critical study of film also support this notion.

My goal here is to explain the legitimation of film as an art form. Through an examination of the history of film in the United States, I highlight the major developments within the film world that contributed to this change. In addition, I explore social forces in the wider society that helped to shift perceptions of film. Although attempts to valorize film began in film's first decades, major advances in the promotion of film's artistic potential occurred through a series of interrelated events that coincided in the United States in the 1950s and particularly the 1960s. In explaining the promotion and diffusion of this idea, the role of a legitimating ideology for film as art merits particular attention. A second goal here is to provide a method for measuring subtle, long-term changes in critical discourse.

Not all film is considered art, just as not all music (e.g., country music or a commercial jingle) and not all painting (e.g., finger painting by children) are indisputably art. The important development, however, is the popular acceptance of the idea that film *can* be art and that it has certain recognizable characteristics that justify the honorific title of "art." Although the idea that film can be art was conceived soon after the advent of the cinema, this idea was not taken seriously by the vast majority of American film critics or American audiences for approximately the first 60 years. I explain the acceptance of this idea in the post-1960 era.

## Creating Artistic Status: Opportunity, Institutions, and Ideology

Sociologists of culture rely on three main factors to explain the public acceptance of a cultural product as art. The first factor is the *changing opportunity space* brought about by social change outside the art world. DiMaggio (1992:44) contends that whether a cultural genre succeeds in earning recognition as art "has depended on the shape of the opportunity space," which is defined by the appearance of "competitors," "substitutes," and the formation of a pool of high-status "patrons" who can act as sponsors. A newly popular substitute or competitor can act as a foil against which a cultural genre's artistic status is enhanced. In addition, a cultural product's association with a high-status audience can help to legitimate the product as art. These developments, which are essentially rooted outside the art world, help explain the timing of "aesthetic mobility" (Peterson 1994:179).

The second factor crucial to explaining the creation of artistic status is the *institutionalization of resources and practices* of production and consumption by members within the art world. Becker (1982) provides a thorough analysis of the importance of organizations and networks in art. Although the artist is at the center of the art world, the participation of many different collaborators is essential for art to maintain its status as art. In this light, Becker (1982:301) explains the creation of an art world as an instance of successful collective action, of winning "organizational victories" and creating the "apparatus of an art world".

The third main factor is the grounding of artistic worth in a *legitimating ideology*. Ferguson (1998) makes the case for the crucial role of the intellectualization of a cultural product in the development of a cultural field. Bourdieu's (1993) concept of a "field" of cultural production focuses on the relations between cultural producers and consumers. A cultural field (also applicable to intellectual endeavors outside the boundaries of art) comes into being when cultural production begins to enjoy autonomy from other existing fields in the type of capital available to cultural producers. In any given field, actors engage in competition for capital. To the extent that there is a distinct form of symbolic capital available to consecrate cultural products of a particular genre, the field is more autonomous. For example, the literary field has achieved a high degree of autonomy—it offers prestigious prizes and critical successes that constitute the symbolic capital that may serve as an alternative to economic capital for authors. Ferguson (1998:600) argues that it is through texts that a field of cultural production is established and a cultural product is transformed into an "intellectual phenomenon." The development of a field-specific set of aesthetic principles provides a rationale for accepting the definition of a cultural product as art and offers analyses for particular products.

---

. . . Through a content analysis of 468 film reviews over a 65-year period, I explore the creation and dissemination of an artistic mode of analysis in film. Content analysis is useful for documenting change over time in particular elements of intellectual discourse. Through a careful accounting of the means by which critics developed a legitimating ideology for film, I show how critical discourse played a crucial role in the creation of the art world for film.

---

## Film Critics Provide an Intellectualizing Discourse

A classification as art rather than entertainment implies that the artistic value of a cultural product can be justified according to a set of conventions. The intellectualization of film involved the application of aesthetic standards and so was a crucial development in the promotion of film to the status of art. Film reviews available to the public in popular periodicals provide evidence for the evolution of an aesthetic in the field of film. Film reviews are therefore an ideal data source. Not only do they document the intellectualization of film, they also explain how the new aesthetic for film was disseminated to the public.

Content analysis of film reviews is well suited to identifying the important elements of an ideology of film as art and showing that this critical aesthetic became prevalent in the 1960s. My sample of film reviews consists of reviews beginning in 1925 and ending in 1985. By 1925, film had existed as a medium for more than 25 years, giving critics and audiences time to become familiar with its basic characteristics and potential. Furthermore, film technology now allowed filmmakers to make films that were long enough to maintain a narrative structure and that had sufficiently good picture quality that reviewers could focus on interpreting the films as art rather than as merely technical works. The end date of 1985 allows ample time after the change in the opportunity space for critics to develop a new film aesthetic. For every fifth year from 1925 to 1985, the first film reviewed each month by 3 popular periodicals (the *New York Times*, the *New Yorker*, and *Time*) was selected because: (1) They are among the few periodicals that published film reviews continuously during the period under study; (2) they are mass-circulation periodicals that are widely available and reach a large public, targeting a wide middle-brow audience; and (3) they are thought to be trendsetters and hence other film critics are likely to adopt their practices. This method generated 13 time periods, with 36 film reviews in each period, yielding a total of 468 film reviews. Two variables serve as evidence that a change in film reviewing has occurred: (1) the use of specific terms associated with artistic criticism in other highbrow artistic genres; and (2) the use of critical devices and concepts that facilitate an analytical, interpretive approach to film rather than a facile, entertainment-minded approach. For example, the following passage is from a 1931 *New Yorker* film review of *City Lights*, directed by Charlie Chaplin, a film currently considered a "classic" of great artistic value:

> Occasionally, you know, strange and unfortunate things occur to persons of such acclaimed place when they settle back for a while to enjoy their triumphs. There is the constant headiness, anyhow, of the great public's applause, and also so many excited little articles appear in various select journals spiced richly with such terms as "genius" and "artist" that the

reading of them may cast a sad spell over the subject. To be sure such journals have a small circulation as a rule, yet I suspect that the persons so dealt with usually contrive to unearth them and ponder on their arguments. The results may be disastrous. There grows an inclination to be more dramatically an artist, one with a mission, a significant message, an interpretation, and that aspiration has killed many a delightful talent. . . . I might wax eloquent about the meaning of his clowning, its relation to the roots of human instincts, had I at all the official vocabulary for that kind of thing, and did I not suspect that it tired many people the way it does me. (*New Yorker*, February 21, 1931, p. 60)

The reviewer's comments show that the idea of film as art existed in 1931, but that this idea was mainly confined to avant-garde journals with a "small circulation" waiting for filmmakers to "unearth" them. For a reviewer in the *New Yorker* to ridicule the idea of film as art, the idea could not have had wide currency. The more mainstream opinion, as represented by this *New Yorker* reviewer, was opposed to the notion that Charlie Chaplin could be an "artist," that words such as "artist" and "genius" could be applied to a filmmaker, and that films should attempt to convey a message or allow for interpretation. Films, the reviewer is saying, do not serve that purpose, and are better for it.

## Changing Language

A vocabulary of criticism is a common feature of artistic commentary. Measurement of the changing language used in film reviews requires identifying a manageable number of elements of that vocabulary. Reviews from the *New York Times*, the *New Yorker*, and *Time* of classical music performances and recordings and of painting exhibitions from the year 1925 provided a sample vocabulary from which a list of "high art" terms was drawn. Using the first music review and the first painting review from each month in 1925, a primary list was compiled for each publication. (Only the first six months of music reviews were available for the *New York Times*, but their music reviews were, on average, twice as long.) Each primary list included any term considered to be characteristic of highbrow art criticism from that publication.

The final list of terms was created by including any term that appeared on at least two primary lists (i.e., at least two publications' reviews of painting and/or music in 1925). The list of terms was then pared down to include those words thought to have the strongest "high art" connotations. (The list of terms is available from the author on request).

Using reviews from 1925 avoids the tendency to generate a list that includes terms that resonate with a contemporary knowledge of critical terminology, which would have led to finding more such terms in later periods independent of any change or lack of change in the nature of film reviews before that. If there is any bias, it is against finding these terms in later periods. Three additional terms pertaining to the interpretive analysis of a narrative structure were added to the list: genre, irony, metaphor. Two other terms were also counted: the mention of a proper name followed by the suffix "ian" (e.g., Hitchcockian) or by the suffix "esque" (e.g., Felliniesque), as an indication of setting an academic tone. Appearances of these terms were then counted in the film review sample. Accurate counts of each term were achieved by scanning the reviews into a computer and then using the "find" function in a word processor. Each review was, of course, corrected for spelling errors that occurred in the scanning process. All variants of a term were also counted. For instance, "art," "artist," "artistry," "artistic," and "artistically" would each be counted as "art." A term was counted only if it was used in a sense that relates to art commentary. If a film as a whole or some aspect of the film was described as "brilliant," the term "brilliant" was counted. If a bright light, something shiny, or any concrete object was described as "brilliant," the term was not counted. The term "work" was counted only if it applied to the film as a production, not if it was being used to denote labor or in any other nonartistic sense, and so on. The terms were divided into two groups. The first group is designated as "high art" terms and includes words that have a rhetorical effect in the context of the evaluation of cultural products. They imply an erudite assessment and expert judgment. These words are: art, brilliant, genius, inspired, intelligent, master, and work. In addition, as mentioned above, the use of a proper name followed by the suffix "esque" or "ian" was counted. Such usage indicates the tendency to set a serious, weighty tone. The second group is designated as "critical" terms and includes words that are used in the analysis of texts. These words are: composition, genre, irony, metaphor, satire, symbol, and tone.

Table 1 reports the total number of "high art" and "critical" terms by year. (The results for each term by year are available from the author on request.) There is a statistically significant tendency for occurrences of these terms to increase over time, which supports the view that it became more common for reviewers to incorporate a more sophisticated and analytical vocabulary in their reviews in more recent decades.

In addition to using specialized terms, critics who take film seriously will also write lengthier reviews. Long reviews allow them to provide fully elucidated analyses, as opposed to the more superficial treatments. The second column of Table 1 confirms that the fewest words per review were

**TABLE 1  Analysis of "High Art" and "Critical" Terms Used in Film Reviews: 1925 to 1985**

| Year | Total Number of "High Art" and "Critical" Terms Used | Mean Number of Words per Review | Number of Terms Divided by Total Number of Review Words |
|---|---|---|---|
| 1925 | 19 | 337.2 | .0016 |
| 1930 | 18 | 395.8 | .0013 |
| 1935 | 21 | 414.0 | .0014 |
| 1940 | 5 | 339.1 | .0004 |
| 1945 | 21 | 434.1 | .0013 |
| 1950 | 9 | 371.4 | .0007 |
| 1955 | 12 | 396.8 | .0008 |
| 1960 | 31 | 450.5 | .0019 |
| 1965 | 32 | 447.0 | .0020 |
| 1970 | 107 | 898.2 | .0033 |
| 1975 | 69 | 978.3 | .0020 |
| 1980 | 103 | 1,132.3 | .0025 |
| 1985 | 78 | 950.4 | .0023 |
| Rho | .88*** | .86*** | .70** |

*Note:* Twelve reviews were sampled for each year from the *New York Times*, the *New Yorker*, and *Time* magazine; N = 468.

**p < .01  ***p < .001 (one-tailed tests)

written in 1925—a review in this year averaged 337.2 words. This amount remained relatively constant until 1955, followed by a slight increase in 1960 and 1965. After 1965 the average number of words per review increased dramatically, peaking in 1980 at 1,132.3, and then decreasing somewhat in the final time period to 950.4.

———

The use of a specialized vocabulary is not merely a reflection of the increase in the length of reviews. Instead, the data suggest that the proportionate increase in the number of "high art" and "critical" terms is the effect of a nascent tendency to treat film as an art form, and that the use of a specialized vocabulary necessitated contextualization and more explanations, resulting in lengthier reviews.

## Changing Techniques and Concepts

The second measure of the change in film reviews is the use of critical devices and concepts. These devices and concepts are the comparisons and distinctions that critics use and the thought modes that critics employ when reviewing films. Eight techniques were defined.

### (1) POSITIVE AND NEGATIVE COMMENTARY.

It is thought that high art is complex and does not lend itself to easy interpretation or appreciation. The first technique is the appearance of both positive and negative commentary in the same review. Reviews that address film as art are expected to have a more complex, in-depth approach to film involving evaluation of many aspects on different levels, resulting in more mixed reviews. Such a mixture of commentary exists, for example, when a reviewer praises the actors for their interpretations but finds fault with the tone that the director gave to the material.

### (2) DIRECTOR IS NAMED.

The second technique is referring to the director by name in the review. Serious art forms require recognition of the artists by name, and in film this means the director (Blewitt 1993). Furthermore, occurrences of this technique are expected to increase in the 1960s, due to the introduction of auteurism.

### (3) COMPARISON OF DIRECTORS.

The third technique in the content analysis is the comparison of one director to another director. Discussion of high art very often places a given work in the context of other works so that the work can be evaluated in a more sophisticated and informed manner (Eitner 1961).

### (4) COMPARISON OF FILMS.

Comparison of the film to other films is also expected to increase. Making connections between different works allows critics to justify their analyses and to display their cinematic erudition.

### (5) FILM IS INTERPRETED.

A defining characteristic of "art" as opposed to "entertainment" is that art is thought-provoking and a form of communication through metaphor. Examples include, "It seems reasonably clear that she means her movie to be a wry and sometimes anguished parable of political corruption and betrayal" (*Time,* October 6, 1975, p. 65) or "she bends this material onto a statement about how women are trapped and self-entrapped in our society" (*New York Times*, November 1, 1975, sec. 1, p. 17). Such statements are subject to debate and require creative inference on the part of the critic. Bordwell (1989), considering the role of interpretation in film criticism, explains that when film criticism became an academic endeavor, it was adopted by intellectuals in the humanities. "As a result, cinema was naturally subsumed within the interpretive frames of reference that rule those disciplines" (Bordwell 1989:17). "Interpretation-centered" criticism prevails in film studies because of its association with other types of cultural criticism.

### (6) MERIT IN FAILURE.

Viewing a given aspect of a film in different ways indicates a complex, multifaceted approach to film. A multifaceted approach is typical for highbrow art, which relies on resolving tensions between beauty and harshness to achieve its effect (Eitner 1961). Seeing merit in failure, requiring evaluation on two levels, is the sixth technique. An example of this is, "If Pontecorvo's film is flawed throughout, it is nevertheless an amazing film, intensely controversial even in its failures" (*New Yorker*, November 7, 1970, p. 159).

## (7) ART VERSUS ENTERTAINMENT.

Critics develop a canon and then must justify why a film is good (serious art) or bad (commercial entertainment). A fault line appears between "real art" and film that is motivated by profit or obviously and intentionally oriented toward a mass market (Bourdieu 1993, chap. 1).[1] "There are times when the movie teeters on the edge of commercial cuteness" (*Time*, February 3, 1975, p. 4) is an example of such a distinction. Distinguishing between "popular" film and "serious" film allows critics to define a canon that excludes standard Hollywood productions. Creating a canon delineates a subgroup of the art form that critics can refer to as representative of their ideas concerning what is good art (DiMaggio 1992). The canon provides a set of exemplary works to which critics can appeal to defend their ideological ground. The identification of these "serious" works also allows critics to dismiss other films as a different kind of cinema, thereby maintaining the artistic integrity of "real" cinema.

## (8) TOO EASY TO ENJOY.

A distinction similar to "art versus entertainment" should appear more often in later periods based on a "disgust at the facile" (Bourdieu 1984: 486). Real art requires effort to be appreciated and cannot be enjoyed on a superficial level (Canaday 1980). Treating film as art encourages disdain for films that are "too immediately accessible and so discredited as 'childish' or 'primitive'" (Bourdieu 1984: 486), while finding value in complexity and subtlety. Two reviews appearing 45 years apart in the *New Yorker* show how critics at different times differed in how they held films to this standard:

> I don't like movies about people who work, and I don't like movies about people who have things the matter with them. (I work and all my friends work, and we all have things the matter with us. We go to movies to forget). (*New Yorker*, April 6, 1935, p. 77)

> I don't mean it as a compliment when I venture . . . that it will prove to be her most popular picture so far. It is an easy movie to enjoy, which is the whole trouble. (*New Yorker*, March 3, 1980, p. 112)

1. Verdaasdonk (1983) discusses the importance critics place on the incompatibility of commercial and artistic values and the consequences for aesthetic legitimacy as applied to the literary field. Verdaasdonk refutes the validity of this dichotomy.

**TABLE 2  Percent of Reviews Using Specific Critical Techniques, 1925 to 1985**

| Year | | Technique[a] | | | | | | | (9)[b] | (10)[c] |
|---|---|---|---|---|---|---|---|---|---|---|
| | (1) | (2) | (3) | (4) | (5) | (6) | (7) | (8) | (9)[b] | (10)[c] |
| 1925 | 36.1 | 47.2 | 2.8 | 8.3 | 2.8 | 0 | 11.1 | 0 | 8.3 | .000686 |
| 1930 | 33.3 | 33.3 | 2.8 | 8.3 | 2.8 | 0 | 0 | 0 | 2.8 | .000195 |
| 1935 | 52.8 | 19.4 | 0 | 16.7 | 13.9 | 0 | 2.8 | 2.8 | 5.6 | .000373 |
| 1940 | 33.3 | 50.0 | 0 | 5.6 | 16.7 | 0 | 2.8 | 0 | 5.6 | .000455 |
| 1945 | 52.8 | 36.1 | 2.8 | 5.6 | 25.0 | 0 | 5.6 | 0 | 5.6 | .000356 |
| 1950 | 61.1 | 50.0 | 0 | 16.7 | 19.4 | 2.8 | 2.8 | 2.8 | 11.1 | .000831 |
| 1955 | 50.0 | 52.8 | 2.8 | 2.8 | 13.9 | 2.8 | 0 | 8.3 | 11.1 | .000778 |
| 1960 | 63.9 | 72.2 | 0 | 5.6 | 41.7 | 11.1 | 5.6 | 5.6 | 30.6 | .001884 |
| 1965 | 52.8 | 80.6 | 0 | 16.7 | 41.7 | 2.8 | 11.1 | 8.3 | 36.1 | .002244 |
| 1970 | 52.8 | 86.1 | 16.7 | 30.6 | 69.4 | 16.7 | 13.9 | 5.6 | 58.3 | .001804 |
| 1975 | 63.9 | 97.2 | 11.1 | 33.3 | 72.2 | 11.1 | 8.3 | 11.1 | 66.7 | .001893 |
| 1980 | 77.8 | 100.0 | 11.1 | 41.7 | 69.4 | 25.0 | 19.4 | 8.3 | 80.6 | .001976 |
| 1985 | 52.8 | 100.0 | 16.7 | 27.8 | 55.6 | 5.6 | 22.2 | 13.9 | 50.0 | .001461 |
| Rho | .67** | .95*** | .54* | .61* | .91*** | .88*** | .66** | .89*** | .90*** | .80*** |

[a]Techniques 1 through 8 are defined as follows: 1 = presence of both positive and negative commentary in review; 2 = director is named; 3 = director is compared with another director; 4 = film is compared with another film; 5 = presence of interpretation; 6 = merit is seen in failure; 7 = opposition drawn between serious versus commercial film or art versus entertainment; 8 = film is criticized for being "easy" or for lacking subtlety.

[b]Column 9 shows the percentage of reviews in which at least 3 of the techniques are used.

[c]Column 10 equals column 9 divided by total words in all reviews.

*p < .05  **p < .01  ***p < .001 (one tailed tests)

Table 2 presents the percentage of reviews in each year that include each of the eight techniques. Results for technique 1 show the increase in the use of mixed, rather than exclusively positive or negative, commentary. Spearman's rho between year and the number of reviews using mixed commentary is .67 and is significant. Results for technique 2 show that the director is named in 100 percent of the reviews in the last two time periods, an increase from less than 50 percent in 1925. The high rank-order correlation (rho = .95) attests to the increase in the practice of naming the director in reviews. The substantial increase of approximately 20 percentage points between 1955 and 1960 conforms to expectations concerning the influence of *auteurism*. Results for technique 3 show that comparisons between directors is not common in film reviews, reaching a high of 16.7 percent in 1970 and 1985. However, a moderate correlation exists (rho = .54). Similar results obtain for technique 4—comparisons between the film under review and another film. Although this device never appeared in more than a minority of reviews in the sample, peaking at 41.7 percent in 1980, there is evidence of a moderate increase over time (rho = .61).

Is there evidence of an increase in attempts to find an implicit message in films as a whole or in certain aspects of films? Results for technique 5 show that the interpretation of film is associated with later time periods (rho = .91). Starting at merely 2.8 percent, interpreting film became the dominant mode of review by the 1970s, peaking in 1975 (72.2 percent). This result provides strong evidence for the shift in the nature of film reviews. Despite the existence of other types of interpretive criticism such as literary criticism, early film reviewers were not likely to find a message in the films they saw. Such a development apparently awaited the adoption of film as subject matter by academic-minded critics.

The increase in viewing a given aspect of a film as both a success and a failure (technique 6) is statistically significant (rho = .88). Although the device was not widely used, it was most popular in reviews from 1980 (25.0 percent). The increase over time in drawing a distinction in film between serious art and commercial entertainment (technique 7) is statistically significant (rho = .66). There is a slight but significant increase over time in reviews distinguishing between films that are too easy or too obvious in their intentions and films that are subtle, difficult, or complex (rho = .89). While not used at all in the beginning of the study period, the distinction was drawn most often in 1985 (13.9 percent).

Although each of these techniques can contribute to an intellectual, sophisticated approach to film review, the use of multiple techniques changes the nature of reviews to a greater extent. Column 9 presents the percentage of reviews in which at least three of the techniques were used. Until the 1960s, relatively few reviews used at least three of the critical devices. After 1960, the percentage steadily rose, reaching its highest value in 1980 of 80.6 percent. Apparently, critics were using multiple critical concepts and techniques in their reviews beginning in the 1960s. . . .

# Conclusion

Film was valorized through the institutionalization of various resources and practices by a range of actors in the art world for film, beginning soon after film's emergence and intensifying in the late 1950s to late 1960s. Between the 1920s and the early 1950s, this process occurred only in isolated instances. But in the 1960s the coincidence of factors described above created the thrust necessary for a major turning point in perceptions of the artistic status of film.

The coincidence of these factors highlights the reciprocal influences among them. The changing opportunity space not only facilitated the success of efforts to valorize film but also encouraged the movement to treat film as art. The increased population with a post-secondary education provided a larger potential audience for film as art as more film patrons read the new criticism, attended the newly founded festivals, and enrolled in the emerging field of film studies in universities. The financial troubles of American studios caused by the popularity of television and by industry restructuring in the 1950s and 1960s allowed festivals to play a larger role in determining which films and directors succeeded in the United States (Mast 1981:333). Film festivals granted prestige and exposure to many foreign and independent films whose popularity had increased among a more educated audience for film at a time of decreased Hollywood output. Financially troubled Hollywood studios, eager to participate in and profit from the trend, hired many foreign directors to make films for American distribution. The film companies encouraged a view of film as art by entering festivals and promoting their films as artistic products. The growth in the number of academic courses and programs on film not only helped legitimate the idea of film as art, but also aided in the development of a more sophisticated language and style of reviews. Although most critics writing for major publications in the 1960s and 1970s (including those writing for the publications sampled here) attended college before the emergence of film programs and thus did not have academic backgrounds in film, they had the opportunity to read academic work and to communicate with like-minded admirers of film. A developing art world gathers momentum, cooperation begets further cooperation, and the seizing of opportunities creates further opportunities.

Some of the factors that contributed to the recognition of the artistic possibilities of film, such as the advent of television, the demise of the studio system, and the increase in post-secondary education, cannot be linked to actors who had an interest in promoting film as art. However, an identifiable group of symbolic capitalists can be credited with the creation of film festivals and academic programs for film study and the criticism of films using an aesthetic that treated film as art. Academics, journalists, and other believers in the artistic value of film undertook film's promotion in a social environment in which film's image was more malleable. The symbolic capitalists seized the moment when those qualities consonant with existing norms defining art could be emphasized. Relative to television, which strayed further from the field of art as it was then defined (and as it is now), many films *were* artistic. The new social context of film appreciation promoted a focus on the existing artistic characteristics of films and "forgotten" masterpieces were reevaluated. To understand how art forms are situated within a cultural hierarchy we must recognize the importance of both structural factors and human agency.

As was the case with other art forms, critics have played an important role in creating a legitimating ideology for film. While they were the primary disseminators of the discourse, they were not its only creators. The legitimating ideology for film as art was the product of many participants in the film world including critics, academics, filmmakers, and other intellectuals involved with the organization of festivals, programs, and institutes. Film reviews, while the most visible and influential, were not the sole site for the development of this ideology.

Although many scholars point to the key role of a legitimating ideology, few have documented and analyzed the emergence of that ideology. The present analysis provides a general model for analyzing discourse in other cultural and intellectual fields. Critics influenced how film was viewed and whether film could be discussed as art after they began using a sophisticated, interpretation-centered discourse in film reviews. This discourse employed a vocabulary that resembled the vocabulary used in other highbrow artistic criticism. No critic would claim that all films merited the status of art. However, by devoting serious attention, analyses, and a specialized discourse in their writing on film for a popular audience, critics, in conjunction with academics and other intellectuals in the film world, asserted that artistic value was possible in films. While I argue that the intellectualization of film did not *require* an increase in the artistic nature of film content, it is impossible to prove that such an increase did not occur and did not encourage the development of a legitimating ideology. The evidence suggests that the content of films is not the only determinant of whether and to what degree it is intellectualized. Further research may establish the nature of the link between the changing aesthetic features of film as a genre and film's intellectualization.

The medium of film does not rank among the highest arts in the cultural hierarchy. One reason for this may be that there has not been a purification of genres as there has been in music or in literature. There has been some purification in film; for example, foreign films are often set above the rest. Importation from Europe may have substantiated film's artistic claims. But the presentation of "serious" dramas in the same theaters with lighter Hollywood productions has hindered a clear conception of film as art. Few art theaters exist. This lack of genre distinction has suppressed artistic claims because many films do not possess the qualities that audiences believe are characteristic of art. Many films are not challenging or difficult—they are designed to appeal to a wide audience. Furthermore, films have not enjoyed the near-exclusive elite patronage typical of opera and symphonic music. DiMaggio (1982, 1992) and Levine (1988) point to the sponsorship of wealthy patrons in elevating the status of a variety of art forms, but this was not a factor in the case of film. Finally, the image of film as a business is pervasive. Unlike art that is under the direction of trustee-governed nonprofit organizations, profit-oriented studios and executives are deeply involved in film production. Even independent filmmakers are often portrayed as vitally concerned with securing large box office results for minimal financial investments. To be credible, artists should profess a degree of "disinterestedness" in economic matters.

Because most films are made within the Hollywood system, tension exists between the claims of film's artistic status and the norms concerning the appropriate conditions of artistic production. Although some Hollywood films could be labeled art, it is difficult to convincingly argue that blockbuster action films should be interpreted for their social significance. Critics who try to find messages and meaning in commercial films are often mocked, but new films by respected directors are often approached on the level of art. Prior to the 1960s, such an approach would have been seen as a strained application of a legitimate disposition to an illegitimate field. Today the approach is acceptable because of the critical and institutional maturation of the film world.

# References

Basinger, Jeanine. 1994. *American Cinema: One Hundred Years of Filmmaking*. New York: Rizzoli.

Becker, Howard. 1982. *Art Worlds*. Berkeley, CA: University of California Press.

Blewitt, John. 1993. "Film, Ideology and Bourdieu's Critique of Public Taste." *British Journal of Aesthetics* 33:367–72.

Bordwell, David. 1989. *Making Meaning: Inference and Rhetoric in the Interpretation of Cinema*. Cambridge, MA: Harvard University Press.

Bordwell, David and Kristin Thompson. 1986. *Film Art*. New York: Alfred A. Knopf.

Bourdieu, Pierre. 1984. *Distinction: A Social Critique of the Judgment of Taste*. Translated by R. Nice. Cambridge, MA: Harvard University Press.

———. 1993. *The Field of Cultural Production*. Edited by R. Johnson. New York: Columbia University Press.

Canaday, John Edwin. 1980. *What Is Art?: An Introduction to Painting, Sculpture, and Architecture*. New York: Knopf.

Canby, Vincent. 1971. "Introduction," *The New York Times Film Reviews*. vol.1. New York: New York Times.

DiMaggio, Paul. 1982. "Cultural Entrepreneurship in Nineteenth-Century Boston." *Media, Culture and Society* 4:33–50.

———. 1992. "Cultural Boundaries and Structural Change: The Extension of the High Culture Model to Theater, Opera, and the Dance, 1900–1940." Pp. 21–57, in *Cultivating Differences: Symbolic Boundaries and the Making of Inequality*, edited by M. Lamont and M. Fournier. Chicago, IL: University of Chicago Press.

Eitner, Lorenz. 1961. *Introduction to Art: An Illustrated Topical Manual*. Minneapolis, MN: Burgess Publishing.

Ferguson, Priscilla Parkhurst. 1998. "A Cultural Field in the Making: Gastronomy in 19th Century France." *American Journal of Sociology* 104:597–641.

Giannetti, Louis. 1981. *Masters of the American Cinema.* Englewood Cliffs, NJ: Prentice-Hall.

Levine, Lawrence W. 1988. *Lowbrow/Highbrow: The Emergence of Cultural Hierarchy in America.* Cambridge, MA: Harvard University Press.

Lounsbury, Myron Osborn. 1973. *The Origins of American Film Criticism 1909–1939.* New York: Arno Press.

Mast, Gerald. 1981. *A Short History of the Movies.* 3d ed. Chicago, IL: University of Chicago Press.

Peterson, Richard A. 1994. "Culture Studies through the Production Perspective: Progress and Prospects." Pp. 163–89 in *The Sociology of Culture: Emerging Theoretical Perspectives*, edited by D. Crane. Cambridge, MA: Blackwell.

Quart, Leonard and Albert Auster. 1984. *American Film and Society Since 1945.* London, England: Macmillan.

Sinyard, Neil. 1985. *Directors: The All-Time Greats.* London, England: Columbus Books.

Sultanik, Aaron. 1986. *Film: A Modern Art.* Cranbury, New Jersey: Rosemont Publishing and Printing.

Verdaasdonk, H. 1983. "Social and Economic Factors in the Attribution of Literary Quality." *Poetics* 12:383–95.

# STUDY QUESTIONS

1. Why does Baumann focus on critics' film reviews to make his argument?
2. How might one use the sort of content analysis that Baumann performs here to describe changes over time in attitudes about rock music as an art form?

# 22

# STUDYING OPRAH

EVA ILLOUZ

Scholars who study television are sometimes regarded by other academics to be less than serious, and in academia, seriousness is not just considered a key virtue, but a quality that separates the amateurs from the professionals. Furthermore, studying something as ephemeral and superficial as daytime television talk shows can increase the risk of being stigmatized as frivolous.

Cultural studies (See Introduction, p. xiii) has long grappled with this stigma and has fought back by showing how important media are in shaping everyday consciousness, if not behavior, and by focusing on the agency that viewers bring to their encounters with their favorite TV shows. Fans aren't passive receptors of ideology; they sometimes resist the dominant cultural messages, both explicit and implicit, that travel through the airwaves.

Illouz acknowledges the cultural studies tradition, but seeks to move the sociology of popular culture onto different theoretical ground. For her, the best way to view popular culture is through the lens of "moral sociology"—a branch of the discipline traditionally concerned with the role of culture in meaning-making and binding us to common values and goals. She reviews some of the important contributors to this tradition, many of whom appear in this reader, but her approach to studying popular culture is unique, as she blends theories and methods usually set in opposition to each other. Her goal is not just to help her readers understand popular culture, but also to develop what she calls "ethical criticisms" of both the medium and the messages. She concludes that what made *The Oprah Winfrey Show* such compelling TV (and such a unique cultural icon) was that it did much more than simply reflect or shape conventional moral wisdom. Instead, the show offered practical strategies for living in a complex and uncertain world. And what, we may ask, could be more serious than that?

# OPRAH WINFREY AND THE GLAMOUR OF MISERY

O prah Winfrey is not only a famous character—a condition shared by many others. She is a cultural phenomenon. As an article published in *Ebony* put it: "From the beginning, her show has captured the American television psyche like nothing the industry has seen before or since. The fact is, since her show went national in 1986, it has remained head and shoulders above the others. All of them."[1]

Her talk show has won thirty Daytime Emmy Awards, and, at the rather young age of 44, Oprah garnered the Lifetime Achievement Award. In 1994, she was named by *Forbes* as the highest paid entertainer (winning over such male media figures as Bill Cosby and Steven Spielberg). Oprah Winfrey is more than a taste maker; she not only embodies values that many Americans revere but also has invented a cultural form that has changed television and American culture. In 2000, anyone logging in at the world-famous Amazon.com bookstore could find a rubric entitled "Oprah Winfrey Books," along with such general rubrics as "Fiction" and "Nonfiction." These books were the novels chosen by Oprah Winfrey to appear in her famous monthly Book Club. Her choices alone have been decisive for the careers of numerous authors and publishing houses. Why? Because Oprah Winfrey has been one of the most important commercial forces in the U.S. publishing industry. In April 2000, Oprah even established a new magazine, O *Magazine*, which *Newsweek* called "the most successful magazine start-up in history."[2]

An article in *Vanity Fair* put the point aptly: "Oprah Winfrey arguably has more influence on the culture than any university president, politician, or religious leader, except perhaps the Pope."[3] Or, as writer Fran Lebowitz put it, "Oprah is probably the greatest media influence on the adult population. She is almost a religion."[4] I would even go a step further. In the realm of popular culture, Oprah Winfrey is one of the most important American cultural phenomena of the second half of the twentieth century, if we measure "importance" by her visibility,[5] the size of the fortune she has managed to amass in one decade, the size of her daily audience,[6] the number of imitations she has generated, the innovativeness of her show, and her impact on various aspects of American culture—an effect that some have called, somewhat derogatively, the "Oprahization of culture." In 2001, the "Top Ten Words of 2001 Announced by Your Dictionary.Com" defined "Oprahization" facetiously but tellingly as follows: "Describes the litmus test of political utterances: if it doesn't play on Oprah, it doesn't play at all."

The obvious cultural visibility and economic size of the Oprah phenomenon should provide a good enough reason to undertake a study of its meaning. Indeed, Oprah has such influence that she is an ideal example of those collective "big" cultural phenomena that sociologists of culture love to analyze because they reveal a society's mindset.

But there is another reason why Oprah Winfrey is a compelling object of study. In spite of her popularity, or perhaps because of it, Oprah Winfrey has been the object of disdain on part of the "old" intellectual and cultural elites. In a 1993 *Chicago Magazine* article, Ms. Harrison, an essayist and fiction writer who in 1989 had written an in-depth profile of Oprah, was quoted as saying: "Her show . . . I just can't watch it. You will forgive me, but it's white trailer trash. It debases language, it debases emotion. It provides everyone with glib psychological formulas. These people go around talking like a fortune cookie. And I think she is in very large part responsible for that."[7]

This echoes a more general disparaging view, aptly represented by Robert Thompson, director of Syracuse University's Center for the Study of Popular Television, who said that talk shows exemplify the fact that "TV has so much on it that's so stupid."[8] Like so many other elements of popular culture, Oprah Winfrey and her talk show have generated ritual declarations of disdain from public intellectuals, political activists, feminists, and conservative moral crusaders. Precisely for this reason, Oprah is of great value to the student of culture. The cultural objects that irritate tastes and habits are the very ones that shed the brightest light on the hidden moral assumptions of the guardians of taste.[9] Such cultural objects make explicit the tacit divisions and boundaries through which culture is classified and thrown into either the trash bin or the treasure chest. Indeed, the criticisms of Oprah Winfrey offer a convenient compendium of the very critiques that are ritually targeted at popular culture. If talk shows systematically blur boundaries constitutive of middle-class taste, Oprah offers a privileged point from which to examine such boundaries, partly because she herself manipulates them in a virtuoso fashion.

—————

## A Comprehensive Approach to Culture

Broadly, the analysis of culture can be approached along three paths. The first is concerned with what we may call the realm of the "ethical": that is, the ways in which culture bestows on our actions a sense of "purpose" and "meaning" through a realm of values or through powerful symbols that motivate and guide our action "from within." This perspective approaches culture as the force that binds us to the social body through values, rituals, or morality plays.[10] "Meaning" implies here a kind of energetic engagement of the self in a social and cultural community through the upholding, defense, and performance of those values, core symbols, and morality plays.

The second approach is indifferent to the ways culture informs our moral choices. It approaches culture as an arena in which different groups struggle to define what is worthy and legitimate and that establishes mechanisms of exclusion and inclusion to institutionalize such definitions. Popular culture is viewed as a terrain in which strategies of resistance, empowerment, and symbolic violence are exerted. In this view, meaning is a resource mobilized by actors to bestow legitimacy on their actions or to deny the legitimacy of others' culture.[11]

Finally, a third approach views "meaning" as the outcome of social forces mirrored and/or distorted in a text. These forces can be institutional, economic, legal, social, or organizational. They "explain" meaning in the sense that the text is examined in terms of its context of production. By whom, how, and for whom a text is produced constitute the main parameters of a text's production and will be used to explicate its "meaning."[12]

—————

These three approaches to culture—the ethical, the critical, and the institutional—should be juxtaposed and articulated with, rather than opposed to, one another. For example, as I shall show, we cannot wage an adequate critique of popular culture unless we have devised strategies to find out just what the text intends to perform. Moreover, the critiques that have been proferred about and against Oprah Winfrey have become incorporated in Oprah's textual strategies, in such a way that it becomes difficult to disentangle the moral critiques of the text from the text itself. Analytically, then, I have three broad intents. One is to clarify the historical and cultural meanings that the persona of Oprah Winfrey and her show incarnate, articulate, stage, and perform. The second is to understand the moral enterprise of Oprah Winfrey in the context of a social order that severely strains the capacity of the self to make sense of its social environment; in that respect, my analysis takes very seriously Oprah's therapeutic vocation. The third is a critique of the moral and therapeutic role that Oprah Winfrey has assumed.

## INTERPRETATION

Oprah Winfrey's popularity and success are so spectacular that they compel us to ask, with anthropologist Dan Sperber, a simple question: "Why are some representations more catching than others?" To address this question, we must have a robust method of interpreting texts. But when the sociologist inquires about the meaning of a contemporary text, she is likely to be as perplexed as the historian of the remote past. Both scholars are left with the unnerving job of trying to explicate why certain cultural objects are more efficient and efficacious than others in capturing the social imagination while using tools that make their results too often resemble guesswork. The study of meaning should produce more than an educated guess. No matter how "thick" our study is, it does not excuse us from the methodological obligations to weigh our interpretations against those of others and to ground them as best we can in the social context that has given rise to them.

If the interpretation of a Balinese cockfight was to show how a small incident branches out to "the enormous complexities of social experience,"[13] in the case of Oprah, the challenge is the opposite: she contains and addresses such a wide variety of experiences, stories, and institutions that it is difficult to simplify this labyrinthic cultural form without sacrificing depth and complexity. Indeed, Oprah Winfrey and her show belong to the category of texts that are much "thicker than others."[14] The phenomenon contains multiple cultural forms that demand a variety of tools and sites of study: Oprah's biography, the autobiographical discourse of her guests, the codes of speech used by the talk show to produce an ephemeral but nonetheless powerful reality, the prescriptive speech of the experts invited on her show, the literary formula of the novels she chooses for her readers monthly, the critical articles written about Oprah in the popular press, her Web site, O Magazine. These form a complex and overlapping, mixed-media structure that poses a formidable challenge to textual analysis. Thus the first methodological difficulty is to draw the boundaries of the text(s) we are studying. Where does the talk show text start and end? If "O Magazine is an Oprah Winfrey show that one can hold in one's hand"—as the initiators of the concept claimed—then there is at least contiguity, if not continuity, between the electronic and print versions of The Oprah Winfrey Show, and our analysis cannot be based on the technological differences between the two.

The second difficulty is to figure out the best strategy for analyzing the megatextual structure of The Oprah Winfrey Show. Indeed, if "the study of television is the study of effects,"[15] then focusing on "texts" would seem either injudicious or lazy unless one is hoping, ultimately, to extrapolate to effects. Textual analysis is notoriously problematic, for it is vulnerable to the hermeneutic fallacy of "discovering" in texts the meanings that researchers brought with them. Moreover, the study of reception seems to have marked such a breakthrough in our understanding of the impact of the media that the study of texts has come to seem an imperfect substitute. In the context of the preeminence of audience ethnographies, "textual analysis" seems a flawed method through which to grasp the ways meanings are incorporated into daily life. Because audience analysis seems to have become the royal road to study the meaning of media, a word of explanation on my choice is appropriate. A basic justification for a study of texts is offered by Liebes and Katz: "Content analysis is clearly an essential prerequisite for defining what's on television."[16] To study reception, one needs a frame of reference, which is best provided by the rigorous analysis of the content of television. But this justification is not a real one, for it makes the study of texts ancillary to the study of reception.

The study of texts as texts is all the more warranted in Oprah's case, because the very distinction between texts and users is so blurred that it calls into question the distinction between "author" and "reader" that is at the core of traditional literary and communication theory. Ironically and paradoxically, because we have become the uninterrupted "audiences" of various cultural institutions (advertising, marketing, art, television, radio, newspapers, popular psychology, best-selling books, street posters, fashion designers, and body shapes), the distinction between texts and their interpretation has become somewhat artificial and problematic. As historian of the book Roger Chartier has argued, there is actually a continuity between the mental or cultural schemata that structure a text and the mental or cultural categories through which viewers grasp the world of a text. If this was true in the history of sixteenth-century books, it is all the more pertinent in an era where creators of texts are themselves audiences of other texts, and where media technologies and texts have become so closely intertwined. For example, the code of "family communication," so pervasive in talk shows, is the joint product of the publishing industry's self-help manuals and the psychological professions that have elaborated throughout the twentieth century such descriptive and prescriptive models of family relations. This code also structures the cultural world of talk show guests, producers, and viewers, as well as the narratives of family situation comedies and dramas that populate prime-time TV—often centered around disruptions in family communication (*Thirtysomething*, *All in the Family*), satires of family communication (*The Simpsons*), and idealized versions of family communication (*The Brady Bunch*, *The Cosby Show*).

This does not mean that the two kinds of schemata—that of the text and that of its reader—are similar or reducible to each other. (Indeed, texts are usually self-contained within space and time and have a stylistic structure, whereas experience flows in an unstructured way.) But it does mean that we can—if provided with the adequate tools—learn a great deal about the mental and cultural worlds of their users through texts and that the relationship between texts and audiences is both circuitous and circular.

There is a final reason talk shows do not lend themselves well to the traditional division between "texts" and their "audiences." The very format of the talk show mixes in a highly perplexing fashion an authorial design with the oral testimonies and stories of the show's numerous and varied guests. In this respect, talk shows make the dichotomy between texts and their "reception" crumble, for the raw material of the show's text is made of the live and natural discourse of "real" actors. Indeed, a main characteristic of *The Oprah Winfrey Show* is that it telescopes the production of the text and the response to it. Audience and guest reactions to the show before, during, and after are intrinsic to the genre . . . The genre itself incorporates the response to it, forcing us to move away from the classical production/reception dichotomy.

———

While it does not undertake a systematic analysis of viewer responses to Oprah Winfrey, this study nonetheless incorporates analyses of cultural responses to the show through two main bodies of data. One is her Web site, which contains thousands of messages that provide extensive information on the cultural frameworks within which her show and persona are interpreted. The second comes from an extensive (albeit not exhaustive) search of responses to the show by commentators and journalists in popular magazines. If the Web site provides information on the schemata and cultural frameworks of women from working-class to middle-class backgrounds, the popular and highbrow magazines provide extensive information on the reception of Oprah Winfrey by "cultural specialists" such as journalists, essayists, and academics.

These two forms of reception differ in many obvious ways. While journalists, commentators, and academics attend to a cultural object by self-consciously using formal principles of classification (aesthetic or moral), viewers visiting the Oprah Web site are more immediately implicated in the meaning of the show and are less often in a position to examine the principles that animate their stories, commentaries, and responses to it. In other words, cultural commentators of all persuasions attend to the normative fabric of a text—i.e., which values it conveys, which norms it breaks—much better than viewers or Web site users, who are more attentive to their involvement in the economy of personal meanings enacted by the text. Thus, my hermeneutic strategy pays a great deal of attention to the reception of Oprah Winfrey, but in a different way from what is conventionally dubbed "reception analysis": it is not the readers' way of making sense of *The Oprah Winfrey Show* that interests me as much as the ways in which readers and viewers—who are located at different points of the cultural hierarchy and who approach cultural material with different forms of reflexivity—activate norms, values, and aesthetic criteria to approach cultural material. When examining the readers' and viewers' responses on the Web site, I am less interested in their literal interpretations of any specific show than in the ways in which the show—as a genre—generates discussion, prayer groups, and reflexive self-management. Similarly, my study of the reception of Oprah Winfrey by cultural specialists focuses on the normative and aesthetic criteria underlying the critique and on the ways it is used to defend a certain conception of culture . . .

This study, then, is based on a mass of texts in which I almost sank: close to one hundred transcripts of shows made available by a commercial company (Burelles); a year and a half of watching the show regularly; some twenty books from the Oprah Winfrey Book Club; a dozen self-help guides discussed during her show; a critical mass of articles about Oprah from the popular press; a number of biographies of Oprah Winfrey; fifteen issues of *O Magazine*; and, finally, several hundred messages responding and reacting to the show on the Oprah Winfrey Web site (in the Book Club rubric, "Heal your spirit," and "Angel Network").

## CRITIQUE AND UNDERSTANDING

A cultural object such as Oprah, both popular and offensive to highbrow taste, presents a conundrum for sociological analysis. If sociologists do not want to condemn themselves to reconfirming their own (usually highbrow) tastes or to promoting their own (usually progressive) political agendas, they will want to understand this text from "within," without condescension and without a merely patronizing tolerance for whatever pleasures its audience finds in it. But in adopting this democratic stance, the sociologist becomes ill-equipped to criticize the politics of pleasure. Indeed, endorsing the "pleasure" generated by certain texts leaves us unable to probe further and question the nature of that pleasure. On the other hand, when the sociologist turns to the tradition of critical theory, which has mustered a formidable arsenal of critiques of the culture industries, she seems also condemned to a certain intellectual paralysis that derives from the unswerving assumption that culture and commodity ought to remain in irrevocably separate realms.

I wrestle precisely with the antinomy between understanding and critique in the context of the intensely commodified "political economy" of sentiments offered by Oprah Winfrey. . . . As I understand it, the task of cultural critique is to enhance human practices by treading a fine line between the "real" and the "ideal," the "is" and the "ought to be." Indicting the critical evaluation of popular culture as "elitist" is theoretically and politically disempowering, as it does not enable us to discuss and distinguish between regressive and emancipatory trends in popular culture.[17] A critical evaluation of popular culture can properly take place only after we have elucidated its meanings.

The task of analyzing the Oprah Winfrey phenomenon must be done within the tension between understanding and critique, because she contains highly perplexing contradictions. There is no doubt that Oprah has perfected with an uncanny talent the exploitation of private sorrow for television profits, and there is no doubt that she blatantly flouts the prohibition against mixing the private realm of sentiments with the market. But she also represents one of the most decisively democratic cultural forms to date in the medium of television.

Understanding and critique need not be in conflict. For powerful critiques derive from an intimate understanding of their object and appeal to its very moral code. This book relies on this simple insight. I am as skeptical of the Olympian critique of the Frankfurt School as I am of the glib postmodernist endorsement of "carnivalesque" consumerism. An Olympian critique will not do because it does not articulate critique from an intimate understanding of the object of critique. I am equally wary of postmodern sociology, which views popular culture as either meaningless background noise or a carnivalesque mockery of hierarchy; in both cases, mass media, and television in particular, are viewed as "sensory machines" with little or no cognitive content. Yet Oprah Winfrey is a powerful example of the resources of ordinary language when it is engaged in the activities of "meaning making" and reflecting on our condition. She is a blatant counterexample to the postmodern view that popular culture is benign, meaningless, or cacophonic.

Thus, if I take popular culture seriously, it is not for the same reasons or in the same ways as postmoderns do. It is less the "transgressive" or "playful" character of popular culture that makes it valuable than the ways in which it connects to the activities of "ordinary language," particularly to the ways in which it discusses our obligations to others, dilemmas, and ordinary moral commitments.

Such an approach to popular culture draws on philosophical claims by Wittgenstein, Stanley Cavell, Martha Nussbaum, Alexander Nehemas, Robert Pippin, and Richard Rorty. These philosophers claim in various ways that ordinary language, stories, morality plays, literature, and metaphors are powerful ways of interrogating reality. These philosophers have claimed that literature and art articulate and even clarify important philosophical questions; I would like to extend this view to popular culture.

Indeed, in her exceptional ability to depict and reflect on the predicaments of the self, Oprah Winfrey, no less than tragic plays, novels, or movies, compels us to ask questions fundamental to modern and postmodern existence: How is autonomy to be reached? What is and what ought to be the relationship between individuals and institutions? What is the meaning of marriage and sexuality for men and women in the contemporary era? These and other such questions structure the symbolic world of the text of Oprah Winfrey. . . . The persona of Oprah Winfrey and her show are symbolic devices no less powerful than works of art that ask what it means to have a self in an era where having an "authentic" self (her term) has become a highly elusive project. This approach will not only give us a richer understanding of popular culture but also make us better equipped to simultaneously understand and criticize it.

Following Wayne Booth and Martha Nussbaum, I call the kind of critique I apply to texts "ethical criticism." Ethical criticism tries to understand how texts enhance our "general aim to live well" and interrogates the text from the standpoint of values and the moral fabric of our lives. It tries to understand what kinds of deliberations are involved in a text, what terms it uses to define a problem, and how a text contributes to practical dilemmas and orientations. The practice of ethical criticism demands that we think differently about the distinction between the "highbrow thought" embodied in philosophy and the realm of unreflective entertainment embodied in popular culture. Oprah Winfrey has placed herself at the heart of the most pressing moral questions of our lives. Indeed, Oprah Winfrey and her show comment on what have become the "hard conditions" of personal life in the late modern era and provide "moral maps" for orientation in such "hard conditions." . . .

# Notes

1. Randolph 1995:22–28.
2. Clementson 2001:44–45.
3. Quoted in Lowe 1998:xi.
4. Ibid., 1.
5. To give one example among many: in 1998 she was named by *Entertainment Weekly* magazine the most powerful person in the entertainment industry. "She topped Steven Spielberg, Rupert Murdoch, George Lucas and the dual listing of Time Warner honchos Gerald Levin and Ted Turner in the Top. 5"

("Oprah Winfrey Named Most Powerful Person in Entertainment Industry," *Jet* 94 (24): 11. In 1998, she was voted the second most admired woman in America, after Hillary Rodham Clinton (Lowe 1998).

6. She is thought to reach 33 million viewers a day throughout the globe. In February 1999, she was rated second in the Nielsen ratings, after Jerry Springer (6.7 Nielsen number).

7. Quoted in G. Mair 156.

8. Quoted in Jane Rosenzweig, "Consuming Passions," *The American Prospect* http://www.prospect.org/archives/v11–2/rosenweig.htm1

9. See Bourdieu 1979; Beisel 1993, 1997.

10. Durkheim 1915 (1969):205–239; Bellah 1985, 1991.

11. This approach contains various strands of thought, ranging from critical theory to Bourdieu (e.g., 1988) via Foucault (1965) and Althusser, *For Mark* (New York: Pantheon, 1969).

12. Proponents of institutional analysis of meaning count historians of the book as Roger Chartier (*Forms and Meanings: Texts, Performances, and Audiences from Codex to Computer* [Philadelphia: University of Pennsylvania Press, 1995]) or Robert Darnton (1979), as well as sociologists as Paul DiMaggio (1982) or Wendy Griswold (1991).

13. Greenblatt 1999.

14. Ibid.

15. Liebes and Katz 1990:8.

16. Ibid., 9.

17. See Radway 1991 or Kellner 1995. for examples of a dual hermeneutic and critical approach to popular culture.

# References

Beisel, N. 1993. "Morals Versus Art: Censorship, the Politics of Interpretation, and the Victorian Nude." *American Sociological Review* 58:145–162.

———. 1997. *Imperiled Innocents: Anthony Comstock and Family Reproduction in Victorian America*. Princeton: Princeton University Press.

Bellah, R. N. 1985. *Habits of the Heart: Individualism and Commitment in American Life*. Berkeley: University of California Press.

———. 1991. *The Good Society*. New York: Knopf.

Bourdieu, P. 1979. *La distinction: critique sociale du jugement*. Paris: Editions de Minuit.

———. 1988. *Homo Academicus*. Stanford: Stanford University Press.

Chartier, R. 1995. *Forms and Meanings: Texts, Performances, and Audiences from Codex to Computer*. Philadelphia: University of Pennsylvania Press.

Darnton, R. 1979. *The Business of Enlightenment: A Publishing History of the Encyclopedia, 1775–1800.* Cambridge: Belknap.

DiMaggio, P. 1982. "Cultural Entrepreneurship in Nineteenth-Century Boston: The Creation of an Organizational Base for High Culture in America." *Media, Culture and Society* 4:33–50.

Durkheim, E. 1915 (1969). "Origins of These Beliefs (End)—Origin of the Idea of the Totemic Principle or Mana." In *The Elementary Forms of Religious Life,* 205–239. New York: Free Press.

Foucault, M. 1965. *Madness and Civilization: A History of Insanity in the Age of Reason.* New York: Pantheon.

Greenblatt, S. 1999. "The Touch of the Real." In S. Ortner, ed., *The Fate of "Culture": Geertz and Beyond.* Berkeley: University of California Press.

Griswold, Wendy. 1991. "American Character and the American Novel." *American Journal of Sociology* 86:740–765.

Kellner, D. 1995. *Media Culture: Cultural Studies, Identity, and Politics Between the Modern and the Postmodern.* London; New York: Routledge.

Liebes, T. and E. Katz. 1990. *The Export of Meaning: Cross-Cultural Readings of Dallas.* New York: Oxford University Press.

Lowe, J. 1998/2001. *Oprah Winfrey Speaks: Insight from the World's Most Influential Voice.* New York: Chichester: Wiley.

Radway, J. 1991. *Reading the Romance: Women, Patriarchy, and Popular Literature.* Chapel Hill: University of North Carolina Press.

———. 1997. *A Feeling for Books: The Book-of-the-Month Club, Literary Taste, and Middle-Class Desire.* Chapel Hill: University of North Carolina Press.

# STUDY QUESTIONS

1. Describe Illouz's methodological approach to studying *Oprah* and explain how and why she selected the data she used.
2. What is *ethical criticism*, according to Illouz, and why should cultural sociologists engage in it?

# 23

# RESEARCHING MUSIC WORLDS

DAVID GRAZIAN

"Writing about music," someone once quipped, "is like dancing about architecture." Whether you think this notion is witty, cynical, or perhaps both, you can still see the point: music is an autonomous form of artistic expression. Trying to capture its meanings or its value in words is a bit absurd. After all, if you could capture in words all that music so powerfully evokes you wouldn't actually need music.

Most music critics would probably agree with this sentiment—up to a point. However, they would likely argue that there is much to say about music that music itself cannot say. In particular, if scholars want to know about the social and cultural conditions that give rise to particular kinds of music and musical experiences, or if they want to describe the experiences of audiences as they listen to music, then they need words to do that. And beyond words, sociologists need information (data) and methods that they can use to unearth answers to their questions. Adopting an ethnographic approach—collecting close, direct observations of the social actors involved in the world of music—helps to satisfy the quest for such answers.

David Grazian, an influential cultural sociologist, provides a brief overview of research that relies on this ethnographic method. He surveys work from the Chicago School of American sociology and outlines the work of the Birmingham School of Cultural Studies in the UK, providing a sense of the scope and impact of their findings. Grazian concludes by offering a new research agenda for those interested in pursuing ethnographic research on music—one that could illuminate how changes in the contemporary music scene are affecting artists, producers, and fans. Most importantly, Grazian suggests, ethnography can provide what few other methods can: thick descriptions of the personal, emotional, and embodied experience of listening to music.

# OPPORTUNITIES FOR ETHNOGRAPHY IN THE SOCIOLOGY OF MUSIC

E thnography literally refers to the art of writing about people. Within the social sciences it has come to refer to a broad set of practices through which scholars attempt to observe and interpret the cultural beliefs and practices of social groups by engaging them in some kind of interpersonal encounter. Traditionally, sociological ethnography has referred specifically to the task of the participant observer who "gathers data by participating in the daily life of the group or organization he studies" (Becker, 1958: 652). However, in recent years the term has been appropriated by researchers who employ a broader range of qualitative methodologies, such as open-ended interviewing and biographical narrative collection. In this article I examine how these methodological tools have been employed in the sociological study of music, from the early ethnographic work of the Chicago school to more recent explorations of music-making in the contemporary city.

## The Ethnographic Tradition in Sociology

A founder of the Chicago school of urban sociology during the early decades of the 20th century, Robert E. Park introduced ethnographic fieldwork into the department's curriculum (Abbott, 1999; Anderson, 2001). Park himself was a former journalist, and under his guidance both graduate students and faculty alike researched and wrote ethnographic accounts of the otherwise hidden lives of Chicago's immigrant families, homeless men, working-class gangs, and juvenile delinquents.

Among these monographs, three in particular give an account of how popular music scenes operate within a larger cultural ecology of urban nightlife. In *Vice in Chicago*, Walter C. Reckless (1933) provides a detailed cartography of the city's Prohibition-era jazz venues, public dance halls, and vaudeville houses. In his analysis of the black-and-tan cabarets located in Chicago's segregated black neighborhoods, Reckless (1933: 102–103) uses ethnographic data to emphasize how consumers attach symbolic importance to the neighborhood context in which they experience live blues and jazz music: "To a slumming white patronage the Black Belt location of cabarets offered atmosphere and the colored man's music and patronage added thrill."

Like much of the Chicago school research on urban life, a moralistic social agenda informs *Vice in Chicago*. Similarly, Paul G. Cressey (1932) critically explores the underworld represented by the taxi-dance hall, a type of club popular during the 1920s where men could purchase three-minute dances with attractive female companions at ten cents per song. Cressey relies on close participant observation and in-depth interview data with dancers as well as their male patrons, the latter typically Asian immigrants who relied on these dance halls and their live music as entry points into the social world of American life. Another prominent Chicago researcher, Harvey Warren Zorbaugh, fills *The Gold Coast and the Slum* (1929) with anecdotes about the importance of music for the diverse residential communities of the city's Near North Side. In a chapter on the fashions of high-society, status-seekers measure their social worth in "invitations to certain box parties at the opera," exclusive balls and benefit concerts held for charity (Zorbaugh, 1929: 50–51). His account of the unmarried residents who inhabit the area's furnished rooming-house district includes a sad tale of an aspiring young pianist who flees Kansas for a chance to perform professionally in Chicago. (After a year, her music lessons grow more and more expensive until her teacher finally convinces her of the hopelessness of her ambition.) And in his research on Towertown, the city's bohemian entertainment zone, Zorbaugh (1929: 102) discovers the jazz musicians and "singing waiters" employed within its highly commercialized world of nightclubs and "Paris revues."

The legacy of these Chicago school investigations lies in (1) their use of the case study as a legitimate form of sociological inquiry; (2) an attention to participant observation and other types of ethnographic fieldwork; and (3) an emphasis on the interactional fields in which urban culture is produced, marketed and consumed. These examples would continue to influence ethnographic work in the sociology of music over the course of the twentieth century.

# Producing Music

While the contributions of the Chicago school add to our knowledge of how music cultures operate in the urban milieu, it is clear that the study of music was always tangential to a more general examination of social organization and human ecology in the context of the American city. In contrast, the next wave of ethnography in music focused specifically on the world of musicians in the settings in which they lived and labored. The earliest of this research was conducted not by sociologists, but by folklorists and ethnomusicologists interested in capturing the indigenous musical cultures of the rural South. Through a variety of techniques, including extensive participant observation, interviewing, and recording songs and oral narratives, fieldworkers such as Alan Lomax (1993), Paul Oliver (1965), and David Evans (1982) created vivid and illustrative portrayals of the Mississippi Delta and its folk blues culture. This ethnographic work emphasized how blues musicians in that context drew on the reality of their surroundings, particularly chronic poverty and institutionalized racism, to infuse their songs with both ironic reflection and emotional intensity. In a similar vein, Charles Keil (1966) studied Chicago blues and soul singers, and Samuel Charters (1981) researched West African tribal performers (or *griots*) thought to be the originators of what would come to be the American blues tradition.

While productive, the ethnomusicological approach to blues research suffered from a number of related weaknesses: its presentation was generally impressionistic, rather than systematic; its intellectual goals were descriptive and explanatory, but not theoretical; and its orientation was romantic instead of critical. As a result, classic ethnomusicology evaded an analysis of how more contemporary professional, economic and institutional forces structure the production of popular music.

Sociology, on the other hand, was much better equipped to compensate for these gaps, and from the mid-1950s onward ethnographers explored the commercial contexts in which musicians produce their craft not only as inspired artists, but as employed professionals as well (Becker, 1982). These ethnographic studies developed out of three related paradigms made popular within sociology at this time: the influence of Everett C. Hughes and his work on occupations; the rise of symbolic interactionism; and the strengths of labeling theory and the social construction of deviant behavior. In *Outsiders* (1963), Howard S. Becker (a student of Hughes) examines how jazz musicians negotiate between the demands of their audiences and their own artistic aspirations and establish career identities within an unstable job market. According to Becker (1963: 114–119), jazz musicians labored in a low-status profession regarded as "unconventional," "bohemian" and downwardly mobile by the reigning middle-class norms of the 1950s and 1960s, and this impacted how they conducted themselves in their domestic relationships as well as their professional lives. Becker demonstrates how close participant observation can yield both systematic empirical data and theoretical insight.

Becker's analysis of jazz players as an occupational group propelled future work on the professional lives of other types of musicians. Robert R. Faulkner (1971, 1973) explores the higher-brow world of classically trained orchestral musicians, particularly those who transition from live concert performance to studio recording for film and television. Like Becker, Faulkner's chief emphasis concerns how musicians organize and emotionally experience their careers as workers laboring in an inherently unpredictable field. The economics of musical work require that participants manage their ambitions and definitions of success accordingly, taking into account the challenges of finding employment as well as the benefits and costs of "going commercial."

In contrast to Faulkner, H. Stith Bennett (1980) researches the world of local rock musicians; however, like his predecessors, he addresses a wide range of their occupational strategies, including instrument acquisition, gig procurement, set programming, and techniques of performance. A student of Becker's, Bennett also performs as a musician and relies on his contact with fellow players as his primary source of data about not only professional practices, but the set of meanings that musicians attribute to those practices. Like Becker and Faulkner, Bennett draws on ethnographic methods in order to better understand how musicians develop subjectivities within a set of material constraints, commercial demands and professional expectations.

## Subcultures and Style

Until the mid-1970s, ethnography in the sociology of music focused almost entirely on production. Why? In part, musicians made fitting case studies for research on occupations and on the social construction of deviance, two fields that exponentially grew in popularity among sociologists during the 1960s (Abbott, 2001). But this focus was also due to an abandonment of ethnographic work on music *consumption*. The rise of the Frankfurt school's critique of mass culture, particularly Adorno's work on jazz and the "regression" of listening, contributed to growing attacks on the commodification of popular music by American public intellectuals during the 1940s and 1950s (Macdonald, 1953; Hayakawa, 1955; Adorno, 1989, 1997; also see Rosenberg and White, 1957). By portraying consumers of popular music as alienated, neurotic and childlike simpletons rather than discriminating human agents, this critique ultimately rendered such consumers unworthy of close ethnographic attention.

Perhaps on the strength of this critique of popular culture, research on music consumption tended to employ varied approaches such as content analysis and survey methods but rarely ethnography (i.e. Clarke, 1956; Horton, 1957; Johnstone and Katz, 1957). David Riesman (1950) provided an exception to this rule by conducting lengthy open-ended interviews with his students and a sample of younger teenagers. He found that American youth could be divided into two groups. The majority followed conventional adolescent tastes while a minority of active listeners exhibited their distaste for commercial music and celebrity performers. These latter consumers developed their musical preferences within the context of peer groups who expressed a disdain for conformity to the cultural mainstream.

Two decades later, observations like Riesman's would become the basis for an entire wave of ethnographic research on the consumption of music. Drawing on a amalgam of British social history, neo-Marxist theory and French post-structuralism, fieldworkers associated with the Centre for Contemporary Cultural Studies at the University of Birmingham produced accounts of how youth subcultures actively incorporate music into their overall lifestyles (Hall and Jefferson, 1975; McRobbie and Garber, 1975; Willis, 1978; Hebdige, 1979). In colorful studies of punks, skinheads, bikers, hippies, Rastafarians and other bohemian groups, researchers explored how young people rely on the creative potential of music to develop symbolic and aesthetic practices in concert with other elements of style, including fashion, body adornment, dance, drug use and slang. Reacting to the mass culture critique, these scholars argued that the consumption of music represented a class-conscious form of rebelliousness, or "resistance through rituals" (Hall and Jefferson, 1975). By appropriating commodified forms of music for their own stylistic and expressive ends, music *consumers* could refashion themselves as *producers* as well.

While path-breaking in its own right, some of the research of the Bir-mingham school unfortunately emphasized the development of theory without empirical verification from ethnographic data, sometimes at the cost of substituting armchair sociology for the rigors of fieldwork. In con-trast, more recent studies of subcultures and style employ intensive partici-pant observation to reveal how young consumers use music to shape a set of collective identities and experiences in everyday life. In her late-1980s ethnography *Teenage Wasteland*, Donna Gaines (1991) hangs out in conve-nience store parking lots with working-class hard rock fans from suburban New Jersey, and details the enthusiasm with which they worship the songs and totemic symbols of their favorite bands—Led Zeppelin, Metallica, Bon Jovi, Suicidal Tendencies, the Grateful Dead. Through the consumption of heavy metal and glam rock, kids labeled as so-called "burnouts" invest their socially marginalized lives with meaning and affirmations of self.

Whereas previous accounts of youth subcultures explained how the con-sumption of music could also help foster in-group solidarity and integra-tion, during the 1990s ethnographers began emphasizing how music tastes and rituals of consumption could lead to increased internal differentiation *within* subcultures. In her ethnographic study of British dance clubs, Sarah Thornton (1996) found that established acid house and techno music fans vie for subcultural status by mocking their less experienced counterparts within the scene. Clubbers criticize these novice thrill-seekers for exhibit-ing what they consider an amateurish lack of sophistication and style, and refer to the mainstream clubs that cater to them as "drunken cattle mar-kets" where "tacky men drinking pints of best bitter pull girls in white high heels" (Thornton, 1996: 99). Similarly, Ben Malbon (1999) explores how London dance clubs employees invoke the criteria of "coolness" to restrict entry into their establishments, thereby replicating the racist and sexist social norms of exclusion found in more mainstream cultural settings.

For Malbon's chatty informants, the achievement of "belonging" depends on their ability to negotiate among the various front and back stages of the club. Also with an ethnographic eye toward differentiation and spatial practices within music scenes, Wendy Fonarow (1997) draws on field obser-vations and interviews to provide a mapping of the three spatial regions of British indie rock clubs inhabited by consumers during live shows. The youngest and most enthusiastic fans jump and shout at the front of the stage and in the mosh pit; older fans congregate on the floor behind the pit, where they can enjoy the performance without distraction; and industry personnel and other music professionals linger in the back regions near the bar, coolly consuming the whole scene with bemused detachment. Fonarow demonstrates how the participants of music performances differentiate themselves by engaging in varied strategies of consumption. At the same time, as these consumers get older they alter their affiliation with the band and their place within the club so that they eventually "move back through space until they are aged out of the venue all together" (Fonarow, 1997: 369).

## The Consumption of Music and the Self

While these accounts of music subcultures and scenes focus on collective processes and in-group interaction, other recent ethnographic research within the sociology of music emphasizes how consumers employ music to create more personal and individualized experiences for themselves. In *Common Culture* Paul Willis (1990) emphasizes the meanings and practices that young people attach to popular music. According to Willis's informants, music serves as a resource for generating meaning through the selective interpretation of memorable lyrics and styles of performance. He argues that through activities such as home recording and creating a "personal soundscape" inside one's head with the help of Walkman earphones, listening to music presents opportunities for developing a political consciousness, gaining spiritual nourishment, and making sense of pivotal milestones and life experiences (Willis, 1990: 64).

The work of Tia DeNora (1999, 2000) offers a sophisticated framework for thinking about how individuals consume music. She argues that music operates as a "technology of the self," a resource for managing one's everyday life. Through open-ended interviews and ethnographic fieldwork conducted in sites such as aerobics classes and fashionable clothing shops, DeNora scrutinizes how consumers use music to orchestrate their daily routines from waking up to working out. In bedrooms and offices, music serves a variety of personal functions: it supplies mental preparation for the workday, encourages concentration during important tasks, alleviates stress, and acts as a device of organizing one's memory of key moments with romantic partners, family members or other intimates. In ethnographic forays into the world of music therapy and physical fitness, DeNora (2000) emphasizes the elemental relationship existing between music and the body. In aerobics, music operates not as background, but as *foreground*, as a tool employed to explicitly define the rhythm, pacing and progression of the workout, from warm-up to cool-down. Similarly, Rob Drew (2001) relies on fieldwork conducted in thirty karaoke bars to examine how individuals use their bodies to publicly express themselves musically. Through elaborate performances that attempt to imitate, embellish or parody the recordings of well-known entertainers, amateur crooners experience music in an earthly manner through their intensely drawn facial expressions, exaggerated dance styles and strained vocals.

Drew draws on his own experience as a participant observer to enrich his account, and in doing so he subjects himself to his own analysis. This may not be surprising, given that the last two decades have given rise to the postmodern critique of ethnography emanating from within the worlds of anthropology, gender studies and critical theory. This critique challenges traditional ethnography on several grounds, including (but not limited to): its unfair characterization of politically subjugated groups, including women and racial minorities; the false claim to objectivity made by fieldworkers; the inherent power discrepancies between researchers and subjects; and the resistance of ethnographers to reflect upon these issues and candidly introduce them into their written accounts from the field (Clifford and Marcus, 1986; Clifford, 1988; Rosaldo, 1989; Abu-Lughod, 1993; Behar and Gordon, 1995; Marcus, 1998).

This attention to reflexivity in ethnography has prompted a number of studies by researchers who examine their own experiences as music listeners and/or performers. In *Race Music*, Guthrie P. Ramsey, Jr. (2003) produces what he refers to as an "ethnographic memoir" by drawing on his own first-hand recollections as an African-American child growing up in Chicago, and his experiences as a professional jazz pianist and gospel performer. In addition, he draws on interviews with his immediate and extended family members who provide oral histories of their migration to Chicago from the Deep South and remembrances of life in the city's segregated black neighborhoods. Ramsey elegantly weaves together these materials to describe the relationship between music and memory as it thrives in the spaces of black urban culture, including its house parties, jazz clubs, churches, and roller-skating rinks.

Meanwhile, Stacy Holman Jones (2002) uses her field research as an opportunity for self-analysis. She combines her observations and a brief interview with a cabaret performer with her own musings on torch singing and fantasies about Sarah Vaughan to produce an ethnographic medita-tion on music and desire. Jones (2002: 739) herself refers to the piece as "a fiction and an autoethnography, an analysis and an argument, an irony and a literal rendition, a scrapbook and a fan letter." While these highly personal studies may lack the empirical reliability of more traditional field research, they emphasize the subjective and interpretive quality of ethno-graphic practice (see Geertz, 1973).

## Opportunities for Ethnography in the Sociology of Music

As demonstrated by past research, the promise of ethnographic methods presents a bounty of opportunities for the sociological study of music. Like music, ethnography is an interpretative practice it requires participation and improvisation; its presentation invites a multiplicity of meanings as well as self-reflection. For these reasons, I conclude with three suggestions for new foci in ethnographic research in the sociology of music: the use of popular music in the marketing of urban areas; the production process within the culture industries; and the consumption of music in real time and space.

First, the contemporary literature on urban sociology proposes that elites often appropriate the local culture of their cities for political and entrepreneurial ends (Zukin, 1995; Suttles, 1984; Logan and Molotch, 1987; Lloyd and Clark, 2001; Lloyd, 2002). In Chicago and Memphis, civic boosters promote blues clubs within their cities as a means of increasing tourism and generating revenue for their local economies, just as Nash-ville, New Orleans, and Liverpool rely on their own roots-oriented music heritages for their financial vitality (Grazian, 2003). Ethnographic meth-ods can help sociologists better understand these complex relationships existing between the political economy of urban areas and their music cultures. Specifically, by relying on three techniques—conducting partici-pant observation at city sponsored music festivals and other tourist attractions, engaging in open-ended interviews with civic leaders and the programmers of local cultural organizations, and collecting accounts of how musicians, residents, boosters and out-of-towners creatively employ images of "authenticity" to represent the city, ethnographers can add empirical weight to the more abstract paradigms indicative of much post-modern urban theory.

Second, ethnographic methods can enhance the historical and quantitative research currently conducted on the music industry itself. Over the past thirty years, the sociology of music has greatly benefited from the scholarly efforts made by those attempting to combine the fields of cultural production and organizational behavior. By treating the production of music as a commercial enterprise undertaken by large industrial conglomerates, sociologists have helped demystify the processes through which record labels and other media companies manufacture, market and distribute culture as a commodified form (Hirsch, 1972; Peterson and Berger, 1975; Peterson, 1978, 1997; Frith, 1978, 1981; Dowd and Blyler, 2002).

In recent years, ethnographic work has contributed to this project as well by increasing our knowledge of how corporate cultures impact particular music genres; identifying the diverse artistic and economic interests that drive the production of music videos; uncovering how hip-hop impresarios rely on ideological considerations to successfully promote rap music; discovering how music critics organize themselves within the context of professional journalism; and exploring how the chaotic careers of session musicians are structured (Peterson and White, 1979; Negus, 1992, 1999; Regev, 1997; McLeod, 1999; Klein, 2003). In future endeavors, ethnography may prove to be particularly useful for developing our understanding of how support personnel experience occupational marginality and gender segregation within the music industry; how the employees of independent record companies create alternative identities and professional presentations of self; and how ideologies that shape the industrial production of music eventually filter down to the level of the local music subculture or scene.

Finally, ethnographic methods provide an especially handy tool for sociologists interested in examining how people consume music in real time within spatial contexts of social interaction. To their credit, sociologists of culture have relied on sophisticated techniques to examine the tastes and participation rates among music consumers, and have identified the relationship between music genre appreciation and social class, race, educational background, and occupational status (Bourdieu, 1984; DiMaggio and Ostrower, 1990; Peterson, 1992; Bryson, 1996, 1997; Peterson and Kern, 1996). But even the most rigorous quantitative studies of consumption can fail to account for how individuals actually experience music in their moments of consumption, whether during public concerts, small cabaret shows, or candlelit dinners. Of course, certain questions regarding the consumption of music can only be reliably answered by making inferences based on large population samples, and in these cases ethnography may only be appropriate as a complement to ongoing statistical data analysis. However, the pleasure (and occasional displeasure) produced by music rarely registers at the level of mere approval, but is often experienced in an emotional and visceral manner as expressed through bodily gestures, spontaneous applause, and welled tears of longing (see Malbon, 1999; DeNora, 2000; Drew, 2001; Grazian, 2003). Whether through participant observation, open-ended interviewing, or oral narrative collection, live performance and experiences provide among the most appropriate opportunities for ethnography in the sociology of music.

# References

Abbott, Andrew. 1999. Department and Discipline: Chicago Sociology at One Hundred. University of Chicago Press, Chicago.

———. 2001. *Chaos of Disciplines.* University of Chicago Press, Chicago.

Abu-Lughod, Lila. 1993. *Writing Women's Worlds: Bedouin Stories.* University of California Press, Berkeley.

Adorno, Theodor W. 1989. Perennial Fashion—Jazz. In: Stephen Eric Bronner, Douglas MacKay Kellner, eds. *Critical Theory and Society.* Routledge, New York.

———. 1997. On the Fetish-character in music and the regression of listening. In: Andrew, Arato, Eike, Gebhardt, eds. *The Essential Frankfurt School Reader.* Continuum, New York.

Anderson, Elijah. 2001. Urban ethnography. In: Neil J., Smelser, Paul B., Baltes (Eds.), *International Encyclopedia of the Social & Behavioral Sciences.* Elsevier Science, New York.

Becker, Howard S. 1958. Problems of inference and proof in participant observation. *American Sociological Review* 23, 652–660.

———. *Outsiders: Studies in the Sociology of Deviance.* Free Press, Glencoe.

———. *Art Worlds.* University of California Press, Berkeley.

Behar, Ruth and Deborah Gordon, eds. 1995. *Women Writing Culture.* University of California Press, Berkeley.

Bennett, H. Stith, 1980. *On Becoming a Rock Musician.* Amherst, University of Massachusetts Press, MA.

Bourdieu, Pierre. 1984. *Distinction: A Social Critique of the Judgment of Taste* (Richard Nice, trans.). Harvard University Press, Cambridge, MA.

Bryson, Bethany. 1996. Anything but heavy metal: symbolic exclusion and musical dislikes. *American Sociological Review* 61, 884–899.

———. What about the univores? Musical dislikes and group-based identity construction among Americans with low levels of education. *Poetics* 25, 141–156.

Charters, Samuel. 1981. *The Roots of the Blues: An African Search.* Da Capo Press, New York.

Clarke, Alfred C. 1956. The use of leisure and its relation to levels of occupational prestige. *American Sociological Review* 21, 301–307.

Clifford, James. 1988. *The Predicament of Culture: Twentieth-Century Ethnography. Literature and Art.* Harvard University Press, Cambridge.

Clifford, James and George E. Marcus, eds. 1986. *Writing Culture: The Poetics and Politics of Ethnography.* University of California Press, Berkeley.

Cressey, Paul G. 1932. *The Taxi-Dance Hall.* University of Chicago Press, Chicago.

DeNora, Tia. 1999. Music as a technology of the self. *Poetics* 27, 31–56.

———. *Music in Everyday Life.* Cambridge University Press, Cambridge.

DiMaggio, Paul and Francie Ostrower. 1990. Participation in the arts by black and white Americans. *Social Forces* 63, 753–778.

Dowd, Timothy J. and Maureen Blyler. 2002. Charting race: the success of black performers in the mainstream recording market 1940–1990. *Poetics* 30, 87–110.

Drew, Rob. 2001. *Karaoke Nights: An Ethnographic Rhapsody.* Alta Mira, Walnut Creek, CA.

Evans, David. 1982. *Big Road Blues: Tradition and Creativity in the Folk Blues.* University of California Press, Berkeley.

Faulkner, Robert R. 1971. *Hollywood Studio Musicians.* Aldine Publishing Company, Chicago.

———. 1973. Career concerns and mobility motivations of orchestra musicians. *Sociological Quarterly* 14, 147–157.

Fonarow, Wendy. 1997. The Spatial Organization of the Indie Music Gig. In: Ken Gelder and Sarah Thornton, eds. *The Subcultures Reader.* Routledge, London.

Frith, Simon. 1978. *The Sociology of Rock.* Constable, London.

———. *Sound Effects: Youth, Leisure, and the Politics of Rock 'n' Roll.* Pantheon, New York.

Gaines. Donna. 1991. *Teenage Wasteland: Suburbia's Dead End Kids.* Pantheon, New York.

Geertz, Clifford. 1973. *The Interpretation of Cultures.* Basic, New York.

Grazian, David. 2003. *Blue Chicago: The Search for Authenticity in Urban Blues Clubs.* University of Chicago Press, Chicago.

Hall, Stuart and Tony Jefferson, eds. 1975. *Resistance Through Rituals: Youth Subcultures in Post-War Britain.* Routledge, London.

Hayakawa, S. I. 1955. Popular songs versus the facts of life. *Etc* 12, 83–95.

Hebdige, Dick. 1979. *Subculture: The Meaning of Style*. Routledge, London.

Hirsch, P. M. 1972. Processing fads and fashions: an organization set analysis of culture industry systems. *American Journal of Sociology* 77, 639–659.

Horton, Donald. 1957. The dialogue of courtship in popular songs. *American Journal of Sociology* 62, 569–578.

Johnstone, John and Elihu Katz. 1957. Youth and popular music: a study in the sociology of taste. *American Journal of Sociology* 62, 563–568.

Jones, S. H. 2002. Emotional space: performing the resistive possibilities of torch singing. *Qualitative Inquiry* 8, 738–759.

Keil, Charles. 1966. *Urban Blues*. University of Chicago Press, Chicago.

Klein, Bethany. 2003. *Dancing about Architecture: Popular Music Criticism and the Negotiation of Authority*. MA Thesis. Annenberg School for Communication, University of Pennsylvania (unpublished).

Lloyd, Richard. 2002. Neo-bohemia: art and neighborhood redevelopment in Chicago. *Journal of Urban Affairs* 24, 517–532.

Lloyd, Richard and Terry N. Clark, 2001. The city as an entertainment machine. *Critical Perspectives on Urban Redevelopment* 6, 359–380.

Logan, John R. and Harvey L. Molotch. 1987. *Urban Fortunes: The Political Economy of Place*. University of California Press, Berkeley.

Lomax, Alan. 1993. *The Land Where the Blues Began*. Delta, New York.

Malbon, Ben. 1999. *Clubbing: Dancing, Ecstasy and Vitality*. Routledge, New York.

Marcus, George E. 1998. *Ethnography Through Thick and Thin*. Princeton University Press, Princeton.

McDonald, Dwight. 1953. A theory of mass culture. *Diogenes* 3, 1–17.

McLeod, Kembrew. 1999. Authenticity within hip-hop and other cultures threatened with assimilation. *Journal of Communication* 49, 134–150.

McRobbie, Angela and Jenny Garber. 1975. Girls and Subcultures. In: Stuart, Hall and Tony Jefferson, eds. *Resistance Through Rituals: Youth Subcultures in Post-War Britain*. Routledge, London.

Negus, Keith. 1992. *Producing Pop: Culture and Conflict in the Popular Music Industry*. Edward Arnold, London.

———. *Music Genres and Corporate Cultures*. Routledge, London.

Oliver, Paul. 1965. *Conversation with the Blues*. Cambridge University Press, Cambridge.

Peterson, Richard A. 1978. The production of cultural change: the case of contemporary country music. *Social Forces* 45, 292–314.

———. 1992. Understanding audience segmentation: from elite and mass to omnivore and univore. *Poetics* 21, 243–258.

———. 1997. *Creating Country Music: Fabricating Authenticity*. University of Chicago Press, Chicago.

Peterson, Richard A. and David G. Berger. 1975. Cycles in symbol production: the case of popular music. *American Sociological Review* 40, 158–173.

Peterson, Richard A. and Roger M. Kern. 1996. Changing highbrow taste: from snob to omnivore. *American Sociological Review* 61, 900–907.

Peterson, Richard A. and Howard G. White. 1979. The simplex located in art worlds. *Urban Life* 7, 411–439.

Ramsey, Guthrie P., Jr., 2003. *Race Music: Black Cultures from Bebop to Hip-Hop*. University of California Press, Berkeley.

Reckless, Walter C. 1933. *Vice in Chicago*. University of Chicago Press, Chicago.

Regev, Motti, 1997. Who does what with music videos in Israel. *Poetics* 25, 225–240.

Riesman, David. 1950. Listening to popular music. *American Quarterly* 2, 359–371.

Rosaldo, Renato. 1989. *Culture and Truth: The Remaking of Social Analysis*. Beacon, Boston.

Rosenberg, Bernard and David Manning White. 1957. *Mass Culture: The Popular Arts in America*. Free Press, New York.

Suttles, Gerald D. 1984. The cumulative texture of local urban culture. *American Journal of Sociology* 90, 283–304.

Thornton, Sarah. 1996. *Club Cultures: Music, Media and Subcultural Capital*. Wesleyan University Press, Hanover.

Willis, Paul E. 1978. *Profane Culture*. Routledge, London.

———. *Common Culture: Symbolic Work at Play in the Everyday Cultures of the Young*. Westview, Boulder, CO.

Zorbaugh, Harvey Warren. 1929. *The Gold Coast and the Slum: A Sociological Study of Chicago's Near North Side*. University of Chicago Press, Chicago.

Zukin, Sharon. 1995. *The Cultures of Cities*. Blackwell, Cambridge.

# STUDY QUESTIONS

1. How does Grazian define ethnography and how is his definition different from (or similar to) other definitions found in this reader?
2. What has the ethnographic approach revealed about how music is both produced and consumed?

# PART FIVE

# GROUPS, NETWORKS, AND IDENTITIES

I N THE COEN brothers' movie *O Brother, Where Art Thou?*, set in the 1930s, a dim-witted trio of escaped convicts journeys through rural Mississippi, one step ahead of the law. They happen across a radio station and make a live recording of a song that, unbeknownst to them, quickly becomes a big hit. Their impromptu band—The Soggy Bottom Boys—is suddenly in high demand. The storyline unfolds in the Coen brothers' trademark convoluted, weird way, but the film accurately depicts an era when popular music was loosely organized around radio stations and their listeners. People were exposed to new songs and bands through live performances on the radio and then paid to see those new bands play when they were in town. By the 1960s, the music industry was tightly organized around a studio production model and musicians largely acquired new fans through albums played on the radio. Musicians and record companies no longer made most of their money from concerts and live performances, but from vinyl album and (in the 1980s) CD sales.

Then in the 1990s came the MP3 and the era of Napster. The ability to produce and share digital copies of songs at no cost revolutionized the way popular music is consumed. Peer-to-peer file sharing technology enabled fans to send songs to friends and friends of friends and eventually, with the advent of file sharing networks like Kazaa and Grokster, to find new friends who shared similar tastes in music. In an important sense, the social media of today grew out of our seemingly limitless public hunger for and love of popular music, especially when it is free, as it was in the radio-driven days of the past. Without the Internet showcasing people's desire to connect around their tastes in music, Facebook might never have come about as it did.

Ironically, the MP3 revolution has come full circle: the technology eventually unwound the production system of the recording industry and led to sharp declines in recorded music sales. Musicians now make their money the old-fashioned way—selling live concert tickets and merchandise to groups and networks of avid fans. And new bands build audiences by giving away their music with free downloads just as past musicians gained fans by giving away their music over the airwaves.

All of this raises some important questions for cultural sociologists. For example, what are social groups and networks, and how and why are they formed? What is it that binds members together or tears them apart? What causes individuals to come together in the spirit of cooperation and strategic alliance (and alternatively, what drives conflicts between them)? More fundamentally, do individuals choose their groups and networks or vice versa? How do groups and networks help or hinder people in finding their place in society? That is, how do they shape people's sense of identity, the sense of who they are, not only in their own eyes, but also in the eyes of others?

To answer these questions, sociologists ask how society is organized. What are its fundamental units and building blocks and what forms do they take? Sociologist Dalton Conley notes that for much of the twentieth century, the most common form of social organization in American society was that of concentric circles. "By way of analogy," he writes, "think of Russian nesting dolls: children were nested in families; each family had one breadwinner; that breadwinner worked for a single employer; those employers were firmly rooted in the United States; and, to top it all off, the vast majority of people living in the country were citizens" (Conley 2008). This was a form of social organization that encouraged a strong consensus about what families and individuals needed most, as well as a consensus about the role of government in providing for people in times of need. The result was broad, popular support for a bargain between American citizens and their government: we will work hard to support ourselves and our families and when we need help in doing so, the government will be there to give us a hand until we are back on our feet.

By contrast, Conley goes on to say, the most common form of social organization in the early twenty-first century is not the nested social circle, but the cross-cutting network. Instead of the analogy of Russian dolls, we need the analogy of—you guessed it—Facebook. Social networking sites connect people in casual and intimate ways, even when they are separated by great geographic distances or cultural or generational rifts. Living in a particular community, or having a particular class background or racial identity still matters a great deal, but these may matter less than they once did, since new social networks link people across older social divides. Social identity and a sense of self appear to be more fluid today than under the twentieth-century model. Social networks provide more reference points with which to make sense of who we as individuals are, more opportunities than we as individuals would otherwise have, and therefore, a wider range of aspirations of what we as individuals might become.

Cultural sociologists focus on the role that culture plays in all of these processes. A fundamental theme is that the processes are circular: Culture plays a role in producing and fostering group membership and social network formation, but groups and networks also produce local cultures of their own, called subcultures. The readings in this section pay close attention to subcultures and the small groups that generate and sustain them. They show how individuals sometimes use their membership in groups to differentiate themselves from others, creating both auras of belonging and stigmas of exclusion. The readings show how cultures can become racialized—as is the case when one talks about black or Latino culture—and what some of the consequences of those racializations can be. They also show how everyday practices like amateur sports, talking about politics, and listening to music can and do generate subcultural styles, giving rise to groups and networks that shape the identities and social selves of their members.

## References

Conley, Dalton. 2008. "Network Nation." *New York Times*, June 22.

# 24

# GROUP CULTURE

GARY ALAN FINE

When you were growing up, did your parents ever worry that you might be hanging out with the wrong crowd? Did they seem to take an unusual interest in new friends you made? If so, they weren't just being overly anxious or nosy. They were giving expression to a well-founded concern: our peers and friends have a great deal of influence on us, especially when we are younger. The influence can be positive ("He's such a nice kid!") or negative ("She's a bad influence on you!"), but either way, you've probably learned as many behaviors from your friends as you have from your parents. And, of course, peers influence more than just your behaviors; they shape your thoughts, values, and ideas about the world.

In this classic article, Fine explores how small groups create idiocultures—"sub-universes of meaning"—that emerge in very natural ways out of small group life. He chooses youth baseball teams for his case study, as they vividly show how groups form, build up shared cultural meanings and practices, and dissolve at the end of the season. It's a bit like watching the life cycle of flowering plants in their natural habitat—the process is shaped by the local elements, yes, but it also has a structure all its own. Fine's goal is to remind sociologists to pay attention to small-scale cultural forms, employing the method of microethnography to do so. Such forms not only illuminate how group cultures shape individual identities and behaviors (the issue your parents were worried about), but also shed light on how groups distinguish themselves from other groups, leading to larger and more complex patterns of social differentiation.

# SMALL GROUPS AND CULTURE CREATION: THE IDIOCULTURE OF LITTLE LEAGUE BASEBALL TEAMS

B lumer (1969) has argued that meaning derives from interaction, and culture, a set of shared understandings, is clearly implicated in Blumer's premise. While culture is defined, created, and transmitted through interaction, it is not interaction itself, but the content, meanings, and topics of interaction. In Herskovits's (1948:625) definition:

> though a culture may be treated by the student as capable of objective description, in the final analysis it comprises the things that people have, the things they do, and what they think.

Sociologists and anthropologists who have examined culture have found specifying the cultural patterns of an entire society to be an insurmountable task. While the attempts have been noble, the size of the undertaking has produced disappointing results for the goal of understanding the dynamics of cultural creation and tradition. If we take Blumer's premise seriously, it may be more suitable to begin our examination with interaction, and therefore to consider culture creation as an outcome of this interaction (e.g., Hare et al., 1965:v). The prototype of these interacting units is the small group, and the prevalence of groups in society suggests that it may be useful to conceive of culture as being part of the communication system of these interacting units (Spector, 1973). Despite the focus on the group, we recognize that this does not imply that shared understandings which transcend interactive networks do not exist; however, models are necessary to indicate how information diffuses from the originating group (see Fine and Kleinman, 1979). Although cultural elements can transcend the boundaries of interacting groups, it frequently occurs that cultural elements are experienced within the context of the small group. Thus, one may argue that most culture elements are experienced as part of a communication system of a small group even though they may be known widely.[1] The experience of knowing and using culture is inevitably tied to situational contexts of group life. To understand the dynamics of cultural creation and cultural change, we must analyze this knowledge within the context of its mode of transmission.

In focusing on the interacting unit. I argue that every group has to some extent a culture of its own, which I shall term its *idioculture*.[2] Idioculture consists of a system of knowledge, beliefs, behaviors, and customs shared by members of an interacting group to which members can refer and employ as the basis of further interaction. Members recognize that they share experiences in common and these experiences can be referred to with the expectation that they will be understood by other members, and further can be employed to construct a social reality. The term, stressing the localized nature of culture, implies that it need not be part of a demographically distinct subgroup, but rather that it is a particularistic development of any group in the society.

## Little League Idiocultures

In order to explicate how an idioculture develops, it is necessary to base the discussion on empirical observations. While the examination of any set of continuing small groups could provide the material for this analysis, the data discussed in this paper derive from three years of participant

---

1. Cultural elements disseminated by the mass media (television, radio) or in crowd settings (rock concerts, rallies, sports events) are exceptions. However, even in these isolated or mass settings Fine (1977) suggests that audiences are not composed of discrete individuals, but of a collection of small groups. These small groups help to structure the meaning of the event for individuals in attendance. Printed matter generally is notable for the noninteractional acquisition of cultural knowledge—although even here the material is often discussed with others.

2. *Idio* derives from *idios*, the Greek root for *own* (not *ideo*). It was felt necessary to coin a new term because the most logical phrase, that of *group culture*, has been used previously with several quite different meanings.

observation research conducted with Little League[3] baseball teams in five communities in New England and Minnesota. Little League baseball teams were chosen for observation because they combine the two major elements of group life: task orientation (winning games) and socioemotional orientation (peer friendship). In addition, because Little League is seasonal, the creation, development, and dissolution of the team culture could be observed. While some traditions continue from year to year, as approximately one-half a team's personnel returns, each year essentially represents the creation of a new idioculture.

The teams examined consisted of 12 to 15 preadolescents, coached by one to three adults. Over the course of a three-month season, teams play 14 to 21 games and, including practice time, spend about ten hours a week together. During the seasons the author (and, in one league, a research assistant) interacted with players and coaches (Fine and Glassner, 1979), although the observer had no formal role, such as coach or umpire. Within each league two teams were observed in detail, and during practices and games the observer remained with the team in the dugout or on the field. The five leagues examined were: (1) Beanville,[4] an upper middle-class professional suburb of Boston, Massachusetts; (2) Hopewell, an exurban township outside the Providence, Rhode Island metropolitan area— consisting of small towns, beach-front land, farms and a campus of the state university; (3) Bolton Park, an upper middle-class professional suburb of Saint Paul, Minnesota, similar to Beanville except for geographical location; (4) Sanford Heights, a middle- to lower middle-class suburb of Minneapolis, consisting primarily of developers' tract homes; and (5) Maple Bluff, an upper middle-class neighborhood within the city limits of Saint Paul, Minnesota. The latter teams were examined by a research assistant. In Beanville participant observation was conducted during two seasons, while in the other sites observation was confined to a single season.

---

3. The Little League organization was established in 1939 for the purpose of allowing boys to play organized baseball under the supervision of qualified adults. The organization has grown enormously since then to the point where it now has over 600,000 players between the ages of nine and 12, and about 5,000 leagues. As a result of court suits from equal rights groups, the League changed its policy in 1974 to admit both boys and girls into its programs. However, the ten teams examined in-depth in this project consisted only of boys.

4. All names included in the report of the Little League research are pseudonyms.

# Rationale for the Idioculture Construct

Because discussions of culture have not been grounded in observation of interaction or conceived of in terms of behavioral dynamics and needs of groups, culture has not been represented adequately. By recognizing that groups develop a culture of their own, some of the sterility of much current small-group research can be avoided. Five arguments are proposed here for the utility of the construct of idioculture in sociological research.

## 1. SPECIFICITY OF CULTURES

Since small groups are observable and are capable of being questioned, culture need not remain the amorphous phenomenon which it tends to be in social anthropology and macrosociology. The relatively limited extent of the particularistic aspects of small-group culture lends itself to examination by the participant observer, and thus idiocultures can be specified by the researcher to a much greater extent than is true for either societal cultures or subcultures. Within our Little League study it is possible to compose a relatively complete description of the culture of a team, although the depiction of a culture of a small group of small boys is a rather extensive undertaking (Fine, n.d.). Such a compilation will include the particular team rules developed by the group of boys and their coaches, the regular joking topics, nicknames, and modes of appropriate behavior adopted by the boys. A comprehensive attempt to compile preadolescent culture is an impossible task, although several useful partial collections have been published (e.g., Opie and Opie, 1959).

## 2. COMPARATIVE ANALYSIS OF GROUPS

The concept of idioculture allows for the development of a cultural anthropology of small groups (McFeat, 1974). Social scientists typically have little understanding of how closely related groups differ from each other. These groups may appear to have common goals (winning baseball games), comparable memberships (chosen by means of a player draft in which all adult coaches take turns selecting players), and similar environments (playing and practicing in the same locations), yet groups develop unique cultures and different styles of behavior. Here, again, the examination of differences among groups requires considerable space, more than is possible in this article. However, it is clear that the cultures that teams develop are a result of social and environmental contingencies, combined with the social definitions which emerge in group interaction. Once the idioculture is developed (a process occurring from the beginning moments of the group), it shapes future actions and collective meanings. By comparing groups in terms of their experiences and shared meanings as influencing their culture, one is able to explicate the process of cultural differentiation—a process Fischer (1968) has termed *microethnography*. In our Little League research early victory or defeat (a social contingency) and the definition of that outcome have a considerable effect on structuring the team culture. Teams that perceive themselves as successful typically develop a more robust culture of baseball-related items than the culture of early losers.

## 3. CULTURAL CREATION AND DIFFUSION IN SOCIETIES AND SUBSOCIETIES

Understanding the dynamics of the creation of an idioculture may have significant implications for understanding cultural creation in larger social units. In observing a small group one can pinpoint precisely and with confidence the circumstances under which an item of culture was created. This cultural creation process may be similar to that for cultural products which reach a wider audience. Many cultural products are created in group situations (e.g., scriptwriters' conferences, theatre ensembles or scientific research groups) (Fine, 1977). Informal cultural products, such as jokes, slang, or superstitions, can develop in the course of natural interaction in a group, and subsequently may "catch on," spread beyond the boundaries of the group to which it originally belonged, and become part of a culture or subculture (Fine and Kleinman, 1979). Such mass diffusion does not occur very frequently, and our research does not allow us to cite any example in which a cultural object created by one of the observed teams entered into the national preadolescent subculture, but on several occasions cultural traditions crossed team lines. One team in Bolton Park, for example, started standing on the dugout bench and cheering. This practice subsequently was adopted by two of the other six teams, through acceptance by the high status players on those teams, and the diffusion rapidly spread to their teammates. Such examples of diffusion suggest general processes of cultural transmission (e.g., the two-step flow of communication) (Katz and Lazarsfeld, 1955).

## 4. GROUPS AS CULTURAL UNITS

The idioculture construct indicates that groups do not exist in a content-free context, but are continuously engaged in the construction of a social reality, a history (McBride, 1975), and a sense of meaning (Berger and Luckmann, 1967). Small-group research typically portrays groups as data points, and examines group dynamics divorced from the content of talk or action. Following interactionist theory, we assume that cultural content derives its shared social meaning through interaction, rather than through an a priori assignment of meaning. Groups negotiate meanings, and this ongoing negotiation structures the culture of groups. The content of talk and behavior is thus central to the comprehension of group dynamics, and this understanding can occur only through a contextual examination of culture. The nicknames of Little Leaguers—Big Rides, Shrimppo, Thunderfoot, Train, or Maniac—imply that shared meanings of players exist and the replacement of nicknames over time suggests that these meanings are not necessarily static. Without a consideration of meaning, behavior is "meaningless"—a point experimental examinations of small groups ignore or downplay.

## 5. CULTURE AS MEDIATION BETWEEN ENVIRONMENT AND ACTION

Idioculture is proposed as a mediating element between constraints external to the group and the behavior of the group in dealing with these constraints. It is the process by which collective decisions are selected, and thus permits an understanding of how a group increases its sense of "groupness," cohesion, and commitment. Further, as Berger and Luckmann (1967:87) suggest, sub-universes of meaning (idiocultures) provide for the differentiation of group members from outsiders. Differences in behavioral response to social stimuli and social integration have been shown convincingly to relate to the cultural values of small communities (Vogt and O'Dea, 1953; Rogers and Gardner, 1969; DuWors, 1952). The culture of a group provides a set of behavioral options for the group to choose after the meaning of an external event has been determined. Thus, in this Little League research, teams responded idiosyncratically to potential victory (by special cheers) and defeat (by personalized insults). The team achieves consensus on whether the game is close, is being lost or won; then members choose from the group's repertoire of cultural options available given a situational definition.

## The Social Production of Idioculture

At the inception of any group, an idioculture does not exist; however, the formation of a culture may occur from the opening moments of group interaction. When individuals meet, they begin to construct a culture by asking for names and other biographical points which can be referred to subsequently (Davis, 1973). Eventually idioculture becomes self-generating, and direct solicitation and reciprocal inquisition are no longer necessary for social solidarity. Over time, rules are established, opinions expressed, information exchanged, and members experience events together. Sherif and Sherif (1953:236–7) suggest that:

> When individuals having no established relationships are brought together in a group situation to interact in group activities with common goals, they produce a group structure. . . . This group structure implies positive in-group identifications and common attitudes and tends, in time, to generate by-products or norms peculiar to the groups, such as nicknames, catchwords, ways of doing things, etc.

To be sure, not every element of a group's conversation or behavior will be part of the idioculture. Idioculture is augmented if an experience occurs or a piece of information is transmitted *within* the group (i.e., in the presence of more than one group member) and is perceived as an event or statement which can be referenced legitimately and meaningfully (see Garfinkel, 1967:38–41)—i.e., the occurrence is worthy of retrospective notice. Thus, in Little League, a routine hit or catch, being "taken for granted," usually will not make an impact on the group's idioculture, but may become notable if the situational constraints give the event a significance beyond its expected lack of impact (e.g., a catch by a poor outfielder at a crucial point in a game—an event which did produce a nickname in one Little League scenario).

The specific elements of an idioculture are not generated randomly through chance statements and events, but are accessible to sociological analysis. However, it would be inaccurate to suggest that the cultural elements of a group are inevitably produced by external determinants over which members have no control. Members construct meanings given a set of social constraints which are perceived as affecting the boundaries of permissible behavior. While the content of cultural elements needs to satisfy five analytical criteria to become incorporated into an idioculture, these five criteria are not external stimuli which inevitably shape the behavior of individuals or groups. Rather, these are components of the sense-making systems of individuals; the specific implications of these criteria are negotiated in group interaction. These processes essentially operate as filters (Siman, 1977), which constrain cultural options. They provide strictures within which freedom of selection operates.

The five filtering elements are proposed to explain the selection and continued salience of any given item in a group's idioculture—that the item be perceived as Known, Usable, Functional, and Appropriate in terms of the group's status system, and Triggered by some experienced event. These factors can be schematized roughly in an ordered relationship by a Venn diagram according to the number of *potential* items which meet each criteria: K>U>F>A>T. The manner in which each of these filters will be interpreted is a situational achievement for members, and although I shall take for granted their operation in this discussion, I recognize that the interpretation of each of them is grounded in their own set of situational negotiations.

*Known culture.* The first constraint on whether a potential culture element will become part of the group idioculture is that the item or components of the item be known previously by at least one member of the group. This pool of background information I shall term the *known culture* of the group.

This perspective is congruent with Becker and Geer's (1960) argument that the manifest culture of a group will be derived from the latent cultures of members. While the culture content emerges from group interaction, latent culture or the recall of prior knowledge will affect the form of these culture elements, although not the specific content. Culture content is synthesized from remembrances of past experiences. Since members have access to other idiocultures (or latent cultures) through previous or concurrent memberships, the range of potentially known information may be extensive.

Among Sanford Heights teams, a ball which was hit foul over the backstop was known as a "Polish Home Run." Such a cultural item would have been meaningless had it not been for latent cultural items—what a home run is, and the symbolic opposition of hitting a ball straight over the out-field fence and hitting it backward over the backstop. In other words, hitting the ball over either *end* of the field was a home run (and this was not said of balls which curved outside a foul line). The existence of the item also required a knowledge of social stereotypes—that "Polish" is an ethnic slur—implying backwardness or incompetence. Without this cultural knowledge such an identification of this type of foul ball would not have become a part of the culture of these preadolescents. Likewise, referring to other players on the basis of their uniform color as a "green bean" or "Chiquita," as was done in Hopewell, suggests that cultural elements are dependent upon prior knowledge derived from external sources.

Creativity poses no particular problems for this perspective since created items are not developed de novo; rather, they are novel combinations of previously familiar elements (e.g., Hebb, 1974). These combinations may be given meanings different from that of any constitutive element by the members of the group. Thus, players on the Maple Bluff White Sox developed a dress code which was loosely modeled on observation of major leaguers, although not identical to it. Before one practice in Sanford Heights several players were hanging on the backstop at the practice field while one of their teammates shook the fence as hard as possible, an activity he termed the *Chinese pain shake*, a term apparently created spontaneously. While the term may never have been uttered before, its antecedents exist in that speaker's latent culture: notably the association of Chinese with torture (e.g., the Chinese water torture), and the earthquakes which had affected China during this period and to which this activity was similar. Thus, the creation of this cultural item, although seemingly an idiosyncratic construction, can be interpreted in terms of previous knowledge. The term for that behavior "makes sense" in terms of the web of meanings accessible to those individuals.

The larger the percentage of boys who share a latent cultural element (e.g., the behavior of certain professional baseball players in wearing their hats or socks in a particular style), the more likely will this knowledge or some transformation of it come to characterize the group. This unstated shared knowledge allows newly "created" cultural items to be more readily meaningful for the group.

*Usable culture.* The second criterion for inclusion in a group's idioculture is that a potential item be perceived as part of the members' *usable culture*—

that is, mentionable in the context of group interaction. Some elements of the latent or known culture, although shared by members of a group, may not be shared publicly because of sacred or taboo implications.

The usability of a cultural element is not a result of absolute criteria, but of the social meanings supplied by the group members. Members' personalities, religion, political ideology, or morality may influence the situational viability for a cultural item. Thus, in Bolton Park one star player objected strongly to another player's reference to the "fucking umps"; another player on that team chastised a teammate for uttering the epithet "Jesus Christ" and taking the Lord's name in vain. On other teams, however, such usage was legitimate and was not sanctioned. Observation suggests that teams do have different moral standards for propriety; this is due to their adult and child personnel, and the extent to which these personnel are willing to express their beliefs to shape public behavior.

In Beanville, one of the two teams examined placed a heavier emphasis on religion than did the other, although both teams were largely Catholic. Possibly because of the players or as a reification of the team name, the Angels indicated a greater interest in religion than did the Rangers. Members of the Angels inquired of each other why they missed church. The Rangers never publicly mentioned church, but on several occasions players did joke about abortions. While only a weak inference exists that similar jokes could not have occurred among the Angels, the presence of such jokes seems unlikely and inappropriate. "Dirty" or sexual jokes were only spread among groups of Rangers (outside the earshot of their coach), and not in my observation among the Angels.

Similarly, on one team in Hopewell, racial epithets were common; one player made reference to blacks as "jungle bunnies," while another commented "all the people who live around me are niggers," and a third termed a Puerto Rican adolescent "half nigger and half white." While many of the boys in the League were undoubtedly aware of these terms, only on this one team were they spoken with any regularity, and as part of the normative order of the team. It is difficult to pinpoint why these comments were usable here and not elsewhere, but two years previously this team had a black manager who apparently was not well-liked, and this may have accounted for the public expression of racial resentment after he left. This is compounded by the situation that the two adults who coached this team did not appear to be greatly upset when this language was used. For example, we find this disquieting colloquy:

> (A black boy pitching for the opposing team has just hit one of their batters)
> *Justin*: "Come on, you nigger."
> *Coach*: "Don't be stupid."
> *Justin*: "That's what he is."
> *Assistant Coach*: "You'll get thrown out of the game."
> *Justin*: "I don't mind if he calls me whitey."
> (Field notes)

The issue here is the reaction of the coaches in establishing a definition of usability. In this situation, and others, these adults see racial abuse as a *strategic* problem. Boys should not use these terms because other adults will sanction them, or because (on other occasions) it was said the targets may attack the speaker. The reactions of the adults, while not encouraging these comments, do not make them unusable, and they remained a central part of the team's culture throughout the summer.

Tied to usability is situational appropriateness. Norms for prescribed and proscribed behavior tend to be contextually bounded. An item of culture may be appropriate only in certain circumstances, such as when the coach is absent. Typically, when group members are in the presence of outsiders the expressible elements of the team's idioculture are curtailed. This is evident in regard to preadolescents who refrain from telling "dirty" jokes in the presence of adults or strangers. Jokes comparing aborted babies to ripe, red tomatoes among the Beanville Rangers were limited to situations in which adults, other than the author, were not present. Likewise, one boy on the Sanford Heights Dodgers was called "Mousey" by his affectionate mother. This nickname was used by peers in his absence, since he was a high status team member and it was a nickname he particularly disliked. This dislike only made the nickname more precious for his teammates.

*Functional culture.* A third factor influencing the likelihood of an item being incorporated into a group's idioculture is its perceived congruence with the goals and needs of some or all group members, and whether it is defined as facilitating the survival and successful operation of the group as a unit (Pellegrin, 1953). Items which are consistent with these ends are termed the *functional culture* of the group. Thus, potential cultural elements which are known and usable by members may not become part of the group's idioculture if not recognized as supportive of the needs of the group or its members. In some cases of cultural innovation, especially in regard to competing cultural elements related to task goals, a cultural process metaphorically akin to natural selection may operate.

Some interactionists argue that culture develops as a response to shared problems (Becker and Geer, 1960; Hughes et al., 1968; Spector, 1973); they claim that group culture is functional, and that much of culture production is directly related to group problem solving. This proposition is supported by an examination of group culture in a laboratory setting which indicates that problem-solving strategies that continue across time are those which have been most effective (Weick and Gilfillan, 1971).

Among Little League baseball teams, the rules and restrictions which team members enforce indicate the functional properties of group culture. The Beanville Rangers originated and enforced an operating procedure that the team would take batting practice (a desirable activity for the players) in the order that players arrived. This procedure encouraged promptness and, on occasion, the entire Ranger team arrived at the field before any members of the opposing team. The Rangers particularly were characterized by team spirit and friendships, as players knew each other informally through this pregame activity; it served as a mechanism for minimizing arguments about the batting practice order. The preadolescents, rather than the coaches, structured the team's behavior, and the procedure strengthened the position of the team's preadolescent leader who lived a block from the field and always arrived early. Prior to the establishment of this procedure, batting order was determined haphazardly—mostly by whomever was most insistent at the moment, rather than by a systematic ordering procedure by the coach. It was because the ordering of batting practice had been problematic for the Rangers that such a rule was functional as a problem-solving mechanism.

A Hopewell team prohibited chewing gum on the playing field because one of their players had almost choked on a piece of gum after he ran into another outfielder when attempting to catch an unexpected fly ball. Other teams in the league did not have a similar rule, because the issue was never salient. For an item of culture to be overtly functional to a group, the group must define itself, either implicitly or explicitly, as having a problem, and then the cultural item may be proposed as a solution to the problem.

Some cultural items do not directly address problems in a group, but still may be said to be functional in that they achieve group goals such as entertainment or social solidarity. While they may not be proposed in response to interactional difficulties, these idiocultural items facilitate group functioning. The creation of cultural prescriptions and proscriptions is tied directly to their functional character. The origins of nonovertly functional culture items may not be related directly to the needs of the group, but their continued usage is.

*Appropriate culture.* Some potential elements of a group's culture, while functional for satisfying group goals or personal needs, do not occur or continue because they undermine the group's social structure in not supporting the interpersonal network and power relations in the group. Those potential cultural elements which are consistent with the patterns of interaction of the group are the *appropriate culture* of the group. A cultural item which expresses hostility toward a well-liked or legitimately powerful individual may be known, usable, and even functional (in that hostility may need to be expressed), yet may be inappropriate unless the group structure is altered (see Hollander, 1958).

This becomes clear in the case of nicknames. Many nicknames are evaluative in content, and a nickname must fit the target's defined status in the group. During the first year of observation of the Beanville Rangers, one team member, Tom, acquired the nickname "Maniac," based upon a linguistic play on his last name, and on his physical awkwardness on the baseball diamond. That year he was an eleven-year-old substitute outfielder. When the team members were asked to name their three best friends on the team during the middle of the season, Tom was named only by one of the 12 other boys answering the sociometric questionnaire (with 15 players on the team). According to sociometric ranking and formal status, Tom is a low-status team member. The question formulated that season was: What would happen the following year when he was 12 years of age, and presumably would be one of the better players on the team? The following year, Tom started most of the Rangers' games at third base, was one of the best batters on the team, and was located in the middle of the team's status hierarchy. In sociometric ratings both at the beginning and the end of the season, Tom was named by four of the 14 other players as one of their three best friends on the team. His previous nickname, "Maniac," was no longer in circulation, although Tom and other team members recalled its presence during the previous year. Tom's new nickname was "Main Eye," again a play on the boy's last name, though with dramatically different symbolic connotations.

A similar example occurred the following year in Sanford Heights. One of the eleven year olds on the Giants was known as a particularly poor baseball player, having gone hitless in his previous year in the league. As a function of his weak baseball skills and his somewhat isolated position on the team, he was called "Smell-ton," again a play on a surname. During the first week of the season, much to everyone's surprise—his own included—he hit a Grand Slam home run. His nickname "Smell-ton" was forgotten and, for the rest of the season, his teammates called him Jim. Status can be usefully conceived of as constraining the creation of nicknames, although the labeling effect of nicknames and other culturally identifying information on group position cannot be denied. Nicknames are not the only cultural items subject to status considerations; pranks and practical jokes may only be performed on low status members, and rules may be constructed so that they support the prerogatives of the older players—such as determining who should coach on the bases (high status boys) or who should go to the refreshment stand for water (isolates).

In addition to being affected by status inappropriateness, acceptance of a cultural item may be contingent on the nature of sponsorship. Potential cultural items are more likely to be accepted into a group's idioculture when proposed by a high status member (Sherif and Sherif, 1953:252). This clearly applies when the coach proposes some cultural element; while these are not invariably accepted by his preadolescent charges, they do stand a comparatively greater likelihood of acceptance. Thus, in Hopewell, one set of coaches suggested that before a game their team should form a circle, that team members place their hands in the middle of the circle and, when the coach said "Let's go," that players should buoyantly raise their arms in unison. This ritual characterized the team throughout the season. Another coach in Maple Bluff ritually asked his team what three things they needed to win, and they vigorously responded, "Hustle, pride and class;" a third coach in Beanville would refer to a weak hit as something which his grandmother could hit better than, and so the comic image of this middle-aged man's grandmother entered the team's culture.

High status players, like coaches, find their personal status accorded the traditions they wish to establish. Several members of the Beanville Rangers got wiffles (short haircuts) after Wiley, the second most popular boy on the team, got one and was proud of it. This fad continued (with one or two boys newly shaved each day) until Rich, the most popular boy on the team, publicly claimed that he thought the haircut looked stupid, although he deliberately excluded Wiley from this evaluation, saying that he looked good. After Rich's announcement, only one low status boy had his hair cut in that fashion, and the team, highly critical of his tonsorial style, said it looked horrible and, further, it was not a *real* wiffle. Similar sociometric processes affected clothing conformity, such as wearing wristbands or sneakers at games, and wearing shorts or removing one's shirt at practice.

*Triggering event.* The range of *potential* cultural items which qualify as known, usable, functional, and appropriate is extensive, and some interactional mechanism (or filter) is necessary to account for which items enter the group's cultural repertoire. The concept of a *triggering event* is postulated as an explanatory device to determine selection. Some bit of interaction will provide a "spark" which produces the specific content of the idioculture. This event can consist of any action or statement which produces a response in the group, similar to Smelser's (1962) concept of a precipitating factor for collective behavior. A member's new haircut may be sufficient to spawn a new nickname ("Kojak," "Buzz Conroy," "Peach Fuzz"). A miscue may provide the impetus for a joking sequence that remains part of group lore. A threat to the group may produce a legend, new norm, or a prescription for group action.

While any triggering event may theoretically produce idioculture, some events recur and, in those cases, items of idioculture are particularly likely to be produced and, once produced, will more likely be relevant to the group as they are repeatedly functional and appropriate. Thus, the superior batting of one Beanville youngster led to him being called "Superstar," and the opposite talent of a boy in Bolton Park produced his nickname: "Strike Out King." These nicknames are sociometrically appropriate, as well as being frequently triggered, because of the differential athletic achievements of these two youngsters.

In addition, triggers which are notable or unusual are especially likely to produce idioculture. Support for this assertion is provided by Gmelch (1971) in an examination of baseball superstitions in the professional leagues; he discovered that rituals emanated from particularly good performances, while behavioral taboos resulted from notably poor performances. One Bolton Park coach's old Impala was called a "Cadillac" after a foul ball nearly hit it in practice and he jokingly told them not to hit his Cadillac. The term caught on, and the rusty car was called a "Cadillac" from that point on—the notable event of a wayward foul ball structured the culture creation of the team. As Gmelch notes, notable events also effect taboos. One Hopewell coach brought his team red, white, and blue wristbands on opening day, in order to give the team some sense of unity and specialness. However, the team, which was expected to win the championship that year, lost its first game by the embarrassing score of 12–3. After the game, the players decided that the wristbands were unlucky and from that day no member of the team wore a wristband, and the team eventually won the league championship.

Triggering events and their effects are difficult to predict in advance in natural settings, as they are emergent from social interaction. However, in an experimental setting, triggering events can be systematically arranged by the researcher and their effects upon the content of group culture examined. This constitutes a valuable direction for research in this area.

*Summary.* Five elements—the known culture, the usable culture, the functional culture, the appropriate culture, and the triggering event—influence the specific content of a group's idioculture. Different configurations of these five factors suggest how groups come to differ in their culture, and why specific forms appear and remain in particular groups. To this point, cultural forms have been analyzed using a single characteristic; in order to indicate the combined impact of all five we shall examine the creation and usage of one particular cultural item considering all factors.

During the middle of the season, the Beanville Rangers created and enforced a rule that no player could eat ice cream while sitting on the bench during a game. This rule was triggered by a combination of circumstances: it occurred in the context of a game in which the Rangers, by that time accustomed to victory, were being beaten. On the bench, one of the nonplaying low status players was eating an ice cream cone. This situation triggered the decision by the high status, older players (not the coach) that ice cream could not be eaten on the bench (although gum could be chewed). The rule was known in that it was compatible with the policy and perspectives of professional sports teams. It was usable in that it did not deal with any tabooed or threatening areas of children's culture, and it is comparable to the rules that children frequently make in interaction with each other (Piaget, 1932; Cooley, 1902). The rule was functional in relieving the frustration that the older players felt during that game, and in tending to get the attention of the younger members on the team. Further, the presence of a set of rules or rituals may create a sense of group cohesion (Cartwright and Zander, 1953) and satisfaction (Borgatta and Bales, 1953). Finally, it was appropriate in that it was propounded by the high status members to control the low status members. Later in the season an older, high status player did eat ice cream on the bench, and was not criticized by other team members, although the rules remained for other team members.

# References

Becker, Howard S. and Blanche Geer. 1960. "Latent culture: a note on the theory of latent social roles." *Administrative Science Quarterly* 5:304–13.

Berger, Peter and Thomas Luckmann. 1967. *The Social Construction of Reality*. New York: Anchor.

Blumer, Herbert. 1969. *Symbolic Interactionism*. Englewood Cliffs: Prentice-Hall.

Borgatta, Edgar G. and Robert Freed Bales. 1953. "Task and accumulation of experience as factors in the interaction of small groups." *Sociometry* 16:239–52.

Cartwright, Dorwin and Alvin Zander, eds. 1953. *Group Dynamics*, Evanston: Row, Peterson.

Cooley, Charles H. [1902] 1964. *Human Nature and the Social Order*. New York: Schocken.

Davis, Murray S. 1973. *Intimate Relations*. New York: Free Press.

DuWors, Richard E. 1952. "Persistence and change in local values of two New England communities." *Rural Sociology* 17:207–17.

Fine, Gary Alan. 1977. "Popular culture and social interaction." *Journal of Popular Culture* 11:453–66.

Fine, Gary Alan and Barry Glassner. 1979. "Participant observation with children: promise and problems." *Urban Life* 8:153–74.

Fine, Gary Alan and Sherryl Kleinman. 1979. "Rethinking subculture: an interactionist analysis." *American Journal of Sociology* 85:1–20.

———. 1987. *With the Boys: A Little League Baseball and Pre-adolescent Culture*. Chicago: University of Chicago Press.

Fischer, J. L. 1968. "Microethnology: small-scale comparative studies." Pp. 375–87 in J. A. Clifton, ed. *Introduction to Cultural Anthropology*. Boston: Houghton Mifflin.

Garfinkel, Harold. 1967. *Studies in Ethnomethodology*. Englewood Cliffs: Prentice-Hall.

Gmelch, George J. 1971. "Baseball magic." *Trans-Action* 8:39–41, 54.

Hare, A. Paul, Edgar Borgatta, and Robert Freed Bales, eds. 1965. *Small Groups*. Rev. ed. New York: Random House.

Hebb, Donald O. 1974. "What psychology is about." *American Psychologist* 29:71–87.

Herskovits, Melville. 1948. *Man and His Works*. New York: Random House.

Hollander, Edwin P. 1958. "Conformity, status, and idiosyncrasy credit." *Psychological Review* 65:117–27.

Hughes, Everett C, Howard S. Becker, and Blanche Geer. 1968. "Student culture and academic effort." Pp. 372–85 in R. R. Bell and H. R. Stub, eds. *The Sociology of Education*. Rev. ed. Homewood: Dorsey Press.

Katz, Elihu and Paul F. Lazarsfeld. 1955. *Personal Influence*. New York: Free Press.

McBride, Glen. 1975. "Interactions and the control of behavior." Pp. 415–23 in A. Kendon, R. Harris, and M. Key, eds. *Organization of Behavior in Face-to-Face Interaction*. The Hague: Mouton.

McFeat, Tom. 1974. *Small-Group Cultures*. New York: Pergamon Press.

Opie, Iona and Peter Opie. 1959. *The Lore and Language of School Children*. London: Oxford University Press.

Piaget, Jean. [1932] 1962. *The Moral Judgment of the Child*. New York: Collier.

Pellegrin, Roland J. 1953. "The achievement of high status and leadership in the small group." *Social Forces* 32:10–6.

Rogers, William B. and R. E. Gardner. 1969. "Linked changes in values and behavior in the Out Island Bahamas." *American Anthropologist* 71:21–35.

Sherif, Muzafer and Caroline Sherif. 1953. *Groups in Harmony and Tension*. New York: Harper.

Siman, Michael L. 1977. "Application of a new model of peer group influence to naturally existing adolescent friendship groups." *Child Development* 48: 270–4.

Smelser, Neil J. 1962. *Theory of Collective Behavior*. New York: Free Press

Spector, Malcolm. 1973. "Secrecy in job seeking among government attorneys: two contingencies in the theory of subcultures." *Urban Life and Culture* 2:211–29.

Vogt, Evan Z. and Thomas O'Dea. 1953. "Cultural differences in two ecologically similar communities." *American Sociological Review* 18:645–54.

Weick, Karl and D. P. Gilfillan. 1971. "Fate of arbitrary traditions in a laboratory microculture." *Journal of Personality and Social Psychology* 17:179–91.

# STUDY QUESTIONS

1. Briefly describe the five rationales Fine provides for the usefulness of the concept of *idioculture*.
2. In order for an *idioculture* to emerge, Fine explains, it must combine five kinds of group meaning-making. Identify and explain them.

# 25

# MUSIC AND SYMBOLIC EXCLUSION

BETHANY BRYSON

In the contemporary United States, one of the hallmarks of being an educated person is to demonstrate wide-ranging appreciation of different cultures. Cultural sociologists describe such Americans as cultural omnivores: they consume everything and express few strong dislikes. Omnivores pride themselves on their knowledge of different kinds of ethnic cuisine; they enjoy talking about their cross-cultural travels abroad; and they often take a special interest in the arts and culture of some other continent. Asian, African, or South American artifacts are high on the list of collectible goods, since they are material embodiments of the omnivores' eclectic desires.

The same is true for music. According to survey data, the more educated a person is, the more likely he is to have a broad range of taste in musical genres. Education appears to foster tolerance, at least when it comes to the kind of music individuals prefer. This finding challenges the stereotype of the snooty, upper-class person who only listens to classical music, although some musical genres still don't make the cut. Gospel, country, rap, and heavy metal—genres that tend to attract the least-educated fans—continue to remain unpopular among well-educated Americans. What are we to make of that?

Bethany Bryson has a theory. One of her implicit arguments is that when people express their likes and dislikes about different kinds of music, they are doing much more than simply identifying what sounds good to them or what musical experiences they think are worthwhile. Individuals may also be giving voice to intolerant feelings about the kinds of people they think are worth relating to as fellow fans. Musical tastes reach beyond auditory preferences and reflect something about a person's self-image, group identity, and those groups she would like to exclude from her social worlds.

# "ANYTHING BUT HEAVY METAL": SYMBOLIC EXCLUSION AND MUSICAL DISLIKES

## Background

### MUSIC AS A SYMBOLIC RESOURCE

Music has long been considered an important part of social life. Its symbolic and ritual powers are used to explain both social cohesion and cultural resistance (Willis 1977; Hebdige 1979; Rose 1994). Furthermore, music is an important cultural and communicative medium. For instance, Cerulo (1995) describes how national anthems represent identity and communicate a nation's position in the world system. Likewise, Weinstein (1991) demonstrates that heavy metal music generates community and solidarity among fans while sending an unmistakable message to its detractors.

Music contains a complex set of dimensions, sounds, lyrics, visual cues, social relations, and physical acts (DeNora 1991: Dowd 1992). Music also permits many levels of engagement, from humming to oneself to screaming above the music with 30,000 fans. Given its symbolic and social potency, it is no wonder that music is such an important part of human society, that nearly every nation has an anthem, that most religious ceremonies involve music, and that singing is so frequently a part of political rallies. The importance of music to group identity and social differentiation, then, suggests that musical taste provides a good test for questions about symbolic boundaries. Therefore, I use musical taste to examine a more general theory of cultural exclusion.

## HIGH-STATUS EXCLUSIVENESS

Most sociologists of culture agree that some forms of cultural consumption serve as markers of social status (Weber [1968] 1978). For instance, knowledge of fine arts, literature, and upper-class etiquette signals wealth and prestige. Such knowledge may also serve as a passkey for entrance into elite social life. Bourdieu (Bourdieu 1984; Bourdieu and Passeron 1977) calls this passkey *cultural capital* because it is cultural knowledge that can be translated into real economic gains, for example, by allowing access to elite social networks and clubs where business deals often are made (Kanter 1977).

By restricting access to resources, social status can be translated into market position and political status. This process can be seen as the result of two interrelated levels of exclusion. First, *social exclusion* is a process of social selection that is based on a previously determined set of cultural criteria and is exercised by people with high levels of income, education, and occupational prestige (Bourdieu and Passeron 1977). Social exclusion occurs at the level of social relations and is the sort of "social closure" that Weber ([1968] 1978: 342, 933, 935) addresses as the monopolization of resources and inclusion in social intercourse.

The second level, *symbolic exclusion*, is the source of those "previously determined cultural criteria." Whereas social exclusion refers to the monopolization of human interactions, symbolic exclusion depicts the subjective process that orders those social interactions—taste. This process, then, is a form of "boundary-work" (Gieryn 1983; Lamont 1992) that continuously recreates the positive, negative, and neutral attitudes toward cultural cues and that define these cues as more or less acceptable in various situations. The present study focuses on symbolic exclusion. The analytical distinction between social exclusion and symbolic exclusion highlights an important empirical difference between behavior and attitudes. Note, however, that symbolic systems are social and that social exclusion can occur without physical interaction.

Music is one type of cue that can be used to construct symbolic boundaries between groups or individuals. Therefore, I analyze *musical exclusion* as a type of symbolic exclusion and operationalize it as dislike for various music genres. I use the terms *musical tolerance* or *cultural tolerance* to refer to the absence of dislike for a cultural cue or music genre. Musical tolerance, then, is operationalized as the complement of musical exclusiveness—not its opposite.

The crux of symbolic exclusion is dislike, and according to Bourdieu, the exercise of dislike and exclusion is more important to high-status individuals than to others:

> Tastes (i.e., manifested preferences) are the practical affirmation of an inevitable difference. It is no accident that, when they have to be justified, they are asserted purely negatively, by the refusal of other tastes. In matters of taste more than anywhere else, all determination is negation; and tastes are perhaps first and foremost distastes. . . . The most intolerable thing for those who regard themselves as the possessors of legitimate ["highbrow"] culture is the sacrilegious reuniting of tastes which taste dictates shall be separated (Bourdieu 1984:56–57).

For Bourdieu, the relationship between the symbolic level and the social level is reciprocal (Bourdieu and Wacquant 1992). While they shape each other, other material and subjective factors intervene to prevent the two levels from being perfectly aligned. Symbolic exclusion and social exclusion are assumed to work in a manner similar to another pair of terms more familiar to American sociologists—prejudice and discrimination.

Bourdieu's (1984) main exposition on what I have called "symbolic exclusion" argues that knowledge about fine arts is a status cue while popular taste is rejected. "The higher the level of education, the greater is the proportion of respondents who, when asked whether a series of objects would make beautiful photographs, refuse the ordinary objects of popular admiration . . . as 'vulgar' or 'ugly'" (Bourdieu 1984:35). Bourdieu's perspective, then, expects high-status individuals to be the most culturally exclusive. That is, they distinguish themselves with an exclusive culture that rejects the cultural patterns and tastes of other groups.

## EDUCATED TOLERANCE

When the well-documented finding that education increases political tolerance (Adorno et al. 1950; Stouffer 1955; Davis 1975; Nuno, Crockett, and Williams 1978; Lipset 1981) is extended to cultural tolerance, the predicted effect of education is the opposite of that expected by theories of high-status exclusiveness.

To the extent that political tolerance is a belief that civil liberties should be extended to nonconformist groups (Stouffer 1955), political intolerance is a measure of symbolic exclusion. That is, political tolerance refers to the willingness to include specified groups within the boundary of "citizen"— or "us" as opposed to "them" (Gamson 1995). In the realm of public opinion, then, the term "political tolerance" can be seen as a general reluctance to symbolically exclude nonconformists from the category "citizen."

To link these two literatures, I propose that dislike of social groups is associated with dislike of music genres. My specific expectations are two-fold. First, political intolerance—the general tendency to exclude social groups symbolically—should be positively related to musical exclusiveness— the general tendency to exclude music genres symbolically. Second, because I see both political intolerance and musical exclusiveness as forms of symbolic exclusion, contra Bourdieu's prediction, I expect education to reduce musical exclusiveness, just as it reduces political intolerance, and income and occupational prestige are expected to have little or no effect on musical exclusiveness when the impact of education is held constant (Davis 1975).

## SYMBOLIC RACISM

Kinder and Sears (1981) propose a two-stage description of racism and public opinion. Termed *symbolic racism*, the model suggests, first, that racism shapes cultural (value) orientations and, second, that racism and the resulting set of orientations together may explain public opinion about interracial issues. Whites' stereotypes about African Americans, which can be considered symbolic exclusion, may be good predictors of Whites' discomfort with residential integration, which can be considered an estimate of social exclusion (Farley et al. 1994).

I provide a theoretical foundation and an empirical test for the relationship between racism and cultural orientations that has been named *symbolic racism*. Here, "stereotypes" are understood as symbolic boundaries between social groups that reinforce simple dislike. These "stereotypes" or cultural differentiations are, furthermore, extended from the realm of values (usually relating to work, family, and economics) to the field of musical taste. Thus, racism is expected to predict dislike for the types of music that are disproportionately liked by Hispanic Americans or African Americans.

## PATTERNED TOLERANCE

Recent research on political tolerance raises new questions about the reason for and universality of education's liberalizing effect (Phelan et al. 1995). Jackman and Muha (1984) critique the earlier assertions of Stouffer (1955), Davis (1975) and others that education increases democratic liberalism through simple enlightenment. Jackman and Muha claim that highly educated people have only a superficial commitment to the rhetoric of democratic liberalism, and oppose real social changes if the changes threaten their status. Jackman and Muha show that the strong effects of education on abstract beliefs about the importance of racial equality are not present for attitudes about concrete actions intended to foster racial inequality. Their work suggests that the political tolerance displayed by educated respondents is, in fact, only a carefully cultivated status symbol.

In a new formulation of the superficial ideology explanation, Schuman and Bobo (1988) show that opposition to neighborhood racial integration may be based on perceived class differences between Whites and African Americans rather than a lack of commitment to racial equality. In abstract form and when the class status of an African American family is at least equal to that of the respondent, racial integration is approved, but in concrete form, respondents often see residential integration as the entrance of lower-class families into middle-class neighborhoods. Thus, respondents displayed a commitment to democratic liberalism with respect to racial integration but continued to resist class integration.

If my proposition that dislike of a social group is evidenced by dislike of that group's perceived culture is correct, Schuman and Bobo's (1988) findings suggest that the apparently tolerant tastes of educated respondents may mask a systematic dislike of music genres whose audiences have lower than average levels of education. This prediction has important implications for our understanding of the wide-ranging tastes of highly educated cultural "omnivores" (Peterson 1992; Peterson and Simkus 1992; Peterson and Kern 1996). That is, rather than being indiscriminately broad, omnivorous taste may include high-status types of music that are popular among non-Whites, especially "world music" (Peterson 1990) genres like reggae and Latin music, while excluding low-status genres like gospel and country regardless of their association with race or ethnicity. (See DiMaggio and Peterson 1975 for a discussion of country music's status and audience.) Identifying boundaries around broad taste would allow us to more confidently interpret Peterson and Kern's (1996) findings as a specific pattern of taste, rather than as evidence against the existence of high-status culture (Halle 1993).

A tendency for patterns of broad taste to exclude low-status genres would suggest that cultural breadth, or tolerance, could itself be a source of cultural capital. Unlike the refined form of cultural capital that Bourdieu (1984) documented in France, however, this contemporary American emphasis on breadth and tolerance would be more accurately described as *multicultural capital*—the social prestige afforded by familiarity with a range of cultural styles that is both broad and predictably exclusive. I add the term "multi" to "cultural capital" in order to specify a content of cultural capital, not to modify its meaning. That is, multicultural capital should not be included in a list of "types" of capital (e.g., social capital, cultural capital, and economic capital). However, the term could be used in an as yet nonexistent list of types of *cultural* capital (e.g., multicultural capital, high-cultural capital, counter-cultural capital, techno-cultural capital, etc.). (See Lamont 1992 and Erikson 1991 for work in this direction.)

This specific pattern of broad taste can be considered a form of cultural capital to the extent that it meets three criteria (Lamont and Lareau 1988). First, cultural tolerance and openness are widely recognized as symbols of social status among upper-middle-class Americans (Lamont 1992), and that recognition is evident, though less pervasive, in the working class (Lamont 1997). Second, familiarity with this cultural style must, nevertheless, be at least somewhat restricted. Using Bourdieu's (1984, chap. 8) methodology, then, the frequency of "don't know" responses to questions about musical taste is expected to decrease with education. The third characteristic of cultural capital is that it can serve as the basis of social exclusion. In this case, the potential for exclusion would be evidenced by a class-based distribution of cultural tolerance, on one hand, and a predictable pattern of symbolic exclusion (more dislike of low-status genres), on the other.

# Hypotheses

**HIGH STATUS EXCLUSIVENESS**

$H_1$: People with high levels of education, income, and occupational prestige dislike more types of music than do people with low levels of education, income, and prestige.

### EDUCATED TOLERANCE

$H_2$: People with high levels of education dislike fewer types of music than do people with medium and low education, controlling for income and occupational prestige.

$H_3$: People who are reluctant to extend civil liberties to stigmatized groups dislike more types of music than do people with more tolerant political attitudes.

### SYMBOLIC RACISM

$H_4$: Whites who have high racism scores dislike the types of music that are disproportionately liked by people of color more than do people who report less racist attitudes.

### PATTERNED TOLERANCE

$H_5$: People who dislike few music genres will dislike those types of music that are liked by people with low levels of education more than other types of music, when education is controlled.

$H_6$: People who have high levels of education are less likely to report that they are unfamiliar with any music genre.

## Measures

### DEPENDENT VARIABLES

The General Social Survey (GSS) is a nearly annual survey of noninstitutionalized adults in the United States conducted by the National Opinion Research Center using a stratified random sampling method. The 1993 GSS includes a set of questions about culture, including musical tastes as well as leisure activities and values (Davis and Smith 1993; Marsden and Swingle 1994). These new data make information on musical *dislikes* available for the first time. Like other surveys of taste and participation in the arts, this survey presented respondents with a list of musical categories, but rather than having them choose their favorite or mark all they like, the GSS asked all 1,606 respondents to evaluate each of 18 music genres on a five-point Likert scale ranging from "like very much" to "dislike very much." Using these data, I derive a measure of musical exclusiveness by counting the "dislike" and "dislike very much" responses given by each respondent.

This method highlights the interesting responses and avoids the flattening effect of averages. If a respondent gave pop music a 1 and classical music a 5, the average score would be 3—the same as a response of 3 for each genre. By counting only negative responses, the exclusiveness of the score is preserved. "Don't know" responses are treated as missing and those respondents are eliminated from the analysis, leaving 912 valid cases. The exclusiveness scale has a mean of 5.78 and a standard deviation of 3.76, with a possible range of 0 to 18.

# Conclusion

*Summary.* I seek to resolve the contradiction between two widely accepted theories of culture by highlighting the neglected notion of cultural *exclusion* or dislike. The first perspective posits that people with high social status are the most culturally exclusive and intolerant. The second perspective claims that education increases tolerance, openness, and cultural acceptance. If the most highly educated Americans were ever the most culturally exclusive, this clearly is not the case today.

By analyzing dislikes of 18 types of music, I show that education significantly decreases exclusiveness in musical taste. Thus, the *high-status exclusion* hypothesis (Hypothesis 1) does not accurately describe the distribution of musical taste in the contemporary United States: Respondents with high levels of education reported more tolerant musical taste than those with less education. This supports the first *educated tolerance* hypothesis (Hypothesis 2).

Furthermore, I show that cultural exclusiveness is associated with political intolerance (Hypothesis 3) and that negative attitudes toward social groups result in negative attitudes toward the types of music associated with that group (Hypothesis 4). These findings not only demonstrate that some theories of political tolerance may be extended to cultural attitudes, they also show that patterns of taste are related to group conflict. However, I do not assume that rising levels of education will decrease cultural exclusiveness, as Stouffer (1955) did when he predicted that rising education would obliterate political intolerance. Instead, I draw on recent developments in the study of political tolerance to scrutinize musical tolerance.

I find that highly educated people in the United States are more musically tolerant, but not indiscriminately so. I provide evidence of class-based exclusion in that the genres most disliked by tolerant people are those appreciated by people with the lowest levels of education. Therefore, I suggest that *cultural tolerance should not be conceptualized as an indiscriminate tendency to be nonexclusive, but as a reordering of group boundaries that trades race for class.* If a person with average taste were injected with a serum to encourage broad taste, the first three genres that would disappear from that person's list of dislikes (Latin music, jazz, and blues/rhythm and blues) are significantly associated with non-dominant racial or ethnic groups, while the types of music that are most likely to remain on that person's list of musical dislikes (rap, heavy metal, country, and gospel music) are the four most strongly associated with low education. Furthermore, two of those four most excluded genres—gospel and rap—lie at the intersection of race and education. Their fans tend to be Black and have less education than the general population.[1]

Together with the finding that less educated people more frequently reported being unfamiliar with one or more of the 18 genres, results show that cultural breadth has become a high-status signal that excludes low-status cultural cues and is unevenly distributed by education in the United States. Therefore, I suggest that the phenomenon be understood as *multicultural capital.*

*Limitations.* With this large data set, I have demonstrated a connection between inter-group affect and musical taste. However, the proportion of variance explained is relatively modest. Therefore, I do not argue that musical dislike is *only* a tool of symbolic exclusion. Cultural taste may also be shaped by the extent to which a particular work or genre resonates with the cultural orientations of its listeners (Griswold 1992). This can cause taste for the genre to be patterned by social location that, in turn, would reinforce the tendency for the genre to appeal to one group more than others. Also, symbolic exclusion treats cultural cues as "tools" (Swidler 1986), but music can be *used* in other ways as well. Anderson (1990), for example, shows how young African American men use rap music (at high volumes) to gain control of public spaces.

1. See Binder (1993) for an analysis of how dislike for heavy metal and rap music has been cultivated in the popular press. Her comparison of rap and heavy metal is particularly useful for understanding the way race and class intersect in the framing of musical exclusion.

A second limitation of this study is that these data cannot tell us what respondents have in mind when they think of each genre. One of the categories, for instance, is labeled "new age/space music." While 18.2 percent of the respondents reported that they didn't know much about the genre, we cannot tell how the remaining respondents understand the category. Are they thinking of Vangelis and music with an electronic sound from the early 1980s (such as the themes from *Star Wars* and *Chariots of Fire*), or music like that of the group Enigma (whose eerie sound and sometimes disturbing lyrics won a spot in the movie *Sliver*), or are they thinking of the "new age" music produced by artists on the Windham Hill label? (These nearly qualify as "easy listening.") I assume that respondents would not agree about the type of artists belonging in each category. Therefore, although the lack of a clear understanding of what these musical categories mean to respondents is regrettable, it makes the fact that significant patterns emerge even more striking.

As with most survey data on opinions and attitudes, the GSS imposes cultural categories on respondents (Marsden and Swingle 1994). The bias introduced by this method may be unimportant when "real world" choices are constrained ("For whom do you plan to vote in the upcoming election?"), but an important task in the sociology of culture is to *discover* salient cultural categories rather than assume them. The list used by the GSS vaguely resembles the major categories of music used by popular music distributors, but we cannot be sure how the results would differ if the list were altered. If, for example, it contained six varieties of "rock," the tendency to be musically exclusive might be largely driven by the factors that determine attitudes toward the larger category—rock. The validity of the measure could have been greatly improved if a prior study had determined the most common categories of musical classification.

Finally, it is unclear whether the inconsistency between my findings and Bourdieu's (1984) are due to differences in time, national culture, or methodology. Peterson and Kern (1996) show that the status value of cultural breadth has increased over time in the United States, but Lamont (1992) finds that upper-middle-class Americans are much more reluctant than their French counter-parts to draw class boundaries on the basis of cultural taste. Likewise, Weil (1985) finds that the effect of education on anti-Semitism is not constant cross-nationally. In either case, Bourdieu (1984) does not provide much evidence that educated respondents were more *or less* exclusive because, with one exception, he does not ask them about their distastes. His finding that the upper classes have more knowledge about and appreciation for high culture does not contradict the concept of a tolerance line. In fact, support of multiculturalism is positively associated with—rather than opposed to—an appreciation for traditional high culture (DiMaggio and Bryson 1995). Cross-national research is needed to separate theoretical generalities from local strategies of symbolic exclusion.

*Contributions.* By exploring the connections between literatures on cultural taste, political tolerance, and racism, this analysis contributes to each field. In the political tolerance literature, I address the central question of why there is a relationship between education and democratic liberalism. Researchers have suggested that political tolerance in the United States may be part of an official culture learned through the educational system (Weil 1985; Phelan et al. 1995), but no one had explored the application of status culture theories to this problem. By conceptualizing political intolerance as a set of symbolic boundaries, I separate inter-group affect from beliefs about civil rights. Sullivan et al.'s (1979:792) suggestion that political tolerance is not related to education when tolerance presumes dislike might be better understood if the importance of the negative relationship between *dislike* and education is considered. It is not the sophisticated understandings of democratic liberalism that vary, as Jackman and Muha (1984) suggest, but the dislike of cultural (and presumably political) "otherness."

This study also contributes to our understanding of racism by lending support to Schuman and Bobo's (1988) finding that educated respondents resist racial integration only when it means class integration. The correlation between race and class is an important feature of modern industrialized societies. The relationship creates substantial room for ideological confusion and provides an opportunity to study how two types of symbolic boundaries interact. Therefore, research into strategies of self-definition and symbolic exclusion may be crucial to an understanding of class and ethnic relations as well as of the way these cultural categories interact (Lamont forthcoming).

I also find that class is not the only important basis of cultural exclusion—musical dislikes parallel racial group conflict as well. This finding challenges Bourdieu's (1984) description of taste as rooted in class and caused by varying levels of freedom from necessity. The underlying notion that one's experiences shape cultural taste can be applied more broadly, but the way this process shapes other group boundaries remains to be specified.

Finally, this analysis shows how Bourdieu's (1984) theory of high-status cultural exclusiveness may still be useful despite strong evidence that patterns of cultural appreciation in the contemporary United States are inconsistent with his description of cultural capital's *content* (Peterson and Simkus 1992; Halle 1993). Increasing tolerance has undoubtedly made high-status culture more open to racial and ethnic cultural differences. However, tolerance itself may separate high-status culture from other group cultures. This *tolerance line* recreates the pattern of high-status (cosmopolitan) culture in opposition to non-high-status (group-based) culture. Thus, it provides a new criterion of cultural exclusion.

———

# References

Adorno, Theodore W., Else Frenkel-Brunswick, Daniel J. Levinson, and R. Nevit Stanford, 1950. *The Authoritarian Personality.* New York: Harper.

Anderson, Elijah. 1990. *Streetwise: Race, Class and Change in an Urban Community.* Chicago, IL: University of Chicago Press.

Binder, Amy. 1993. "Media Depictions of Harm in Heavy Metal and Rap Music." *American Sociological Review* 58:753–67.

Bourdieu, Pierre. 1984. *Distinction: A Social Critique of the Stratification of Taste.* Cambridge, MA: Harvard University Press.

Bourdieu, Pierre and Jean-Claude Passeron. 1977. *Reproduction in Education, Society and Culture.* Beverly Hills, CA: Sage.

Bourdieu, Pierre and Loïc J. D. Wacquant. 1992. *An Invitation to Reflexive Sociology.* Chicago, IL: University of Chicago Press.

Cerulo, Karen A. 1995. *Identity Designs: The Sights and Sounds of a Nation.* Rose Book Series of the American Sociological Association, New Brunswick, NJ: Rutgers University Press.

Davis, James A. 1975. "Communism, Conformity, Cohorts, and Categories: American Tolerance in 1954 and 1972–73." *American Journal of Sociology* 82:491–513.

Davis, James and Tom Smith. 1993. *General Social Surveys, 1972–1993: Cumulative Code-book.* Chicago, IL: National Opinion Research Center [producer]. Storrs, CT: Roper Center for Public Opinion Research [distributor].

DeNora, Tia. 1991. "Musical Patronage and Social Change in Beethoven's Vienna." *American Journal of Sociology* 97(2):310–46.

DiMaggio, Paul and Bethany Bryson. 1995. "Americans' Attitudes Towards Cultural Diversity and Cultural Authority: Culture Wars, Social Closure or Multiple Dimensions." General Social Survey Topical Report No. 27. National Opinion Research Center, Chicago, IL.

DiMaggio, Paul and Richard Peterson. 1975. "From Region to Class, the Changing Locus of Country Music: A Test of the Massification Hypothesis." *Social Forces.* 53(3):497–506.

Dowd, Timothy J. 1992. "The Musical Structure and Social Context of Number One Songs, 1955–88: An Exploratory Analysis." Pp. 130–57 in *Vocabularies of Public Life: Empirical Essays in Symbolic Structure*, edited by R. Wuthnow. London, England: Routledge.

Erickson, Bonnie H. 1991. "What is Good Taste Good For?" *Canadian Review of Sociology and Anthropology* 28:255–78.

Farley, Reynolds, Charlotte Steeh, Maria Krysan, Tara Jackson, and Keith Reeves. 1994. "Stereotypes and Segregation: Neighborhoods in the Detroit Area." *American Journal of Sociology* 100:750–80.

Gamson, William A. 1995. "Hiroshima, the Holocaust, and the Politics of Exclusion: 1994 Presidential Address." *American Sociological Review* 60:1–20

Gleryn, Thomas F. 1983. "Boundary-Work and the Demarcation of Science from Non-Science: Strains and Interests in Professional Ideologies of Scientists." *American Sociological Review* 48:781–95.

Griswold, Wendy. 1992. "The Writing on the Mud Wall: Nigerian Novels and the Imaginary Village." *American Sociological Review* 57:709–24.

Halle, David. 1993. *Inside Culture: Art and Class in the American Home.* Chicago, IL: University of Chicago Press.

Hebdige, Dick. 1979. *Subculture: The Meaning of Style* New York: Methuen.

Jackman, Mary and Michael Muha. 1984. "Education and Intergroup Attitudes: Moral Enlightenment, Superficial Democratic Commitment, or Ideological Refinement?" *American Sociological Review* 49:751–69.

Kanter, Rosabeth. 1977. *Men and Women of the Corporation.* New York: Harper.

Kinder, Donald R. and David O. Sears. 1981. "Prejudice and Politics: Symbolic Racism versus Racial Threats to the Good Life." *Journal of Personality and Social Psychology* 40:414–31.

Lamont, Michèle. 1992. *Money, Morals and Manners: The Culture of the French and American Upper-Middle Class.* Chicago, IL: University of Chicago Press.

———. 1997. "Colliding Moralities: Boundaries and Identity among Black and White Workers." *Sociology and Cultural Studies*, edited by E. Long. New York: Blackwell.

Lamont, Michèle and Annette Lareau. 1988. "Cultural Capital: Allusions, Gaps, and Glissandos in Recent Theoretical Developments." *Sociological Theory* 6:153–68.

Lipset, Seymour Martin. 1981. *Political Man*. Baltimore, MD: Johns Hopkins University Press.

Marsden, Peter and Joseph Swingle. 1994. "Conceptualizing and Measuring Culture in Surveys: Values, Strategies, and Symbols." *Poetics* 22(4):269–89.

Nunn, Cyde Z., Harry Crockett, Jr., and J. Allen Williams, Jr. 1978. *Tolerance for Nonconformity*. San Francisco, CA: Josey-Bass.

Peterson, Richard A. 1990. "Audience and Industry Origins of the Crisis in Classical Music Programming: Toward World Music." Pp. 207–27 in *The Future of the Arts: Public Policy and Arts Research*, edited by D. B. Pankratz and V. B. Morris. New York: Praeger.

———. 1992. "Understanding Audience Segmentation: From Elite and Mass to Omnivore and Univore." *Poetics*. 21:243–58.

Peterson, Richard A. and Roger M. Kern. 1996. "Changing Highbrow Taste: From Snob to Omnivore." *American Sociological Review* 61:900–907.

Peterson, Richard A. and Albert Simkus. 1992. "How Musical Tastes Mark Occupational Status Groups." Pp. 152–86 in *Cultivating Differences: Symbolic Boundaries and the Making of Inequality*, edited by M. Lamont and M. Fournier. Chicago, IL: Chicago University Press.

Phelan, Jo, Bruce G. Link, Ann Stueve, and Robert E. Moore. 1995. "Education, Social Liberalism, and Economic Conservativism: Attitudes Towards Homeless People." *American Sociological Review* 60:126–40.

Rose, Tricia. 1994. *Black Noise: Rap Music and Black Culture in Contemporary America*. Hanover, MA: Wesleyan University Press.

Schuman, Howard and Lawrence Bobo. 1988. "Survey-Based Experiments on White Racial Attitudes Toward Residential Integration." *American Journal of Sociology* 94:273–99.

Stouffer, Samuel A. 1955. *Communism, Conformity, and Civil Liberties*. New York: Doubleday.

Sullivan, John L., James Pierson, and George E. Marcus. 1979. "An Alternative Conception of Political Tolerance: Illusory Increases 1950s–1970s." *American Political Science Review* 73:781–94.

Swidler, Ann. 1986. "Culture in Action: Symbols and Strategies." *American Sociological Review* 51:273–86.

Weber, Max. [1968] 1978. *Economy and Society*. Translated by G. Roth and C. Wittich. Berkeley, CA: University of California Press.

Weil, Frederick. 1985. "The Variable Effects of Education on Liberal Attitudes: A Comparative-Historical Analysis of Anti-Semitism Using Public Opinion Survey Data." *American Sociological Review* 50:458–74.

Weinstein, Deena. 1991. *Heavy Metal: A Cultural Sociology.* New York: Lexington.

Willis, Paul. 1977. *Learning to Labor: How Working-Class Kids Get Working-Class Jobs.* Farnborough, England: Saxon House.

# STUDY QUESTIONS

1. According to Bryson, what can musical preferences tell sociologists about symbolic group boundaries?
2. As a general rule, more education leads to greater musical tolerance. What are the exceptions to this general pattern and how does Bryson explain both the exceptions and the rule?

# 26

# POLITICAL MICROCULTURES

ANDREW J. PERRIN

Do you consider yourself a political person? If so, what would you say has been the biggest influence on your politics? Your religion or worldview? Your outlook on life? Your family's politics? Your friends?

If you said friends, you are on to something. As Andrew Perrin's research shows, non-political small groups—and the political talk that flows through them—strongly influence people's political viewpoints. Perrin studied church groups, labor unions, business groups, and sports leagues, and found that the microcultures of these small civic organizations influence a range of outcomes related to politics. The groups function, he found, like incubators of citizenship, molding individuals' level of involvement and engagement and priming them for discussion of topics directly related to American politics. In these discussions, group members were guided by a common set of principles and logics that were intrinsically related to the group setting. For instance, church groups relied heavily on moral logics about doing the right thing (however that was defined), while labor union members often expressed the logic of self-interest to justify their political arguments.

This research suggests that not only do the cultures of the small groups to which people belong shape the course and content of their political discussions, but these microcultures also help to account for whether individuals find themselves acting on their political values or not. This finding ties Perrin's research to important questions about the basic foundations of democratic life and the social conditions that foster democracy. Perrin suggests that without the cultural ingredients for civic engagement—such as voluntary organizations that bring like-minded individuals into contact and conversation— fledgling democracies may not be able to mature into thriving democratic states.

# POLITICAL MICROCULTURES: LINKING CIVIC LIFE AND DEMOCRATIC DISCOURSE

## Introduction

A core principle of democracy is citizens meaningful participation in public decisions. This principle requires both the presence of institutional mechanisms for citizens to pursue their ideals and Interests (Bollen 1990) and citizens' cultural ability to discuss and come to judgment on (Warren 2001, pp. 70–93) those interests and ideals.

Deliberation, then, lies at the core of democratic citizenship. While there has been much research on the concepts (Ferree et al. 2002a; Mansbridge 1996), history (Habermas 1962 [1989]), function (Marcus and Hanson 1993: Gamson 1988), and capacity (Conover et al. 1991; Page 1996; Dutwin 2003) of political deliberation, there has been little attempt to examine empirically structural influences on the form of deliberation or to determine the consequences of variations in that structure.

Separately, recent investigations into the relationship between "civil society" and political participation (e.g., Putnam 1995a, b; Verba et al. 1995) have developed arguments that citizens' involvement in nonpolitical organizations underlies their political engagement. Robert Putnam—the most adamant defender of this position—claims that declines in civil society involvement constitute a threat to democracy because ". . . the health of our public institutions depends, at least in part, on widespread participation in private voluntary groups." (Putnam 2000, 338) Indeed, there is substantial evidence that citizens with more civic experiences are also more likely to engage in a variety of political behaviors (Leighly 1991; Verba et al. 1995), although membership in different kinds of associations is associated with different levels and kinds of political activity (Verba et al. 1995; Perrin 2001).

In this paper, I establish one mechanism for observed differences in association members' political mobilization. I introduce the concept of political microcultures: social environments that vary in the quality and quantity of their political discourse and, therefore, offer different resources for political thought and action. I present evidence that some of the keys to political evaluation, discussion, deliberation and engagement lie in political microcultures. Associational life plays two distinct roles in democratic citizenship. As others (e.g., Lin 2001; Verba et al. 1995) have shown, membership in associations fosters network connections and civic skills to enable participation. In addition, it works to structure citizens' political imaginations by constituting civic contexts that, in turn, foster political microcultures. These microcultural effects are important, independent pieces of organizations' contribution to mobilization. They may play a part in influencing the framing of issues and so-called "cognitive liberation" (McAdam 1982; Voss 1996) in social movements.

## The Culture of Politics

Substantial research has demonstrated the impact of group contexts on citizen deliberation. Gamson (1992) showed that groups of citizens came to different conclusions by "framing" the same issues differently. Eliasoph (1998) showed that social contexts can encourage or discourage citizens from wearing different "hats," including their "democratic citizenship hats" (p. 231) by, in part, licensing and forbidding certain modes of talk.

Recent thinking in cultural sociology suggests that cultures provide their participants with structures for interpreting and participating in social life by defining a set of rules, strategies and resources available in social settings (Swidler 2001. 30). Contemporary frameworks for understanding culture such as those of Swidler (1986), Bourdieu (1990) and Sewell (1992), see culture as providing a repertoire of resources and guidelines, thereby at once enabling and constraining the available choices for social action. Cultural sociology suggests that we look for the rules, strategies and resources mobilized in groups, and that we use specific settings and contexts (Mische and Pattison 2000) as units of cultural analysis.

Access to public-sphere discourse helps generate citizenship resources by enriching the cultural repertoire from which they may be drawn. Furthermore, different civic contexts (organizational activities as well as family, neighborhood and workplace encounters) offer access to different types and degrees of such public-sphere discourse. These different civic contexts are therefore a promising place in which to look for cultural influences on why some forms of civic involvement mobilize more broadly than do others. The evidence in this paper demonstrates that the cultural quality of deliberation varies across different kinds and parts of civil society.

Voluntary organizations constitute one context wherein the raw material for citizens' political imaginations is generated (Hart 2001). I use the term "context" here in a more specific, micro sense than have others (e.g., Boltanski and Thévenot 1999, 1991; Bourdieu 1990). I am not referring to the cultural or social environment (the "discursive opportunity structure" in Ferree et al. 2002) within which groups operate, nor to the set of ideas, habits and concerns their individual members bring to the table. Rather, "context" refers here to the particular setting in which citizens are interacting at a particular time. A complete theory of contextual effects on deliberation should certainly account for both nesting (subgroups within groups within regions, etc.) and cross-classification (e.g., race within groups) of contexts. Furthermore, it should account for contexts other than those in civic associations: for example, in mediated public spheres (Clayman 2004), informal discussions (Walsh 2004), and workplaces. This paper presents evidence for one piece of such a complete theory.

Because involvement in organized civic life predicts political participation (Putnam 2000: Verba et al. 1995), and different kinds of civic organizations mobilize their members differently (Verba et al. 1995; Perrin 2001), if political culture is an important contributor to political participation, then different civic contexts should display different cognitive repertoires of politics. This paper demonstrates that they do. It does not claim that group context is more important than individual characteristics or the substance of the issues being discussed. The claim, rather, is that the group context matters in addition to such factors.

# Methods

I use the results of 20 focus groups to understand what kinds of groups foster different kinds and degrees of citizenship talk. In March–June 2000, I conducted focus groups in four civic organizations of each of five types: Presbyterian churches (chosen to represent mainline Protestant churches; see Steensland et al. 2000), Catholic churches, labor unions (one manufacturing union, two service unions and one white-collar union), business organizations (such as local Chambers of Commerce), and organized sports groups (two bowling leagues, one softball team and one cycling club). The organizations were all based in southern Alameda County, California.

———

I presented each of these focus groups with the same series of four scenarios designed to probe variations in the groups' approaches to political problems.

Focus group participants filled out a short questionnaire containing questions about demographics, political ideas and organizational affliations. Individuals filled out the questionnaire before any group discussion began. The group then gathered at a table or in a meeting room to address the scenarios by deciding whether they would want to get involved in the situation, and if so, by deciding what they would do about it. Groups were told that they should attempt to come to agreement, but that they could move on if they were unable to do so. The following introduction is typical:

> Moderator: I'm going to give you, as a group, four scenarios that could face your community. They're not scenarios that have faced this community, but they're all ones that have faced other communities elsewhere. . . . What I'd like you to do with these scenarios is discuss among yourselves and decide first of all if it's an issue that you would like to get involved in. . . . And then if so, what would you want to do about the issue. And I would like you to try to convince one another that your approach to this is right. Either that you think it's not important and they also should think it's not important, or you think that it is important and they also should see it as important. . . . I have a lot more information about each scenario, and so what you should do as well is as you're deciding is this something you'd like to do about it, you should ask me questions about the surrounding details and information about the scenario. And I will tell you as much as I can about each one. (P3)

The four scenarios presented to the focus groups were:

1. **Profiling,** on alleged racial profiling by local police.
2. **Halfin,** in which the groups' U.S. senator. Joan Halfin, took questionable campaign contributions and changed key positions related to the interests of the contributors.
3. **Chemco,** on a local chemical company's violations of EPA regulations and the possibility of its being shut down.
4. **Airport,** on excessive neighborhood noise from a recent airport expansion.

## Group Context and Political Culture

In analyzing the focus groups, I concentrated on the logics that participants used to defend their positions. I was also interested in what information the groups felt they needed in order to make decisions. When different groups asked the same question, the same answer was provided to ensure comparability among the sessions.

Of course, the group context in which a participant took part in a focus group is often not the only context to which he or she had access. Focus group participants were members of, on average, 3.7 organization types. This does not include contexts such as work, family and school, from which citizens might derive skills and cognitive resources.

However, what individuals say in a group context is likely to be structured as much by what they expect to be effective as by the resources they have at their disposal (Eliasoph and Lichterman 2002; Calhoun 1999; Goffman 1959, p. 223). Participants operate within what Ferree et al. (2002b, p. 62) call a "discursive opportunity structure." The relationship between individual participants' resources and the group context is bidirectional: groups gain resources from members' other experiences, but they also constrain and structure members' resources and the ways in which they maybe used. Hypothetically, any participant might have used a different set of resources or used them differently in a different group context. This method captures the political culture of groups, not the ideology of the individuals within them. I seek to minimize this concern by including individuals' group memberships in the multivariate models.

# Coding

I divided the themes emerging from the discussions into three categories: argumentative logics, methods of participation and argumentative resources. Argumentative logics compose the repertoire of ways of interpreting a situation and options for addressing it. Methods of participation, by contrast, are actions participants can imagine taking. Strategic comparisons and sources of information are resources used by participants to bolster arguments and provide content to positions. These themes are based on the transcripts of the conversations; this is not a comprehensive scheme for interpreting political discussions, but rather a set of categories specific to these data.

These categories correspond roughly to the framing tasks contemplated in the framing literature: diagnostic framing, prognostic framing and frame bridging, respectively (Benford and Snow 2000, pp. 615–616, 624). Where social movement framing is engaged in an attempt to present existing information in a way that encourages mobilization, though for the most part, the non-movement-participating focus group members often used logics, methods and resources to discourage participation and to introduce new information. Therefore, despite the clear affinities between these categories and the framing literature, I have used more generic terminology here.

There are several codes within each theme (table 2). Each conversational turn was coded with the presence or absence of each code. The codes are essentially qualitative in nature; they represent themes that emerged from the ways these groups discussed these issues. (See Strauss and Corbin 1990). The codes are not mutually exclusive; a single turn can contain, for example, logics of capacity and of morality alongside comparisons with other historical situations. I identified more codes in the data than are analyzed here; table 1 presents codes that are relevant to this paper's argument.

# Argumentative Logics

I identified and coded for three major groups of logics participants used in the focus groups: Morality- or ideology-based logics, interest-based and other pragmatic logics, and capacity-based logics.

## MORALITY- OR IDEOLOGY-BASED LOGICS

These are most easily viewed as "political." Speakers employing a morality or ideology logic argue for a position because they see it as intrinsically right; their arguments are not based on logics of self-interest or on the feasibility of action. Others have called this mode of reasoning "abstract rules." (Bellah et al. 1986, pp. 151–2). I do not differentiate between arguments based on morality and those based on ideology because they function similarly in arguments; each argues that a course of action is simply right rather than proposing debatable standards such as "interests" by which to judge the action.

A member of a Protestant church (a 59-year-old white woman) approached the profiling scenario this way:

> VK: I don't like the idea of any group being targeted . . . even though the consensus is that it makes for a safer society. Too often not only are people targeted, but their treatment is also different than groups of another nationality or group. So . . . I would feel that we should do something about it. (P3)

VK establishes a standard for judgment about the profiling scenario beyond the possibility of debate: "I don't like the idea of any group being targeted." Unlike an interest-based argument, this opinion could be rejected by another participant, but it cannot be disproved as a matter of logic.

Similarly, a 29-year-old Latino male union member approached the Chemco scenario this way, considering it a matter of moral status:

> PD: Jesus, it's just the only place we've got. Somebody's got to do something about it, and whether it's something small or large, you know, somebody's got to say this is it. (U4)

Much as Sandman (1986) suggests, PD considers environmental protection a matter of moral value. Again, there is an important contrast: PD is concerned with institutions' moral failure to protect the environment, while others (see EV's comment below) address the ineffective use of institutional policies.

Ideological rhetoric need not be focused on consensus. Indeed, cynicism and ideological logics are often mixed in the focus groups. Consider

## TABLE 1  Focus Group Coding Categories

### Argumentative Logics

| | |
|---|---|
| Ideological/Moral | ideological or moral argument |
| Pragmatic | |
|    interests | self-interested motivation |
|    other pragmatic | what works, what's most effective |
|    expanded | children and/or community interests |
|    capacity | ability to make a difference |

### Methods of Participation

| | |
|---|---|
| Governmental | |
|    bureaucratic | ask the appropriate personnel to fix |
|    electoral | vote, don't vote, etc. |
|    legislative | pass laws |
|    donate | give money |
| Public | |
|    educate | spread a message, partic, when seen as non-threatening |
|    letter | write letters to either media or government |
|    organize | build/use group capacity to address |
|    petition | circulate a petition |
|    protest | demonstrations, parades, pickets, etc. |
|    revolution | violent, radical solution |
| Private | |
|    exit | individually remove self from situation |
|    explore | find out more about the situation |

### Argumentative Resources

| | |
|---|---|
| Narratives | |
|    anecdote | a personal story told to illustrate a point or concept |
|    comparison | comparing the situation to another well-known situation |
|    entertainment | comparison with movies, TV, etc. |
|    history | discussion of past situation similar to this one |
| Doubt | |
|    two sides | unreliability of expert sources |
|    suspicion | questioning the text's reliability |

the following passage, from a 39-year-old Latino male Catholic church member considering the Halfin scenario:

> QJ: This second scenario here I think is completely indicative as to why people don't get involved in the political arena. And this is what, see, this controversy seems to come up with every election in some form or another and so for us it leaves us with little faith and so as long as we in a family structure are doing okay, we tend to close our eyes to this type of scenario. When somebody who runs for public offce either rides the fence or changes position from one side of the fence to another after they've been elected, it is very detrimental to the people who have initially supported the individual. I think this is where when you have this kind of immorality it changes the belief of the American people in the American system. (C5)

This speaker is not concerned about the impact the senator's betrayal might have on his personal interests. His concern is aimed instead at the moral damage done by Senator Halfin's apparently self-serving political shift. He combines a cynical approach to politics (". . . it leaves us with little faith . . .") and moral indignation.

## PRAGMATIC LOGICS

These are based on the speaker's or group's self-interests (interest logics) or on the expectation that others act principally out of self-interest (pragmatic logics). For example, consider the following interest-based reaction to the racial profiling scenario, by a 54-year-old white, male Protestant church member:

> JL:. . . if you treat public officials as using their time in our best interest, then I want them to go after criminals more so then non-criminals. And if this is a profile that they have, or a demographic or whatever it is, then I want them to use it. (P3)

JL rejects the idea of a broadly political or moral approach to racial profiling, arguing instead that his interests are served by police being allowed to use whatever methods they consider best. Indeed, JL avoids asking the question of the effectiveness of profiling, arguing more generally that his best interests are served by allowing public officials to use their discretion and latitude.

Other pragmatic logics deal similarly with the politics of interest, but they are more broadly stated to include the interests of others instead of only those of the speaker. For example, a 46-year-old white female union member worried about the job losses that might be associated with shutting down the plant in the Chemco scenario:

> EV: There must be better ways to do things. Why aren't we doing that? Why aren't they spending this money that they're fining them, making them find a different way to do something so that these people are still employed? (U3)

Note that pragmatic logics need not be crass or uncaring. Indeed, this speaker uses implied self-interest to argue for meeting the needs of others. The call for "better ways of doing things" displays a pragmatist logic; the EPA fines are being used ineffectively.

### CAPACITY-BASED LOGICS

These are based on a discussion of whether successful involvement is feasible or not. They consider an individual's or a group's ability to participate effectively in a public-sphere activity. For example, a Catholic church member (a 52-year-old white woman) rejected action on the Halfin scenario for this reason:

> WK: I mean, I guess I can't see exactly a solution to this for me. I don't know where to go with it, and so it wasn't one of the higher priorities of things that trouble me. (C3)

WK decides not to become involved in the situation because she doesn't "know where to go with it." She skips over the process of determining the intrinsic importance of the issue, noting immediately that it seemed impossible to solve. She was therefore unwilling to become involved.

## Methods of Participation

I broke down the methods of participation into three categories:

1. Government-oriented methods, including bureaucratic methods (finding officials responsible for a policy arena and requesting their involvement);

electoral methods (voting, refusing to vote, working on campaigns); legislative methods (seeking to have bills introduced, passed or defeated); and "check writing" (making political donations).

2. Public methods, including educational campaigns, letter writing, organizing groups, circulating petitions, protests and revolution.

3. Private methods, including "learning more about the situation" (a common suggestion on how to participate) and exit: simply withdrawing from the situation.

This typology emerged from participants' discussions in the groups. Decisions about these modes of participation are structured by groups' interpretations of the scenarios in general; they offer additional clues as to how groups understood the relationship between interpretation and political participation.

### ARGUMENTATIVE RESOURCES

If logics make up the form of these political discussions, comparisons to other situations and evaluations of information make up their content. I call these elements argumentative resources: they are mobilized strategically to provide authenticity and substance to political arguments.

To make their cases more convincing, participants used ideas and knowledge available from elsewhere. One of the most common strategies was to compare scenarios with stories of other events related by participants. These comparisons included anecdotes (individually-known stories about the participant or a friend or family member); entertainment (comparisons with television, movies or other fictional stories); history (comparisons with earlier, well-known events); and other comparisons. These three resources are similar to one another in that they are stories told in strategic context, and as such, unpacking their meaning in the group is a significant interpretive task for other members of the group. In addition to personal stories, participants turned to outside sources for comparisons: the news media, scientists and other experts, and well-known popular fiction such as movies and television shows.

In addition to such story resources, participants used two other types of talk in similar ways: factual questions and a general attitude of mistrust. I also include mistrust of information (doubt) in the resources section because, in many of the discussions, participants mobilized doubt precisely as a way to counter claims of information and comparison. The two most common ways participants did this were: (1) the suggestion that experts had no privileged access to the truth; rather, there are two sides to every story; and (2) suspicion of the truth of the scenario itself.

## Conclusion

I have shown in this paper that different civic contexts are associated with different ways of talking about and imagining political action around similar issues. Beyond simply connecting individuals with social networks that breed greater political skills and participation (Putnam 2000; Lin 2001), civic contexts foster environments that may encourage, stifle and direct political thought. Citizens' civic experiences (presumably alongside non-civic experiences such as work, family and friendship networks) provide their members with a web of available resources for political thought. These resources, in turn, can be used for a variety of purposes in the public sphere.

Nina Eliasoph's (1998, p. 231) concern with which contexts encourage citizens to wear their "democratic citizenship hats" is well-placed; the organizational, civic contexts of citizenship do structure citizens' political imaginations. If political culture is a schematic web of interconnected ideas, styles, habits and evaluations that structures and enables citizens' political views (Boltanski and Thévenot 1991; Swidler 2001), associational life is a crucial territory for building citizenship, as others (e.g., Putnam 2000) have suggested.

... The character of political discourse is crucially social. Citizens' choices about what elements of a situation to discuss, how to evaluate them, and how to seek to convince their fellow citizens are structured by the civic contexts in which they are embedded. To be sure, they share some important sensibilities across civic contexts. But beyond matching discussion tactics to the situation under discussion, citizens match their political discourse to the setting in which they find themselves.

The independent importance of context suggests that political microcultures may be one mechanism by which associational involvement affects citizenship. These findings should spur further research to determine how the contours of microcultures develop and to what extent political-cultural elements developed in one context can be mobilized in another. For current problems of democratic theory and practice, they suggest closer attention to the character of group interactions, since different contexts may foster dramatically different political microcultures. Engaging in rich dialogue on public-sphere issues is, in itself, a way of doing politics. Political activity cannot be separated from political talk. Nevertheless, attention should be paid to the likelihood that citizens who think and talk differently may also behave differently in domains such as voting, letter-writing and other citizenship techniques.

# References

Bellah, Robert, Richard Madsen, William M. Sullivan, Ann Swidler, and Steven M. Tipton. 1988. *Habits of the Heart: Individualism and Commitment in American Life*, Harper & Row.

Benford. Robert D. and David A. Snow. 2000. "Framing Processes and Social Movements: An Overview and Assessment." *Annual Review of Sociology* 26:611–39.

Bollen, Kenneth A. 1990. "Political Democracy: Conceptual and Measurement Traps." *Studies in Comparative International Development* 25:7–24.

Boltanski, Luo and Laurent Trévenot. 1991. *De La Justification: Les économies de la grandeur.* Paris: Gallimard.

———. 1999. "The Sociology of Critical Capacity." *European Journal of Social Theory* 2:359–377.

Bourdieu, Pierre. 1984. *Distinction: A Social Critique of the Judgment of Taste* (Richard Nice, Trans.). Harvard University Press, Cambridge, MA.

———. 1990. *The Logic of Practice.* Stanford University Press.

Calhoun, Craig. 1999. "Nationalism, Political Community and the Representation of Society; Or, Why Feeling at Home Is Not a Substitute for Public Space." *European Journal of Social Theory* 2:217–231.

Clayman, Steven E. 2004. "Arenas of Interaction in the Mediated Public Sphere." *Poetics* 32:29–49.

Conover, Pamela Johnston, Ivor M. Crewe, and Donald D. Searing. 1991. "The Nature of Citizenship in the United States and Great Britain: Empirical Comments on Theoretical Thames." *The Journal of Politics* 53:800–832.

Dutwin, David. 2003. "The Character of Deliberation: Equality, Argument, and the Formation of Public Opinion." *International Journal of Public Opinion Research* 15:239–264.

Eliasoph, Nina. 1998. *Avoiding Politics: How Americans Produce Apathy in Everyday Life.* Cambridge University Press.

Eliasoph, Nina and Paul Lichterman. 2002. "Culture in Interaction," *American Journal of Sociology* 108:4, 735–794.

Ferree, Myra Marx, William A. Gamson, Jürgen Gerhards, and Dieter Rucht. 2002a. "Four Models of the Public Sphere in Modern Democracies." *Theory and Society* 31:289–324.

———. 2002b. *Shaping Abortion Discourse: Democracy and the Public Sphere in Germany and the United States.* Cambridge University Press.

Gamson, William A. 1988. "Political Discourse and Collective Action." *International Social Movement Research* 1:219–244.

———. 1992. *Talking Politics.* Cambridge University Press.

Gibson, David R. 2000. "Seizing the Moment: The Problem of Conversational Agency." *Sociological Theory* 18:368–382.

Goffman, Erving. 1959. *The Presentation of Self in Everyday Life.* Doubleday.

Habermas, Jürgen. 1962 [1989]. *The Structural Transformation of the Public Sphere: An Inquiry into a Category of Bourgeois Society.* MIT Press.

Hart, Stephen. 2001. *Cultural Dilemmas of Progressive Politics: Styles of Engagement Among Grassroots Activists.* University of Chicago Press.

Leighly, Jan. 1991. "Participation as a Stimulus of Political Conceptualization." *The Journal of Politics* 53:198–211.

Lin, Nan. 2001. *Social Capital: A Theory of Social Structure and Action.* Cambridge University Press.

Mansbridge, Jane J. 1996. "Using Power/Fighting Power." *Democracy and Difference.* Seyla Benhabib, editor. Princeton University Press.

Marcus, George E. and Russell L. Hanson, eds. 1993. *Reconsidering the Democratic Public.* Pennsylvania State University Press.

McAdam, Doug. 1982. *Political Process and the Development of Black Insurgency, 1930–1970.* University of Chicago Press.

Mische, Ann and Phillppe Pattison. 2000. "Composing a Civic Arena: Publics, Projects, and Social Settings." *Poetics* 27: 163–194.

Page, Benjamin I. 1996. *Who Deliberates?: Mass Media in Modern Democracy.* University of Chicago Press.

Perrin, Andrew J. 2001. *Civil Society and the Democratic Imagination.* Ph.D. thesis, University of California, Berkeley.

Putnam, Robert D. 1995a. "Bowling Alone: America's Declining Social Capital." *Journal of Democracy* 6:65–78.

———. 1995b. "Tuning In, Tuning Out: The Strange Disappearance of Social Capital in America." *PS: Political Science and Politics* 28:664–683.

———. 2000. *Bowling Alone: The Collapse and Revival of American Community.* Simon & Schuster.

Sandman, Peter. 1986. "Explaining Environmental Risk." (Pamphlet) Washington: U.S. Environmental Protection Agency, Office of Toxic Substances. Available: http://www.psandman.com.

Sewell, William H., Jr. 1992. "A Theory of Structure: Duality, Agency, and Trans-
    formation." *American Journal of Sociology* 98:1–29.
Strauss, Anselm L. and Juliet Corbin. 1990. *Basics of Qualitative Research:
    Grounded Theory Procedures and Techniques.* Sage Publications.
Swidler, Ann. 1986. "Culture in Action: Symbols and Strategies." *American Socio-
    logical Review* 51:273–286.
———. 2001. *Talk of Love: How Culture Matters.* University of Chicago Press.
Verba, Sidney, Kay Lehman Schlozman, and Henry E. Brady. 1995. *Voice and
    Equality: Civic Voluntarism in American Politics.* Harvard University Press.
Voss, Kim. 1996. "The collapse of a social movement: The interplay of mobilizing
    structures, framing, and political opportunities in the Knights of Labor." Pp.
    227–259. *Comparative Perspectives on Social Movements: Political Opportunities,
    Mobilizing Structures, and Cultural Framings.* Doug McAdam, John D. McCar-
    thy and Mayer N. Zald, editors. Cambridge University Press.
Walsh, Katherine Cramer. 2004. *Talking About Politics: Informal Groups and Social
    Identity in American Life.* University of Chicago Press.
Warren, Mark E. 2001. *Democracy and Association.* Princeton University Press.

# STUDY QUESTIONS

1. What does Perrin mean by *political microcultures* and why does he
   think these are important for cultural sociologists to study?
2. Why is group context so important in shaping political talk? Why is
   political talk important to democracy?

# 27

# CULTURAL PREFERENCES AND PERSONAL NETWORKS

OMAR LIZARDO

It's easy to see how peer groups and social networks influence people's preferences and cultural tastes. Almost everyone has had a friend or a friend-of-a-friend introduce them to a new band, fashion trend, or TV show that they grow to like or even love. Put simply, *who* people like ends up influencing *what* they like.

But do individuals' cultural preferences shape their networks? Does *what* someone likes end up influencing *who* they like? Omar Lizardo says that yes, it does. Drawing on the theories of Pierre Bourdieu and Paul DiMaggio (see pages 495 and 92), Lizardo uses network analysis to demonstrate the special power of popular culture to connect individuals who share enthusiasm for the same kinds of movies, TV shows, sports, and music. People don't just find fellow fans to connect with in their local social settings. Pop culture has the power to connect individuals who reside in diverse social settings and worlds, bridging social distances and linking people who share only weak social ties. In sociological terms, individuals convert the cultural capital (cultural knowledge and tastes) into social capital (friendships and connections). Interestingly, while popular culture has this power, "highbrow" cultural tastes (like a love of the opera, the symphony, or poetry readings) do not.

The big sociological idea here is that culture has the power to shape social structures in directly observable ways. Lizardo's research

**encourages researchers to look beyond simple models, which show how individuals' cultural tastes are based on the preferences of their peers, to a model that also acknowledges how individuals select peers based on cultural tastes and preferences.**

# HOW CULTURAL TASTES SHAPE PERSONAL NETWORKS

M ost treatments of the relation between culture and social structure—
going all the way back to the classic statements by Marx and Engels
(1939) and Durkheim ([1933] 1997:215, 276)—aim at explaining the connection between these two domains by highlighting the ways in which
patterns of social relations affect the composition and structure of cultural
systems (Bearman 1993; Douglas 1978; Martin 2002). Some of the more
ambitious projects, such as formulations in which large-scale cultural formations are linked to social structure broadly conceived (i.e., Swanson
1967), have been criticized for positing an unwarranted "reflection model"
of the relation between culture and society (Wuthnow 1985), in which
culture is seen as somehow being isomorphic with social structure but the
mechanisms that produce this convergence are left unspecified (Martin
1997:5). Bourdieu, for instance, dismissed this stance as the "short-circuit
fallacy" (quoted in Wasquant 1989:33), whereby a "direct link" is sought
between what are in fact "very distant terms."

Dissatisfaction with this state of affairs prompted a conceptual turn
from conceiving of culture as disembodied ideas toward thinking of culture as grounded in practice (Bourdieu 1990a; Ortner 1984; Peterson
1979), moving empirical research to focus on the study of concrete fields
of social relations (Anheier, Gerhards, and Romo 1995; Kay and Hagan
1998). This shift was coupled with a revitalized view of culture as useful in
practical strategies of social-boundary drawing (Bourdieu 1984; Lamont
1992; Lamont and Lareau 1988; Lamont and Molnar 2002; Peterson 1992,
1997). On the side of social structure, attention now focused on how *social
networks* affect individual and collective tastes, preferences, and patterns of
cultural involvement (DiMaggio 1987; Erickson 1996; Mark 1998a, 2003).
Nevertheless, this line of research has for the most part treated cultural
practices and patterns of culture consumption and taste as being primar-

ily *shaped* and *determined* by social networks (DiMaggio 1987; Erickson 1996; Mark 1998a; McPherson 2004; Relish 1997), but never as being able in turn to have an effect on these networks.

We can refer to this pervasive assumption in the recent literature in the sociology of culture as the "traditional network model" of taste formation and taste transmission (Erickson 1996; Mark 2003, 1998b). Unquestioned allegiance to the traditional network model has precluded investigation of the question of whether cultural tastes and practices themselves have an independent effect on social structure (conceived as patterns of network relations), and if they do, *how* are different profiles of cultural tastes linked to variations in network characteristics. Exploring the implications of this alternative stance on the culture-networks link is important on both empirical and theoretical grounds. If cultural tastes can be shown to have autonomous effects on the composition of personal networks, then the simple model that sees cultural tastes and practices as *contents*, and that sees network relations as the *conduits* through which these contents are transmitted, will have to be revised. Further, shedding light on the question of reciprocal effects of taste on social networks will allow us to conceptualize more clearly the dynamic relation between cultural knowledge and social structure in both small and larger social collectivities (Carley 1991, 1995; DiMaggio 1987; Mark 1998b; Collins 1988). This in its turn may help to connect those dynamics with research and theory on the practical use of cultural resources to create and transform network relations, as part of the situated conversational rituals that constitute the micro-interactional order (Collins 1988; DiMaggio 1987; Long 2003; Mische 2003; Mische and White 1998).

This article opens a path in this direction. Using nationally representative survey data for the United States, I examine the effects of two different styles of culture consumption, what have been traditionally referred to in the literature as "popular" and "highbrow" (Blau 1989; DiMaggio 1987; Emmison 2003; Katz-Gerro 2002; Van Eijck 2001), on outcomes related to the properties of personal networks. In this manner I follow DiMaggio (1987:442) by focusing "on the ways that people use culture to make connections with one another" and Bourdieu ([1986] 2001) in clarifying the way that cultural and social capital are "transubstantiated" into one another and mobilized in practical action to attain desirable resources. In this way I aim to contribute to research and theory on the connection between cultural competences and network relations, a link that while receiving a great deal of recent theoretical attention, continues to be a relatively understudied topic in the sociology of culture (DiMaggio 2003). I draw theoretical motivation from Bourdieu's ([1986] 2001) original statement on the forms of capital and on network theory in order to show how dispositions toward certain broad forms of taste are connected to patterns of density in different components of the personal network.

## Theoretical Background

### BOURDIEU AND THE FORMS OF CAPITAL

A prominent statement highlighting the mutual interconnection among economic assets, cultural dispositions, and access to social resources in the forms of network connections is Bourdieu's ([1986] 2001) classic essay "The Forms of Capital." Here Bourdieu presents a convincing argument for the fungibility among economic, cultural, and social resources. This is done through the *conversion hypothesis*, whereby economic capital is construed as capable of being transformed into cultural and social capital during the course of socialization into different class strata. Accrued social and cultural capital can then be partially transformed into economic capital throughout the life-course trajectory of individuals who originate from relatively privileged class factions.

Social capital allows the individual to accrue benefits by facilitating the formation of durable networks of acquaintance, obligation, and recognition—Bourdieu's (1986] 2001:103) definition of social capital—and providing access to membership in prestigious groups. Cultural capital on the other hand, provides the person with the symbolic recognition afforded by mastery of specific dispositions toward collectively valued cultural goods (Mohr and DiMaggio 1995). More importantly, *embodied* cultural capital (Holt 1997)—in the form of specific "pieces" of knowledge that can be exploited and exchanged in conversational rituals (Carley 1991; Collins 1988:360; DiMaggio 1987)—allows the individual to enter prestigious groups and to participate in exclusively bounded networks, helping in the formation of social connections with other individuals endowed with similar tastes.

From this perspective, all of the forms of capital—social, cultural, and economic—are at least *in principle* convertible into one another. As Bourdieu ([1986] 2001:107) notes, "The convertibility of the different types of capital is the basis of the strategies aimed at ensuring the reproduction of capital (and the position occupied in social space) by means of the conversion work." Bourdieu, however, did not fully theorize the directional link going from cultural to social capital, focusing instead on the conversion of cultural into economic capital by way of the acquisition of "institutionalized" markers of the former, especially in the form of educational credentials ([1986] 2001:99–100, 102) and the analogous conversion of social into economic capital (Bourdieu 1996:329–30). In this article I am specifically interested in the alternative process of conversion of informal cultural knowledge (associated with different kinds of taste) into social connections. Recent research at the intersection of cultural sociology and network theory has indirectly dealt with the issue of conversion of cultural—defined as those portable parts of the culture that the person can deploy in interaction—into social capital.

## THE CONSTRUCTURAL MODEL

The Carley-Mark (Carley 1991; Mark 1998b, 2003) "constructural" model can be interpreted as an elementary schema of how culture can be translated into social connections, and how social structure (the distribution of chances to interact across persons in the system) and cultural structure (the distribution of cultural forms across persons) can be defined in an interdependent manner. The authors use a simple assumption of similarity (homophily), which postulates that the likelihood of a social tie increases with the cultural similarity between any given dyad (a dynamic process similar to the one proposed by Homans [1950: 108–121]). In this way the probability that two persons will interact is driven by their cultural similarity. Interaction, in this positive feedback loop, in its turn increases cultural similarity as individuals exchange their stocks of knowledge with one another.

While the constructural model breaks with the one-side view of the traditional network model by explicitly modeling both the acquisition of culture by way of social connections and the formation of new social ties by way of cultural similarity (because it is explicitly concerned with the conversion of cultural knowledge into social connections), it fails to specify *which* types of cultural knowledge can convert into *what* kinds of social connections. This objection notwithstanding, the constructural model opens a promising theoretical avenue beyond the one-sided concern with the effects of social structure on culture of conventional network theory, by providing a plausible mechanism through which cultural information can be transformed into network relations.

## CULTURE CONSUMPTION, THE ARTS, AND SOCIABILITY

A more detailed formulation of how the process of conversion of cultural into social capital might operate can be found in DiMaggio's influential article "Classification in Art" (1987). For DiMaggio, the most significant change in modern, (post)industrial societies consists of the rising role of the arts, and mass-produced culture in general, in providing the "baseline" forms of cultural capital necessary to maintain interaction across different types of network ties. This process acquires more importance as these network ties have been transformed in the contemporary context of increasing geographic mobility and the decline of the traditional bonds characteristic of primordial local communities (Wellman 1979), which used to be centered around kinship and spatial contiguity (DiMaggio and Mohr 1985).

Personal networks are now more fluid, discontinuous, and less tied to geography and family (Castells 2000; Wellman 1979; Wellman and Wortley 1990), and popular culture and the arts increasingly serve as the "default" forms of knowledge that connect people across different "foci" of interaction (Feld 1982). Thus in contrast to material goods, which are "physically present and visible," cultural consumption is "invisible once it has occurred. This evanescent quality makes artistic experience, described and exploited in conversation, a portable and thus potent medium of interactional exchange" (DiMaggio 1987:442–43). This leads to the conclusion that *"[i]f there is a common cultural currency [in contemporary society], the arts (supplemented by fashion, cuisine and sport) constitute it"* (DiMaggio 1987:443, emphasis added).

DiMaggio not only notes the role of the arts as a generator of cultural knowledge, and as one of the most important facilitators of informal interaction—or "sociability" in Simmel's (1949) sense of social interaction for its own sake—but also suggests that culture consumption may play different roles in either helping foster ties that lead to social closure or social bridging. DiMaggio remarks that in the modern system, "as Douglas and Isherwood write of goods, artistic tastes are neutral, *their uses are social, they can be used as fences or bridges*" (DiMaggio 1987: 443, emphasis added). The consumption of arts and popular culture is therefore distinctive in this sense because it "provides fodder for least-common denominator talk, infusing conversation within local, socially oriented groups with time to spend on interaction for its own sake" (DiMaggio 1987:43). More generally, the consumption of cultural goods and performances thus can serve as a bridge not only to sustain current network connections but also to gain and cement new ones. This is because the consumption of arts-related culture and other aesthetic products "gives strangers something to talk about and facilitates the sociable intercourse necessary for acquaintanceships to ripen into friendships" (DiMaggio 1987:443).

Communication theorist John Fiske (1987) concurs with DiMaggio's assessment of the pivotal role that arts and popular culture consumption play in facilitating social interaction—by way of serving as topic for conversation—in contemporary industrial societies. For Fiske, while there has been much critical attention devoted to "the mass media in a mass society," he notes that most analysts have tended to ignore "the fact that our urbanized, institutionalized society facilitates oral communication at least as well as it does mass communication." Although the household is new the primary site of leisure culture consumption, it is important not to forget that most individuals "belong to or attend some sort of club or social organization. And we live in neighborhoods or communities. And in all of these social organizations we talk. Much of this talk is about the mass media and its cultural commodities." For Fiske, these cultural commodities take on primarily expressive functions, enabling the representation of "aspects of our social experience in such a way as to make that experience meaningful and pleasurable to us. These meanings, these pleasures are instrumental in constructing social relations and thus our sense of social identity" (Fiske 1987:77–78).

Fiske's and DiMaggio's framework is useful because it allows us to see how the consumption of publicly available and mass-produced cultural goods results in the acquisition of cultural capital when individuals endowed with the requisite dispositions consume those objects (Bourdieu 1984). This cultural capital can then be linked to the relative prevalence—or comparative lack—of different types of network relations (fences or bridges). This conversion of cultural into social capital functions in the same manner as would be expected by Bourdieu: it is transformed into social and (later on) material resources that are beneficial for the individual concerned: "taste then, is a form of ritual identification and a means of construction [of] social relations. . . . It helps to establish networks of trusting relations that facilitate group mobilization and the attainment of such social rewards as desirable spouses and prestigious jobs" (DiMaggio 1987:443).

In the following section, I begin the task of outlining a model of how such a transformation of different types of cultural capital into alternative kinds of social capital might take place.

## The Conversion of Cultural into Social Capital

### WEAK TIES AND STRONG TIES

Do different types of cultural tastes lead to the formation and sustenance of different types of network relations? To gain empirical and theoretical purchase on this question, I adopt the fundamental distinction in network theory between *strong* connections related to frequent, local interactions (and that are relatively more probable to cover a short distance in socio-demographic space—connecting people with individuals similar to them) and *weak* connections characterized by relatively infrequent, extra-local interactions (and that are more likely to span a larger distance in socio-demographic space—connecting people to dissimilar others) (Chwe 1999, Granovetter 1973, Lin, 2001). This distinction is helpful in bringing much needed specificity to the starting idea (Jasso 1988:4) built around a process of "conversion" of cultural into social capital, and in helping us begin to theorize the link between types of culture consumption with more specific forms of network composition.

### HIGHBROW AND POPULAR TASTE

In the context of taste for cultural products associated with the artistic sector, tastes and consumption practices appear to cluster around two dominant styles (or forms) of taste (Katz-Gerro 2002: 217–218) that have come to be referred to as *highbrow* and *popular*. As Van Eijck (2001:1168) notes, highbrow taste is characterized by an emphasis on the consumption experience as helping to foster an attitude of "transcendence" and is thus infused with the classical Kantian aesthetic in which cultural products are seen as a conduit for intellectual and emotional impressions that reflect "higher" moral and aesthetic values. Popular taste, on the other hand, is geared toward a more superficial hedonic engagement with culture, with "fun" and "pleasure" as the primary goals of cultural involvement. This is essentially the same distinction made by Blau (1989:433), who differentiates between an "elite culture" with a productive and distributive infrastructure centered around art museums, galleries, opera, theaters, symphony orchestras, and ballet and dance companies, and a "culture with broad popular appeal" that is primarily conveyed through live popular music concerts, general-interest museums, cinemas, and commercial bands. In a similar way, Emmison (2003:220) in a study of culture consumption in Australia notes, "Our analysis of the results for attendance at cultural venues suggests that two distinct factors are operative here. One set of venues, orchestral concerts, chamber music, ballet, musicals, opera and theatre, commonsensically can be grouped as 'high culture.' Another set, comprising rock concerts, movies, night clubs, pub music and theme parks, we regard as popular culture."

Most of the attention in the sociology of consumption focuses on the class fractions that are characterized by different combinations of these taste styles (popular, highbrow, and a third style that Van Eijck [2001] terms "folk"). Indeed, it is easy to show that these two contrasting forms of taste occupy distinct—but increasingly overlapping (Peterson 1997)—positions in sociodemographic space. Popular taste is more likely to be found among younger individuals who are either still in the process of acquiring educational credentials or who have not yet established themselves in a permanent occupation (or who are occupied in a sector of the artistic field that specializes in the production of popular culture), and among some segments of the working class and routine service sector (Bourdieu 1984:32–34). The highbrow aesthetic is more likely to be found among the older, more established upper-middle class, who engage in more difficult and demanding forms of aesthetic consumption with an eye toward using these objects to express more abstract values. The primary ideal commitment here is to approach culture as "cultivation"—what Bourdieu (1984:28) refers to as the "aesthetic disposition"—and the consumption of certain cultural goods as requiring effort, commitment, and a "distance from necessity" in order to be "properly" appreciated (Bourdieu 1984:28–30, Waterman 1998:56).

## TWO TYPES OF CONVERSION

Using the distinction between two types of culture consumption ("highbrow" versus "popular") and two types of network ties (strong and weak) it is possible to formulate a more specific model of the conversion of cultural into social capital. In the very same way that weak ties are construed as beneficial because they traverse wider portions of social space, I propose that consumption of popular cultural forms is beneficial because it provides the appropriate form of cultural capital that is more likely to flow through those types of (weaker) social connections. As DiMaggio (1987:444) notes, "popular culture provides the stuff of everyday sociability." That is, precisely because popular culture has a broader distribution in social space, it will thus tend to be associated with having connections that have a wider reach in that space. Conversely, the consumption of more demanding and arcane forms of culture—such as highbrow culture—because of its relatively stronger correlation with social position, should be more likely to be used to sustain local connections that do not reach far in social space and that are therefore more likely to be "strong" ties (Mark 1998a; McPherson, Smith-Lovin, and Cook 2001).

This differentiation between two different types of cultural capital is roughly in line with (although not strictly homologous to) Collins's (1988:360) distinction between *generalized* cultural capital and *particularized* cultural capital, and with Basil Bernstein's (1964) analogous differentiation between *restricted* and *elaborate* codes as the two primary forms through which cultural knowledge is produced and conveyed within and across status groups (see also Emmison 2003:217 on the distinction between inclusive and restricted "modes of cultural practice").[1] For Bernstein (1964:61), restricted codes are more likely to be used when "the form of the social relation is based upon some extensive set of closely shared identifications by the members." The elaborate code on the other hand is more likely to come into play when "role relations receive less support from shared expectations. The orientation of the speaker is based upon the expectation of psychological [or in our terms, *relational*] difference." In Collins's formulation, generalized cultural capital is primarily composed of "symbols which have come loose from any particular person and which simply convey a general sense of group membership [such as talking to friends about a popular sitcom or the local sports team]," which "can be

---

1. Bernstein's original typology of restricted and elaborate codes was initially developed as a way to contrast the flexible styles of speech displayed by members of the affluent middle class with the more context-bound linguistic practices of the working class which would make my claim that highbrow culture is a restricted code appear to be the reverse of his original intent. Bergesen (1984:189–91), however, has shown that we can think of restricted codes in a more general way: the difficult styles of communication developed in exclusive artistic communities or scientific "thought collectives" can, and do function as a restricted code.

widely used (as a topic of conversational exchange) even with strangers." Particularized cultural capital, in contrast, is that which is only "useful in keeping up a conversational ritual but only with certain people." Particularized cultural capital is much more important in Collins's view (1988:406) in solidifying networks of power and authority (Collins 1975).

Combining Bourdieu's, Bernstein's, and Collins' terms, we can say that popular culture has *generalized conversion value:* it may be more easily converted into weak-tie connections with heterogeneous others, or used to nourish existing connections of this type, because of its relatively low correlation with position in sociodemographic space (Erickson 1996). Elite (highbrow) culture, on the other hand, has *restricted conversion value:* it should be more likely to sustain recurrent, strong-tie networks and function in the long-established-status boundary-maintaining role identified by analysts from Weber (1946:187) to Veblen ([1912] 1945) and more recently Bourdiou (1984) and Collins (1988), because of its tighter connection to social position. The reason for this has to do (in part) with (1) the normatively constrained matching of cultural content to the type of network relation (and ultimately the local situation [Mische and White 1998]), and (2) the added ritual and emotional outcomes that derive from sharing more "selective" forms of culture in an intimate (and thus more trusting) social context (Collins 1988; DiMaggio 1987). As DiMaggio (1987:443) puts it, in contrast to the consumption of popular and mass media culture that simply serves to provide "fodder for least-common denominator talk . . . conversations about more arcane cultural forms— [such as] opera, [or] minimalist art . . . enable individuals to place one another and serves as rituals of greater intensity." In this way, social interaction involving the exchange of knowledge about relatively scarce cultural goods "bind[s] partners who can reciprocate, and identify[ies] as outsiders those who do not command the required codes," with "investors in specialized tastes" joining together in "the joy of sharing names."

Without losing sight of the ultimately heuristic nature of all economic metaphors (Bourdieu 1990b:92–93)—including that of capital—when applied to culturally mediated social interaction, it is possible to envision an informal social "transaction" between two individuals that makes use of highbrow culture as one that is accompanied by a high degree of asset specificity in Williamson's (1981) sense. It therefore makes sense to embed that social transaction under a governance structure that will ensure its successful completion; this case would require a "strong-tie" or a close, recurrent relationship that is charged with emotional value and associated cognitive salience (DiMaggio 1987; Erickson 1996; Granovetter 1973, Uzzi 1999). Social exchanges that make use of more popular cultural forms, on the other hand, are of a more general, less asset-specific nature, and thus do not need to be necessarily embedded in a strong-tie governance structure, but may occur under a looser, more "arms-length" type of social relationship (Uzzi 1999), one that would be consonant with the idea of a weak tie (Granovetter 1973). This will lead us to expect that generalized cultural tastes should increase the relative prevalence of these types of ties in an individual's social network.

## ARE CULTURAL TASTES ALWAYS AN EFFECT OF NETWORK TIES?

A crucial concern when examining the dynamic interplay between cultural taste and personal network characteristics—such as the number of social ties currently possessed by the individual—is the issue of reciprocal causation. Do cultural tastes produce larger networks or do larger networks drive tastes? Not surprisingly, most sociological research and theory that draw on network imagery (Erickson 1996; DiMaggio 1987; Mark 1998a) has assumed that the principal influence flows *from* networks *to* cultural tastes. Because of this widespread consensus, the empirical and theoretical propriety of this assumption has seldom been called into question. One reason why this has been the case might have to do with habitual patterns of inference drawn from entrenched metaphors (Lakoff and Johnson 1999), and theoretical commitments that construe networks as the infrastructure of society (and thus these networks are "hard" and casually efficient), cultural tastes as fleeting, and cultural content as simply objects that flow through these social pipes.

Recent research (i.e., Wellman et al. 1997; Burt 2000, 2002), however, has shown that networks are hardly stable, and that change and volatility in personal networks appear to be the rule rather than exception. Current dyadic contacts are constantly being deleted and new ones being formed throughout the adult life course. As Wellman and his collaborators (1997:47) conclude, "The most striking thing about our findings is how unstable intimacy is." This volatility is even more pronounced for weak ties or "bridging" connections (Burt 2000). Even personal networks studied in relatively delimited foci of interaction for comparatively short periods of time (less than a year) experience large amounts of turnover and change (see the review in Burt 2000:5, Table 1).

There has been little empirical research on the dynamic stability of tastes through time. However, there is good reason to suppose that tastes are more stable than current network theory leads us to believe. For instance, most studies on the role that early-family and school experiences play in the development of cultural capital have shown the strong influence of arts participation, education, and after-school training during adolescence on adult tastes even after controlling for subsequent educational attainment (Kracman 1996). Bourdieu's (1984) model of the habitus as a system of *durable* dispositions acquired in the family environment assumes the same stability, of tastes through time. Smith (1995), for instance, shows that musical tastes are developed early in youth and are fairly stable across the life course, and Dumais (2002) shows evidence of stable dispositions toward certain types of culture already present in early adolescence.

Thus, it is not unreasonable to suppose that the received picture of a steady and temporally continuous social structure determining soft and malleable tastes might be a bit one-sided, if not empirically inadequate. Given the observationally established instability of social connections and the relative stability of tastes, an alternative model consistent with the idea of conversion of cultural into social capital can be proposed, one in which comparatively stable patterns of taste drive the cultural contents more likely to be deployed in interaction, which in their turn affect the composition of personal networks. While the notion of cultural tastes "having an effect" on network ties may seem relatively counterintuitive at first, this possibility should not be very surprising if these tastes are construed as "foci", or cultural structures that serve to organize social interaction around commonly shared knowledge and interests, such as fan clubs, reading groups, or internet hobby sites (Feld 1982).

## Empirical Implications

The model of conversion of cultural into social capital that I have outlined so far leads to a series of important empirical implications. First, we should expect that in contrast to the traditional network model that posits a one-way avenue of conversion of social into cultural capital, we should also expect to observe a reciprocal process of conversion of cultural into social capital. This implies that in comparison to those who are not involved in the consumption of arts-related culture, those individuals with a taste for either popular or highbrow culture should also have larger and wider spanning networks. Thus, in the very same way that tastes are seen as resulting from the network ties that transmit them, we should also find that large networks are a result of the possession of the wide variety of tastes that help to sustain them.

Furthermore, if the conversion model is on the right track, highbrow and popular culture should be subject to different conversion dynamics: we should expect that those individuals who are more likely to have mastery of the highbrow-culture restricted code should also be more likely to have personal networks rich in social ties of a more intimate nature (strong ties):

*Hypothesis 1*: Highbrow culture taste leads to a denser network of strong ties.

Popular culture taste, on the other hand, should be subject to a different conversion regime, whereby those individuals who have a greater degree of familiarity with these types of cultural goods being more likely to possess personal networks relatively richer in less intimate, "arms-length" ties, which, while not useful for purposes of intimacy and emotional support, provide access to nonredundant sources of information and other forms of instrumental resources (Lin 1999; Granovetter 1973):

*Hypothesis 2*: Popular culture taste leads to a denser network of weak ties.

## Measures

To test the foregoing hypotheses, I use data from the culture and network modules of the 2002 General Social Survey (GSS) (Davis, Smith, and Marsden 2002). The GSS is administered biannually by the National Opinion Research Center (NORC) to a nationally representative sample of non-institutionalized, English-speaking American adults. The 2002 wave of the GSS contained a recurring module on participation in the arts (similar to ones fielded in 1993 and 1998), along with a new module related to social networks and social support. To my knowledge, this represents the first time that sociometric measures of network size and reach as well as measures of cultural taste have been present in a high-quality, representative dataset of the American population, which also contains relevant socio-demographic variables, thus representing a unique opportunity to evaluate empirically the adequacy of the conversion model outlined earlier.

## CULTURAL TASTE INDICATORS

Respondents were asked to report whether they had engaged in the following activities during the past year: (1) seen a movie in a theater, (2) gone to a live performance of popular music like rock, country, or rap, (3) attended a live performance of a nonmusical stage play, (4) watched a live ballet or dance performance, (5) heard a classical music or opera performance, (6) visited an art museum or gallery, and (7) read a novel, poem, or play. The variables are coded one if the respondent engaged in that activity in the past year and zero otherwise.

## SUMMARY

Three conclusions emerge from these analyses: (1) net of sociodemographic factors, highbrow taste is more likely to be converted into a denser network of strong ties, and popular taste leads to an increasing number of weak ties; (2) the net effect of highbrow (popular) taste on the size of the portion of the network composed of less-intimate (more-intimate) contacts is largely null, as would be expected if this type of cultural competence were not useful for the sustenance of these types of network connections; and (3) the positive effect of institutionalized forms of cultural capital (such as education) and of economic capital (as measured by occupational earnings) on the size of the personal networks is largely mediated through embodied forms of cultural capital displayed in the form of cultural taste.

# Discussion

The basic thrust of the results reported in this article can be summarized in a succinct way: individual tastes for different types of culture help to create and sustain different types of network relations. In a general manner, this finding supports the basic proposition that the primary use of the knowledge gained through cultural tastes—especially those connected with the arts and sports (and other cultural pursuits)—are *social* (DiMaggio 1987). Thus, the consumption of widely available cultural goods serves as one of the primary ways in which individuals become connected and integrated into the social structure. Individuals who are not involved in culture consumption are therefore more likely to be disconnected from others and forgo all of the benefits that come from network relations and that have been glossed under the banner of social capital. In this way the often-noted but seldom-explained association between high socioeconomic status and personal network density can be explained. Insofar as high-status occupants are also the more avid culture consumers, they will also be the ones capable of sustaining larger social networks.

An important implication of the findings reported here is that the likelihood that certain forms of cultural knowledge will serve as either "fences or bridges" depends on their appeal and ease of incorporation. Cultural pursuits that have a steep learning curve or that require extensive training and experience to be consumed (i.e., the "acquired tastes" of the dominant classes, the "niche" tastes developed around newly emerging technologies, or a strong interest in nineteenth-century social theory) are more likely to be used as fences, simply because people are likely to exploit that type of knowledge to sustain network relations already imbued with multiple meanings and emotional salience (multiplex ties), in relatively exclusionary interaction foci. Popular cultural forms, on the other hand, connect individuals to more distant segments of the social structure. In this way the consumption of widely available cultural forms serves as the "default" form of portable cultural knowledge that helps to keep a minimal level of integration even in large and complex social structures such as those characteristic of contemporary postindustrial societies (Watts 2004).

# References

Anheier, Helmut K., Jurgen Gerhards, and Frank P. Romo. 1995. "Forms of Capital and Social Structure in Cultural Fields: Examining Bourdieu's Social Topography." *American Journal of Sociology* 100:859–903.

Bearman, Peter. 1993. *Relations into Rhetorics*. New Brunswick, NJ: Rutgers University Press.

Bergesen, Albert. 1984. "The Semantic Equation: A Theory of the Social Origins of Art Styles." *Sociological Theory* 2:187–221

Bernstein, Basil. 1964. "Elaborated and Restricted Codes: Their Social Origins and Some Consequences." *American Anthropologist* 66:55–69.

Blau, Judith R. 1989. *The Shape of Culture*. Cambridge, England: Cambridge University Press.

Bourdieu, Pierre. 1984. *Distinction*. Cambridge, MA: Harvard University Press.

———. [1986] 2001. "The Forms of Capital." Pp. 96–111 in *The Sociology of Economic Lift*, edited by Richard Swedberg and Mark Granevetter. Boulder, CO: Westview.

———. 1990a. *The Logic of Practice*. Cambridge, England: Polity Press.

———. 1990b. *In Other Words*. Stanford, CA: Stanford University Press.

———. 1996a. *The State Nobility*. Cambridge, England: Polity Press.

Burt, Ronald S. 2000. "Decay Functions." *Social Networks* 22:1–28.

———. 2002. "Bridge Decay." *Social Networks* 24:333–63.

Carley, Kathleen M. 1991. "A Theory of Group Stability." *American Sociological Review* 56:331–54.

———. 1995. "Communication Technologies and Their Effect on Cultural Homogeneity, Consensus, and the Diffusion of New Ideas." *Sociological Perspectives* 38:547–571.

Castells, Manuel. 2000. *The Rise of the Network Society*. 2nd ed. Oxford, England: Blackwell.

Chwe, Michael Suk-Young. 1999. "Structure and Strategy in Collective Action." *American Journal of Sociology* 105:128–56.

Collins, Randall. 1975. *Conflict Sociology*. New York: Academic Press.

———. 1988. *Theoretical Sociology*. San Francisco, CA: Harcourt, Brace, and Jovanovich.

Davis, James Allan, Tom W. Smith, and Peter V. Marsden. 2002. General Social Survey 2002. Chicago, IL: National Opinion Research Center; Storrs, CT: The Roper Center for Public Opinion Research, University of Connecticut.

DiMaggio, Paul. 1987. "Classification in Art." *American Sociological Review* 52:440–55.

DiMaggio, Paul and John Mohr. 1985. "Cultural Capital, Educational Attainment, and Marital Selection." *American Journal of Sociology* 90:1231–1261.

Douglas, Mary. 1978. *Cultural Bias*. London, England: Royal Anthropological Institute.

Dumais, Susan A. 2002. "Cultural Capital, Gender, and School Success: The Role of Habitus." *Sociology of Education* 75:44–68.

Durkheim, Emile. [1933] 1997. *The Division of Labor in Society.* New York: Free Press.

Emmison, Michael. 2003. "Social Class and Cultural Mobility: Reconfiguring the Cultural Omnivore thesis." *Journal of Sociology* 39:211–230.

Erickson, Bonnie H. 1996. "Culture, Class, and Connections." *American Journal of Sociology* 102:217–52.

Feld, Scott. 1982. "The Focused Organization of Social Ties." *American Journal of Sociology* 86: 1015–1035.

Fiske, John. 1987. *Television Culture: Popular Pleasures and Politics.* New York: Methuen.

Granovetter, Mark S. 1973. "The Strength of Weak Ties." *American Journal of Sociology* 78:1360–80.

Holt, Douglas B. 1997. "Distinction in America? Recovering Bourdieu's Theory of Tastes from Its Critics." *Poetics* 25:93–120.

Homans, George C. 1950. *The Human Group.* New York: Harcourt Brace.

Jasso, Guillermina. 1988. "Principles of Theoretical Analysis." *Sociological Theory* 6:1–20.

Katz-Gerro, Tally. 2002. "Highbrow Cultural Consumption and Class Distinction in Italy, West Germany, Sweden, and the United States." *Social Forces* 81:207–29.

Kay, Fiona M. and John Hagan. 1998. "Raising the Bar: The Gender Stratification of Law Firm Capital." *American Sociological Review* 63:728–43.

Kracman, Kimberly. 1996. "The Effects of School-Based Arts Instruction on Attendance at Museums and the Performing Arts." *Poetics* 24:203–18.

Lakoff, George and Mark Johnson. 1999. *Philosophy in the Flesh: The Embodied Mind and Its Challenge to Western Thought.* New York: Basic Books.

Lamont, Michèle. 1992. *Money, Morals, and Manners.* Chicago, IL: University of Chicago Press.

Lamont, Michèle and Virág Molrár. 2002. "The Study of Boundaries in the Social Sciences." *Annual Review of Sociology* 28:167–95.

Lamont, Michèle and Annette Lareau. 1988. "Cultural Capital: Allusions, Gaps and Glissandos in Recent Theoretical Developments." *Sociological Theory* 6:153–68.

Lin, Nan. 1999. "Social Networks and Status Attainment." *Annual Review of Sociology* 25: 467–487.

———. 2001. "Building a Network Theory of Social Capital." Pp. 3–30 in *Social Capital: Theory and Research*, edited by Nan Lin and Karen S. Cook. New York, Hawthorne: Aldine de Gruyter.

Long, Elizabeth. 2003. *Book Clubs: Women and the Uses of Reading in Everyday Life.* Chicago: University of Chicago Press.

Mark, Noah P. 1998a. "Birds of a Feather Sing Together." *Social Forces* 77:453–85.

———. 1998b. "Beyond Individual Differences: Social Differentiation from First Principles." *American Sociological Review* 63:309–30.

———. 2003. "Culture and Competition: Homophily and Distancing Explanations for Cultural Niches." *American Sociological Review* 68:319–45.

Martin, John Levi. 1997. "Power Structure and Belief Structure in 40 American Communes." Ph.D. diss. University of California at Berkeley.

———. 2002. "Power, Authority, and the Constraint of Belief Systems." *American Journal of Sociology* 107:861–904.

Marx, Karl and Friedrich Engels. 1939. *The German Ideology: Parts I and II.* New York: International Publishers.

McPherson, Miller. 2004. "A Blau Space Primer: Prolegomenon to an Ecology of Affiliation." *Industrial and Corporate Change* 13:263–80.

McPherson, Miller, Lynn Smith-Lovin, and James M. Cook. 2001. "Birds of a Feather: Homophily in Social Networks." *Annual Review of Sociology* 27:415–44.

Mische, Ann. 2003. "Cross-talk in Movements: Reconceiving the Culture-Network Link." Pp. 258–80 in *Social Movements and Networks: Relational Approaches to Collective Action*, edited by Mario Diani and Doug McAdam. London, England: Oxford University Press.

Mische, Ann and Harrison White. 1998. "Between Conversation and Situation: Public Switching Dynamics Across Network Domains." *Social Research* 65:695–724.

Mohr, John W. and Paul DiMaggio. 1995. "The Intergenerational Transmission of Cultural Capital." *Research in Social Stratification and Mobility* 14:167–199.

Ortner, Sherry. 1984. "Theory in Anthropology since the Sixties." *Comparative Studies in Society and History* 26: 126–166.

Peterson, Richard, A. 1979. "Revitalizing the Culture Concept." *Annual Review of Sociology* 5:137–66.

———. 1992. "Understanding Audience Segmentation: From Elite and Popular to Omnivore and Univore." *Poetics* 243–58.

———. 1997. "The Rise and Fall of Highbrow Snobbery as a Status Marker." *Poetics* 25:75–92.

Relish, Michael. 1997. "It's Not All Education: Network Measures as Sources of Cultural Competency." *Poetics* 25:121–39.

Simmel, Georg. 1949. "The Sociology of Sociability." *American Journal of Sociology* 55:254–61.

Smith, Tom W. 1995. "Generational Differences in Musical Preferences." *Popular Music and Society* 18:43–59.

Swanson, Guy E. 1967. *Religion and Regime.* Ann Arbor, MI: University of Michigan Press.

Uzzi, Brian. 1999. "Embededness in the Making of Financial Capital: How Social Relations and Networks Benefit Firms Seeking Financing." *American Sociological Review* 64:481–505.

Van Eijck, Koen. 2001. "Social Differentiation in Musical Taste Patterns." *Social Forces* 79:1163–85.

Veblen, Thorstein. [1912] 1945. *The Theory of the Leisure Class.* New York, Viking.

Wacquant, Loïc J. D. 1989. "Towards a Reflexive Sociology: A Workshop with Pierre Bourdieu." *Sociological Theory* 7:26–63.

Waterman, Stanley. 1998. "Carnivals for Elites? The Cultural Politics of Arts Festivals." *Progress in Human Geography* 22:54–74.

Watts, Duncan. J. 2004. "The 'New' Science of Networks." *Annual Review of Sociology* 30:243–70.

Weber, Max. 1946. *From Max Weber: Essays in Sociology.* Edited by Hans Gerth and C. Wright Mills. New York: Oxford University Press.

Wellman, Barry. 1979. "The Community Question: The Intimate Networks of East Yorkers." *American Journal of Sociology* 84:1201–31.

Wellman, Barry, Renita Yuk-Lin Wong, David Tindall, and Nancy Nazer. 1997. "A Decade of Network Change: Turnover, Persistence and Stability in Personal Communities." *Social Networks* 19:27–50.

Wellman, Barry and Scot Wortley. 1990. "Different Strokes from Different Folks: Community Ties and Social Support." *American Journal of Sociology* 96:558–88.

Williamson, Oliver E. 1981. "The Economics of Organization: The Transaction Cost Approach." *American Journal of Sociology* 87:548–77.

Wuthnow. Robert. 1985. "State Structures and Ideological Outcomes." *American Sociological Review* 50:799–821.

# STUDY QUESTIONS

1. What is the difference between *weak ties* and *strong ties* and why does this matter to sociologists?
2. Why would a preference for highbrow culture lead to a denser network of strong ties? According to Lizardo, is this hypothesis correct?

# 28

# COMMUNES AND COMMUNITY

STEPHEN VAISEY

In his 2003 novel, *Drop City*, American author T. C. Boyle describes life in a northern California commune. Teeming with characters drawn from the pantheon of 1960s counter-cultural hippies, political revolutionaries, radical feminists, and other utopians, Boyle's tale charts the demise of the communal ethos as it mutated and fractured in the more conservative 1970s. Few novelists have managed to depict so vividly or sympathetically the slightly mad efforts of the small bands of cultural pioneers who sought to reimagine society as existing without hierarchies or human exploitation. Boyle is adept at illustrating how these utopian longings crashed and burned against the structural realities of the era: law-and-order neighbors who would not tolerate communes in their communities; unfair divisions of chores that left some members bone tired and disgruntled and others fat and happy; and harsh environmental conditions that threatened the physical survival of even the strongest members of the tribe. Given the many structural constraints imposed by society, Boyle seems to question whether or not utopian communes could ever be expected to survive.

Stephen Vaisey, in his research on "the search for belonging," asks a different question: What are the cultural conditions that helped some communes not only survive, but thrive? To answer that, he turns to a dataset containing detailed information on 1970s communes in six different American cities. He finds that while structural features are an important predictor of commune vitality, a sense of shared moral order is essential. Indeed, it is this search for a shared moral order, Vaisey concludes, that leads people to experiment with intentional community in the first place. When they find it, they find a place to feel at home in the world.

# STRUCTURE, CULTURE, AND COMMUNITY: THE SEARCH FOR BELONGING IN 50 URBAN COMMUNES

Few concepts have generated as much theoretical speculation and as little scientific payoff as "community." While Tönnies's ([1897] 1988) distinction between *gemeinschaft* and *gesellschaft* resides at the heart of sociology—or at least at the heart of sociology's historical origins—it has produced little generalizable knowledge about the social world. This has not, however, stopped community from playing an important role in social, scientific, and political discourse. Among classical theorists, Durkheim's notions of anomie and solidarity, Weber's warnings about the "iron cage" of rationalization, and Marx's concerns about alienation from our "species being" all spoke to a greater or lesser degree to the disappearance of "authentic" relational life in modernity (see Delanty 2003). Although the nostalgic narrative of "Community Lost" seemed to fade among sociologists in the years following World War II (see Smith 2003), there is ample evidence of resurgent interest. Recently, for example, there has been a renaissance of concern for community under the auspices of social capital theory (see Field 2003). Though he is ostensibly not fond of the term "community," Putnam nevertheless chose "The Collapse and Revival of American Community" as the subtitle for *Bowling Alone* (2000), suggesting that the social capital literature deals with many of the same issues, albeit under a different name.

Community can be a slippery term and I do not seek to solve its conceptual problems once and for all. My goal is more modest: to explore the structural and cultural mechanisms that lead to the experience of community in communal groups. I begin with the simple observation that individuals and groups subjectively *experience* their social relationships in different ways, and that an important dimension of this variation tracks along Tönnies's distinction between "natural" and "rational" will. To investigate the structural and cultural origins of differing relational experiences in communal settings, I rely on data from the Urban Communes Project (UCP), a collection of ethnographic, network, and survey data collected in 1974 and 1975 from 60 urban communes in the United States.

Communes are not of course representative of all attempts to create face-to-face community. Nevertheless, as Kanter (1972) and Zablocki (1980) have pointed out, communes are strategic sites for engaging with important sociological questions about alienation, anomie, and solidarity. Despite their limitations, communes as bounded social entities offer the rare opportunity to observe mechanisms of interaction, solidarity, and social conflict on a scale that is more tractable than with larger, less clearly defined, and less intentional units of analysis such as neighborhoods. The UCP data are particularly valuable because they contain information on groups that were much more varied than one might expect given popular stereotypes. Some UCP communes, for instance, were intense and demanded large investments of time, resources, and ideological commitment. Others were little more than "crash pads" organized around a vague desire for communal life. Such heterogeneity facilitates meaningful analysis and comparison, and also a valuable opportunity to observe basic social processes at work in discrete, clearly bounded entities (Zablocki 1980).

To understand how and why some of these groups led to an intense experience of *gemeinschaft* while others did not, I rely on various social and political theories of community to suggest plausible causal mechanisms. I distinguish between two general types of explanation—the structural (i.e., mechanisms grounded in organizational factors) and the substantive (i.e., mechanisms grounded in cultural meanings). This division is by no means novel; it corresponds roughly to the historic divide between formal theories of community that have their origins in Plato, Hobbes, and Rousseau and the more spiritual or emotional theories of community linked to Augustine and Johannes Althusius (see Keller 2003:16–36). While this debate has typically been about how to best *define* community, I treat these perspectives as alternative theoretical frameworks for generating testable hypotheses. Each tradition proposes different mechanisms that may be responsible for generating what Kanter (1972) has called the "we-feeling"—a sense of group identification and solidarity.

While the regression analyses below suggest that substantive theories of community are generally more consistent with these data than structural theories, fuzzy-set techniques shed light on important ways in which cultural and structural factors work together to produce—or prevent—the presence of *gemeinschaft*. I argue that this two-method strategy is essential for capturing both proximate mechanisms and "the duality of structure" simultaneously (Sewell 1992). In addition to highlighting a novel analytic approach, the analyses in this article supply two main substantive contributions: first, an improved account of the factors that produce the we-feeling in communal groups; and second, some empirical evidence that suggests the value of reconsidering culture's role in producing community in face-to-face groups.

## Theoretical Foundations

### COMMUNITY AS EXPERIENCE

Both Tönnies ([1897] 1988) and Weber ([1922] 1978) relied on the experience of particular kinds of relationships to get leverage on the community concept. Tönnies contrasted the "natural will" (i.e., bonds based on affect and trust) with the "rational will" (i.e., associations based on mutual advantage or contract). Weber ([1922] 1978:40–43) relied on a similar, though not identical, division between motivational orientations, with substantive rationality underlying communal action and instrumental rationality underlying "associative" action (see Brint 2001, note 3). I discuss issues of definition and measurement below, but in general terms the outcome of interest here could be called "the experience of *gemeinschaft*," we-feeling, a sense of collective self, or the feeling of natural belonging (Bender 1978; Kanter 1972; Keller 2003).

Some scholars have criticized this subjective view as insufficiently grounded in specific patterns of interaction (e.g., Calhoun 1980; see also Wuthnow 1989). They usually base their criticism on the fact that some social patterns co-occur with the experience of the "natural will." This is of course true, and if one were simply interested in providing yet another definition or typology of community, the categories of experience or "will" would indeed be inadequate. As Keller (2003:*xi*) notes, though, the original impetus for studying community emerged out of the question: "Where can I be at home?" Durkheim's anomie and Marx's estrangement, for example, while grounded in macrostructures of collective representations or material production, become salient in our *experience* of them as persons.

Like the study of income inequality or racial discrimination, the study of community ultimately derives its importance from its consequences for human lives (Sayer 2005:11–12). Though studying community-as-experience does not capture all dimensions of the concept, it does encompass a theoretically justifiable and subjectively important aspect of human life.

Two principal schools of thought have been used to explain the experience of *gemeinschaft:* the structural and the substantive. Though the distinction between the two is not hard and fast, it is nevertheless highly useful. Structural theories explain community in terms of a set of organizational properties such as power relations, "dynamic density," the built environment, or other formal characteristics. Substantive theories, on the other hand, explain *gemeinschaft* as a product of moral order.

## STRUCTURAL THEORIES OF COMMUNITY

One exemplary structural theory comes from the social networks and social capital tradition. Though rarely stated explicitly, Putnam (2000:19) has come closest to giving a formal articulation of this view: "Social capital refers to connections among individuals—social networks and the norms of reciprocity and trustworthiness *that arise from them*" (emphasis added). On this account, the norms and trust that constitute major aspects of community emerge from the "infrastructure" of the social networks that underlie them (for a review of this literature, see Field 2003). The relationship between networks and culture here is one of "structural determinism" (Emirbayer and Goodwin 1994).

This network-influenced view is not only widespread among those who want to understand community, but also among those who seek to promote it. Putnam (2000) and Brint (2001), for instance, have focused on the importance of physical space, advocating the creation of "well-traveled paths and common meeting places" that would provide "opportunities for interaction" (Brint 2001:19). An emphasis on the vital importance of physical space also underlies New Urbanism, an enormously influential planning philosophy that is behind the creation of hundreds of planned communities in the United States (Calthorpe 1993; Katz 1994). All of these theories assume that shared identity and meaning *emerge from* the spatiotemporal organization of social life. They take for granted that solidarity is a by-product of interaction.

Another important strand of structural theory to come out of network theory has had its clearest incarnation in the work of McPherson and colleagues (e.g., McPherson and Rotolo 1996). This compelling research has shown that the distribution of individuals in "Blau space" (that is, the multidimensional space defined by various sociodemographic variables) influences the relative growth of voluntary organizations. The presumed engine behind this phenomenon is homophily—that actors who are alike in their education, income, or other sociodemographic characteristics tend to gravitate toward and interact with each other (McPherson, Smith-Lovin, and Cook 2001). While McPherson and colleagues have not specifically addressed the issue of community in Tönnies's sense, their work suggests that social homogeneity may be an important factor leading to the experience of community.

Finally, Brint's (2001) work on community can also be placed squarely in the structural camp. I already noted his focus on interaction as a catalyst for *gemeinschaft*. He has gone further, however, drawing on the work of Kanter (1972) and others to suggest other mechanisms that can serve as "instruments of community-building" (Brint 2001, Table 2). He classified these mechanisms into two groups: voluntaristic and sacrificial (see also Kanter 1972:68–74). Voluntaristic mechanisms include well-traveled meeting places, regular times for gathering, ritual occasions, and "socioemotional leadership." The first three are variants on the spatiotemporal themes already discussed. (Ritual, while not merely spatiotemporal, is certainly structural in that it is based in Durkheim's [(1912) 2001] later sociology of religion, which largely disregards substantive content.) "Socioemotional leadership," according to Brint, means that a group's leader organizes the group's culture "out of the materials of personality and experience" rather than out of shared beliefs or moral commitments (p. 19).

Sacrificial mechanisms are meant to separate individuals from out-groups by demanding sacrifices. Unlike voluntaristic mechanisms, which are (largely) grounded in the shared, elective use of spatiotemporal resources, sacrificial mechanisms imply strong authority and high levels of investment. The four mechanisms Brint (2001, Table 2) outlined were: hazing, the renunciation of pleasure(s), investment of time and/or money, and enforced changes in appearance and expression. The organizing principles of these mechanisms are *authority* and *investment*—that is, group leaders set controls on entry and on the required behavior of members. There is a strong parallel here to rational choice theories of religion, which identify "strictness" as a primary mechanism behind variation in organizational success (see Iannaccone 1994). Advocates of this view hold that by screening out free-riders, strict groups create higher levels of average investment, creating a better shared experience for participating members.

In general, then, the proposed mechanisms of structural theories can be grouped under four headings: (1) spatiotemporal interaction, (2) homophily, (3) authority, and (4) investment.

## SUBSTANTIVE THEORIES OF COMMUNITY

The overriding concern of substantive theories is that ideas, culture, and identity matter at least as much as social structure for the development of particular forms of social interaction. Etzioni (2001) has been particularly critical of structural theories, stating that while Putnam (2000) and others are correct that interactions are a necessary part of community they are not in and of themselves sufficient to produce it. He has argued, "Without shared values, communities are unable to withstand centrifugal forces. . . . For these reasons, the mainstays of community cannot be bowling leagues, bird watching societies, and chess clubs" (Etzioni 2001:224). According to Etzioni, these types of organizations are not adequate because they are not formed around shared moral cultures (see also MacIntyre 1981; Sandel 1996, 2000).

Charles Taylor shares with communitarian, theorists a focus on moral order. Taylor has argued that both individual and group identity are firmly grounded in what actors intersubjectively hold to be good or valuable in life (see Taylor 1989, 1991, 2003). Taylor is not an idealist; he has simply claimed that practices (such as those posited by structural theories) can have no social power unless they are interpreted through the "hermeneutic key" of shared moral order. According to this view, interpretive understanding "makes possible common practices and a widely shared sense of legitimacy" (2003:23). In other words, without a common understanding about what a given practice *means* in the context of a group's day-to-day interactions, it cannot provide a basis for solidarity.

Taylor's work has been imported into sociological theory primarily through the writings of Craig Calhoun (1991) and Christian Smith (1998, 2003). While Calhoun has stressed in a general way the importance of moral horizons for grounding individual and collective selves, Smith has adapted these ideas for empirical inquiry. Smith's (1998) subcultural theory of religious strength maintains (*contra* rational choice theory) that "strict churches" are not strong because they require investments, but rather because they inspire a shared and morally salient group identity.

Proposition 1 of Smith's (1998:90) theory holds that "the human drives for meaning and belonging are satisfied primarily by locating human selves within social groups that sustain distinctive, *morally orienting* collective identities" (emphasis added). In contrast to the structural mechanisms considered previously, these substantive theories possess a common core—the importance of the mechanism of *shared moral order* for generating a sense of belonging in face-to-face groups.

## Data

I test these theories of community using data from the Urban Communes Project, a stratified sample of urban communes collected in six U.S. metropolitan areas—Atlanta, Boston, Houston, Los Angeles, New York, and the Twin Cities—in 1974 and 1975. To be included in the sampling frame, groups had to have at least five members and at least one member of each sex (or resident children). (This design was meant to exclude monasteries and convents.) The sample was drawn using a clustered quota design. To maximize geographical diversity, the investigators chose six large Standard Metropolitan Sampling Areas from different regions across the United States to analyze. Fieldworkers in each city first compiled a comprehensive census of communes within the SMSA. They then selected 10 communes in each SMSA on the basis of certain key variables such as ideological type, population size, and year founded (see Zablocki 1980). The study design included several different methodologies. Participant observers went to each of the communes and filled out a standardized form based on their observations. These observers also asked the members of each group to fill out a variety of survey instruments on attitudes, beliefs, and communal relationships (see Zablocki 1980 and Martin, Yeung, and Zablocki 2001). These data present a rich picture of life in a number of groups that were attempting to achieve the *gemeinschaft* experience. Because of missing data on some theoretically important variables, the analyses in this article are restricted to 50 groups.

Though the questions that motivate this analysis concern the broader issue of "community," the data are of course limited by their specificity. Communes are not representative of all attempts to build face-to-face community. Yet because producing the phenomenological *experience* of belonging was a major objective of these groups, they serve as valuable self-imposed experiments that permit testing predictions or recipes offered by very different theories in well-defined settings.

Though the communes were demographically very similar—whiter, younger, and more educated than the general population—they also differed from one another in many ways. At the individual level, Zablocki (1980:194) concluded, commune members were "almost maximally heterogeneous," with the major difference between them and noncommunal samples being the former's relatively high rates of survey non-response. There were also group differences in ideology. The original research team devised a seven-part typology they deemed most useful for coding each group's ideology (Zablocki 1980). Among the 50 groups examined in this analysis, there are 14 Eastern religious, eight Christian, six political (revolutionary), seven countercultural (hippie), five alternative family, seven cooperative living, and three "psychological" communes. Of more relevance for this particular investigation, these 50 groups varied markedly in their degree of *gemeinschaft* as well as in their levels of spatiotemporal interaction, social homogeneity, authority structures, investment, and strength of moral order. This variation is not simply an artifact of measuring relative differences between nearly identical groups; . . . This leaves plenty of scope for testing links between the we-feeling and the various factors that might give rise to it.

## Measures and Methods

### MEASURING THE EXPERIENCE OF COMMUNITY

One way to think of *gemeinschaft* is as a kind of phenomenological experience characterized by what Tönnies ([1897] 1988) called the "natural will" or what Kanter (1972) referred to as the we-feeling. This refers to human relations based primarily on emotion and trust rather than on instrumentality. It is doubtful that a single measure could capture this multivalent concept (see Loomis and McKinney 1956). While I also conduct replications using single measures. I rely primarily on a scale of six different measures, one of which comes from ethnographic observation and the others from the survey data. A UCP ethnographer rated each commune's level of "feeling of community," with possible values of (1) "no feeling of 'We the commune' apparent among members, just feelings of a collection of individuals;" (2) "minimal feeling of 'We the commune,' more dominant feelings of 'I' among the members;" (3) "feeling of 'We the commune' on certain occasions;" and (4) "strong feeling of a sense of 'We the commune' among members." I also use each group's mean response to a number of individual-level survey questions. The measures used to construct the *gemeinschaft* scale (recoded if necessary so higher values are more *gemeinschaft*-like) are as follows:

- "I feel the members of this commune are my true family" (five-point scale from "agree strongly" to "disagree strongly").
- "Most people in this commune are more inclined to look out for themselves than to consider the needs of others" (same coding).
- "No one in this communal household is going to care much about what happens to me" (same coding).
- "I think there is a very good chance I will still be living communally 10 years from now" (same coding).
- "If you were offered $10,000 in cash by an anonymous donor to leave this commune, and never again live communally in this house or with any of these same people (spouse, children, relatives excepted) would you: (1) definitely accept the offer, (2) have to think about it, (3) definitely reject the offer."

These measures each tap different but related dimensions of the community experience. The first three deal with the affective quality of relations within the group, specifically the extent to which the members were attached to each other in a noninstrumental way. The fourth question assesses each group's average degree of commitment to a communal lifestyle. The last captures whether each group's communal relationships were reducible to instrumental value, directly capturing Weber's and Tönnies's distinction between natural (substantive) and instrumental motivations for interaction. To construct the overall measure of *gemeinschaft*, I compute a scale from the ethnographers' rating, the average value of the first four survey questions, and the proportion in each group who responded "definitely reject" to the hypothetical cash offer. (As with all scales in this study, the individual variables are standardized before summing to give equal weight to each component.) A factor analysis using varimax rotation (not shown here) confirms that all of these measures load on a single factor. Cronbach's alpha for this scale is .84 and would not be improved by eliminating any of the individual measures.

## MEASURING STRUCTURAL MECHANISMS

Above, I outlined four basic types of structural mechanisms—spatiotemporal interaction, social homogeneity, authority, and investment. Fortunately, the UCP data contain multiple measures in each of these categories. In the primary analysis, I use standardized scales to measure these concepts. . . .

*Spatiotemporal interaction* refers to the frequency that members of the commune interacted with each other as members of the group. To assess the degree of interaction, I consider the following three measures: (1) the number of meetings per month, ranging from 0 to 30; (2) the frequency of eating meals together, measured on a five-point scale—never, special occasions only, one meal per day, two meals per day, three meals per day; and (3) the log interpersonal density of the commune (log[persons/ rooms]). Meetings and meals provided opportunities for ritual occasions and "collective effervescence" within the group, and interpersonal density increased the necessity of physical interaction. When combined into a scale of spatiotemporal intensity, Cronbach's alpha equals .72.

*Social homogeneity* reflects the degree of social similarity between members of each commune. I consider potential homophily effects on three axes: age, education, and father's occupational prestige. (There is no available question about individual race or income.) As noted above, these measures figure prominently in McPherson's work on organizational growth and vitality (e.g., McPherson and Rotolo 1996). I measure age similarity by the group's standard deviation in age. Because of the original question's categorical response scale, I measure educational similarity by the probability that any two group members picked at random will have the same degree status (college versus no college). Finally, I measure "class" similarity using the group's standard deviation of father's occupational prestige (based on 1970 Census occupational codes). Since the differing forms of social homogeneity are conceptually very different, they are never combined into a single scale.

*Authority* refers to the degree to which communal life was regulated by leader(s) with coercive power. To construct this measure, I rely on reports by the UCP participant observers. The first measure is the "extent of authority" in the commune, which varies on a four-point scale from "no authority recognized" to "high degree of authority." The second reports the "extent of rules" in the commune, which varies on a four-point scale from "no rules" to "many rules governing conduct and behavior." The final measure of authority comes from a series of five variables reported by UCP ethnographers. The observers reported on the way the group made decisions in five areas: "the executive sphere," defining values, making judgments, setting policy, and making specific house decisions. I include the number of these areas (0 to 6) in which leaders made decisions without consulting the group as a whole through either democratic or consensual processes. When all three measures are combined in an authority scale, Cronbach's alpha equals .87.

*Investment* refers to the amount of scarce resources a member or prospective member was required to devote to the commune. This construct is meant to assess how "demanding" the group was in terms of time, economic resources, and personal freedom. To construct this measure, I use three ethnographer reports and one survey item. The ethnographic variables are: the degree of economic communism (a four-point scale ranging from "no communism" to "virtually total communism"), and two dichotomous variables representing whether the group assigned chores to its members (rather than using a volunteer system) and whether a trial membership or novitiate was required to join the group. The survey-based measure is the number of hours the average member spent in the commune during the preceding three days. When combined into a scale of investment, Cronbach's alpha equals .85.

## MEASURING SUBSTANTIVE MECHANISMS

Following Smith (1998, 2003) and Taylor (1989), I define moral order as a group possessing a belief structure with two characteristics: *sharedness* and the capacity for *orienting action*. To get at these aspects of moral order, I rely on two ethnographic measures and two survey measures. Participant observers rated the "degree of consensus about commune's ideology, values, and beliefs among members" using a four-point scale with the options "much diversity," "some homogeneity," "great homogeneity," and "ideological unity." This reflects sharedness of beliefs. They also rated the "importance of ideology, values, and beliefs in [each] commune's life" on a three-point scale, which reflects the extent to which these shared beliefs were capable of being translated into action. To supplement these ethnographer-reported indicators, I also look to the individual-level data for indicators of morally-orienting beliefs. I take the average value of two survey measures (both measured on a five-point scale from "agree strongly" to "disagree strongly") that indirectly tap the morally-orienting character of the group's beliefs. I use the mean value of the survey question, "With respect to relations between husband and wife these days there are no clear guidelines to tell us what is right and what is wrong," because it asked about a common dilemma for organizing communal life. Individuals in groups with morally-orienting cultures should have had a clear sense of how marital relations ought to be organized, whether along traditional or egalitarian lines (Smith 1998:90). The next survey-based item is the group's mean value for the question: "I am skeptical of anything that tries to tell me the right way to live." Again, following the definition of moral orders as orienting, groups with strong moral orders should have had clear beliefs about the "right" way to live, whatever that may be. When combined into a scale, Cronbach's alpha for these four items is .91.

While measures of belief unity and moral orientation capture the overall sharedness, importance, and morally-orienting character of the group's ideology, the general *type* of organizing ideology may itself have played a role. This is measured by dummy variables that reference the group typology decided on by the study investigators (e.g., Eastern religious or countercultural; Zablocki 1980).

## ADDITIONAL VARIABLES

There are a few other factors that may be related to the overall level of *gemeinschaft* in these groups that are not directly addressed by either structural or substantive theories. Several control variables are therefore included in the multivariate analyses. Group size may not matter here since even the largest communes were quite small in absolute terms. Nevertheless, the number of members in the group (age 15 or over), is included as a control variable. I also consider the age of the group (in years) since we might expect that groups with a longer history would have developed a stronger sense of community. Finally, I include a dummy variable coded 1 if the group derived from a prior organization or organized group, since it represents a prior association between at least some current commune members and may reflect a preexisting stock of we-feeling independent of measured group characteristics.

This investigation does not include some factors other studies of communes (e.g., Zablocki 1980) have examined: (1) the presence of "charisma" and (2) the character of sexual relations in the group. I do not include these variables in the analysis because they do not fit well into either the structural or substantive theories of community that guide this study. Of course, I cannot simply exclude these variables without testing if their exclusion might bias the results. While ethnographer-coded charisma is positively associated with *gemeinschaft* ($\rho = .314$) and "shifting sexual relationships" are negatively associated with it ($\rho = -.653$), neither is significant in the multivariate model below ($p > .10$) and are, thus, not included in the findings reported here.

## HYPOTHESES AND A NOTE ON CAUSALITY

The bivariate hypotheses suggested by the theories are straightforward. High levels of spatiotemporal interaction, social homogeneity, authority, investment, and moral order should be positively related to the overall level of *gemeinschaft* in these groups. Moreover, since these theories go beyond positing associations and offer specific mechanisms for producing the experience of community, we should expect their effects to persist net of other factors. For example, if specific mechanisms of investment (such as the exclusion of free riders) were really operative in these groups, then the association between investment and we-feeling should persist even when other factors are controlled statistically. Otherwise, we would have to conclude that the bivariate relationship between investment and the experience of community exists because investment produced another phenomenon (or was itself produced by another phenomenon) that was the "real" (i.e., proximate) culprit that led to the outcome. Multivariate analysis will thus also be necessary to try to isolate the specific mechanisms at work in the production of community (see Ron 2002). The theories outlined above would lead us to hypothesize that *interaction, homogeneity, authority, investment,* and *moral order* will all be positively related to the experience of *gemeinschaft* net of other factors.

Finally, implicit in these hypotheses is that these mechanisms *produce* a sense of community instead of somehow being produced by it. Although theories of community treat the feeling of belonging as a "dependent variable," it is possible that a group of people who already (for whatever reason) share a sense of community might come to desire and pursue more interaction or increased investment, or might be more willing to submit themselves to an authority or develop a shared moral vision. Perhaps more plausibly, causality may operate in both directions—certain mechanisms may lead to greater *gemeinschaft* that in turn may lead to an increased intensity of (or willingness to accept) the original mechanism. Even though qualitative work and empirically-driven theory points to the *causal* importance of these factors (e.g., Brint 2001; Kanter 1972), there is no way to rule out alternative explanations in this investigation. The goal of this study is thus to test which theoretical perspectives are most consistent with these particular cases and the empirical data at hand.

―――――

## Discussion

. . . The findings strongly support the hypotheses advanced by substantive theories of community: there is good evidence that moral order was a vital dimension of producing the experience of *gemeinschaft* in these groups. Conversely, there is little evidence that interaction, authority, or (to a lesser extent) investment could—on their own—produce the experience of community.

Second, it may be that moral order intervenes to explain the bivariate association between we-feeling and the structural variables in communes because interaction, investment, and authority tend themselves to co-occur with moral order. Strong authority may appear to "work," for example, because its indirect positive relationship to we-feeling via its association with moral order is greater than its direct alienating effects. Both Martin (2002) and Sewell (1999) have argued that social power has the ability to organize cultural beliefs, which would account for the co-occurrence of authority and moral order, but other explanations are certainly plausible. It may be, for example, that groups with strong moral orders are willing to accept stricter authorities because they see them as legitimate. Ultimately, however, because we cannot isolate causal order with any precision, any specific interpretation must remain speculative.

―――――

While the existence of moral order was not sufficient in and of itself to produce we-feeling in these groups, the absence of moral order was sufficient to prevent it. A plausible interpretation of this result can be found in the work of Charles Taylor (2003), who has argued that moral orders provide "hermeneutic keys" for interpreting practices—that is, for answering the common query: "Why are we doing this again?" Though it is not always the case, communal life can be particularly demanding in terms of time, resources, freedom, and other generally valued goods. If actors don't have some shared, collective sense of why they are going to meetings, making food for other people, submitting to authority, and so on, how can they continue to feel that these efforts are worthwhile? Authority, in particular, appears to be alienating in the absence of shared moral order, at least in these groups.

====

## Conclusions

This article seeks to contribute to debates in the literature on intentional communities, community studies, and the social capital literature by disentangling some of the processes at work in the creation of the experience of community. Since the findings are based on a study of communes in a particular time and place, the results are not necessarily generalizable to other face-to-face groups, much less to nonlocalized forms of community such as race or ethnicity. In important ways, communes are different from other kinds of organizations. They typically (but not always) demand higher investments than other forms of association; they are more face-to-face and personal than, for example, nations, professions, or religious traditions; and these particular groups arose out of a particular culturally- and historically-specific time in U. S. history (Zablocki 1980). I argue, however, that the groups under consideration here were far more diverse than one might expect given the stereotype of "commune," and that they therefore serve as a fruitful window for exploring some general processes that previous work has linked theoretically to the we-feeling. On the face of it, one might expect face-to-face, bounded, and voluntary groups with solidarity as an explicit goal (like religious congregations or social movement chapters) to be more like communes than would other organizations, but this remains speculative. Ultimately, generalizability is, strictly speaking, an empirical question. Future research will have to determine the extent to which these findings are applicable to other settings.

Despite their limitations in scope, these findings do lend credibility to Etzioni's (2001) claims about the moral underpinnings of trust and social capital. More empirical research is needed, but these analyses suggest that cultural al theories emphasizing moral order may be an important corrective to the structuralist determinism that seems to pervade the social capital and network literature (see Emirbayer and Goodwin 1994). In the case of these communes, at least, the key point is this: contrary to Putnam

(2000:19) and others, *reciprocity and trust-worthiness do not simply "arise" from social networks, except, perhaps, as that interaction is either animated by or productive of shared moral understandings.* Even in previous studies of communes, this fact has been surprisingly underappreciated.

To the extent that these findings can be generalized to religious congregations as a related form of face-to-face community, this article also casts some doubt on the "strictness" theory of religious vitality (e.g., Iannaccone 1994), at least insofar as it offers a *mechanism* for actually producing satisfying group life. The level of required investment did not appear to matter as much (at least directly) to the communal life of these groups as the presence of "morally orienting collective identities" (Smith 1998:90). This article, then, has taken a small step toward adjudicating between two theories that produce very similar predictions at the denominational level. While the results show that high investment and strong moral orders usually co-occur, the regression analyses suggest that moral order is a more likely candidate mechanism for directly producing the experience of community. If sociologists are to move beyond the description of empirical regularities to explanatory theory in this area, more empirical research is needed that can isolate the specific processes at work (see Danermark et al. 2002; Hedström and Swedberg 1998).

In emphasizing the importance of moral order, my objective is not to imply that cultural belief structures are determinative of structures or practices, nor to suggest that moral orders are static, immutable things that hegemonically define meanings for social actors. Because of the need for resources to enact and sustain moral orders, they are subject to influence through the exercise of economic or political power (see Sewell 1999; Smith 2003; Wuthnow 1989). Furthermore, social structures themselves are inherently polysemous—that is, in their relationship with human actors they contain an interpretive flexibility that allows (even requires) cultural improvisation and change that can in turn affect the distribution of resources (Sewell 1992). The structure-culture relationship is one of complexity and dualism rather than determinism.

———

Finally, the substantive issues in this study go beyond mere academic interest. It is the human experience of alienation and anomie that inspires social theorists and lay people alike to ponder—and attempt—the creation of community. Since Tönnies and Durkheim wrote about these issues more than a century ago, the problem of modernity's "Great Dis-embedding" has not gone away (Taylor 2003:50). Human beings are still left to attempt to "re-embed" themselves in ways that will not do undue violence to their freedom or autonomy, while simultaneously trying to find sources of shared meaning and purpose. As the experience of these communes shows, this is not a simple or straightforward process. Yet perhaps work in this area will help us find better answers to a foundational sociological—and human—question: "Where can I be at home?"

# References

Bender, Thomas. 1978. *Community and Social Change in America.* Baltimore, MD: Johns Hopkins University Press.

Brint, Steven 2001. "Gemeinschaft Revisited: A Critique and Reconstruction of the Community Concept." *Sociological Theory* 19:1–23.

Calhoun, Craig. 1980. "Community: Toward a Variable Reconceptualization for Comparative Research." *Social History* 5:105–29.

———. 1991. "Morality, Identity, and Historical Explanation: Charles Taylor on the Sources of the Self." *Sociological Theory* 9:232–63.

Calthorpe, Peter. 1993. *The Next American Metropolis: Ecology, Community, and the American Dream.* New York: Princeton Architectural Press.

Danermark, Berth, Mats Eksröm, Liselotte Jakobsen, and Jan Ch. Karlsson. 2002. *Critical Realism in the Social Sciences.* New York: Routledge.

Delanty, Gerard. 2003. *Community.* New York: Routledge.

Durkheim, Emile. [1912] 2001. *The Elementary Forms of Religious Life.* New York: Oxford University Press.

Emirbayer, Mustafa and Jeff Goodwin. 1994. "Network Analysis, Culture, and the Problem of Agency." *American Journal of Sociology* 99:1411–54.

Etzioni, Amitai. 2001. "Is Bowling Together Sociologically Lite?" *Contemporary Sociology* 30:223–24.

Field, John. 2003. *Social Capital.* New York: Routledge.

Hedström, Peter and Richard Swedberg, eds. 1998. *Social Mechanisms: An Analytical Approach to Social Theory.* New York: Cambridge University Press.

Iannaccone, Laurence. 1994. "Why Strict Churches are Strong." *American Journal of Sociology* 99:1180–1211.

Kanter, Rosabeth Moss. 1972. *Commitment and Community: Communes and Utopias in Sociological Perspective.* Cambridge, MA: Harvard University Press.

Katz, Peter, ed. 1994. *The New Urbanism: Toward a New Architecture of Community.* New York: McGraw-Hill.

Keller, Suzanne. 2003. *Community.* Princeton, NJ: Princeton University Press.

Loomis, Charles P. and John C. McKinney. 1956. "Systemic Differences Between Latin-American Communities of Family Farms and Large Estates." *American Journal of Sociology* 61:404–12.

MacIntyre, Alasdair. 1981. *After Virtue.* Notre Dame, IN: Notre Dame University Press.

Martin, John Levi. 2002. "Power, Authority, and the Constraint of Belief Systems." *American Journal of Sociology* 107:861–904.

Martin, John Levi, King-To Yeung, and Benjamin Zablocki. 2001. "The Urban Communes Data Set: A Gold Mine for Secondary Analysis." *Connections* 24:54–59.

McPherson, J. Miller and Thomas Rotolo. 1996. "Testing a Dynamic Model of Social Composition Diversity and Change in Voluntary Groups." *American Sociological Review* 61:179–202.

McPherson, J. Miller, Lynn Smith-Lovin, and James M. Cook. 2001. "Birds of a Feather: Homophily in Social Networks." *Annual Review of Sociology* 27:415–44.

Putnam, Robert D. 2000. *Bowling Alone: The Collapse and Revival of American Community.* New York: Simon and Schuster.

Ron, Amit. 2002. "Regression Analysis and the Philosophy of Social Science: A Critical Realist View." *Journal of Critical Realism* 1:119–42.

Sandel, Michael J. 1996. *Democracy's Discontent: America in Search of a Public Philosophy.* Cambridge, MA: Harvard University Press.

———. 2000. "Democracy's Discontent: The Procedural Republic." Pp, 269–303 in *The Essential Civil Society Reader*, edited by D. E. Eberly. New York: Rowman and Littlefield.

Sayer, Andrew. 2005. *The Moral Significance of Class.* New York: Cambridge University Press.

Sewell, William H., Jr. 1992. "A Theory of Structure." *American Journal of Sociology* 98:1–29.

———. 1999. "The Concept(s) of Culture." Pp. 35–61 in *Beyond the Cultural Turn*, edited by V. E. Bonnell and L. Hunt. Berkeley, CA: University of California Press.

Smith, Christian. 1998. *American Evangelicalism: Embattled and Thriving.* Chicago, IL: University of Chicago Press.

———. 2003. *Moral, Believing Animals.* New York: Oxford University Press.

Taylor, Charles. 1989. *Sources of the Self: The Making of the Modern Identity.* Cambridge, MA: Harvard University Press.

———. 1991. *The Ethics of Authenticity.* Cambridge, MA: Harvard University Press.

———. 2003. *Modern Social Imaginaries.* Durham, NC: Duke University Press.

Tönnies, Ferdinand. [1897] 1988. *Community and Society.* New Brunswick, NJ: Transaction.

Weber, Max. [1922] 1978. *Economy and Society.* Berkeley, CA: University of California Press.

Wuthnow, Robert. 1989. *Meaning and Moral Order: Explorations in Cultural Analysis.* Berkeley, CA: University of California Press.

Zablocki, Benjamin. 1980. *Alienation and Charisma: A Study of Contemporary American Communes.* New York: Free Press.

# STUDY QUESTIONS

1. Communes are a particular kind of group. How are they like other groups and how, according to Vaisey, are they unlike other groups?
2. What is meant by *shared moral order* and why does Vaisey argue for its importance in cultural sociology?

# 29

# CULTURE AND RACIAL AND ETHNIC GROUPS

JOHN D. SKRENTNY

As numerous sociologists in this volume have argued, studying culture is arduous and challenging. It's also controversial: not all sociologists think a science of culture is really possible or desirable, while others insist that such a science should be foundational for the discipline. And if studying *culture* is controversial, studying *race* is even more so. In part, this is because the assumptions and theories of much early sociological research on race strike many modern sociologists as downright racist. But it is also due to the fact that, in American society and elsewhere, race is often a highly charged political issue, swirling with fiery emotions and passionate viewpoints that give off more heat than light.

Given the combustible nature of culture and race, how does one study the intersection of the two? It's a fair question, but for the past few decades, sociologists have all but ignored it. Since the infamous 1968 Moynihan Report, which John Skrentny discusses below, sociologists have shied away from analyzing the relationships between race, ethnicity, and culture, not because we found these relationships uninteresting, but rather, Skrentny insists, because we were afraid of the political backlash our answers might provoke.

In this article, Skrentny chastises sociologists for being timid and urges us to embolden ourselves and to dig deeper and more broadly into this long-fallow field. There are fascinating but unanswered

questions about race and culture—questions regarding the role of culture in shaping patterns of assimilation and acculturation; how experiences of discrimination and prejudice shape racial meanings and
identities; and how, thanks to globalization, immigrants may be Amer-
icanizing before they ever reach U.S. shores. Answers won't come
easily, but if researchers don't begin to tackle the questions, answers
won't ever come at all.

# CULTURE AND RACE/ETHNICITY: BOLDER, DEEPER, AND BROADER

## Explaining Achievement: Culture Is the Last Resort

Studies of ethnic or racial variations in economic or educational achievement have long been at the center of the sociology of race and ethnicity.
With a few exceptions, such as the study of ethnic variations in entrepreneurship (e.g., Light 1972), however, cultural analysis in this area has lagged
behind other subfields of research since the 1960s. This is primarily for
political rather than sociological reasons. However, scholars have made
important recent attempts to bring culture in while avoiding political
pitfalls.

### THE POLITICAL IMPLICATIONS OF CULTURAL EXPLANATION

Orlando Patterson (2006) has argued that scholars avoid cultural explanations of racial inequality because of misconceptions: that cultural explanations blame the victim; that they are deterministic, turning people into
robots; and that culture does not change. Although Patterson singled out
scholars in economics and political science, the ghost of Oscar Lewis (1969),
the originator of the "culture of poverty" argument, has haunted the sociology of poverty (Lamont and Small forthcoming) and also the sociology of
ethnicity and achievement. Most simply put, Lewis argued that cultural
practices and values of the poor—especially a lack of value on achievement—
kept them in poverty.

The misconceptions Patterson noted arose in part from political commitments. The politics of cultural explanations of black poverty exploded in 1965 when the so-called Moynihan Report, named after the author, Daniel Patrick Moynihan, a social scientist and assistant secretary of labor, was leaked to the press. Moynihan argued that slavery had destroyed the black family and that stable families were key to upward mobility. Press accounts created an angry backlash from those who believed Moynihan was calling for policy to remake black families (and thus black culture) rather than simply provide jobs (Rainwater and Yancey 1967). The controversy showed that for many, identifying ethnic or racial cultural beliefs and practices that contribute to poverty is bad because it blames the victim, and blaming the victim is bad because it implies there is no shared responsibility for ethnic inequality (Patterson 1997).

One might add another reason to those listed by Patterson for the marginality of culture in this subfield: some early attempts to invoke ethnic culture were very weak. Steinberg (1981/1989) used comparative analysis to attack cultural arguments that he called "ethnic myths" (e.g., that Jews are academically oriented and Catholics are not). He showed that many cultural theories of achievement were based on faulty assumptions that different groups are similar in skill and education levels.

In this view, culture was only a trait that people had in varying types, rather than a constitutive force that defined groups themselves or elements of their ethnic worlds. This view fit well with quantitative analyses of inequality, where culture is often a residual variable. Sociologists thus learned to appeal to culture only as a last resort—*after* controlling for all ostensibly noncultural factors to explain variation in achievement, such as human capital, economic opportunities, social capital, and other "structural" variables. Mostly neglected by the Left, cultural explanations of black or Latino poverty became the province of the Right (Patterson 1997; Hein 2006).

## ANALYZING CULTURE WITHOUT BLAMING THE VICTIM

In this environment, it was a bold move when Wilson (1987), a supporter of a generous welfare state, acknowledged the reality and independent effects of certain cultural traits, such as a tendency toward tardiness or absenteeism at work, when explaining the poverty of the black "underclass." In a later work, Wilson (1996) used sophisticated cultural sociological concepts to show that detrimental behavior can become entrenched and self-reproducing. However, Wilson also argued that culture was externally created and uninteresting from the point of view of race and ethnicity. He explained that "culture is a response to social structural constraints and opportunities" (Wilson 1987, 61) and that "group variations in behavior, norms and values often reflect variations in group access to channels of privilege and influence" (Wilson 1987, 75).

This view—that culture has effects but is decoupled from ethnicity or race, is not a fundamental cause, and thus is not appropriate as a focus of social policy—can be found in other works. For example, Anderson (1990, 3) discussed new role models in the black inner city who, contemptuous of low-status jobs, arose due to the lack of good jobs; and Waters (1999) presented a study of recent black immigrants, whose proachievement culture withered away in the face of continual experiences with discrimination. This approach represents a sociological as well as political move: it takes cultural explanations back from the Right, and then banishes them from policy discussion because culture is epiphenomenal. Why talk about culture, or direct policy toward "fixing" cultures of poverty, if those cultures are simply a response to social and material conditions? Moreover, this theory of culture avoided blaming the victim by denying that racial or ethnic cultures were in play at all. Rather, a culture of blocked opportunity (somehow) arises in any poor group to shape behavior (Tyson, Darity, and Castellino 2005).

Prominent in this approach is the theory of "segmented assimilation" (Portes and Zhou 1993; Portes and Rumbaut 2001), where immigrants vary in three background factors, including human capital, family composition (e.g., whether both parents are present), and context of reception (e.g., whether a group faces significant racism or whether it receives assistance as refugees). Low human capital, broken families, and racism make it more likely that an immigrant group will experience "dissonant acculturation," where the children—but not the parents, who find their children difficult to understand and control—assimilate into the "oppositional cultures" of poorer American minorities. Although this may appear to be a culture of poverty argument, in fact the stress here is on how cultures are *not* brought to America by particular groups but are created by or learned in structural conditions in the United States.

Is a theory of ethnic or racial culture (as opposed to a culture of class and blocked opportunity) possible in this context that does not appear to blame the victim? Carter's (2005) work suggests that it is. Focusing on the school context and using a variety of concepts from cultural sociology, including cultural capital, cultural tool kits, and symbolic boundaries, she examined the distinctions between the cultures of low-income African American and Latino students and the cultures of public schools. She argued that these students develop positive cultures of solidarity and distinction, creating cultural boundaries between themselves and others. School success depends in part on how they do this. In Carter's analysis, the most successful are the "cultural straddlers" who are able to deploy tools to play by the cultural rules of the school as well as the cultural rules of the peer group. Carter distinguished her approach from those who view cultures as epiphenomenal: "For many African American and Latino youths, their ethno-racial cultures are important sources of strength and are not merely reactive or adaptive by-products of their positions in a stratified opportunity structure" (p. vii).

Another way to use cultural analysis and avoid blaming the victim is to discuss the role of culture in ethnic or racial group *success*. Kao and Thompson (2003) noted that cultural theories are prominent to account for Asian American educational success, which remains distinctive even after controlling for human capital variables. Neckerman, Carter, and Lee (1999) assessed the cultures of middle-class African Americans, showing that these groups exhibit "minority cultures of mobility," or cultural strategies and tools for getting along and moving upward in a predominately white world that may misjudge and repress them. Using techniques such as "caucusing" for solidarity and support, or conspicuously dressing and speaking in particular ways that signal their class status, they minimize the impacts of negative treatment from whites.

———

Sociologists, then, are making more attempts to understand the cultures of ethnic groups in the contexts of inequality and poverty. Politically, it is a delicate endeavor, and even the most explicitly cultural accounts often avoid describing any intrinsically ethnic cultures, internally generated or traceable to ancestral homelands, that impact achievement.

## Studies of Racial Domination

Scholars of racial domination, and specifically discrimination and racism, typically make cultural arguments without acknowledging that they are doing so. "Prejudice" and "stereotypes" have cognitive components, but studies rarely analyze them explicitly as cultural phenomena or systems of meaning. Similarly, studies defining discrimination and racism as part of a system of power share with neoinstitutional theory the notions of taken-for-granted meanings, rules, and scripts, but these studies seldom engage neoinstitutionalism (see, for example, Feagin 1991; Feagin and Sikes 1994).

We can also find unacknowledged cultural arguments in public opinion studies of discrimination and racism, which typically see attitudes as social-psychological phenomena (Edles 2002). Consider "symbolic racism" theory in public opinion studies. In this view, white Americans view black Americans as lacking in traditional values such as work ethic, individual responsibility, and ability to defer gratification. These attitudes—or more precisely, these *meanings* many European Americans perceive in African Americans—are correlated with opposition to policies to benefit blacks (Kinder and Sanders 1996). In Bobo's (2001) view, the driving force behind white opposition to policies to benefit blacks is not a liberal ideology but a perceived threat to white status. Although Bobo's view seems to emphasize group interests, it still has a strong cultural component because it is *perceptions* of threat—a cognitive, cultural phenomenon—that drive white interests and attitudes (p. 206).

Explicitly cultural approaches to racial domination are more common in historical work. Omi and Winant (1994) focused on the process of "racial formation," itself based on "racial projects," which they defined as "simultaneously an interpretation, representation, or explanation of racial dynamics, and an effort to reorganize and redistribute resources along particular racial lines" (p. 56). Edles (2002) put culture front and center in her definition of racism, which is "a specific kind of racialized system of meaning . . . in which (implicitly or explicitly) physical 'racial' differences between groups are assumed to reflect internal (moral, personality, intellectual) differences, and that these differences are organized both biologically and hierarchically, i.e., racist systems of meaning suppose that on the basis of genetic inheritance, some groups are innately superior to others" (p. 101, emphasis removed).

Similar models of culture play a prominent role in big-picture, comparative-historical studies of racial domination. Glenn's (2002) study of racial and gender domination through citizenship and labor in the American South, Southwest, and Hawaii captured this approach well and showed how the creation of racial meanings through domination is an interactive process. She structured her comparative analysis with three main dimensions—representation (symbols, language, and images that express race and gender meanings), micro-interaction (focusing on social norms), and social structure (rules regulating power; p. 12), showing the different ways employers used race and gender to control labor and the ways subordinated groups resisted. Patterson (2005) presented a framework for understanding race stratification in different parts of the African diaspora, including in his analysis a variety of interacting factors, such as the kind of slave system present, geography, African cultural background, the ethnic demography of the host society, and the nature of European culture. His approach shows why, for example, North America produced a "binary mode" characterized by the one-drop rule as an instrument of oppression, while the Afro-Caribbean mode has race as continuum, where black and brown people dominate politics and the professions and play a significant role in business in a culturally pluralistic society.

## The Social Construction of Race

Work on the *construction* of racial categories and identities, which may or may not have a domination component, is also strongly cultural in orientation (e.g., Nagel 1994; Cornell and Hartmann 2007). These studies typically see the construction of race and racial or ethnic identity as an interactive process—part assertion and part ascription—through which race gains meaning or significance. Brubaker, Loveman, and Stamatov (2004, 45) invited us to think of ethnicity as a cognitive phenomenon: "Race, ethnicity, and nationality exist only in and through our perceptions, interpretations, representations, classifications, categorizations, and identifications. They are not things in the world, but perspectives on the world—not ontological but epistemological realities."

The state may be a key actor in the categorization process. Skrentny (2002, 2006) has shown how policy makers' cultural, cognitive process of analogizing some racial categories (Latinos, Asian American, American Indians) and even nonracial (women, the disabled) as similar to African Americans, while excluding others (white ethnics, gays/lesbians) shaped the political dynamics of inclusion in minority rights programs. Regarding race/ethnicity, this process created panethnic categories that became the American state's "official minorities." The state may also play the role of institutionalizing categories that are the result of political or even scientific contestation. In his analysis of how political pressure led the U.S. government to require that members of different races be included as research subjects in medical studies, Epstein (2007) showed how the categories of racial belonging and political mobilization also came to serve as categories for scientific purposes. At the same time, he considered how this new attention to the biology of racial difference alters the broader meanings of race in U.S. society.

However, works such as these are mostly about how political processes—movements and the state—create racial meanings, Lamont's (2000) analysis of black and white working-class men in the United States and France shows how in everyday life these men draw symbolic or moral boundaries that specify position in relationships and assign moral meanings to racial markers. In the U.S. case, she found that blacks and whites both use moral criteria to distinguish themselves from others. Whites are more likely to use a standard of "the disciplined self," which emphasizes integrity and work ethic. Blacks, on the other hand, are more likely to use "the caring self" as a standard, looking with disapproval on those they consider exploitative or lacking in compassion.

———

## New Frontiers for Cultural Analysis: Bolder, Deeper, and Broader Approaches to Ethnic Cultures

A bolder, deeper, and broader questioning of ethnic and racial cultures would bring cultural analysis to new or understudied topics. Especially ripe for more energetic analysis are assimilation, the racial/ethnic mapping of American culture on "existential" questions, attention to sending state cultures to understand ethnic cultures in the United States, and the impacts of globalization on ethnic culture.

## BOLDER APPROACHES TO CULTURAL ASSIMILATION
## AND AMERICAN CULTURE

For several years, "assimilation" was almost a dirty word as scholars preferred to study "acculturation" or "transnationalism." But it has made a
comeback, partly on the strength of Portes's work (Portes and Zhou 1993;
Portes and Rumbaut 2001) and that of Alba and Nee (2003), and partly
because it is undeniable that there is a process whereby ethnic differences
disappear. That is, ethnic groups become *assimilated*. What has been surprising is how easily "culture" can be written out of a concept that seems
to have a significant cultural component—"cultural assimilation" was a key
idea in the early sociology of race and ethnicity (Gordon 1964). More typically, sociologists today measure assimilation quantitatively in statistics
of residential patterns, language use, employment, and marriage partners
(e.g., Waters and Jiménez 2005).

Recently, however, sociologists have taken the assimilation concept into
new, explicitly cultural directions. Alba (2005), for example, building on work
in cultural sociology, has moved toward conceptualizing assimilation as a
process of movement across or movement of cultural boundaries. Examining
language acquisition and religion as cultural phenomena, as well as citizenship and race, Alba showed how boundaries separating immigrant groups
from the majority may be "bright" (unambiguous) or "blurry." Individuals
may cross boundaries by assimilating, or the boundaries themselves may
shift, redefining formerly immigrant practices as part of the mainstream.

The more expressive aspects of ethnic culture, however, and the ways
these fit into the wider American culture, are relatively understudied. Yet
there is promising work in this direction. Building on work on symbolic ethnicity (Gans 1979; Waters 1990) that emphasized the ways white ethnics
have maintained ties to their ethnic background through rituals, foods, and
elective ties after leaving their ethnic neighborhoods, Jiménez (2004)
explored the identities and cultural lives of multiethnic Mexican Americans
(individuals with one Mexican-descent parent and one white, non-Hispanic
parent). He showed how their Mexican side is continually replenished
through contact with Mexican neighborhoods, political movements, and
celebrations whereas the "cultural stuff" of their non-Mexican ancestry,
which is typically a European ethnicity or a mix of European ethnicities,
tends to be in short supply. Following Cornell (2000), who used the cultural concept of narrative to understand ethnic identity, Jiménez (2004)

documented the tensions of mixed-background Mexican Americans' participation in the "Mexican American narrative" that is only partially their own.

A related area of inquiry is the distinctively American yet still divergent cultures developed by ethnic groups in the United States. Here, scholars address not just culture as cognitive patterns but also art, fashion, and other forms of representation. Lee and Zhou's (2004) edited volume on young Asian Americans shows the potential of this approach. Bringing an American-style sociological sensibility to the Birmingham School theorists, they showed how Asian American youth have created a new hybrid culture—not clearly American, not clearly Asian—out of American and Asian elements. Their authors examined such cultural forms as beauty contests, import car racing, gangs, consumer culture, and campus religious groups and revealed their meaning and significance within ethnic cultures.

A full understanding of ethnic culture would need to be comparative—ethnic minority cultures must be understood in relation to majority cultures. Too often, research on race and ethnicity is only on racial and ethnic *minorities* (the American Sociological Association has a Section on Racial and Ethnic Minorities, rather than simply on Race and Ethnicity). Note, for example, that Portes and Rumbaut's (1996) study of second-generation assimilation makes a strong argument about the impact of nonwhite race yet contains no data on non-Latino white Americans. But if we do not know what white culture or "American" culture looks like, how can we know what is distinctive about nonwhite groups, or about immigrant groups?

Alba's (2005; Alba and Nee 2003) and Lamont's (2000) works on boundaries are important steps toward an approach that takes American culture seriously. We can conceive of American society and culture as a set of boundaries that define some groups as "in" and others as "out," But we can know more of the cultural stuff within the boundaries. For example, if we are to claim that import car racing makes Asian American youth culture distinctive, we need to be able to describe the practices of comparable white or black youth. But a bolder approach to ethnicity, race, and American culture would also need to get deeper.

## GETTING DEEPER: AN EXISTENTIAL CULTURAL SOCIOLOGY
## OF RACE AND ETHNICITY

We should also know more about the subjective experiences and meanings, as well as distinctive practices, that might profoundly shape experience. This is the key contribution of cultural sociology: showing how culture shapes interests. Of course, mapping American culture is a daunting task to say the least. Given the class and regional differences in the United States, does it even make sense to search for a mainstream American culture—and its relation to ethnic and racial cultures?

One useful place to start might be the classic study of how Americans find meaning in their lives, *Habits of the Heart* (Bellah et al. 1985). Bellah and his colleagues (1985) limited their focus to white, middle-class Americans but provided unprecedented depth and sophistication in their analysis. They showed how American cultural traditions of "utilitarian individualism" (the belief in self-improvement through individual initiative) and "expressive individualism" (the cultivation of the self) are manifested and, in particular, in the ways white, middle-class Americans think about success, justice, and freedom. In other words, they showed how culture can shape interests.

What is needed is a truly comparative *Habits of the Heart:* an analysis of different ethnic or racial (or indeed class) groups within the United States. Wary of blaming victims or casting cultures negatively, many sociologists of ethnic achievement emphasize or assume similarities, or even uniformity, in what different ethnic groups, on average, want out of life. They assume all ethnic and racial groups have the same interests. But is this a credible assumption? To be sure, studies indicate similarly high educational aspirations of nonwhite and white youth. But it is far from clear if it means the same thing when individuals from different ethnic or racial cultures say they want to go to college or graduate from school (Kao and Thompson 2003). Given all of the variation in ethnic cultures, and the cultural diversity so often celebrated in the American mosaic, is it likely, or even possible, that all groups on average want all the same things out of life, in the same degree, and balance competing demands in the same ways? Does everyone see the same meaning in life?

Lamont (2000) offered a start toward a multicultural *Habits of the Heart.* As discussed above, she specifically compared black and white working-class men on a variety of factors—including definitions of success. And she found some variation. "Compared to whites," she wrote, "blacks are more likely to define success in financial terms (half of blue-collar blacks compared to a third of their white counterparts) and to praise ambition (a third of black workers compared to a fourth of whites). In fact, more black workers value standards of evaluation associated with the upper half, such as money" (p. 117).

Variations in the meaning of life likely can be found between ethnicities within racial groupings. For example, Kao (1995) found strong evidence of cultural effects in explaining Asian American educational patterns showing high achievement. Even after controlling for human capital factors, Asian Americans earn higher grades than whites. After adding variables for ethnicity, however, she found variation between Asian subgroups. Only Chinese, Koreans, Southeast Asians, and South Asians earned higher grades than did whites. Filipinos, Japanese, and Pacific Islanders earned grades similar to whites, and Pacific Islanders showed more signs of education disadvantage than other groups typically considered "Asian." Desmond and Turley (2007) showed the importance of "familism" among Hispanics, particularly Mexican Americans, and specifically the importance of remaining at home during college years—a choice that often leads to lower levels of achievement.

These variations suggest the need for more debate on what is going on—is it possible that ethnic and racial groups vary in their career preferences and what they consider to be a satisfying or meaningful life, including a satisfying marital or personal life? If so, how do they vary? Most important, how does behavior correspond to perceptions of the meaning of life? Sociologists of race and ethnicity are uniquely situated to offer insights on the nature of U.S. culture and should take nothing for granted on the existence and nature of ethnic cultures within racial groupings and a diversity of "habits of the heart" for different populations. Doing so would hardly be a radical move. From the view of cultural sociology, the point is simple: culture can shape interests.

### BROADENING HORIZONS: HOW DO IMMIGRANTS' NATIONAL CULTURES AND GLOBALIZATION MATTER?

Scholars of race and ethnicity give little attention to the connection between ethnic cultures in the United States and how they originally appeared in their sending states. Despite growing interest in transnationalism, it is more common for scholars' attention—and thus their theorizing—to begin and end at the U.S. borders. This is perhaps most explicit in the theory of segmented assimilation, which places great importance on "contexts of *reception*." Immigrants might bring human capital, or intact or broken families, but that is pretty much all they bring. Inattention is also apparent in attempts to understand the effort and success of East and South Asian students in American education. Typically, scholars either emphasize strategies to counteract discrimination in the United States or casually invoke Asian values on education to explain the relative success of Asian Americans (see Kao and Thompson [2003] for a review).

There are of course exceptions. Some sociologists know well the source countries of the immigrants and/or consider their impacts on immigrants when they come to the United States (e.g., Massey, Durand, and Malone's [2002] work on Mexico; Waters's [1999] attention to conditions in the West Indies; and Morawska's [1985] study of Eastern European immigrants at the turn of the past century). Studies of Asian immigrant entrepreneurs note their importation of rotating credit associations to finance business ventures (Lee 2002). But attempts to systematically theorize the impact of sending state experience or culture on immigrants in the United States are far rarer.

Hein's (2006) study of Cambodian and Hmong refugees in the American Midwest offers a model on which to build. He developed an "ethnic origins hypothesis" to understand how homeland experiences affect patterns of integration and assimilation. There are four elements: religious values (including individualism vs. collectivism), norms of constraint and choice in networks, effects of inequality in national institutions, and effects of intraethnic and interethnic political conflicts. Hein stressed that ethnic culture is not primordial but that cultural norms emerge from interactions of cultural and noncultural factors in the homeland and destination state. This approach gives prominent place to culturally shaped cognition: "Immigrants use memory and imagination to continuously tap into the histories, politics, and culture of their homelands" as they create lives in the new context (p. 31).

More can be done in this area. First, we can use cultural theory to understand the mechanics of this process. Hein (2006) distinguished between cultural factors (values and norms) and other "effects" that arise from experiences in sending states. But these are easy to conceptualize as cultural. Scripts or schemas shape behavior in institutional contexts.

Immigration provides an excellent opportunity to study how reactions to the United States are conditioned by experiences in sending states. Immigrants do not come with a tabula rasa. They come with habits, understandings, and perceptions of meaning ingrained over years.

Second, sociologists can explore sending states to understand how these contexts matter. For example, consider again Asian American educational achievement. The substantial effort and money devoted to education by Asian immigrants to the United States, as well as the building of institutions such as "cram schools" (Kao and Thompson 2003), appear much less as immigrant-only phenomena and much more as transported cultural and institutional arrangements from sending states. Cram schools are a major industry in Korea, Japan, Taiwan, and elsewhere in Asia, and the importance of educational success, as well as the status gained from the most prestigious schools or occupations, are common themes in everyday life and popular culture (Skrentny 2007). In 2007, Korean society was rocked by a major scandal involving political leaders and celebrities who inflated their educational credentials to get ahead. A popular Korean soap opera, *Catch a Gangnam Mother*, showed the value on status and education differently. It details the sacrifices of a mother in the Gangnam section of Seoul, known for mothers who are particularly obsessed with their children's education. She works in a gentlemen's club to earn money to send her son to private tutoring school in the hopes that one day he will earn a place in a prestigious university. Great sacrifices for children's education are in fact common in Asia, including mothers living with children abroad— sometimes for years—so that the children can gain useful language and other educational benefits (Douglass 2006). Similar educational beliefs and practices of Asians in the United States and in Asia suggest not all behavior patterns are a response to the U.S. context.

## NATIONAL CULTURES, GLOBALIZATION, AND ASSIMILATION

Another way to broaden the use of cultural analysis in the study of race and ethnicity is to consider the opposite dynamic: immigrants may be bringing distinctive national cultural patterns to the United States, but they also may be taking on American cultural patterns before they even arrive. In other words, sending state cultures are changing due to globalization, and this may be affecting the dynamics of assimilation. Because of the narrow vision in much of the research on race, ethnicity, and immigration, as well as the inattention to cultural assimilation, studies of assimilation typically do not consider how globalization is changing sending states before their emigrants even depart their shores. Sociologists of immigration often seem to assume an anachronistic image of immigrants moving between discrete and disconnected national societies. But most sending states are awash in images of the United States, and American styles are popular, if not dominant, in all regions of the world.

=====

The notion of immigrants coming to America's shores and then "acculturating" and "assimilating"—as if they are extraterrestrials—seems quaint at best. There is room here for sociologists of race, ethnicity, and immigration to join with cultural sociologists in a project of tracing how and which culture moves from the United States to other states, is reinterpreted and reproduced, and is reintroduced to the United States. Assimilation can occur *before* immigrants reach American shores, shaping how immigrants behave and adapt to U.S. society when they arrive. In short, an international sociology of assimilation and acculturation can show that immigrants sometimes transport distinctive national cultural patterns to the United States *and* that their Americanization may begin even before they arrive to our shores.

=====

# References

Alba, Richard. 2005. Bright vs. blurred boundaries: Second-generation assimilation and exclusion in France, Germany and the United States. *Ethnic and Racial Studies* 28:20–49.

Alba, Richard and Victor Nee. 2003. *Remaking the American mainstream: Assimilation and contemporary immigration.* Cambridge, MA: Harvard University Press.

Anderson, Elijah. 1990. *Streetwise: Race, class, and change in an urban community.* Chicago: University of Chicago Press.

Bellah, Robert N., Richard Madsen, William M. Sullivan, Ann Swidler, and Steven M. Tipton. 1985. *Habits of the heart: Individualism and commitment in American life.* Berkeley: University of California Press.

Bobo, Lawrence D. 2001. Race, interests, and beliefs about affirmative action: Unanswered questions and new directions. In *Color lines: Affirmative action, immigration and civil rights options for America*, ed. John D. Skrentny, 191–213. Chicago: University of Chicago Press.

Brubaker, Rogers, Mara Loveman, and Peter Stamatov. 2004. Ethnicity as cognition. *Theory and Society* 33:31–64.

Carter, Prudence L. 2005. *Keepin' it real: School success beyond black and white*. New York: Oxford University Press.

Cornell, Stephen, 2000. That's the story of our life. In *Narrative and multiplicity in constructing ethnic identities*, ed. P. R. Spickard and W. J. Burroughs, 41–53. Philadelphia: Temple University Press.

Cornell, Stephen and Douglas Hartmann. 2007. *Ethnicity and race: Making identities in a changing world*. 2nd ed. Thousand Oaks, CA: Pine Forge.

Desmond, Matthew and Ruth N. López Turley. 2007. Staying home for college: An explanation for the Hispanic-white education gap. Paper presented at the annual meeting of the American Sociological Association, August, New York.

Douglass, Michael. 2006. Global householding in Pacific Asia. *International Development Planning Review* 28 (4): 421–45.

Edles, Laura Desfor. 2002, *Cultural sociology in practice*. Malden, MA: Blackwell.

Epstein, Steven. 2007. *Inclusion: The politics of difference in medical research*. Chicago: University of Chicago Press.

Feagin, Joe R. 1991. The continuing significance of race: Antiblack discrimination in public places. *American Sociological Review* 56:101–16.

Feagin, Joe R. and Melvin P. Sikes. 1994. *Living with racism: The black middle-class experience*. Boston: Beacon.

Gans, Herbert J. 1979. Symbolic ethnicity: The future of ethnic groups and cultures in America. *Ethnic and Racial Studies* 2:1–20.

Glenn, Evelyn Nakano. 2002. *Unequal labor: How race and gender shaped American citizenship and labor*. Cambridge, MA: Harvard University Press.

Gordon, Milton. 1964. *Assimilation in American life*. New York: Oxford University Press.

Hein, Jeremy. 2006. *Ethnic origins: The adaptation of Cambodian and Hmong refugees in four American cities*. New York: Russell Sage Foundation.

Jiménez, Tomás R. 2004. Negotiating ethnic boundaries: Multiethnic Mexican Americans and ethnic identity in the United States. *Ethnicities* 4:75–97.

Kao, Grace. 1995. Asian Americans as model minorities? A look at their academic performance. *American Journal of Education* 103 (February): 121–59.

Kao, Grace and Jennifer S. Thompson. 2003. Racial and ethnic stratification in educational achievement and attainment. *Annual Review of Sociology* 29:417–42.

Kinder, Donald R. and Lynn M. Sanders. 1996. *Divided by color: Racial politics and democratic ideals*. Chicago: University of Chicago Press.

Lamont, Michèle. 2000. *The dignity of working men: Morality and the boundaries of race, class and immigration*. Cambridge, MA: Harvard University Press.

Lamont, Michèle and Mario Luis Small. Forthcoming. How culture matters for poverty: Thickening our understanding. In *The colors of poverty*, ed. David Harris and Ann Lin. New York; Russell Sage Foundation.

Lee, Jennifer. 2002. *Civility in the city*. Cambridge, MA: Harvard University Press.

Lee, Jennifer and Min Zhou, eds. 2004. *Asian American youth: Culture, identity and ethnicity*. New York: Routledge.

Lewis, Oscar. 1969. *A death in the Sanchez family*. Berkeley: University of California Press.

Light, Ivan. 1972. *Ethnic enterprise in America: Business and welfare among Chinese, Japanese and blacks*. Berkeley: University of California Press.

Massey, Douglas S., Jorge Durand, and Nolan J. Malone. 2002. *Beyond smoke and mirrors: Mexican immigration in an era of economic integration*. New York: Russell Sage Foundation.

Morawska, Ewa T. 1985. *For bread with butter: The life-worlds of east central Europeans in Johnstown, Pennsylvania, 1890–1940*. New York: Cambridge University Press.

Nagel, Joane. 1994. Constructing ethnicity: Creating and recreating ethnic identity and culture. *Social Problems* 41:101–26.

Neckerman, Kathryn M., Prudence Carter, and Jennifer Lee. 1999. Segmented assimilation and minority cultures of mobility. *Ethnic and Racial Studies* 22:945–65.

Omi, Michael and Howard Winant. 1994. *Racial formation in the United States: From the 1960s to the 1990s*. 2nd ed. New York: Routledge.

Patterson, Orlando. 1997. *The ordeal of integration: Progress and resentment in America's "racial" crisis*. Washington, DC: Civitas.

———. 2005. Four modes of ethno-somatic stratification: The experience of Blacks in Europe and the Americas. In *Ethnicity, social mobility and public policy: Comparing the US and UK*, ed. Glenn C. Loury, Tariq Modood, and Steven M. Teles, 67–121. New York: Cambridge University Press.

———. 2006. A poverty of mind. *New York Times*, March 26.

Portes, Alejandro, and Ruben Rumbaut. 1996. *Immigrant America: A portrait*. Berkeley: University of California Press.

———. 2001. *Legacies: The story of the immigrant second generation*. Berkeley: University of California Press.

Portes, Alejandro and Mín Zhou. 1993. The new second generation: Segmented assimilation and its variants. *Annals of the American Academy of Political and Social Science* 530:74–96.

Rainwater, Lee and William L. Yancey, 1967. *The Moynihan Report and the politics of controversy.* Cambridge, MA: MIT Press.

Skrentny, John D. 2002. *The minority rights revolution.* Cambridge, MA: Harvard University Press.

———. 2006. Policy-elite perceptions and social movement success: Understanding variations in group inclusion in affirmative action. *American Journal of Sociology* 111:1762–1815.

———. 2007. The benefits of comparison: New challenges to race and ethnicity research. *Ethnicities* 7:135–41.

Steinberg, Stephen. 1981/1989. *The ethnic myth: Race, ethnicity and class in America,* Boston: Beacon.

Tyson, Karolyn, William Darity Jr., and Domini Castellino. 2005. It's not "a black thing": Understanding the burden of acting white and other dilemmas of high achievement. *American Sociological Review* 70:582–605.

Waters, Mary C. 1990. *Ethnic options: Choosing identities in America.* Berkeley: University of California Press.

———. 1999. *Black identities: West Indian immigrant dreams and American realities.* Cambridge, MA: Harvard University Press.

Waters, Mary C. and Tomás R. Jiménez. 2005. Assessing immigrant assimilation: New empirical and theoretical challenges. *Annual Review of Sociology* 31:105–25.

Wilson, William Julius. 1987. *The truly disadvantaged: The inner city, the underclass, and public policy.* Chicago: University of Chicago Press.

———. 1996. *When work disappears: The world of the new urban poor.* New York: Knopf.

# STUDY QUESTIONS

1. Why have sociologists avoided cultural explanations for poverty and inequality over the last forty years? What are the indications that this may be changing?

2. What does Skrentny mean by, "culture shapes interests," and why is this idea important for his argument?

# PART SIX

# INEQUALITY, POLITICS, AND POWER

I F, AS READINGS in the previous section argued, groups, networks, and identities are crucial agents in the production of culture, as well as being products of culture themselves, how can we best observe this circular development? If culture is a machine for reproducing social structures, how does it work? What are its mechanisms and linkages? What gives culture its power to structure our social worlds and how does that power operate?

Cultural sociologists are all grappling in one way or another with these central questions. Finding a way to answer them is simpler if researchers make it less abstract and more concrete. Consider *The Matrix* film trilogy, which portrays a world in which humans are trapped in womb-like pods. They live and die within these pods, but their subjective experience of the world—what they think, feel, and see—is almost exactly like our own. They work, they eat, they sleep and drink. They make families and friends, they grow old and die. What they do not know, however, is that their experiences of the world are part of an elaborate illusion, crafted by creepy, self-aware, superintelligent machines that have come to rule the earth. Humans, safely ensconced in their biopods, "live" in the matrix, a virtual world of computer-generated reality that masks the harsh objective reality, which is that the machines are harvesting the bio-electrical activity and heat from human bodies to power both their own civilization and the Matrix itself. Fortunately for humanity, not everyone is taken in by the machines' ruse and there are humans who have unplugged from the Matrix and entered back into the real world, where they fight to destroy the machines and liberate humanity from these virtual and material chains.

Like all good science fiction, *The Matrix* series raises questions about existing social arrangements and cultural and political realities by contrasting them with those one might encounter in a futuristic and more technologically advanced world. One of the questions raised by the series is whether individuals' perceptions of reality can be trusted. What if the present social reality, as most people experience it, is a false reality designed to prevent people from realizing that their lives are being controlled by others seeking to exploit humanity for their own gain? What if everyone was so entranced by this simulated reality that they became perfectly docile and content with the status quo? And if this were the case, how would anyone know? Unlike Neo, Morpheus, and the other heroic humans in the Matrix universe, you and I don't have a red pill we can take to instantly awaken us to the machinations of our computer overlords.

What we have instead are our own minds. We have to think our way out of the false realities that seduce us. We have to dig deep below appearances to find the structures that trick our senses and deceive us. It's easy to believe the matrix *is* reality. It seems so natural and so well suited to who we are that we seldom question it. But cultural sociology offers ways to analyze the matrix, to question its functions, observe its effects, and judge who is served by it and who is not. The readings in this section offer ideas and strategies to help us understand how the cultural matrix works to deepen social stratification and inequality, to divide and conquer groups that might otherwise form powerful alliances, and to pacify and amuse us while more powerful members of society take advantage of us.

If it seems like I'm saying that culture can be a war zone, then you understand correctly. As noted in the Introduction, some cultural sociologists envision culture as a vast social space where different groups fight for the right to control the production of meaning and values. Like the machines in *The Matrix*, the most powerful groups in society seek to impose their versions of reality on everyone else. In authoritarian societies, for example, ruling groups exercise the hard power of coercion, utilizing guns and violence to lock up and silence all dissenters. However, this kind of hard power is difficult to maintain over the long term: it has to constantly justify the political repression it rests upon, and many authoritarian regimes eventually fail because they can no longer legitimate themselves in the eyes of the masses (witness what began happening across the Arab world in 2011).

Hard power of this kind flies in the face of what modern-day democracies are supposed to represent, which is a stable relationship of power sharing, where ordinary citizens have a voice in government. Rather than the hard power of coercion, modern democratic societies favor the soft power of consent. Dominant groups dominate in large part by their ability to impose their reality on the rest of us. They control us most completely not by controlling our bodies, but by controlling our aspirations, tastes, and desires. They get us wanting what they already have and in so doing, win half the battle because we no longer see them as overlords, but as idols. It makes sense: rulers have an easier time governing when they have gained the consent of the governed. If they can win the hearts and minds of the masses, they can put away their guns and shutter their gulags.

But how exactly do rulers do that? How do they win hearts and minds? How do they gain the consent of the governed? In *The Matrix*, it was done by installing a virtual simulation of the real world as it once was. In the real world—our world—it is accomplished by installing and instilling cultural values and morals, habits and practices that, once accepted in general fashion, tend to benefit elites by reinforcing—or at least not challenging—the existing social hierarchy. For example, working hard, staying out of trouble, and being loyal to the flag are core values that most Americans espouse. Is it merely a coincidence that these values are directly supportive of the current economic system of capitalism, the current legal system, and the ongoing demand for willing soldiers who will volunteer to fight the nation's wars? Cultural sociologists of the Marxist and Frankfurt Schools would say, no, it's not a coincidence at all. Culture, they would insist, plays a crucial role in helping society reproduce itself from one generation to the next. The thinkers represented in this section would likely agree, but would add that culture is not simply a conspiracy foisted by elites onto the hapless masses. Ordinary people use elements of the same culture to resist becoming resigned to exploitation and to resist assimilation into the mainstream. Groups create their own cultures to produce meanings and values they can live with and abide by. Individuals use culture to create dignity for themselves and to demand respect for the groups to which they belong.

Culture is presented by these sociologists as a multifaceted social force that is not only capable of producing conformity and reproducing the status quo, but also capable of providing innovative ideas, values, and practices that challenge the status quo and make for gradual social change or social revolution.

# 30

# CULTURE, CAPITALISM, AND THE WORKING CLASS

## PAUL WILLIS

Paul Willis's *Learning to Labor: How Working Class Kids Get Working Class Jobs* is one of the classic books to come out of the Center for Contemporary Cultural Studies (CCCS) in Birmingham, England. Founded in 1964, CCCS, also known as the Birmingham School, was an interdisciplinary research center devoted to understanding the role of culture in everyday life. Combining theories and methods from literary criticism, sociology, and anthropology, CCCS exerted a major influence on the field of Cultural Studies as it spread around the globe. The center was closed due to budget cuts in 2002, despite protests by faculty and students.

In this excerpt, Willis summarizes some of the theoretical implications of his study, which was an ethnographic examination of a group of rebellious high-school-aged boys from working-class families. As his title indicates, he wanted to know what role culture played in "social reproduction"—the process whereby societies replicate and reproduce themselves with each successive generation. While it was obvious to everyone that generation after generation of working-class kids ended up in working-class jobs as adults, no one knew exactly how or why this occurred. It was particularly puzzling given massive-scale efforts to provide those kids with the educational opportunities that would help them rise above their parents' occupations into middle-class careers.

Willis noted that the culture of opposition to authority and the resistance to schooling demonstrated by the boys in their behavior, speech, and attitudes bore a close resemblance to the masculine culture of the factory. While the similarity of these cultures is not a mere coincidence, neither is it the result of some overwhelming force like class structure. As you read, you can observe Willis working out, in sometimes complicated language, the vexing relationship at the heart of every social theory between structure and agency, and order and action.

# NOTES TOWARDS A THEORY OF CULTURAL FORMS AND SOCIAL REPRODUCTION

Though we have only looked at one of the specific forms of the reproduction of labour power and of the subjective attitudes which allow it to be applied to the production process, there are some broad guides in this study for the development of a more general theory of cultural forms and their role in social reproduction, or more exactly for their role in maintaining the conditions for continued material production in the capitalist mode.

In the first place it warns against a too reductive or crude materialist notion of the cultural level. It is not true, for instance, that the manpower requirements of industry in any direct sense determine the subjective and cultural formation of particular kinds of labour power. Nor is it true that designated institutions such as the school produce—or could produce if in some way better run—classless, standardised packages of labour power. In its desire for workers of a certain type the reach of the production process must pass through the semi-autonomous cultural level which is determined by production only partially and in its own specific terms. Its own terms include consciousness, creativity of collective association, rationality, limitation, unintentionality and division. Its particular contributions to the formation of manual labour, for instance, are a particular kind of affirmation of manual activity and a penetration and transference of sets of divisions (principally manual/mental and male/female).

In a more general sense it cannot be assumed that cultural forms are *determined* in some way as an automatic reflex by macro determinations such as class location, region, and educational background. Certainly these variables are important and cannot be overlooked but *how* do they impinge on behaviour, speech and attitude? We need to understand how structures become sources of meaning and determinants on behaviour in the cultural milieu *at its own level*. Just because there are what we can call structural and economic determinants it does not mean that people will unproblematically obey them. In some societies people are forced at the end of a machine gun to behave in a certain way. In our own this is achieved through apparent freedoms. In order to have a satisfying explanation we need to see what the *symbolic* power of structural determination is within the mediating realm of the human and cultural. It is from the resources of this level that decisions are made which lead to uncoerced outcomes which have the function of maintaining the structure of society and the status quo. Although it is a simplification for our purposes here, and ignoring important forms and forces such as the state, ideology, and various institutions, we can say that macro determinants need to pass through the cultural milieu to reproduce themselves at all.

In the case of job choice amongst the unqualified working class, for instance, we can *predict* final employment quite well from class background, geographical location, local opportunity structure, and educational attainment. Certainly these factors will give us a better guide than expressed intention from individuals, say, during vocational guidance counselling. But what is it to say in any sense that these variables *determine* job choice? We are still left with the problem of the forms of decision taking and of the apparent basis of willing acceptance of restricted opportunities. To quote the larger factors is really no form of explanation at all. It does not identify a chain or set of causalities which indicate particular outcomes from many possible ones. It simply further outlines the situation which is still in need of explanation: *how* and *why* young people take the restricted and often meaningless available jobs in ways which seem sensible to them in their familiar world as it is actually lived. For a proper treatment of these questions we must go to the cultural milieu which has been studied in this book and we must accept a certain autonomy of the processes at this level which both defeats any simple notion of mechanistic causation and gives the social agents involved some meaningful scope for viewing, inhabiting and constructing their own world in a way which is recognisably human and not theoretically reductive. Settling for manual work is not an experience of absolute incoherence walled from enlightenment by perverse cultural influences, nor is it that of atavistic innocence deeply inscribed upon by pre-given ideologies. It has the profane nature of itself, neither without meaning nor with other's meaning. It can only be lived because it is internally authentic and self made. It is felt, subjectively, as a profound process of learning: it is the organisation of the self in relation to the future.

If a distinctive level of the cultural is to be argued for then, how are we to specify its scope and nature? In my view it is misleading to attempt such a specification in mechanical or structural terms. Culture is not static, or composed of a set of invariant categories which can be read off at the same level in any kind of society. The essence of the cultural and of cultural forms in our capitalist society is their contribution towards the creative, uncertain and tense social reproduction of distinctive kinds of relationships. Cultural reproduction in particular, always carries with it the *possibility* of producing—indeed in a certain sense it really lives out—alternative outcomes. The main relationships which cultural forms help to reproduce are those of its members to the basic class groupings of society and with the productive process. Though the cases vary markedly I do not mean to imply that the main class cultures are conceptually different at this formal level.

Within this larger specification of process it is possible to outline three specific characteristics of the cultural level in our society which help to accomplish this main purpose. In the first place the basic material of the cultural is constituted by varieties of symbolic systems and articulations. These stretch from language to systematic kinds of physical interaction; from particular kinds of attitude, response, action and ritualised behaviour to expressive artefacts and concrete objects. There are likely to be distinctions and contradictions between these forms, so that for instance, actions may belie words, or logics embedded within cultural practices and rituals may be quite different from particular expressed meanings at the level of immediate consciousness. It is these stresses and tensions which provide the text for the more interpretative analysis required "beneath" ethnography if the account of a culture is to be in any sense full.

In the second place I suggest that these things are produced at least in part by real forms of cultural production quite comparable with material production. Indeed in such areas as the generation of a distinctive style in clothing or changes made in the physical environment the production *is* material production. The basis for, and impetus of, this production is the informal social group and its collective energies at its own proper level. These energies I suggest are expressed in two connected forms. One is direct. It is the attempt to develop some meaningful account and representation of the world (often in an antagonistic relationship with language) of cultural members' place within it and to experiment with possibilities for gaining some excitement and diversions from it. The other is the profane investigation, the unconsciously revellatory probing of the world and its fundamental organisational categories, made in the course of the first process. The symbolic construction of the cultural world and of possibilities within it (the first) involves work on materials which—especially where they are new, only partially used or not properly ideologically incorporated—can bring real and unexpected results. These importantly derive from the nature of the materials, and the construction of the world, as they are worked upon by human agency for its own purpose. The first process is relatively intentioned—though not on an individual basis. The second can be quite decentred from the particular culture and implies no particular teleology though it importantly influences direct cultural activity and is the basis for its long term relevance and resonance for particular individuals.

Finally I suggest that cultural forms provide the materials towards, and the immediate context of, the construction of subjectivities and the confirmation of identity. It provides as it were the most believable and rewarding accounts for the individual, his future and especially for the expression of his/her vital energies. It seems to "mark" and "make sense" of things. I suggest in particular that the individual identity is importantly formed by the culturally learned sense, and subjective inhabitation, of labour power, and, in the reverse moment, that cultural forms themselves are importantly articulated, supported and organised by their members' distinctive sense of labour power and collective mode of effectivity in the world.

These are some of the main forms, functions and distinctive practices to be found at the cultural level. Their basic nature and their own full reproduction can only be understood, however, with respect to the way in which they help to produce the major relationships of the social group to itself to other classes and to the productive process. We might think of this process of reproduction as having two basic "moments." In the first place, outside structures and basic class relationships are taken in as symbolic and conceptual relations at the specifically cultural level. The form of this, I suggest, is of cultural (i.e. not centred on the individual or conscious practice) penetrations of the conditions of existence of the social group who support the culture. Structural determinations act, not by direct mechanical effect, but by mediation through the cultural level where their own relationships become subject to forms of exposure and explanation. In the second "moment" of the process, structures which have now become sources of meaning, definition and identity provide the framework and basis for decisions and choices in life—in our liberal democracy taken "freely"—which taken systematically and in the aggregate over large numbers actually helps to reproduce the main structures and functions of society. That is: the factories are filled on Monday morning and on every Monday morning with workers displaying the necessary apparent gradations between mental and manual capacity and corresponding attitudes necessary to maintain, within broad limits, the present structure of class and production. The processes which interact with the penetrations of the first "moment" to produce a cultural field such that life-decisions are made to reproduce and not refuse or overthrow existing structures I call limitations. Where the penetrations tend towards an exposure of inequality and the determining relationships of capitalism and the construction of a possible basis of collective action for change by the social group concerned, the limitations break up and distort such tendencies and apply them to different ends. The limitations are specific to the cultural level, prevent any essentialist reading of cultural forms, cannot be derived from the production process itself, and include both inherent functional weaknesses of cultural process, the effects of relatively independent meanings systems such as racism and sexism, and the actions of powerful external ideologies. In the case we have studied cultural penetrations of the special nature of labour in modern capitalism become a strangled muted celebration of masculinity in labour power. Cultural penetrations stop short of any concrete resistance or construction of political alternatives in an unillusioned acceptance of available work roles and a mystified use of them for a certain cultural advantage and resonance—especially concerning sexism and male expressivity. We should not underestimate the surviving degree of rationality and insight here. That working situation is given only the minimum of intrinsic interest and involvement. The self-abnegation of living subordination as equality, and in the terms of the official ideology, in the face of daily evidence and experience to the contrary, is at least denied.

The argument here, then, is that cultural forms cannot be reduced or regarded as the mere epiphenomenal expression of basic structural factors. They are not the accidental or open-ended determined variables in the couplet structure/culture. They are part of a necessary circle in which neither term is thinkable alone. It is in the passage through the cultural level that aspects of the real structural relationships of society are transformed into conceptual relationships and back again. The cultural is part of the necessary dialectic of reproduction.

This view of cultural forms and reproduction is both pessimistic and optimistic. It is pessimistic in suggesting the irony that it is in the form of creative penetrations that cultures live their own damnation and that, for instance, a good section of working class kids condemn themselves to a future in manual work. It is optimistic, however, in showing that there is no inevitability of outcomes. Subordination and failure is not unanswerable. If there are moments when cultural forms make real penetrations of the world then no matter what distortions follow, there is always the possibility of strengthening and working from this base. If there has been a radical genesis of conservative outcomes then at least there exists a *capacity* for opposition. We have the logical possibility of radicalness. Structuralist theories of reproduction present the dominant ideology (under which culture is subsumed) as impenetrable. Everything fits too neatly. Ideology always pre-exists and preempts any authentic criticism. There are no cracks in the billiard ball smoothness of process. All specific contradictions and conflicts are smoothed away in the universal reproductive functions of ideology. This study suggests on the contrary, and in my view more optimistically, that there are deep disjunctions and desperate tensions within social and cultural reproduction. Social agents are not passive bearers of ideology, but active appropriators who reproduce existing structures only through struggle, contestation and a partial penetration of those structures. Quite apart from a particular society's structural characteristics, it is the type of this contested settlement which helps to give it its special nature. A society, for instance, is deeply marked by the specific forms in which its labour power is prepared.

This warning against too closed or pre-emptive a notion of cultural forms and reproduction is also a case for recognising a necessary uncertainty. Too often it is assumed that capitalism implies thoroughly effective domination of the subordinate class. Far from this, capitalism in its modern, liberal democratic forms *is* permanent struggle. What is accommodating in working class culture is also what is resistant so that capitalism is never secure. It can never be a dynasty. Insofar as it has a stability it is the dynamic one of risking instability by yielding relative freedoms to circles of unintention in the hope of receiving back a minimum consent for rule. There is thus a deep uncertainty and changing balance of ever-heightening contradictions at the heart of capitalism. Full contested cultural reproduction is more important to capitalism than to any other system but the conditions for its own survival are also the conditions for its replacement.

Capitalist freedoms are potentially real freedoms and capitalism takes the wager, which is the essence of reproduction, that the freedoms will be used for self-damnation. The dominant class could never batten down the hatch on these freedoms without help from below. And if these freedoms are not used at this time for their full subversive, oppositional or independent purposes capitalism will not take the blame. It makes its own wager on uncertainty, others can make theirs.

The profound—though not limitless—uncertainty at the heart of the system should also warn against too functionalist a view of class cultural processes. Certainly, for instance, the circles of contradiction and unintention described in this book "work" for capitalism at this point in time. But so must any system "work" which is stable enough to be studied. There must therefore always be a functional level of analysis in reproduction. But this must not be allowed to obscure the struggles which through uncertainties motor the working parts. Many aspects of "the lads" culture, for instance, are challenging and subversive and remain threatening. There are many breaks, lags, antagonisms, deep struggles and real subversive logics within and behind cultural processes of reproduction which fight for outcomes other than those which satisfy the system for the moment.

This uncertainty also warns against any simple teleological notion of capitalist development. The huge growth of the state in welfare and education, for instance, is not necessarily in any "best" interests of capitalism. It has to some extent been forced on it by competing groups using their own real freedoms for self-advancement as they have seen it. Of course state agencies have been utilised and modified to help cool out, or drive out, problems which capitalism produces but cannot solve. But whilst they help to solve problems these institutions cannot wholly be absorbed back into capitalism. They maintain spaces and potential oppositions, keep alive issues, and prod nerves which capitalism would much rather were forgotten. Their personnel are in no simple sense servants of capitalism. They solve, confuse or postpone its problems in the short term very often because of their commitment to professional goals which are finally and awkwardly independent from the functional needs of capitalism. They may help, unconsciously, in unintended tended forms of class reproduction but all the same this may also involve the heightening of opposition and criticism which the dominant class could well do without. State agencies and institutions often take contradictions further, and faster, and in stranger, more displaced and disoriented forms, than any pure capitalism could dream of. The bureaucratic educational welfare state machine so characteristic of Western capitalism must be seen in part as the result of a cumulative encrustment which capitalism manages to turn to its advantage rather than as the expression of its own will or straightforward domination. Its own uncertainty makes it prone to mutation and further gives it life in mutation.

## Reproduction and State Institutions

This study gives more precise suggestions, especially concerning the significance of systematic misrecognition and unintended consequence, for conceptualising the role of institutions in cultural and social reproduction.

In the first place we must not expect particular kinds of reproduction to take place tidily in discrete kinds of institution. Just as the school and its formal timetable lies tangential to the real processes of learning and of the preparation of manual labour power, other kinds of institution may lie awkwardly against real social functions. The particular meaning and scope of the role of institutions in reproduction may be less to do with their formal nature and manifest communications than with the unintended and often unseen results of their relationships and habituated patterns of interaction with located and informal cultures. Furthermore, the same institution may play very different roles in different kinds of reproduction, so that, for instance, the school is more central to the preparation of mental labour power than to manual labour power.

In the second place it suggests that institutions cannot be studied as simple unities. They have at least three levels which we might describe as the official, the pragmatic and the cultural. At the official level an institution is likely to have a formal account of its purpose in relation to its view of the main structural and organisational features of society and how they interrelate (or might be made to interrelate). In a liberal democratic society such as ours, it would be quite wrong to assume that state institutions like the school are run in any obvious or intentional way for the benefit of the dominant class (as are private schools for instance) Their conscious and centrally directed aim is not to promote two very different kinds of ideology suited to the needs of acknowledged inferior and superior classes. Their educated, concerned and honest liberal agents would not countenance that. Furthermore, this level of institutional practice is most directly related to the political realm proper and all the determinants and interests which operate there. Part of the dominant social democratic political pressure since the war has been to equalise provision, or at least to equalise access to provision through the reform and development of institutions. Convergence, not divergence, has been the main official tendency.

It is, of course, an absolute requirement for the existing social system that the same standards, ideologies and aspirations are not really passed on to all. The success of the official ideology, or what amounts to the same thing the demise of its oppositional cultural reproduction, in many institutions would be catastrophic for social reproduction in general. The "transition" from school to work, for instance, of working class kids who had really absorbed the rubric of self-development, satisfaction and interest in work, would be a terrifying battle. Armies of kids equipped with their "self-concepts" would be fighting to enter the few meaningful jobs available, and masses of employers would be struggling to press them into meaningless work. In these circumstances there would indeed be a much greater "problem" of "careers guidance" than we have now. Either a gigantic propaganda exercise of wartime proportions or direct physical coercion would be needed to get the kids into the factories. Since this is not yet required, and since social reproduction of the class society in general continues despite the intervention of the liberal state and its institutions, it may be suggested that some of the real functions of institutions work counter to their stated aims. This misrecognition, it can be suggested, helps to maintain many of the cultural processes taking place within particular institutions which contribute towards social reproduction. At the second, the pragmatic level, official ideologies and aims are mediated to the agents and functionaries of particular institutions. They are likely to appreciate something of the more theoretical rationale for the prevailing or coming "official" ideology, but they are also mainly interested in their own face to face problems of control and direction and the day to day pressures of their own survival within the inherited institution. They run a practical eye over "official" ideology. They will adopt newly sanctioned ideologies, for instance, only when they seem to offer real and practical help—though they may well justify the change, even to themselves, with the rubric of the purer received ideology. It is this practical engagement which very often prevents the agents from seeing what is happening below them.

At the third level "below" the others are the cultural forms of adaption of the institution's clients as their outside class experience interacts with the practical exigencies and processes of the institution as they strike them. One of the important variants of this is likely to be an oppositional informal culture which may well actually help to accomplish the wider social reproduction which the official policy has been trying to defeat or change. As we have seen in this book, where they occur at a cultural level the destruction of official myths and illusions and a canny assessment of the world do not stop incorporation into that world. They can aid it. If the specificity of the institution and vulnerability of its ideology help to promote certain kinds of oppositional cultures and their characteristic penetrations it also helps to disorientate them into their accommodative mode by providing or strengthening powerful limitations. In particular it is likely to generate divisions especially in the area of its own proper concerns and also between the formal and informal. Though the school, for instance, is not effective in the way it hopes to be, it is an extremely important location, and proximate cause of renaissance of oppositional class culture experienced by a good percentage of working class boys during their 3rd, 4th and 5th years at school. This renaissance leads to changes and refinements in the subjective inhabitation of labour power which lead to very concrete outcomes. In contradictory and unintended ways the counter-school culture actually achieves for education one of its main though misrecognised objectives—the direction of a proportion of working kids "voluntarily" to skilled, semi-skilled and unskilled manual work. Indeed far from helping to cause the present "crisis" in education, the counter-school culture and the processes it sponsors has helped to prevent a real crisis.

I suggest that all major changes in institutional organisation might be thought through in terms of these three levels. In the case of education, for instance, progressivism has been developed and theorised as an official ideology by academics in conjunction with wider social democratic, political and institutional movements to increase educational provision and access for the working class. At the pragmatic level, however, progressivism is taken up in schools mainly as a practical solution to practical problems without any real shift in basic philosophies of education. At the cultural level it can be argued that often "progressivism" has had the contradictory and unintended effect of helping to strengthen processes within the counter-school culture which are responsible for the particular subjective preparation of labour power and acceptance of a working class future in a way which is the very opposite of progressive intentions in education. It is this strengthened cultural reproduction in relation to the school which of course guarantees the future of educational experiment by always limiting the scope of its success.

This is no simple argument against, or criticism of, progressivism or other kinds of institutional reform. Any kind of educational, or other, change will encounter its own forms of unintention, contradiction, and unseen forms of reproduction in complex links to class cultures and the objective requirements of the outside system. This is rather the point: that no institutional objectives, no moral or pedagogic initiative, moves in the clear still air of good intention and Newtonian cultural mechanics. Every move must be considered in relation to its context and likely circles of effectiveness within the netherworld (usually to institutional and official eyes) of cultural reproduction and the main world of social class relationships.

# STUDY QUESTIONS

1. According to Willis, cultural forms are marked by both *limitations* and *penetrations*. What does he mean by these terms and what purposes do they serve in his argument?
2. Willis says that institutions like schools have three important levels: the official, the pragmatic, and the cultural. What does he mean by this and how does it shape his conclusions?

# 31

# NAMING AS POWER

PIERRE BOURDIEU

In the book of Genesis, God creates man and places him in a garden. "And God said, Let us make man in our image, after our likeness: and let them have dominion over the fish of the sea, and over the fowl of the air, and over the cattle, and over all the earth, and over every creeping thing that creepeth upon the earth." From the perspective of cultural sociology, what happens next is telling: "And out of the ground the Lord God formed every beast of the field, and every fowl of the air; and brought *them* unto Adam to see what he would call them: and whatsoever Adam called every living creature, that *was* the name thereof." So says the King James Version of the Bible.

What's interesting about this myth is how clearly it shows the power of naming—of classifying things—as a way of having dominion and power over the world. Adam alone carries out the task of naming and does so with complete and unchallenged authority: he does all the naming before Eve is even created. If it had been otherwise, the Garden of Eden might have been the scene of some serious lovers' quarrels.

In this excerpt, Pierre Bourdieu (1930–2002), one of most influential sociologists of the twentieth century, revives a classical sociological theme: the ability to impose one's system of classification on the world is a fundamental form of social power (See Durkheim and Mauss pp. 12–21). Unlike the Bible story where Adam possesses absolute control, the process of installing classification and naming schemes on the world is never carried out alone and is seldom if ever unchallenged. Different groups with different agendas battle for the authority to impose their worldview as *the* legitimate view. In the modern era, science has gained this authority, which Bourdieu calls "the monopoly of *official naming,*" in large part because it is backed by the power of the state. The task of social science is not just to question this authority by exposing how it serves the interests of particular groups (scientists, for example), but also to expose the way it operates as a kind of symbolic violence—coercing other groups to accept the logic and classification schemes of science or risk exclusion and marginalization if they refuse.

## The Perception of the Social World and Political Struggle

The most resolutely objectivist theory must take account of agents' representation of the social world and, more precisely, of the contribution they make to the construction of the vision of this world, and, thereby to the very construction of this world, via the *labour of representation* (in all senses of the term) that they continually perform in order to impose their own vision of the world or the vision of their own position in this world, that is, their social identity. The perception of the social world is the product of a double social structuring: on the "objective" side, this perception is socially structured because the properties attached to agents or institutions do not make themselves available to perception independently, but in combinations whose probability varies widely (and just as feathered animals have a greater chance of having wings than furry animals, so the possessors of a substantial cultural capital are more likely to be museum visitors than those who lack such capital); on the "subjective" side, it is structured because the schemes of perception and evaluation susceptible of being brought into operation at a given moment, including all those which are laid down in language, are the product of previous symbolic struggles and express, in a more or less transformed form, the state of symbolic relations of power. The fact remains, none the less, that the objects of the social world can be perceived and expressed in different ways because, like the objects of the natural world, they always include a certain indeterminacy and vagueness—because, for example, the most constant combinations of properties are never founded on anything other than statistical connections between interchangeable features; and also because, as historical objects, they are subject to variations in time and their meaning, in so far as it depends on the future, is itself in suspense, in a pending and deferred state, and is thus relatively indeterminate. This element of risk, of uncertainty, is what provides a basis for the plurality of world views, a plurality which is itself linked to the plurality of points of view, and to all the symbolic struggles for the production and imposition of the legitimate vision of the world and, more precisely, to all the cognitive strategies of *fulfilment* which produce the meaning of the objects of the social world by going beyond the directly visible attributes by reference to the future or the past. This reference may be implicit and tacit, through what Husserl calls protension and retention, practical forms of prospection or retrospection excluding the positioning of past and future as such; or it may be explicit, as in political struggles in which the past, with the retrospective reconstruction of a past adjusted to the needs of the present . . . and especially the future, with the creative foresight associated with it, are continually invoked, in order to determine, delimit, and define the ever-open meaning of the present.

To point out that perception of the social world implies an act of construction is not in the least to accept an intellectualist theory of knowledge: the essential part of one's experience of the social world and of the labour of construction it implies takes place in practice, without reaching the level of explicit representation and verbal expression. Closer to a class unconscious than to a "class consciousness" in the Marxist sense, the sense of the position one occupies in the social space (what Goffman calls the "sense of one's place") is the practical mastery of the social structure as a whole which reveals itself through the sense of the position occupied in that structure. The categories of perception of the social world are essentially the product of the incorporation of the objective structures of the social space. Consequently, they incline agents to accept the social world as it is, to take it for granted, rather than to rebel against it, to put forward opposed and even antagonistic possibilities. The sense of one's place, as the sense of what one can or cannot "allow oneself," implies a tacit acceptance of one's position, a sense of limits ("that's not meant for us") or— what amounts to the same thing—a sense of distances, to be marked and maintained, respected, and expected of others. And this is doubtless all the more true when the conditions of existence are more rigorous and the reality principle is more rigorously imposed. (Hence the profound realism which most often characterizes the world view of the dominated and which, functioning as a sort of socially constituted instinct of conservation, can appear conservative only with reference to an external and thus normative representation of the "objective interest" of those whom it helps to live or to survive.)

If the objective relations of power tend to reproduce themselves in visions of the social world which contribute to the permanence of those relations, this is therefore because the structuring principles of the world view are rooted in the objective structures of the social world and because the relations of power are also present in people's minds in the form of the categories of perception of those relations. But the degree of indeterminacy and vagueness characteristic of the objects of the social world is, together with the practical, pre-reflexive and implicit character of the patterns of perception and evaluation which are applied to them, the Archimedean point which is objectively made available to truly political action. Knowledge of the social world and, more precisely, the categories which make it possible, are the stakes *par excellence* of the political struggle, a struggle which is inseparably theoretical and practical, over the power of preserving or transforming the social world by preserving or transforming the categories of perception of that world.

The capacity for bringing into existence in an explicit state, of publishing, of making public (i.e. objectified, visible, sayable, and even official) that which, not yet having attained objective and collective existence, remained in a state of individual or serial existence—people's disquiet, anxiety, expectation, worry—represents a formidable social power, that of bringing into existence groups by establishing the *common sense*, the explicit consensus, of the whole group. In fact, this labour of categorization, of making things explicit and classifying them, is continually being performed, at every moment of ordinary existence, in the struggles in which agents clash over the meaning of the social world and their position in it, the meaning of their social identity, through all the forms of speaking well or badly of someone or something, of blessing or cursing and of malicious gossip, eulogy, congratulations, praise, compliments, or insults, rebukes, criticism, accusations, slanders, etc.

It is easy to understand why one of the elementary forms of political power should have consisted, in many archaic societies, in the almost magical power of *naming* and bringing into existence by virtue of naming. Thus in traditional Kabylia, the function of making things explicit and the labour of symbolic production that poets performed, particularly in crisis situations, when the meaning of the world is no longer clear, conferred on them major political functions, those of the war-lord or ambassador. But with the growing differentiation of the social world and the constitution of relatively autonomous fields, the labour of the production and imposition of meaning is performed in and through struggles in the field of cultural production (and especially in the political sub-field); it becomes the particular concern, the specific interest, of the professional producers of objectified representations of the social world, or, more precisely, of the methods of objectification.

If the legitimate mode of perception is such an important stake in different struggles, this is because on the one hand the movement from the implicit to the explicit is in no way automatic, the same experience of the social being recognizable in very different expressions, and on the other hand, the most marked objective differences may be hidden behind more immediately visible differences (such as, for example, those which separate ethnic groups). It is true that perceptual configurations, social *Gestalten*, exist objectively, and that the proximity of conditions and thus of dispositions tends to be re-translated into durable links and groupings, immediately perceptible social units such as socially distinct regions or districts (with spatial segregation), or sets of agents possessing altogether similar visible properties, such as Weber's *Stände*. But the fact remains that socially known and recognized differences exist only for a subject capable not only of perceiving the differences, but of recognizing them as significant and interesting, i.e., exists only for a subject endowed with the aptitude and the inclination to *establish* the differences which are held to be significant in the social world under consideration.

In this way, the social world, particularly through properties and their distribution, attains, in the objective world itself, the status of a *symbolic system* which, like a system of phonemes, is organized in accordance with the logic of difference, of differential deviation, which is thus constituted as significant *distinction*. The social space, and the differences that "spontaneously" emerge within it, tend to function symbolically as *a space of lifestyles* or as a set of *Stände*, of groups characterized by different life-styles.

Distinction does not necessarily imply, as is often supposed, following Veblen and his theory of conspicuous consumption, a quest for distinction. All consumption and, more generally, all practice, is *conspicuous*, visible, whether or not it was performed *in order to be seen*: it is distinctive, whether or not it was inspired by the desire to get oneself noticed, to make oneself conspicuous, to distinguish oneself or to act with distinction. Hence, every practice is bound to function as a *distinctive sign* and, when the difference is recognized, legitimate and approved, as a *sign of distinction* (in all senses of the term). The fact remains that social agents, being capable of perceiving as significant distinctions the "spontaneous" differences that their categories of perception lead them to consider as pertinent, are also capable of intentionally underscoring these spontaneous differences in life-style by what Weber calls "the stylization of life" (*Stilisierung des Lebens*). The pursuit of distinction—which may be expressed in ways of speaking or in a refusal to countenance marrying beneath one's station—produces separations which are meant to be perceived or, more precisely, known and recognized as legitimate differences— most frequently as differences of nature (in French we speak of "natural distinction").

Distinction—in the ordinary sense of the word—is the difference written into the very structure of the social space when it is perceived in accordance with the categories adapted to that structure; and the Weberian *Stand*, which people so often like to contrast with the Marxist class, is the class adequately constructed when it is perceived through the categories of perception derived from the structure of that space. Symbolic capital— another name for distinction—is nothing other than capital, of whatever kind, when it is perceived by an agent endowed with categories of perception arising from the incorporation of the structure of its distribution, i.e. when it is known and recognized as self-evident. Distinctions, as symbolic transformations of *de facto* differences, and, more generally, the ranks, orders, grades and all the other symbolic hierarchies, are the product of the application of schemes of construction which—as in the case, for instance, of the pairs of adjectives used to express most social judgements—are the product of the incorporation of the very structures to which they are applied; and recognition of the most absolute legitimacy is nothing other than an apprehension of the everyday social world as taken for granted, an apprehension which results from the almost perfect coincidence of objective structures and incorporated structures.

It follows, among other consequences, that symbolic capital is attracted to symbolic capital and that the—real—autonomy of the field of symbolic production does not prevent this field from remaining dominated, in its functioning, by the constraints which dominate the social field as a whole. It also follows that objective relations of power tend to reproduce themselves in symbolic relations of power, in visions of the social world which contribute to ensuring the permanence of those relations of power. In the struggle for the imposition of the legitimate vision of the social world, in which science itself is inevitably involved, agents wield a power which is proportional to their symbolic capital, that is, to the recognition they receive from a group. The authority which underlies the performative effectiveness of discourse about the social world, the symbolic force of visions and pre-visions aimed at imposing the principles of vision and division of this world, is a *percipi*, a being known and recognized (*nobilis*), which allows a *percipere* to be imposed. It is the most *visible* agents, from the point of view of the prevailing categories of perception, who are the best placed to change the vision by changing the categories of perception. But they are also, with a few exceptions, the least inclined to do so.

## The Symbolic Order and the Power of Naming

In the symbolic struggle for the production of common sense or, more precisely, for the monopoly of legitimate *naming* as the official—i.e. explicit and public—imposition of the legitimate vision of the social world, agents bring into play the symbolic capital that they have acquired in previous struggles, in particular all the power that they possess over the instituted taxonomies, those inscribed in people's minds or in the objective world, such as qualifications. Thus all the symbolic strategies through which agents aim to impose their vision of the divisions of the social world and of their position in that world can be located between two extremes: the insult, that *idios logos* through which an ordinary individual attempts to impose his point of view by taking the risk that a reciprocal insult may ensue, and the *official naming*, a symbolic act of imposition which has on its side all the strength of the collective, of the consensus, of common sense, because it is performed by a delegated agent of the state, that is, the holder of the *monopoly of legitimate symbolic violence*. On the one hand, there is the world of particular perspectives, of individual agents who, on the basis of their particular point of view, their particular position, produce namings—of themselves and others—that are particular and self-interested (nicknames, insults, or even accusations, indictments, slanders, etc.), and all the more powerless to gain recognition, and thus to exert a truly symbolic effect, the

less their authors are *authorized*, either personally (*auctoritas*) or institutionally (by delegation), and the more directly they are concerned to gain recognition for the point of view that they are seeking to impose. On the other
hand, there is the authorized point of view of an agent who is personally
authorized, such as a great critic or prestigious preface-writer or established author (Zola's "*J'accuse*"), and above all the legitimate point of view
of the authorized spokesperson, the delegate of the state, the official naming, or the *title* or qualification which, like an educational qualification, is
valid on all markets and which, as an official definition of one's official
identity, saves its bearers from the symbolic struggle of all against all, by
establishing the authorized perspective, the one recognized by all and thus
universal, from which social agents are viewed . . . The truth is that scientific analysis does not have to choose between perspectivism and what has
to be called absolutism: indeed, the truth of the social world is the stake in
a struggle between agents who are very unequally equipped to attain
absolute, that is, self-verifying, vision and pre-vision.

> One could analyse from this point of view the functioning of an institu-
> tion such as the French national statistics office, INSEE, a state institute
> which, by producing the official taxonomies that are invested with a
> quasi-legal authority, and, particularly in the relations between employ-
> ers and employees, that of a qualification capable of conferring rights
> independent of actually performed productive activity, tends to fix hier-
> archies and thereby to sanction and consecrate a relation of power
> between agents with respect to the names of professions and occupa-
> tions, an essential component of social identity. The management of
> names is one of the instruments of the management of material scarcity,
> and the names of groups, especially of professional groups, record a par-
> ticular state of struggles and negotiations over the official designations
> and the material and symbolic advantages associated with them. The
> professional name granted to agents, the title they are given, is one of the
> positive or negative retributions (for the same reason as one's salary), in
> so far as it is a *distinctive mark* (emblem or stigma) which takes its *value*
> from its position in a hierarchically organized system of titles, and which
> thereby contributes to the determination of the relative positions between
> agents and groups. As a consequence of this, agents resort to practical or
> symbolic strategies aimed at maximizing the symbolic profit of naming:
> for example, they may give up the economic gratifications assured by a
> certain job so as to occupy a less well paid position, but one which is

endowed with a more prestigious name; or they may orient themselves towards positions whose designations are less precise, and thus escape the effects of symbolic devaluation. In the same way, in the expression of their personal identity, they may give themselves a name which includes them in a class which is sufficiently broad to include agents occupying positions superior to their own, such as the "instituteur" or primary-school teacher who calls himself an "enseignant" or teacher, without specifying the level at which he teaches. More generally, agents always have a choice between several names and they may play on the uncertainties and the effects of vagueness linked to the plurality of perspectives so as to try to escape the verdict of the official taxonomy.

But the logic of official naming is most clearly demonstrated in the case of the *title*—whether titles of nobility, educational qualifications or professional titles. This is a symbolic capital that is socially and even legally guaranteed. The nobleman is not only someone who is known, famous, and even renowned for his good qualities, prestigious, in a word, *nobilis*: he is also someone who is recognized by an *official* authority, one that is "universal", i.e. known and recognized by all. The professional or academic title is a sort of legal rule of social perception, a being-perceived that is guaranteed as a right. It is symbolic capital in an institutionalized, legal (and no longer merely legitimate) form. More and more inseparable from the educational qualification, by virtue of the fact that the educational system tends more and more to represent the ultimate and unique guarantor of all professional titles, it has a value in itself and, although we are dealing with a common noun, it functions like a great name (the name of some great family or a proper name), one which procures all sorts of symbolic profit (and goods that one cannot directly acquire with money). It is the symbolic scarcity of the title in the space of the names of professions that tends to govern the rewards of the profession (and not the relation between the supply of and demand for a certain form of labour). It follows that the rewards associated with the title tend to become autonomous with regard to the rewards associated with the work. In this way, the same work can receive different remunerations depending on the titles and qualifications of the person doing it (e.g. a permanent, official post-holder as opposed to a part-timer or someone acting in that capacity, etc.). The qualification is in itself an *institution* (like language) that is more durable than the intrinsic characteristics of the work, and so the rewards associated with the qualification can be maintained despite changes in the work and its relative value: it is not the relative value of the work which determines the value of the name, but the institutionalized value of the title which acts as an instrument serving to defend and maintain the value of the work.

This means that one cannot establish a science of classifications without establishing a science of the struggle over classifications and without taking into account the position occupied, in this struggle for the power of knowledge, for power through knowledge, for the monopoly of legitimate symbolic violence, by each of the agents or groups of agents involved in it, whether they be ordinary individuals, exposed to the vicissitudes of everyday symbolic struggle, or authorized (and full-time) professionals, which includes all those who speak or write about social classes, and who can be distinguished by the extent to which their classifications involve the authority of the state, as holder of the monopoly of *official naming*, of the right classification, of the right order.

While the structure of the social field is defined at each moment by the structure of the distribution of capital and the profits characteristic of the different particular fields, the fact remains that in each of these arenas, the very definition of the stakes and the trump cards can be called into question. Every field is the site of a more or less openly declared struggle for the definition of the legitimate principles of division of the field. The question of legitimacy arises from the very possibility of this questioning, from this break with the doxa which takes the ordinary order for granted. That being said, the symbolic force of the parties involved in this struggle is never completely independent of their positions in the game, even if the specifically symbolic power of naming constitutes a force which is relatively independent of the other forms of social power. The constraints of the necessity inscribed in the very structure of the different fields still weigh on the symbolic struggles which aim to preserve or transform that structure. The social world is, to a great extent, something which agents make at every moment; but they have no chance of unmaking and remaking it except on the basis of a realistic knowledge of what it is and of what they can do to it by virtue of the position they occupy in it.

In short, scientific work aims to establish an adequate knowledge both of the space of objective relations between the different positions which constitute the field and of the necessary relations that are set up, through the mediation of the habitus of those who occupy them, between these positions and the corresponding stances, i.e. between the points occupied in that space and the points of view on that very space, which play a part in the reality and development of that space. In other words, the objective delimitation of constructed classes, of *regions* of the constructed space of positions, enables one to understand the source and effectiveness of the classificatory strategies by means of which agents seek to preserve or modify this space, in the forefront of which we must place the constitution of groups organized with a view to defending the interests of their members.

Analysis of the struggle over classifications brings to light the political ambition which haunts the gnoseological ambition to produce the correct classification: an ambition which properly defines the *rex*, the one who has the task, according to Benveniste, of *regere fines* and *regere sacra*, of tracing in speech the frontiers between groups, and also between the sacred and the profane, good and evil, the vulgar and the distinguished. If social science is not to be merely a way of pursuing politics by other means, social scientists must take as their object the intention of assigning others to classes and of thereby telling them what they are and what they have to be (herein lies all the ambiguity of forecasting); they must analyse, in order to repudiate it, the ambition of the creative world vision, that sort of *intuitus originarius* which would make things exist in conformity with its vision (herein lies all the ambiguity of the Marxist conception of class, which is inseparably both a being and an ought-to-be). They must objectify the ambition of objectifying, of classifying from outside, objectively, agents who are struggling to classify others and themselves. If they do happen to classify—by carving up, for the purposes of statistical analysis, the continuous space of social positions—it is precisely so as to be able to objectify *all* forms of objectification, from the individual insult to the official naming, without forgetting the claim, characteristic of science in its positivist and bureaucratic definition, to arbitrate in these struggles in the name of "axiological neutrality." The symbolic power of agents, understood as a power of making people see—*theorein*—and believe, of producing and imposing the legitimate or legal classification, depends, as the case of *rex* reminds us, on the position they occupy in the space (and in the classifications that are potentially inscribed in it). But to objectify objectification means, above all, objectifying the field of production of the objectified representations of the social world, and in particular of the legislative taxonomies, in short, the field of cultural or ideological production, a game in which the social scientist is himself involved, as are all those who debate the nature of social classes.

# STUDY QUESTIONS

1. What does Bourdieu mean by the *labor of representation?* How is this concept central to his argument about the power of naming?
2. Bourdieu argues that social scientists struggle to impose classification systems on the world and that this is what makes their work political. What, according to him, must social scientists do to avoid politics?

# 32

# CULTURE, CLASS, AND RACE

JAY MACLEOD

As an undergraduate student, Jay MacLeod worked as a youth coun-
selor for impoverished kids in a housing project. He worked with two
different groups of young boys, aged eleven to thirteen, and observed
two very different sets of attitudes about the future. One group, which
he dubbed the Hallway Hangers, expressed deep pessimism and hopelessness about the American Dream of upward mobility, the fabled
idea that anyone who works hard and gets an education can climb the
ladder of success. The other group of boys, The Brothers, were much
less skeptical. For the most part, they embraced the idea of individual
achievement and were hopeful about their chances for success.
MacLeod was puzzled by what he saw: how could two groups of
young kids from the same low-income neighborhood hold such different perspectives on their life chances? Maybe it had something to
do with race? One group was white and the other black. If race did
play a role in shaping kids' expectations about the future, it was not
the role we might expect: The hopeful kids were black, the pessimistic kids, white.

MacLeod's unanswered questions led him to conduct an ethnographic study, which became an instant sociological classic when it was
published in 1987. Eight years later, he revisited his field site and followed up with the boys—now young men—he had previously studied.
The excerpt included here reflects on the ways in which the cultural
attitudes and mindsets of The Brothers and the Hallway Hangers did
and did not prepare them for life after high school. In MacLeod's

view, the American ideology of achievement plays an important role in shaping both aspirations and attainment of low-income youth, but in the end, neither group of boys was well-served by the attitudes and behaviors they adopted in response to the achievement ideology.

# CONCLUSION: OUTCLASSED
# AND OUTCAST(E)

One afternoon, while hitchhiking to the city, I was picked up by a motorist in a BMW. The charitable middle-aged man chatted away for an hour about his teenage children. As we drove into the city and past Clarendon Heights, however, he peered at the young men lounging in the project's doorways, shook his head in disgust, and dismissed them as ignorant, lazy losers. That sort of causal simplicity is attractive: Losers lose; wanting individuals lead to wasted lives; poverty is self-generated. What we see on the streets, however, is actually complex. Once we push beneath the surface texts of individual lives, we discover the hard contours of structural inequality.

Our society is *structured* to create poverty and extreme economic inequality. There are simply not enough good jobs to go around. For every boss there are many workers, and the gap in their pay is unparalleled among industrialized nations. Chief executives of large U.S. companies made 160 times as much as the average blue-collar worker in 1989.[1] Indeed, while Juan, Mokey, Stoney, and Shorty struggled to survive on earnings of five dollars per hour, top corporate executives routinely raked in up to $5,000 per hour (including stock options and other income).[2] By 1993 the median pay package for the chief executive officers of the Fortune 1,000 largest companies was worth over $2.4 million. By comparison, the median annual earnings for everyone over fifteen years of age in 1992 was $17,696.[3] Our occupational structure is shaped much like the Eiffel Tower. There is little room at the top, a larger but still limited number of tolerably well-paid positions in the middle, and near the bottom a wide band of inferior positions (with no "positions" at all for the unemployed). This roughly pyramidal structure ensures that even if everyone excels in school and strives ceaselessly for the top, the great majority are automatically bound to be disappointed.

The occupational structure guarantees a vast divide between rich and poor. In 1989, 1 percent of the population owned 37 percent of the wealth and 10 percent of the population owned 86 percent of the wealth.[4] By the end of Reagan's second term, 32 million Americans were living below the poverty level and the gap between rich and poor was at an all-time high.[5] Consider not only the sheer magnitude of inequality between winners and losers but also the fact that most losers have had to play on a field slanted against them. The pyramid isn't shaken up and recast from scratch for each generation; rather, families tend to occupy similar locations in the social division of labor over time. Families at the top of the class structure can use their superior status and resources to stay there, while other families, low on options, languish at the bottom. We are all born into a social class, and most of us die in the one into which we were born. Although a few working-class individuals with dedication and ability will rise to the top of the heap, most (including many who are just as conscientious and able) will remain close to where they started.[6]

The United States has a remarkably stable class structure, albeit one that is obscured by the rhetoric of classlessness. To be sure, social mobility does exist—just enough to maintain the myth of America as the land of opportunity. Whereas a completely closed society cannot maintain a semblance of openness, a society that allows some mobility, however meager, can always hold up the so-called self-made individual as "proof" that barriers to success are purely personal and that the poor are poor of their own accord. And so most Americans, the denounced teenagers often as much as the denouncer in the BMW, see poverty in purely individual terms rather than as structurally induced.

—————

## Poverty: A Class Issue

. . . Poverty is not a black issue. In absolute terms, most poor people are white, although a disproportionate number of African Americans are impoverished. Many of the black poor live in ghettos: urban neighborhoods that are racially segregated, economically devastated, socially stigmatized, and politically abandoned. As government and civic institutions have crumbled and the labor market has declined, the vacuum has largely been filled by "the blossoming of an underground economy dominated by the only expanding employment sector to which poor minority youths mise-ducated by public school can readily accede: the retail trade of drugs."[7] As a result, these enclaves of concentrated and pernicious poverty have become virtual war zones where terror, despair, and death are common-place. To much of the American public, however, the state of the ghetto signifies not the gross inadequacy of the welfare state but its overgeneros-ity to a black underclass that is morally dissolute, culturally deprived, and socially undeserving. The underclass has been twisted into a racial rather than a class formation, and poverty has become a black issue.

By bringing the white poor into view, our story dissolves the mistaken connection between African Americans and behavior associated with poverty—crime, family disruption, substance abuse, and so on. The Broth-ers and Hallway Hangers fail to follow the script penned by journalists, academics, politicians, and policy analysts. Because criminality is almost completely confined to the Hallway Hangers, this study debunks stereo-types about the black poor. Even in the case of white youths, what appears to be a tangle of pathology and purely self-destructive behavior turns out to have an underlying social rationality. Far from being a distinctive breed apart, the urban poor are ordinary human beings struggling to cope as best they can under oppressive circumstances. Poverty is not a moral problem, much less a black moral or cultural problem.

The underclass debate in the popular media divides the poor along racial lines, focuses the spotlight on African American poverty, and largely ignores the socio-economic context in which the drama is set. This book draws the white poor out of the shadows, widens the debate beyond race, and recovers the common class basis of exploitation that bedevils all the urban poor—black, white, Latino, Asian, or Native American.

Industrial restructuring—the decline of manufacturing, the suburban-ization of blue-collar employment, and the ascendancy of the service sector—has hit all the urban poor. Real wages and job security have fallen dramatically, as the experiences of the Hallway Hangers and Brothers illustrate, Layoffs, seasonal cutbacks, closings, and abrupt dismissals have been widespread for both groups of men. The economic recession of the late 1980s has exacerbated the instability of the low-wage labor market, and so has the weakening of labor unions and the absence of government regulation—both matters of public policy. It may be that insecurity and volatility are structural features of the new urban economy.

The experiences of both the Brothers and the Hallway Hangers also indicate that "career tracks" are sparse for uncredentialed individuals. The jobs these men manage to obtain seldom lead to a sequence of ascending positions with increased wages, responsibility, and security. Movement, when it occurs at all, tends to be lateral or between firms but not along an occupational ladder. Disappointed, workers like Mokey and Jinks move rapidly between dead-end jobs, a strategy that ends up reinforcing irregularity because they become even less attractive to employers. Contrary to popular perception, none of the Hallway Hangers or Brothers shun employment in low-wage entry-level positions as working for "chump change."

*Jm:* You're looking for a job now?

*Boo-Boo:* Yeah.

*Jm:* And how's that going?

*Boo-Boo:* Not that good. Not that good at all. I just gotta keep on looking. I'd even work at McDonald's or something. Just so I can get some money together, just til I can find something a little bit better. . . . I'll work at McDonald's if I have to. I need something. Sell newspapers, anything.

Boo-Boo's stated willingness to accept any job is no empty declaration: Among other places, he applied for work at car washes, grocery stores, and fast-food chains. Mokey, Shorty, and Slick echo Boo-Boo's willingness to accept poorly paid menial employment. What they and the others object to are so-called entry-level positions that lead nowhere.

Both groups of men have been stuck in the secondary labor market with low wages, infrequent raises, awkward working hours, minimal training, and high turnover. Only James has earned a family wage, and he was soon laid off. Only a couple of these men have held jobs with basic health and retirement benefits. Most cannot afford to own a car, let alone a home. Stable employment is the crucial pivot for social and cultural transitions into adulthood. Without it, many of these young men have been unable to contemplate settling down, marrying, or establishing households independent of parents. Their physical mobility has been minimal, and they have generally been excluded from leisure pursuits that most Americans take for granted. In short, the lives of both the Brothers and the Hallway Hangers have been severely circumscribed by their subordinate position in the class structure.

## Racial Domination: Invidious but Invisible

Both the Brothers and the Hallway Hangers are victims of class exploita-tion, but the African Americans among them have had to cope with racial oppression as well. Sometimes this oppression is brutally direct, as Shorty and Boo-Boo's contrasting experiences attest. Shorty assaulted several police officers after ransacking his girlfriend's apartment, but he was let off.

> *Shorty:* I had fucking, I coulda' been doing at least twenty years
> for that, right there. Three counts of mayhem, I had like eight
> assault and batteries on police officers, each one carries two
> and a half years to four and a half years. Mayhem alone carries
> fifteen to twenty. I had three of 'em for biting three cops. Lucky
> my brothers were cops. If I didn't have no brothers that are
> cops, I'd be, I'd be doing at least forty fucking years right now.
> *Jm:* So no charges were ever pressed?
> *Shorty:* Yeah, they pressed 'em at first, but then I got 'em all
> dropped. The judges were pissed off about that; they didn't like
> that. None of the cops showed up to court. I fucking lucked
> out big time then.

Contrast Shorty's experience with that of Boo-Boo when he was stopped by the police for reckless driving.

> *Boo-Boo:* I was drinkin' and drivin'; I was cheatin' on my girl-
> friend with this other girl, Josie, from the Heights. We were
> drivin' around. The cops, they beat me up and they called me
> nigger and black bastard and all this stuff, y'know. It was crazy.
> And they put me in jail. . . . They broke my nose and cracked
> my jaw, y'know, and ripped all my chains off my neck and
> scarred up my arms and all that stuff like that.

Racial domination is seldom as graphic and straightforward as police bru-tality, although some police officers are openly racist. Standing in front of Clarendon Heights one evening, I was asked by an officer in a cruiser, "Seen a carload of niggers drive by just now?" Doubtless, Boo-Boo was beat up largely because he is black. Yet there is also a history of police violence against white residents of Clarendon Heights: In the 1970s a white youth from Clarendon Heights was beaten by police in front of the project and died in custody. Moreover, black police officers can be just as brutal as their white colleagues. Even police violence cannot be explained in purely racial terms. Racial oppression, though it often takes the form of direct discrimination, is also more subtly embedded in the social order.

As African Americans, the Brothers are not as connected as the Hallway Hangers to informal networks that can provide access to jobs. Consider a string of three jobs Frankie held when he returned to the area from out of state.

*Frankie:* Then I moved back. I had my son. So I come back down here. I tried a little floor-laying.

*Jm:* How did you get in?

*Frankie:* Mutual friends, y'know. . . . Got the floor-layin' job. That didn't kick out. So I started seein' people, y'know, that I knew, guys that had jobs, and I went on to a few city jobs and state jobs—they were real good jobs, but doin' my drinkin'— like I had one job as a custodian up the high school, and it was a real good job. And I screwed that up by drinkin'. Y'know, it's a job where you got so much to do and then you can slack. And my slackin', I was leavin' the premises, goin' to the bar and playing the dogs, y'know. I just got in the way of fuckin' goin' to the bar and goin' to the dogs. So I left that. And when I left that I got another job through the same guy—a politician—and I was over to the big convention center and they made me crew chief. I was over there, I was a crew chief, and I didn't have a fuckin' inkling of what I was doin'. They have a cleanin' crew, just Spanish guys. Y'know, they couldn't even understand me. So I didn't show up much, evidently. But I was still gettin' paid. They paid me hours I didn't work. Y'know, I did eighty hours one week, and I was lucky to have worked ten, y'know. These were set jobs. And I couldn't even hold them. I know why today: cuz I was drinking.

Apart from access to jobs, personal connections provided some job security for Frankie. During roughly the same period, Juan, Mokey, and James all lost their jobs on account of minor infractions of bureaucratic rules in their workplaces. Frankie's experience also underlines the poor prospects of promotion for people of color. When people like Frankie come in at a supervisory level, people like the Brothers and Frankie's Spanish crew are robbed of opportunities for advancement. It is instructive that Frankie was able to exploit personal contacts to secure employment in the public sector, the area where antidiscrimination policies should most improve the prospects of racial and ethnic minorities. If Frankie can leapfrog over others in government jobs, it is no wonder that industries with informal hiring and training practices are virtually closed to the Brothers. Jobs in construction are a notorious case in point.[8] Slick, Shorty, Steve, and Jinks have all landed jobs in the construction industry through informal social networks. Jobs like roofing are hardly prestigious, secure, or highly paid; nevertheless, they are jobs for which white ethnic networking has given the white Hallway Hangers an edge over their black counterparts.

Their exclusion from occupational networks handicaps the Brothers, but they also have special tensions to negotiate if they do manage to get a job. In the new postindustrial service economy, both the Hallway Hangers and the Brothers are in closer contact with supervisors and clients than they would be in manufacturing jobs. The members of neither group have much social space in which to express their class and cultural identities. Frankie finds it difficult to interact with young, bossy, bourgeois supervisors, gossiping middle-aged colleagues, and the upper-class consumers whom his catering job served. But the Brothers must also deal with racial prejudice that stereotypes them as hoodlums. The interpersonal experiences of black jobholders, especially those who do not convey a mastery of middle-class cultural conventions, are a special source of tension in service jobs. Busing tables in a posh restaurant, Mokey will find it more difficult than Frankie to put customers at ease simply because his black skin evokes so many stereotypes.

For the black Brothers, race is so much a part of life that it figures only tangentially in their expressed worldviews. But to say that race is inscribed in the social scenery is not to denigrate its importance. On the contrary, the experiences of the Brothers and Hallway Hangers since 1984 beg the question of whether race is a more fundamental cleavage than class in American society.

# Race Versus Class: Can They Be Untangled?

On the face of it, race appears to have taken on heightened importance as these young men have sought jobs. Racial inequality seems to account for differences in outcome both between and within the two groups. Given their ambition, schooling, and skills, the Brothers could have been expected to leave the Hallway Hangers in the dust. They haven't. Indeed, the Brothers are only marginally better off than the Hangers. Moreover, the African Americans within each group have fared poorly relative to the whites. Of the Hallway Hangers, the two black members—Boo-Boo and Chris—are in the most desperate straits. And of the Brothers, the sole white member—Mike—has been far and away the most successful on the job market. Does race matter as much as (or more than) class in determining the economic fate of African Americans in Clarendon Heights?

. . . Class and race introduce objective structural contraints that individuals must face. The bricklayer's child has barriers to overcome that the banker's child need never negotiate. And blacks face limits on opportunity relative to whites. These are real differences rooted in objective material conditions.

On the subjective side, individuals can make of these objective conditions what they will in forging their identities. The bricklayer's son may look across his high school desk at the banker's boy sitting in front of him, shake his head dismissively, and silently wager that the other can't change the oil in his Volvo. Or he may see in the banker's son an effortless ease with girls, grades, and teachers and shake his head despairingly at his own oil-stained fingers. Or he may do both, depending on the context—which peers are around, who the teacher is, and whether the class is algebra or technical drawing. Both attitudes are subjective articulations of class identity that are ultimately rooted in objective economic inequality. But neither attitude can easily be traced to that source. The subjective refuses to be reduced to a reflex of the objective.

In fact, the Hallway Hangers completely invert objective reality in their subjective rendering of it. Their racial and gender identities as white working-class men are actually assets on the job market, whereas their class background puts them at a disadvantage. But most of the Hallway Hangers see exactly the reverse: They complain not about class oppression but about discrimination against white men. Here again, the views of the Hallway Hangers point to the potency, pervasiveness, and persuasiveness of neoconservative ideology and the historical slough of class analysis in the United States. Perhaps the Hallway Hangers fail to see class as a variable because they grew up so ensconced in their own class culture. Just as the Brothers do not consider race an issue, the Hallway Hangers fail to see class as constraining.

Like class, race has an objective dimension rooted in the structure of opportunities. Educational attainment, annual earnings, rates of employment, and a host of other measures confirm that African Americans are disadvantaged relative to whites. Yet race exists not just in material differences in power and resources but also in its subjective dimension—in individuals' minds as a category that shapes the way they view themselves and the social world. As with class, the subjective articulation of race seldom lines up with its objective dimension. Thus, although race is a central category by which both the Brothers and the Hallway Hangers understand themselves, neither group underscores the objective constraints faced by African Americans. Structural constraints on opportunity, whether rooted in race or class, are largely invisible to the young men in this study. The Hallway Hangers and the Brothers, like almost all Americans, tend to interpret their situation in individual rather than structural terms.

## Structure Versus Agency: "No One to Blame but Me"

Every individual in this study holds himself acountable for his condition. . . . The Brothers blamed themselves for their academic mediocrity. The Hallway Hangers were less self-critical but still reproached themselves for screwing up in school. Eight years later, for both groups, the verdict is similar. The previous chapter shows how the Brothers variously chastise themselves for being lazy, unmotivated, indecisive, unrealistic, overly opportunistic, fickle, and generally inept. Juan is straightforward: "I really screwed up." Super is equally succinct: "I just fucked everything up." The Hallway Hangers, it turns out, are also hard on themselves.

*(all in separate interviews)*

*Jinks:* I could kick myself in the ass, because if I stayed in school, I'd probably have a better job, and I'd be doing better in life right now.

*Chris:* I fucked up. I regret everything. I feel real bad about my mom. I just fucked up, man, fucked everything up. I'd like to regain back the trust of my family. Man, I wouldn't wish this situation on anyone.

*Stoney:* I was doing good for a while. Running this pizza place over in Medway. He gave me the keys, the boss did. I was running it, doing a good job, too. The money wasn't great but still. I ended up fucking the guy over. He vouched for me when I was in the pre-release center. I burned that bridge. About two months after I got out I said, "Here, here's the key, I'm fuckin' through, I'm sick of this." Shoulda stayed. Shoulda stuck it out. He might've given me more money, who knows? My judgment sucks sometimes.

*Frankie:* I know today I wasted a lot of my life. I had a lotta fun but I wasted a lot of it. Lotta guys went to jail, lotta guys were just fucked up, man. And I was fucked up in my own way.

*Boo-Boo:* I should never have got into drugs. I dunno, if I could do one thing, start all over again, I'd just go right back to school, I'd do my thing, wouldn't get tied up in all this bullshit I got tied up in.

*Steve:* I've been fucking up big time, Jay, no lie. Going away [to jail] too much, man. Fighting with my girl. I left her, and she called up and said I was doing drugs and drinkin' and all that other shit. Which I was. Called my probation officer and ratted me right out. . . . I dunno, dude, I guess I've got no one to blame but me.

Both the Brothers and the Hallway Hangers hold themselves responsible for their plight. Like most Americans, they point to personal vices and individual shortcomings to account for their subordinate position in the class structure.

But this is not the whole story. We have already seen that, apart from Mike and Derek, the Brothers blame not only themselves but also the socio-economic order for their failure to get ahead. James argues most forcefully that the economic system is also to blame. He acknowledges constraints on economic opportunity, holds the government accountable, and sympathizes with those who turn to illegal activity. But James also contends that lower-class culture prevents people from developing proper ambition.

> *Jm:* What do you think about the white kids at Clarendon Heights? Steve, Slick, Frankie, Jinks?
>
> *James:* They, er, gee, what can I say about that? They reached a certain level in their life and then they just stayed at that level. They just said, "Oh well, this is my life. This is what my life's gonna be." But it's all attitude, it's all if you wanna go farther than you are. They're gonna be in the Heights all their life. It's like back to, if you grow up in a certain environment, then that's what you gonna live. That's what you're gonna live all your life. That's what you're used to. And that's how their life is. It's the same as the Coopers next door. The Coopers next door are always gonna be the same. They're never gonna change. Fifty years from now a new set of Coopers will be the same exact as these Coopers. Because they've reached a certain level, and they're always gonna be at that level. I'm not down on them, that's all they know. They're gonna just say, "I stopped at that level." But you can't say that. You have to want more for your kids and for your grandkids.

Like social theorists, both the Brothers and the Hallway Hangers wrestle with the roles of structure, culture, and agency in the reproduction of social inequality.

. . . All three levels of analysis—the individual, the cultural, and the structural—play their part in the reproduction of social inequality. Had Slick been born into a middle-class family, he probably *would* be sitting in an office with a suit and tie on. Had his peer group been into Shakespeare and square roots rather than beer balls and bong hits, Slick might not be so blistered and dirty. Finally, Slick would be in better shape had he made different choices himself. Although all three levels have explanatory power, the structural one is primary because it reaches down into culture and individual agency. The culture of Clarendon Heights—with its violence, racism, and other self-destructive features (as well as its resilience, vitality, and informal networks of mutual support)—is largely a response to class exploitation in a highly stratified society. Similarly, Slick's individual strategies have developed not in a social vacuum but in the context of chronic social immobility and persistent poverty. To be sure, individual agency is important. Causality runs in both directions in a reflexive relationship between structure and agency. Structural constraints on opportunity lead to leveled aspirations, and leveled aspirations in turn affect job prospects. Contrary to popular belief, structure is still the source of inequality.

## Notes

1. J. Castro, "How's Your Pay?" *Time*, 15 April 1991, pp. 40–41.
2. "Corporate Executives Go to the Trough," *Dollars and Sense* 138 (1988):10–11. Cited in Thomas R. Shannon, Nancy Kleniewski, and William M Cross, *Urban Problems in Sociological Perspective* (Prospect Heights, Ill.: Waveland Press, 1991), p. 104.
3. David R. Francis, "Executive Pay in the U.S. Just Goes Up and Up," *Christian Science Monitor*, May 20, 1994, p. 9.
4. Cornel West, *Race Matters* (Boston: Beacon Press, 1993), p. 6.
5. Manning Marable, *Race, Reform, and Rebellion* (Jackson: University Press of Mississippi, 1991), p. 207.
6. Leonard Beeghley, "Individual and Structural Explanations of Poverty," *Population Research and Policy Review* 7 (1988):207.
7. Loïc J. D. Wacquant, "Morning in America, Dusk in the Dark Ghetto: The New 'Civil War' in the American City," *Revue française d'études américaines* 60 (May 1994):97–102.
8. See Roger Waldinger and Thomas Bailey, "The Continuing Significance of Race: Racial Conflict and Racial Discrimination in Construction," *Politics and Society* 19:3 (1991):291–323.

## STUDY QUESTIONS

1. How, according to MacLeod, is American society structured to create inequality and what role, if any, does culture play in this?
2. MacLeod examines both structural and cultural factors to explain the lack of mobility in the lives of the young men he studied. What does he conclude about the relative weight of these factors in explaining outcomes?

# 33

# FAMILIES, INSTITUTIONS, AND INEQUALITIES

ANNETTE LAREAU

In the small, rural, working-class town where I grew up, the neighborhood kids and I roamed around quite a bit. After school, we did homework and chores, then ventured out into the woods behind our houses or down to the riverbank to skip stones. On hot days, we rode our bikes out to the swimming hole, and in the winter we went sledding on the hill. Often, we just stayed in and watched whatever was on TV, filling the hours until our parents came home from work. Most of the time, there was no adult supervision, nor were there many organized sports to play.

In the urban, middle-class neighborhood where I live now, most families would never allow their kids to grow up the way I did. It's not just that they think it is unsafe to let their ten-year-olds roam around unsupervised (although many do), they also worry that the kind of unstructured play my friends and I engaged in would not be enriching enough. Without providing a steady stream of music lessons, sports leagues, after-school classes, and adult-supervised play dates, they fear they are somehow selling their kids short and failing to do what good parents do.

Annette Lareau, in a landmark study, observed middle-class and blue-collar families to get a better sense of how such families differ in their approach to parenting. Children from middle-class families, she

**notes, are beneficiaries of all kinds of enriched learning. Middle-class parents raise their kids to have a sense of entitlement and individuality— qualities that prepare them to see adults as equals and help them navigate a variety of social institutions, such as schools, that reward such characteristics. Children from working-class families, on the other hand, are raised with less supervision and instruction. Their parents teach them to respect and defer to their elders and to rely on peers and kin for support. This often leads to distance from (or even distrust of) authority figures such as teachers, and makes it harder for working-class kids to succeed at school. In this way, Lareau argues, the cultural values that adults hold about parenting can have a direct impact on the social structure of opportunities available to their kids.**

In the United States, people disagree about the importance of social class in daily life. Many Americans believe that this country is fundamentally *open*. They assume the society is best understood as a collection of individuals. They believe that people who demonstrate hard work, effort, and talent are likely to achieve upward mobility. Put differently, many Americans believe in the American Dream. In this view, children should have roughly equal life chances. The extent to which life chances vary can be traced to differences in aspirations, talent, and hard work on the part of individuals. This perspective rejects the notion that parents' social location systematically shapes children's life experiences and outcomes. Instead, outcomes are seen as resting more in the hands of individuals.

In a distinctly different but still related vein, some social scientists acknowledge that there are systemic forms of inequality, including, for example, differences in parents' educational levels, occupational prestige, and income, as well as in their child-rearing practices. These scholars, however, see such differences within society as a matter of *gradation*. To explain unequal life outcomes, they see it as helpful to look at, for example, differences in mothers' years of education or the range of incomes by households in a particular city. These different threads are interwoven in an intricate and often baffling pattern. Scholars who take this perspective on inequality typically focus on the ways specific patterns are related (e.g., the number of years of mothers' schooling and the size of children's vocabularies, or the number of years of mothers' education and parental involvement in schooling). Implicitly and explicitly, social scientists who share this perspective do not accept the position that there are identifiable, categorical differences in groups. They do not believe that the differences that do exist across society cohere into patterns recognizable as social classes.

. . . I have challenged both views. Rather than seeing society as a collection of individuals, I stressed the importance of individuals' social structural location in shaping their daily lives. Following a well-established European tradition, I rejected analyses that see differences in American families as best interpreted as a matter of fine gradations. Instead, I see as more valuable a *categorical* analysis, wherein families are grouped into social categories such as poor, working class, and middle class. I argued that these categories are helpful in understanding the behavior of family, members, not simply in one particular aspect but across a number of spheres. Family practices cohere by social class. Social scientists who accept this perspective may disagree about the number and type of categories and whether there should be, for example, an upper-middle-class category as well as a lower-middle-class one. Still, they agree that the observed differences in how people act can be meaningfully and fruitfully grouped into categories, without violating the complexity of daily life. My own view is that seeing selected aspects of family life as differentiated by social class is simply a better way to understand the reality of American family life. I also believe that social location at birth can be very important in shaping the routines of daily life, even when family members are not particularly conscious of the existence of social classes.

Thus, I have stressed how social class dynamics are woven into the texture and rhythm of children and parents' daily lives. Class position influences critical aspects of family life: time use, language use, and kin ties. Working-class and middle-class mothers may express beliefs that reflect a similar notion of "intensive mothering," but their behavior is quite different. For that reason, I have described sets of paired beliefs and actions as a "cultural logic" of child rearing. When children and parents move outside the home into the world of social institutions, they find that these cultural practices are not given equal value. There are signs that middle-class children benefit, in ways that are invisible to them and to their parents, from the degree of similarity between the cultural repertoires in the home and those standards adopted by institutions. . . .

# The Limits of Social Class

Among the families we observed, some aspects of daily life did not vary systematically by social class. There were episodes of laughter, emotional connection, and happiness as well as quiet comfort in every family. Harold McAllister and his mother laughed together as he almost dropped his hot dog but then, in an awkward grab, caught it. After a baseball game, Mr. Williams rubbed Alexander's head affectionately and called him "handsome." Ms. Handlon gave her daughter a big squeeze around her shoulders after the Christmas Eve pageant, and Melanie beamed. One summer afternoon, Mr. Yanelli and Billy played cards together, sitting cross-legged on the sidewalk. These moments of connection seemed deeply meaningful to both children and parents in all social classes, even as they take different shape by social class, in terms of language, activity, and character.

All the families we observed also had rituals: favorite meals they often ate, television programs they watched, toys or games that were very important, family outings they looked forward to, and other common experiences. The content of their rituals varied (especially by social class); what did not vary was that the children enjoyed these experiences and they provided a sense of membership in a family. Also, in all social classes, a substantial part of the children's days was spent in repetitive rituals: getting up, making the bed, taking a shower, getting dressed, brushing hair and teeth, eating breakfast, finding school books and papers, and waiting for adults to get ready. These moments were interspersed with hours, days, and weeks of household work, tedious demands, mundane tasks, and tension. This was true for all families, regardless of social class. Nor were any families immune to life tragedies: across all social classes there were premature deaths due to car accidents or suicides. Across all social classes children and parents had different temperaments: some were shy and quiet; some were outgoing and talkative. Some had a sense of humor and some did not. The degree of organization and orderliness in daily life also did not vary systematically by social class. Some houses were clean and some were a disaster. Some of the messiest ones were middle-class homes in which the entryway was a paragon of order but the living spaces, particularly the upstairs, were in a tumble. Despite the formidable differences among the families detailed in the previous chapters, in each home, after a few visits, the research assistants and I found that the surroundings felt normal, comfortable, and safe. Put differently, they all felt like home.

# Concerted Cultivation and the Accomplishment of Natural Growth

Despite these important areas of shared practices, social class made a significant difference in the routines of children's daily lives. The white and Black middle-class parents engaged in practices of *concerted cultivation*. In these families, parents actively fostered and assessed their children's talents, opinions, and skills. They scheduled their children for activities. They reasoned with them. They hovered over them and outside the home they did not hesitate to intervene on the children's behalf. They made a deliberate and sustained effort to stimulate children's development and to cultivate their cognitive and social skills. The working-class and poor parents viewed children's development as unfolding spontaneously, as long as they were provided with comfort, food, shelter, and other basic support. I have called this cultural logic of child rearing the *accomplishment of natural growth*. As with concerted cultivation, this commitment, too, required ongoing effort; sustaining children's natural growth despite formidable life challenges is properly viewed as accomplishment. Parents who relied on natural growth generally organized their children's lives so they spent time in and around home, in informal play with peers, siblings, and cousins. As a result, the children had more autonomy regarding leisure time and more opportunities for child-initiated play. They also were more responsible for their lives outside the home. Unlike in middle-class families, adult-organized activities were uncommon. Instead of the relentless focus on reasoning and negotiation that took place in middle-class families, there was less speech (including less whining and badgering) in working-class and poor homes. Boundaries between adults and children were clearly marked; parents generally used language not as an aim in itself but more as a conduit for social life. Directives were common. In their institutional encounters, working-class and poor parents turned over responsibility to professionals; when parents did try to intervene, they felt that they were less capable and less efficacious than they would have liked. While working-class and poor children differed in important ways, particularly in the stability of their lives, surprisingly there was not a major difference between them in their cultural logic of child rearing. Instead, in this study the cultural divide appeared to be between the middle class and everyone else.

Across all social classes, child-rearing practices often appeared to be natural. Like breathing, child rearing usually seemed automatic and unconscious. Parents were scarcely aware that they were orienting their children in specific ways. For example, the Handlon and the Tallinger children had cousins their own ages who lived within a twenty-minute drive. They saw their cousins, however, only on special occasions, not several times per week as did children in the Driver and McAllister families. While firmly committed to the strategy of concerted cultivation, Mr. and Ms. Williams did not seem especially conscious of their approach. Although both parents mentioned the pleasure they experienced from knowing that Alexander was curious, they did not appear to link that trait to their own extensive use of reasoning with him. Nor did they analyze their failure to use directives. The fact that most of Alexander's time was spent with other children his own age, rather than with his cousins (in part because they lived so far away), also was not a subject of reflection or discussion. Parts of their lives, of course, did reflect conscious choices and deliberate actions, including Ms. Williams's vehement objections to television and both parents' commitment to furthering Alexander's musical talents. The scarcity of time was also a subject of discussion. Even here, however, the focus was on the details of life (e.g., missing a baseball game to take part in a school play) rather than on the overall approach to child rearing.

Similarly, in families using the accomplishment of natural growth, there was tremendous economic constraint and almost constant talk about money. But there was a "taken for granted" character to daily life that presumed a focus on natural growth rather than concerted cultivation. Ms. McAllister stressed her strengths as a mother. As she fed, clothed, and cared for her children, took them on picnics, and watched out for them, she compared her actions favorably to the behavior of mothers living nearby, including those who took drugs. She did not compare herself to the Ms. Tallingers or Ms. Williamses of the world.

## The Intersection of Race and Class

In *Race Matters*, Professor Cornel West reports his frustration in trying to hail a cab to get to a photo shoot for the cover of his latest book. As he waited and waited, ten taxis without passengers passed him by, stopping (often within his vision) instead to pick up people whose skin color was not black. Furious, he gave up, took the subway, and was late for the appointment. Professor West and other middle-class African Americans report feeling enraged over this inability to signal their class position in social interactions with strangers. In these situations, race trumps social class.

The middle-class Black fathers in this study told similar tales. One father reported white women clutching their purses and looking terrified as he walked briskly one evening to use the cash machine in an upscale shopping district. Also, as I have shown, the mothers and fathers of middle-class African American children kept a keen eye out for signs of racial problems. Their worries were confirmed, as when a first-grade boy told Alexander Williams (son of a lawyer) that he could only be a garbage man when he grew up, or when Fern Marshall, the only Black girl in a camp of a hundred white girls, had fun during the morning basketball activities but at lunchtime found it more difficult (than if she had been white) to blend into the groups of girls chattering away. Although they moved heavily within white worlds, parents sought to avoid having their children be the only Black child at an event. In addition, parents sought to have their children develop a positive self-image that specifically included their racial identity. Thus, for example, they attended all-Black middle-class Baptist churches every Sunday.

Given this evidence, it would be a mistake to suggest that race did not matter in children's lives. It did. Nevertheless, the role of race was less powerful than I had expected. In terms of the areas this book has focused on—how children spend their time, the way parents use language and discipline in the home, the nature of the families' social connections, and the strategies used for intervening in institutions—white and Black parents engaged in very similar, often identical, practices with their children. As the children age, the relative importance of race in their daily lives is likely to increase. Most African Americans do not date or marry outside their own racial and ethnic groups. Housing markets are heavily segregated for Black homeowners, regardless of their income. African Americans also are likely to encounter racism in their interpersonal contact with whites, particularly in employment settings. In fourth grade, however, in very central ways, race mattered less in children's daily lives than did their social class. Black and white middle-class children were given enormous amounts of individualized attention, with their parents organizing their own time around their children's leisure activities. This prioritizing profoundly affected parents' leisure time. In these situations, race made little to no difference. Mr. Williams, after a week of working until midnight preparing for a trial, spent Sunday driving Alexander to baseball practice, home for a quick shower and change, and then off to a school play. Mr. Tallinger flew across the country on a red-eye, had a short nap, went to work, and then was out late at a soccer practice on a chilly spring evening, yearning for the event to be over so that he could get home and sleep.

Similarly, it was the middle-class children, Black and white, who squabbled and fought with their siblings and talked back to their parents. These behaviors were simply not tolerated in working-class and poor families, Black or white. Still, the biggest differences in the cultural logic of child rearing in the day-to-day behavior of children in this study were between middle-class children on the one hand (including wealthy members of the middle class) and working-class and poor children on the other. As a middle-class Black boy, Alexander Williams had much more in common with *white* middle-class Garrett Tallinger than he did with less-privileged Black boys, such as Tyrec Taylor or Harold McAllister.

## How Does It Matter?

Both concerted cultivation and the accomplishment of natural growth offer intrinsic benefits (and burdens) for parents and their children. Nevertheless, these practices are accorded different social values by important social institutions. There are signs that some family cultural practices, notably those associated with concerted cultivation, give children advantages that other cultural practices do not.

In terms of the rhythms of daily life, both concerted cultivation and the accomplishment of natural growth have advantages and disadvantages. Middle-class children learn to develop and value an individualized sense of self. Middle-class children are allowed to participate in a variety of coveted activities: gymnastics, soccer, summer camps, and so on. These activities improve their skills and teach them, as Mr. Tallinger noted, to be better athletes than their parents were at comparable ages. They learn to handle moments of humiliation on the field as well as moments of glory. Middle-class children learn, as Mr. Williams noted, the difference between baroque and classical music. They learn to perform. They learn to present themselves. But this cultivation has a cost. Family schedules are disrupted. Dinner hours are very hard to arrange. Siblings such as Spencer and Sam Tallinger spend dreary hours waiting at athletic fields and riding in the car going from one event to another. Family life, despite quiet interludes, is frequently frenetic. Parents, especially mothers, must reconcile conflicting priorities, juggling events whose deadlines are much tighter than the deadlines connected to serving meals or getting children ready for bed. The domination of children's activities can take a toll on families. At times, everyone in the middle-class families—including ten-year-old children—seemed exhausted. Thus, there are formidable costs, as well as benefits to this child-rearing approach.

Working-class and poor children also had advantages, as well as costs, from the cultural logic of child rearing they experienced. Working-class and poor children learned to entertain themselves. They played outside, creating their own games, as Tyrec Taylor did with his friends. They did not complain of being bored. Working-class and poor children also appeared to have boundless energy. They did not have the exhaustion that we saw in middle-class children the same age. Some working-class and poor children longed to be in organized activities—Katie Brindle wanted to take ballet and Harold McAllister wanted to play football. When finances, a lack of transportation, and limited availability of programs conspired to prevent or limit their participation, they were disappointed. Many were also deeply aware of the economic constraints and the limited consumption permitted by their family's budget. Living spaces were small, and often there was not much privacy. The television was almost always on and, like many middle-class children growing up in the 1950s, working-class and poor children watched unrestricted amounts of television. As a result, family members spent more time together in shared space than occurred in middle-class homes. Indeed, family ties were very strong, particularly among siblings. Working-class and poor children also developed very close ties with their cousins and other extended family members.

Within the home, these two approaches to child rearing each have identifiable strengths and weaknesses. When we turn to examining institutional dynamics outside the home, however, the unequal benefits of middle-class children's lives compared to working-class and poor children's lives become clearer. In crucial ways, middle-class family members appeared reasonably comfortable and entitled, while working-class and poor family members appeared uncomfortable and constrained. For example, neither Harold nor his mother seemed as comfortable as Alexander and his mother had been as they interacted with their physician. Alexander was used to extensive conversation at home; with the doctor, he was at ease initiating questions. Harold, who was used to responding to directives at home, primarily answered questions from the doctor, rather than posing his own. Unlike Ms. Williams, Ms. McAllister did not see the enthusiastic efforts of her daughter Alexis to share information about her birthmark as appropriate behavior. Ms. Williams not only permitted Alexander to hop up and down on the stool to express his enthusiasm; she explicitly trained him to be assertive and well prepared for his encounter with the doctor. Harold was reserved. He did not show an emerging sense of entitlement, as Alexander and other middle-class children did. Absorbing his mother's apparent need to conceal the truth about the range of foods in his diet, Harold appeared cautious, displaying an emerging sense of constraint.

This pattern occurred in school interactions, as well. Some working-class and poor parents had warm and friendly relations with educators. Overall, however, working-class and poor parents in this study had much more distance or separation from the school than did middle-class mothers. At home, Ms. McAllister could be quite assertive, but at school she was subdued. The parent-teacher conference yielded Ms. McAllister few insights into her son's educational experience.

Other working-class and poor parents also appeared baffled, intimidated, and subdued in parent-teacher conferences. Ms. Driver, frantically worried because Wendy, a fourth-grader, was not yet able to read, resisted intervening, saying, "I don't want to jump into anything and find it is the wrong thing." When working-class and poor parents did try to intervene in their children's educational experiences, they often felt ineffectual. Billy Yanelli's mother appeared relaxed and chatty when she interacted with service personnel, such as the person who sold her lottery tickets on Saturday morning. With "the school," however, she was very apprehensive. She distrusted school personnel. She felt bullied and powerless.

There were also moments in which parents encouraged children to outwardly comply with school officials but, at the same time, urged them to resist school authority. Although well aware of school rules prohibiting fighting, the Yanellis directly trained their son to "beat up" a boy who was bothering him. Similarly, when Wendy Driver complained about a boy who pestered her and pulled her ponytail, and the teacher did not respond, her mother advised her to "punch him." Ms. Driver's boyfriend added, "Hit him when the teacher isn't looking."

The unequal level of trust, as well as differences in the amount and quality of information divulged, can yield unequal *profits* during a historical period such as ours, when professionals applaud assertiveness and reject passivity as an inappropriate parenting strategy. Middle-class children and parents often (but not always) accrued advantages or profits from their efforts. Alexander Williams succeeded in having the doctor take his medical concerns seriously. The Marshall children ended up in the gifted program, even though they did not qualify.

Overall, the routine rituals of family life are not equally legitimized in the broader society. Parents' efforts to reason with children (even two-year-olds) are seen as more educationally valuable than parents' use of directives. Spending time playing soccer or baseball is deemed by professionals as more valuable than time spent watching television. Moreover, differences in the cultural logic of child rearing are attached to unequal currency in the broader society. The middle-class strategy of concerted cultivation appears to have greater promise of being capitalized into social profits than does the strategy of the accomplishment of natural growth found in working-class and poor homes. Alexander Williams's vocabulary grew at home, in the evenings, as he bantered with his parents about plagiarism and copyright as well as about the X-Men. Harold McAllister, Billy Yanelli, and Wendy Driver learned how to manage their own time, play without the direction of adults, and occupy themselves for long periods of time without being bored. Although these are important life skills, they do not have the same payoff on standardized achievement tests as the experiences of Alexander Williams.

These potential benefits for middle-class children, and costs for working-class and poor children, are necessarily speculative, since at the end of the study, the children were still in elementary school. Still, there are important signs of hidden advantages being sown at early ages. The middle-class children have extensive experience with adults in their lives with whom they have a relatively contained, bureaucratically regulated, and somewhat superficial relationship. As children spend eight weeks playing soccer, baseball, basketball, and other activities, they meet and interact with adults acting as coaches, assistant coaches, car pool drivers, and so on. This contact with relative strangers, although of a different quality than contact with cousins, aunts, and uncles, provides work-related skills. For instance, as Garrett shakes the hand of a stranger and looks him or her in the eye, he is being groomed, in an effortless fashion, for job interviews he will have as an adult (employment experts stress the importance of good eye contact). In the McAllister home, family members have great affection and warmth toward one another, but they do not generally look each other in the eye when they speak; this training is likely to be a liability in job interviews. In settings as varied as health care and gymnastics, middle-class children learn at a young age to be assertive and demanding. They expect, as did Stacey Marshall, for institutions to be responsive to *them* and to accommodate their individual needs. By contrast, when Wendy Driver is told to hit the boy who is pestering her (when the teacher isn't looking) or Billy Yanelli is told to physically defend himself, despite school rules, they are not learning how to make bureaucratic institutions work to their advantage. Instead, they are being given lessons in frustration and powerlessness.

# STUDY QUESTIONS

1. Why does Lareau focus on different parenting styles as a way to understand inequality in American life?
2. Reflect on your own upbringing. How was it similar to and different from each of the major parenting styles Lareau observed?

# 34

# CULTURE AND HEALTH

PETER A. HALL AND MICHÈLE LAMONT

In 2006, a team of health researchers painstakingly compared the health status of older residents in England and the United States by analyzing datasets that collected comparable measures of health, income, and education levels from representative samples of individuals in both countries. Given that the United States spends considerably more money on health care than England, the findings were striking: Americans were sicker than their English counterparts for a wide range of illnesses, including cancer, heart and lung diseases, stroke, and diabetes. These differences were not due to health issues among American blacks or Latinos, as these populations were excluded from the analysis. Nor were results explained by differences in health behaviors between Americans and the English, as the study controlled for smoking, overweight, obesity, and alcohol use. It remains a puzzling fact: Americans spend so much money to be healthy, but end up being sicker. What gives?

Peter Hall and Michèle Lamont argue that the answer can be found by comparing how culture shapes the "wear and tear of daily life" from one society to the next. Some societies, they contend, are more successful than others in equipping members with abilities to manage the many challenges life throws in their paths. In cultural contexts where life challenges exceed a person's ability to cope with them, normal wear and tear turns into toxic stress: depression, anxiety, and anger take a toll on the health and happiness of citizens, resulting in higher levels of illness and early death. Central to their argument is the notion that successful societies breed cultures that feature shared moral orders and symbolic boundaries that are broadly inclusive rather than exclusive. Successful societies also find ways to minimize the distance between high- and low-status members, and, moreover, they provide meaningful ways for minorities to see themselves as full participants in citizenship and national belonging. Without these characteristics, Hall and Lamont note, societies fail to protect the well-being of all of their inhabitants.

## FROM *SUCCESSFUL SOCIETIES: HOW INSTITUTIONS AND CULTURE AFFECT HEALTH*

Across time and space, the social fabric is woven differently. How do differences among societies affect the well-being of those who live in them? Are some types of societies more successful than others at promoting individual lives and the collective development of the community? How might the character of a society have such effects, and how are such societies built? These are large questions of classic interest to the social theorists of modernity, such as Comte, Tocqueville, Durkheim, Weber, and Marx, with a pedigree that stretches back to the utopian writings of Bacon, More, and Saint-Simon.

In recent years, however, social science has been more reluctant to tackle such questions. There are good reasons for caution. Post-Enlightenment thought observes that the success of a society is difficult to define independently of complex normative issues, not least because trade-offs must often be struck between goals or groups. Assessing the multifaceted web of social relations connecting members of society also poses major empirical challenges. Even the most promising studies in contemporary social science usually fasten onto one or two dimensions of it to the exclusion of others. Their formulations reflect a balkanization among disciplines that has seen some scholars focus on strategic interaction, while others concentrate on symbolic representations or psychosocial processes, each construing institutions and human motivation in different terms.

There is something becoming in the modesty of contemporary social science. It has made focused empirical inquiry more practicable. But something has also been lost. There are good reasons for believing that well-being is conditioned by many dimensions of social relations, but we do not know enough about how those dimensions interact with one another, whether some are substitutes or complements for others, and by what standards some societies can be said to be more successful than others.

This book steps into that breach. We define societies as patterns of social relations structured by institutional practices and cultural repertoires. We are especially interested in understanding how institutions and cultural structures combine to advance (or limit) collective well-being. If this scope connects us to a classic literature, for conceptual tools we draw on contemporary arguments about social networks, identity, social hierarchies, collective action, boundaries, and social capital. Our objective is not to supersede such perspectives but to build on them. We are especially interested in understanding the effects of institutions, organizations, and available cultural repertoires and how they interact with one another.

Our premise is that some societies are more successful than others but, unlike some of the modernization theories of the 1960s, we do not claim there is a single path to success, and, precisely because institutions interact with local cultures, we are skeptical about proposals to identify "best practices" that can readily be transferred from one society to another. There may well be more than one way to solve similar problems. Nevertheless, the contributions the structures of society make to social welfare should be investigated.

A wide range of outcomes can be associated with successful societies, including nonviolent intergroup relations, open access to education, civic participation, cultural tolerance, and social inclusion. We see each as desiderata. However, the priority each should be assigned is open to debate, and engaging in that debate could easily absorb much of this volume, leaving little room to consider the issues that most concern us, namely, how institutional and cultural structures feed into such outcomes. Therefore, the empirical outcomes on which we have decided to focus the book are those of population health, taken as a proxy for social well-being. We concentrate on the health status of those living in a particular country, region, or community and what we sometimes describe as "health plus."[1]

This is an appropriate choice. On the one hand, a focus on population health fits well with our understanding of successful societies. A successful society is one that enhances the capabilities of people to pursue the goals important to their own lives, whether through individual or collective action, and, as we will argue later, population health can be seen as an indicator of such capabilities.[2] On the other hand, health is a relatively uncontroversial measure of well-being—longer life expectancies and lower rates of mortality can reasonably be associated with the success of a society—and it provides measurable outcomes to explain.

In these outcomes are many sets of puzzles for social scientists. Consider three examples. When the communist regimes of Eastern Europe fell after 1989—in a set of developments some described as the "end of history"—one might have expected life to improve for those people who had been given new freedoms, and for some it did. After dipping amidst the transition, male life expectancy in the Czech Republic, for instance, began to improve more rapidly than under the previous regime, to reach 72 years by 2001. But male life expectancy in Russia dropped sharply during the transition and remained so low that it was barely 59 years in 2001. Why did a historic development improve collective well-being in one nation and erode it in another?

Recent gaps in the trend lines for life expectancy in the United States and Canada are equally puzzling. In the two decades after World War II, Canadians and Americans gained years of life at about the same pace. However, life expectancy has been increasing more slowly in the United States since the 1970s, such that the average Canadian now lives two years longer than his American neighbor. Moreover, women, who live longer than men, are losing their relative advantage at a faster pace in the United States than in Canada. These gaps translate into millions of years of productive life. Why are they occurring?

1. We owe this term to James Dunn who uses it to indicate that good health is usually accompanied by higher levels of self-esteem and associated with many other valued social outcomes, including fruitful employment and a satisfying family life.

2. For an influential argument that associates development with the promotion of capabilities, see Sen (1999), although the meanings we associate with "capabilities" are more specific than his.

Some of these puzzles have policy implications. As sub-Saharan Africa copes with a devastating AIDS epidemic, some governments have had much more success than others. Uganda brought its rate of HIV infection down from about 20 percent of adults in 1992 to less than 8 percent a decade later, while Botswana has seen the rate of infection climb toward 38 percent. By most conventional measures, however, Botswana is much better governed than Uganda. How can one explain these differences in the success of AIDS prevention strategies? These are the types of puzzles this book tackles. For answers, we look to new ways of understanding the relationship between institutional frameworks, cultural repertoires, and population health.

## From the Material to the Social in Population Health

What accounts for variation across countries and communities in the health of the population? Although they loom large in popular conceptions, variations in the quality and availability of medical care do not fully explain such differences. New vaccines, diagnostic procedures, and treatments have reduced the incidence and effects of many diseases, but comparisons over time and countries show that this type of innovation explains only a small portion of the variance in population health.[3] Much more can be attributed to the economic prosperity of a country or community and corresponding improvements in sanitation, housing or basic utilities.[4] But material factors alone do not provide complete explanations. Among the developed countries with annual per capita incomes greater than about US$11,000, there remain wide variations in population health that bear no relationship to national income. The United States has the world's highest income per capita, for instance, and spends more on health care per person than any other country in the world, but it ranks only forty-first in terms of average life expectancy. Population health is clearly conditioned by factors that go well beyond the medical or material.

Much the same can be said about the distribution of health inside each society. . . . In all countries, people of lower socioeconomic status tend to

---

3. For a classic statement, see McKeown (1965) and the controversy published in the *American Journal of Public Health* (2002). Compare Cutler, Deaton, and Lleras-Muney (2006).
4. Pritchet and Summers (1996).

have worse health than those in higher socio-economic positions—a relationship so pervasive that some describe social inequality as the "fundamental cause" behind disparities in population health.[5] But how is this gradient to be explained? Some of it turns on the distribution of material resources: people with higher incomes are likely to be able to purchase the housing, health care, and opportunities for relaxation that contribute to better health. Nothing in our analysis disputes this basic point. However, there is more to one's position in a social structure than the material resources associated with it, and some of these other dimensions are likely to be consequential for health. Even studies of baboons show that position within a social hierarchy engenders physiological effects that impinge on health.[6] One of the objectives of this book is to explore how such dimensions of social relations can affect the distribution of health across the population. We are looking for the social sources of the health gradient.

Of course, this is a problem central to social epidemiology, a field on whose findings we build. One of our objectives is to integrate work in social epidemiology with the concerns of a wider range of social sciences, and to that task we bring a distinctive perspective, which emphasizes the impact on health of institutional structures and cultural repertoires. Many social epidemiologists share these concerns, but they tend to focus on a limited range of social relations and to conceptualize explanations based on them in terms of relatively undifferentiated categories, such as the "psychosocial." We look at the impact of a broader range of institutional structures and cultural repertoires with special emphasis on how they relate to one another.[7] This perspective allows us to identify a number of dimensions of social relations consequential for population health that deserve more

5. Link and Phelan (1995; 2000). For overviews of the large literature on this topic, see Adler and Newman (2002); Lynch et al. (2004); Wilkinson (2005); Leigh and Jencks (2006).

6. Sapolsky, Alberts, and Altmann (1997).

7. Social relations broadly construed are the day-to-day interactions, informal (left to the subject's agency) or formalized (into structures, institutions, traditions), between individuals and groups, along with their various correlates: symbolic, material and social *stricto sensu* (hierarchies, networks, solidarities, and so on). Our analysis focuses on cultural structures and institutions rather than other dimensions of social relations. Cultural structures are representations (identities, scripts, frames, myths, narratives, collective imaginaries) that feed into behaviors and social boundaries. Institutions are defined as a set of regularized practices, whether formal or informal, with a rule-like quality in the sense that the actors expect those practices to be observed.

attention than they have received and to deepen our understanding of the ways in which the effects of institutional structures can operate through the cultural frameworks they sustain. Although grounded in ongoing research projects, all the chapters in this book are exploratory. Our objective is to widen the lens through which issues of population health can be seen.

## Pathways from Institutions and Culture to Health

. . . Some consider the challenges to health posed by contemporary developments. Others address problems associated with policies to improve health. Some focus on the impact of collective representations or symbolic boundaries. However, all are concerned with the roles played in such processes by institutional and cultural structures, which affect health through many routes.

Among these routes, this book accords special importance to the health effects that follow from what is sometimes called the "wear and tear of daily life." Although less dramatic than a virus that decimates the population, the toll taken by the stresses of everyday life may be just as great, given the number of people they affect. Many studies show that the emotional and physiological responses generated by the challenges people encounter in daily life condition not only their risk behaviors but also their susceptibility to many of the chronic illnesses that have become the dominant causes of mortality in the developed world, including stroke and heart disease.

Biological pathways link the anger, anxiety, or depression generated in daily life to a person's health. Chronic exposure to high levels of stress has been associated with cumulative developments in the neuroendocrine system that inspire hypertension and poor health. Negative emotions such as depression, resentment, and anxiety appear to raise all-cause mortality, as well as the risk of coronary heart disease, through their effects on the sympathetic-adrenal-medullary (SAM) system, hypothalamic-pituitary-adrenocortical (HPA) system, and immune system. In many cases, these effects seem to operate, much as aging does, to induce progressive increases in the physiological costs of meeting new challenges from the social environment, thereby reducing resilience to health threats over time. Moreover, there can be interaction along these pathways. The development of reflective consciousness, widely associated with the growth of the prefrontal cortex during adolescence, for instance, can condition the levels of stress experienced later in life.

To understand how institutional practices and cultural frames impinge on health, we develop a particular conception of how the wear and tear of daily life is generated. We suggest that wear and tear depends crucially on the balance between the magnitude of the *life challenges* facing a person and his or her *capabilities* for responding to such challenges. We use the term "life challenges" to refer to the tasks a person regards as most important to life, ranging from basic efforts to secure a livelihood and raise a family to others whose importance will vary across individuals—such as securing material goods, companionship, or social prestige in specific arenas of activity.

We conceptualize "capabilities" in terms that borrow from psychology as well as sociology. To some extent, these are constituted by basic attributes of personality associated with reflective consciousness and emotional resilience, which are conditioned by the experiences of childhood and refined in the contexts of adulthood. But a person's capabilities depend on much more than personality. They include the ability to secure cooperation from others, which invokes a person's capacities for meaning-making and self-representation and the recognition he receives from the community, as well as the institutional frameworks that allow for recognition and effective cooperation. Ultimately, they depend on access to the range of resources that can be used to resolve life's problems. The import of this equation should be apparent. As the life challenges facing a person loom larger relative to his or her capabilities for coping with them, we expect that person to experience higher levels of wear and tear in daily life, feeding into feelings of stress, anger, anxiety, and depression that take a toll on health.

The impact of material circumstances on health is readily captured by this model. In general, people with higher incomes face fewer—and generally different—challenges than those with low incomes. Even more important, however, is the contribution economic resources make to a person's capabilities. In most societies, income is a multipurpose instrument that can be deployed to meet many kinds of challenges, ranging from securing housing to finding a partner. In short, the balance between life challenges and capabilities is a function of material resources. We acknowledge the important impact economic inequality has on the distribution of health across populations and nations.

However, the advantage of our model is that it also illuminates the role played by institutional practices and cultural frameworks in the determination of population health. The core point is that a person's capabilities can be augmented (or attenuated) not only by his access to material resources but also by his access to social (including symbolic) resources. A number of scholars have suggested that the correlates of social class constitute such resources.[8] However, existing attempts to enumerate them remain limited. Our analysis can be read as an effort to specify in more detail how resources are constituted and how they work their way into health. We focus on the ways in which institutional structures and cultural frames are constitutive of such resources, and we explore the ways in which those resources affect peoples' health by conditioning their capabilities for coping with life challenges.

The results are informative for comparisons across communities. Some societies seem to have more symbolic and social resources than others. However, the analysis also illuminates the familiar relationship between socioeconomic status and health, revealing pathways through which social inequalities impinge on health. Moreover, instead of assuming that the distribution of resources corresponds exactly to the distribution of economic resources, we look into that relationship, allowing for the possibility that social and symbolic resources may not be as tightly coupled to income inequality as some studies imply.[9]

## Bringing Culture Back In

Social epidemiologists have shown, in repeated studies, that social relations matter to people's health. Broadly speaking, the field has emphasized three types of relationships. The first is the set of social networks to which people belong. There is substantial evidence that people with close ties to others, through marriage, friendship, or social networks, tend to enjoy better health and to recover more effectively from illness than those who have relatively few such ties. Research shows that the level and intensity of contacts with

8. Giddens (1975); Pearlin and Schooler (1978); Weber (1978); Bourdieu (1984); Link and Phelan (1995, 2000); Kristenson (2006); among others.
9. For a theoretical model spelling out the determinant role of semiotic practices in relation to material resources, see Sewell (2005).

others affect all-cause mortality, self-rated health, and rates of recovery from illnesses such as myocardial infarction. Membership in networks offers resilience against depression, illness, and addiction.[10]

A second body of work emphasizes the secondary associations and trust in others they are said to promote, arguing that such associations provide a community with multipurpose "social capital" that can be used to mobilize collective action, especially to press governments to address the needs of the community. Studies show relatively strong correlations between the density of membership in secondary associations and average levels of health across communities. Those who belong to such associations also appear to be healthier, even when factors such as age, income, and social class are controlled.[11]

If the concept of social capital highlights symmetrical relations among people, a third set of studies stresses the asymmetrical relationships found in hierarchies. Pioneering studies of British civil servants, for instance, have found differences in their health, corresponding to their rank within the employment hierarchy, and others find a relationship between the level of autonomy people enjoy in their job and their health.[12] Others suggest that society-wide status hierarchies may have health effects based, in particular, on the feelings of relative deprivation that high levels of income inequality may engender.[13]

[We are] inspired by these lines of research. They blaze important paths. However, we think those paths are still too narrow, notably in the range of social relationships they consider and how they construe the causal linkages to population health. One of the objectives of this book is to broaden prevailing conceptions of how social relations impinge on health, and we think one of the principal ways to do so is to bring the cultural dimensions of such relationships into fuller focus. Doing so reveals new causal logics and enriches understanding of the pathways to which social epidemiology has pointed.

Scholars who look at the impact of social networks on health have been the most expansive in their formulations. They argue that networks provide logistical support for important tasks, such as rearing children, securing

10. See the pioneering work of Berkman and Syme (1979); Berkman (1995); Berkman et al. (2000); Smith and Christakis (2008).

11. Kawachi, Kennedy, and Wilkinson (1999: Chapters 22 and 23).

12. Marmot (2004).

13. There is controversy about some of these points. See Wilkinson (1996; 2005) and Kawachi (2000).

employment, and managing illness; information about how to approach these tasks; and social influence useful for securing the cooperation of others. Close contacts provide the emotional support that wards off feelings of isolation or depression.[14] This is congruent with our model. In each of these ways, membership in social networks can improve a person's health by enhancing her capabilities for meeting life challenges.

However, these formulations stop short of capturing the full meanings people give to their relations with others. What is missing is a sense of the moral valence people attach to people around them. Long ago, sociologist Max Weber made the point that there is no action and social relationship without meaning. Building on this insight, recent network analysts have observed that the social connectedness of a society is not specified simply by the structural properties of networks, such as their density or even the instrumental functions they serve, but by the meanings those networks produce and convey. For those who belong to a network, membership is often associated, not only with arrangements of mutual convenience, but with value-laden judgments about the self and others, defined at its limits by a sense of who belongs, who should be defended and respected, and who is only at the margins. People use these meanings to derive purposes for their actions as well as a sense of what they can reasonably expect in moral terms from each other. Those meanings constitute social resources. The research of Sampson and his colleagues underlines this point. They find that variations in the level of violence present across Chicago neighborhoods are best explained, not by the presence of social networks per se but by whether people in each neighborhood believe it appropriate for them to admonish their neighbors' children.[15]

Studies of the relationship between health and social capital take an even more restricted view of social relations and how they condition behavior. By and large, they emphasize relationships built on a logic of mutual exchange, whereby face-to-face encounters in associations or networks create generalized trust and a diffused reciprocity that can be mobilized for collective action.[16] There is evidence that relations of this sort can improve the ability of communities to press governments to address local problems. But this perspective misses many of the contributions that organizations make to a

14. See, for instance, the nice formulations in Berkman et al. (2000).
15. Sampson, Raudenbausch, and Earls (1997).
16. Putnam (1993).

community's capacities for collective mobilization through the cultural frames they promote.[17]

Social organizations do not simply foster a diffuse sense of reciprocity. In many cases, they contribute important moral visions, identities, symbols, and historical narratives to the collective representations of a community, thereby influencing how individuals or groups see themselves and their relationship to the community as a whole. They convey information about the relative status of groups within the community. They communicate boundaries, defining inclusion or exclusion, and visions of what it means to belong to the community as a whole, which can promote specific models for action. These visions can be more crucial to mobilization, whether individual or collective, than the diffuse reciprocity engendered by associational life. . . .

The literature linking health to social status is especially important for its attentiveness to the distributional implications of social structure. However, there is no consensus in this literature about how social position affects health. Much of it relies on a vague concept of status or links status to health through a concept of relative deprivation that implies status derives mainly from income. In some instances, of course, status inequalities can give rise to a sense of deprivation, which affects a person's health by inspiring feelings of anger and resentment.

However, we think there is room for more multifaceted approaches to the relationship between status and health. On the one hand, differences in status may be grounded in a variety of sources. People may secure status in their local community and in their own eyes, not only from their material possessions but also from their commitment to collective solidarity or from their role in raising a family.

On the other hand, the effects of status may not operate entirely through feelings of relative deprivation. Hall and Taylor argue that social status conditions the toll daily life takes on people's health by affecting their capacities to secure the cooperation of others. Social status can condition a person's self-image in ways that increase the anxiety or stress he feels—what Giddens calls "ontological security"—without necessarily engaging feelings of relative deprivation.[18] Psychologists have noted that the stereotypes embedded in status systems can influence the self-confidence

---

17. For an illustration of this point, see Small (2004). For relevant critiques, see Hall (1999) and Offe (1999).

18. Giddens (1991).

and competence people bring to particular tasks, even if they are not conscious of it doing so.[19] Recognition influences self-efficacy independently of access to material resources. Being defined as able to achieve or as a valuable member of the community has to be a component of how inequality penetrates under the skin. In short, we need a more expansive conception of the mechanisms through which status works its way into health, notably by affecting the capabilities people bring to life challenges.

We should also acknowledge that the status order is a cultural construct whose shape varies across societies. Status is not determined exclusively by material affluence or position within formal hierarchies. The extent to which status corresponds to income will depend on the available cultural frames. Michèle Lamont's comparison of the French and the American upper-middle class, for instance, shows how much these two societies vary with respect to the value or prestige attached to money, culture, and morality. In another study, she finds that French and American workers employ quite different matrices for assessing the value of various groups, such as blacks, immigrants or the poor, which means that blacks and the poor are regarded in more inclusive terms in the French than American context.[20] Because the status or social recognition accorded such groups varies across national contexts, the social opportunities available to them do so as well, with important implications for their health.

The study of population health can be enriched by taking into account the meaning-laden dimensions that permeate all social relations, even when the latter might seem solely interest-based. Those who belong to a society are tied together by ideas of who they are and what they can do that are as evaluative as they are factual. These ideas underpin the judgments we make about others and ourselves. They provide resources for our imagination and specify its limits. In some respects, these "webs of meaning" constitute moral orders. They are organized around group boundaries that have negative (exclusive) aspects as well as positive (identity-bearing) aspects and embodied in hierarchies that assign status or prestige. They find voice in collective narratives grounded in tales about the historic struggles of the tribe or nation, redolent with implications about what a member can or should do—providing definitions of "possible selves" for individuals and aspirations for the collectivity.

19. Shih, Pittinsky, and Ambady (2002).
20. Lamont (1992; 2000; 2006).

For the purposes of this book, we put special stress on three dimensions of culture, which are often embodied in institutional forms. The first is the set of *symbolic boundaries* that define who is at the center of the community and who is at its margins.[21] Boundaries of this sort construct ethnicity and the other social categories that structure the transactions of daily social life. They may be more or less permeable. Closely associated with them are sets of evaluative criteria, which attach more or less opprobrium to one side of a boundary and give rise to the stereotypes that influence views of ourselves as well as others.[22]

The second dimension consists in the *status hierarchies* of a society, understood as implicit sets of principles for distinguishing among social positions and a distribution that assigns varying amounts of social prestige to those positions. We are concerned with the steepness of the relevant status hierarchies, namely, the distance in status between positions at the top and bottom, and in the multidimensionality of status distribution. As Max Weber argued, where status can be secured in several different ways, the social disadvantages experienced by those who lack status on one hierarchy may be offset by the status they gain through alternative means. Relevant to such processes are the terms on which a society assigns status, whether on the basis of citizenship, learning, income, or some other criteria.

Finally, we are attentive to the *collective imaginaries* that portray a society and its members in particular ways. If nations are "imagined communities," as Benedict Anderson has suggested, it matters how they imagine themselves. Collective imaginaries are sets of representations composed of symbols, myths, and narratives that people use to portray their community or nation and their own relationship as well as that of others to it. By virtue of their contributions to collective identity, these imaginaries condition the boundaries and status hierarchies to which we have just referred. In addition, by presenting a community's past in a particular way, collective narratives influence the expectations of its members about the future, suggesting paths of collective development available to the community and "strategies of action" feasible for individuals within it. The moral valence of such representations lends them influence, but they have cognitive and emotional impact as well, conjuring up templates for action from the past.

21. On the literature on boundaries, see Lamont and Molnár (2002).
22. See Steele (1988); Steele and Crocker (1998); Krieger (2000); Son Hing et al. (2002).

These cultural frameworks condition the health of individuals and its distribution across the population in multiple ways. As noted later, they provide blocks on which effective policies to promote healthy behaviors can be built and underpin the collective mobilization central to securing more healthy living conditions in many societies. However, we want to emphasize the ways in which cultural frameworks affect health by conditioning peoples' capabilities for coping with life challenges and, hence, the amount of daily wear and tear they experience.

Social recognition can feed directly into capabilities.[23] As we have noted, it can affect a person's capacities for securing cooperation from others. Those who belong to low-status groups or occupy positions with low social respect may find it more difficult to secure such cooperation. Research on racial discrimination indicates that social recognition is also likely to affect self-confidence and the effectiveness with which tasks are performed.[24] Here, there are important life course effects: the recognition one achieves in childhood has durable importance for the self-concept and health. Even with the most auspicious upbringing, however, in the absence of cultural templates that sustain a sense of social recognition, adults can rarely sustain the self-esteem that feeds directly into health.[25]

The predominant models of cultural citizenship, social boundaries, and status hierarchies of a society will influence whether social recognition is available and who will receive it. Where the status hierarchy is relatively flat or there are diverse paths toward status, those in the lower rungs of the social ladder should be healthier on average than their counterparts facing steeper or dominant hierarchies. Much may depend on whether status is driven by income.

# Bibliography

Adler, Nancy E. and Katherine Newman. 2002. "Socioeconomic Disparities in Health: Pathways and Policies." *Health Affairs* 21 (2): 60–76.

Berkman, Lisa F. 1995. "The Role of Social Relations in Health Promotion." *Psychosomatic Medicine* 57 (3): 245–54.

23. On social recognition, see Taylor (1993) and Lamont and Bail (2005).
24. Steele (1999). Also Steele and Aronson (1998).
25. Steele (1988); Pyszczynski et al. (2004).

Berkman, Lisa F. and S. Leonard Syme. 1979. "Social Networks, Host Resistance, and Mortality: A Nine-year Follow-up of Alameda County Residents." *American Journal of Epidemiology* 109 (2): 186–204.

Berkman, Lisa F., Thomas Glass, Ian Brissette, and Teresa E. Seeman. 2000. "From Social Integration to Health: Durkheim in the New Millennium." *Social Science and Medicine* 51: 843–57.

Bourdieu, Pierre. 1984. *Distinction: A Social Critique of the Judgement of Taste*, translated by R. Nice. London: Routledge.

Cutler, David M., Deaton, Angus S., and Lleras-Muney, Adriana. 2006. "The Determinants of Mortality." National Bureau of Economic Research working paper no. W11963.

Giddens, Anthony. 1975. *Class Structure of the Advanced Societies*. New York: Harper and Row.

———. 1991. *Modernity and Self-Identity: Self and Society in the Late Modern Age*. Stanford, CA: Stanford University Press.

Hall, Peter A. 1999. "Social Capital in Britain." *British Journal of Political Science*. 29 (3): 417–61.

Kawachi, Ichiro. 2000. "Income Inequality and Health." In *Social Epidemiology*, edited by Lisa Berkman and Ichiro Kawachi. New York: Oxford University Press.

Kawachi, Ichiro, Bruce P. Kennedy, and Richard G. Wilkinson, eds. 1999. *The Society and Population Health Reader: Income Inequality and Health, Vol. I*. New York: The New Press.

Krieger, Nancy. 2000. "Discrimination and Health." In *Social Epidemiology*, edited by Lisa F. Berkman and Ichiro Kawachi. New York: Oxford University Press.

Kristenson, Margareta. 2006. "Socio-economic Position and Health: the Role of Coping." *Social Inequalities in Health*, edited by Johannes Siegrist and Michael Marmot. Oxford: Oxford University Press.

Lamont, Michèle. 1992. *Money, Morals, Manners: The Culture of the French and American Upper-Middle Class*. Chicago: University of Chicago Press.

———. 2000. *The Dignity of Working Men: Morality and the Boundaries of Race, Class, and Immigration*. Cambridge, MA: Harvard University Press.

———. 2006. "How French and American Workers Define Cultural Membership." In *Inequalities of the World*, edited by Goran Therborn. London: Verso.

Lamont, Michèle and Christopher Bail. 2005. "Sur les frontières de la reconnaissance. Les catégories internes et externes de l'identité collective." *Revue Européenne des Migrations Internationales* 21 (2): 61–90.

Lamont, Michèle and Virág Molnár. 2002. "The Study of Boundaries Across the Social Sciences." *Annual Review of Sociology* 28: 167–95.

Leigh, Andrew and Christopher Jencks. July 2006. "Inequality and Mortality: Long-Run Evidence from a Panel of Countries." KSG working paper no. RWP06–032. Available at SSRN: http://ssrn.com/abstract=902381.

Link, Bruce G. and Jo Phelan. 1995. "Social Conditions as Fundamental Causes of Disease." *Journal of Health and Social Behavior* 35: 80–94.

Link, Bruce G. and Jo C. Phelan. 2000. "Evaluating the Fundamental Cause Explanation for Social Disparities in Health." In *Handbook of Medical Sociology*, edited by Chloe E. Bird, Peter Conrad, and Allen Fremont. Upper Saddle River, NJ: Prentice Hall.

Lynch, John W., George D, Smith, Sam Harper, Marianne Hillemeier, Nancy Ross, George A. Kaplan, and Michael Wolfson. 2004. "Is Income Inequality a Determinant of Population Health? Part 1. A Systematic Review." *The Milbank Quarterly* 82: 1–77.

Marmot, Michael G. 2004. *The Status Syndrome: How Social Standing Affects Our Health and Longevity.* New York: Times Books.

McKeown, Thomas. 1965. *Medicine in Modern Society.* London: Allen & Unwin.

Offe, Claus. 1999. "How Can We Trust Our Fellow Citizens?" In *Democracy and Trust*, edited by Mark E. Warren. New York: Cambridge University Press.

Pearlin, L. I. and C. Schooler. 1978. "The Structure of Coping." *Journal of Health and Social Behavior* 19: 2–21.

Pritchett, Lance and Lawrence H. Summers. 1996. "Wealthier Is Healthier." *Journal of Human Resources* 31 (4): 841–68.

Putnam, Robert D. 1993. *Making Democracy Work: Civic Traditions in Modern Italy*, with Robert Leonardi, and Raffaella Y. Nanetti. Princeton, NJ: Princeton University Press.

Pyszczynski, Tom, Jeff Greenberg, Sheldon Solomon, and Jamie Arndt. 2004. "Why Do People Need Self-Esteem? A Theoretical and Empirical Review." *Psychological Bulletin* 130 (3): 435–88.

Sampson, Robert J., Stephen W. Raudenbush, and Felton Earls. 1997. "Neighborhoods and Violent Crime: A Multilevel Study of Collective Efficacy." *Science* 277 (5328): 918–24. doi: 10.1126/science.277.5328.918.

Sapolksy, R. M., S. C. Alberts, and J. Altmann. 1997. "Hypercortisolism Associated with Social Subordinance or Social Isolation among Wild Baboons." *Archives of General Psychiatry.* 54 (12): 1137–43.

Sen, Amartya. 1999. *Development as Freedom.* New York: Alfred A. Knopf.

Sewell, William H., Jr. 2005. *Logics of History: Social Theory and Social Transformation.* Chicago: University of Chicago Press.

Shih, Margaret, Todd Pittinsky, and Nalini Ambady. 2002. "Stereotype Susceptibility: Identity Salience and Shifts in Quantitative Performance," *Psychological Science* 10 (1): 80–3.

Small, Mario. 2004. *Villa Victoria: The Transformation of Social Capital in a Boston Barrio.* Chicago: University of Chicago Press.

Smith, Kristen P. and Nicholas A. Christakis. 2008. "Health and Social Networks," *Annual Review of Sociology* 24: 405–29.

Son Hing, Leanne S., Winnie Li, and Mark P. Zanna. 2002. "Inducing Hypocrisy to Reduce Prejudicial Responses among Aversive Racists." *Journal of Experimental Social Psychology*, 38: 71–8.

Steele, Claude M. 1988. "The Psychology of Self-Affirmation: Sustaining the Integrity of the Self." *Advances in Experimental Social Psychology, Vol. 21: Social Psychological Studies of the Self: Perspectives and Programs.* San Diego: Academic Press.

———. "Thin Ice: 'Stereotype Threat' and Black College Students." *The Atlantic Monthly* 284 (2): 44–7; 50–4.

Steele, Claude M. and Joshua Aronson. 1998. "Stereotype Threat and the Test Performance of Academically Successful African Americans." In *The Black-White Test Score Gap*, edited by Christopher Jencks and Meredith Phillips. Washington, DC: The Brookings Institution Press.

Steele, Claude and Jennifer Crocker. 1998. "Social Stigma." In *Handbook of Social Psychology*, edited by Daniel T. Gilbert, Susan. T. Fiske, and Gardener Lindzey. Boston: McGraw-Hill.

Taylor, Charles. 1993. *Multiculturalism and the Politics of Recognition.* Princeton, NJ: Princeton University Press.

Weber, Max. 1978. *Economy and Society, Vols. 1 and 2.* Berkeley: University of California Press.

Wilkinson, Richard G. 1999. "Health Hierarchy and Social Anxiety." *Annals of the New York Academy of Sciences* 896 (1): 48–63.

———. *The Impact of Inequality: How to Make Sick Societies Healthier.* New York: Free Press.

# STUDY QUESTIONS

1. How, according to the authors, is the "wear and tear of daily life" associated with inequality? How is it associated with health? And why is culture an important factor in these relationships?

2. What are *status orders* and *symbolic boundaries* and how are they related to health outcomes?

# CREDITS